Dublin's Great Wars

For the first time, Richard S. Grayson tells the story of the Dubliners who served in the British military and in republican forces during the First World War and the Irish Revolution as a series of interconnected 'Great Wars'. He charts the full scope of Dubliners' military service, far beyond the well-known Dublin 'Pals', with at least 35,000 serving and over 6,500 dead, from the Irish Sea to the Middle East and beyond. Linking two conflicts usually narrated as separate stories, he shows how Irish nationalist support for Britain going to war in 1914 can only be understood in the context of the political fight for Home Rule and why so many Dubliners were hostile to the Easter Rising. He examines Dublin loyalism and how the War of Independence and the Civil War would be shaped by the militarisation of Irish society and the earlier experiences of veterans of the British army.

Professor Richard S. Grayson, of Goldsmiths, University of London, authored *Belfast Boys: How Unionists and Nationalists Fought and Died Together in the First World War* (2009), edited *At War with the 16th Irish Division: The Staniforth Letters, 1914–18* (2012), and co-edited *Remembering 1916: The Easter Rising, the Somme and the Politics of Memory in Ireland* (2016). He is an associate member of the Northern Ireland WWI Centenary Committee, contributed to the BBC's series *Ireland's Great War*, co-edits www.irelandww1.org and works closely with community groups and museums on historical projects. He is both a British and an Irish citizen.

Dublin's Great Wars

The First World War, the Easter Rising and the Irish Revolution

Richard S. Grayson

CAMBRIDGE
UNIVERSITY PRESS

CAMBRIDGE
UNIVERSITY PRESS

University Printing House, Cambridge CB2 8BS, United Kingdom

One Liberty Plaza, 20th Floor, New York, NY 10006, USA

477 Williamstown Road, Port Melbourne, VIC 3207, Australia

314–321, 3rd Floor, Plot 3, Splendor Forum, Jasola District Centre, New Delhi – 110025, India

79 Anson Road, #06–04/06, Singapore 079906

Cambridge University Press is part of the University of Cambridge.

It furthers the University's mission by disseminating knowledge in the pursuit of education, learning, and research at the highest international levels of excellence.

www.cambridge.org
Information on this title: www.cambridge.org/9781107029255
DOI: 10.1017/9781139248877

© Richard S. Grayson 2018

First published 2018

Printed in the United Kingdom by TJ International Ltd. Padstow Cornwall

A catalogue record for this publication is available from the British Library.

Library of Congress Cataloging-in-Publication Data
Names: Grayson, Richard S., 1969–
Title: Dublin's great wars : the First World War, the Easter Rising and the Irish Revolution / Richard S. Grayson, Goldsmiths, University of London.
Description: Cambridge ; New York, NY : Cambridge University Press, [2018] | Includes bibliographical references and index.
Identifiers: LCCN 2018008863 | ISBN 9781107029255
Subjects: LCSH: World War, 1914–1918 – Ireland – Dublin. | Ireland – History – Easter Rising, 1916. | Ireland – History – War of Independence, 1919–1921. | Soldiers – Ireland – Dublin (Ireland) – History – 20th century. | Dublin (Ireland) – History, Military – 20th century.
Classification: LCC DA995.D75 G734 2018 | DDC 941.8/350821–dc23
LC record available at https://lccn.loc.gov/2018008863

ISBN 978-1-107-02925-5 Hardback

This book is produced with the generous assistance of a grant from Isobel Thornley's Bequest to the University of London

Contents

Figures

Maps

Tables

Abbreviations

ANZAC	Australian and New Zealand Army Corps
ASC	Army Service Corps
ASU	Active Service Unit
BEF	British Expeditionary Force
BET	*Belfast Evening Telegraph*
BMH	Bureau of Military History, Dublin
CWGC	Commonwealth War Graves Commission
DCLA	Dublin City Library and Archive
DCM	Distinguished Conduct Medal
DEM	*Dublin Evening Mail*
EH	*Evening Herald*
ET	*Evening Telegraph*
FJ	*The Freeman's Journal*
FS	(Irish) Free State
GAA	Gaelic Athletic Association
GPO	General Post Office
GR	Georgius Rex (Irish Association of Volunteer Training Corps)
HC Deb	House of Commons Debates
HM	His Majesty's
HMS	His Majesty's Ship
HMT	His Majesty's Trawler
HS	Hospital Ship
ICA	Irish Citizen Army

II	*The Irish Independent*
IN	*Irish News*
IPP	Irish Parliamentary Party
IRA	Irish Republican Army
IRB	Irish Republican Brotherhood
IT	*The Irish Times*
IV	*The Irish Volunteer*
IWM	Imperial War Museum Archive, London
LDV	Loyal Dublin Volunteers
MA	Military Archives, Dublin
MBE	Member of the Most Excellent Order of the British Empire
MC	Military Cross
MP	Member of Parliament
MSPC	Military Service Pensions Collection
NAA	National Archive of Australia
NAI	National Archives of Ireland, Dublin
NAM	National Army Museum, London
NAOIRA	National Association of the Old IRA
NLI	National Library of Ireland, Dublin
NV	*The National Volunteer*
RAF	Royal Air Force
RAMC	Royal Army Medical Corps
RCS	Royal College of Surgeons of England Archives, London
RDF	Royal Dublin Fusiliers
RDFA	Royal Dublin Fusiliers Association
RFA	Royal Field Artillery
RFC	Royal Flying Corps
RGA	Royal Garrison Artillery
RIC	Royal Irish Constabulary
RMS	Royal Mail Ship
RNAS	Royal Naval Air Service
SDU	South Dublin Union
SF	Sinn Féin
SH	*Saturday Herald*
SI	*Sunday Independent*
SS	Steam ship
TCD	Trinity College Dublin
TNA	The National Archives, Kew
UB	*U-Boot (Unterseeboot)*

UCD	University College Dublin
UK	United Kingdom of Great Britain and Ireland
UVF	Ulster Volunteer Force
VAD	Voluntary Aid Detachment
VC	Victoria Cross
WIT	*Weekly Irish Times*

INTRODUCTION

This book offers a new military history of the city and county of Dublin in the era of the First World War and the Irish Revolution, setting the narratives of British soldiers and Irish republicans alongside each other. Much of the writing of Dublin's history between the start of the Home Rule crisis in 1912 and the end of the Irish Civil War in 1923 has been dominated by the Easter Rising of April 1916, along with its causes and consequences. There are certainly important studies of the city (less so the county) which recognise the interconnections between the two conflicts in terms of their impact on society, politics and the economy.[1] Meanwhile, excellent material on the Rising and the wider Irish Revolution has emphasised how the war created 'the long-awaited opportunity for rebellion' and made Irish republicans believe that an attempt at revolution was necessary to seize the political initiative.[2] Yet the war raging in Europe and elsewhere in 1914–18 is generally treated as a backdrop to this turning point in Irish history. From the end of mass commemorations of the war in the 1920s until the 1990s, much First World War service by men and women from what is now the Republic of Ireland was forgotten, their story overwhelmed by that of different heroes and heroines: the rebels of 1916.

Similarly, Dublin's First World War narrative tends to pay little attention to the Rising and the wider Irish Revolution. Indeed, it has long been dominated by the story of part of one battalion: D Company of the 7th Royal Dublin Fusiliers, the 'Dublin Pals', at Gallipoli. Just as the Somme overshadows all in Belfast, the Pals and August 1915 loom largest in knowledge of Dublin's contribution to the war effort,[3] despite work in recent decades to broaden the story.[4] Consequently, the full extent of Dublin's role in the British military during the war is narrowly told, and the crossovers between the military history of the Irish Revolution and the course of the First World War are rarely considered.[5] There is little sense in historical writing that telling the stories of the First World War and the Irish Revolution as one can shed light on how we understand Irish history at this time. Yet as Keith Jeffery argued, it is better to treat the Irish Revolution 'not as some completely separate narrative distinct from the world war' because in addressing Ireland's future political settlement 'paths diverged during the war, and *because* of the war'.[6]

This book offers a new narrative of this period, focused on people from the Irish capital and its surrounding county who were involved in military conflict, arguing that between 1912 and 1923, their history is best understood not as a series of separate events. Instead of one narrative leading from Home Rule to Civil War, and another dealing with the First World War, it argues that these events can best be understood as a series of interconnected 'Great Wars'. Irish nationalist support for *the* Great War can only be understood in the context of the political fight for Home Rule, while the Rising could not have happened without the outbreak of war in Europe.[7] Later, the War of Independence could not have occurred without the militarisation of Irish society which flowed from the 1914–18 war, while the Civil War would not have happened as it did without the earlier experiences of men in the British army. So this book does not intend to be a social or economic history of Dublin at this time, or an analysis of its 'home front'. It focuses on Dubliners serving in the British military and republican forces, and is fundamentally about the experiences of people in those roles and the conflicts in which they took part. Social, economic and political issues appear regularly when they relate to those subjects, but for such matters readers already have plenty of other books to which they can turn.[8]

Three themes run through the book. The first is about contexts: Dublin's Great Wars of 1912–23 should be placed within broad contexts of imperial and political conflict, and of Dublin's strong military and naval traditions. The former means that Ireland's fight for independence and its expressions of loyalty to the British Empire brought Dubliners of this era into violent conflict with each other far from Ireland and well before 1916, at least as far back as 1899 in the

South African War. Traditions of military service meant that Dublin was strongly embedded in the British military. Consequently, as soon as war broke out in 1914, Dubliners were thrown into action as members of the Royal Navy and of the regular army. Service was not simply about membership of volunteer units (whether Pals or political) recruited from the outbreak of war. The second theme is that the story of British volunteers goes far beyond the Pals of the 7th Dublins. That is seen vividly in other units of the 10th (Irish) Division at Gallipoli, in particular the 6th Dublins who recruited heavily in the city and county but received relatively little attention compared to the 7th Dublins. Service can also be seen in regular battalions and in Ireland's two politically aligned divisions. At least two thousand Dubliners joined the 16th (Irish) Division which attests to the strength of Dublin's willingness to follow John Redmond and parliamentary Irish nationalism prior to the Rising. Meanwhile, membership of the 36th (Ulster) Division points to a forgotten history of Dublin loyalism, as do public responses to pre-war royal visits. The third theme is that the events of the Irish Revolution must be set alongside the events and experiences of the First World War if we are to understand the causes and contexts of each. For the Easter Rising, that means understanding how, from the streets closest to where the Rising was fought, over a thousand men came to serve in the British military in the war. The vast majority were already serving by April 1916, while 121 had already been killed before the Rising.[9] That does much to explain how the Rising was received by Dubliners and as it took place, men of the 8th and 9th Royal Dublin Fusiliers were suffering heavy losses on the Western Front. Indeed, across the Monday to Saturday of the Rising, nearly three times as many Dubliners were killed serving in the British army in the First World War, as the total number of rebels killed in Dublin. Though news seeped through slowly, such levels of service and sacrifice explain much of the initial reception of the Rising among Dublin's people. Later, links between the events of the Revolution and service in the First World War can be seen in service by former British soldiers in the Irish Republican Army (IRA) fighting against the British, and in the use of British artillery during the Civil War. Such crossovers point to intimate links between the conflicts.

In offering a new narrative of Dublin's Great Wars of 1912–23, this book utilises the 'military history from the street' methods developed for my 2009 book *Belfast Boys*. In simple terms, the method involves trying to use every source possible to draw in the military service of everyone from a given area. The gold standard used to establish that someone is 'from' an area (in this case the city or county of Dublin) is that an address for them can be verified during the relevant years, or in the absence of an address for the individual themselves, that a next-of-kin in the area can be identified. Simply having been born in a location is not enough to place them there during the relevant period, so my numbers will always tend to err on the side of caution.[10] Despite that, my estimate is that at least 35,000 Dubliners served in the British military during the First World War.[11]

The methods are described in some detail in an appendix to *Belfast Boys* and in a journal article.[12] Newspapers and service records have been particularly rich sources of information.[13] But there are some differences between the approach used in that book and the approach used for Dublin, in five key areas. First, many new sources for the British military have appeared in a searchable form since 2009 and that has allowed the inclusion of, for example, more sailors and airmen. More specific data on which infantry battalion men served with has come from newly digitised regimental medal rolls.[14] Second, some use of the 1911 Census has been made in ways not done in *Belfast Boys* but it is worth noting that, if rigorous standards are applied to its use, this source is not quite the key to all mythologies which it might at first appear to be.[15] Third, through the British Red Cross Society, there is now publicly available data on the Voluntary Aid Detachment which enables the scope of volunteering, especially by women, to be assessed. Fourth, since this book addresses involvement in republican units of various types, full use has been made of the Irish government's IRA pensions and medal records, along with witness statements from the Bureau of Military History, and other material on republicans such as arrest records.[16] Finally, since I was not only interested in a specific part of one city as I was for *Belfast Boys*, I have been able to make use of records (in particular casualty lists printed in newspapers) where simply a general reference is made to 'Dublin' as being the residence of the next-of-kin. For the same reason, I have drawn in war memorials from across the city and county.[17] I remain of the view that the gold standard for viewing someone as being from Dublin during its 'Great Wars' of 1914–19, 1919–21 and 1922–3 should be an address, but I have presented my overall figures by including all possible information.[18]

Central to the book is the question of how Dubliners fared on the battlefield during the First World War. In its approach it is broadly 'revisionist' in the sense of being influenced by the approach of writers over a period of decades but most prominently those such as Gary Sheffield and William Philpott.[19] It is tempered by 'post-revisionist' analyses which accept the broad thrust of revisionism but point to 'patchiness' and 'inconsistencies' in the British army's performance rather than a steady learning curve,[20] and also consider the complexities of the processes by which the army learned.[21] Revisionism has offered significant challenges to widely and deeply held popular perceptions of the war by making a number of arguments: once the war broke out, the stakes were so high that the UK was right to be involved; the vast majority who fought returned; even infantry soldiers spent most of their time out of trenches and fought rarely; the generals learned as the war went on and became highly effective at what they did; on the Western Front the war was, eventually, won on the battlefield with German soldiers driven back to whence they came. These views are consensus ones among most academic historians and I count myself a revisionist.

However, there is a danger that revisionism is misunderstood as meaning that those who hold such views are somehow dismissive of the effects of the war. One case I uncovered in writing this book made me realise the necessity of explaining that this is not the case. In May 2016 I visited the archives at the Royal College of Surgeons in London to use the plastic surgery records of a First World War officer from Dublin. What I saw there had a profound effect on me. The photos in the file of Captain Robert Callaghan of the 7th Royal Dublin Fusiliers were stark (see p.342). The first showed a man without any eyes. One eyelid was almost completely closed. It looked as if it had been damaged then healed as if closed. The other eyelid was partially sewn up, possibly some eyelashes remaining – or perhaps sutures – creating a sense of prickliness in a wound still open and sore and hinting at the empty eye-socket. I saw a general sense of bewilderment in the photos of Callaghan, of him not knowing where he was or what was happening, and a sense of hoping for help. Everyone has their own private fear and mine has long been to lose my eyesight. So I was immediately struck by the life that Callaghan was now facing when these photos were taken and found it hard to begin my research. Of course, I did carry on – telling myself that I had no troubles compared to Callaghan – but I shed tears when I got home.

A month later I followed up Callaghan's story in the National Archives at Kew. His file is an unusually weighty one because his correspondence with the War Office about his pension took twists and turns.[22] In 1921 it was found that he had been overpaid his pensions by £305 (around £14,000 now). This was because at the time of his injury, Callaghan had only been a captain for ten days rather than the required fifteen for a captain's pension, but he had still been paid a captain's dues. He was in no position to repay the amount overpaid to him and he was later let off some of it, but not all. Poignantly, the file began with his last letter to the War Office, written in 1938. It said that although he was blind, he was now a medical masseur and a medical electrician. He wrote to offer his services to the army in the event of another war.

Historians are not often emotional in the archives. We use small individual cases to build up a big picture and the individual can be lost. But that does not mean that we are oblivious to individual suffering, nor that we overlook how mistakes were made in diplomacy prior to the war. Yes, 'only' 12 per cent of those who served in the British forces were killed, but that 12 per cent amounted to three-quarters of a million. Of the 88 per cent who returned, millions bore mental and physical scars. It is correct that the majority of time at war was spent behind the lines,[23] but even one day in the firing line was not something anybody in their right mind would wish on themselves or others. Certainly, I believe that the UK was right to fight the war once it broke out as it did, and that the primary fault for that outbreak lies with the Central Powers – Germany and Austria-Hungary. But if the Union of Democratic Control were correct in their critique of 'secret diplomacy'[24] – and I am inclined to think that they were – then this was a war which could and should have been avoided. Then there would not have been the lives cut short, the children who never knew their fathers, and the parents who spent the best part of their remaining lives mourning the loss of a son or daughter – perhaps more than one, and sometimes an only child.

The photographs of Captain Callaghan were a stark reminder to me that the effects of the war were, literally, bloody terrible. It brought home to me what had long been a nagging doubt about the dangers of the public perceiving revisionist history and its proponents in a certain way. Simply because revisionist historians seldom talk about the horrors of war, it does not mean that we are not horrified by them. So it needs to be said: the achievement of the victory came with a human cost which impacted millions just in the UK, and many millions elsewhere. Nobody should ever forget that, whatever they have to say about the broad sweep of history, though it should be no surprise that so many veterans wanted to do precisely that – forget – when they came home. For those from Dublin, this book attempts to tell the story of the Great Wars of the revolutionary period in as complete a manner as possible, recognising the full scope of their service – in the British army and as Irish republicans – and the horrors they endured.

1 PRELUDE: DUBLIN AND CONFLICT, 1899-1914

. . . we were at war with England, and . . . all our political and social ills were due to her occupation of our country.
Helena Molony, Inghinidhe na hÉireann, on anti-recruiting campaigns of the early 1900s[1]

Southern Africa, 1899

Ireland's conflict of 1912–23 grew from such deep roots that those involved in it were fighting long before then and far from Ireland. Recognising that broad context is essential for understanding the motives which made Dubliners fight on different sides in 1912–23. Of course, one can trace the origins of the problems back to Norman times, the Reformation, 1798, or the Act of Union, to name just a few. But for some of those who were the active participants of 1912–23, the first chance to show what they would do in the name of 'freedom', or to become part of a British military tradition, came in southern Africa over a decade before.

In late October 1899, Tom Byrne, a Commando in the Irish Transvaal Brigade, set up camp just outside Ladysmith, in the British southern African colony of Natal. He had been on horseback for much of the past three weeks (since the beginning of the South African War, then commonly known as the Boer War) along with around 300 other men of the Brigade allied to the Boer forces. They had seen action in the earliest days of the war, crossing into Natal as war broke out on 11 October. Among the British prisoners they captured in the war's first days were Royal Dublin Fusiliers.

Born in Carrickmacross in County Monaghan in 1877, Thomas Francis Byrne had moved to Dublin with his family five years later, spending his formative years in the city until departing for South Africa in 1896. The 19-year-old émigré found mining work in Johannesburg. Over the summer of 1899 it became clear that there was a strong risk of war between Britain and the two 'Boer' (Afrikaans-speaking) states, the South African Republic (known as the Transvaal) and the Orange Free State. Ostensibly the conflict was about voting rights for British settlers in these areas. However, underpinning the dispute were concerns that British settlement had grown so much that if such settlers were given the vote the two states would be likely to opt to join the British Empire. Only war could save the Boer states from losing their independence.

On a broader canvas, this quarrel was a struggle between a small nation and the might of the British Empire – a struggle which foreshadowed later events in Ireland. So radical Irish nationalists saw common cause with the Boers and over the summer of 1899 Byrne organised 'an Irish contingent with the Boer army' along with Richard McDonagh from Listowel, County Kerry. Closely involved from the start was County Mayo-born Irish Republican Brotherhood member John MacBride, described by Byrne as 'the only outstanding Irishman in the Transvaal at this time'. In late September 1899, Byrne's organising was complete and the Irish Transvaal Brigade mobilised. Former US Cavalry officer John Blake was elected as colonel, with MacBride as major. With war imminent, the Brigade was given horses and rifles and entrained at Johannesburg for the Transvaal–Natal border. On arrival, around two weeks were spent learning to ride.[2]

Crossing into Natal on 12 October as the Boer states launched pre-emptive attacks on British positions, the Brigade 'rode on without opposition'[3] and entered Newcastle with other Boer forces on 15 October. MacBride would later criticise cautious Boer tactics, which meant that the advance only covered sixty to seventy miles in its first week.[4] It was not until 20 October, in an advance on Dundee that they saw any fighting. Byrne described how in their 'first brush with the enemy' they captured horses and

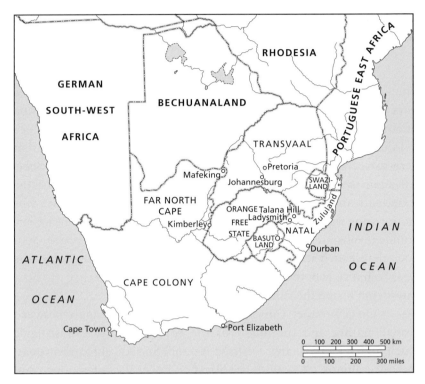

Map 1.1: Key locations of the South African War. Drawn by David Cox.

a heliograph and, he said, two hundred British prisoners. Among them were members of the Dublin Fusiliers. MacBride wrote, 'A number of the prisoners had been at school in Ireland with members of the Brigade.' These were men from the 2nd Dublins and 'Talana Hill' was not only the first major encounter of the Boer War but also the first ever hostile action for the 2nd Dublins since the formation of the Royal Dublin Fusiliers in 1881.

Despite these early Boer successes, the Battle of Talana Hill eventually saw the British forces successfully drive the Boers from a defensive position on high ground, though the British suffered heavy casualties. In a reference to an earlier British defeat in the first Boer War two decades before, the 2nd Dublins' official history described Talana Hill as 'Majuba reversed'. It showed it was possible to take high ground in the face of modern rifle fire, even though that would not be a regular occurrence for the British in the Boer War. MacBride had a different view, writing several years later that 'the British showed themselves absolutely incapable' and lamented the failure of Boer generals to engage more directly with the enemy.[5]

Proceeding on to Ladysmith, the Irish Transvaal Brigade took part in the battle there on 30 October as the British attacked growing Boer positions. Three of them were killed while Blake was among ten wounded, so MacBride took command. Ladysmith was besieged by the Boers until the end of February 1900 when the British managed to break through. By then, the Irish Transvaal Brigade had taken part in several operations, including the Battle of Colenso on 15 December.[6] Through 1900 the Brigade fought in several more encounters with the British and during a retreat in the Orange Free State blew up bridges, stations and anything else they thought might help their enemy. Byrne recalled, 'We always left a notice "With the compliments of the Irish Brigade", which was read by the British fifteen minutes afterwards.' At Machadodorp station Byrne encountered prisoners of the Irish Imperial Yeomanry and 'recognised a few of them, but I did not go near them.' In late September, Byrne and MacBride were among retreating Boer troops who crossed the border into Mozambique and surrendered to the Portuguese. They were soon shipped to Europe or the USA with Byrne winding up in New York with fifty to sixty others. MacBride went to Paris. Byrne stayed in America until returning to Dublin in 1913.[7] Three years later, he – and MacBride – would play their part in the most momentous events in the city's history.

While Byrne was preparing to cross the border into Natal, Michael Tracey of the 1st Royal Dublin Fusiliers was with his battalion at the Curragh in County Kildare. Born in Rathmines in 1877, Tracey was working as a labourer when he enlisted in the regiment in the summer of 1895, three weeks after his eighteenth birthday. Mobilised on 7 October 1899 to form part of the 5th (Irish) Brigade in South Africa, the battalion left Ireland a month later. Reaching Cape Town on 28 November after nearly three weeks at sea, they acclimatised before being thrown into the war at Colenso on 15 December, some companies attached to the 2nd Dublins. They had little sight of the Boers but heard 'one ceaseless rattle of Mausers, and a constant hum of bullets only drowned by the screams of the shells'.[8] Losses were heavy, though Tracey escaped injury. He served through the South Africa War with the 1st Dublins, seeing action at places like Alleman's Nek and Volksrust. The Peace of Vereeniging brought the war to an end in May 1902, and the 1st Dublins departed for Malta in November. Tracey's time in the army effectively ended in April 1903 when he was transferred to the army reserve, in which he remained until September 1911, having married in Dublin in 1906. The army had done little for his education as he was unable to read and write when he signed the 1911 Census with his mark. By that point, he was working as a builder's labourer, had one daughter, and was living in Francis Street in Dublin's Wood Quay area. Yet there must have been something about army life which appealed to him for in January 1912, he again enlisted in the Dublin Fusiliers, this time as a reservist in the 4th battalion.[9] That decision took him on a journey which meant that in April 1916, he, like Thomas Byrne, was in a fight, though many miles away and for a different cause.[10]

In 1907 a triumphal arch was erected at St Stephen's Green commemorating 250 Dublin Fusiliers killed during the South African War. Though such commemoration of British imperialism was controversial, opposition represented minority opinion in the city, only that of 'advanced nationalists'.[11] Dublin's connection to the British army was strong and popular, and many of those who fought in the Boer War would play their part in Britain's next war. It is hard to identify exactly how many South African War veterans from Dublin joined the British army in the First World War, but it is likely to number in the hundreds.[12] Among the most notable to serve in both wars was Thomas Crean, who was born in Dublin's Northbrook Road in 1873 and won nine Ireland rugby caps. Serving with the Royal Army Medical Corps as a Surgeon Captain, he won the Victoria Cross at Tygerkloof on 18 December 1901. He had tended the wounded under heavy fire, despite already being wounded himself. Only a second wound, initially thought to be mortal, stopped his work. He would serve in France in the First World War, winning the Distinguished Service Order.[13] Crean's story, like that of Tracey and Byrne hints at the deep-running Dublin traditions of support for, and resistance to, British rule which would again come to the fore in its Great Wars of 1914–19, 1919–21 and 1922–23.

Dublin and the Military

That a Dubliner like Thomas Byrne was fighting in South Africa during the Boer War was not unusual. Yet the army in which he fought was far from typical. Michael Tracey's case was far more representative. Dublin's contribution to the British army came most visibly through the Royal Dublin Fusiliers, founded in 1881 under the Childers Reforms which reorganised the army. Though new, the regiment drew on long traditions, being the result of a merger between the 102nd and 103rd regiments of foot, the Royal Madras Fusiliers and the Royal Bombay Fusiliers. The 102nd Regiment had roots in the mid-eighteenth century, and the 103rd a century before. The new regiment recruited both in Dublin and from adjoining counties, Carlow, Kildare and Wicklow. Three reserve battalions supported two regular battalions, the 1st and the 2nd. The theory was that one of the latter two would be at 'home' (Britain or Ireland), while the other was overseas (often India). In the reserves, Ireland's long amateur military tradition was represented through the 3rd, 4th and 5th Royal Dublin Fusiliers, and the Dublin City Artillery. Pre-war, the men who joined these units were predominantly labourers, but over one-third were skilled members of the working class. In general, recruits had a higher standard of education than the population as a whole, in contrast to the pattern in Great Britain of relying more on the 'underemployed'. Officers were disproportionately Protestant, but since labourers comprised the bulk of recruits, the rank and file of the militia in Dublin was disproportionately Catholic.[14] Meanwhile, from 1910, students at Trinity College had the Dublin University Officer Training Corps, which was nearly 90 per cent Protestant.[15]

Yet as in every other part of the United Kingdom, men from Dublin could and did enlist in any part of the British army or Royal Navy. That might mean other Irish regiments, but often they joined English, Scottish or Welsh regiments, or units such as the Royal Engineers or Army Service Corps. Pre-war, the county and city of Dublin dominated Irish recruitment for the British Army. With a population of just under 11 per cent of the island as a whole, Dublin supplied around 30 per cent of the army's Irish recruits. Over two-thirds of those who enlisted for the regular army in the Dublin recruiting area did *not* join the Dublin Fusiliers.[16] In this, Dublin trailed behind all other parts of Ireland except the recruiting area of the Royal Irish Rifles around Belfast in its devotion to the local regiment. All other areas saw a majority of their infantry volunteers head for a local regiment, and in most areas over three-quarters did so. Consequently, the story of Dublin's involvement in the First World

War goes far beyond the Royal Dublin Fusiliers, including some connection to an Irish Section of the Black Watch, and also the Royal
Welsh Fusiliers, both of which had been stationed at Dublin's
Portobello Barracks in the early 1900s.[17] Part of this diversity of
enlistment destination is explained by where Dubliners enlisted.
Sample data exists for nearly 7,000 men in First World War service
records (Table A5.5) showing that nearly 87 per cent of army recruits
from Dublin enlisted in Dublin. Nearly 6 per cent enlisted in other
parts of Ireland, with 5.5 per cent in England.

The city of Dublin's imperial connection – it was often described
as being the 'Second City' of the British Empire – was seen far beyond
the military in its fabric and nomenclature, as a symbol of the 1801 Act
of Union between Great Britain and Ireland, and as the centre of British
power in Ireland. Big houses in the wider county were bastions of the
Anglo-Irish ascendancy. Viceregal ceremony was exhibited in Phoenix
Park, redesigned from the 1830s to plans set by a London landscape
architect. Military might was seen not only in several barracks but in the
Ordnance Survey, the Royal Military Hospital and the Hibernian
Military School. Dublin Castle offered an imposing image of political
power. Meanwhile, as Ireland's 'capital', Dublin was the centre of
newspapers, most prominently the conservative *Irish Times*, the
Freeman's Journal aligned to the Irish Parliamentary Party (IPP), and
the nationalist but (as its name suggested) more independent, *Irish
Independent*, plus a range of evening publications. Dublin was also
important in the re-emergence of Gaelic culture, and the growth of
national consciousness through culture, not least with the formation
of the Gaelic League in 1893 in Lower Sackville Street and the opening
of the Abbey Theatre in 1904. Political Irish nationalism had its sites of
power too, particularly through control of the Dublin Corporation, and
the election of Westminster MPs across the city. Both nationalists and
the Dublin Anglo-Irish establishment knew the signifying power of
statuary and of naming streets and places. Nationalists' local power
manifested itself in the naming of bridges in 1879 and then 1880, first
after Isaac Butt and then Daniel O'Connell. At a similar time, an attempt
to rename Sackville Street after O'Connell was not successful and would
have to await revolution to come to fruition formally, though the name
was used by some before then. In almost every case, the naming of
streets remained reflective of British, royal and imperial history, rather
than of Irish nationalism, and in particular the late nineteenth-century

and Edwardian dominance of Irish nationalism was not reflected in Dublin's geography: there would be no Redmond Street or Redmond Square.[18] In later years, that absent geography of Parliamentary nationalism was lost alongside something else: that of recruitment into the British army, overwritten by the memory of Easter 1916.

As for the people, Dublin City's population of nearly 305,000 was more Catholic than Ireland as a whole (83.1% compared to 73.9%). It had broadly the national percentage of Protestant Episcopalians (principally Church of Ireland), but considerably fewer Presbyterians (1.4% compared to 10% nationally, mostly in Ulster). Despite their minority status, Protestants controlled key businesses from Jacob's to Guinness and occupied many positions of power in the city, while the Church of Ireland had an important place at official events.[19] Meanwhile, the city's population was less likely to have any Irish-language skills (3.9% compared to 13.3% across the island). Ireland's agriculture employed 43% of the workforce but as a city Dublin obviously had very few working in the sector (just 1.7%). Instead, over half the workforce was industrial, compared to an all-Ireland figure of around one-third, while nearly twice the proportion of people were employed in professions and nearly three times in commerce. Consequently, with a larger middle class, it also had a larger domestic workforce. Some of these city patterns were broadly matched in the wider County Dublin.[20] There, far higher numbers were employed in the professions and in commerce than across Ireland. However, numbers working in industry were roughly the national figure, while domestic workers were considerably higher at 24.1%. Meanwhile, the county was a little less Catholic (71%) than the island as a whole, and considerably more Anglican (22.8%). Where the city truly stood out, though not as anyone would have wished, was in overcrowded housing. Across Ireland, 6.4% of families lived in just one room. The county figure was close to that but in the city it was over one-third. A further one-fifth lived in just two rooms, and three-quarters overall lived in fewer than five rooms. Of one-room dwellings, over half were occupied by families of two to four, and one-fifth were home to five to seven people.[21] In these cramped conditions disease spread. In 1906, though its death rate had fallen significantly in previous decades, Dublin had the worst mortality rate of any city in western Europe and twice that of London. Little had changed by 1913 when Dublin's mortality rate was 23.1 per thousand compared to 18.4 in Belfast and 14.3 for

London. A Local Government Board report on housing published in early 1914 proposed radical measures but was roundly rejected by those in power in the city, not least because so much of Dublin's middle class earned rent from letting tenements.[22] Dublin was a poor and squalid city, ripe for recruitment into the army, and ripe for political discontent.

Ceremony and Political Conflict

As Ireland's largest city and capital, Dublin was a centre of national ceremony and politics. The King and Queen's visit to Dublin over 8–12 July 1911 highlighted the city's connection to the monarchy, which was no weaker due to desire for Home Rule (which of course meant devolution to Dublin but within the UK, not independence). Indeed, the monarch's visit was possibly better received than previous ones in 1900 and 1903.[23] The *Dublin Evening Mail* reported 'EIGHT MILES OF CHEERS'. The *Saturday Herald* described the 'Streets Filled by Cheering Thousands'.[24] The military were ever-present throughout the proceedings, especially at the Royal Review of 15,000 troops in Phoenix Park involving several Irish regiments. The *Mail* commented, 'The Dublin populace dearly love the regiments in which many of their kith and kin are serving.'[25]

The IPP-aligned *Freeman's Journal* cautioned that the 'cordial welcome' should 'not be misconstrued for political purposes' by those opposed to Home Rule. They presented the welcome as being in line 'with the traditions of the Irish people for generosity and hospitality'.[26] Yet there was also a clear nationalist position on the visit, stemming from the fact that the King was, in the words of the *Evening Telegraph*, 'the Head of the Constitution under which the powers of self-government are denied to us'. The Dublin Corporation 'declined to discuss the visit', leaving its individual members free to participate if they wished. Pembroke Urban Council decided not to present an address to the King, and instead placed a banner on the town hall at Ballsbridge saying 'Welcome. We want Home Rule.'[27] A small minority opposed the visit more vociferously. Rose McNamara and Helena Molony were members of Inghinidhe na hÉireann, the 'Daughters of Ireland'. The group was radically nationalist in wanting an independent Ireland, and also promoted Gaelic Irish culture. Formed in 1900 in response to Queen Victoria's visit to

Dublin, they were, in Molony's words, 'a counterblast to the orgy of flunkeyism which was displayed on that occasion'.[28] The key figure in their foundation in 1900 was Maud Gonne, who married the Irish Transvaal Brigade's John MacBride three years later.[29] Molony joined in 1903 and McNamara in 1906. Their activities included anti-recruiting work: Molony described distributing leaflets 'addressed to Irish girls appealing to them not to consort with the armed and uniformed enemies of their country, telling them that 'we were at war with England, and that all our political and social ills were due to her occupation of our country'.[30] During the royal visit, McNamara was instructed to 'give out handbills denouncing England' at Leeson Street Bridge where the royal couple entered the city centre. Returning from 'an anti-loyalist demonstration' at Smithfield Helena Molony was travelling in a brake with fellow republican Countess Constance Markiewicz. At the bottom of Grafton Street, Molony threw a stone at illuminated pictures of the King and Queen, smashing one. Markiewicz 'whipped up the horses' but they did not escape far. Molony was arrested and fined. Such actions had little support. McNamara described the crowds in the streets as being 'entirely composed of "loyalists"', adding 'I may say it comprised practically the whole population of Dublin.'[31]

However, the strength of mainstream nationalist feeling was soon seen on Dublin's streets. After decades campaigning for Home Rule John Redmond's IPP was clear by the spring of 1912 that it was about to achieve its goal. The Unionist-dominated House of Lords had blocked Home Rule in both 1886 and 1893, but in 1911 its powers were greatly reduced so that it could only delay and no longer block the will of the House of Commons. So when the Liberal government, whose majority in Parliament depended on the support of the IPP, introduced a third Home Rule bill in 1912 the Lords could no longer prevent it becoming law. They could, and would, delay it, but the IPP believed their cause had won.

There was some public opposition to Home Rule in Dublin. Unionists met at the Fowler Memorial Hall in mid-February 1912 and asserted that 'the vast majority of Irishmen of intelligence and industry refuse their sanction to the plans which are being carefully formed to place their lives and liberties under the tyrannous leagues which have been permitted to usurp the Government of Ireland'.[32] But they could never summon large numbers for public action. In contrast, on Sunday

31 March 1912 a mass demonstration supporting Home Rule was held in Dublin with John Redmond speaking at the Parnell Monument in what the *Evening Telegraph, Evening Herald, Irish Independent* and *Freeman's Journal* called 'O'Connell Street'. The *Herald* said, 'There was but one voice in Dublin yesterday, and that was the voice of Home Rule – the voice of over 100,000 Irishmen and Irishwomen proclaiming their loyal adherence to the National demand.' The *Evening Telegraph* believed numbers had approached 300,000. Among many speakers was the former nationalist MP, Professor Thomas Kettle, who called on 'the sturdy people of Ulster' to back Home Rule. He said, 'They have a world to gain, they have nothing to lose but the claims of political superstition.' However, a discordant note was sounded by the refusal of admission to suffragettes trying to enter a Home Rule meeting at the Mansion House. After the events were over, presumably overnight, suffragettes decorated the platforms erected for speakers with the words 'Votes for Women' daubed in red paint.[33]

The Home Rule campaign continued both in Dublin and across Ireland in 1912 and into 1913, but it was far from being the only focus of politics in the city. Arguably more important was the labour unrest of the Dublin 'Lockout' which ran from August 1913 to January 1914. The workers on strike, led by James Larkin and former British soldier James Connolly, were fighting for the right to unionise.[34] The Lockout represented a challenge to nationalism, partly because the main opponent among employers was the former IPP MP, and owner of the *Irish Independent*, William Martin Murphy. However, the Lockout also promoted a politics in which capitalism – not simply British rule – was said to be the cause of working people's problems, offering a different way of thinking about how to improve the lot of Ireland. As Helena Molony recalled, 'All the sympathy of the Irish Ireland movement was with the strikers but not all of us were in sympathy with James Larkin, or his outlook, which was that of a British Socialist. He attacked the "Nationalist" outlook, which he dubbed "Capitalist".' However, during the strike, the Irish Citizen Army (ICA) was formed to defend workers. This would have a key role in the future of Irish nationalism.[35] In popular memory, the Lockout also drove recruitment to the British army in 1914 as strikers found it difficult to get commercial work at home, having been blacklisted.[36]

Further turmoil with implications for Dublin was simultaneously taking place in Ulster. In September 1912, a quarter of a million men had pledged their willingness to use 'all means which may be found necessary' to defeat Home Rule when they signed the Solemn League and Covenant. A similar number of women had signed a declaration pledging to support them. In early 1913, the Ulster Volunteer Force (UVF) was formed. Around 90,000 men joined, eventually armed and uniformed.[37] In Dublin, an associated organisation, the Loyal Dublin Volunteers (LDV), was founded and came to number around 2,000 men.[38] While the strength of support for Home Rule in the city meant that the LDV was marginal, with the formation of the UVF it was clear that elsewhere in Ireland armed resistance to Home Rule was likely.

Such concerns led to a meeting at Dublin's Rotunda Rink on the evening of Tuesday 25 November 1913 when as many as 7,000 people attended the formation of Óglaigh na hÉireann, the Irish Volunteers.[39] Tom Byrne, formerly of the Irish Transvaal Brigade, who became known as 'Byrne the Boer', was among those who joined.[40] Later in the year and into 1914 local companies were formed outside the city in the towns and villages of County Dublin.[41] For some of those joining, the militarisation of nationalism was the logical next step of a journey they had been making for many years. Dubliner Patrick O'Kelly described 'lads of the more advanced national views' making a 'natural graduation' from playing Gaelic football and hurling, to joining the Gaelic League and Sinn Féin and then the Irish Volunteers.[42] Meanwhile, in keeping with its strategy of seeking to control as many groups as possible, in a covert manner, the shadowy Irish Republican Brotherhood (IRB) were involved in the formation of the Irish Volunteers.[43]

However, one did not have to be as radical as Sinn Féin nor envisage revolution to join the Volunteers. The brothers Thomas and Laurence Kettle, IPP supporters, were both involved at the outset.[44] The Irish Volunteer manifesto proclaimed that they would drill, learn to use weapons and act in a disciplined manner in order 'to secure and maintain the rights and liberties common to all the people of Ireland.' They would be 'defensive and protective' and would 'not contemplate either aggression or domination'. Though disrupted by trade unionists who supported the ongoing Lockout, the meeting drew together broad nationalist opinion. Presided over by Professor Eoin MacNeill of

University College, Dublin, those present argued for Ireland to organise under arms, showing, in MacNeill's words 'courage, vigilance and discipline'. The advanced nationalist Pádraig Pearse even said that he could imagine 'circumstances in which it would be desirable and feasible' for the Irish Volunteers and UVF 'to fraternise and co-operate'. He recognised that there was a division within those assembled as to whether Ireland could achieve freedom within the British Empire. But he argued 'Ireland armed, would, at any rate, make a better bargain with the Empire than Ireland unarmed.' This was not because, he said, of any threat to Britain, but 'the moral effect' on Ireland.[45]

The Volunteers attracted around 170,000 members across Ireland, with former British soldiers playing a crucial part in training and drilling at locations throughout Dublin, and with a headquarters at 206 Great Brunswick Street.[46] In April 1914, at Wynn's Hotel in Dublin, a women's organisation, Cumann na mBan was formed to work alongside the Irish Volunteers, subsuming the Inghinidhe.[47] The Fianna Éireann (an Irish nationalist group for boys) founded in 1909 by Constance Markiewicz and Bulmer Hobson also supported the Volunteers.[48] The movement's growth led to alarm on the part of John Redmond that it might undermine constitutional politics. In June 1914, Redmond requested the Provisional Committee to take twenty-five of his nominees to ensure that the Irish Volunteers were under the IPP's control. This was initially rejected, but Redmond's supporters mounted a successful takeover of the organisation. They organised local resolutions which made clear the extent of support for Redmond within the wider movement in the country and the Executive backed down.[49]

On taking over the Volunteers, Redmond sent Thomas Kettle to Belgium to try to buy arms for the movement. He did not know that Sir Roger Casement and others had already initiated a purchase in secret.[50] Sunday 26 July 1914 signalled how the Home Rule campaign might develop in months to come. In the morning, 900 rifles and 29,000 rounds of ammunition, purchased in Hamburg by Casement, were landed from the *Asgard* (piloted by Erskine Childers[51]) at Howth by the Irish Volunteers, joined by members of the Fianna and Cumann na mBan.[52] Gerald 'Gerry' Byrne was there as a member of the 4th Dublin Battalion of the Irish Volunteers. His company was stationed at the entrance to the pier at Howth and prevented police and coastguards interfering with the landing. They were then handed rifles (though no

Figure 1.1: The Howth gun-running, 26 July 1914. Members of Fianna Éireann and the Irish Volunteers transporting guns in a cart. (Image Courtesy of the National Library of Ireland, NPA ASG2).

ammunition) and marched into the city.[53] Patrick Egan, also of the 4th battalion, recalled 'wild cheers' as the guns were landed and then 'singing ourselves hoarse' on their way to the city.[54]

In parading towards the city centre the Volunteers assumed, according to the *Evening Herald*, 'that they could do as had been done by the Ulster Volunteers, who parade openly in the streets of Belfast with machine guns and rifles'. However, the 2nd King's Own Scottish Borderers had other ideas and intercepted the Volunteers at Clontarf. A scuffle ensued, with shots fired, until the Volunteers dispersed. Inside the city, tensions were high as news spread. The Borderers were jeered by crowds as they returned to barracks and missiles were thrown at them. In Bachelors Walk, they charged with bayonets and fired shots, hitting between fifty and a hundred, killing three outright. The *Herald* condemned an 'unparalleled outrage committed by British soldiers in the streets of the Irish capital'. The *Evening Telegraph* said 'there never has been, in the history of Dublin, a greater outrage'.[55] The *Dublin Evening Mail*, though talking of the soldiers firing on a 'Dublin Mob', drew a distinction between how the British army treated parading by Ulster Volunteers and how it treated Nationalists. It condemned the government's policy roundly as being a 'remarkable discrimination', symptomatic of a 'policy of drift, with strange intervals of waking up and going to sleep again'. The *Irish Independent* argued that 'In all the annals of British misgovernment in this country nothing has ever happened transcending in sheer brutality the murders committed by the military yesterday in the streets of Dublin.' Even the Unionist *Irish Times* could not find any reason to condemn the Volunteers since they were only seeking to do what the UVF did in Belfast. Instead, the paper blamed 'an attack on His Majesty's troops' by a 'slum crowd'. Some policemen refused orders to disarm Volunteers and rumours spread that the 5th (Royal Irish) Lancers had been ordered on to the streets to quell disorder but had refused.[56]

That rumour fed the distinction between 'British' and 'Irish' soldiers, which grew further when it emerged that one of those killed, Mary Duffy, had a son, Thomas Tighe, serving in the Dublin Fusiliers. He wrote to the *Herald* calling on members of his regiment and 'all other Irish soldiers in Dublin' to attend her funeral.[57] The *Freeman's Journal* was also keen to ensure that opprobrium for the Borderers did not spread to the other regiments stationed in Dublin.[58] The funerals continued to grab the front pages as the threat of European war grew. With the strength of the UVF in Ulster, and the action they could take if the Westminster government passed Home Rule, prospects of a civil war in Ireland were greater in the minds of many Irish people than the likelihood of a conflict on the continent. However, news first of Russian mobilisation and then a German declaration of war changed everything.[59]

2 DUBLIN GOES TO WAR

It was certainly a novel and hopeful sign of the times to hear each mention of the King's name greeted with cheers by an audience composed in the main of Irish Nationalists.
> The Irish Times on Asquith and Redmond at the Mansion House, 25 September 1914[1]

Difficulties, Opportunities

In the early months of the First World War, Dublin mobilised on a massive scale. Regular soldiers were already serving, while reservists were called to the colours. Volunteers joined many units of the British army, of which the best known were the 7th Royal Dublin Fusiliers, even though most went elsewhere. Women (and some men) joined the British Red Cross Society. Voluntary enterprise was unleashed in support of men at the front. In Dublin, some of this was only possible because of the dominance of Parliamentary nationalism and its decision to back the war effort. When the United Kingdom formally went to war with Germany at 11pm on 4 August 1914, in response to German threats to Belgian neutrality, mainstream nationalist politics might have been thrown into turmoil, threatening the unity in its ranks. A traditional nationalist view, associated first with Daniel O'Connell in the 1850s, was that 'England's difficulty is Ireland's opportunity'.[2] Indeed, almost as soon as the war began the IRB started to plan, dependent on German support, for what would become the Easter Rising.[3]

Yet the mood among most in Ireland was supportive of the British war effort. In Dublin the strength of Parliamentary nationalism significantly influenced recruiting. On 3 August, speaking in the House of Commons on the likelihood of war and the challenges facing the UK, the foreign secretary, Sir Edward Grey, said, 'The one bright spot in the whole of this terrible situation is Ireland.'[4] This was partly fuelled by agreement from the unionist leader Edward Carson on 30 July to suspend discussion of the Amending Bill which sought to exclude Ulster from Home Rule, followed by his statement that the UVF were 'willing and ready to give their services for home defence, and many will be willing to serve anywhere they are required'.[5] John Redmond responded to Grey in extremely supportive terms in the Commons, saying,

> In past times when this Empire has been engaged in these terrible enterprises, it is true ... the sympathy of the Nationalists of Ireland, for reasons to be found deep down in the centuries of history, has been estranged from this country. Allow me to say that what has occurred in recent years has altered the situation completely.

He offered the Irish Volunteers for the defence of Irish shores, saying that the government

> may to-morrow withdraw every one of their troops from Ireland. I say that the coast of Ireland will be defended from foreign invasion by her armed sons, and for this purpose armed Nationalist Catholics in the South will be only too glad to join arms with the armed Protestant Ulstermen in the North.[6]

This tone was echoed in the national press which stated – as nationalists would always be prone to imagine – that such co-operation in war offered hope for political unity in peace.[7]

However, unity was threatened as the government decided what to do about the main Home Rule Bill. Carson imagined it would be postponed with the Amending Bill, while Redmond believed it would be passed rapidly. That did not happen until 18 September with Royal Assent, but also suspension for the duration of the war.[8] The passage of Home Rule allowed Redmond to address head-on the fact that nationalist enlistment appeared sluggish because they were not, unlike the UVF, enlisting in one division.[9] Redmond had announced in mid-

September that he wanted to see an 'Irish Brigade' to keep Irish soldiers together, deliberately using a phrase that was resonant of previous Irish service in war.[10] Two days after Home Rule's Royal Assent he took a further step, at Woodenbridge, County Wicklow. He told a meeting of the East Wicklow Irish Volunteers that the Irish Volunteers had a 'two-fold duty' to defend Ireland and also to take up arms 'wherever the firing line extends in defence of the right of freedom and religion in this war'.[11]

There had been no sign of hostility within the Irish Volunteers to Redmond's statement that the Volunteers would defend Irish shores.[12] However, by late August some were opposing calls for Volunteers to join the British army. With Home Rule yet to be passed, the editorial of *The Irish Volunteer* on 29 August said it was not clear whether or not it would be and 'The only active service for a Volunteer is active service if necessary to rout out the current invader first and then defend our country at any cost.'[13] That attitude did not change once Home Rule was placed on the Statute Book. A meeting of the Irish Volunteers' Provisional Committee at the headquarters of the Irish Volunteers in Kildare Street was called by Eoin MacNeill for 24 September. Stating that Redmond had not consulted with any part of the Volunteer movement before making his Woodenbridge speech, the committee expelled Redmond's nominees from the Provisional Committee because Redmond had advised the Volunteers 'to take foreign service under a Government which is not Irish'. That, the committee argued, was a violation of the aims of the Irish Volunteers.[14]

A series of meetings followed around Ireland. These resulted in approximately 93% of the Volunteers across Ireland backing Redmond (158,360 to 12,306), and immediately forming the National Volunteers. Meanwhile, the prospect of an 'Irish Brigade' was opened up by Kitchener's decisions first to form the 16th (Irish) Division from troops recruited in Ireland, and then to clear space in one brigade (the 47th) for men from the National Volunteers to be drafted into battalions together.[15] By the end of October, with the National Volunteers working from offices in Parnell Square while the Irish Volunteers remained in Kildare Street, the split's impact became clear.[16] Despite the vast majority of volunteers across Ireland backing Redmond, a sizeable proportion in Dublin city did not do so: 4,850 supported Redmond, and 1,900 (28%) were for MacNeill. There was even a majority for

MacNeill in two of the battalions: 500 to 230 in the 1st and 750 to 100 in the 2nd.[17] Oscar Traynor was a Dublin-born former Belfast Celtic footballer, working as a printer and living in Jones Road. He recalled that 'The division took place immediately' and the men simply continued as they had done, but in different organisations. In the Irish Volunteers, Traynor was elected as a lieutenant.[18]

Both the strength and vulnerability of Redmond's position were seen on the evening of Friday 25 September when he was joined by Prime Minister Herbert Asquith and the Lord Mayor of Dublin at a public meeting in Dublin's Mansion House. Showing a united front to boost the war effort, Asquith and Redmond spoke of the end of animosity between Britain and Ireland. *The Irish Times* commented, 'It was certainly a novel and hopeful sign of the times to hear each mention of the King's name greeted with cheers by an audience composed in the main of Irish Nationalists.' Redmond's speech focused on the 'fight for small nations' saying that Ireland had 'been profoundly moved by the horror and sufferings of Belgium'. Faced with this, he said, 'there never was a war in which higher and nobler issues were at stake'. However, rumours had circulated that suffragettes and Labour or militant nationalists might disrupt the meeting and a guard of 400 Redmondite Irish Volunteers combined with police were needed to ensure that the meeting was secure.[19] Two days later the funeral took place of a victim of the Bachelors Walk shooting who had died of wounds after being in hospital since July. It was a stark reminder of how little unity there had been only recently.[20]

Beyond the split in the Volunteers, signs of outright nationalist opposition to the war were limited. Francis and Hanna Sheehy-Skeffington organised anti-war meetings in Dublin, but they attracted little support and some violent opposition. The *Freeman's Journal* described how on the day of Asquith's visit, Francis Sheehy-Skeffington had handed out leaflets at St Stephen's Green and attempted to make a speech after climbing up on railings. The paper said the crowd was hostile and that the police, 'for Mr. Sheehy Skeffington's own protection, placed him in a cab, and drive him off to the College Street police station, amid the jeers and laughter of the crowd'.[21] Anti-recruiting leaflets were distributed in Howth on 18 September and Dundrum on 26 September.[22] At a meeting of the Dublin Corporation on 2 November some councillors voiced opposition to Redmond when asked to pass a resolution congratulating him on the passage of Home Rule. Alderman Thomas Kelly argued that the Home Rule Act 'was a disgraceful and sorrowful ending to fifty years of parliamentary action'. Another called Home Rule 'a recruiting dodge to fight for a flag which had floated over and caused the misery of Ireland'.[23] Yet the mood within nationalism was firmly with Redmond. The police concluded at the end of August that 'general opinion', as with that of the IPP, was 'on the side of the Government in the War'.[24]

Encounters

As the war began and developed, it was encountered by Dubliners in a series of events and experiences. Some changes were immediate. In the first days of the war, Thomas Moylan, who worked in an asylum, noticed how civilian wireless telegraphy installations on the corner of Abbey Street and Sackville Street were dismantled in keeping with government restrictions. He also noted that 'horses are being collected by the Government from all and sundry' with the Lucan Dairy losing seven immediately. Meanwhile, newspapers 'sold like wild-fire', while '"Soldiers" is the one and only game of all the youth in the City at present' and there was panic-buying.[25] In little more than a week it became apparent that censorship was preventing much news of the activities of the army and navy. A belief that newspapers were not telling the full story meant that rumours could circulate, such as one 'that the Black Watch and some Irish regiments had been wiped out'. Other rumours included one 'that the Cossacks are being brought round by seas from Archangel to Aberdeen, there to be entrained for the South of England' from where they would cross the Channel 'so as to take the Germans in the rear'. That claim circulated for about three weeks.[26] None of these rumours came from newspapers, but later in the year heavier restrictions were placed on reporting under the terms of the Defence of the Realm Act. In Dublin, seven newspapers were felt to be 'of doubtful loyalty'. Three closed themselves, two fell into line, and two were shut.[27]

Germans in Dublin faced immediate problems. Around one hundred were arrested over 12 and 13 August and held 'pending explanations as to their bonafides, or the giving of guarantees that they will do no illegal act or render any assistance to the enemy'. Such a declaration needed to be supported by an undertaking from two British subjects that they would be responsible for the behaviour of a specific German.[28] On 15 August there were attacks on pork butchers' shops owned by George Reitz in South Circular Road and Frederick Lang in Wexford Street. The police arrested those responsible, charging them with malicious damage and being part of 'a riotous and disorderly mob'.[29] However, when appeals were made by Lang and Reitz for compensation under the Local Government (Ireland) Act of 1898, their cases were dismissed on the basis that they were enemy aliens and any rights they might have were suspended for the duration of the war. Lang's lawyer argued that he had been in Ireland for twenty-three years, during which time he had paid rates on his property. Lang had an Irish wife and children, and planned to remain in Ireland. Though not a British subject he had rights of domicile and was not subject to being called for service in the German army. The lawyer for the Dublin Corporation argued that it was clear that no enemy alien had rights to sue in a British court, and that Lang could have applied for naturalisation but had chosen not to do so. In dismissing the case, the court's Recorder said that 'I deprecate the attack' and said that it was 'an unfortunate circumstance' that it had happened. However, 'at the time I suppose there was a good deal of feeling, and certainly it is very mild compared with what occurred in Berlin'. He went on to say that the authorities had ensured that the premises were 'protected ever since' and that Lang 'had been able to carry on with his business'. In dismissing Reitz's case the Recorder stressed that 'While carrying out the law, he strongly disapproved of the slightest want of fair play towards alien enemies.'[30] Two weeks later, several of those charged were convicted of riot and unlawful assembly. The court Recorder argued, 'Whether a man was a German or an Austrian, if he was in this country for some time, he was entitled to protection.' The prosecuting barrister said he was glad that it would be 'understood that the property of Germans could not be attacked. It is not cricket.' The sentence was, in theory, one of two years' hard labour for those found guilty, but that was clearly meant as a deterrent to others since it was suspended for two years. Moreover, although the Recorder made it clear that 'if there was the slightest interference by these accused with Mr. Lang or Mr. Reitz' the sentence would be imposed, it was only held over the guilty until 19 November.[31]

Meanwhile, the courts pursued 'enemy aliens' vigorously when they were said to be evading regulations. Adolphus Atter had been reporting to the police every second day as required since the outbreak of war, but in October 1914 he had changed his residence from Chelmsford Road to Fitzwilliam Square without telling the police. He was discharged with a £5 fine. The case of Edward Taverner of Rathgar Road raised the question of whether he was German or French. Having been born in Germany to French parents, British courts technically viewed him as German. However, his solicitor argued that German law granted citizenship by descent, while French law said that someone was French if they had French parents wherever they were born. During the hearing his lawyer won laughter by saying that he 'was fairly driven to the conclusion that the man was of no nationality at all'. Pointing out that Taverner spoke no German, but did speak French and had a French name, he successfully argued that both German and French law should apply and Taverner was discharged as a 'friendly alien'.[32]

Such cases were heard while newspapers presented stories of German atrocities on the Western Front, some of them coming from the former nationalist MP Thomas Kettle.[33] The first big story was the burning of Louvain in late August 1914. Buildings destroyed by the flames included churches and an ancient library in what the *Freeman's Journal* described as an 'unpardonable act of barbarity and vandalism'. An eyewitness described how 'The beautiful town, with its noble buildings, was a sea of flame. Dead bodies lay thick in the streets. Dreadful cries came from many of the houses.' Stories of anarchy circulated, with tales of looting, and of people burned to death in their homes and shot in the streets. Fifty civilians (men and women) were said to have been shot in one batch by firing squad.[34] Stories from the front line included accounts of violence against civilians and prisoners. Private 9577 Andy Ford of the 2nd Dublins had been working on a dairy farm at the war's outbreak but was called up as a reservist. He told the *Irish Times* how after his battalion's first encounter with German troops 'they saw the villages all around them in flames and the frightened peasants running for their lives'. Ford described a hospital at St Quentin which 'was destroyed by a German shell, though it contained three hundred wounded soldiers at the time'. Ford claimed this was not untypical as he had 'heard of several instances where the Germans had shelled hospitals, and the convents of the Nursing Sisters, even though they had the Red Cross flying'. Meanwhile, he said members of the Royal Army Medical Corps 'were attacked the same as ordinary soldiers, and he was told, though he did not see it – that members of this corps had their hands cut off by the German soldiers'.[35] Many of these stories implied that Germans were specifically attacking the Catholic church. That sense was amplified in September with the burning of Rheims cathedral, described by the *Freeman's Journal* as a 'German crime against civilisation'. Again, this story included references to violence against nuns who were said to be 'dead on the floor of the Cathedral their white faces set with the sublimity of their Faith'.[36]

These stories might well have influenced the welcome given to Belgian refugees with the Mansion House, Sandymount Castle and Stradbrook Hall all opening their doors early on. By the end of 1914, Joseph Halpin of Glasthule was receiving wounded Belgian soldiers at Gowran Hall. In time, 3,000 Belgian refugees were welcomed to Ireland across the war, a relatively small proportion of the 250,000 who found their way to the UK as a whole.[37] A flag day for the 'Belgian Relief Fund' was held in Dublin on 18 September.[38] Around eighty refugees reached Dublin by boat from England on 20 October. The day before, a Belgian Refugees Committee had met to make arrangements and it continued to meet for at least the next year.[39] On arrival, the refugees were given breakfast by a railway company before being dispatched to different locations – around fifty to Laytown in County Meath, twenty to Sandymount Castle and the rest to a range of different places. A report in the *Irish Times* stressed that the refugees were clean and well-dressed (having been furnished with basics in England) but had very few possessions. They were accompanied by Belgian priests and were said to be keen to return home eventually. The refugees brought further tales of horrors with them. One from Termonde told of how four civilians 'had their feet smashed by the butt-ends of rifles by the Germans, who did not kill them till they had put their eyes out'.[40]

Hosting refugees was not without problems and in January 1915 the Belgian Refugees Committee considered complaints from two hosts 'in regard to the unsatisfactory conduct of certain refugees'. The unspecified problems appear to have been dealt with and they did not come up again at future meetings.[41] Later efforts to support Belgian refugees included the opening of a gift shop in Grafton Street in July 1916.[42] However, there was a steady decline of numbers in Ireland at any one time as the war progressed: 1,426 in March 1915, 938 a year later, around 600 in March 1917 and 527 by March 1918. This decline was probably due to Belgians returning home, some to enlist and others just trying to rebuild their lives, possibly driven back by some general hostility to foreigners in general. Others took up war work in Britain. Only ninety appear to have remained in Ireland after the war.[43]

In addition to help for refugees, Dubliners supported the war effort in other practical ways. Some of that related to the war's first Christmas, with the Royal Dublin Fusiliers' Bureau in Kildare Street collecting donations from individuals and organised groups. These ranged from clothing and cigarettes to plum puddings.[44] Similar work was done in 1915 by the 'Women's Branch' of the City and County of Dublin Recruiting Committee.[45] By late January 1915 plans were being put in place for copies of the *Weekly Freeman*, enclosing sprigs of shamrock, to be sent to soldiers at the front for St Patrick's Day two months later.[46] Munitions production grew steadily, bringing some limited work to the city though across Ireland, National Shell Factories would employ little more than 2,000.[47] The requisitioning of hay by the military caused problems for County Dublin farmers.[48]

Dublin also soon encountered the war through wounded soldiers. By early 1915 large batches of men were arriving by boat, five hundred or more at a time. They were dispatched to a range of hospitals in the city, principally Richmond War Hospital, King George V Hospital, Dublin Castle Hospital and (from May 1916) the Portobello Military Hospital. Another eighteen hospitals in the city took in wounded military.[49] German prisoners also passed through the city,[50] but the visitors who were most celebrated were medal winners. No Dubliner won a Victoria Cross during the war but the city found a connection with Lance Corporal Frederick Holmes of the King's Own Yorkshire Light Infantry. Marking Holmes' award of the VC in January 1915, the *Irish Independent* pointed out that 'Prior to the war he was stationed in Dublin, and married a Dublin girl.'[51] The city also hosted events for Victoria Cross winners visiting Ireland. Egyptian-born Corporal Issy Smith of the Manchester Regiment found himself in the Dublin University Voluntary Aid Detachment (VAD)

Auxiliary Hospital in August 1915, having been gassed about a month after winning his VC. Smith was Jewish and the *Evening Mail* told how 'the Jews of Dublin' were proud of him as 'the first Jew in the British Isles to win such a distinction', and made it their business to visit and entertain him during his stay in the city.[52] 2nd Lieutenant Arthur Boyd-Rochfort of the 1st Scots Guards arrived at the North Wall on his way home to Westmeath and was greeted by a small but enthusiastic crowd: '"One does not meet a V.C. every day," joyously declared one of the ladies as the vessel swung into her berth.'[53]

The highest-profile Irish Victoria Cross was Lance Corporal 3556 Michael O'Leary, from Macroom, County Cork. He won the VC serving in the 1st Irish Guards at Cuinchy in February 1915, storming a German position during an attempted advance, killing eight and capturing two.[54] As he travelled home on leave in Ireland in June he was hailed as a hero at Dublin's North Wall.[55] On his return through Dublin he was greeted with a civic reception, a theatre visit and meetings with local dignitaries. At this point, O'Leary spurned requests to take part in recruiting meetings. It was said that he was 'no speaker' and that 'if there is anything he could be said to fear it is attending a public meeting'.[56] However, in December, by then promoted to be a lieutenant in the Connaught Rangers, O'Leary spoke at a recruiting meeting in Kingstown (now Dún Laoghaire) and featured on a recruiting poster which said '1 Irishman defeats 10 Germans'.[57]

Joining Up

Regular soldiers from Dublin were already serving as war broke out, particularly in the 1st and 2nd Royal Dublin Fusiliers, with the 1st in India and the 2nd at Gravesend. Dubliners who were members of the Army Reserve or Special Reserve joined their battalions over 4–6 August. Thomas Moylan noted how on 5 August, 'during a performance at the Theatre Royal, when the cinema pictures were on, there was thrown on the screen an order that reservists in the building should immediately start for head quarters'. That same evening, 'an immense body of reservists left the City to rejoin; they were accompanied to the North Wall by a crowd estimated at 50,000 people'.[58] Many of those, like Irish Volunteer Private 7360 James Gosson who had led the Skerries branch of the Irish Volunteers in their drills in 1914, joined regulars in the 1st and 2nd Dublins.[59] There was an immediate impact on the ranks of the Irish Volunteers. The police reported on 1 September that 'nearly all the instructors are ex-army men. A good number of these have now gone to the war' with the result that by the end of September there was 'a great falling off in enthusiasm' for Volunteer drilling and marching.[60]

Recruiting offices were open initially in Great Brunswick Street (targeting ex-soldiers)[61] and then another in late September at 86 Grafton Street in the wake of Asquith's Mansion House appearance. On its first day of business, recruiting was said by the *Irish Times* to be slow. Indeed, immediately after the Mansion House meeting 'a crowd of considerable dimensions' gathered outside and 'When the first young man entered to have his name enrolled he was boohed by the crowd.' The *Dublin Evening Mail* reported that some of the crowd 'were shouting for the Kaiser and the Germans'.[62] However, the office became busier within a few days, initially recruiting only for the 8th Dublins. The *Irish Times* described how, following medical examinations on the building's top floor, those who had met the requirements completed paperwork:

> Then, with Testaments in their hands, they swore allegiance to the King and his heirs, repeating the oath phrase by phrase after a stalwart sergeant. A few words were then addressed to the new soldiers by Colonel Cronin, who reminded them of the traditions of the Royal Dublin Fusiliers, and exhorted them to do credit to "the old Toughs", and deal adequately with the Prussians.[63]

Recruitment levels did not satisfy all. The *Irish Times* reported on 16 October that although setbacks for the allies had usually led to an increase in recruitment, that had not been the case in Dublin following the fall of Antwerp. A possible reason was that 'The circulation of anti-enlistment handbills is again in evidence, and "peaceful persuasion", it is reported, is threatened for those who go to enlist.' The newspaper also reported that 'the toll of rejections of medical grounds was heavy' and cited one case where a man had passed his medical but withdrew when his friends did not do so.[64] At both Grafton Street and Great Brunswick Street valvular disease of the heart was said to be leading to 'an extraordinary number' of rejections.[65] As recruitment continued into 1915 public meetings were held under the auspices of the City and County of Dublin Recruiting Committee, with politicians and businessmen, as well as serving soldiers and military bands.[66] Following the establishment of the Central Council for the Organization of Recruiting in Ireland in early 1915, generic UK-wide posters and adverts were replaced with messages more specific to Ireland.[67] These called for men to join the army (note the 'army' and not the 'British army') to defend the rights of small nations with particular reference to the trials of the Belgians.[68]

Beyond the cause for which men were said to be fighting, Dubliners were appealed to on the basis of joining specific units. The most prominent was the 7th Dublin Fusiliers, the 'Pals', and specifically its D Company. Pals battalions were the norm for recruitment in the north of England, with groups of men who knew each other enlisting together, but the 'Pals' label was not otherwise used in Ireland. D Company's origins lay in the Irish Rugby Football Union Volunteers, first mooted on the war's second day by Francis Henry Browning, the Irish Rugby Football Union's President.[69] Initially conceiving of the unit as being for home defence, Browning urged members to join the army where their circumstances allowed. In August there was no plan for mass enlistment in the army with men instead drilling and taking part in basic military instruction after work. They drilled first on 24 August, then at 6pm and 8pm every evening.[70] However, in early September with numbers at around 250,[71] Lieutenant Colonel Geoffrey Downing, a former Monkstown rugby player and newly appointed as commander of the 7th Dublins, issued a public appeal to the Irish Rugby Football Union Volunteers. He said that he would keep D Company of his battalion for them, 'but I cannot keep open long'. At the same time he stressed that the 1st City of Dublin cadets were joining the battalion 'as a body', raising the idea of mass enlistment.[72] Meanwhile, a newspaper appeal was made to the 'Young Men of Dublin' to join the 'Dublin "Pals" Battalion'. Headed 'Dublin Men Serve with your Friends', the advert claimed that 'Lord Kitchener is very disappointed at the slowness with which the Irish Division in the New Army is filling up.' It was said that 'Friends who wish to serve together may enlist by Sections, Platoons, or Companies, and so far as possible they will be kept together in the Seventh Battalion.'[73] Such an appeal was even heard by men who had already enlisted: Richard Patrick 'Paddy' Tobin was a student at Trinity College when he enlisted on 6 August, applying for a commission and specifically

Figure 2.1: 1st Dublin Battalion, Irish Association of Volunteer Training Corps, autumn 1914. Volunteers in civilian clothes, rifles over shoulder, on a country road, possibly south County Dublin. The officer in front is probably Francis Henry Browning. (Image Courtesy of the National Library of Ireland, NPA FID).

requesting that he join the East Kent Regiment, known as 'the Buffs'. Yet he too joined the Pals later that month.[74] Enlistment in the Pals was unusually middle-class for an infantry battalion.[75] It was also a clear example of men choosing to join a battalion along with friends from a sense of 'collective sacrifice' and belonging.[76]

The first departure of men came on 16 September when 110 rugby players assembled on Trinity College's parade ground before marching to Kingsbridge Station for a train journey to the Curragh.[77] The *Evening Mail* reported that 'A very stirring spectacle was witnessed in College Green, where a vast crowd had assembled. Union Jacks were vigorously waved, and the cheering was incessant ... while at Kingsbridge the sturdy athletes were greeted with a remarkable ovation.' Much was made of the men assembled being 'our famous footballers'.[78]

Among the Pals was Poole Henry Hickman. He was born in Kilrush, County Clare, but had been living in Dublin for several years due to his work as a barrister. Hickman was a well-known rugby player as captain of the Wanderers 1st XV in 1908–9. He had enlisted on 14 September 1914 as a private but just a few days after leaving Dublin with the Pals was commissioned in the battalion. He became a captain on 7 January 1915 and was given command of D Company.[79] An even bigger rugby star in the battalion was Private 14160 Jasper Brett, who had played once for Ireland against Wales during the 1914 Five Nations tournament. Played at Belfast's Balmoral Showgrounds, Ireland's final match in the competition had become known as 'The Battle of Balmoral' due to violent conduct by several players.[80] Brett was from Kingstown – he was born there and lived at 18 Crosthwaite Park – and enlisted on 14 September 1914, while working as a clerk in his father's firm of solicitors.[81]

The 7th Dublins dominated all coverage of the 10th (Irish) Division which was the first volunteer division to be recruited in Ireland.[82] The division drew from across the island, but it did contain another battalion of the Royal Dublin Fusiliers, the 6th. Among those joining the 6th was Noël Drury of Swift Brook House, Saggart, County Dublin, and a former student of Trinity College. He had applied for a commission twice in October, after joining the Dublin University Officers' Training Corps in September, only for both applications to be lost. He then applied again in late November 1914, simply requesting 'Some Irish Regiment' though a month later he expressed a preference for the Connaught Rangers and briefly joined the 5th Connaughts before being transferred to the 6th Dublins.[83] He became that battalion's most important chronicler through a personal diary kept throughout the war.[84]

The newspaper attention to the 7th at the expense of the 6th would later become a cause for complaint by some in the latter battalion.[85] The 6th Dublins had a looser connection to the Dublin area than the 7th,[86] its social background was less middle-class than the 7th,[87] and it did not have the glamour of rugby stars joining, which perhaps influenced the newspaper coverage. From the start, all but one of its companies had at least two captains who had served in the army or the police, including several who were ex-Dublin Fusiliers.[88] Perhaps those different backgrounds also affected relationships between the 6th and 7th Dublins: Drury noted in mid-1915, 'It is an interesting fact that our battalion, officers and men, are far more chummy with the 6th Munsters than with our own sister battalion, the 7th R.D.F., but so it has been since the start.'[89]

Figure 2.2: Noël Drury, 6th Royal Dublin Fusiliers. (Image Courtesy of the Council of the National Army Museum, NAM 1976–07-69–1).

Statistics of Service

Across the war as many as 210,000 Irishmen served in the British forces. Among these, around 21,000 were regular soldiers, already in the armed forces as war began. Another 30,000 were members of the Army Reserve or Special Reserve who were mobilised at the outbreak.[90] As many as 6,500 of the regulars and 6,900 of the reservists could have been from Dublin.[91] In Dublin (the city only[92]), police figures suggest that 26,538 men volunteered for the British army by the end of the war. Of over 23,438 who had joined by mid-January 1918, 13,254 were known to be Catholic, 3,432 known to be Protestant, while the denomination of the remaining 6,752 was not known. Also up to mid-January 1918, National Volunteers accounted for 3,012 with Ulster Volunteers another 16, meaning that the vast bulk, 20,410, had no known volunteer background. The peak month for army recruitment across the UK and also in Dublin was September 1914 when 3,091 enlisted. In the rest of the war, only April 1915 would top a thousand. Wednesday 2 September 1914 was the busiest day of the entire war for joining the army in Dublin: 222 men enlisted. By mid-December, one-quarter of the total of Dublin's total wartime recruits had enlisted, and 40% by June 1915. Two-thirds had enlisted by the middle of April 1916. By the end of the war, Dublin's total recruits for the army represented around one-fifth of Ireland's total of 123,724, almost twice its share of the population.[93]

In other branches of the services, the Royal Navy and Royal Naval Reserve secured 1,978 recruits from the Dublin Metropolitan Police District from 4 August 1914 to 15 August 1917 which was 32% of those recruited across Ireland in that time. Another 250 joined the Navy in 1918 along with 830 joining the air force. As war broke out there were 5,100 recruited in Ireland already serving in the navy and if the same percentage had been recruited in Dublin as during wartime then of those, 1,632 would have been from Dublin.[94] Meanwhile, a small number of men served far beyond British forces. One unusual case, Alexandre Raoult, had lived in Dublin since 1901 and was a member of the Leinster and North-End Flying Club and Dublin Pigeon Society. He was described as having 'answered France's mobilisation call' on 10 August 1914 and served in the 28th Infantry of the French army's 53rd Brigade.[95]

In the research for this book, 38,714 individual records of British military service[96] were identified overall. Of the total, certainly 12,225 are duplicates (of 6,980 individulals). Another 1,541 are possible duplicates, which means that between and 24,948 and 26,489 individuals were identified. All but twenty of these were men. Due to the destruction of around two-thirds of service records in the London Blitz,[97] it is likely that there were roughly another 10,321 who served and who could not be identified elsewhere, putting levels of service by

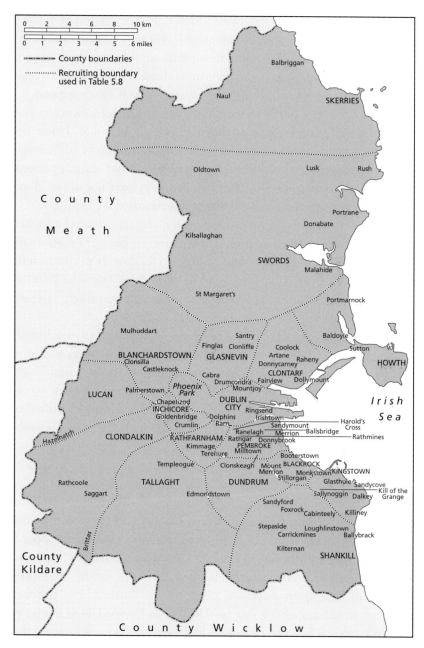

Map 2.1: County of Dublin – key places and areas for recruiting (See Table A5.8).
Drawn by David Cox.

Dubliners at around 35,000 at least.[98] That is without factoring in army officers beyond those already identified whose records cannot be searched by place, and also some naval and air records which cannot be similarly searched or do not include an address.[99] These would nudge the total of 35,000 towards official figures, which reach 40,000.[100] Otherwise, the gap is partly in the nature of any project seeking to find 'all' who served, simply because they will not all be found. However, even at the time it was believed that police figures might be inaccurate. As a 1916 parliamentary report said, police figures 'may include persons who have left home ostensibly to enlist, but who have not in fact done so, or have been rejected, and who have not returned'.[101]

As part of the county of Dublin, the city contributed a higher share of the recruits than its population share. In the 1911 Census its population was 63% of the county (Table A1.1), but its proportion of recruits was just over 70%. Nearly 13% more came from the suburbs south-east of the city, in the 'Pembroke' area, and another 7% from Kingstown, meaning that just under 10% came from the rest of the County (Table A5.8). Of those Dubliners who served in the British military, 6,568 have been verified as killed or died in service, from the outbreak of the war until the Commonwealth War Graves Commission stopped considering deaths as 'war deaths' at the end of August 1921. The figure might be around 10% higher with over 600 more identified as possibly dead but not possible to verify through the most reliable sources.[102] The heaviest losses were seen in 1916, with 1,656 dead. Across the war, the 'France and Flanders' theatre accounted for 4,517, nearly 70% of the total. Nearly 10% died at 'home' somewhere in the UK, often in hospitals suffering from wounds. Gallipoli accounted for nearly 500 and almost 400 died at sea. Dublin's worst month of the war was May 1915, with 387 dead, principally because of the Second Battle of Ypres, but also due to Gallipoli. Another month saw over 300 deaths: September 1916, which included the 16th (Irish) Division's involvement in a more successful phase of the Battle of the Somme. The worst single day of the war for Dublin, as for the UK as a whole, was 1 July 1916, when 116 Dubliners lost their lives, 111 of those on the Somme. Many were part of the 36th (Ulster) Division. Losses reached one hundred on one other day of the war: 21 March 1918, the first day of the German spring offensive. Other costly days included 24 May 1915 (75), through a combination of the Second Battle of Ypres and Gallipoli, and 16 August 1917 (87) because of

Passchendaele.[103] Fifty-eight civilian Dubliners were killed because of the war (seventeen of them women). Forty-four of them were killed in one day, 10 October 1918, as the RMS *Leinster* was sunk, and another five in the sinking of a fishing vessel.[104]

Details of the type of British unit in which individuals served are available for 23,957 people (Table A2.1). Around 55% of these served in Irish infantry regiments, and another 9% in English, Scottish or Welsh infantry regiments. The remaining one-third saw service in a range of branches of service, around 21% in non-infantry units of the British army, principally the Artillery, Army Service Corps, Royal Engineers and Royal Army Medical Corps. Those who flew or who served at sea were around 4% each. Half of those who served in Irish infantry regiments (Table A2.2) served in the Royal Dublin Fusiliers, followed by nearly 12% in the Royal Irish Rifles. The first division of service is known for nearly 8,500 of these men (Table A2.3), of whom one-quarter were in the 16th (Irish) Division, and approximately 15% each in the 4th and 10th (Irish) divisions. At least 177 Dubliners served in the 36th (Ulster) Division as originally formed. A specific Irish infantry battalion in which a soldier first served is known for over 10,000 men (the number being higher than that for divisions because the data includes reserve battalions). They served in 94 different battalions, with 50 or more Dubliners identified in each of 44 different battalions, covering every Irish infantry regiment. Over 1,000 served in the 2nd Royal Dublin Fusiliers, and nearly 800 in the 1st Dublins. The volunteer battalion with the largest number of Dubliners was the 8th Dublins at 708, followed by the 9th Dublins at 540. Both battalions were part of the 16th (Irish) Division on the Western Front. Marginally more men who were identified served in the 2nd Royal Irish Rifles than in Dublin's most famous battalion, the 7th Royal Dublin Fusiliers (438 to 430).[105]

While many men enlisting afresh joined the Dublin Fusiliers, many others would join a wide range of units (Tables A2.1 and A2.2). Meanwhile, the Dublin Fusiliers were supplemented by men joining up throughout the UK. Figures exist for recruitment to specific regiments across the army between January and October 1915. Over that time, nearly half of 4,508 who enlisted in the regiment joined in Dublin, and another quarter in other areas of Ireland. But Scotland accounted for 14%, with Glasgow looming large, and England's 'Western' area contributing 8%, the largest number in Liverpool.

London gave a further 5%.[106] Of course, some of these men could have been from Dublin and were briefly away from home, enlisting wherever they were. Others might have been part of the wider Irish diaspora, perhaps specifically a Dublin diaspora, and for them enlistment in the Dublin Fusiliers might have represented a homecoming of sorts. Pointers to what was taking place in recruitment to the regiment can be seen in a sample of 3,045 men from service records whose first war service was with the Dublin Fusiliers. Of those, 1,810 were living in Dublin and all but 76 of them had enlisted in the city or county. Another 89 were not living in Dublin but had enlisted there. Of the remaining 1,146 (over one-third), there is information on both place of enlistment and place of birth for 428 (Table A5.7). Strikingly, only 8% were born in Dublin, and another 45% in other parts of Ireland. Yet the limit of the statistics is that we cannot know how many of those born outside Ireland were second-generation migrants who attached some significance to joining an Irish regiment.

As men enlisted, a vast amount of information was gathered on their service records. This included hair and eye colour, even complexion, plus any marks or distinguishing features. Among the latter were descriptions of tattoos, almost all on forearms, the most popular being anchors, crosses, female figures, initials, hearts, and two traditional Irish designs: two hands clasped around a heart, and a harp and shamrock combination. Religious denominations were found on the army records of over 5,600 men joining the ranks (Table A5.6). Roman Catholics were nearly 89% of these recruits (compared to a population of 83% in the city and 71% in the country). However, since it is not possible to gather comprehensive and reliable data for officers, who were more middle-class and therefore more likely to be Protestant, the difference between share of the population and recruitment by religious denomination is likely to be smaller, and possibly even more in favour of Protestants joining.[107]

Service records also noted physical measurements. The average height of army recruits was 5 feet, 5 and 4/5 inches (Table A3.1). Members of the Irish Guards were, on average, three inches taller than the rest of the army. An average Body Mass Index (BMI) of 20.8 puts men on the lean side of what today would be regarded as healthy (18.5 to 24.9, Tables A3.2 and A3.3). Members of the artillery were the stockiest, being more than an inch shorter than the average but having the highest average BMI (Tables A3.1 and A3.3).

The information on civilian occupations which was gathered for this book does not generally include army officers, so overstates in particular the presence of unskilled labourers in the army overall and understates white-collar workers. Yet the data gives a clear illustration of the situation in the ranks of the military (Table A4.1). For example, unskilled workers were nearly 41% of recruits to the ranks overall, but nearly 55% of Irish infantry regiments. White-collar workers were 10.5% of the total, but nearly 20% of airmen and nearly 30% of Irish cavalry units. Men who had worked with animals were just over 6% of the total, yet they were nearly one-quarter of the cavalry and over 10% in other units which worked extensively with horses, the artillery and Army Service Corps (ASC). Transport workers were 7% of the total but over one-quarter of the ASC, where they would have worked driving or maintaining vehicles. People who had worked with food and drink were less than 3% of recruits but 10% of the ASC. Of 84 bakers who enlisted, 47 joined the ASC. Most markedly, communication workers (such as line telegraphists and messengers) were just under 15% of the total but nearly 70% of the Royal Engineers. Within the battalions of the Royal Dublin Fusiliers (Table A4.2), the ranks of some units were more white collar than others. Such jobs accounted for 10% of Dublin Fusiliers, but they were over one-fifth of the 7th Dublins and nearly half of the 10th 'Commercial' battalion. Unskilled workers were just under 60% of the regiment, yet they were over three-quarters of the 6th Dublins and only 4% of the 10th Dublins. Notably, the 7th Dublins, widely seen as a middle-class unit, still had over half its ranks filled with the unskilled.

Beyond the military, others, mainly women, volunteered for the British Red Cross Society. Nearly 4,000 offered their services over the course of the war, nearly 90% of them women. 1914 saw 367 join, with a rush in August and then in October. A steady stream of volunteers followed through the war, with 1917 outstripping both 1915 and 1916 for recruits. Nearly 40% of those who volunteered went into the nursing Voluntary Aid Detachment. Nearly 30% worked at the Irish War Hospital Supply Depot at 40 Merrion Square. Just over 20% were in work parties, principally knitting and sewing. Around 5% worked for the Irish Sphagnum Moss Association, harvesting moss to use in wound dressings, and a similar number were involved in fundraising and administration. Handfuls of people worked in a range of activities including driving, entertainment, and as 'hospital searchers' who travelled seeking out the wounded who might not be easily identified. Some of these occupations were very heavily gendered: 98% of those picking sphagnum were women, as were 99% of those at 40 Merrion Square. Hospital searchers were 95% men. Drivers were roughly equally split. Of 1,301 VADs, nearly one-quarter were men, but within those numbers were clearly roles for men (ambulance drivers, hospital orderlies) and women (nursing, cooking). Across the UK most of these volunteers came from middle- and upper-class backgrounds[108] and Dublin was no different. Whereas Dublin's notoriously poor Coombe looms large in lists of army privates, it is barely present as an address for Red Cross volunteers. Instead, they came from the same places as so many officers, the elegant houses of places like Ailesbury Road, Fitzwilliam Square and Merrion Square, along with the city's suburbs and the county's small towns and villages. Lady Boyd and her three daughters (Ida, Ena and Alice) of 66 Merrion Square worked at the hospital supply depot close to home, and made clothing. Norah Hollwey of Ardfallen, Dalkey, age 27, had two brothers serving when she enlisted as a nurse in August 1915. She served until April 1919, running her own ward at 24 General Hospital, Étaples.[109]

Among Irish republican forces, we already know that at the time of the Truce in 1921, a total of 5,464 were serving in the IRA's 2nd Eastern Division, better known as the Dublin Brigade. They were part of a total IRA strength of 115,446.[110] Numbers for service in republican forces (predominantly the Irish Volunteers) during the Rising are less clear. However, research for this book, drawing on recently available sources including pensions, medals and prison records, and on excellent granular studies of the Rising's personnel, identified 2,122 (233 women and 1,889 men) from Dublin with service.[111] Another 481 were arrested who had probably not been involved in the Rising.[112]

The occupations of Dublin republicans were examined by Peter Hart who concluded that in Dublin across the revolutionary period, skilled workers constituted a high proportion of republican activists. Since his work was published over a decade ago many more sources have become available which allow more detailed interrogation of who Irish republicans were, not least in 1916 for which Hart did not have substantial figures.[113] There are some difficulties in making direct comparisons between the data used here and Hart's figures.[114]

Moreover, just as interesting as examining the proportion of republicans in certain jobs is to compare them with those in the British forces using the same categories as used for the latter. In 1916, around one-quarter of the ranks of the Irish Volunteers and ICA were unskilled, and just over 10% of the officers (Table A4.3). Nearly one-fifth of the ranks were in white-collar jobs, alongside just over two-fifths of the officers. Skilled workers constituted one-third of the ranks and one-quarter of the officers. Comparing republican ranks with British ranks, the one-quarter unskilled among republicans contrasts to just over 40% among the British. The gap widens if the Irish regiments of the British infantry are considered where nearly 55% were unskilled (Table A4.1) and the figure is slightly higher for members of the Dublin Fusiliers (Table A4.2). However, Hart points out that in later stages of the revolution, unskilled workers became steadily even less important in the ranks.[115] This all points to the working class of Dublin being far more rooted in the British military than in republican ranks, a factor which would help to dictate some reactions to the Easter Rising.[116]

Training

Once men had enlisted, volunteers had extensive training before they even left Ireland, let alone went to the front. The 7th Dublins' D Company trained initially at the Curragh and was given the unusual privilege of electing from their number non-commissioned officers and two junior commissioned officers. For the latter they chose Ernest Julian (a barrister and Reid Professor of Law at Trinity[117]) and Robert Douglas whose sporting connections commended him. That these were different types of recruits was seen in the way they reacted to their first military pay at the end of September. Rather than spending it on essentials, or viewing it as a rare bonus, or sending it home for the care of families, 'many were the humorous scenes and discussions as to how it would be spent. Some of them kept it as a memento and marking the first stage of their career.'[118] Training at the Curragh continued for nearly eight months: a mix of drilling, marching, musketry and divisional manoeuvres, with the route marches steadily more intensive.[119] In the 6th Dublins, Noël Drury described a typical day in late 1914: rising at 6am, an hour's drill at 6.30am then half an hour breakfast; 45 minutes in orderly rooms checking kit; parades from 9am until 12.30pm; two hours for lunch; drills and exercises until 4pm; a half-hour break for tea; two hours in the gym or bayonet practice from 4.30pm; a short rest until 7.15pm for dinner; finally, lectures from 8.30pm to 10pm. Saturdays were generally finished by 4pm, with Sunday as rest. Drury recorded that all the exercise initially made him lose weight, but he then gained about a stone 'although I was as hard as nails'. He noticed similar changes across all ranks of the battalion.[120]

Training in early 1915 and into spring focused more on the rifle range and on brigade field days in which mock operations were carried out. There was also more specialised training for some, with Drury spending two weeks on a signalling course in Carlow.[121] One special event in the 6th Dublins challenged some patterns of behaviour with Drury describing how on St Patrick's Day it was a regimental custom for all officers, regardless of denomination to attend a Catholic service with the men. He reflected,

> Good Presbyterians like myself paraded and marched off to the tunes of the "Boys of Wexford" and "A Nation Once Again" and went to chapel for the first and, probably, the only time in our lives. What a change the war has brought over things to be sure. If anyone had told me a year ago that I would have marched to a R.C. chapel to a rebel tune, I would have said they were potty to say the least of it. It was rather disconcerting to find oneself standing up or sitting down at the wrong time through ignorance of the ritual but nobody seemed to mind.[122]

Practical jokes were played by some of the officers on each other. Drury noted how he and others had driven sheep into the rooms of two officers while asleep, locking the doors and leaving the key hanging. Drury noted, 'They slept through the ceremony, apparently, and it was only the next morning when their batmen arrived and asked what they "wanted with them sheep" that they found out the trick.'[123]

The Pals continued to interest the newspapers until they left Ireland at the end of April 1915, with their basic training complete, for further training in England *en route* to deployment.[124] The rest of the 10th Division, including the 6th Dublins, went at the same time. They were stationed in Basingstoke, but used rifle ranges at Aldershot.

Training was considerably tougher than in Ireland: trench digging was regular; route marches were longer; divisional manoeuvres lasted for several days at a time, under war conditions of equipment and food. Despite their sporting prowess, one member of D Company recalled after a march, 'The muscles of my thighs were simply worn out. I never experienced anything like it before, and, in fact, all the other fellows were in much the same state.' This went on for most of May – with an inspection by the King in late May – and into June before they left for Gallipoli in July.[125] On departure, Drury noted, 'Strange emotions these few days – delight at being about to be put to the test at last, mingled with regret for the hard lines of those who have to stay behind and think, also a vague wonder whether we would see them again.'[126]

A further opportunity for Dublin men to join as 'Pals' (though without the term being used) came in the autumn of 1915 through a new 'Commercial' company. It was described as 'a generous effort on the part of the military authorities to meet the wishes of the business men to join the army, and, at the same time, to preserve as far as possible, their old associates.' The *Evening Mail* said that 'it is invariably found that men who are known to each other and are bound together by ties of long friendship, train better, fight better, and hold together with greater determination than otherwise could be reasonably expected'. A club was opened in Grafton Street for the use of men enlisting and it was stressed – by mentioning a range of businessmen who supported the initiative – that the new company 'will not be tinged with any particular shade of politics or religion'. Initially associated with the 5th Dublins, recruiting went so well that by early 1916 it had become clear that there were enough men for a battalion rather than just a company, and the unit became the 10th Dublins.[127]

A further Dublin connection to a specific battalion came with the 9th Royal Inniskilling Fusiliers, part of the Ulster Division. Its core was formed from the Tyrone UVF, but men from Dublin joined in a group from the LDV.[128] Numbering around 2,000 at the war's outbreak, around 600 LDVs had enlisted within a year, around 200 of these having rapidly joined the 9th Inniskillings.[129] The link between the LDV and the battalion can be seen by the application for a commission from William Crozier, a barrister of Stephen's Green in October 1914. On his application he stated that he had been drilling with the LDV and that 'if appointed he will be serving with and commanding some of the men he has trained during the last year'.[130] Crozier was granted a commission in the 9th Inniskillings and he and his men were kept together in a 'Dublin Company' which would later see action on the Somme.[131]

Beyond these units, the 16th (Irish) Division, initially formed on 11 September 1914, attracted significant attention in Ireland once it became clear later that month that it would take men from the National Volunteers and it was regularly referred to as the 'Irish Brigade'. As a bastion of Parliamentary nationalism, Dublin made a major contribution. 'Brigade' was not accurate in relation to how the British army was organised, with a 'brigade' consisting of four infantry battalions and being one of three brigades in a division. However, in the autumn of 1914 'Irish Brigade' was used in discourse in Ireland to denote something approaching an Irish army. The *Irish Times* reported on a planned parade of the Royal Irish Rifles through Dublin in early October saying that the formation of the Irish Brigade 'may possibly extend into an Irish Army Corps'.[132] This grand scheme did not materialise and the term 'Irish Brigade', initially also used for units of the 10th Division,[133] soon became synonymous with the 16th Division.[134] Despite that, there were many men in the division who had not been involved in nationalist paramilitarism. Orlando Beater was living and working in England at the outbreak of the war but he came 'home' to enlist (his parents lived in Rathgar) and was posted to the 9th Dublins.[135] The 16th Division went through similar training to the 10th, though for longer, and spending more time in Ireland. Once the division's core had been formed in October they spent nearly a year training at Fermoy in County Cork, before moving to Aldershot in September 1915. From there, they went to France in December.[136] As they left, Orlando Beater expressed the relief that men felt at heading for the front. 'At last!' he wrote in his diary. After more than a year of training in 'hail, rain, heat and snow', the men had begun to wonder if they would be kept in England for the duration of the war. Now, however, 'that was all done with ... and this day was for us the beginning of a new chapter in the Great Adventure'.[137] Plenty of Dubliners had already experienced that 'adventure', not least the 6th and 7th Dublins at Gallipoli, and from the very first in regular battalions on the Western Front.

3 OUTBREAK, 1914

I will never forget my first experience of being under fire. Words cannot describe it. All I know is that I fixed my bayonet and rushed forward. All around me men kept dropping and the cries of the wounded were awful.

Private John Soloman, 2nd Royal Irish Regiment, on the Battle of Mons, August 1914[1]

HMS *Amphion* and the War at Sea

With much of Dublin's memory of the First World War focused on the 7th Royal Dublins Fusiliers at Gallipoli in August 1915, the central role of so many more Dubliners in the first days of fighting in August 1914, and in the rest of that year, has been neglected. There is a substantial story to tell of those regular soldiers and reservists, from the Battle of Mons and the subsequent retreat, via the First Battle of Ypres to the solidifying of the trench lines by the end of the year. Yet even before there was fighting on the Western Front, maritime Dubliners felt the effects of the war. Merchant sailors in Hamburg on four steamers were detained as war was declared. In 1918, many were still held in Germany.[2] Then when war death came to Dublin, the British Empire's second city shared in its very first losses. They came at sea more than a week before the British Expeditionary Force (BEF) arrived on the continent.

Throughout the Edwardian years Anglo–German naval rivalry had been a cause of anxiety on both sides of the Channel and a focus of thinking for military strategists. However, in August 1914 neither side believed it had a chance of winning a decisive battle at sea. The Royal Navy's Grand Fleet had the advantage over the German High Seas Fleet in terms of dreadnoughts and battle cruisers, but was significantly below par in the competition over destroyers. Consequently, full-scale naval battles were unlikely. Instead, skirmishes would be the norm.[3]

The first salvoes of the United Kingdom's war were fired on its second day, 5 August 1914, when three British ships ran into a German minelayer, *Königen Luise*, off Harwich. Two of the ships were destroyers, the *Lance* and the *Landrail*, along with a cruiser, the *Amphion*. The *Königen Luise* was disguised in the colours of a Great Eastern Railway steamer, but the mines it carried betrayed its true purpose. A chase over thirty miles ensued with four shots fired by the Royal Navy, one missing and the other three hitting the bridge, bow and propeller. As the *Königen Luise* sank, taking as many as 80 of her crew with her, around 50 German sailors were rescued by the Royal Navy.[4] No casualties were incurred by the Royal Navy, but as the *Amphion* returned to Harwich the next day, 6 August, it struck a mine which exploded: 148 crew were killed, plus around 20 German prisoners taken from the *Königen Luise*. A further two of the *Amphion*'s crew died in hospital; around 150 were saved, along with about 30 further German prisoners.[5] Announcing the losses in the House of Commons, the first Lord of the Admiralty, Winston Churchill, offered one of the first public claims of what became labelled as 'Hun frightfulness' or 'Hun bestiality', condemning 'the indiscriminate use of mines' as a risk to merchants and neutrals, and a matter which should 'be attentively considered by the nations of a civilised world.'[6] Perhaps the British had been caught off-guard by the 1907 Hague Convention's prohibition of mining in international waters, though by early 1915 the Royal Navy was itself actively mining.[7]

Dublin's loss on the *Amphion* came in the figure of 25-year-old Signalman Joseph Pierce Murphy, known to his family as Pierce. His death was marked by a personal notice in the *Evening Herald* on 13 August:

> **MURPHY** – Pierce, beloved son of John Murphy, jun., Cambridge Road, Ringsend, who was killed on H.M.S. Amphion. R.I.P. Sacred Heart of Jesus, have mercy on his soul.[8]

Such notices became a crucial way for the death of a loved one to be recorded, often with a standard verse or religious text as part of the

notice. Newspaper stories on individuals or the publication of photographs had not yet become the norm and Murphy's death went otherwise unremarked in the press despite him being the first Dubliner killed
in the war. Not until October 1915 was his photograph published.[9]
As with every other 'lost at sea' death, Murphy has no grave and is
instead remembered on the Plymouth Naval Memorial along with over
7,000 others from the First World War.

Murphy's death at sea was shortly followed by others which
highlighted a new naval threat: the U-Boat. *U-9* sank the *Aboukir* and
Hogue off the Dutch Coast on 22 September 1914 and the *Hawke*
off the east of Scotland on 15 October.[10] Dubliners were also lost on
Royal Navy submarines: *D5* off Great Yarmouth to a mine on
3 November 1914 and *D2* sunk by a German torpedo boat off the
Dutch coast on 25 November.[11] An ammunition explosion on the
Bulwark off Sheerness on 26 November 1914 resulted in 738 deaths
and just 12 survivors, making it the second largest single explosion in
terms of the number of deaths in British history. Seven Dubliners were
among them.[12]

Other naval events far from Irish shores emphasised
that this was a *world* war. At the outbreak, German Admiral
Maximilian Graf von Spee commanded a naval squadron in the
Far East centred in Tsingtao in China, with which the Germans
planned to threaten trade routes. The Japanese declaration of war
against Germany on 23 August meant that relying on Tsingtao for
supplies was problematic. Spee was forced to head eastwards for
coaling. The wisdom of that decision became apparent in
early September as it became clear that the Japanese, supported
by the British, would try to take Tsingtao.[13] The British Empire's
military contingent at Tsingtao was limited to the 2nd South Wales
Borderers and the 36th Sikhs, and two ships: the *Triumph* and the
Usk. Serving on HMS *Triumph* was 28-year-old Able Seaman
Edward Swords, whose brother Patrick lived in the Summerhill
area of Dublin. Born in Dublin, Swords had only been on the
Triumph since the end of July 1914, but had served for ten years
on other ships. At some point, whether before he had enlisted or
during his service he enthusiastically embraced the sailors' tradition
of tattooing: his record notes 'Design of flowers and woman's bust'
on his right forearm, along with a butterfly on the back of his right
hand and a wreath of flowers around his neck.[14]

On 14 October 1914, during a naval bombardment of German forts the *Triumph* was hit. A German eyewitness recalled 'a joyful, triumphant "Hurrah" burst from our lips for one of our explosive shells had hit the English warship *Triumph* plumb in the middle of her deck. *Triumph* veered at once and ran away for all she was worth.'[15] Two were wounded, and Swords was killed. He was buried at the Liukungtao Naval Cemetery at Weihaiwei but was later added to the Sai Wan Memorial in Hong Kong, opened in 1974 after the cemetery was destroyed during China's Cultural Revolution.[16]

By the time Spee neared South America, the British had gathered enough intelligence to ensure that he would be met by a squadron under the commend of Rear Admiral Christopher Cradock. On 1 November, Spee engaged with four ships off the Chilean port of Coronel: the *Glasgow, Good Hope, Monmouth* and *Otranto*. With the sun setting in the west, by around 7pm the British ships were visible against the final glimmers of the horizon but the German ships in the east (the *Dresden, Gneisnau, Leipzig, Nürnberg* and *Scharnhorst*) were not. The superior gunnery of the German ships soon told. Both the *Good Hope* and the *Monmouth* were sunk in the first British naval defeat for a century. However, of the five German ships involved all except the *Dresden* were sunk a month later in the Battle of the Falkland Islands, while the *Dresden* itself surrendered and was scuttled in March 1915.[17] Coronel cost the lives of at least twelve Dubliners, six on each of the *Good Hope* and the *Monmouth*.

Mons and the Retreat, August to September 1914

A week after Pierce Murphy's death on the *Amphion* the first units of the BEF arrived in France on the night of 12/13 August. The first Irish battalion to land was the 1st Irish Guards on 13 August as part of the 4th (Guards) Brigade in 2nd Division. That battalion's official history is unusual in being written not by a former officer but by Rudyard Kipling, whose son served and was killed in it. Kipling used accounts of those who had served in the battalion, as well as official records, and he had more eye for colour than the usual official history writer. On landing at Le Havre on 13 August, 'a fiercely hot day', the battalion 'received an enthusiastic welcome from the French, and were ... introduced to the wines of the country, for many maidens lined the steep road and offered bowls of drinks to the wearied'.

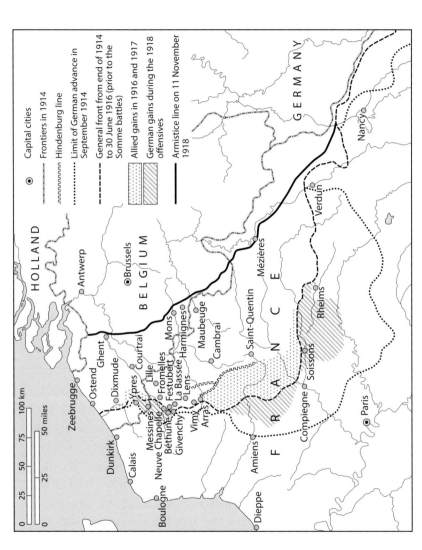

Map 3.1: Western Front 1914–18. Adapted by David Cox from the map drawn by David Appleyard in Grayson, *Belfast Boys*, xiv.

The next day the men looked 'at this strange, bright France with strange eyes, and bathed in the sea'.[18]

The 1st Irish Guards were followed on 14 August by the second battalions of the Royal Munster Fusiliers (1st Division), Connaught Rangers (2nd Division), Royal Irish Regiment and Royal Irish Rifles (both in 3rd Division) the next day. By the end of August 1914, all the regular Irish infantry and cavalry units (plus the North and South Irish Horse) based in the UK were in France, with the exception of the 2nd Leinsters who arrived on 12 September. As for those units stationed overseas at the war's outbreak, all regular Irish battalions except the 1st Royal Inniskilling Fusiliers, Dublins and Munsters (all of whom would be deployed at Gallipoli in April 1915) had landed in France by the end of 1914.[19] This meant that Irish regiments, with Dubliners spread throughout them, took a significant part in the war on the Western Front in 1914, in particular at Mons, Le Cateau, La Bassée and Ypres. Over half of those in the original BEF were reservists, called up as war broke out.[20] Many had 'softened up during their years of civilian life' and the demands of war did not fall easy on them.[21] The BEF was initially concentrated at Maubeuge, about thirteen miles south of Mons, in line with pre-war plans to protect the French army's left flank.[22] As it opened its operations, the BEF was dogged by animosities among generals which meant that it had 'a high command team not fully fused together by mutual confidence and respect'.[23]

The very first death during the war of a soldier with possible Dublin connections came on 20 August 1914, but not on the Western Front: Private 4485 James Ryan of the 4th Royal Irish Regiment. His battalion was a training unit which was then based in Queenstown (now Cobh), where he was buried in the Old Church Cemetery. He is recorded as 'died home' with 'home' meaning simply within the UK rather than being 'at his home', and this is likely to mean from illness. Born in Kilkenny, his father was living at 31 Richmond Street South in Dublin by the time the Commonwealth War Graves Commission came to record his details after the war, but it is not clear where the family was in 1914 or indeed when the 1911 Census was taken.[24]

The BEF saw its first major action (after a skirmish on 22 August) at the Battle of Mons on 23 and 24 August, as part of the wider Battle of the Frontiers.[25] As German troops sought to sweep all before them, Sir John French commanding the BEF initially planned counter-attacks at the Mons Canal but ended up taking defensive positions. From the morning of 23 August until the early hours of the 24th around 70,000 British soldiers faced approximately 160,000 Germans before beginning what became known as the 'Retreat from Mons'. The story of such unequal numbers, and the fact that the German army appeared to have been held back gave rise to the 'Mons myth' in which British total casualties of around 1,600 (with 282 dead on 23 August[26]) were contrasted with German losses of anything from 2,000 to 10,000 (but most likely at the lower end of that scale). Rapid rifle fire by the British was a central element of this narrative, though it later became apparent that where the Germans had been significantly delayed artillery fire was decisive.[27]

Certainly three men with some Dublin connection were killed on that first day of battle.[28] Private L/12712 Edward Clow, killed in action serving in the 4th Royal Fusiliers (City of London Regiment), may have had only tenuous links to the city.[29] His battalion was positioned at Nimy, north of Mons, where, with 'orders to hold on to this position as long as possible' they faced fierce rifle and artillery fire. Most of their machine gunners on a bridge over the canal were killed before the battalion withdrew from 1.10pm on 23rd.[30] Clow was one of 28 of his battalion lost that day.[31] Facing similar pressures near to Nimy were the 2nd Royal Irish Regiment. They began the battle as the reserve troops for 8th Brigade and when called into the fray after 1pm to support the 4th Middlesex Regiment found themselves pinned down and unable to reach the front line. The 4th Middlesex had already lost the Nimy salient by this time and both battalions were withdrawn at around 4.30pm.[32] Private Thomas Whelan of Chancery Street reported, 'The fighting was terrific. You could not recognise your own brother the next morning.'[33] Private 10550 John Soloman, described in the press as 'A young Dublin Jewish soldier', wrote, 'I will never forget my first experience of being under fire. Words cannot describe it. All I know is that I fixed my bayonet and rushed forward. All around me men kept dropping and the cries of the wounded were awful.'[34] Among the 20 dead in the 2nd Royal Irish Regiment were men from across the UK, including England and Wales, and from different parts of Ireland. Mainly these men came from the regiment's recruiting area in the south-east of Ireland, but at least two had Dublin connections. Lance Corporal

10255 John Corre was born and had enlisted in Dublin, with his parents then residing in Great Brunswick Street.[35] Private 4517 Thomas Ward, born in Dundalk, resided in the city.[36] Their contrasting resting places illustrate the agonising wait for news to reach home. Ward is buried at St Symphorien Military Cemetery. Established by the Germans for the British losses at Mons, it houses the first and last British Empire fatalities of the war.[37] That Ward's body was found and buried by the Germans means that he would first have been declared missing and it could have been many months until his family received definite news. That was almost certainly the case for John Corre, who is remembered on the La Ferté-sous-Jouarre memorial along with nearly 4,000 others lost in 1914 whose bodies were never identified. That news of his death did not appear in newspapers until September 1915 is an indication of how long hope could be held.

If Mons was a success of sorts for the allies, it was also the beginning of a retreat in which a swath of France and Belgium was given up to Germany, much of it for four years. Yet that 'Retreat from Mons' is, like Dunkirk in 1940, remembered as a type of victory: the action during the retreat meant that the Germans were prevented from reaching Paris. While the retreat itself ended in early September, it was followed by a French counter-attack on the Marne,[38] and the beginning of trench warfare on the Aisne over 12–15 September as the Germans dug in to fend off British attacks. Later in the month the Germans then failed to outflank the allies and reach the Channel ports which were essential if Germany was to dominate in the war of supplies. The Retreat from Mons and the battles which followed did not necessarily mean that Germany would be defeated on the Western Front, but it did make it very hard for Germany to win.

The first Dublin Fusiliers to reach France were the men of the 2nd battalion. That battalion would carry the standard for the city of Dublin on the Western Front throughout the entire war. Many other units containing Dubliners came and went but none contained so many as the 2nd.[39] They left England on 22 August, as part of 10th Brigade in the 4th Division, via Southampton on the SS *Caledonia*, disembarking at Boulogne at 5am the next day. Spending the day camped until 9pm, they then travelled by train to Le Cateau, and marched just over four miles to Beaumont where they spent most of the next day resting. On 25 August, at 2am, the battalion marched another four miles to a position one mile south of St Python. At 6am gunfire was heard before the battalion marched a short way east to a farm at Fontaine-sur-Tertre where at 6pm the unit was shelled from German positions to the north-east. Rapid movement around the French countryside was disorienting for soldiers who had only just arrived in the country, many of whom were reservists without previous war experience. Private 11078 John Dowling told the *Evening Herald*:

> We didn't know where we were going to. We were just going round and round, moving night and day. None of us, or very few anyhow, had been at war before, and the very first night we got to the front we came into the full blaze of the German guns. 'Twas hell, sir; not war at all, but just hell and murder.[40]

Three hours later, two German soldiers were spotted and shot, before the unit marched overnight eight miles to the south-east, reaching the village of Haucourt at 5am on 26th.

There, they took part in the key British action of the retreat, the Battle of Le Cateau. The 2nd Dublins' 4th Division was part of II Corps commanded by Lieutenant General Horace Smith-Dorrien who took a decision to stand at Le Cateau before retreating. Smith-Dorrien had expected to be covered by I Corps, commanded by Lieutenant General Douglas Haig, but contact between I and II Corps had been broken and that help never materialised. Nevertheless, a ferocious stand took place and was hailed as having saved the BEF.[41] Later in the war, much was made of the 1917 Battle of Messines which saw the 36th (Ulster) and 16th (Irish) divisions fight alongside each other. Yet Le Cateau was an early but now forgotten example of men from the north and the south joining together in battle: the 2nd Dublins served with the 1st Royal Irish Fusiliers (whose recruiting area was around Armagh) in 10th Brigade of the 4th Division, while the 2nd Royal Inniskilling Fusiliers were in another brigade in the same division.

During Le Cateau, the 2nd Dublins clung on to their position at Haucourt with all that they could. Fire was opened by the enemy at 6.15am. At this point, two companies held high ground while two others were in reserve. They were on the extreme left of the allied flank, so the Germans were trying to work their way around the British line. From 2pm shell fire rained down. At 5pm it became apparent that the artillery was withdrawing and it transpired that this was part of a brigade-wide withdrawal. However, on enquiring as to whether they should also withdraw, the battalion adjutant was told by divisional staff 'that nothing was known of the Battn., and that it had better retire'. This chaos was a common product of retreat. The battalion withdrew in small parties which became separated, and when it reformed at Roisel at 5am on 27th, only 100 Dublins (from perhaps around 800) were in formation.

These were desperate times for the 2nd Dublins. With nothing more than snatched moments of sleep for days, they were at the limits of what could be endured by soldiers. The battalion war diary was silent – as would the regimental history be – on one consequence of this, which became a matter of scandal: the attempted surrender by the battalion commanding officer, Lieutenant Colonel Arthur Mainwaring, and his subsequent court martial. Mid-afternoon on 26 August, Mainwaring found himself in the town of St Quentin with a party of men from his own battalion, along with several hundred soldiers from other units but very few officers. Mainwaring and his men were exhausted and believed they were surrounded by advancing Germans. Fearing the destruction of the town and the slaughter of civilians, Mainwaring (acting with Lieutenant Colonel John Elkington of the 1st Warwickshires) began to arrange the surrender of all the British soldiers in St Quentin. However, a cavalry officer arrived, informing them that they were not surrounded. Retreat took place but this did not save Mainwaring and Elkington from courts martial a fortnight later under charges of cowardice and scandalous conduct. Though acquitted of cowardice, they were stripped of their rank and cashiered. Elkington sought to reclaim his reputation, joining the French Foreign Legion and later regaining his rank in the British army after a royal pardon. Mainwaring never made the same journey and died in obscurity in 1930.[42]

As Mainwaring led his men back from St Quentin, fragments of the 2nd Dublins continued to pull back from across the front line. The battalion continued to retire for the remainder of August and into early September but took no major part in any fighting during the rest of the retreat. During this time many were 'physically incapable' of marching with equipment, which was partly down to it not being fitted correctly. Problems had also been found with boots, with those issued to reservists having 'to be cut before they could get them on.'[43] Temporarily, the 2nd Dublins were down to no more than eighty men, and formed a composite battalion with the 1st Warwickshires. Only by 6 September, the day the retreat ended, had the battalion received enough reinforcements and returned stragglers to take on its own identity.[44] Some stragglers told their stories to the press. Thirteen Dublin Fusiliers arrived in Boulogne in early September having spent six days hiding from advancing Germans in the barn of a chateau. From there, 'aided by friendly peasants' they crossed German lines making a 'run for it, while the bullets were flying round us'.[45] A larger party of forty-seven led by Captain Alfred Trigona spent a week eluding the Germans before being shipped back to the UK. At night they rested in barns and farmhouses, aided by French civilians, while 'By day they hid in barns, in stacks of corn, or in the branches of trees, and frequently German soldiers passed close to their place of concealment.'[46]

Over 26 and 27 August the 2nd Dublins lost forty-one men dead. Three of those deaths came on 26 August, including the first Dubliner killed in the battalion, Private 9578 William Clarke, whose parents lived at 94 Lower Dorset Street.[47] Among the thirty-eight to lose their lives on 27 August, at least thirteen were Dubliners. That 'only' forty-one were dead and yet the battalion was down to such low numbers was because hundreds had been taken prisoner. None of that was known even in late September – though it would have been suspected – when the battalion war diary noted '513 were missing after this battle & up to the present date it is not known what happened to them or what casualties they suffered.'[48]

Cavalry had also been in significant action at this mobile stage of the war. The mobility of the war meant that the enemy could easily spring a surprise. Trooper 3999 John Ryan of Parnell Street was serving in the 5th (Royal Irish) Lancers in September 1914. The *Evening Herald* reported that on 3 September his squadron had been cut off for four days when,

> while on scout duty with a corporal, Ryan saw a barn in front of them and went forward to get some fodder for themselves and their horses. They were entering the building when they were suddenly attacked by a force of Germans from inside. Ryan ... killed four of them, and was getting away on his horses, when a bullet struck his left shoulder and exploded his remaining cartridges. Man and horse fell and both were killed.[49]

Private 4511 Peter Harvey was killed on 24 August in partly dismounted action against German infantry at Elouges, serving in the same unit.[50] Four days later, Privates 1561 Charles Coote and 1746 Hugh Nolan were killed serving in the 12th (Prince of Wales's Royal) Lancers. This action was also partly dismounted, with fire exchanged with German Dragoons. However, a charge was made and the war diary noted the 12th Lancers 'killed the lot with the exception of 4 prisoners'. Around 70 Germans were killed in the charge, which would have been a bloody affair involving lances and sabres.[51]

More curious is the case of the 9th (Queen's Royal) Lancers at Audregnies on 24 August. In mid-October a story appeared in the *Evening Herald*, carrying an interview with 'Sergeant Jimmy O'Brien', said to be from Mark's Alley off Francis Street. The interview gave a detailed account of the capture of eleven guns by the 9th Lancers at Mons in an encounter which the paper said 'will become as memorable in history and literature as the famous charge of the Light Brigade at Balaclava'. The mission described was to recapture twelve guns of the Royal Field Artillery of 61 and 64 Brigades which had been taken by the Germans. O'Brien described how 960 Lancers charged 'like demons' at 2,000 Uhlans. He told how his two brothers – Peter and Christy – were both killed, 'run through the stomach with Uhlan lances'. Despite heavy loses in 'a howling raging inferno', O'Brien described how 'We cleared out the Uhlans, and with swelling chests our chaps took possession of the guns', then followed this by taking another eleven German guns.[52]

This was a stirring tale. But did it actually happen and who was O'Brien? The 9th Lancers certainly charged at Mons, at German lines, on 24 August 1914. The story was rapidly told in heroic terms in newspapers, and there was undoubtedly great heroism, with Captain Francis Grenfell winning the Victoria Cross. In most stories 'saving guns' featured somewhere. But at first there was no mention of capturing guns, merely charging at eleven.[53] The story soon became embellished. A poem in the London *Times*, 'The Charge of the Ninth Lancers', talked of how the cavalry 'slew the gunners beside their guns, And captured the cannon, the roaring eleven'.[54] Where saving guns had been a genuine feature of the story is seen in both the unit war diary and in a story from a corporal in the battalion. This told how, on returning from the attack, four British guns had been abandoned after the gunners were mown down, and the men of the

9th Lancers had dragged them back to safety.[55] But the idea of guns being captured or Uhlans made to flee is not borne out by the evidence. As Adrian Gilbert argues, while the charge has been written about in epic terms, 'The only thing epic about it was its folly.'[56] Meanwhile, as for the three O'Briens, no Peter or Christy O'Brien (or any names similar) were killed at that time in the 9th Lancers or indeed in the entire war. Indeed, no O'Brien seems to have served in the 9th Lancers at the front at this time.[57]

Trench Warfare and First Battle of Ypres

The BEF's retreat ended on 5 September, by which time they had covered nearly two hundred miles in thirteen days, and found themselves fifteen miles south-east of Paris. At that point, the French army attacked the German right flank, which was exposed along the River Marne, and the BEF joined the next day. By mid-September, the Germans were forced back across the Aisne, but the allies found it difficult to deal with the German superiority in artillery, and dug in.[58] Although the 2nd Dublins were operational as a unit by mid-September 1914, it was not until April 1915 that they would again see major action. During the Battle of the Aisne (12–15 September 1914), temporarily commanded by Captain T. H. C. Frankland, the battalion played a supporting role losing just three men.[59] As four days of fighting drew to a close it became clear that the German army was now focusing on defensive positions, having lost around fifty miles of ground since early September. British attentions also turned to constructing sound defences. The 2nd Dublins' war diary noted, 'that trenches on the reverse slope of a hill are most satisfactory. They cannot be seen by searchlights at night as they only show up the crest of the hill, & are also not subjected to such heavy shelling by day.'[60]

Finding such a favourable position was a rare luxury. More common – and pressing – was the need to make adequate arrangement for sanitation. Latrines were dug, reaching four feet below the bottom of the trench and 'At night empty biscuit tins are placed in recesses specially cut in rear wall of fire trench to serve as urinals.'[61] Across the war, battalions of the first wave of the BEF spent less than half their time at the front, but there were significant exceptions in the early months when a battalion might be at the front for much longer.[62] From the end of the Battle of the Aisne until the attack at St Julien on 25 April 1915, the 2nd Dublins spent 142 days (or 64 per cent of their time) in the front line and a further 64 days (29 per cent) resting, usually in billets. Seven days were spent moving between different sectors (rather than rotating shorter distances between the front and billets) and on a further seven the battalion was held ready for action, not at the front but in brigade or divisional reserve positions. Just one day was spent being involved in attack. These overall figures for a period of just over seven months mask the fact that the most intense period at the front was from mid-September to mid-November. During this time, the battalion was first in trenches along the Aisne, at La Montaigne Farm and then at Chivres. Although only part of the battalion was at the front at any one time, rotation of companies only saw them move to reserve positions and the period from 16 September to 5 October was very much a life in the trenches. At that point, the battalion was moved to billets for two days, before spending four days travelling northwards to new positions, marching, in trucks and on trains. This was part of the broad movement of the BEF to the left of French lines, closer to the English Channel. On 12 October, at St Omer, the 2nd Dublins faced aerial bombing for the first time when 'German aeroplanes dropped two bombs apparently aimed at us. They killed two women and injured two children.' Arriving in Flêtre, close to Bailleul on 13 October the battalion took part in a small attack on the village of Meteren, which was captured without any deaths in the 2nd Dublins.[63]

The battalion would now stay in the Bailleul-Armentières area until late April. From mid-October to mid-November the battalion spent all of its time at the front around Armentières. The pattern was for two companies to be in the front line, with two others in reserve trenches. But from 18 November a new pattern emerged. On that day the 2nd Dublins went to billets for a week, first in Ploegsteert then Armentières. From that point on there was rotation between billets and trenches, and they were never at the front for more than seven days at a time. More commonly, it was five, with three to four days spent in billets between each front-line posting. Conditions were tough in this wet and cold winter, and the battalion was regularly under both shell and sniper fire. On 5 December the battalion war diary noted, 'Trenches in an appalling state, some parts had to be evacuated owing to the water, others were filled with debris from crumbling parapets.' Christmas was spent in billets, so the battalion had no part in the truce. Casualties were relatively low but persistent. In December the battalion lost sixteen killed through shell and sniper fire.

Dubliners were also serving far beyond the Dublin Fusiliers. On the Aisne, clusters of Dubliners were killed in different battalions, four in the 2nd Connaughts and two in the 1st Irish Guards on 14 September. In the 2nd Royal Irish Rifles, four Dubliners were killed on the Aisne. One of these, Rifleman 9749 Constantine Murray, of Ross Road, had enlisted aged 18 in 1911, having worked as a bootmaker. Serving in the battalion's A Company he was declared wounded and missing from 15 September, but his parents were only advised in late October that he was wounded. A flow of letters ensued from his family, trying to find out news of where he was. Not until late April 1915 was Murray's father told that he was missing. This followed a letter in early April from his sister, Mary Costello, who wrote to the War Office, 'His mother and I are broken hearted about him. His mother cannot rest night or day thinking of him. If we only knew his whereabouts. What a relief to us all if he be dead, living or a prisoner.' In November 1915, his death was accepted for official purposes and he would later be listed on the La Ferté-sous-Jouarre Memorial.[64]

Following the Aisne, and before the 2nd Dublins' engagement at St Julien in late April 1915, there were two battalions in which more Dubliners would be killed than in the 2nd Dublins. Fifty-eight lost their lives in the 2nd Royal Irish Rifles and fifty-three in the 1st Irish Guards. This did not mean that there were more Dubliners serving in those battalions – the Royal Irish Rifles recruited most heavily in its Antrim and Down recruiting area – rather that these battalions were involved in heavier fighting. However, the numbers do indicate that in understanding the impact of the war on any area one needs to go far beyond the units obviously linked to that area.

Some of the fifty-eight Dubliners killed in the 2nd Royal Irish Rifles between mid-September 1914 and late April 1915 died on relatively quiet days when the battalion found itself under German fire from artillery or snipers. But there were other occasions on which the battalion faced more major action. The first was during a series of German counter-attacks on the Aisne following the battle over three days on 19–21 September. On 19 September, there was long and heavy bombardment, followed by a raid for about an hour and a half in the evening. More followed the next day. In his post-war memoirs,

Lieutenant Gerald Lowry, a regular officer from Belfast, recalled that on the morning of the 20th, a Sunday, 'We heard music from the German lines and thought that "Jerry" was going to church, but within a few minutes he started one of the most deadly attacks he had made on our line.'[65] This 'severe attack' by infantry was supported by artillery and continued for two hours. The same happened the next day around dusk, before the battalion was relieved on 22nd. Each time, the 2nd Royal Irish Rifles repelled the attack, supported by detachments from the 3rd Worcestershires and 2nd South Lancashires. But losses were heavy, with thirty-nine dead,[66] at least nine of them Dubliners.

The German counter-attacks on the Aisne were part of an effort to try to outflank the allies, known as the 'Race to the Sea'. This had the twin aim of trying to get behind allied troops and also securing important Channel locations, At the Battle of Armentières, twelve Dubliners were among 139 deaths in the 2nd Leinsters over 18–20 October. Based at Premesques the battalion endured both heavy shell fire and an attack by German infantry, but held their ground.[67] Much worse came a few days later at Neuve Chapelle during the Battle of La Bassée which had begun on 12 October. The 2nd Royal Irish Rifles' main involvement followed their arrival at Neuve Chapelle from 22 October. By this stage of the battle, despite some early hopes, there seemed little question of pushing the German lines back and so the battalion focused on holding positions. When the first casualties came the next day they were not from German guns but from night patrols being fired on by units elsewhere in the battalion's brigade. Similar incidents over the next days punctuated a bloody and chaotic battle. Lines were regularly changing and the artillery's intelligence rapidly became out of date. Only word of mouth could stop this as the telephone wire back to HQ was cut by shelling. On the night of 24/25 October, the 2nd Royal Irish Rifles successfully defended against a German attack with bayonets in 'a hand-to-hand struggle'.[68] On 25 October the battalion was 'practically without officers'. By the time the battalion went to billets on 27 October, its strength was down to 5 officers and about 250 men.[69] Corporal John Lucy later described Neuve Chapelle as 'the place of our destruction'.[70] Among 203 dead were at least 32 Dubliners.

The Race to the Sea ground to a halt by the end of November with trench lines becoming ever more set. By this time, the Germans

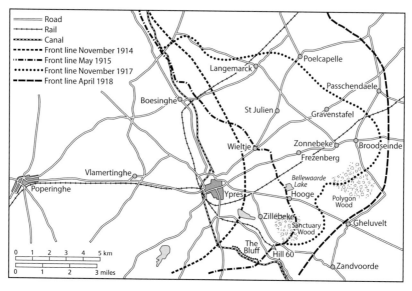

Map 3.2: Ypres, 1914–18. Drawn by David Cox.

were already attempting to break through British lines at Ypres. The town holds a special place in the UK's war. It was briefly occupied by German cavalry on 7 October 1914. They confiscated supplies, and more random looting occurred. However, after hearing of a British landing at Zeebrugge, the German high command believed that there was a risk of the cavalry becoming detached from the main German force and they were withdrawn the next day.[71] For the next four years, the British held the town, which meant that it occupied a place like no other in the British experience of war, even if by mid-1915 the town was little more than rubble with its civilian inhabitants evacuated. That connection has continued for a century with the town playing a central role in commemoration of the war, not only through the daily Last Post ceremony at the Menin Gate, but also practically, as a base for feeding, watering and hostelling visitors to Western Front sites. In 1914–18 Ypres' strategic significance lay in it being at the centre of a 35-mile-long salient which bulged into German lines.[72] That made it a position from which to launch attacks into German-held Belgium, and it was thus a key target for German counter-attacks.

From mid-October 1914 the Germans sought to take the town, launching a furious onslaught on 29 October in what became known as the First Battle of Ypres. At the same time the British artillery was being supplied with high-explosive shells which it used for the first time on 23 October. The advantage of these over shrapnel was that while shrapnel was effective against troops out in the open, it did little against those hidden in dugouts. For that, high-explosives were necessary.[73]

The 1st Irish Guards arrived in the Ypres area on 20 October.[74] Kipling noted that the matter-of-fact battalion war diary did not deem it 'worth while to record how the people of Ypres brought hot coffee to the Battalion as it passed through ... and how, when they halted there a few hours, the men amused their hosts by ... dancing Irish jigs on the clattering pavements while the refugees clattered past'.[75] Heavy losses came on 1 and 2 November near Zillebeke, with a total of 103 Irish Guards dead of whom at least 15 were Dubliners.[76] In some parts of the line the trenches were completely blown in with very few escaping. Kipling wrote in heroic terms of how the battalion held on for as long as it could on 1 November:

> The line was near breaking-point by then, but company after company delivered what blow it could, and fell back, shelled and machine-gunned at every step, to the fringe of Zillebeke Wood. Here the officers, every cook, orderly, and man who could stand, took rifle and fought; for they were all that stood there between the enemy and the Channel Ports.[77]

On 2 November, while trying to erect barbed wire along the front they were holding, 'they received several wounded men of the day's fight as they crawled into our lines; they heard one such man calling in the dark, and they heard the enemy turn a machine-gun on him and silence him'.[78] On the same two days the 2nd Connaughts at Molensaarlhoek lost 34 of whom at least 12 were from Dublin.[79] The 2nd Connaughts suffered from heavy German artillery fire after reinforcing a Gurkha battalion.[80] Further losses in the 1st Irish Guards came on 6 November when at 2pm the French position to the right of the Guards was attacked by German infantry. The French 'at once retired' which left the Guards' right flank open to attack. One company withdrew but this left another open to enfilade fire from the Germans. The position was only strengthened – and lost ground retaken – when reinforcements came from the Household Cavalry and the Life Guards.[81] That day 89 men died in the battalion, among them 12 Dubliners including Private 3258 William

Brennock of South Lotts Road.[82] He was the first of three brothers to be killed in the war.[83] The bodies of 78 of the dead, including Brennock, were never found or, if they were, never identified, for they are all listed on the Menin Gate which records the dead of the Ypres salient who have no known grave.[84]

A very different memorial for the first Battle of Ypres was found in the name of a child: Lillian Ypres Roberts. She was born during the battle and named after it because her father, William, was serving as a sergeant in the 1st Royal Welch Fusiliers and was captured. Roberts had married a Dublin woman while stationed in the city and his wife (Marie) and daughter were living at Ringsend Road. Her photo and his were reproduced in the *Evening Herald* under the headline 'PAPA HAS NOT YET SEEN BABY'. Tragically, Roberts never did see his daughter, as he died, still being treated as a prisoner though in the neutral Netherlands, four days after the armistice was signed in 1918. He was buried in The Hague's Roman Catholic Cemetery.[85]

Some comfort for bereaved families could be found in letters sent home by those who had served with the dead. As the war developed these were increasingly published in newspapers, containing, as they always did, only positive stories. In March 1915, the *Evening Herald* published a particular extensive set of letters sent to the family of Company Sergeant Major Patrick Kenny of the 1st Leinsters, killed in action on 15 March at Neuve Chapelle. Many wrote to his sister, Nurse McAlpine, who had been involved in sending gifts to the Leinsters. Captain W. Bates wrote, 'He was a splendid soldier, of high principles, and would have risen much higher had he not given up his life while defending his trench.' Lieutenant A. J. M. Pemberton wrote that Kenny has been 'a regular father to me ... He was one of the best soldiers and best loved men of the regiment.' Colour Sergeant J. W. Holden provided the all-important words about the moment of death: 'He died without pain about half an hour after being wounded.' That he was without pain for thirty minutes was highly unlikely but was the sort of consolation regularly offered to and, one imagines, clung on to by, the bereaved.[86] Such letters were repeated in newspapers throughout the war, even more common than stories of men saved from death by something in their pocket which stopped a bullet.[87] As 1914 closed, the BEF was facing a series of problems: it did not have enough shells for the rate at which the artillery could fire, and basic equipment such as boots, entrenching tools and sandbags were in short supply. Casualties had been heavy, outnumbering the original total of 84,000 men which had arrived in August, and the BEF was only still in the field because the system of reinforcement had delivered over 109,000 fresh men, along with Territorials and the Indian Corps. Meanwhile, the army had never prepared for the war without flanks which trench warfare had initiated.[88] Perhaps only the professionalism of the officers and men of the BEF had saved it as it 'tottered but never crumbled'.[89] In Dublin, with nearly five hundred from the city and county already dead,[90] the cost of the war was becoming ever more clear.

4 STALEMATE, 1915

I suddenly saw about a quarter of a mile to our left a heavy yellow mist coming from the German trenches towards ours.

Corporal J. E. Simpson of the 90th Winnipeg Rifles, on the use of gas by the Germans at Ypres in April 1915[1]

The Second Battle of Ypres

During the winter of 1914–15, two aspects of the war became apparent at a time when Dublin's presence on the Western Front was still through the regulars and reservists. The first, seen through the war at sea, was that losses could strike far from the Western Front and close to home. Dubliners died as the HMS *Viknor* hit a mine off the coast of Donegal on 13 January 1915. HMS *Bayano* was torpedoed by a U-Boat in the Irish Sea while heading to Liverpool on 11 March 1915.[2] A traditional enemy of the sailor, the weather, accounted for the *Clan McNaughton* which foundered in a gale off the coast of north-west Scotland on 3 February 1915.[3] Eight Dubliners died on the HMS *Formidable*, another U-Boat victim, off Portland on the English south coast on New Year's Day 1915. It was the first battleship to fall victim to a U-Boat in the war and the sinking caused Vice-Admiral Sir Lewis Bayly to be relieved of his command of the Channel Fleet. This was because *Formidable* and other ships on exercise had not been zig-zagging which would have been normal when there was a threat of enemy action from submarines. Bayly claimed that he had no warning from the Admiralty that he might expect to find U-Boats so far to the west.[4]

The second lesson of the winter was that the war was not ending soon. During the winter of 1914–15 neither side made any effort to shift the front and fighting was limited. 2nd Lieutenant Wilfrid Colyer was from Catford in London and was posted to the 2nd Dublins in January 1915 as they spent the winter in the line around Bailleul and Armentières.[5] He wrote how in early 1915:

> During the day there was nothing much doing in our section of trench. Every morning at breakfast time, as regularly as possible, the Boche used to send over six little shells of the brand familiarly known as "Little Willies." They were very startling, as they came without warning; the report of the gun and the burst of the shell were practically simultaneous. But they did not do much damage.

Colyer also reported that there was little sniping in his section of the line due to an agreement made during the 1914 Christmas Truce that 'if you don't fire at me, I won't fire on you'.[6]

The 2nd Dublins' winter and early spring at the front ended on the evening of 11 April, when they went into billets at Bailleul. The next day, they spotted a Zeppelin over the town. It dropped bombs killing civilians – three women and a child – plus seven horses. The battalion's next ten days were spent resting, their longest time in billets as yet.[7] From the Aisne to that point in April, the 2nd Dublins lost 113 officers and men. Of these, 31 appear not to have been Dubliners, coming mainly from other parts of Ireland with a few from England and Scotland. Certainly 51 were from the city or county of Dublin, while the remaining 31 are harder to identify, but in all likelihood they probably came from either Dublin or the rest of Ireland in similar proportions to those who can be identified. This means that in the early stages of the war, around one-third of those in the 2nd Dublins had strong links to the immediate recruiting area, with the vast bulk of the rest coming from elsewhere in Ireland.

In the spring of 1915 the Ypres area was the location of a terrifying new experiment by the Germans: the use of poison gas. Though banned by the 1907 Hague Convention, both sides considered using it, with the Germans trying unsuccessfully to discharge gas shells on the eastern front in January 1915. In subsequent months they experimented with cylinders emitting gas through a pipe with the prevailing wind taking it towards enemy lines. On 22 April, along more than four miles of the Ypres salient 6,000 cylinders released 168 tons of chlorine gas. The effect was devastating, creating in minutes a gap along the whole front as allied troops fled. As much as three miles was seized by the Germans in about five hours. However, hindered by a lack of reserves they did not push as far as they might have done and instead dug in on their main target, the Pilckem Ridge.[8] Such failures to press an advantage would dog all armies on the Western Front highlighting 'the problem of the attacker'.[9]

The following day British forces counter-attacked, only to be thrown back by heavy artillery and machine-gun fire. On 24 April, Canadian troops came under a further gas attack.[10] Writing to his mother in Dublin, Corporal J. E. Simpson of the 90th Winnipeg Rifles described how the Canadians still held their part of the line:

> I suddenly saw about a quarter of a mile to our left a heavy yellow mist coming from the German trenches towards ours . . . I saw the Germans climbing over their parapet, so I called to all who could to get up and 'fire rapid'. We killed all who got over, and no more attempted, but away on our left the Germans broke through, and soon thousands were swarming.[11]

On 24 April the allies sought to hold St Julien but it was taken by the Germans with gas and a storm of artillery fire. The next day, the 2nd Dublins joined the fray. At 4am they took up a position west of the Wieltje–St Julien road where they stayed until moving at dusk on 5 May to bivouacs behind the lines. On their first night at the front the German attack was seen vividly from a distance. Colyer recalled, 'Whole streets are burning now, the great red flames curving and leaping up into the gloom.'[12]

During this time at the front the 2nd Dublins twice endured gas attacks on 28 April and 2 May. The first attack consisted of gas shells which were far less effective than piped and wind-blown gas. On the second occasion, piped gas was used as cover for a German attack. Colyer recalled 'a big yellow cloud rolling slowly towards us along the ground'. With the gas rapidly upon the 2nd Dublins Colyer found that 'Putting a handkerchief over one's mouth evidently doesn't improve matters much.'[13] However, the attackers did not reach the Dublins' lines.

On 8 May, after three days resting, the 2nd Dublins were thrown back into the line in a counter-attack north of Potijze Woods which was eventually repelled. The battalion then held the line until 12 May. Attempts were made to repair the trenches but persistent heavy shelling made that difficult.[14] Four days' rest were followed by two days in support trenches before the battalion was again at the front, close to where they had been on 25 April along the Wieltje–St Julien road. From 13 May there had been a lull in German attacks, and this gave the British some time to strengthen their lines, but the onslaught was renewed on 24 May. A detailed report was produced by Captain Thomas Leahy who was the only officer left with the battalion when it withdrew from the line the next day. He noted that at 2.45am on 24 May he had been standing outside the HQ dugouts (about 400 yards behind the front line) with the battalion commander, Lieutenant Colonel Arthur Loveband, when 'a dull roar was heard ... and we saw the gas coming'. The battalion was by now equipped with rudimentary respirators and fortunately everyone was awake for a rum issue so these went on speedily. The Germans used the gas cover to gain a foothold in Shell Trap Farm, following which heavy artillery and machine fire was opened on British lines. By midday the Dublins' lines were almost completely overrun and Leahy noted there was 'no quarter given or accepted'. Battalion headquarters withdrew at 9.30pm with Leahy and just 20 other ranks from that morning's strength of 17 officers and 651 other ranks.[15]

The fate of those lost was initially unclear. Soon after the end of operations a report showed that between 25 April and 25 May the battalion had lost 24 officers and 103 other ranks killed, with 13 officers and 291 men wounded. But an incredible 1,094 other ranks, plus 2 officers, were recorded as missing.[16] Among them was Private 9312 Thomas Quigley of James Street. He recalled how,

> Our men had bandaged me. After their retirement I lay alone for about two hours, when the Germans came up. One of the German privates on coming up jumped on me – one foot landing on my wounded knee – exclaiming "Englander". I was left in the trench where I was wounded with only a coat to cover me for 3 days and 3 nights. The Germans opened a tin of our own meat and left it beside me, and gave me three water bottles full

of water and a slice of their own bread. My leg was shattered and I was unable to move off my back.

Quigley added that the Germans had their own wounded to deal with and that although a German sergeant had wanted to move him, the stretcher-bearers would not as he was a British soldier. Eventually, he was taken to a German field hospital.[17]

It later became clear that the total number of deaths in the battalion during that time was 416. Of these 120 were on 25 and 26 April and 174 on 24 and 25 May.[18] Such fatality levels match those of units which fought on the Somme on 1 July 1916 and made the Second Battle of Ypres the most costly battle of the war for the 2nd Dublins. Aside from the immediately known dead, the eventual total of 416 accounts for another 289 of the missing, meaning that over 800 of those unaccounted for were not dead. These men either steadily returned to the battalion having been lost in the chaos of battle, or were taken prisoner. Lists of the latter gradually appeared in newspapers.[19] In what proportions these two possibilities occurred is unclear, but since the battalion records never noted any large-scale return of lost men – with numbers instead being stated as increasing due to fresh drafts – it is likely that most were taken prisoner.

Among the 416 dead were at least 199 Dubliners, eighty-two of those being on 24 and 25 May. One family particularly suffered: among the 2nd Dublins' dead were three brothers, privates 8982 John, 9443 Peter and 8848 Patrick McDonnell. Ten years separated each when they died. Peter, the eldest at 42, was killed first, on 26 April 1915. John, age 22 and Patrick, age 32, lost their lives on the same day, 24 May, although John was still officially missing in August.[20] Their parents, Edward and Anne, lived at 46 Bride Street, while Patrick left a widow, Elizabeth, a few doors away at number 38. None of their bodies were ever identified so all are remembered on the Menin Gate.[21] It is not clear whether their other brother, Edward, served, but at least there is no sign of him being killed.

The 2nd Dublins were not the only unit serving at Second Ypres in which Dubliners lost their lives. In the 1st Royal Irish Fusiliers 16 were killed, and 23 in the 1st Leinsters. Later in the year, the 2nd Royal Irish Rifles fought two costly battles in the Ypres area at Bellewaarde, first in June and then in September.[22] Elsewhere, the 1st Royal Irish Rifles lost 11 men at Fromelles on 9 May as part of an unsuccessful attack at Aubers Ridge.[23] In the 1st Irish Guards 16 Dubliners were killed by shells and machine-gun fire a few weeks later, 'in wreaths of driving rain and mist' at Festubert.[24] However, the Second Battle of Ypres stands out as one of the war's most destructive battles for the people of Dublin with around 370 Dubliners dead in a month. Beyond the Irish regiments, they lost their lives scattered through English, Scottish, Welsh and Canadian regiments, along with formations such as the Royal Field Artillery. On the Western Front, only the Somme and Passchendaele would see more Dubliners killed than at Second Ypres.

Prisoners

Those captured at Second Ypres were among 192,000 British Empire captives across the war, including at least 859 Dubliners.[25] Men who returned home during the war – usually due to being badly wounded – were cross-examined by the Committee on the Treatment of British Prisoners of War about their experiences.[26] Others gave detailed accounts during the trial of Roger Casement about his attempts to form an 'Irish Brigade' to fight alongside the Germans.[27] A significant amount of information flowed between the prison camps and home, beyond what could be conveyed in censored letters. Priests played an important role. Father Crotty, sent by the Vatican to the Limburg camp, wrote in detail to Father Hickey of Halston Street Church in Dublin describing the way Christmas 1915 was spent. He even wrote about plans – to which the Germans had apparently agreed – for a monument to those who died in the camp to be made in Ireland and transported to Limburg.[28] One newspaper, the *Herald*, tried to play an important role in helping to determine whether men thought to be dead were actually prisoners. It printed group or individual pictures of prisoners and asked if people recognised them. In November, 1915 the *Herald* claimed to have secured information on over a hundred missing Irish soldiers. However, in both of the cases it reported on in detail where a relative had identified a photo, the man did in the end turn out to be dead, so it might be that such work only provided false hope.[29]

For some, capture did not last long. Sergeant Francis Taite of the 1st Irish Guards was captured on 1 September 1914 and held for a week, only to be liberated by the French.[30] John Dowling of the 2nd Dublins was captured retreating from Mons, finding himself and several others surrounded by German cavalry. He told the *Herald*, 'They put a rope around each man and hitched us to a motor car, and in that way we were hurled along like cattle to Cambrai.' Overnight, a captured French officer said he suspected they would all be shot so the men decided to escape. After prisoners assaulted the guards Dowling and two others escaped. They were taken in by French farmers and worked on the land for sixteen days in disguise as German soldiers passed. Then a French officer asked them to try to break through German lines with him. Soon separated from the officer they nevertheless managed to make it through by stealth.[31]

There was a risk of being killed on capture. Dalkey man Private 4968 Edward 'Ned' Richardson was serving in the 17th Lancers on an advance patrol on 12 October 1914. Writing to Richardson's mother, fellow Dalkey resident Sergeant 6458 Henry Drew of the 5th Lancers relayed a story he had been told by a comrade in the 17th:

> Ned was captured and made go along the road as a sort of hoax to get another patrol into the trap. When Ned saw what they were up to he sacrificed his life to save his comrades by putting up his hand for them not to come any further, which they perceived, and halted. But the Germans struck poor Ned with his own bayonet several times, killing him.[32]

However, killings or evasions were not the norm. Private 6713 James Wilson of Richmond Place was among the first to be captured, on 27 August 1914 at Ligny, serving with the 2nd Dublins. Wilson was a regular soldier who had served from age 18 in 1899 until 1907, seeing service in the South African War from July 1900 for a year. Having married Martha Kavanagh in 1909 he re-enlisted in the reserve in 1911 and was mobilised on the outbreak of war. On his return, Wilson made a lengthy statement to the War Office, the interviewing officer noting, 'Struck me as being a very intelligent and reliable fellow. Not prone to exaggerate.'[33] Wilson was wounded when captured due to a shell whizzing close to his eyes, causing problems which would mark his time in captivity. He was part of a group which spent seven days with scant food, marching from Ligny to Mons (about thirty miles). They slept mainly in chapels. After initial treatment at Ligny no medical attention was given to any of the wounded, with first-aid packs having been taken from them when 'All our men were robbed by the German soldiers *en route.*' At Mons the men were put in railway cattle trucks on 5 September: 'The floor of the truck was thick with horse manure.

We had to take it in turns to sit down.' When another Dublin Fusilier asked for something to clean the floor he was told, 'it's good enough for swine'. On 7 September the men arrived at Sennelager camp, roughly equidistant between Dortmund and Hanover. For six days they had no shelter or blankets, only straw to sleep on. Then, steadily, tents and blankets arrived.

Fresh clothing was slower to appear. Wilson recalled, 'I kept my shirt on for five weeks after I was captured, and then I had to throw it away as it was nearly alive with lice.' That was on 2 October and no new shirt appeared until early December. Men who complained were routinely tied to a tree for several hours. Washing was a challenge with no soap for the first two months of incarceration, although hot showers appeared in late November. Food was limited, a pint of chicory 'coffee' in the morning, with a pint and a half of boiled cabbage plus occasional bits of meat in the evening. Each night, aside from more coffee, three men shared two pounds of stale rye bread. Occasionally white bread was brought from France but it was days old and mouldy. Food parcels from home arrived from mid-November. Wilson said, 'I can't say anything as to the Germans stealing parcels of food, but all the Germans were smoking English cigarettes.' As for work, days were long, beginning with a 7am march of five miles, then a 9am to 12pm shift. The 'lunch' break was rest but no food, before more work at 12.30pm to 4.45pm. They arrived back at camp at about 6.15pm. Wilson's work for seventeen days was carrying timber for the construction of a light railway and he estimated that he walked twenty miles each day. There were no games in the camp, but from mid-October a German Roman Catholic priest held a weekly mass on Sunday.

Wilson left Sennelager on 22 December 1914 for Limburg by which time the camp had grown from its initial 900 British and 400 French to 4,500 British and 28,000 French. The Germans had begun to treat Irish prisoners differently. In early December the building of two wooden huts was complete and around 2,000 Irish were the first to move in. Following fatigues one day the Commandant said, 'All Irish step forward.' Wilson said, 'he told us that we were not going to work any more as we were the friend of the Germans, and the English must do the work'. While conditions were basic, and food did not change, the huts were at least warmer than tents. The move to Limburg was part of an attempt to give the Irish better conditions, which seems to have been reflected in lighter work plus better washing, lavatories and clothing, but not food. Wilson's work was particularly light because towards the end of his time at Sennelager his eye wound caused him serious problems and he could not even see his own feet clearly. Other men, however, carried out heavier work even at Limburg including work in mines, quarries and factories.

From early 1915 representatives of neutral powers such as Sweden and the USA visited camps for inspections, while letters and parcels did reach the men at Limburg. However, Wilson's sight was deteriorating and in early March 1915 he was admitted to hospital. A German doctor, who had worked in Liverpool, gave him dark glasses to wear. The German doctor advised 'that my sight was greatly affected and that ... I would not get it back for six or seven years.' Wilson remained in hospital until August 1915 but as early as April he was told by a Swedish representative that he would be repatriated in an exchange of disabled prisoners. That process had begun from March 1915[34] with severely wounded or ill prisoners sent home via Switzerland or Holland, or interned in either country if it was felt they might return home and pursue some kind of military service. Wilson returned in February 1916, still wearing his dark glasses. Arriving home, he was discharged in April 1916 as no longer physically fit for war service. He was awarded a pension of 9d per day for life.[35] Thomas Quigley, captured in the 2nd Dublins at Ypres on 24 May 1915 had his left leg amputated by German doctors after it had been wounded in three places by shrapnel. He recalled eight operations 'and on one occasion they began to operate before I had become unconscious. I think they were pressed for time, but did not intend cruelty.' In February 1916 he was sent home via Holland.[36] Violence against prisoners was common.[37] However, in general, Dublin soldiers reported good medical treatment from doctors, indifferent or no nursing, and conditions which were strict but not cruel.[38]

Just before going into hospital Wilson had become of interest to recruiters for the Irish Brigade.[39] Arriving at Limburg, Wilson met two priests from Rome, Fathers Crotty and O'Gorman. In early March 1915, O'Gorman was recalled to Rome and replaced by Father Nicholas or Nicholson, Leitrim-born but an American citizen. After mass Nicholas 'drew a small crowd round him and 'started by reminding the men of the injustice of England to Ireland'.

He said that if they joined the Irish Brigade they would be given their freedom and 'have a fine time in Berlin'. A few days later Roger Casement arrived citing '1798, our rotten Government, and what our forefathers bled for'. He promised money (£20), free passage to the USA and work after the war. Wilson recalled that Casement 'only got growled at' with one Irish soldier asking 'Are we going to fight against our fellow countrymen?' After Casement left, Nicholas and a German priest continued to try to recruit telling them their oaths in the British army were 'a passing fancy'. However, Crotty did not support their cause and advised Wilson that 'an oath is binding and you will be committing a sin if you break your oath of allegiance'. Others reported being offered similar inducements to Wilson's.[40]

Undoubtedly, an unwillingness to fight against Irish soldiers was a factor in men not joining Casement's Irish Brigade. There was also an issue of how those men saw their national allegiance. Michael McGuirk saw the Brigade as being at odds with his own Irish nationalism, telling one man who had joined that 'I was a Nationalist at heart and would take up no arms for the Germans.'[41] Wilson, a Roman Catholic Dubliner with long service in the British army including the South African war said to a member of the Brigade, 'I'm a Britisher and shall still like to be one.'[42] Michael Kehoe, Casement's assistant and the Recruiting Officer of the Brigade put it down to more practical factors, with various support groups such as what he called the 'Ladies Society in Dublin', ensuring that far more parcels reached the Irish soldiers at Limburg than others, although there is no compelling evidence of that from interviews with returning prisoners. There were, though, fears about what might happen to families at home if it became known that men were backing the Germans.[43]

However, some Irish prisoners did join: a total of fifty-six.[44] Wilson and McQuirk described visits to Limburg from some, either wearing civilian clothes or Irish Brigade uniforms (grey with green trim), telling how good their conditions were.[45] In late May these men were sent to a German barrack at Zossen and attached to the 203rd Brandenburgers, with whom they were to be organised into machine-gun teams. The plan was that they would, in due course, land in Ireland with German officers to support revolution at home. That eventually happened in April 1916, but with just two men, both Dubliners, Robert Monteith and Daniel Bailey, joining Casement.[46]

For the remainder of the Irish Brigade the war amounted to little. In August 1915 they moved to Danzig with the 2nd Schlawe Battalion. Some took up civilian employment, twenty joined the German army and were given barrack duties, with three sent to a machine-gun company in Munich. Most of the rest of the Brigade followed there by the end of the war. Kehoe tried to secure passage to America for anyone who wanted to go but failed. Around a dozen agreed to be repatriated as British prisoners of war, while the rest remained in Germany. Kehoe noted in 1952, 'Some of them married German girls and a few Irishman are still living there in Germany.' Kehoe himself returned to Ireland in 1920 to serve with the IRA.[47]

Aside from Bailey and Monteith, there were nine other men in the Brigade with a Dublin connection.[48] Among them, Michael O'Toole had been a Lance Corporal in the Irish Guards when captured, but before the war had been a civil servant. As a fluent Irish speaker and a member of the IRB, it is unlikely that he needed any persuading to join the Brigade. Indeed, he was the only exception to the rule that only unmarried men could join for fear of pressure which might be exerted on families at home.[49] Harry Burke, who had been captured on 27 August 1914 in the 2nd Dublins, was tailor to the Irish Brigade and was trying to find a route home in early 1919. It was reported that he was in Berlin and had been involved in post-war political fighting there on the government side, but that: 'This man now wants to go home, and is anxious to know whether he will be court-martialled. "I am willing to take my punishment", he said.'[50] It is not clear whether he did come back to the UK but in 1952 he was said to be living in America.[51]

The *Lusitania* and the *Arabic*

While attempts were made to recruit the Irish Brigade, Ireland faced the war's highest-profile U-Boat attack on a civilian vessel, Cunard's RMS *Lusitania*. The liner was hit off the south coast of Ireland on 7 May 1915, carrying nearly 2,000 people from New York to Liverpool.[52] 1,201 people lost their lives. The Germans justified the attack partly on the basis of the allied blockade of the Central Powers.

Although it was a civilian vessel it was British – and therefore belonged to the enemy – and it was carrying ammunition which caused a second explosion after the ship was hit by a torpedo. But among the passengers were 128 American citizens, and the response from the public and politicians in the USA was fierce. Germany was forced to limit its submarine war against passenger liners, even those carrying enemy flags. However, a more thorough cessation of U-Boat attacks only took place after the sinking of the White Star liner SS *Arabic* on 19 August 1915, about fifty miles off the Old Head of Kinsale.[53] Nearly 400 were saved, but 44 lost their lives, including more American citizens. Following this, all U-Boat warfare against merchants and liners in the Channel and west of the UK was stopped, and would not start again until early 1917.[54]

Dublin was affected by the sinking of both ships. The city saw survivors at first hand, with about 300 passing through Kingsbridge (now Heuston) station on their way from Cork to various destinations.[55] Among the dead on the *Lusitania* were two Dublin-born crew members: Fireman W. Barry and a waiter, Martin Geraghty. The parents of two other men resided in Dublin: Fireman John Orange and a passenger, William Winter.[56] Another crewman, Fireman James Murphy, a native of Swords, survived the attack. He was pictured in the *Sunday Independent* and told how he had been jammed between two lifeboats in the water and was rescued.[57] The *Freeman's Journal* headline was typical in describing the sinking as a 'crime' and a 'fiendish deed', with the coverage similar to that of 'Hun frightfulness' in the early months of the war.[58] Vivid stories of escape added to the horror. One Dubliner, Dr Mecredy, explained that after being hit the ship 'listed so heavily to the starboard that the port boats could not be launched.' George Scott from Clontarf described how 'When we were about half way through our lunch, we heard a terrible crash. The vessel trembled first and then listed to one side. Every one jumped from their seats and rushed on deck. The women and children shrieked wildly, and when we got on deck there was a great deal of panic.' Scott was on the ship until the deck went below the water, pulling him with it. He continued, 'On coming to the surface I felt very much exhausted and was entangled in a mass of wreckage.' Soon he was on an upturned boat, then taken on a lifeboat which was towed by a fishing smack before the survivors were put on a trawler to Queenstown. Scott concluded, 'The whole thing appears to me now to be a terrible nightmare. The agonising cries of the hundreds struggling with death in the sea were distressing beyond all description.'[59] An Irish jury which met at Kinsale on 10 May declared the sinking an act of 'wilful and wholesale murder' in a verdict against 'the officers of the German submarine, the German Emperor, and the Government of Germany'. In doing so, the *Freeman's Journal* said, 'The jury simply gave voice to the verdict of the civilized world.'[60]

On the *Arabic* there were nine Dublin passengers, all survivors.[61] They included John Day and his sister, Lelie, both of Dundrum. John Day was manager of the National Benefit Insurance Company in Dame Street and assistant secretary of the Dublin Motor Club. Later that year he was commissioned into the Royal Flying Corps.[62] His time on the *Arabic* was far from the only time in which he would have a close brush with death in the First World War, before losing his life in another conflict.[63]

Home Comforts

Following the Second Battle of Ypres, set-piece battles on the Western Front involving many Dubliners were scarce for well over a year until an attack was made on the Somme from 1 July 1916. Indeed, the British army as a whole was only involved in one major battle during that time: Loos in September 1915, which marked the arrival of Kitchener's New Army on the Western Front.[64] Of course, the relative absence of set-piece battles did not mean that fighting was not taking place, but it was in skirmishes designated as 'actions' rather than battles. These actions had their cost: over 70,000 dead in the British army as a whole, and over 800 Dubliners lost their lives on the Western Front in 1915.[65] However, casualties in some battalions were relatively light compared to what had gone before. By the end of March 1916, the 2nd Dublins could count 18 killed, 89 wounded and one missing in the 7 months since the battalion left the Ypres area in late July 1915.[66] That was far less than in just one fighting day's losses at Ypres.

Insight into the 2nd Dublins' lives at this time comes from letters to Monica Roberts, a well-off Stillorgan woman who had organised sending comforts to the troops. Roberts organised the 'Band of Helpers to the Soldiers'. Not only did that involve sending items ranging from tobacco and chocolate to socks and boot-laces, but Roberts herself became a regular correspondent with many men. They wrote making special requests and telling something of their lives (subject to censorship) and she wrote on life back in Ireland.

From late July 1915 the 2nd Dublins were based in the Somme area, holding trenches variously at Serre, Auchonvillers, Beaumont-Hamel and Bienvillers into the spring of 1916. Rotation between the front and billets was regular, rarely with more than five days spent in the line. The battalion paraded in front of the King and the French President on 25 October. Private 18178 Joseph Elley of the 2nd Dublins wrote to Monica Roberts, 'He did not say anything to the troops, but we were pleased to see that the King [was] taking so much interest in the men so we cheered with all our might.'[67] Christmas Day 1915 was spent partly at the front, with the 2nd Dublins relieving the 9th Royal Irish Rifles in the line that day. The 9th had been formed from the West Belfast UVF though no record was passed down of any banter between the Dubliners and the northerners.[68] Perhaps there was none; of a visit to the front by John Redmond, who spoke to the Ulster Division, Elley wrote there was 'no bad feeling amongst us fellows out here & I think it will end such feelings forever'.[69] Elley had earlier written, 'The Dublins get on well with all the Reg[imen]ts, especially the Jocks.'[70] After they were relieved from their Christmas duty at the front on 29 December the men were still given goose, turkey and Christmas pudding.[71]

Letters to Monica Roberts reveal hugely varied levels of literacy among the men, and in so doing offer vivid accounts, often as if spoken by the men. One regular correspondent was Private 8723 Edward Mordaunt who wrote of the Germans in September 1915:

> i seen them slay innocent women and children and also young Girls it was something shamefull it brought the tears to most of our eyes who seen what they did and i think it is our turn now to revenge the death of those poor innocent people and also our poor comrades who died on the field of battle for those we love i am not afraid to die to-morrow because i know i am doing it for a good cause.[72]

The men's persistent gripe was over the weather, hardly surprising since they were partly living out of doors during winter months. Sergeant John Brooks wrote in late November 1915, 'the snow is at least a foot on the ground and is also freezing very hard for the past week' which made it 'rather bad for anyone lying sick'. At the same time Joseph Elley wrote, 'the trenches are simply unbearable with the rain washing them in'. He continued, 'The trenches we hold were up to our knees after the rain, but we are all looking forward to our leave, so we just have to grin and bear it.'[73]

Providing cigarettes and tobacco was a key task for Roberts. The importance of smoking was explained in a letter to the *Evening Mail* by William Armstrong Pratt, who had been working for the newspaper when commissioned. Pratt served in the 1st King's Liverpool Regiment and wrote:

> One is inclined necessarily to smoke more out here than at home. In the trenches cigarettes are a Godsend and a necessity. For instance, in most places I have been to there were thousands of dead buried all round, and in many instances only a couple of feet under ground. In places, therefore, the stench is oppressive. Then there was a huge number of mosquitoes and flies, which are kept away by tobacco.[74]

He was killed in August 1918, serving as a captain and having won the Military Cross.[75]

Beyond Roberts' organisation there were also efforts more officially connected to the Royal Dublin Fusiliers. A regimental bureau operated from the house of businessman Sir Stanley Cochrane, 45 Kildare Street, personally funded by Cochrane. There were four arms to the organisation: the Bureau provided comforts except clothing; the Women's Branch dealt with clothing and comforts; Lady Arnott's group dealt with items for prisoners at Limburg, while Lady Mayo did the same for prisoners in other camps. Tuesday 28 September 1915 was designated as a regimental 'Flag Day' across the county. It was estimated that around 1,500 volunteers sold flags and rattled collection tins. 200,000 flags were made (though it is not clear how many were sold), and 2,000–3,000 collection boxes distributed. Two types of flag were offered: one in regimental colours (blue, green and red) and the other green with a harp and crown.[76]

Other events supported causes beyond the Dublin Fusiliers, including St John's Ambulance Brigade, Italian soldiers' families, and blind veterans.[77] By the end of 1915 plans were being made for a Central

Soldiers' Club in the old police station in College Street, to provide soldiers with a place to stay when travelling through Dublin to or from home leave.[78] By this time, Dubliners had become well aware of the war far beyond the Western Front, as blood had been shed throughout the summer of 1915 at Gallipoli.

5 GALLIPOLI: HELLES

... the landing was a great triumph for the British soldier, and will go down to history as a wonderful military achievement.
The Freeman's Journal on Cape Helles[1]

A Byword for Failure

Revisionist historians have challenged the popular view of the war as one of futile slaughter. The Somme was, for William Philpott, a 'Bloody Victory'.[2] While A. J. P. Taylor called Passchendaele 'the blindest slaughter of a blind war', Gary Sheffield argues that Taylor's 'blanket condemnation of the campaign ... is a travesty of the truth'.[3] But no such case is made for Gallipoli, or more formally the 'Dardanelles' campaign. Its aim was extremely laudable: the naval destruction of Turkey's defences along the Dardanelles passage at the entrance of the Sea of Marmara which led to Constantinople. Through a mix of land and sea power, the Turkish capital would be seized and the Central Powers would lose a key ally. The idea was the brainchild of Winston Churchill, then the First Lord of the Admiralty. As Gary Sheffield points out, a senior officer who served towards the end of the campaign said, 'Mr. Winston Churchill's conception was magnificent' while also 'the most damnable folly that ever amateurs were enticed into'. Moreover, the campaign took place at the beginning of the British army's learning curve: 'At Gallipoli in 1915, the British troops lacked experience, artillery, ammunition, scientific gunnery, aircraft, Lewis guns, Stokes mortars, technical and tactical know-how – everything, in short, that contributed towards the success of the 1917–18 offensives.'[4]

Meanwhile, recent research on Ottoman records suggests that the Turkish generals exerted far more effective 'command and control' over their operations at Gallipoli than did the British. Their approach encouraged initiative, and was based on effective reporting, while commanders were willing to intervene in operations when they went wrong. In contrast, the British commanders had poor information, left too much to relatively junior commanders, and were unwilling to intervene when they should have done.[5] The end result was around 46,000 allied dead (38,000 British and Empire, 8,000 French) and a similar number of Turkish. The British suffered around 44,000 wounded and another 90,000 evacuated with sickness. Total allied casualties were around 390,000.[6]

The popular memory of Dubliners at Gallipoli is dominated by part of one battalion: D Company of the 7th Royal Dublin Fusiliers, the Dublin Pals. Yet there is a much wider and deeper story to tell: Dubliners served far beyond that battalion and suffered heavily. The 1st Dublins were part of the bloody landings in late April 1915. At Suvla Bay in August 1915 the 6th Dublins were in the same division as the 7th. Yet their social background meant that they were of far less interest to the newspapers than the rugby stars of the Pals.

The Naval Campaign

It was not initially intended that soldiers should set foot on the Gallipoli peninsula until Turkish defences were subdued by naval guns. An attack from the sea was authorised in principle by the British War Council on 13 January 1915. After further discussions it began on 19 February, but an eight-hour onslaught destroyed no guns. Bad weather intervened and the next bombardment took place nearly a week later. Over the next three weeks a series of attacks took place, sometimes including landings by marines who were more successful at hitting Turkish guns than the naval bombardment was. However, simply not enough guns were destroyed, and Turkish forces not only held the forts but mined the Dardanelles straits. An attempt to force through on 18 March failed to sweep any mines and destroyed only one gun, with around a third of the British–French force of sixteen ships out of action

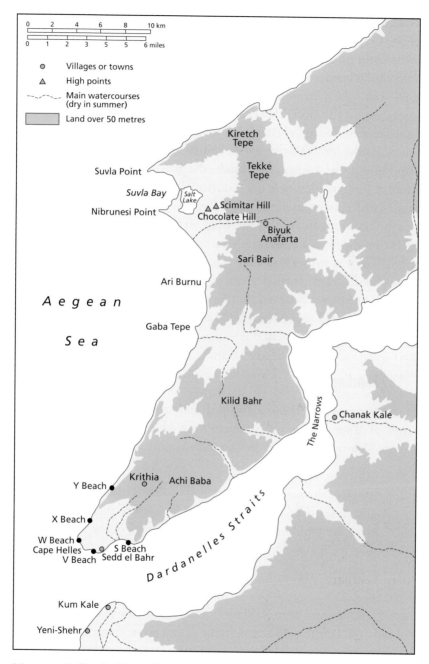

Map 5.1: Gallipoli. Adapted by David Cox from the map drawn by David Appleyard in Grayson, *Belfast Boys*, 50.

in one way or another.[7] Dublin's first death at Gallipoli came a few days before. On 15 March 1915 Leading Stoker Joseph O'Brien of Skerries was serving on the light cruiser HMS *Dartmouth* in the Dardanelles campaign, when he was scalded to death in a boiler explosion.[8] Earlier in the war, the *Dartmouth* saw action in East Africa pursuing the *Königsberg* in the Rufigi River, and then in the Adriatic, before going to the Dardanelles in February 1915.[9]

By the time O'Brien was killed, troops had already been sent to form the core of an invasion force: the Royal Naval Division, 29th Division (which included the 1st Royal Dublin Fusiliers) and two divisions of Australians and New Zealanders. This force of around 50,000 was consolidated as the Mediterranean Expeditionary Force under General Sir Ian Hamilton's command. In an example of 'mission creep',[10] it was now clear that a full invasion would take place on the peninsula. This, rather than naval bombardment was how the British government believed that Constantinople would be taken, yet a decision to send troops had been taken before it was clear that the naval operation had failed.[11]

Landing

Serving on HMS *Cornwallis* and involved in the landing of troops at Cape Helles on 25 April was Able Seaman Ernest 'Dick' Rickus. Writing to his sister in Croydon in early May Rickus described how

> we went through the gates of hell ... The Turks waited until we got close in & then fired a murderous fire the troops which were the Dublins started to fall like leaves in the autumn anyway we managed to get them ashore & went back for another Boat load ... the poor old Dublins their is about 100 left out of 1000.[12]

The 1st Dublins had been at Madras at the outbreak of war, arriving in England just before Christmas 1914. They were then mostly in the Nuneaton area until late March when they set sail for the Dardanelles via Alexandria and Lemnos.[13] Their destination was Cape Helles on the Gallipoli peninsula's southern edge. The shoreline was mainly surrounded by steep sandy cliffs, rising to between 100 and 300 feet, broken occasionally by gullies and ravines. Landings were to be made on five beaches (S, V, W, X and Y) by British troops, while two diversionary attacks took place, one involving French troops. The main landings were at three beaches: V and W, where the slopes were not so steep as elsewhere, and X, where it was believed that the shape of the land would provide shelter from artillery. 29th Division's eventual target was to take the Kilid Bahr plateau, specifically the village and fort of Sedd-el-Bahr, hills 114, 138, 141 and 472, and Achi Baba, securing forts which overlooked the straits.[14] The 1st Dublins' war diary for April to June 1915 did not survive, perhaps because parts of it were lost or just never made, due to the losses they suffered. However, their story can be pieced together from a detailed regimental history compiled soon after the war, brigade records and the war diary of the 1st Royal Munster Fusiliers with whom the 1st Dublins landed.[15]

V Beach was narrow and sandy, 350 yards long and 10 yards deep. One company of the 1st Dublins was on the collier SS *River* Clyde, which beached at the start of the landing, with three other companies on barges towed by pinnaces (small rowing boats).[16] An unnamed officer in the 1st Dublins wrote a lengthy description to his father in Dublin which appeared in the *Irish Times*. He described how the Dublins had been towed on the pinnaces from 5am. Their journey over water was to be three miles. About half-way in, Turkish shells began to hit the water

Figure 5.1: Sedd el Bahr fort photographed from the SS River Clyde. A party of Dublin Fusiliers are sheltering on land, and wounded men of the Munster Fusiliers are lying on board a lighter in the foreground. (©IWM, Q 50473).

around them, but he said that 'with my field glasses I could see many of the Turks running for their lives. I thought then that we would have no difficulty in landing.'[17]

However, Turkish soldiers were concealed on the cliffs and in trenches in front of the village of Sedd-el-Bahr which was the Dublins' initial target. Such was the ferocity of the fire that the British landing at V Beach believed the Turks had machine-guns though they did not.[18] The three companies on barges (X, Y and Z) were to land at 6am with the *River Clyde* following half an hour later containing one company (W).[19] But the currents were strong and slowed the barges so much so that the *Clyde* and the barges arrived at roughly the same time, attempting to land from 6.25am. Captain Alexander Molony, on the *Clyde*, later wrote home that the boats 'were met by a terrific tornado of fire, many men killed and wounded in the boats, and wounded men were knocked over into the water and drowned, but they kept on, and the survivors jumped into the water in some cases up to their necks, and got ashore; but the slaughter was terrific'.[20] Others had more trouble even attempting the leave the boats. Set free by the pinnace, one unnamed officer's boat collided with another just as men were disembarking, and came under heavy fire:

> I was covered with dead men. Not knowing that they were dead I was roaring at them to let me up for I was drowning a wounded man under me (there was half a boat-full of water then, the boat having been pierced with bullets). The machine guns still played on us when we were towed back to a minesweeper. I was simply saturated all over with blood, and I could feel the hot blood all over me all the way across. When they pulled those poor fellows off me they were all dead, and the poor fellow under me was dead.

Though wounded in the arm the officer attempted another landing, in a new boat. But that too was badly hit and he ended up being taken back to a ship and sent to Malta.[21] An official report from Captain Guy Geddes of the 1st Munsters echoed the officer's account, noting how on landing, two companies of the Dublins 'were met with a terrific rifle and machine-gun fire. They were literally slaughtered like rats in a trap.' Men shot in the water but not killed instantly fell and drowned. Geddes noted, 'Captain French of the Dublins told me afterwards that he counted the first 48 men to follow me, and they all fell.'[22] Of the 700

Dublins who had tried to land from barges only around 300 made it there at all.[23] Matters were so bad that W Company was ordered to remain on the *Clyde*.[24]

How had this happened? Poor decisions were made at command level about where the best opportunities for attack could be found.[25] Meanwhile, the British had seriously underestimated the strength of the Turkish defences. Kitchener had said, 'Suppose one submarine pops up opposite the town of Gallipoli and waves a Union Jack three times – the whole Turkish garrison on the peninsula will take to their heels.'[26] Not even the maps were very accurate. Geddes noted, 'The maps issued were indifferent, and painted but a poor picture of the topographical features.' As a consequence, an unexpectedly steep cliff meant that those who succeeded in landing found the climb rendered difficult by the weight of their packs. Within two hours so many officers had been lost that 86th Brigade's task became not to advance but 'to prevent any forward movement of the Turks'. Mixed groups of Munsters and Dublins formed up as they could, taking leadership from whichever officers had survived. From mid-morning they had little option but to dig in as best they could.[27] The Dublins had borne the brunt of the Turkish defence in a battle which resembled the kind of attack launched on the Western Front. Elsewhere, more successful landings had taken place, by the ANZACs at Ari Burnu, and by other British units either side of V Beach. The French had landed on the Asian side of the Dardanelles at Kum Kale. However, even though the Anzacs' initial landing encountered relatively light opposition (they landed 4,000 men in the first fifteen minutes), they soon faced a fierce fight as they worked their way inland.[28]

With around 300 of the 1st Dublins having landed, the day of 25 April and overnight into 26 April were desperate hours in which men sought to secure the beachhead and make some inroads into Turkish positions. Captain David French was one of a few officers who made it to the beach though he was hit by a bullet in the left arm, and the bullet had forced parts of his wrist-watch into him.[29] The battalion commander, Lieutenant Colonel Richard Rooth, was shot dead, according to Molony, 'at the edge of the water'.[30] The battalion chaplain, Father Finn, who insisted on being at the very front with the men fell at the same stage, the first British chaplain to be killed in action in the war.[31] French later recalled how, 'I could find only 30 or 40 men intact & we commenced to dig into the low cliff. Why the Turks with their vast preparations did not level this bank of earth down I cannot imagine. Had they done so not one of us would have escaped.' French and the men he had gathered took shelter when they had dug in and 'lay there all day'.[32] 2nd Lieutenant Cuthbert Maffett was with French and later told how, 'We had a man near us with a pocket periscope, which we put over the top of the bank from time to time to see if the Turks were coming down on us, but there was no move on their part.'[33] French described the overnight conditions: 'Heavy rifle fire incessantly. Drizzling with rain. Wounded groaning on all sides, &, surrounded by dead, I admit I thought it was all up.'[34] The 1st Dublins' regimental history – never the sort of publication to talk easily of failure – recorded that on the evening of 25th the situation was grim:

> The landing at "V" Beach had failed ... "W" Beach was held, though the position of the partially entrenched troops on the plateau above it was precarious; "X" Beach was fairly safe; at "Y" and "Z" Beaches the diminishing companies clung desperately to their gains ... while at Kum Kale the French were fulfilling their task but were under orders to withdraw.[35]

But strengthened by the remaining company of the Dublins from the *Clyde* at around 7pm on the evening of 25th (though they also faced fire on landing) the situation on V Beach began to improve.[36] Men from a range of units were consolidated. Supported by a bombardment from HMS *Albion* both the 'Old Fort' and the village of Sedd-el-Bahr had been taken by 1pm. A successful move was made against Hill 141 (north-west of Sedd-el-Bahr) in the afternoon, but over the course of 25 and 26 April, 88 of the 1st Dublins were dead[37] and at least 300 wounded.

Krithia

Having secured a beachhead, the next task was to try to take Achi Baba, a high point between Cape Helles and the village of Krithia. Three attempts (the three Battles of Krithia), all involving the 1st Dublins, were made between late April and early June. On 28 April a Turkish counter-attack repelled a joint British–French operation which suffered from poor intelligence, inadequate artillery, an over-complex plan and too few reserves.[38] The Dublins were in reserve during this operation and losses were relatively light: three dead that day and two

died of wounds a day later.[39] On 30 April, the Dublins had 374 men and
had been commanded for two days by the only officer left: Lieutenant
Henry O'Hara, who had begun the landings in command of a platoon,
only to find himself steadily in command of a company and then the
whole battalion. The Munsters stood at 596 men and 12 officers, so the
two battalions were temporarily merged. They became known as the
'Dubsters' or 'Dubster Battalion'.[40]

A Turkish counter-attack soon followed, almost certainly on
the night of 1/2 May, with the Dublins losing 100 men and the 1st
Munsters another 62 as the Turks broke into the Dubsters' line.[41] Of the
fighting on 1/2 May, which took place from 10.30pm to 5am, Henry
O'Hara wrote:

> The Turks were simply driven on to the barbed wire in front of
> the trenches . . . and shot down by the score. At one point they
> actually got into the trenches, but were driven out by the
> bayonet . . . The fighting is of the most desperate kind – very
> little quarter on either side. The men were absolutely mad to
> get at them, as they mutilate our wounded when they catch
> them.[42]

These losses suffered by the Dublins were devastating following those
during the landings at Cape Helles. They were exacerbated by the fact
that, as David French wrote, 'The wounded had a ghastly time – none of
the Dublins being attended to – except with field dressings – by a medical
man for 36 hours.'[43] A further reorganisation within 29th Division was
necessary as 86th Brigade was temporarily broken up and the Dubsters
moved to 87th Brigade until 6 June.[44]

Between 6 and 8 May at Second Krithia there was again no
breakthrough against strongly held Turkish positions after insufficient
artillery fire.[45] The Dubsters were initially in reserve, but after a short
advance of 200 yards at 5pm on 7 May, they faced machine-gun and
shell fire from Turkish lines. There was little more to do than hold their
position, which they did until being relieved at 7pm the next day. Losses
were much lighter at this second attempt on Achi Baba, the 1st Dublins
losing eight men. O'Hara described 'a most awful time – fighting by day
and night – appalling casualties'.[46] The Dubsters were eventually withdrawn to Y Beach on 9 May to reorganise and then to Gully Beach
where they were split into separate battalions again on 19 May.[47]
O'Hara wrote, 'The fighting has now developed into trench warfare

just the same as in France.' He added, 'I don't expect to survive long myself – a Captain on the staff here said the first fortnight was incomparably worse than Mons or La Bassee, so you see we have had a rough time.'[48]

One more attempt was made, on 4–6 June at Third Krithia, when artillery fire was once again inadequate, ceasing two minutes before the main attack began and also missing the centre of the area to be attacked. On 4 June, 'The attack fizzled out by about 4pm when it appeared inadvisable to make further efforts.' Some fighting and exchanges of fire continued over the next two days, and there was a Turkish counter-attack on the 6th, but there was no further attempt at advance by the British. Over the three days, the 1st Dublins lost thirty-five men.[49] From this point on, no major advance was attempted from Helles, with the British instead focusing on divisional-scale operations in the area.[50]

Between the landings on 25 April and the end of Third Krithia the 1st Dublins lost 268 men dead.[51] At least 114 of these were from Dublin. Echoing how some Belfast streets would be affected by the Somme, some Dublin streets were particularly affected by Gallipoli. Summerhill, Lower Gardiner Street, Parnell Street and Stafford Street (now Wolfe Tone Street) each lost three men. Many others lost more than one. In Stafford Street, two sets of grieving parents lived close to each other. Private 10010 Patrick Dillon's parents Richard and Teresa lived at number 9, while the parents of Private 8891 Denis Walsh were at 8. Dillon was probably killed on 1 May, while Walsh lost his life on 4 June.[52] They might also have had another grieving neighbour at the time, and certainly would do later, widowed Alice Fagan at number 18. She had already lost a son, Private 8197 Simon Fagan, in the 1st Connaught Rangers on 23 November 1914, when news came that her son Private 11233 Christopher Fagan had been killed on 8 May 1915.[53] These men were among thirteen linked to Stafford Street killed during the war.

The Mounting Cost

News of the full extent of the heavy losses took about three weeks to reach the newspapers at home. On 18 May the *Evening Mail* headlined 'A TERRIBLE DEATH-ROLL', talking of only 115 in the 1st Dublins answering the roll call on the evening of 25 April. The next day, the unnamed officer's letter in the *Irish Times* said that 'nearly all' the officers were killed or wounded.[54] However, the Dublin newspapers also presented the actions of the 1st Dublins alongside the 1st Munsters in heroic terms. An artist's impression of the Helles landings printed in the *Irish Independent* on 22 May showed the men making steady progress up a steep incline. Its description implied that the two battalions had been specially chosen: 'The Dublin Fusiliers and the Munster Fusiliers were the troops selected to lead the way in the landing of the Expeditionary Force on the Gallipoli Peninsula. Their devoted heroism on the occasion is one of the most glorious features of the war, and, at the same time, one of the saddest, as their losses are very severe.' It went on to say that the 'This picture is an impressionist sketch of the scene at the landing.' It was indeed highly impressionistic since it showed large groups of men making their way up a gentle slope with some ease, with no hint of the heavy losses which the newspaper itself was clear had been incurred.[55] Later stories in newspapers talked of 'Stories of Gallantry', 'The Dash of the Irish', the 'Thrilling' story of the fight on V Beach and 'Unparalleled Feats of Arms'.[56] Underpinning this view was the fact that despite very heavy costs, the landing had been made and a beachhead established. It was remarkable that one story in the *Freeman's Journal*, after recounting how those landing heard body after body fall into the water wounded, said that the soldiers interviewed 'concur in the opinion that the landing was a great triumph for the British soldier, and will go down to history as a wonderful military achievement'.[57] A tribute to heroism it certainly was, but 'triumphs' like this would not secure the peninsula.

Although the landing at Cape Helles, and the battles at Krithia which followed, remain the most well-known aspects of the 1st Dublins' time at Gallipoli these events were not the end of their story on the peninsula. Indeed, they lost even more men between 9 June and their withdrawal in early January 1916. During this time the battalion's total dead at Gallipoli numbered 297. Another 22 succumbed to wounds, having been taken from the peninsula to Egypt, Malta, Greece or Gibraltar. Among them was Lieutenant Henry O'Hara who had briefly commanded the battalion.[58] At least 100 of these dead were from Dublin.

Many of the deaths resulted from small-scale skirmishes or unpredictable shell fire from Turkish lines. However, there were further attempted advances, most notably for the 1st Dublins on 28 June at

Gully Ravine, on the western side of the peninsula near Y Beach, in a fresh attempt to take positions near Krithia. This was preceded by an artillery bombardment which was more effective than previous ones.[59] The goals were also more limited than at Krithia and 29th Division was involved at Gully Spur. The attack was initially led by 87th Brigade with 86th Brigade due to follow and advance through them. Within 86th Brigade the 1st Dublins were in reserve in a hollow south of Geoghegan's Bluff, so their involvement might have involved little more than mopping up. 87th Brigade successfully took their first targets within twenty minutes of their advance at 11am, with 86th Brigade following through at 11.30am. Turkish machine-gun posts were identified by noon and artillery was contacted to shell these. Steady progress was made, but some of that was held up by conflicting reports of whether or not the 1st Lancashire Fusiliers had taken their initial targets – by 3.30pm it became clear that they had, but in small numbers and they had difficulties holding off a counter-attack. Elsewhere in the division the 1st Inniskillings had made a 'gruesome find': the bodies of Dublin Fusiliers who had been killed on 27 April and never buried.[60] The 1st Dublins were moved into position from 5pm for a further advance following more artillery fire. However, by 7.45pm it was clear that the Turks were very well dug in and that the 1st Dublins could not move. Further artillery fire did not allow an advance, and the Dublins dug in and erected a barricade, facing a Turkish counter-attack in the early hours of 29 June, before being relieved at 3.15pm that afternoon.[61] Even if the 1st Dublins had made little progress – and had lost 69 men over 28 and 29 June[62] – this operation overall was an effective example of 'bite and hold' tactics being used at Gallipoli and yielded much better results than the advances attempted in the three Battles of Krithia.[63] One regimental history described it as 'the first material success since the Day of the Landing'.[64]

The battalion was briefly withdrawn from Cape Helles on 16 July by ship to Mudros on the Greek island of Lemnos. Unlike the Western Front where soldiers were rotated behind the lines easily, finding leisure in undamaged towns and villages, there was no such respite at Gallipoli. Rare withdrawals offered the only freedom from the threat of Turkish sniping or shell fire. However, they were back at Gallipoli overnight on 21/22 July, landing at V Beach then marching a few miles westwards to Gully Beach. By this time, the focus of British planning at Gallipoli had shifted north-west to a fresh offensive at

Anzac Cove and Suvla Bay. The aim was to secure high ground at Tekke Tepe and Sari Bair in order to grab the 'waist' of the peninsula, cutting off the Turkish positions attacked from Cape Helles, while also securing the harbour at Suvla Bay. Most of the fighting took place in those areas, but 29th Division, once again at Cape Helles, was tasked with a diversionary attack on 6 August which might gain some ground but was principally aimed at preventing the Turks from sending troops to reinforce their lines at Anzac and Suvla.[65] The attack failed: inadequate artillery fire once again meant that Turkish positions were undamaged and there were 2,000 casualties in the division as a whole and 63 dead in the 1st Dublins from 6 August until their withdrawal from the area on 18 August.[66] At that point they moved to Suvla Bay, where two other battalions of the Royal Dublin Fusiliers, the 6th and the famous Dublin Pals of the 7th, had already seen action, temporarily transferred from the 30th to the 31st Brigade in the 10th (Irish) Division.

6 GALLIPOLI: SUVLA BAY

… we went to Gallipoli without any orders and without any maps.
Lieutenant Noël Drury, 6th Royal Dublin Fusiliers[1]

Landing at Suvla Bay

Dublin's story of the First World War is dominated by memory of the Dublin Pals at Gallipoli, specifically their role at Suvla Bay in August 1915. Yet they were alongside another battalion of the Dublin Fusiliers, and Dubliners also fought in many other units. Any account which only focuses on the 7th Dublins can therefore only partly explain why Gallipoli came to mean so much to Dubliners. In particular, the role of the 6th Dublins should be a central part of Dublin's story of Suvla Bay, which began as both battalions left their camp at Basingstoke for Devonport over 9 and 10 July 1915. They reached Lesbos on 25 and 26 July via Gibraltar, Malta and Alexandria where they saw exotic sights such as 'sailing vessels like those seen in Biblical pictures'.[2] Nearly a fortnight was spent on Lesbos, hearing 'in the olive-trees the locusts making a funny noise like starlings',[3] before the battalions embarked for Suvla Bay on 6 August.[4]

The landings at Suvla Bay were an attempt to open a new front at Gallipoli with fresh troops not struggling with dysentery, as were so many who had been on the peninsula since April.[5] Yet the campaign turned out just as badly as that at Helles. When the Dardanelles Commission – established in 1916 to investigate what had gone wrong at Gallipoli – reported in 1919, it said the failure to make ground at Suvla was due to the attack not being 'pressed' after the initial landings. That was attributed 'in a great measure to a want of determination and competence in the Divisional Commander and one of his Brigadiers'.[6] However, there are strong grounds for believing that the operation was doomed to failure due to a combination of factors: in particular, the goals being too ambitious for the numbers deployed; terrain hindering coordination of movement; communication networks being inadequate; and artillery strength being insufficient.[7]

The landings were led by 11th Division which was ashore by midnight on 6 August without opposition at C and B beaches south of the bay. They then faced more resistance as they captured Nibrunesi Point and high ground at Lala Baba in the first attack of the war by New Army volunteers.[8] Yet losses of officers in the attack left leaderless men unclear as to how to push on. Theoretically, Suvla Bay was highly suitable for an amphibious landing with only a gentle slope up from the shore line and soft sand on which boats carrying soldiers could run ashore.[9] However, although another part of the division had got ashore at A Beach in Suvla Bay itself, unexpected sandbanks had caused vessels to land in places other than those planned in 'one of the worst fiascos in the history of the British army'.[10] Units were mixed up and this slowed the advance inland, even though part of Kiretch Tepe Sirt (a ridge), and Hill 10 were captured.[11]

It became apparent that few officers had clear orders over what to do once they had established a beachhead. In particular, the instructions given by General Frederick Stopford, in overall command of IX Corps during the Suvla Bay landings, acquired a reputation for being brief, unclear and sporadic. He was 'a man appointed for his technical superiority rather than his battle experience. He was old and incompetent.'[12] Stopford was eventually sacked by the overall commander at Gallipoli, General Ian Hamilton, and was much criticised after the war. But it should be noted that he did deliver what he had said he would: the limited goal of a harbour from which to supply the northern part of the Gallipoli peninsula. Hamilton had not insisted on anything more.[13] Yet the fact remained that, as Lieutenant Noël Drury of the 6th Dublins noted in his diary, 'we went to Gallipoli without any orders and without any maps.' This contributed to how Drury was feeling going into action for the first time: 'I felt very nervous, as I am sure the others did, about how I would get on when the real fighting started, and I think the responsibility of leading the men well weighed on us.'[14]

The 6th and 7th Dublins were closely connected throughout their time at Gallipoli and most of both battalions went to the peninsula on the same ship, the HMT *Fauvette*.[15] Writing to his father, Captain Richard Patrick 'Paddy' Tobin of D Company of the 7th Dublins described sleeping on the deck of the *Fauvette* and being 'awakened at 2 a.m. by the booming of guns, and soon after I heard the crack of rifle and machine-gun fire. This was my first intimation and experience of actual war.'[16] Before landing, at around dawn on 7 August, they were transferred to smaller 'lighters', which Drury described in a letter to a friend as 'specially made for the job'.[17] With the 10th Division in reserve to the 11th, the two battalions had been due to land at A Beach, but the problems caused by sandbanks there meant that they were landed at C Beach along with 31st Brigade. The rest of the division landed at A Beach as planned but this complicated divisional communications.[18] The 6th landed first on C Beach from 6am, followed by the 7th. Being in reserve, their landing was nothing like that faced by the 1st Dublins at Cape Helles but it was not without opposition: the 7th in particular faced shrapnel fire, both as they landed and once on the beach. In the 6th, Noël Drury noted,

> we rushed the men up the little beach to a low bank about 6 feet high and piled arms and took off equipment. We then started bringing ashore the tools, machine guns, ammunition, water and food. We had some gunfire but not anything like what I expected ... While this was going on, the Colonel was looking around for someone to give us our orders but no staff were to be seen. I could see no sign of Turks anywhere nor any trenches.[19]

Captain Arthur Preston of the 6th Dublins wrote to his father 'we waited for orders till about 10 o'clock, and we were lucky to get no one hit'.[20] Eventually, they were ordered to advance, taking up a position in reserve at the entrance to Salt Lake, of which Drury noted, 'This isn't really a lake but a sort of marsh in which the salt water has dried up, leaving a coating of glistening salt shining in the sun.'[21] The 7th Dublins took refuge on the slopes of Lala Baba, captured earlier by the 11th Division. Shrapnel was a constant problem as described by Poole Hickman of D Company: 'You hear a whistle through the air, then a burst, and everything within a space of 200 yards by 100 yards from where shrapnel burst is liable to be hit. The wounds inflicted are dreadful – deep, big, irregular gashes, faces battered out of recognition, limbs torn away.'[22]

Hills

Hickman was describing the beginning of the 7th Dublins' advance on Hill 53, which became known as Chocolate Hill due to its colour, and later as Dublin Hill.[23] Much of their day was taken up with a long march to the site of attack. Although less than four miles from the coast, they only reached the hill after a march of ten to twelve miles around Salt Lake, often on soft sand or mud which made walking difficult. On their way, they had to cross a spit of sand, less than 20 yards wide, which the Turks had covered by snipers. Paddy Tobin told his father, 'We had been running along hard, for about a quarter of a mile in heavy sand before this and we had not much energy left ... Well across that neck of land I expected every minute to fall.'[24] Irish rugby international Jasper Brett wrote home, 'When one hears a shell screaming one falls flat; well I fell flat several times, and then one time when I did not, the ground was torn up in front of me; the man in front was wounded in the neck.'[25] Tobin found himself 'under the bank in a paroxysm of fear, and chattering my prayers between my teeth'.[26]

The men had landed with heavy kit: wearing lightweight khaki drill uniforms, in addition to their rifles and two hundred rounds of ammunition, their packs included greatcoats, two blankets, a waterproof sheet, three days' rations, an entrenching tool, and a selection of other items such as a shovel or a kettle. Unsurprisingly, many abandoned the bulkier items such as greatcoats.[27] At around 6.30pm naval guns opened on the Turkish positions at the top of Chocolate Hill. The attacking group initially consisted of the 7th Dublins along with the 6th Inniskillings and two companies of the 6th Royal Irish Fusiliers, with the 6th Lincolns and 6th Borders joining later. The hill was taken by successive rushes – with bayonets fixed – of platoons from the various battalions. Tobin said, 'The Turks ran when we were within about 40 yards of them.'[28] Within the 7th Dublins there seems to have been some rivalry over who could reach the target first. One officer, who had once served in D Company but had been promoted in another company, noted how D advanced, 'with a dash for all the world like a wild forward rush at Lansdowne Road'. He added, 'We were not long till we were upon them, as we had been first up to this and had no desire to be pipped on the post, especially by my old company.'[29]

Chocolate Hill was taken by the 7th Dublins at around 8pm on 7 August as the sun set. There would be some public dispute as to whether they or 6th Royal Irish Fusiliers had taken the position first, but in fact the Irish Fusiliers had secured a nearby target.[30] Despite the summer heat during the day, it was cold at night and those who had dumped their greatcoats regretted it. Douglas Gunning was an Enniskillen man serving with the 7th Dublins alongside his brother, Cecil. He remembered of the first night on Chocolate Hill, 'It was so cold . . . and there we were huddled in the trench with only our light khaki drill uniforms and bare knees.'[31] For some time it would be known by soldiers at Gallipoli as 'Dublin Hill'.[32]

During their time holding Chocolate Hill, the 7th Dublins encountered some gruesome sights. Private 19185 Gilbert Dando of the 7th Dublins was a Richmond Asylum cricketer and a member of the National Volunteers, specifically the 1st Battalion Ambulance Corps of the Dublin City Regiment. He described how, soon after taking the position, 'We were in the evil-smelling trenches of Dublin Hill, where many of the Turks lay buried. As we walked down one trench one after the other we would stumble against a pair of large flabby hands just above the surface.'[33] But they held the hill until 12 August when they were relieved.[34] From the landing to this time the 7th Dublins had lost eighteen men dead, which might be thought a relatively light death toll given the ferocity of the action in which they had fought.[35] Among the dead was Ernest Julian, the Trinity law professor selected by the Pals to be one of their junior officers. He died of wounds on the Hospital Ship *Valdivia* on 8 August.[36]

Following their landing, the 6th Dublins had been taken from reserve positions back to the beaches, taking on duties such as water and ammunition-carrying for the brigade. Aside from a lack of sleep – Drury said there was very little in the first fortnight at Gallipoli[37] – water supplies seriously broke down and were a major problem in the heat of the Turkish summer.[38] Bryan Cooper, an officer with the 5th Connaught Rangers remembered of mid-August, 'It is hard to find words to convey the true state of affairs. No doubt it would be too much to say that at home thirst is unknown, but at any rate the passionate craving for water felt in Gallipoli is seldom experienced.' He went on to describe how when water arrived it had to be distributed very carefully to ensure that men did not drink it all at once. Meanwhile, biscuit rations were dry and bully beef was salty, which only worsened the thirst, as did the dysentery, enteritis and fever from which men were suffering. Cooper continued, 'In such times surface civilization vanishes, and man becomes a primitive savage.' Men crept away to find water wherever they could. Some stole from others.[39] Hickman wrote of the men's desperation saying 'even the dirtiest water was drunk'.[40] This was hardly surprising given that the daily allowance in August was just a quart (approximately one litre).[41]

Back in action on 9 August, the 6th Dublins took part in an attack from Hill 50 towards Ali Bey Chesme meeting fierce opposition. The issuing of orders was again a problem, with Captain Preston saying 'I had only a minute to explain to my platoon commander when off we had to go.'[42] They joined the firing line at 6am that morning. Drury described how 'The firing was worse than I imagined it would be and I felt very scared.'[43] However, later in the day he overcame his fears and described how battalions became mixed up, hiding in 'funk holes' and that members of the Lincolns and Borderers 'started running away like mad, shouting out that they were "cut to ribbons"'. Drury said that he and others 'had a job to prevent them clearing out altogether, and even had to threaten to use our revolvers, even to the officers'.[44] Meanwhile, Ali Bey Chesme was 'almost unapproachable' because snipers had 'the range of it to a yard'.[45] Indeed, throughout the Gallipoli front snipers were a major problem. Drury noted the problems of 'stumpy oak trees with thick bushy tops in which were snipers'.[46] Sergeant 10034 Paul Losty of the 6th Dublins wrote to his mother at Montpelier Hill on Dublin's North Circular Road: 'The snipers here are very daring. They hide themselves in all sorts of places, and pick us off whenever we expose ourselves.'[47] There were even accounts of a female sniper. Douglas Gunning remembered, 'One day some chaps who were trying to knock out some of the snipers in a certain part of the bushes came across the body of a young Turkish girl sniper lying at the foot of a tree. She was dead, and round her neck were fourteen identification discs of the Munster Fusiliers mostly.'[48]

Up to this point at Suvla Bay the 6th Dublins had suffered heavy casualties, with 77 dead between 8 and 12 August, almost all in action on 9 and 10 August, and around another 180 wounded. Consequently, they were far below fighting strength. Yet following the advance, the battalion was in and out of trenches over the next four days, often carrying out work to strengthen the lines.[49] They periodically relieved and were relieved by a range of battalions, gaining hours of rest behind the front line whenever they could.[50] Movement was regularly hindered by 'short prickly scrub and tangled grass'.[51] On a typical day, men stood to arms in response to Turkish fire at 4.45am for a few hours, before breakfast at 7.30am. An inspection took place at 8.30am, with the remainder of the morning involving work to improve and repair trenches. The middle hour or two of the day was free time and lunch. In the afternoon, saps were dug towards Turkish lines, followed by dinner at around 5.30pm. 'Stand to arms' could be called again in the evening and then into the early hours of the morning. Throughout the day a Turkish attack could come at any time, so sentries rotated.[52]

While the ground gained to this point represented progress, the landing was actually a missed opportunity since just 3,000 Turkish soldiers defended the area, compared to the 27,000 British troops who had landed. Because the main aim was to secure the harbour and the high ground close to it, little thought had been given to gaining ground inland which would need to be taken later if the peninsula was to be won. The delay in an attempted advance led to frustration among some. Drury had noted in his diary on 8 August,

> I cannot understand the delay in moving inland. There has been no fighting all day and the Turks haven't fired a shot, and are probably rushing up reinforcements and digging new trenches. The men are all talking about the waste of valuable time. We have quite a lot of old soldiers who know a good deal about this sort of war and they are all grousing like blazes, saying we are throwing away our chance and will pay for it later.[53]

They were right. Turkish forces were reinforced when an advance was attempted on 15 August.[54] On that day the 6th Dublins were in further action at Kiretech Tepe, a steep ridge about 500 feet high, which in the 6th Dublins' sector had a summit of just five to six feet across. Drury described how 'we charged and reaching the top drove out the Turks with the bayonet sending them rushing down the other side'. Drury reflected that 'It was really a marvellous bit of work by men who were very, very tired and who had been short of sleep, food and water for the past 10 days.'[55] The men then moved along the ridge to take Spion Kop, though the eventual target of Kidney Hill was never reached.[56] Though the 6th Dublins managed to clear Turkish trenches there they had to retreat on facing enfilade fire due to a lack of progress around them.[57]

The 7th Dublins had been in reserve during this attack, specifically at Karakol Dagh, and relieved the 6th at the front overnight. Dublin schoolteacher, Private 18584 Reginald Ford described how the battalion 'built up a parapet of rocks along the crest of the hill, for we knew the Turkish counter-attack would begin at dawn'.[58] There, at 3.30am the next morning they faced 'a furious counter-attack' until 9am. While holding high ground would usually make defence easy, the slope down from the ridge they held was so steep that rifle fire was difficult. Meanwhile, the Turkish attackers were expert at finding hiding places on the slope and throwing bombs into the 7th Dublins' lines.[59] Shaped like cricket balls, such bombs could be caught and thrown back. Private Albert Wilkin of the 7th Dublins was mentioned in dispatches for doing so on five occasions before being blown up on his sixth attempt.[60] D Company was on the highest knoll of the hill and the Turks were attacking in large numbers. Captain Poole Hickman was shot dead, and Major Richard Harrison (attached from the 51st Sikhs) was killed by a bomb,[61] so Paddy Tobin took charge. Lieutenant Ernest Hamilton wrote how 'We fought like demons against three times our numbers and held on too. Our knoll came in for at least six attacks.' But the purpose of Hamilton writing, to Paddy Tobin's father, was to explain that 'your son was killed, shot through the head'. Hamilton said, 'His death affected the men so much that I thought all was finished, but spurred by his example they fought for another hour as they never fought before.'[62] The line was held and the 7th Dublins were relieved at 9am on 16 August. In this action overnight the 7th Dublins lost fifty-eight men and the 6th another sixteen.[63]

Trench Warfare

The 6th Dublins were posted to A Beach for rest on 17 August, with the 7th going to divisional rest bivouacs a day later. There they carried out fatigues as the 6th had done a week earlier, this time building mule paths. By this time men of the 7th Dublins – including Douglas Gunning – were being evacuated due to being ill. Gunning had dysentery and would not see Gallipoli nor the 7th Dublins again, being commissioned into the Royal Inniskilling Fusiliers after his recovery, before being killed on the Somme on 1 July 1916.[64] A reorganisation was also necessary because the battalion's commanding officer, Lieutenant Colonel G. Downing had been shot in the foot by a sniper on 15 August, and his second in command, Major M. P. E. Lonsdale, was struck down sick on 18 August. Temporary command went to Captain C. B. Hoey.[65] From 17 August to the end of September D Company had no officers at all.[66]

Both battalions were back in the line on 21 August, the day on which the 29th and 11th Divisions attacked Scimitar and W Hills.[67] The 10th Division did not take a lead, being in reserve, but came under fire as they went to the front to relieve forward units. Drury noted that 'a queer mist or fog' made it difficult to move in the right direction and that 'we got a heavy shelling most of the way up'.[68] The 6th and 7th Dublins would spend much of the next six weeks rotating in and out of trenches every few days. The lines they held could offer significant challenges to defenders because there was no field of fire against attacking troops.[69]

On other occasions when the 6th Dublins took over a line, much of their work involved digging since the positions were not in a very good condition and it was hard for men to take cover.[70] So hard was the work that Drury observed wryly, 'Men all very weary, but have to keep digging. They won't call a spade a spade after this, but a damned torture instrument.'[71] Drury had earlier been very critical of the absence of orders for the landing at Suvla Bay but he was more complimentary about one general's role at the front. Writing of General Nicol of 30th Brigade he said, 'He's a great old chap, and his energy is amazing considering that he must be nearly 60 years old. He is always nosing about and won't be satisfied until he sees every inch of the line himself.'[72]

By this time, British attempts to advance had halted and a pattern of trench warfare had developed just as at Cape Helles.

On 1 September, fighting had become so muted that the 6th Dublins' war diary noted that the men were able to go out into No Mans' Land: 'Buried several bodies in front of our lines. Many others still lying about. Several rifles and sets of equipment brought in.'[73] However, attacks could come at any time. A member of the 7th Dublins wrote of how he had been naked and washing when an attack began:

> Now it is bad enough to be clothed and in one's right mind on these occasions, but to be in one's birthday costume with one's thoughts in Dublin, well, *then* it becomes, to say the least of it, rather awkward; however, I grasped my rifle and bayonet, also some ammunition and began to fire away, then when things had quietened down a bit, I began to dress, and then for the first time the fellows noticed me, and you should have heard them laugh.[74]

There was also time spent at the 'rest camp' on the beach. Bryan Cooper described its name as 'somewhat of a jest' for it was regularly under Turkish fire. However, there was an opportunity to wash in the sea. Beyond that, there were 'none of the distractions sometimes experienced on the Western Front', the only other reliefs being 'the arrival of mail and a visit from a chaplain'.[75]

There were also still episodes of fighting at the front. The 7th Dublins were in action on 21 August, supporting an attack by the 11th and 29th Divisions on a line running from Hetman Chair to Kazlar Chair. That began with a naval bombardment from 2.30pm to 4pm, followed by a successful infantry advance. The 7th took up a front-line position at 11pm and remained there until 4 September. The 6th Dublins were having a very quiet time in their positions. Drury noted on 8 September,

> except for the morning and evening 'hate' there is hardly any shooting ... Once or twice we heard the Turks commence shouting Allah! Allah! Allah! And making a rhythmic noise as if thumping the buts [*sic*] of their rifles on the ground. A few got leisurely out of their trenches as if to attack but a few cunningly laid bursts of M.G. fire send them scuttling back.[76]

Drury even had time to keep 'a little baby tortoise which is only about the size of a penny'.[77] However, on 18 September at 5pm the 6th

Dublins faced a heavy bombardment, followed five minutes later by rifle fire. It was feared that an attack was imminent but by 5.30pm the firing had stopped. Drury noted, 'We heard later that in some places the Turks had left their trenches in a half-hearted way and then went back again.'[78] On 19, 22 and 25 September the 7th faced heavy bombardments but, remarkably, suffered no casualties at all on the 19th or 25th. Only on 27 September did an attack follow such a prelude though it was more raid than full-scale attack. It began just as a wiring party was out in No Man's Land. They were surprised by about fifty Turkish soldiers, armed with bombs. The bombs were thrown into the 6th Dublins' party and the front line. Fire was then exchanged across a distance of as little as 250 yards separating the lines. However, by 9pm the firing had ceased. It later became clear that both sides had thought the other was beginning an attack. Drury described how the Lovat Scouts had heard news of the Battle of Loos (far better news than the battle turned out to deserve) and had begun playing the bagpipes and cheering. The Turks thought this was the beginning of an attack and countered. Drury noted, 'This sort of thing is most infectious and it spread rapidly along the line, and the absence of decent officers and N.C.O.s made it difficult to stop it.'[79]

Two days later, a relief of the 6th Dublins by the 7th was postponed for reasons of which neither battalion was immediately told. Soon after, they learnt the news: both battalions were leaving Gallipoli. By this time the men had become quite settled in their surroundings. On 27 September Drury noted that the 6th Dublins' system of trench-naming had been given official approval. They drew heavily on Dublin with names such as College Green (for battalion headquarters), Dublin Road, Sackville Street and O'Connell Bridge.[80] But news of leaving Gallipoli was inevitably a massive relief and when it first came through, Cecil Gunning remembered men in the 7th Dublins saying 'It's too good to be true. We are just being transferred to Cape Helles.'[81] In contrast, as they left over 30 September and 1 October for Mudros, Drury noted, 'Everyone seemed to have a strange feeling of regret at leaving Suvla. It's hard to say why, as I didn't love the place at all.'[82] The history of the Dublin Pals at Suvla Bay, written in late 1916 drawing on many interviews with the men who served, noted, 'Looking back it still seems to them to have been an impossible task that was set, but they faced it cheerfully and gave of their best to achieve their goal.'[83]

Reputations

Dubliners had also served in small numbers in battalions beyond the 6th and 7th Dublins at Suvla Bay. They were men like Private 2708 Patrick Finn of Dominick Street in Kingstown, serving in the 7th Royal Munster Fusiliers. He was wounded on 20 August and made it all the way back to England before finally succumbing to his wounds at Napsbury Military Hospital near St Albans on 29 October.[84] Lieutenant Henry Greene was the son of George and Emma Greene of St Lawrence Road in Clontarf. He joined the Indian Army in the summer of 1913 immediately after graduating from Trinity College, and was killed in action at Gallipoli on 21 August serving with the 1/6th Gurkha Rifles. He had earlier seen action with the 92nd Punjabis at the Suez Canal in April 1915.[85] Some Dubliners were killed serving in ANZAC forces. Private Frederick Mangan's wife was still living in Dublin when he enlisted in the Australian 9th Battalion, while the same applied to the mothers of Private 1427 Mitchell Ryan and Private 10/1329 Thomas Saunders (in the New Zealand forces).[86] At least another eight men with such connections were killed in the Australian forces during the campaign and another two among the New Zealanders.[87]

Yet all these losses were eclipsed by the story of the Dublin Pals. This was despite the fact that the 6th Dublins suffered more fatalities than the 7th: from landing until the departure on 30 September, 128 men in the 6th were killed or died, while the 7th lost 115.[88] Within D Company, 37 men from the original 286 were killed, though the fact that only 79 from it were evacuated on 30 September means that 170 others had been wounded or were ill and been taken from Gallipoli already.[89] This amounts to a literal decimation of the company, yet it was not unusually high for the Gallipoli campaign. However, it is clear that the 7th Dublins were more closely connected to Dublin than the 6th were.[90] So despite the 6th suffering more, throughout August and September 1915 the extensive newspaper coverage of the Suvla Bay campaign held a particular focus on the men of the 7th Dublins and within that battalion, D Company. Possibly the men of the 7th had a particular propensity to write home in detail. At any rate, the news-papers were certainly willing to cover their news. Poole Hickman's detailed account of fighting was published after news of his death in a number of papers.[91] In addition to information from Lance Corporal

Honeyman, a wide range of pieces came from many other officers and men.[92] For example, Lieutenant Colonel Downing wrote to his wife of the capture of Chocolate Hill and she sent extracts of the letter on to the press for publication.[93] Private 14285 Victor Jeffreson of Rathmines lost his life at Gallipoli on 23 August. Nearly a week later a letter was published in which he told of being unhurt but having 'had some very lucky escapes'.[94] Private 14171 Henry Gibson wrote about fighting just as others did, but also included much information on daily life in late August after the main fighting had ceased.[95]

There were also many similar accounts published into early 1916.[96] As a result, the 7th Dublins' story headlined much coverage which was even noticed and criticised by members of the 7th Dublins. Private 13837 Frederick McCabe, serving in C Company rather than D was pleased that there was some mention of his company in the newspapers because it showed that his company 'were not forgotten, and that the D.Coy. were not the only ones to shine'.[97] Sergeant 13825 Alec Hogg, a 20-year-old Clontarf man, wrote a letter to his father saying, 'To read your papers one would think "D" Company were the only company in our lot. True, they did their bit well, but no better than any other company; and the 6th Dubs. behaved gallantly also, though they got no special note.'[98] For some time, stories of the 7th Dublins dominated newspaper coverage with wider pieces about the 6th Dublins or the 10th Division as a whole being relatively uncommon.[99]

Withdrawal

The evacuation of units which had landed at Suvla Bay in August was a sign of things to come. There was no question of a further attack on the peninsula and the only issue was whether or not there was some strategic value in holding on to part of it. So initially, in a decision taken in early December 1915, only Suvla and Anzac were abandoned, but as powerful voices grew in London for a complete withdrawal, the Cabinet eventually decided to do so towards the end of the month.[100]

By this time, allied troops at Gallipoli had endured months of a hard winter and continued casualties. Following their deployment at Suvla Bay on 18 August, the 1st Dublins lost 101 men over the next four and a half months. During this time the battalion was not close to major action, other than being in support on 21 August during the attack on

Scimitar Hill. They also had some relief by being returned to Imbros from 8 to 21 September. By the end of September, back at Suvla, they were feeling the effects of dysentery which meant that the battalion was down to 15 officers and just over 600 men, even though over 300 drafts from home had recently arrived.[101] As winter set in, heavy rain and violent winds became a significant problem, but the biggest challenge was that there was almost no hiding place from Turkish fire. Writing to Monica Roberts, whose parcels were reaching Dubliners at Gallipoli, Private 19543 Harry Loughlin explained, 'This place does not afford one to say I am safe in any one part as from the Base Hospital to the firing line has every 20 yards found room for the Turkish Shrapnel.'[102] A similar point was made by Captain Andrew Horne of the Royal Army Medical Corps and Dublin's Merrion Square, writing home to his mother about running a dressing station on W Beach during the final phase of the occupation of the peninsula. He told her, 'I could never take my clothes off because immediately I would do so a shell would burst somewhere on Beach with a resulting casualty.'[103]

The 1st Dublins remained at Suvla until 15 December when they were briefly sent to Mudros before being taken back to Helles the next day. There, they spent just over a fortnight before final withdrawal at midnight on 1/2 January 1916, a week before the final evacuation took place. Ironically, this was the most successful phase of the entire Gallipoli campaign.[104] The occupation was over, nothing had been gained, and Gallipoli became a byword for failure. It would also have a profound impact on Dublin's memory of the war as the place where the Dublin Pals – and others – had met their deaths. This would stand in marked contrast to Ulster's memory of the Somme, which became 'instant history' partly because the news travelled home more quickly from France than Gallipoli. There were similarities between the Ulster Division's actions in taking and briefly holding the Schwaben Redoubt, and the 10th Division's advance at Chocolate Hill. Yet the 36th would be lauded for years to come while the 10th would not because the Gallipoli narrative was overtaken by what happened over Easter 1916 in Dublin, not because the public did not care about losses in the Dardanelles.[105]

That they did care was seen in how attention turned to whether Irish regiments had been let down at Gallipoli by decision-making. A lengthy poem with a very unusual tone for the time, critical of the generals, appeared in the *Freeman's Journal* in August 1916.

It applauded Irish military success at Gallipoli, claiming that 'The road to Stamboul opened fair / For Britain's troops – had they been there'. But after presenting the Irish troops as proclaiming 'The East is ours! We've won the war!' it asked:

> But where were their supports? – oh where?
> We only know – they were not there!
> Somewhere inert, aback they lay,
> Nor ever faced that bloody fray.
> By dullard generals thus was lost
> The gorgeous East, won at such cost
> > By the Irish at Gallipoli.[106]

When the Dardanelles Commission presented an initial report into the Gallipoli campaign in March 1917, the *Freeman's Journal* headline described the Dardanelles as the place 'Where Irish Troops Were Sacrificed by Blunders'.[107] It should be no surprise then that when, in 1919, the rebel song *The Foggy Dew* was written it contrasted the Easter Rising not to Irish deaths on the Western Front, but to those at Gallipoli, saying ''Twas far better to die 'neath an Irish sky / Than at Suvla or Sud el Bar.'[108] Drury was being a little understated when he noted in his diary in November 1915 in Serbia, that judging by letters from home, 'Gallipoli meant a lot to Dublin people.'[109]

7 PREPARATIONS

... the air was full of rumours ...
Isaac Callendar, 1st Dublin Irish Volunteers, on Holy Week
1916[1]

Dublin in Early 1916

When the Dublin Fusiliers left Gallipoli, the focus of Dublin's First World War shifted back to the Western Front. The 16th (Irish) Division, the military expression of Ireland's endorsement of Parliamentary nationalism's support for the war, had arrived there in December 1915. It would first see major action in the week following Easter 1916, at Hulluch in Belgium. Coincidentally, plans were being made in Dublin for momentous events which would take place in the same week, not only overshadowing the fighting at Hulluch but dramatically altering the course of Irish history.

Yet in early 1916 Dublin appeared calm. The Home Front activities of war continued as before. Funds were raised for the Royal Dublin Fusiliers,[2] and entertainments were laid on for wounded soldiers in the city.[3] Efforts at recruitment continued as they had done in late 1914 and 1915, even if numbers were reduced.[4] From December 1915 there was a flurry of concern about Ireland being included in the Compulsory Service Bill to introduce conscription. Some in England believed that Ireland was not adequately supporting the war effort. While recognising the enlistment of John Redmond's son and his brother Willie (a nationalist MP) and of another nationalist MP Stephen Gwynn, the *Morning Post* argued that the IPP 'have done absolutely nothing to promote recruiting', a claim which was hardly supported by the evidence of multiple speeches and the direct efforts of Redmond to encourage the National Volunteers to enlist.[5] However, Redmond's actions behind the scenes, and clear statements in Parliament that Ireland could not support conscription, ensured that Ireland was not included, despite an 'Inclusion Motion' from Ulster Unionists.[6]

Meanwhile, recruiting meetings, often including serving soldiers home from the front, took place across the county of Dublin. The focus of some of these was to promote the merits of the voluntary system, ever conscious of the spectre of conscription.[7] A high-profile 'Recruiting Conference' was held at Dublin's Mansion House on 10 February, while local groups provided information on how dependants could claim separation allowances.[8] The tone throughout much of these initiatives was that Irishmen were joining an Irish army – implicitly not a British one. That was clear in a manifesto issued by Redmond in mid-February when he talked of his pride in having 'to-day a huge Irish army in the field', adding that the ongoing challenge was to 'maintain the Irish Army at the front'.[9] In March and April a series of meetings were held in places throughout the city centre and further afield.[10]

There were signs that some of the volunteer movements were losing some momentum by 1916. The Volunteer Training Corps now incorporated the Irish Rugby Football Union Volunteer Corps. It continued to parade, but was depleted by men joining the ranks.[11] From their formation after Redmond's Woodenbridge speech, and well into 1915, the National Volunteers held regular local drills across the city and county, and occasionally held public meetings in support of the nationalist leadership. There were active companies in Clontarf, Donnybrook, Dundrum, Inchicore, Kingstown, Lucan, North Strand, Rathmines and Swords, with city centre battalions operating from Claude Road, Langrishe Place, Lower Baggot Street, Lower Pembroke Street, North Brunswick Street and North King Street.[12] In early 1915 the Dublin units held an inter-battalion rifle shooting competition,[13] while Easter Sunday 1915 (4 April) saw a review of 25,000–30,000 National Volunteers in Phoenix Park.[14] The city and county National Volunteers also held manoeuvres there in September 1915.[15]

However, the numbers involved steadily reduced. In August 1914 Irish Volunteers across the county (outside the city, for which police records have not survived) numbered 4,225, organised in 32 branches. By October, enlistments and the split had left 3,477 supporting Redmond in the National Volunteers and around 200 backing the Irish Volunteers. By the end of 1915 there were only 2,554 in the National Volunteers in 28 branches, and the police reckoned that the Irish Volunteers numbered 186 in four branches, plus another 90 who remained in the National Volunteers but opposed Redmond.[16] Yet despite the disparity in numbers, activity levels were higher in the Irish Volunteers.[17] At the end of March the police reported that across the county 'The National Volunteers exist only in name' and that 'The Irish Volunteers are really of very little account in Co. Dublin', with branches only at Rathfarnham, Balbriggan, Swords and Lusk.[18]

In the city, the situation was very different. From the outbreak of the war, a small group within the IRB had been planning an armed uprising against British rule. They feared that as the war continued, Home Rule might be implemented and any chance of full independence would be lost as Ireland settled in contentedly to autonomy within the UK. Driven initially by Thomas Clarke and Seán Mac Diarmada, the rebellion was planned by the IRB's Military Council from mid-1915. On the council, the two leaders were joined by Pádraig Pearse, Éamonn Ceannt and Joseph Plunkett, then later in 1916 James Connolly and Thomas MacDonagh. In mid-1915 they sought German support in the form of 12,000 men to land on the west of Ireland, plus arms for the Irish Volunteers, but the Germans responded with scepticism and would never commit men.[19]

Nothing of those plans was known to most Irish Volunteers but they continued to be very active in the city of Dublin. From late 1914 the *Irish Volunteer* carried detailed instructions for 'military training' and that was enhanced in February 1915 with an eight-week programme for the Dublin Brigade.[20] By the end of March 1915, a command structure had been established. Pearse, Michael Joseph O'Rahilly (known as 'The O'Rahilly'), Joseph Plunkett and Bulmer Hobson were in overall charge of the Volunteers. In the north of the county, disparate companies operated, not properly gathered into the 5th Fingal Battalion until soon before the Rising, under the command of Thomas Ashe.[21] Within Dublin, commandants were appointed for each battalion: 1st, Edward 'Ned' Daly; 2nd

Thomas MacDonagh; 3rd, Éamon de Valera; and 4th, Éamonn Ceannt.[22] They each covered a specific area, from various meeting halls: 1st Battalion, north of the Liffey, west of Sackville Street; 2nd, north of the Liffey, east of Sackville Street; 3rd, south of the Liffey; and 4th, townships to the south.[23] These areas were simply guidelines and there was considerable flexibility over which units men joined. It is easy to imagine that this would have been affected by factors such as friendships and workplaces. We have some idea of how far men joined their local unit from information on who was active in the Easter Rising. A sample of over 700 men shows that just over 70 per cent of the men of the 3rd battalion were from their area, but the 1st and 2nd each had just over 50 per cent of men from their locality (see Table A5.9).

Thus organised, from spring 1915, exercises took place based on printed orders every bit as detailed as British army orders.[24] In field manoeuvres, units were given mock military targets, for example, 'to seize the cross-roads at Little Finglas'.[25] Such public displays of strength contributed to a sense of growing conflict between the authorities and the Irish Volunteers. Tom Byrne of the 1st Battalion recalled, 'A few months before Easter, 1916, it was generally understood that there would be a fight.'[26] By March 1916 there was increased tension when the Irish Volunteers held a 'field day' in the city on St Patrick's Day, due to which, the *Evening Mail* reported, 'The city's lines of communications were held up for some time, but the trams were only temporarily put out of action.'[27] The day began with parades at various churches before the Irish Volunteers concentrated on College Green at noon for an hour-long military display. The pipers of the 2nd and 3rd battalion played, and Eoin MacNeill inspected the Volunteers. Leaflets were circulated asserting Ireland's rights to self-determination, while arguing that Ireland had not had the power to obtain it. However, the leaflets said, in only a lightly veiled threat, 'In raising, training, arming, and equipping the Irish Volunteers as a military body, the men of Ireland are acquiring the power to obtain the freedom of the Irish Nation.' The Volunteers were mostly in uniform, and carried rifles and bayonets, though the *Mail* commented, 'It is believed that the guns would be more formidable if they had adequate ammunition.'[28]

Two weeks later, on 30 March, there was disorder on the streets, including revolver shots fired, when a crowd of about two thousand gathered at the Mansion House and paraded past the Grafton Street recruiting office on their way to College Green. They were protesting against the deportation from Ireland of two organisers of the Irish Volunteers, Ernest Blythe and Liam Mellows, who had been told a few days before that they must move to the midlands of England within six days.[29] Such events prompted Mr Justice Kenny to make a public statement of his concern at the existence of 'propaganda of an openly seditious character' being circulated against recruitment. He added, 'I believe there is not a single peaceable and law-abiding citizen who would not be very pleased to see the mischievous state of things to which I refer brought to an end.'[30] He might have feared that Dublin was about to witness a little more than mischief.

By April, Volunteers were gathering weapons from any source possible. One of those involved was 15-year-old Michael McCabe of Dolphin's Barn, whose father was a member of the IRB. Young Michael McCabe had joined the Volunteers at the end of 1915, having been in the Fianna since 1912. He obtained weapons – including shotguns and pikes – from a range of sources and stored them at his home.[31] Very specific rehearsals were meanwhile taking place without the Volunteers realising it. James Burke of the 4th battalion described manoeuvres around the South Dublin Union (SDU) four or five weeks before the Rising and said that 'it struck me immediately when we were in position in Easter Week that we had been all over the same ground not long previously'.[32] Dr Richard Hayes of the 5th Fingal battalion recalled that in the first week of April 1916 Thomas Ashe 'was officially informed (verbally) by [James] Connolly that the Rising was fixed to take place on Easter Sunday'.[33] Others had been preparing for longer. The Kimmage Garrison of the Irish Volunteers consisted largely of men who had returned from Britain, of Irish families but brought up elsewhere.[34] Among those were brothers Seán and Ernie Nunan. Their father was from County Limerick but their mother was born in London of Limerick parents and when interviewed in the 1960s Seán had an English accent. Both their parents had been active in Irish movements in London. Seán joined the Volunteers in London in 1913, moving in the same circles as Michael Collins. In late 1915, rumours of a Rising began to spread, and in January 1916 he and his brother decided to head for Ireland. They settled in Rathfarnham and initially joined the 4th battalion of the Volunteers but were transferred to Kimmage along with fifty to sixty other 'exiles' from Liverpool, Manchester, Glasgow and London. There, Seán recalled, 'we busied ourselves, drilling, making explosives and generally preparing for the Rising'.[35]

Western Front, Winter 1915–16

On the Western Front, Christmas 1915 had seen no repeat of the previous year's truce. Writing to his sister, Kitty, in Dublin's High Street, Private Coughlan of the 1st Irish Guards described how the Germans offered friendly moves over Christmas 1915, 'But we always gave the same reply – a couple of rounds rapid.'[36] Coughlan's case was one of many which appeared in the newspapers of Dublin men serving in units beyond the Dublin Fusiliers. Another example was that of Lieutenant Harrie Barron of the Royal Garrison Artillery, whose mother lived in Portobello. He was known in Dublin as a footballer, having played for Trinity College and Shelbourne, and then in England for both Queen's Park Rangers and Sheffield Wednesday. He enlisted in October 1914, and went to the Western Front in August 1915. News came through in March 1916 that he was suffering from serious facial wounds received at Ypres. He had been hit by a rifle grenade and surgery to his lower jaw was carried out in the months to come.[37] However, Dublin's engagement in France and Belgium was about to be dominated once again by the Dublin Fusiliers.

The 2nd Dublins had never left, while the volunteer battalions of the 16th (Irish) Division, including the 8th and 9th Royal Dublin Fusiliers, arrived in France in the early hours of 20 December 1915. They spent two weeks in and out of billets and marching, before taking part in trench instruction at Noeux-les-Mines near Béthune in early January with 'echelons' of each battalion attached to the 1st Division. Such training included being in front-line positions under enemy fire and the first Dubliners to be killed in the 16th Division were lost during this time. Corporal 2270 Thomas Howard of the 8th Dublins was killed in action on 3 January 1916.[38] Aged 38, Howard was a Boer War veteran who had trained the Young Ireland Athletic Club and was secretary of the Brinsley Sheridan Dramatic Society in Dorset Street. He left a widow, Martha, at Baggot Court. In the 9th Dublins, the first Dubliner killed in the battalion was Private 16082 James Gallacher of Kingstown on 2 January 1916.[39] From early January until the end of March the 9th Dublins lost another eleven men, and the 8th Dublins nineteen, as they rotated in and out of trenches at various places around Béthune, before taking over parts of the Loos salient at Hulluch and the area known as Puits 14 bis.[40]

April 1916 was to be a bloody month for the 16th Division. On 1 April, the 8th Dublins assisted 253rd Company of the Royal Engineers working in the Hay Alley mining shafts in the Hulluch sub-sector. In the afternoon, the Germans blew a 'camouflet', an underground bomb designed to destroy tunnels, often accompanied by gas. In the 8th Dublins, seventeen were killed with another twelve gassed and sent to hospital. Five days later while in trenches at Hulluch the battalion faced lengthy German bombardments. The first took place from 9am for about an hour, followed by another from 11am to 2.30pm. Fifteen were dead.[41] It was merely a prelude to what came later in the month.

Holy Week

The 2nd Dublins spent most of Holy Week at the front, deployed there on the Tuesday before Easter, 18 April, staying for seven days. From their arrival they faced steady fire from German field artillery and trench mortars, with damage to trenches worsened by heavy rain. Losses amounted to only four dead in the week, an unusually low total for a period during which fire had been regular, probably explained by men taking effective cover in dug-outs. One death was described to Monica Roberts in heroic terms, that of Private 8660 Patrick Byrne, whose mother lived in Thomas Court.[42] Writing to Roberts on 22 April on events two days before, Private 18369 Joseph Clarke said, 'Byrne was killed while he was endeavouring to rescue wounded comrades who were buried in the debris of a dug-out.' Clarke thought Byrne deserved the Victoria Cross, but Byrne did not win the VC nor any other medal for his actions on 20 April.[43]

In Dublin, rumours of an impending Rising spread among the Irish Volunteers. On Saturday 15 April, Oscar Traynor attended a lecture for Dublin Brigade officers. Pádraig Pearse joined the meeting towards the end, and Traynor recalled, 'The first words he uttered sent a thrill through the persons present':

> "I know that you have been preparing your bodies for the great struggle that lies before us, but have you also been preparing your souls?" These words made such a deep impression on all present that there was dead silence for a considerable period ...

> Most of us left that meeting … with the impression that in a short time we would find ourselves in action in the field.[44]

In the week following, Isaac Callendar of Sarsfield Quay, a member of the 1st Dublin Irish Volunteers recalled, 'the air was full of rumours, at Company meetings there was record attendance, Companies vied with each other in their purchase of arms, ammunition, etc.'[45] Word was more formally spread to those who needed to know. Frank Robbins of the ICA, from North William Street, was called into a meeting with James Connolly on the evening of Tuesday 18 April, with about half a dozen others: 'He informed us of the part each one of us was to act in the Insurrection, which was planned to take place at 6.30 p.m. on Easter Sunday in Dublin, while 7 p.m. was fixed for the country.'[46] Tom Byrne was told by Pearse 'On about Holy Thursday' and dispatched to Kildare to spread the word among the Volunteers' hierarchy there.[47] Harry Colley of the 2nd battalion and a Clonliffe Road resident said that on Thursday 20 April, his battalion was told that there would be 'manoeuvres' on Easter Sunday, to take two days' rations and to be prepared to fight.[48] Anybody watching Liberty Hall, James Connolly's headquarters and the base for the ICA, would have known that something was afoot during Easter Week. Matthew Connolly of the ICA recalled that in the 'weeks immediately preceding the Rising' armed men, many in uniform, were guarding the building which 'resembled a military barracks in everything but in name'.[49] For those who were most in the know, Joseph O'Connor, a company commander in the 3rd Battalion, the whole week leading up to Easter had an atmosphere 'of highly-strung nervous activity'. He saw it as the culmination of a lifetime's work 'and no matter what the cost was I was determined to give of my best'.[50]

Easter Weekend

Over the Easter weekend of 1916, both the Dublin Irish Volunteers and the men of the Dublin Fusiliers had clear signs that the tempo of their respective conflicts was quickening. Maundy Thursday, 20 April, saw the 9th Dublins take over the line from the 8th Dublins at Hulluch. The Easter weekend was relatively quiet, though on Easter Sunday the ominous news came from brigade headquarters that a German gas attack was expected. Patrols were sent out and identified 'great activities and work in German lines'.[51] As they waited in the front line on Good Friday, final preparations for the Rising were put in place in Dublin. James Connolly asked printers of *The Irish Republic* 'to turn out a Bill for Easter Sunday that would be in the nature of a Proclamation'.[52] Countess Markiewicz was staying at 21 Henry Street, the home of Jennie Wyse-Power and the location at which the proclamation was signed. Jennie's daughter Nancy recalled in 1951 how, 'as an act of friendship', Markiewicz 'warned my mother on Good Friday that the neighbourhood would be unsafe in a few days time and advised the removal of any valuables'. Excitement about events to come was shown by Markiewicz who 'That night ... showed me her uniform in which she took childish delight – ladies in trousers were less common then than now.'[53]

However, one part of the planned Rising was already falling apart on Good Friday. Roger Casement, along with Irish Brigade members, Robert Monteith and Daniel Bailey, landed at Bann Strand, County Kerry on the night of 21 and 22 April from German Submarine *U-19*. Monteith was a former British soldier with service in the South African War, who had later joined the Irish Volunteers in Dublin, but did not enlist in the British Army in 1914.[54] Casement recruited him from America in 1915, where he was carrying on Irish republican work, to be Commanding Officer of the Brigade. Private 7483 Daniel Bailey was serving in the 1st Royal Irish Rifles, and was recruited as sergeant in the Irish Brigade. Dublin-born, Bailey's sisters lived in Stanhope Street though he appears to have been away from the city after he enlisted in 1904, serving in India and living in England after being discharged in 1913 and before being mobilised at the outbreak of war.[55] Casement had learned that weapons sought by the IRB from Germany would not be adequate in number, and he managed to send word of that to the Rising's leaders. He urged them to cancel the Rising. However, Casement and Bailey were arrested within hours of landing. Even the weapons which were sent by Germany would play no part in the Rising. On Saturday 22nd, the ship was intercepted by the Royal Navy and scuttled by its crew.[56]

Despite this, the republican leadership was set for an insurrection on Easter Sunday. However, Eoin MacNeill had other thoughts. MacNeill learned of the planned Rising only late on Thursday 20 April, and went to see Pearse in the early hours of Good Friday.[57] MacNeill believed 'that the enterprise was madness, would mean a slaughter of unarmed men and that he felt it to be his bounden duty to try and stop it'.[58] MacNeill placed an advertisement in the *Sunday Independent* cancelling the day's manoeuvres. A state of confusion ensued with prospective rebels trying to find out what was happening – and why. Andrew McDonnell of Rathmines, serving in the 3rd Irish Volunteers but with a brother in the British army since the outbreak of war, arrived at Oakley Road to mobilise at around noon that day. After two hours of waiting around, 'We were dismissed and told to remain at home for 24 hours and await further orders.'[59] Outside the city, with the Swords Company of the 5th Fingal Battalion, Joseph Lawless recalled the effect of the change of plans: 'Such an anticlimax to what might have been an eventful day was more than disappointing, and, as a result, no one took seriously the final injunction – "to be ready for immediate mobilisation at any moment."'[60]

By the time news spread of the cancellation, James Connolly was already planning to launch the Rising a day later. When Michael Molloy arrived at his print works around 9am on Easter Sunday, to meet Connolly and receive instructions on printing the proclamation, Connolly declared 'We are going ahead.' He went on, 'This must take place; we must rise. If not, fathers and sons will be tracked by the British and there will be wholesale massacre. If we are able to hold the Capital for 48 hours we would, in fact, be in a position to declare ourselves a Republic.'[61] Later that day, at 3pm, James Connolly mobilised the ICA, which marched through the main streets of Dublin. At 5pm, recalled Matthew Connolly, in front of Liberty Hall, 'Connolly addressed us, saying that we were no longer the Citizen Army, that we were now merged with the Irish Volunteers, under the title of the Irish Republican Army, that we were to be confined to barracks until further orders, and that nobody was to leave the Hall without permission.'[62] Next day, the most momentous week in Dublin's history began.

8 RISING

The women spat at us and shouted jingo slogans, while the men started to pull down the barricade.

Patrick Egan, 4th Dublin Irish Volunteers, on Dublin civilians outside Roe's Distillery. Easter Monday 1916[1]

Heroes

In the week following Easter 1916, fewer than 2,000 Dubliners, serving with others from across Ireland, went into action in a fight that turned out to be against overwhelming odds. Many would die, many were taken prisoner, but most would survive. For much of the week, they saw little action, with the decisive onslaught coming towards its end. In years to come, some regarded them as heroes. They were the men of the 8th and 9th Royal Dublin Fusiliers of the 16th (Irish) Division. The overwhelming odds were in the form of a German gas attack, and they were fighting at Hulluch in Belgium. Yet for most of Ireland, the true heroes of Easter 1916 were those who fought in a Rising against British rule and whose story could be told in the same way.

The events at Hulluch are not commonly placed alongside those of the Rising, yet only by connecting the two narratives can we fully understand the context of the Rising and why it was initially received as it was. Examination of the places in which the Rising was fought shows how far it antagonised the so-called 'separation women' who were receiving a separation allowance while their husbands were away fighting in the British army, at the same time as inflicting significant damage on the streets from which some of those men were drawn.[2] We can also understand how Dubliners were part of British forces in the city during the Rising, how the Rising had the potential to divide families, and how it posed dilemmas for those serving in the British army. Setting the Rising and First World War narratives alongside each other also shows that across the Monday to Saturday of the Rising, nearly three times as many Dubliners were killed serving in the British army in the First World War, as the total number of rebels killed in Dublin. Thus any reading of 'Easter 1916' which focuses on the Rising only can only offer a partial history of Dublin's experience of that time.

The principal actors of the Rising on the rebel side were six units of the Irish Volunteers along with the ICA and Cumann na mBan. The headquarters at the General Post Office (GPO) was held by both Irish Volunteers and the ICA, among them the Irish Volunteers' Kimmage Garrison. Ned Daly's 1st battalion of the Volunteers was in the Four Courts area. The 2nd battalion, commanded by Thomas MacDonagh, was centred on Jacob's Biscuit Factory on the corner of Bishop Street and Aungier Street. Éamon de Valera's 3rd battalion was in the Grand Canal Street area, centred on Boland's Bakery and Boland's Mills. Éamonn Ceannt's 4th battalion was at the South Dublin Union in James Street. Units of the ICA were centred on City Hall and St Stephen's Green. Outside the city, in the north of County Dublin and into County Meath, was Thomas Ashe's 5th 'Fingal' Battalion. Women from Cumann na mBan were spread throughout these locations.[3]

On the government side, three Irish infantry units were already in Dublin: the reserve 3rd Royal Irish Rifles and the 3rd Royal Irish Regiment, plus one service battalion not yet posted overseas, the 10th Royal Dublin Fusiliers. They were joined by the 6th Reserve Cavalry Regiment, which fed the 5th (Royal Irish) and 12th (Prince of Wales's Royal) Lancers. Altogether there were over 120 officers and 2,265 other ranks in Dublin at the outbreak of the Rising.[4] As the Rising began, the 2/7th and 2/8th Sherwood Foresters arrived from England, while the 5th Leinsters and 5th Dublins came from the Curragh.[5] In time, aside from the police, government forces were bolstered by the 3rd and 4th Dublins, an Ulster Composite Battalion and a detachment of the 12th Inniskillings.[6] Among the 4th Dublins was 2nd Lieutenant Eugene

Sheehy, who was closely connected to leading nationalists through family ties. He was born in County Tipperary but had grown up in Dublin's Belvedere Place, attending Belvedere College and later University College. He was the brother of Hanna Sheehy and therefore brother-in-law of Francis Sheehy-Skeffington, while his younger sister, Mary, was married to Tom Kettle. His father, David, was the IPP MP for South Meath. An uncle, a priest also called Eugene, was more radical, and would be in the GPO during the Rising supporting the rebels. Sheehy had applied for a commission in April 1915 and by the time of the Rising was living in Ranelagh.[7]

The Dublin University OTC played a part in the Rising, with men like Paul Guéret of Strand Road. He was waiting to take up training in July 1916 having successfully applied for a commission in February. Born in Dublin, his family were French Catholics and ran a shop in the city selling religious artefacts, while his father had stood in local government elections as a nationalist.[8] Civilians in a uniformed and armed paramilitary formation, the Irish Association of Volunteer Training Corps, played a role too. Known as the GRs for the 'Georgius Rex' red GR badges they wore, their local nickname was the 'Gorgeous Wrecks'. They included men who had initially joined Frank Browning's rugby volunteer corps but had not enlisted, and also men of the LDV.[9]

Monday 24 April

Rising dead: 55 (26 British military, 15 civilians, 11 rebels, 3 police).[10]
Dublin's war dead: 5 (France and Flanders 3, Home (of wounds) 2).

On Easter Monday, the 9th Dublins were relieved at the Hulluch front at 7.45pm by the 8th Dublins. The 9th went to support trenches, ready to assist if the 8th were attacked.[11] The threatened gas attack did not materialise, yet the 9th did not emerge from their five days in the line unscathed, losing four men, including Private 15784 Bernard Colgan of Dublin's Ormond Market, killed in action on Easter Monday.[12] On the same day, the 2nd Dublins were relieved having faced 'Shells nearly all day' but with 'little damage done'. They were not at the front again until mid-June having begun an intense period of training for the attempted advance at the Somme.[13] None of these Dublin Fusiliers battalions would have known what had taken place in Dublin earlier in the day.

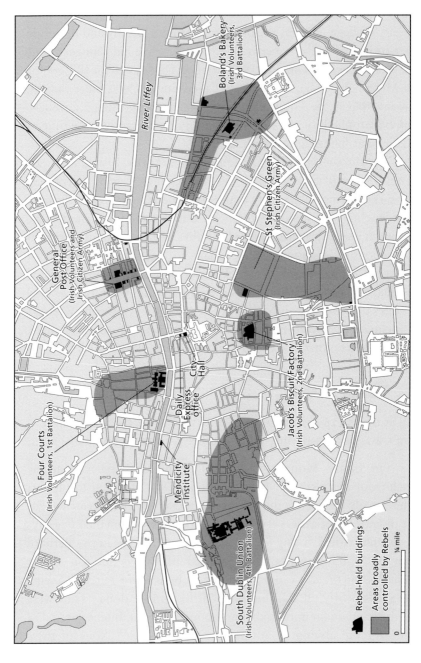

Map 8.1: Easter Rising – key locations. Adapted by David Cox from the map drawn by Charlie Roche and Mike Murphy in Crowley et al., *Atlas of the Irish Revolution*, 242.

When Easter Monday, 24 April came, the role of 'Pivot' was crucial to the mobilisation of the Volunteers. This role was described by Frank Henderson of the 2nd Irish Volunteers as needing 'A very steady reliable man in the Company' who 'was responsible, on receiving a mobilisation order from the Captain, for getting in touch immediately with the men in charge of each mobilisation group and setting the machinery in motion'. The Pivot then relayed news back to the captain.[14] Pivots were among the Volunteers who bore the brunt of the effects of MacNeill's orders of the day before, along with their officers. Captain Simon Donnelly of the 3rd battalion later said, 'It is my opinion that the 3rd Battalion went into action on Easter Monday with a maximum strength of 110 to 120 men, as against the 400 who would have paraded on Easter Sunday.'[15] In the 3rd Battalion's Blackrock Company, Lieutenant Tim Finn paraded in Blackrock Park from 9.30am but his captain did not appear. Confusion followed, and Finn was told there was no mobilisation. Many men went home. Heading for the city with those who remained, Finn failed to connect with his unit and retreated to take up a position at Stillorgan Grove.[16]

Around 11am members of the 2nd Irish Volunteers were told to assemble at Father Mathew Park. Among them were Harry Colley and Oscar Traynor but they were rapidly demobilised: MacNeill's efforts to stop the Rising had continued and a message sent with his secretary said that only the ICA – and not the Irish Volunteers – were out that day. However, at 2pm, Colley received a message to say that the Rising was on.[17] Meanwhile, Traynor had made his own enquiries and joined Volunteers in Fairview who were very clearly in the field. His unit of thirty men was directed to Gilbeys in Fairview Strand, which they would hold until the next evening.[18]

At 11.30am the 1st Irish Volunteers led by Ned Daly paraded at 5 Blackhall Street. Daly addressed the men and Peadar McNulty described how he told them 'that the Irish Republic was to be proclaimed that day at 12 noon.' Daly also said that they were no longer the 1st Irish Volunteers 'but the 1st Battalion Dublin Brigade of the "Irish Republican Army"'.[19] Meanwhile, Liam MacNiamh of the Kimmage garrison had made other plans for the day: 'as we thought that everything was off we decided to go to Fairyhouse Races'. Only a chance meeting that morning with another volunteer in Sackville Street made him change his plans.[20] Among the first into the General

Figure 8.1: Two unidentified Irish Volunteers inside the barricaded GPO during the Easter Rising. (Image Courtesy of the National Library of Ireland, NPA GPO1).

Figure 8.2: British soldiers manning a street barricade during the Rising. This *Daily Sketch* photograph wrongly placed it in 'May' 1916. (Image Courtesy of the National Library of Ireland, EPH A671).

Post Office around noon was Seán Nunan with the Kimmage garrison. He recalled, 'I, with others in the leading files, entered the Post Office by the Henry Street door – the main body entering through the main door in O'Connell Street. All civilians and Post Office staff were evacuated, and we proceeded to barricade all windows.' At 12.45pm, Pearse stood on the step of the GPO, proclaiming 'the Irish Republic as a Sovereign Independent State' and establishing a Provisional Government.[21] Aligning his cause with that of Britain's enemies in the First World War, he claimed support from 'gallant allies in Europe'.[22]

On hearing of the Rising, Patrick Dalton from Upper Gloucester Street and a member of the 1st Irish Volunteers simply made his way to the GPO. On arrival, he was told by James Connolly, 'there are plenty of guns & you can go inside.' He guarded a window until the next morning. He was sixteen and had joined the Volunteers just a few weeks before.[23] Volunteers were making their way into the city centre as best they could. John Doyle, a member of the 2nd Irish Volunteers who had served in the British Naval Medical Auxiliary Service in 1914–15, was held up at Summerhill Bridge by British fire but reached the GPO at about 5pm from where he established medical posts.[24] Thomas Devine of the 3rd Irish Volunteers had gone to work in the morning at a laundry, but around noon when on the way home had heard news of the Rising. Having tried and failed to get into the city via Portobello Bridge, he made progress through Richmond Hill. He recalled that on arriving at the GPO he saw a tricolour flying and 'from inside a tremendous hammering and crashing sounded as the garrison prepared it for defence'.[25] Though an 'Irish Republic' bannerette also flew from the GPO it was the tricolour which, in years to come, the participants were most likely to remember.[26]

Joseph Byrne of Usher's Island received notice of the Rising in a rather different way. He had joined the Fianna in 1911, and then the Volunteers in 1913, but at the end of 1915 had enlisted in the British army. He was stationed at Portobello Barracks in the 3rd Royal Irish Rifles but was home at Usher's Island on compassionate leave over Easter Weekend. Late on Monday morning he was contacted by the police who told him there was trouble in the city and that he should report to the barracks. He said he would go immediately but instead set out to join the rebellion. He made his way to his mother's house in Camden Street, to meet his brothers and they met up with a Volunteer unit. There, they were told to find whatever arms they could. They did so, at his mother's, and agreed to meet the next morning.[27]

Ned Daly's 1st battalion had taken over the Four Courts and the Mendicity Institute at Usher's Island. Meanwhile, they had fired on a party of Lancers, wounding some and taking others prisoner. Member of the 1st Irish Volunteers simultaneously took various positions in the Four Courts area with the aim of covering approaches to the stronghold. Police were initially confused as to what was going on. Seán Prendergast recalled 'a big burly policeman endeavouring to pass through our lines'. He was perhaps confused by the fact that 'We must have looked a strange motley of soldiers there with our miscellaneous array of guns, dressed in various fashions, some in Volunteer uniforms and others in their "Sunday best" attire, accentuated by a not too pronounced military order, deportment or even aggressiveness.' A scuffle ensued and the policeman was shot in the shoulder. Prendergast recounted how, 'In the midst of the melee he could be heard to say, "I'm as good an Irishman as any of ye".' Meanwhile, the 1st Irish Volunteers erected barricades across streets, with Michael O'Flanagan recalling how horse-drays were dragged over to block the junction of Church Street and Chancery Place. Some of these posts would be under very regular British fire though Thomas Dowling, holed up in the Bow Street–Mary's Lane area, 'had very little action' for the first three days.[28]

The 1st battalion men in the Mendicity Institute had orders to slow down any British troops who might make their way to centres of the Rising. Early in the afternoon they spotted a group of the 10th Royal Dublin Fusiliers on the other side of the Liffey. Leading the 10th Dublins was 34-year-old Lieutenant Charles Grant. He was Dublin-born, and had grown up first in Sandymount and then in Rathgar Road where he was living when he enlisted in 1916. Grant had served as a reservist in the South Irish Horse from 1903 for four years. At the outbreak of war, by then qualified as a barrister, he joined the Dublin University Officers Training Corps, being commissioned in November 1915. Soon after noon Grant was ordered to take around fifty men from the Royal Barracks to Dublin Castle which was being attacked, and they came under fire from the Mendicity Institute as they crossed the Liffey at Queen Street Bridge. Grant later recalled that he had 'no inkling that rebellion had broken out'. On crossing the river and reaching Bridgefoot Street 'we received a volley of rifle shots which scattered our party'.

Several British soldiers were killed or wounded. Others hid behind a tram which had been passing and from which passengers had fled. Grant and his men made it to City Hall by a different route and placed snipers in various positions.[29]

One of those killed in Bridgefoot Street was Lieutenant Gerald Aloysius Neilan, a Dublin resident. Born in County Roscommon, he enlisted in the Sherwood Foresters in 1899 and served in the South African War as a private, being wounded and taken prisoner. He then served in the Birmingham police but re-enlisted in the army – and was commissioned in the Northumberland Fusiliers – in December 1914. Transferred to the Dublin Fusiliers in February 1916, his mother had moved back to city in which she was born by 1911, and was living at Mount Harold Terrace on Leinster Road. Two of his brothers, both doctors, were serving in the Royal Army Medical Corps: Captain Alan Neilan and Lieutenant Charles Neilan. However, despite his service in the British army, Gerald Neilan was an Irish nationalist. Indeed, Stephen Gwynn later wrote that he 'was so strongly Nationalist in his sympathy as to be almost a Sinn Féiner'. A further brother certainly was a republican: Arthur. Easter 1916 found him also armed and in Dublin, but with the Irish Volunteers. Formally a member of the 4th Irish Volunteers, he had mobilised on Sunday and then been stood down. Not receiving any mobilisation message on Easter Monday he made his way to Kimmage and then entered Dublin 'under cover of darkness' that night. Reporting to the GPO he was sent to reinforce Ned Daly's 1st Irish Volunteers at the Four Courts rather than go to his own unit. It was men from this unit who had deployed to the Mendicity Institute and killed Arthur Neilan's brother earlier in the day.[30] Neilan was not the only British soldier with Dublin connections to lose his life that day in the city. Also killed in the 10th Dublins was 25244 Private Francis Brennan whose parents lived at Benburb Street. He was possibly killed outside the Mendicity having been wounded there but that is uncertain.[31]

Jacob's Biscuit Factory was occupied by the 2nd Irish Volunteers after mustering at St Stephen's Green around noon.[32] Although the factory was secured easily enough, the volunteers faced hostility from local people, some of whom had been turned out of houses nearby. James (later Seamus) Pounch, a captain in the Sluagh Brian Boru of the Fianna, attached to the 2nd Irish Volunteers, described how 'Some of the people were very antagonistic towards us, partly from the fact of being put out of their homes and mostly because they were of a pro-British type, soldiers' wives and relatives.'[33] The crowd tried to break into the factory. William Stapleton of North Great George's Street described how separation women made their feelings known: 'We were boohed and frequently pelted with various articles throughout the day. We were openly insulted, particularly by the wives of British soldiers who were drawing separation allowance and who referred to their sons and husbands fighting for freedom in France.' At the factory, 'the mob tried to burst the gate in. They kicked and barged it with some heavy implements, but seeing that that was of little effect they tried to set fire to it with old sacking which had been soaked in paraffin and pushed under the door and ignited.' Stapleton was ordered to fire blanks 'in the direction of the mob … and they dispersed after a short time'.[34] However, local opposition made the holding of barricades in the street very difficult, and a male civilian was shot in a struggle, later to die.[35] By the evening some outlying positions had been abandoned for the safer haven of the factory. Thoughts turned to practical matters of how to survive a possible siege. Michael Walker described how, 'At first the catering for the garrison consisted of all kinds of confectionery and rich cakes found on the premises, with tea', but that parties later went out to commandeer food. Members of the Cumann na mBan then 'gave the garrison some substantial meals'.[36]

Éamon de Valera's 3rd Irish Volunteers reached Boland's Bakery around noon, many having gathered at Earlsfort Terrace an hour or so before.[37] Marching from there, Andrew McDonnell 'was still convinced I was going on a manoeuvre'. Indeed, McDonnell was never told directly that they were part of a Rising and only when in the city centre did he have 'doubts about the manoeuvres and was convinced there was something wrong when I was ordered to hold up a tram, my first taste of active service'.[38] Some of the 3rd Irish Volunteers were stationed at railway bridges, but most consolidated at Boland's.[39] Safely dug in, de Valera led men on a mission to confuse the British. McDonnell described how overnight on 24/25 April he was a part of a group of ten led by de Valera to the gas works. Finding workmen at the premises 'he told them to get home as best they could and he would have the place garrisoned shortly. The idea was to let it be known that the Gas works were held, while in actual fact we did not leave a man in it.'[40]

In and around the South Dublin Union hospital, Éamonn Ceannt's 4th Irish Volunteers saw some of the closest fighting of the Rising's first day. One of those there was Gerald Doyle for whom the 'enemy' was close to home. His father joined the British army about a week before the Rising, having been a National Volunteer. Doyle remembered first seeing him in a British uniform 'on the Easter Monday morning as I myself was leaving the house to report ... and we just met and passed each other with a casual "Good Morning!"'[41] Reaching the SDU and other locations, barricades were erected by both the volunteers and patients.[42] Here too the rebels faced local hostility. Patrick Egan was at Roe's distillery and near a barricade at Bowbridge, a noisy crowd had gathered: 'The women spat at us and shouted jingo slogans, while the men started to pull down the barricade ... The butts of the rifles were used on the men; O'Toole knocked out two of them; the crowd then scattered.'[43]

British troops arrived at the SDU itself about 12 noon. In an outbuilding was James Burke along with a handful of other volunteers who later guessed that the British 'must have made a move even before the G.P.O. was properly ready for the Declaration of the Republic'. Rifle fire was exchanged and the Irish Volunteers discovered that the thin walls of the building provided little protection. Burke described how John Traynor 'was killed by a bullet which came through the side of the building, which soon became perforated by bullets'. Gerald Doyle described how 'With a prayer on his lips "Lord Jesus, Mary, Joseph, have mercy on me" he died.' Traynor lived close by in Kilmainham and had worked as a messenger at the Guinness brewery. Easter Monday was his 19th birthday. Burke, along with Willie Corrigan began breaking glass to avoid injury when it was hit by British fire, but both were wounded in doing so. Burke had been told by a volunteer captain that they would receive instructions on where to move, but had never done so, and British troops overran their position. He recalled with some bitterness, 'This was about an hour after we had opened fire. So ended the fight in the union after all our preparations. We were only an hour in action. We should not have been left there at all.'[44]

Among those surrendering that afternoon was Gerald Doyle. Being moved to Kilmainham police station in the afternoon, bystanders 'boohed us and shouted at the soldiers to shoot us out of hand'. He also suggested that more hostility came from the police than from the army: 'The soldiers at no time molested us and when we were locked into cells the police on duty started to shout at us through the grills ... The soldiers on guard would not let the cells be opened.' Late at night they were moved to Richmond Barrack and 'The crowd followed us up to the gate of the Barracks where a woman rushed up with an uplifted jug and hit one of us. The officer knocked her back into the mob shouting at them that they should be ashamed of themselves.' At this stage, rebels probably thought that they would be executed, for a British officer had said when they were captured 'You all know the rules of war where rebels are concerned – they are shot without trial.'[45]

No quarter was given by the British in the evening when Ceannt requested a temporary ceasefire while the Volunteers collected their dead and wounded. According to William Murphy, the store-keeper of the SDU who was co-operating with Ceannt, the response was 'No, they have shot our Major (Ramsay) and we will give them no quarter.' By nightfall, the British occupied all the buildings at the back of the premises, while the Irish Volunteers held those at the front.[46] The Ramsay referred to was a Dubliner, and was in fact a captain rather than a major, Alan Livingstone Ramsay, age 26 and from Ballsbridge. He had been wounded by shrapnel in Belgium at the Battle of Frezenburg, on 9 May 1915, and returned to Dublin to the 3rd Royal Irish Regiment after recovering in England.[47] At the SDU, Ramsay led men in through the narrow Rialto gate but they came under heavy fire and Ramsay suffered a head wound. A temporary ceasefire had allowed his body to be removed but he died shortly after, and his men were forced to retreat. Aside from Ramsay another five members of the 3rd Royal Irish Regiment were killed that day at the SDU, among them Private 9852 Michael Carr from Mulhuddart, County Dublin.[48] Among the British Army's dead elsewhere in the city were two more Dubliners, both serving in the 3rd Royal Irish Rifles: Riflemen 5797 John Mulhern and 8692 James Nolan, of Stephen's Place and Powers Court.[49] Meanwhile, three members of the Dublin GRs were killed: Reginald Clery of Harcourt Terrace, John Gibbs from Rathmines and Thomas Harborne from the Finglas-Glasnevin area. Clery was shot by a sniper on the railway bridge at South Lotts Road while the other two were killed by sniping from outposts in Northumberland Road. Their deaths meant that of the twenty-six British military killed on the Rising's opening day in Dublin, at least nine were from Dublin.[50] Other Irish regiments spent the day learning of the Rising and awaiting deployment in Dublin. The 4th Dublins were at Templemore in County Tipperary. Serving with them was Arthur Killingley from County Wexford. He noted in his diary, that all were confined to barracks following rumours of 'troubles' in Dublin. While there, 'We have a general discussion as to how men will behave if ordered to fire on their fellow-countrymen.'[51]

Outside the city, commanders of the 5th (Fingal) Battalion of the Irish Volunteers received orders from Pádraig Pearse at around 7am to 'Strike at one o'clock to-day'. Their activities were bolstered by the addition of Richard Mulcahy, who was a member of a city Volunteer unit, but was in the Fingal area and unable to reach his battalion. Part of their role was to guard the main road and prevent any British officers coming that way from the Fairyhouse races (though none did so). They were also tasked with blowing up railway bridges so to as to prevent transports by train to Dublin, but had mixed results with only one operation partially successful.[52]

The ICA were active in two locations: around City Hall and on St Stephen's Green. They did not look any more like a formal army than the Irish Volunteers. Helena Molony, who had recently acted at the Abbey Theatre and joined the ICA,[53] recalled:

> The women had no uniform, in the ordinary sense – nor the men either. Some of the men had green coats. They wore an ordinary slouch hat, like the Boer hat and mostly a belt. They insisted that they were citizen soldiers, not military soldiers – at the same time regimented and disciplined. I had an Irish tweed costume, with a Sam Browne. I had my own revolver and ammunition.[54]

Molony's unit's first target was Dublin Castle, because 'It was expected that the psychological effect of attacking Dublin Castle, the citadel of foreign rule for seven hundred years, would be considerable when the news spread through the country.'[55] The ICA were mocked by observers as they marched through Dame Street. Matthew Connolly recalled, 'A voice from the footpath remarked, "Here's the Citizen Army, with their pop-guns!"'[56] On reaching the gates of the castle, a police sergeant appeared and apparently assumed that the ICA were on a parade and would continue past the gates. However, when Captain Seán Connolly (in command of the unit and the brother of Matthew Connolly) tried to get past him 'the Sergeant put out his arm; and Connolly shot him dead.' At that point, the military guard closed the gates and the ICA could go no further. Instead, they diverted to the City Hall where they faced no opposition due to the Bank Holiday.[57]

At about 1.30pm, Molony was sent to the GPO to request reinforcements. On her way there she met Francis Sheehy-Skeffington, who lived in Rathmines. Though he was an advanced nationalist he was also a pacifist and could not support the rebels. Instead, he tried to organise a 'police' force to stop looting. Molony described how he was 'really looking distressed. He was standing in the midst of the bullets, as if they were raindrops. He was a fighting pacifist. He believed one had to suffer for peace – not to inflict peace, but to suffer for it.'[58] However, his efforts had little effect.[59]

Once inside the City Hall, the ICA soon lost their commanding officer, Seán Connolly, at around 2pm. Helena Molony recounted how Dr Kathleen Lynn (a Cumann member serving with the ICA, and one of many Protestants involved in the nationalist movement[60]) tended Connolly: 'She said: "I'm afraid he is gone." He was bleeding very much from the stomach. I said the Act of Contrition into his ear. We had no priest.'[61] His brother, Matthew, tried to reach him at that time but was ordered back to his post by his section leader, though he was later taken off duty and allowed to rest for a few hours.[62] Lynn herself believed that 'Sean Connolly's death had a demoralising effect on the City Hall men.'[63] Soon after his loss City Hall came under heavy attack. Lynn recalled, 'There was no way of escape although we discussed all possibilities.'[64]

Later that evening, British troops entered the building and captured those there.[65] The British assumed that all the women in the City Hall had been taken by the rebels. Helena Molony was asked 'Did they do anything to you? Were they kind to you?'[66] Kathleen Lynn recalled that when she told a British soldier, 'I was a doctor, he thought I had just come in to attend to the wounded. I informed him that I belonged to the Citizen Army which surprised him very much.'[67] Molony and her comrades would spend the next eight days held as prisoners in Ship Street: 'The soldiers were decent enough to us. The Dublin Fusiliers were there. They would bring us in a dish of fried bacon and bread.'[68]

Meanwhile, another party of the ICA commanded by Michael Mallin made its way to St Stephen's Green. Mallin was born in Dublin's

Liberties area in 1874 and served in the British army from 1889 to 1902, first as a 'Boy' in the band of the Royal Scots Fusiliers, including spending time in India, seeing service in the North-West Frontier and Tirah campaigns of 1897–8. Returning to Dublin he became a trade unionist and a socialist, and by 1916 he was Chief of Staff of the ICA.[69] He was certainly not the only ex-British army soldier in the ICA, with Richard McCormick, John J. O'Neill, Christopher Poole and Vincent Poole all having previous service.[70] As they reached the top of Grafton Street, James O'Shea recalled how 'a policeman passed a remark about playing soldiers'. However, 'He got an awful shock when he saw us marching straight into St Stephen's Green Park', because the ICA immediately ordered people out. Trenches were then dug on the Green.[71] Frank Robbins was part of a detachment of the ICA which Mallin ordered to take outlying positions, first at Harcourt Street Station and then in Hatch Street which was to be barricaded.[72] He was later ordered to St Stephen's Green where Mallin instructed him to take control of the College of Surgeons overlooking the Green. That he did at 3pm along with three other men and four women (one of whom was Countess Markiewicz). However, due to a shortage of numbers, the Shelbourne Hotel, which also overlooked the Green, was not garrisoned and was taken by the British later in the day. That made the Green itself impossible to defend as the ICA soon discovered.[73]

Tuesday 25 April

Rising dead: 37 (22 civilians, 8 rebels, 7 British military).[74]
Dublin's war dead: 2 (both Mesopotamia)

On Tuesday 25 April, with the 8th Dublins in front-line trenches at Hulluch and the 9th Dublins in reserve there was still no sign of gas. The 9th Dublins practised what they would do in the event of a gas attack. For protection of personnel, gas helmets made of sacking were available, although these did not offer complete protection.[75] At the front, at 6am, two men of the 8th were killed by a German bomb, Private 14891 Patrick Rourke and Private 14878 George Lloyd. Neither were Dubliners, Rourke being from Clane, County Kildare and Lloyd from Dundalk. Two other men were accidentally wounded firing a rifle grenade which was too strong for the rifle and exploded.[76] Dublin's war dead on Tuesday 25th were both far from Hulluch, in Mesopotamia: Private 8988 Michael Downey of the 1st Connaughts and Lieutenant W. Brabazon Parker of the 8th Cheshires. Both men died of wounds.[77] Downey's wounds were probably incurred at some point between 15 and 18 April when, as part of the ongoing effort to relieve Kut, the 1st Connaughts had taken part in the capture of Turkish positions at Beit Aiessa, and then fought off a counter-attack.[78]

In the city, martial law was declared by Lord Wimborne, the Lieutenant General of Ireland.[79] Even so, some residents tried to go about their business despite the Rising. Thomas Moylan tried and failed to make his way to work at Richmond Asylum. As he did so, he found 'such a lull over the place ... Isolated reports are heard on and off, but the fighting, if there is to be any fighting, has not yet started'.[80] Others were still not fully aware of what was happening. Private 10404 Peter Ennis was home on leave from the 3rd Scots Guards, visiting his mother at Queen's Square. In the morning, he decided to go for a walk. Unarmed, but in uniform, he was on Grand Canal Street when he was shot dead by rebels.[81] Another soldier home on leave was Sergeant Major 15231 Patrick Brosnan of the 3rd Royal Irish Fusiliers, aged 50. He was visiting his wife and children who were in family quarters at Dublin Castle. Offering to help disarm a rebel outside the castle he was wearing civilian clothes and was shot by another soldier who thought him a rebel.[82] Of the five more British soldiers killed that day, one was from Dublin: Corporal 19222 John Humphreys, originally from Clonmel but living in Dublin when war broke out. Serving with the 5th Dublin Fusiliers he was killed in an attack on an ICA outpost in the *Daily Express* offices.[83]

In the absence of definitive news, rumours were rife in Dublin as the rebels strengthened their positions. William Christian of the 3rd Irish Volunteers was told 'there were 20,000 Germans marching to Dublin to help us and were due to arrive at any time'.[84] Isaac Callendar 'was told by a Volunteer at the G.P.O. that thousands had landed at Kerry and were marching on Dublin and had arrived at Kildare'.[85] Mary Martin of Monkstown was writing a diary for her son who was missing at Salonika.[86] On Tuesday 25th she noted the problems of getting news since, she said, newspapers were not being published and the mail was not being delivered. However, 'We also hear there were Risings in Cork, Limerick, Belfast & Derry.'[87] In fact, the

Irish Times was published between 25th and 27 April but it only carried news of the events of the Rising on 25 April when it reported that 'This newspaper has never been published in stranger circumstances than those which obtain to-day.' It described how 'an effort has been made to set up an independent Irish Republic in Dublin. It was well-organised; a large number of armed men are taking part in it; and to the general public, at any rate, the outbreak came as a complete surprise.' The paper went on to carry an accurate report of the key sites of action.[88] It was this term 'outbreak' which the paper used initially to describe the rebellion. A day later it made a brief reference to 'The Sinn Fein Rising', but there was no further news of the Rising in its issues on 26th and 27 April which only carried details of the terms of martial law.[89]

On the previous evening, Eily O'Hanrahan (later O'Reilly) of Cumann na mBan was returning to Dublin having been delivering messages in Wexford. She was born in New Ross in 1889 but the family had later moved to Dublin and was living in Connaught Street. She was told by a passenger on her train that 'the streets are running with blood'.[90] Also returning was Tom Byrne who had found his efforts in Kildare hampered by MacNeill's countermanding order. He left Newbridge, nearly thirty miles from Dublin, by bicycle on the morning of Easter Monday, making some detours on the way. Arriving in the city that evening he visited the GPO and then brought nearly twenty Maynooth Volunteers into the city on the Tuesday morning. Later in the day Byrne's men and some members of the Hibernian Rifles took over a house in Parliament Street, solely with the purpose of preventing the British from gaining a foothold nearby. Having done so, they withdrew to the GPO that evening.[91]

Many of the locations occupied on Monday were relatively quiet on Tuesday, as the British took stock of the situation and began to draft in reinforcements. The 4th Dublins arrived in the city from Templemore late in the morning. Arthur Killingley noted, 'A batch of prisoners soon arrived, and all doubt about the men's behaviour was removed when they booted the prisoners with great gusto.'[92] Joseph Byrne tried to make his way to meet his brothers, finding that his British army uniform helped him cross military barricades. However, when he reached his mother's house his brothers had left without leaving a message. Byrne's mother burnt his uniform and he tried to join a Volunteer unit, but was arrested when he met a sergeant of his own battalion. Byrne spent two days held in the Royal Barracks, only to escape later. He rejoined his battalion after the Rising and was arrested, but in the chaos which followed the Rising the charge was not pressed. Weeks later he was drafted to the Western Front where he stayed until 1918.[93]

In the Dublin countryside, the 5th Irish Volunteers did little of note beyond sending a detachment of twenty men to Dublin.[94] In the city, Isaac Callendar was even sent home to rest and change clothes in the evening as he had been out delivering messages and gathering information all day, and had got very wet as rain fell in the evening. Recruits – though in much smaller numbers – continued to join the Rising. Bernard Byrne had two brothers in the Volunteers and tried to enlist at Father Mathew Hall. However, he was turned away, partly for being too young but also because he had two brothers serving already. Then, 'Somebody took pity on me' and he was recruited to carry out intelligence work which 'consisted mostly of watching enemy movements and concentrations, finding out where new telephone wires were being laid down, etc.'[95]

Prisoners continued to be taken, with Frank Robbins at the College of Surgeons given charge of former Irish Volunteer Laurence Kettle, who was then Chief of the Dublin Corporation Electricity Department and was the brother of Thomas Kettle, the former nationalist MP, by then serving in the British army.[96] Some work was done consolidating positions, for example, with John Doyle establishing a series of medical posts around the GPO in places such as Clery's and a bank in Abbey Street.[97] Among those staffing the posts were women like Aoife de Burca, who was based at Reis's in Lower Abbey Street. On Tuesday, the area was quiet enough for her to 'race across to the G.P.O. to see my brother whom I had learned was stationed there'.[98] Optimism was high in the GPO. Harry Colley had returned there in the evening after being sent to blow up railway track at Clontarf, which he failed to do. He recalled, 'At this time we all had the idea that the whole country had risen in our support and, therefore, under reasonably sanguine conditions, we could make a fight of it.'[99]

At Jacob's factory, the 2nd battalion captured some policemen as prisoners and carried out some sniping on Portobello Barrack.[100] In the 3rd battalion area, some positions were abandoned as having no defensive value.[101] In the SDU area, there were only occasional exchanges of fire,[102] but some evacuations went wrong. Charles O'Grady described how Roe's Distillery was evacuated at about 4pm on Tuesday: 'The men were told to leave in small groups and it was every man for himself. Some of the men got down James' St. and round to Marrowbone Lane without being spotted by the enemy; others walked right into them and were taken prisoner.'[103] Michael McCabe, the 15-year-old who had been in the Fianna and joined the Volunteers in late 1915, left the distillery with a comrade called Paddy Byrne but ran into a British patrol at the Fountain. They managed to hide out until Saturday morning, before being escorted to Marrowbone Lane Distillery by Lily McClean, a member of Cumann na mBan.[104]

The heaviest onslaught by the British was faced by the St Stephen's Green contingent of the ICA as they brought to bear the advantage of holding the Shelbourne Hotel, raking the green with machine-gun fire and forcing withdrawal to the College of Surgeons.[105] Once inside, James O'Shea and a small group were ordered to break through walls in the College of Surgeons and then house by house through to Grafton Street in an ultimately unsuccessful effort to reach and destroy a machine-gun post in the United Services Club.[106]

That evening, Oscar Traynor's unit at Fairview Strand was ordered to evacuate to the GPO. On arrival, they were addressed by Pearse who told them 'that they had done a great and noble work for their country'. He added, 'Be assured that you will find victory, even though that victory may be found in death.' Traynor described that as a 'terribly thrilling moment' before being sent with his men to garrison the Metropole Hotel and buildings adjacent.[107] He perhaps did not guess at the time that it was a clear sign of the blood sacrifice which was in Pearse's mind.[108]

9 FALLING

... a dense cloud of black gas and smoke was between us and the sun and gradually spreading over our lines ...
War Diary, 8th Royal Dublin Fusiliers, 27 April 1916[1]

A City Against Itself

Over Wednesday to Sunday of the Rising, Dubliners continued to be pitched against Dubliners as those in the British army played their part in quelling the Rising. Soldiers home on leave, who might have expected to be safe found themselves in mortal danger. Divided loyalties continued to surface. Some did not know how close they were to their enemies, with British soldiers unknowingly breakfasting alongside rebels.

By the next week, the Rising had collapsed and it initially appeared – from the responses of ordinary Dubliners – that the republican cause would not easily find roots in the city. That was in large part due to the destruction of parts of the city centre, but it was also influenced by levels of British military service among men from the areas where the Rising took place.[2] Many of those men had simultaneously been serving at Hulluch, where the nationalist volunteers of the 16th (Irish) Division had faced a devastating blow.

Wednesday 26 April

Rising dead: 73 (30 British military, 28 civilians, 13 rebels, 2 police).[3]
Dublin's war dead: 7 (France and Flanders 5, Mesopotamia 2).

On the Western Front, preparations for an impending gas attack continued. The 8th Dublins strengthened wires to hinder the German infantry who would follow the gas. Blankets which covered dug-out entrances were soaked in the anti-gas agent Vermorel. Activity was observed in German lines, and a small bombing party was sent out late that night.[4] Five Dubliners died elsewhere on the Western Front. They included Private 7723 Thomas Byrne, age 19, whose mother and sisters lived in Ranelagh. He had enlisted in late April 1915, initially in the Royal Field Artillery, but was killed in action serving with the 2nd Royal Irish Rifles in the Vimy Ridge area which had been mined by the Germans. After exploding a mine on the 2nd Royal Irish Rifles' left flank, the Germans took part of the line but were driven out later in the day, by which time Byrne had been killed.[5] Deaths continued in Mesopotamia, with privates 5050 Thomas Dolan and 7991 Michael Furlong dying in the 1st Connaught Rangers, possibly due to a cholera epidemic which had broken out in the battalion.[6]

In Dublin, Thomas Moylan once again tried and failed to get to work.[7] Some of the British forces found food scarce. In the evening, Arthur Killingley noted that 'We are very hungry, as we have had nothing to eat since our tea and biscuits at 7 a.m.'[8] Meanwhile, the fighting intensified and it was the costliest day of the Rising so far for the British military. Among thirty dead, at least five were Dubliners. It is not certain where Private 5422 William Mulraney of the 8th (King's Royal Irish) Hussars was killed, nor Sergeant 6745 Henry Hare of the 5th Dublins. Hare's wife lived in Meath Street and he was a Boer War veteran and reservist called up in 1914.[9] However, the third death, of Company Quartermaster Sergeant 8833 Robert Gamble of the Royal Irish Rifles' 2nd Garrison Battalion certainly took place on the railway line near Shelbourne Road when trying to capture a rebel outpost on the railway bridge at South Lotts Road. Gamble was sent to Dublin in the summer of 1915 suffering from the effects of a gunshot wound to the right hand, scrotum and left leg, incurred while serving in the 2nd Royal Irish Rifles at Hill 60 in May of that year. His transfer to a garrison battalion indicated that he was no longer fit for front-line service and he might have expected to sit out the war.[10] Commanding him was Lieutenant Edward Gerrard from Donnybrook, serving in the Royal Field Artillery. He had been at Gallipoli in 1915 but was home on leave when the Rising broke out. Gerrard led Gamble and a unit of Sherwood Foresters in the sortie. Years later he recalled, about eight Sinn Féiners advanced from the direction of the city to meet us. I saw them coming towards us, firing. There was what they call a fairly sharp fire fight. These men were standing up, not lying down. They came out of their trenches to meet us. They were very brave, I remember. They did not know how many of us there might be. The first casualty was Q.M. Gamble. He was shot dead, under the right eye.

Gerrard was wounded.[11] Meanwhile, the GRs lost two men. Frank Browning had been wounded in Northumberland Road two days before and finally succumbed to his wounds on 26 April. The other man dead was Joseph Hosford from Rathmines, shot through a window at Beggars Bush Barracks by a sniper while he stood up to put on his overcoat.[12]

One British officer in Dublin sought to avoid the Rising: Robert Barton, from County Wicklow, and a cousin of Erskine Childers who had piloted the gun-running *Asgard* into Howth. Educated at Rugby School and Oxford, he had been a member of the National Volunteers, working as secretary to their commander, Maurice Moore. However, by the autumn of 1915 he had decided 'that the National Volunteers were rather a futile body and that I was not doing anything of much use'. He therefore enlisted as an officer in the British army. Posted to a training camp at Berkhamsted in Hertfordshire, he was then gazetted to the 10th Dublins on Easter Monday and reached Kingstown two days later. He recalled,

> Being unable to get in to the city, I reported to the Provost-Marshal at Kingstown. He told me that, as I had no uniform, I had better go home – my officer's uniform was in Phillips's shop, the tailors in Dame Street. I went to my home in Annamoe, Co. Wicklow, and, as I received no further order, I stayed there as long as I thought proper.

Barton managed to miss the Rising entirely.[13]

In the city, having been sent home the previous evening, Isaac Callendar breakfasted at 6.15am in his mother's restaurant, the Lucan, on Sarsfield Quay. Eating in the same room were two British officers, oblivious to Callendar's role in the previous days. It was a calm prelude to a day which, in Seán Prendergast's words, was one 'of intense activity' due to a significant increase in shooting across the city.[14] In the evening,

Prendergast witnessed from the Four Courts the burning of the Linenhall Barracks about a quarter of a mile away, which was said to be 'destroyed on our Battalion orders and for sound military reasons'. He described the fire as 'a huge burning furnace, a veritable inferno' which 'transformed an otherwise dark night into uncommonly lurid brightness, brighter even than daylight'.[15]

Rumours continued to spread. At St Stephen's Green James O'Shea heard much 'about the Germans coming to help' and a 'mutiny of Dublin Fusiliers'.[16] O'Shea was part of continued efforts to break through buildings into the corner of Grafton Street and South King Street, as was Frank Robbins. As they did so, they came under intense fire from British machine-gun posts A sign of growing British intent was the shelling of Liberty Hall from the *Helga* that morning.[17] One rogue British officer, John Bowen-Colthurst, took matters into his own hands. He had arrested Francis Sheehy-Skeffington the day before on the basis that he was a sympathiser of the rebels. On the morning of Wednesday 26th, Colthurst had Sheehy-Skeffington and two journalists shot at Portobello Barracks, without trial. An eventual enquiry found Colthurst guilty of murder, but insane. He was sent to Broadmoor and is now believed to have been suffering from post-traumatic stress.[18]

At the GPO further barricades were erected in surrounding streets. Thomas Devine described 'probably the best dressed barricades of the Rising – bales of Irish tweed and worsted being the materials we used'.[19] Some began to think about how the Rising might end. Nancy de Paor was working in the GPO kitchen when The O'Rahilly told her 'that there would be a fight to a finish in the G.P.O., that the Volunteers could hold out for a fortnight in the cellars and that the last survivors might escape'. He added that if he was among those, he would shed his uniform and take other clothes from prisoners, but would need a safe house to which to retreat and he asked de Paor to identify such a location.[20]

In the South Dublin Union the 4th battalion had another uneventful day. It was relatively cut off from the rest of the Rising: William T. Cosgrave recalled Ceannt receiving a message from the GPO on Wednesday, 'to say that there were 680 men "out" in Dublin, and that they were holding out successfully' which 'to the best of my belief, was the only message received in the South Dublin Union during the whole Rising'.[21] Rose McNamara of the Cumman described,

'19 chickens captured from messenger boy. Quiet day. We cooked the chickens for dinner, having to take them up out of the pots with bayonets, not having any forks or utensils for cooking.'[22] Elsewhere, Christopher Byrne was posted to Marrowbone Lane and remembered 'We were so free from fighting that Seamus Murphy, the O/C., suggested that we should have a sing-song – to keep the fellows' hearts up.'[23]

In the country, the 5th battalion was more active, seeking to capture the RIC barracks in Swords. Joseph Lawless was one of the first to enter the village and saw

> the R.I.C. Sergeant, Sergeant O'Reilly, standing in a lounging attitude at the barrack door, his tunic half unbuttoned and his hands in his trousers pockets. He looked at us with a kind of mild curiosity as we flashed past him, and made no move to retire within. There was no appearance of defence about the barracks ... I had a feeling that our movements were not taken too seriously by the police, or at any rate they were not unduly worried. Perhaps they could not believe that a lot of boys whom they knew well all their lives would dare invade the sanctity of the local seat of the law.[24]

Thomas Ashe arrived and requested the surrender of the barracks which was given immediately, with its arms and ammunition handed over to the Volunteers. Meanwhile, Richard Mulcahy destroyed telegraph equipment at the Swords post office. Moving on to the Donabate barracks, there was resistance from the police but 'At the end of ten minutes, on one of the besieged policemen being wounded, the remainder surrendered and handed over rifles and ammunition.'[25] Later that day, around dusk, the 5th battalion gained their first news of the Rising from Dublin when Molly Adrian arrived by bicycle, bringing a copy of the Proclamation and concentrated food such as Oxo cubes. Lawless recalled, 'perhaps for the first time we, that is the younger ones of us, began to realise that all was not going well, and that there was no sign of the rest of the country rising in arms'.[26]

In the 2nd battalion's area around Jacob's, 'Nothing of note took place on Wednesday or Wednesday night, but the firing was continuous.'[27] However, the battalion was assisting the 3rd battalion, after a request from de Valera. Their target was a British post at Mount Street Bridge, and it was hoped that by attacking in the morning, the 2nd battalion could relieve some pressure on Boland's. Volunteers with bicycles were chosen for the mission, including Michael and John Walker who had both competed as cyclists in the 1912 Olympics in Stockholm, notionally for Great Britain, but although the formal entry was made by the British Olympic Association, separate English, Scottish and Irish teams entered.[28] The unit dismounted at a corner of Holles Street with a clear sight up to the bridge. Michael Walker recalled 'the noise of our volleys made it difficult to tell whether our fire was returned or not'. However, they were then ordered to remount and returned to base, coming under fire near Grafton Street. One man was fatally wounded, John O'Grady, who died on the return to Jacob's.[29]

Later in the day, Mount Street Bridge saw much heavier fighting and the largest British losses of the week. Troops had been steadily arriving at Kingstown from England: Monica Roberts described the seafront as 'a seething mass of khaki'.[30] Around noon, two entire battalions – the 2/7th and 2/8th Sherwood Foresters – made their way into the city and approached the junction of Haddington Road and Northumberland Road. They were unaware that since Monday rebels had held several positions around Mount Street Bridge and that they were walking into an ambush.[31] The mass of khaki made an easy target for the rebels, who numbered just seventeen in total. Thomas Walsh of the 3rd battalion's B Company was based in Clanwilliam House and described 'blazing away at those in the channels, and after a time as they were killed, the next fellow moved up and passed the man killed, in front of him. This gave one the impression of a giant human khaki-coloured caterpillar.' Repeated charges over the bridge failed and 'By now there was a great pile of dead and dying on the Bridge.' Civilians tried to help the wounded and Walsh later said 'I should mention here the bravery of two girls, who ran up under fire and carried away the wounded. I learned afterwards that their names were Loo Nolan and Kathleen Pierce, and I heard they were presented with medals for valour by the English King.'[32] Once more civilians came on to the bridge. Both sides stopped firing, only for it to resume once the wounded were moved. Walsh described how 'the Bridge was rushed as before but with the same result. Again the Bridge was filled with dead and dying, and again cleared by the civilians who now had white sheets to carry the wounded on.' Walsh recalled being jubilant:

The casualties were so great that I, at one time, thought we had accounted for the whole British Army, in Ireland. What a thought! What joy! What a day! But a lot of their losses was their own fault. They made sitting ducks for amateur rifle men. But they were brave men and, I must say, clean fighters.[33]

British attempts at an advance over the bridge continued until about 7pm, with sporadic firing thereafter. Gradually the rebels were winkled out of their positions. By 8.30pm, Clanwilliam House was burning, and other positions evacuated.[34] However, the comparative death tolls were striking and the 'Battle of Mount Street Bridge' would be remembered as the rebels' major 'success' of the Rising. Volunteers numbering 17 had fought around 1,750 British soldiers, suffering 4 deaths and inflicting 160 casualties (26 of them dead) on the Wednesday of the Rising.[35]

Thursday 27 April

Rising dead: 53 (15 British military, 32 civilians, 7 rebels).[36]
Dublin's war dead: 53 (France and Flanders 49, Mesopotamia 3, Kenya 1)

On Thursday 27th, Nöel Drury noted in Salonika that via divisional signals news came 'that a rebellion has broken out in Ireland'. He felt that it was 'a regular stab in the back for our fellows out here, who don't know how their people at home are'. Drury worried, 'I don't know how we will be able to hold our heads up here as we are sure to be looked upon with suspicion.'[37] Disease continued to account for Dubliners in Mesopotamia with two more dead on 27 April as cholera continued to hit the 1st Connaughts.[38] Further afield, Private G/200 Thomas Jordan of the 1st Garrison Battalion of the Royal Irish Fusiliers died of a fractured skull in Kenya.[39] Meanwhile, at Hulluch, the 16th Division faced the most serious gas attack by the Germans since the Second Battle of Ypres.[40] The 8th Dublins' A Company met the gas first. The battalion war diary noted 'an almost imperceptible breeze from the EAST' which sped the journey of the gas. Soon 'a dense cloud of black gas and smoke was between us and the sun and gradually spreading over our lines'. That was rapidly followed by an artillery bombardment of the 16th Division's front, and then further gas, this time white in colour, coming from sap heads positioned in No Man's Land.[41] Even where gas helmets were worn they often leaked and trapped gas inside. Dalkey-born Father Willie Doyle, the Jesuit Chaplain to the 8th Royal Irish Fusiliers of the 16th Division wrote how, when making his way along a trench, 'I stumbled across a young officer who had been badly gassed. He had got his helmet on, but was coughing and choking in a terrible way. "For God's sake", he cried, "Help me to tear off this helmet – I can't breathe. I'm dying."' Doyle managed to get the officer to an aid post.[42] In such confusion and under cover of the gas, the Germans attacked the 8th Dublins and 'entered a section of our front trench where nearly all the men were killed or wounded'.[43] But reinforcements from the 8th and 9th Dublins drove out the Germans and held the position for the rest of the day, aided by a British barrage at 5pm. The evening was spent evacuating the wounded, 'identifying where possible' and burying the dead.[44] Across the 8th and 9th Dublins, 85 men were dead.[45]

Among the victims of explosives rather than gas was the 8th Dublins' Lance Corporal 15654 William Douglas, of Oxmantown Place. He was captured by the Germans on 27 April having lost his right foot in an explosion. After spending seven hours at a dressing station he was shifted to a hospital about a mile beyond the line and then by hospital train to Douai. Douglas recalled that the German Red Cross tended him on the journey and that 'They were very kind to me.' A month in hospital in Douai was followed by transfer to Cologne on 1 June. Only then was news of Douglas' survival conveyed to his family. In late May the *Freeman's Journal* carried an 'In Memoriam' notice stating that he had been killed in action, but in mid-July it was reported that his family had received a letter from him stating that he was alive and held prisoner in Germany. Just a month later he was sent home due to the loss of his foot.[46]

Outside Dublin, in the early hours of that day, Thursday, the 5th Irish Volunteers raided Garristown post office and police barracks, though the barracks were empty. At the post office they broke telegraph equipment and took money 'for which Dick Mulcahy gave a receipt remarking to the Postmaster at the time "This money is of no longer any value".'[47] For the rest of the day there were 'no special activities'[48] though there was some internal dissent over the failure of most of the country to rebel. Bernard McAllister described how Ashe, Hayes and Mulcahy addressed the battalion. Mulcahy spoke about duty to Ireland, but Ashe said that 'Anybody who is not satisfied to carry on could go home there and then and that they would not be thought the least about.' A few did, leaving their weapons and being instructed not to give any information about the battalion.[49]

In the city, on his third day of trying, Thomas Moylan made it to work at Richmond Asylum.[50] Thursday was the day the British made their move. By this time they were supplemented from units from outside Ireland. The Irish battalions were less regularly in the front line and on this day possibly only one soldier with Dublin connections was killed.[51] Some had had little sleep: Arthur Killingley noted that he had been in bed at 1.30am and up at 3am as a rebel attack was rumoured. His whole battalion stood to at 3.30am.[52] For the moment, the British attack was not pressed in all locations and things were quiet at Jacob's.[53] At St Stephen's Green 'The shortage of food supplies was beginning to cause concern.'[54] In the 1st battalion's area, British guns had found the range of many barricades, forcing the withdrawal of some outposts to the Four Courts itself.[55] That evening, some rebel barricades began to be replaced by British ones as rebel strongpoints were steadily cordoned off. The British were becoming more and more suspicious of those who were essentially boys and had not previously been thought of as likely rebels, as Isaac Callendar found out when he breakfasted early again. He met a Lieutenant Anderson of the Dublin Fusiliers who 'had some suspicion as to my movements. It was quite a long time before I could venture to get away.' Callendar then bumped into a Captain Connolly of the Dublins who 'demanded to know why I was "out", and I said that I heard a rumour that my aunt was seriously ill. He permitted me to proceed.' By this point Callendar, recalled, 'as I was seemingly the only civilian on foot that morning, I considered myself lucky that I had not been made a prisoner'.[56] Meanwhile, at Boland's, although 'we did very little except rest', the bakery was hit by a shell from the *Helga*. It hit a bread van on top of which were a number of grenades, but incredibly, none exploded and nobody was wounded.[57] Within the SDU, William T. Cosgrave remembered 'a sustained attack' by the British on Volunteer positions in the nurses' home. There was a temporary withdrawal before re-occupation by Cosgrave and others later.[58] However, in one attack at the SDU, as James Foran remembered, 'The fighting stopped suddenly. Whatever happened, the British were fired on from behind by their own men. I believe they thought they were surrounded by the Volunteers and got out as quickly as they could. That was that.'[59]

It was the GPO area to which the British turned most attention. From the Metropole Hotel, Oscar Traynor witnessed British shells setting building after building on fire. He recalled, 'I had the extraordinary experience of seeing the huge plate-glass windows of Clery's stores run molten into the channel from the terrific heat.'[60] Harry Colley was across the street from the GPO at the Imperial Hotel and recalled of the evening that 'I was washing myself when the first shells fell at 8 o'clock.' Evacuation of the hotel began. Once outside, Colley tried to access tenement buildings which would usually have been unlocked but had been ordered locked by the British. Colley was hit in the ankle but with a fixed bayonet tried to rush a British barricade, only to be bayoneted in the thigh as he climbed over. A British soldier who assumed Colley was dead used his body as a rest for his rifle and also as a shield. Colley was now unable to move and thought his neck was broken. He fell unconscious and the next he knew, 'there was some R.A.M.C. men carrying flashlights and a stretcher. A Corporal of the R.A.M.C. was stooping over me and he raised himself and said, "Take him gently, boys, he appears to be very badly hurt". I shall always remember the humane and Christian attitude of that R.A.M.C. Corporal.' Colley was taken to a dressing station and then on to Castle Hospital. There

Figure 9.1: Sackville Street burns as the Rising draws to an end. This *Daily Sketch* photograph wrongly placed it in 'May' 1916. (Image Courtesy of the National Library of Ireland, EPH A652).

he was told he would die, and said his prayers to a British army chaplain from County Carlow.[61] Similar thoughts were in the mind of Aoife de Burca in the GPO, who 'could not help thinking our turn would come soon, and that we would be burned like rats in a trap. I tried to prepare myself for the worst by going to confession'.[62]

Outside the GPO, Nancy de Paor saw events unfold from high ground at the top of Parnell Square. She had tried to reach the GPO but found it impossible and saw a procession of women bearing a white flag crossing O'Connell [Sackville] Street at the Parnell monument. These were inhabitants of the Moore Street–Parnell Street areas leaving their homes for safety.[63] Meanwhile, James Connolly was being treated inside after being hit in the leg by a sniper. He was treated by Aoife de Burca, Joseph Doyle and two republican doctors, alongside Lieutenant O'Mahony, an RAMC prisoner. Doyle claimed later to have 'performed the operation' to set the bone (which he said was ultimately not possible), with the assistance of O'Mahony, but de Burca said it was 'ably performed' by O'Mahony 'ably assisted by two of our own young Doctors'.[64]

Friday 28 April

Rising dead: 65 (42 civilians, 8 British military, 8 police, 7 rebels).[65] Dublin's war dead: 11 (France and Flanders 9, Mesopotamia 1, Home (of wounds) 1).

Men continued to die from the previous day's gas attack at Hulluch and the results of other engagements on the Western Front: another six Dubliners in the 8th and 9th Dublins, and one each in the 7th Inniskillings, 2nd Dublins and 2nd Irish Rifles. Private 10781 John Kinahan was yet another to die of illness in Mesopotamia with the 1st Connaughts.[66] However, Friday 28 April was a relatively quiet day at Hulluch. The 8th Dublins faced some shelling but otherwise spent time dealing with the aftermath of the attack on 27 April, repairing trenches and, at night, removing dead bodies. The 9th Dublins assisted.[67] In contrast, the Germans prepared for another gas attack.

In Dublin, Major General Sir John Maxwell arrived at 2am as military governor of Ireland, declaring that only unconditional surrender by the rebels would suffice.[68] Michael O'Flanagan of the 1st Irish Volunteers was in Reilly's Fort in North King Street and recalled that in the morning 'enemy pressure eased somewhat'.[69] But later that day the 2/6th South Staffordshire Regiment attempted an advance in the area. From 6pm that evening until 10am the next day, fifteen civilians, wrongly believed to be rebels, were killed by British troops in what became known as the North King Street Massacre.[70] However, the British became more focused on Friday on the GPO, and in other places such as the SDU, Volunteers just observed 'the great pall of smoke' which 'hung over the city'.[71] Tim Finn's Blackrock Company, holed up at Stillorgan Grove since Monday evening had steadily lost men to desertion in the days since. On Friday morning, Finn 'found himself with only one man; so he quit and went home'.[72] Others also came to the conclusion that the fight was nearing an end. Tom Byrne's unit had been holding various houses one after the other since the day before and by Friday they were holed up in Liffey Street. Byrne recalled, 'There were a couple of young men with me who were deserters from the Dublin Fusiliers and they asked me, seeing that the fight was over, would I give them a chance to make their getaway as it would be very serious for them if they were caught fighting with us.' Byrne 'saw the force of their necessity and let them go'. Later in the evening Byrne said to the rest of his men, 'It is all over now. There's no use trying to retreat to the Post Office. Each one of us can now make his getaway.' Arms were dumped, and Byrne went into hiding in the Liffey Street house for the next two days.[73]

In the country, Friday was a day of some triumph for the 5th battalion of the Volunteers at what became known as the Battle of Ashbourne, about thirteen miles north of the city and just over the border into County Meath. The battalion planned to destroy the railway line at Batterstown, attacking the police barracks at Ashbourne on the way, as part of generally impeding 'enemy troops' from reaching the city. Around thirty-five rebels set out from camp at Borranstown at 11am, reaching the Rath crossroads on the Dublin–Ashbourne–Slane road about 12.30pm. Ashe and Mulcahy led a small group to the barracks about a hundred yards away and called for surrender, but shots were fired in response. Volunteers therefore occupied a ditch and opened fire on the barracks. After half an hour a white cloth was waved from the barracks but as that happened police reinforcements arrived in cars and firing was resumed from the barracks. About five hours of fighting ensued, with small groups of Irish Volunteers – bolstered by half a dozen reinforcements led by Frank Lawless (father of Joseph) – being placed to surround the barracks.[74] The end came with the death of District Inspector Smyth. Joseph Lawless described how his father shot and hit Smyth 'on the forehead and smashed his skull'. As Joseph approached and saw 'his brain matter spattered the grass beside him, he yet lived, his breath coming in great gasps at long intervals, in the minute or so I watched him. Then he was still, and the muscles of his face relaxed.'[75] In later years, Mulcahy's leadership and tactics were credited for the success of the operation.[76] But the encounter had taken so long that the 5th battalion returned to camp rather than go the railway line. Charles Weston described the mood that evening: 'Everyone was now in great spirits as a result of our victory and we felt ready now for anything that might come.'[77]

However, positions around the GPO such as the Metropole Hotel, held by Oscar Traynor's unit, were becoming untenable.[78] As dawn approached that morning, Thomas Devine's outpost received an order from Pearse to return to the GPO. When he arrived he found that in less than a day since he had been there,

> the bombardment had worked havoc in the building, especially in the roof and upper storeys which had got the brunt of the shelling. Daylight was visible in many places, twisted girders hung at queer angles, walls, floors and staircase were in a chaotic state ... Down on the ground floor many wounded lay, sat or stood by, whilst those active went about their tasks.

In the afternoon Pearse gathered together the GPO garrison and Devine described Pearse 'standing up on a table ... his fine head in relief against a sunlit window'. Devine recalled, 'the (prophetic) words: "Win it we will although we may win it in death", and the cheer went up from the garrison'. Pearse then outlined an evacuation plan, which would see a new headquarters established in Moore Street at Williams and Woods Jam factory, while the wounded evacuated through the Coliseum theatre to Jervis Street Hospital.[79] Aoife de Burca took temporary shelter in the Coliseum with the wounded. She and others had an unexpected reaction to the stress of the situation: 'I tried to make an Act of fervent Contrition, but the situation was bordering on the comical as well as tragedy, so I burst out laughing instead. Another girl did likewise, and very soon we were all at it.'[80]

Thomas Devine was part of an advance party leaving the GPO through the Henry Street exit led by The O'Rahilly. Devine recalled,

'The O'Rahilly drew his sword and took his place in front. Then at the words; of command "Quick March – at the double", we moved off along Henry Street and at a brisk trot rounded Moore Street corner.' They faced devastating machine-gun and rifle fire and were forced to take cover in doorways. The O'Rahilly was 'hit from the barricade and he fell face forward, his sword clattering in front of him'. He died shortly after. However, another group had successfully taken positions in Moore Street which meant that the new headquarters could be established.[81]

Among those covering the escape were Seán and Ernie Nunan, who had been among the first to enter the GPO. They were ordered to stay on the first floor and fire at snipers on the other side of Sackville Street. Seán recalled 'We did so, but the fire got so close to us, that I decided to go while the going was good, as it seemed to me that the officer who gave us the order to remain had probably forgotten about us. I had no desire to emulate the Roman legionnaire at Pompeii, and finish up buried in lava!' The Nunans went downstairs and left the GPO when those on the ground floor did so, joining a barricade at the junction of Moore Lane and Moore Street.[82]

Over night, the move of the rebel headquarters caused further civilians to evacuate. Oscar Traynor recalled that moving into a building in the middle of Moore Street, 'we were met by a little family, an old man, a young woman and her children, cowering into the corner of a room, apparently terrified'. The man said that he wanted to leave under a white flag which Traynor advised against, especially when it was dark. Later, just before the surrender, Traynor 'saw the old man's body lying on the side of the street almost wrapped in a white sheet, which he was apparently using as a flag of truce'.[83]

Saturday 29 April

Rising dead: 78 (45 civilians, 21 British military, 12 rebels).[84]
Dublin's war dead: 69 (all France and Flanders)

At 3.30am on Saturday 29 April a second German gas attack at Hulluch began, preceded by a bombardment. The gas reached the 8th Dublins from two separate positions 'and settled down on our trench without wind to move it'. There was no bombardment or infantry attack but 'The casualties from gas poisoning were more severe than on the 27th owing presumably to the gas clouds meeting and remaining stationary and concentrated.'[85] However, a German advance did not follow because, as the 9th Dublins reported, once the gas had settled on British lines, it 'finally blew back over German lines causing them to evacuate their trenches on a 700 yard front'.[86] Both battalions were relieved that evening, by other units of the 16th Division in 47th Brigade.[87]

Across the 16th Division on 27–9 April there were nearly 2,000 casualties. 570 were dead and another 1,410 wounded. The dead in the 8th Dublins included Private 22741 Michael Tracey, the Boer War veteran of Mark's Alley.[88] Gas was responsible for the majority of cases: 338 dead and 922 wounded. It was initially thought by some senior officers outside the division that perhaps poor training in how to deal with gas had been responsible and that the division lacked discipline. However, the official history later concluded that such accusations were unjustified since it was later realised that the sacking gas helmets were simply not effective in thick gas attacks. Moreover, several practices had been carried out before the attacks. Meanwhile, as Terry Denman wrote, 'the Easter Rising had broken out in Dublin only a few days before and it is likely that Irish troops were regarded with particular suspicion at this time'.[89]

Dubliners also served at Hulluch in units beyond the Dublin Fusiliers. One was Private 21316 William Doran of the 7th Royal Irish Fusiliers, part of the 16th Division's 49th Brigade. He had enlisted in the 8th Dublins in October 1914, when his wife was living at Summerhill. His record shows that he was certainly gassed on 29 April but intriguingly (for no Dubliner won the medal in the entire war) his story was elaborated in the *Evening Mail* under the heading 'DUBLIN V.C.' From the King George V Hospital Doran told how, on 29 April, he had been on duty at the top of a mine shaft when the Germans attacked. The story said that he managed to alert around sixty men in the shaft and then 'immediately proceeded to the shaft again, and commenced hurling bombs at the enemy'. Doran said, 'I kept bombing and cutting and slashing away at the Bosches. Men were falling around me from the effects of the gas fumes, but I managed to hold on for a couple of hours and a half, and then I could stand it no longer. I simply fell in a heap.' Yet Doran did not win the VC, nor any other gallantry award. His record does show that he had a poor disciplinary record (sometimes involving drunkenness) and when he was eventually discharged from the army in

1919 as 'no longer physically fit' he was stated as suffering from 'Insanity', aggravated by war service.[90]

The 8th Dublins bore the brunt of the attack at Hulluch and the costs were massive. Their war diary contains a casualty list for other ranks covering 27–9 April, prepared in mid-May, which was unusually detailed for a listing of non-officers, perhaps because it was the battalion's first major action. Overall other ranks casualties were 402. Of these, 93 were known to have been killed in action or died of wounds, 77 were wounded, 97 gassed, and one wounded/gassed. There were 134 missing, of whom 83 eventually turned out to be dead, so the battalion's fatalities over those two days amounted to 176 other ranks. In addition, 2 officers were dead, 6 wounded and 3 gassed. Of the 178 dead, at least 84 were Dubliners. The vast bulk of the other ranks casualties came from two companies A (150) and B (153). A Company was in the front line when the gas attack began, with 46 of their number gassed and survived compared to 51 across the other three companies. In the 9th Dublins, who had provided reinforcements for the 8th, there were another 22 dead over 27–9 April, including at least 13 Dubliners.[91] In other battalions of the 16th Division, principally the 7th and 8th Inniskillings, at least another 28 Dubliners were killed at Hulluch.

Among the dead in the 8th on 29 April was Private 14578 John Naylor. He had lost a brother in the 1st Dublins in March 1915 and another would be killed in October 1918 in the same battalion.[92] Yet his wife, Margaret, living at Great Brunswick Street, never knew of her husband's death since she was shot and fatally wounded on exactly the same day in Dublin. It is not known whether her death was accidental but she was hit while crossing Ringsend Drawbridge. Commonly said to have died on the same day as her husband, her gravestone at Grangegorman confirms that she in fact died two days later on 1 May. Their three daughters under the age of six were taken in by an aunt.[93]

In Monkstown, Mary Martin noted, 'Fighting still continuing as fierce as ever in Dublin & fires were seen during the night & one could hear the big guns going. We hear great rumours of the damage that is being done to the city by the cannonade.'[94] In the Dublin countryside, the 5th Irish Volunteers 'were in great form this day after our victory at Ashbourne. Their morale was very high and looking forward to the next fight. We now had good rifles, the police ones having been issued to us

Figure 9.2: Pádraig Pearse surrendering to General William Henry Muir Lowe and his son John, on Moore Lane, Dublin, 29 April 1916. (Image Courtesy of the National Library of Ireland, NPA POLF234).

and plenty of ammunition.'[95] However, the Rising in the city was coming to an end. The stand at Moore Street did not last long. At 12.45pm on Saturday 29 April a white flag was sent out to a British barricade with a request to discuss terms. The British operational commander, Brigadier General William Lowe would accept only an unconditional surrender and at 3.30pm Pearse was received by Lowe to surrender in person; his son, Lieutenant John Lowe, escorted Pearse to Kilmainham.[96]

Some members of the original GPO garrison had already been mopped up from various points during the morning.[97] Others avoided capture. Aoife de Burca was stopped by a British officer when returning home from Jervis Street hospital. She and other nurses with her were asked if they could help at a British Red Cross station. She described how, 'We politely declined his offer saying we got orders to return to Jervis St. Hospital if not allowed to pass. He smiled, and let us return, and I didn't think he would for I'm sure he knew we came from the G.P.O.'[98]

Other rebel posts had no thought of surrender. At around 4pm the Four Courts garrison heard news that a surrender had been ordered. Michael O'Flanagan passed the news on to Piaras Beaslai, the 1st battalion's second in command, who 'scoffed at the idea, pointing out that the position was "impregnable and could be held for a month"'. However, Daly's men did surrender that evening.[99] Meanwhile, during the day, Joseph Burke had been transferred from Richmond Barracks to Kilmainham Gaol. There, he remembered, 'some drunken soldiery of the Dublin Fusiliers immediately set upon us, kicking us, beating us and threatening us with bayonets'. He added, 'The Dublin Fusiliers were the worst of the lot. The English soldiers were mostly decent. Most of them were young fellows who did not know one end of a rifle from the other as far as I could see.'[100]

This was a sign of things to come for many prisoners in the next days and weeks. But for now, although the headquarters and Four Courts had surrendered, the rebels remained in place and optimistic at the College of Surgeons, Jacob's, Boland's, the South Dublin Union and in the Fingal area.

Sunday 30 April

Rising dead: 19 (14 civilians, 4 British military, 1 rebel).[101]
Dublin's war dead: 8 (all France and Flanders).

Both the 8th and 9th Dublins were in billets at Noeux-les-Mines on Sunday 30 April, having been relieved the night before. However, the death toll from the German attack continued to mount as another eight

Dubliners across battalions of the 16th Division died of wounds that day. One of them was Enniskillen-born Lieutenant Robert Valentine of the 8th Dublins, who had been educated in Dublin and whose parents lived in Lower Beechwood Avenue in Ranelagh. Before the war, Valentine had been a geologist for the Geological Survey of Ireland, working on strata at Hook Head in County Wexford. He was also credited with designing an improvement to the Lewis Gun, his war-grave record stating that he was the 'Inventor of a quick-firing improvement to the Lewis Machine Gun'. Like so many men of his background he had originally enlisted into the 7th Dublins, being transferred later to the 8th on commission. The *Irish Times* lamented, 'He would undoubtedly have made his mark among scientific men in Ireland, and his loss is especially regretted by those who had looked forward to working with him as a colleague.'[102]

Not until Sunday did news of the surrender filter through to the remaining rebel strongpoints. At the College of Surgeons Frank Robbins believed that the news might be a trick, but the garrison reluctantly accepted it. Commandant Mallin had already urged some to escape if they felt they needed to. One of those who took the opportunity was the ICA's Captain Joseph Byrne (not to be confused with the other Joseph Byrne mentioned above), who was a deserter from the British Army and might have been concerned about the treatment he would receive if captured.[103] Yet Robbins described how 'The act of surrender was to each one a greater calamity than death itself at that moment.'[104] At Jacob's, Patrick O'Kelly recalled that he 'saw a few Volunteers hurling their guns away in disappointed rage. For some others there was, I think, a feeling of relief that the strain of the week was over; the strain on us was probably more intense because of our comparative inactivity.' Meanwhile, despite the rumours of German and Irish-American forces coming to their aid, he later conceded 'That the Rising was a gallant but hopeless venture which could not end but in early defeat seemed the general feeling amongst the Jacob's garrison.'[105] William Stapleton remembered rather more 'general dismay and a lot of shouting that we should not surrender but that we should get into bands and go out to the hills and continue fighting'.[106] For some of the men the presence of a priest encouraged them to surrender. Vincent Byrne recalled a Franciscan 'pleading with the men to lay down their arms quietly. I remarked to the reverend father: "Is there no chance of getting out to the hills and

fighting it out?" He said: "No, my son, and come along with me".'
The priest helped Byrne and he made his way home where 'there was
great jubilation and weeping of tears, as my father and mother
believed that I had been killed in Stephen's Green'.[107] The cyclists,
Michael and John Walker, also succeeded in escaping, to their home in
Fairview.[108]

At Boland's, when news of the surrender first arrived in
the morning, Peadar O'Mara recalled: 'Volunteers were shouting
themselves hoarse denouncing everyone who had surrendered; others
were singing songs and some were openly crying.'[109] However, de
Valera stood before the garrison and said it would be possible for
them to leave by the railway and go home quietly, but 'this would not
fulfil the terms of the surrender', so 'as we had gone into battle on an
order, the order to surrender was equally binding'.[110] Seamus Kavanagh
described how 'This announcement met with general disapproval but as
soldiers we felt obliged to comply with the instruction.'[111]

Before noon, two policemen had approached the camp of the
5th battalion and said that there was a general surrender. They said that
Pearse was a prisoner and that someone might wish to visit him to
confirm that. Mulcahy trusted them enough to do so. He returned at
3pm with verification. It was not popular news, but Ashe said to Charles
Weston, 'We fought as soldiers. We came out under Pearse as soldiers
and it is our duty to surrender on his orders.' About a dozen men left,
while the other two dozen or so followed the order.[112]

At the South Dublin Union, there was still a defiant mood
around noon. Rose McNamara recalled a parade when men and
women were asked 'if they were prepared to fight to the last'. She said,
'They all shouted "Yes".' But at 4pm, news of the surrender came and
the garrison marched out. Rose McNamara and other women were
defiant to the last when the men assumed they would go home: 'we
were not going to leave the men we were with all the week to their fate;
we decided to go along with them and be with them to the end whatever
our fate might be'.[113]

As the prisoners marched through the streets Christopher Byrne
recalled, 'When we came out of the Distillery the crowd was cheering
us.' He even believed that 'it took Ceannt all his time to make up his
mind to surrender when he saw the reception outside the Distillery'.[114]
However, it is possible that the crowd was simply cheering the end of
the Rising, for other recorded reactions were mostly very hostile.

Thomas Devine recalled 'the hostile attitude towards us of certain Dubliners – mostly soldiers' dependents from the Coombe and adjacent districts'.[115] As they were marched to Richmond Barracks, Oscar Traynor's group 'passed through a number of hostile groups of people who shouted all sorts of things at us, including calling us "murderers" and "starvers of the people"'.[116] Making the same journey, Frank Robbins saw 'a small number sympathetic towards us, but the vast majority openly hostile'. He concluded that 'the vast majority of the citizens' were against the rebels, on the basis of 'the cheering and waving of hats and Union Jacks for the Staffordshire Regiment as they marched us in to Richmond Barracks, and the cries of encouragement to the young Englishmen in that "Regiment" to "shoot the traitors" and "bayonet the bastards"'. He speculated that 'were the British Army to have withdrawn at that moment, there would have been no need for Courtmartials or prisons as the mob would have relieved them of such necessities'. As it was, the prisoners had no clear idea of what would happen to them and there was some alarm when 'Our party were halted beside a big hole, freshly dug. It brought the wildest ideas into our heads.'[117]

Deaths from the Rising still occurred as it ended. One soldier from the city died of wounds incurred the previous day: Lieutenant Philip Purser of the Army Service Corps. He lived in Blackrock and had tried to enlist in September 1914 only to be discharged as unfit in a month. However, he had re-enlisted later. Serving in France in 1915, he was sent back for home service only, due to a heart condition. During the Rising he worked as a dispatch rider and was returning to Dublin from a mission to Kingstown when he was shot by rebels.[118] But for most, the Rising was now over.

10 CONSEQUENCES

I will show my guards how an Irishman can die for his own country – in his own country. I can die praying. If these men are sent to France they will die cursing. They will die lying on the ground, moaning, and not able to see their mothers and their sweethearts.

Former British soldier, Michael Mallin, 7 May 1916, on the eve of his execution for his role in the Rising[1]

Aftermath

As the Rising ended, there was little sign of support for the rebels in Dublin. A factor which influenced the way the rebels were treated by local people was the level of British military service in the areas around the main sites of the Rising. It is easy to understand how the 'separation women' would have been especially angry. Across the war, 1,082 men from these roads served in the British military. It is not clear when all enlisted, but there are enlistment dates for 658 of them. Of those, 528 were already serving when the Rising began. If those for whom an enlistment date has not survived had joined up at similar times, then we can expect that around 868 of the 1,082 were already serving. Of these, 121 had already been killed before the Rising; 14 were killed at Hulluch between 27 and 29 April 1916, and another 170 later in the war. One street serves as an example of how high levels of military service could be close to the heart of the Rising. Marlborough Street ran parallel to Sackville Street and buildings were destroyed at its southern end. Across the war, 65 men from the street served. The enlistment date is known for 46 of them and of those 33, nearly three-quarters had already served by late April 1916. Of these, 9 had already been killed, so there would be little support in Marlborough Street for rebels whose Proclamation had declared support from 'gallant allies in Europe'.[2] At least some of those rebels would have been known to local residents for they lived there themselves: Patrick Poole and his son John at number 50, and Henry Kenny at 110. Kenny and John Poole were at the GPO while Patrick Poole was on St Stephen's Green with the ICA. The two Pooles ended up at Frongoch in north Wales after capture, but Kenny escaped arrest.

Hundreds of miles away, news of the Rising reached the 16th (Irish) Division. The 7th Leinsters were at Hulluch. Serving with them was Lieutenant John Hamilton Maxwell 'Max' Staniforth, from England but with Irish ancestry. He described how the Germans put up a placard in their trench which read, 'IRISHMEN. GREAT UPROAR IN IRELAND. ENGLISH GUNS ARE FIRING ON YOUR WIFES AND CHILDREN.' Another said, 'ENGLISH GUNS FIRING ON YOUR WIFES AND CHILDREN. ENGLISH DREADNOUGHT SUNK: ENGLISH MILITARY BILL REFUSED. SIR ROGER CASEMENT PERSECUTED. THROW YOUR ARMS AWAY. WE WILL GIVE YOU A HEARTY WELCOME.' The response of the 7th Leinsters was to play 'Rule Britannia and lots of Irish airs on a melodeon in the front trench to show them we weren't exactly downhearted'.[3] Close by, the 8th Munsters responded by singing 'God Save the King'.[4]

Word of the executions might not have reached Father Willie Doyle by the time he wrote home on 13 May, but if it had, he was unsympathetic: 'One good result will follow from what has happened: the ridding of Dublin of a most undesirable element which was doing much harm among our ignorant people.'[5] In weeks to come, Monica Roberts received many letters from serving soldiers expressing anger at the Rising. Joseph Clarke of the 2nd Dublins wrote, 'these men are pro-Germans, pure and simple, and no Irishmen will be sorry when they get justice meted out to them which in my opinion should be Death by being <u>shot</u>'. From the same battalion, Christopher Fox wrote at the end of May, 'When I think of them [the rebels] it makes my blood run cold [to] think of some poor fellows out here fighting for there Country and them murdering cowards I suppose have killed some of their mothers an[d] father or there wives an[d] children as the case may be.'[6]

In Dublin, the fatal effects of the Rising were still being felt after it ended. Private 18259 James Byrne of the Royal Dublin Fusiliers' Depot succumbed to wounds on 1 May. He had briefly served at Gallipoli, arriving there in mid-November 1915, and his aunt, Sarah Conlan, his next-of-kin, lived at Harmony Row. It is not clear where and when he had been wounded but he was the last Dublin solder to die in the Rising.[7] It has been estimated that 41 Irishmen lost their lives in the British military during the Rising, from a total of 177 British military dead.[8] Of those, Byrne's death was the twentieth for a Dubliner. In total, 485 people died as a result of the Rising, the majority (54%) civilians, British forces accounting for about a quarter, the rebels 16% and the police another 4%.[9]

On Tuesday 2 May the city was beginning to get back to normal. Only on that day did Thomas Moylan learn 'definitely that the whole rebellion was practically over'. He noted that 'most of the shops resumed business, cabbies plied for hire, and here and there

Figure 10.1: Damage to Dublin city centre, in this case the Hibernian Bank, Abbey Street corner, became apparent as the public came out on to the streets after the Rising. (Image Courtesy of the National Library of Ireland, KE 118).

a uniformed policeman appeared out. The great crowds vanished, although there were still plenty of people about, but the city was closed except to those with permits.'[10] It took another week for the mail delivery to be re-established and for the search for dead bodies to be over.[11] Those whose property was damaged in the Rising now turned to the question of who would pay for it.[12]

Prisoners held in Dublin had no idea of what awaited them. Some carried out small acts of defiance. Rose McNamara recalled that on reaching Kilmainham Gaol, the women prisoners' names were taken 'which we gave in Irish, which the soldiers couldn't understand'.[13] Prisoners continued to face a hostile reception as they were moved about the city. Bernard McAllister was at the docks for shipment to Britain and 'got a very bad reception from the civil population. They boohed us, called us ugly names and were generally hostile.'[14] Charles Weston had the same experience but observed that rebel leaders were not disturbed by how the situation was developing. He was on a ship to Holyhead on Tuesday evening with Richard Mulcahy, who said, 'I am as happy as the day is long – everything is working out grand.'[15] Other prisoners continued to fear that their fate might be the worst: still in Dublin, Edward O'Neill of the 4th Irish Volunteers left Richmond Barracks (heading for North Wall) and 'got a hostile reception. We were told there were graves dug in the Old Men's Home for us.'[16] They could not know that over the next year there would be a marked shift in attitudes.

Executions

Despite the initial hostile reaction among the populace and troops at the front, the British reaction to the Rising initiated a chain of events in which such hostility for the rebels steadily transformed into support. Martial law began to alienate neutral opinion, part of a British tradition of rule which secured 'the worst of both worlds; of appearing to rest on force while seldom exerting enough force to secure real control'.[17] Writing to Monica Roberts in late June from the Royal Flying Corps, Henry Harrington had already begun to sense a change. He noted, 'I used to get letters from quite a number of people in Dublin before the trouble was on but since then I believe some of the people over there think soldiers are not to be bothered about.'[18] In mid-July, Harry Colley, who had been in Castle Hospital ever since he was wounded, noticed a change as he was moved to Frongoch after a few days in Kilmainham Gaol. As he travelled to North Wall, 'We had on this journey our first real evidence of the change of opinion amongst the people. When we reached the centre of the city crowds cheered us and began to follow us.' He described how some onlookers handed the prisoners food or money.[19] Later that month, Tom Kettle said of the executed rebels, 'These men will go down to history as heroes and martyrs, and I will go down – if I go down at all – as a bloody British officer.'[20] More widely, the Rising had unsettled nationalist officers in the British army, even if only a small number would eventually switch sympathies to republicanism.[21]

Exactly when such a change began to affect many people is hard to gauge but the passage of events which eventually led to a swing in public opinion began almost as soon as the Rising ended. From Wednesday 3 May, the British began to execute the leaders of the Rising, including all seven signatories of the Proclamation, all but two of those who had commanded garrisons, plus others who were judged by the British to be senior figures in the rebellion. By 12 May, fifteen had been executed, all bar one in Dublin at Kilmainham. Roger Casement was the sixteenth in August when he was executed in London.[22]

In the meantime, the difficulties in which the executions placed mainstream Irish nationalism became evident in Parliament. On 11 May, introducing a motion on the situation in Ireland, John Dillon MP called for the government 'to put an absolute and a final stop to these executions'. His speech accompanied a public manifesto issued by the IPP, denouncing martial law and protesting against the executions. Of those involved in the Rising Dillon said, 'I admit they were wrong; I know they were wrong', but that 'the circumstances of these secret military executions are horrible and shocking' and they were alarming the entire population of the city. He also raised the Sheehy-Skeffington case. However, the chamber of the House of Commons became heated when Dillon went on to say of those being held prisoner, 'I am proud of these men', even though 'They were foolish; they were misled'. To cries of 'shame' from other MPs, Dillon continued, 'I say I am proud of their courage, and, if you were not so dense and so stupid, as some of you English people are, you could have had these men fighting for you, and they are men worth having.' While he accepted that murderers should pay the ultimate penalty, 'it is not murderers who are being executed; it is insurgents who have fought a clean fight, a brave fight, however misguided'.[23] Part of Asquith's response was perhaps surprising. He agreed with Dillon that the rebels 'fought very bravely. They conducted themselves, as far as our knowledge goes, with humanity ... That tribute I gladly make, and I am sure the House will gladly make it.' But after saying he wanted to see clemency for most, he could only justify the executions which had taken place.[24] The next day, 12 May, Asquith visited Dublin. It was also the day on which the last two Dublin executions took place, of Seán Mac Diarmada and James Connolly.[25] The military authorities effectively signalled that no more executions were planned when they announced that they 'hoped that these examples will be sufficient to act as a deterrent to intriguers'.[26]

Among the fourteen executed in Dublin were two former British soldiers. One was James Connolly, the other was Dubliner Michael Mallin, the ICA's Chief of Staff. His brother, Thomas, recalled how on the evening of 7 May, a British car arrived at his home in Rutland Avenue with a message that Mallin wanted to see his wife, Agnes, who was staying there. Thomas, Agnes and Mallin's children headed for Kilmainham. On arriving and learning from Michael of the death sentence, Agnes collapsed. When she had come to, Michael gave her a series of instructions, including that their two youngest children (a daughter and one of three boys) should be 'dedicated to the Church'. He said, 'I want them in the service of God for the good of my soul.' Agnes was expecting a fifth child and he advised her on names for the baby. Thomas Mallin then learned that his mother had been there earlier in the day and told an army officer that 'she was delighted to have a son dying for Ireland'. Thomas returned later in the evening, first with the two eldest boys, and then met his brother alone. He asked Michael, 'Is it worth it?', receiving a bitter reply:

> It is worth it. Ireland is a grand country, but the people in it are rotters. The first Irishman to join the British Army was a bastard. The British Army is made up of them and gaolbirds and wasters. Some join through drink and some through lack of work. I will show my guards how an Irishman can die for his own country – in his own country. I can die praying. If these men are sent to France they will die cursing. They will die lying on the ground, moaning, and not able to see their mothers and their sweethearts.

Michael Mallin was executed the next morning.[27]

Figure 10.2: Michael Mallin (centre) under arrest with Constance Markiewicz. (Image Courtesy of the National Library of Ireland, NPA DOCA1).

As the executions continued, Robert Barton, the officer of the 10th Dublins who had managed to see out the Rising at home in County Wicklow, arrived in the city and reported to his battalion. He found that his Colonel 'knew where my sympathies lay', so 'my duties were confined to the Barracks'. However, a few days later he was given a special task – perhaps because of his nationalist views – of gathering the effects of Republican prisoners. This became his task for as long as he remained in the army, until September 1917, when he was released, having requested that he be allowed to return home to run the family farm. That had been run by his sister but she had had a breakdown. On the basis that his presence back in Wicklow could do much to boost agriculture in the area, the War Office discharged him as 'a very special case'.[28] He was later elected to Parliament for Sinn Féin in County Wicklow, and played a role in the negotiations of the Anglo-Irish Treaty.[29]

The final execution took place in London three months later. On 15 May, Roger Casement and Daniel Bailey were charged with high treason and put on trial.[30] Bailey claimed that he had only joined the Brigade so he could try to escape from Germany. While it does seem unlikely that Casement would have brought with him a man who had not shown wholehearted support for the cause, Casement successfully persuaded the court that Bailey was a subordinate who should be discharged. Evidence for what the Irish Brigade had planned to do, and how Casement had led them was strong: some of it had appeared in the newspapers in the summer of 1915. Dubliner Corporal Bernard Thompson of the King's Own Yorkshire Light Infantry was among the first to tell the story on returning home with other disabled prisoners.[31] At the trial itself evidence came from a number of returned prisoners, including a Kingstown man, Private 7635 William Egan, who had been captured in October 1914.[32] Bailey was indeed acquitted but Casement's final appeal failed on 29 July and he was executed on 3 August.[33] Bailey was not fully at liberty since he was still a serving soldier and he saw service in the 3rd Wiltshires and 3rd Loyal North Lancashires before heading for Tanzania and Egypt with the 2nd battalion of the North Lancashires and the Royal Engineers. He was even mentioned in dispatches for his service in Allenby's army in the Middle East. Bailey was eventually discharged in December 1919.[34]

Prisoners

Arrests continued to be made in the weeks following the Rising. Vincent Byrne was picked up at home on Saturday and shipped to England about a week later.[35] Some were not detained for long: Andrew McDonnell was released from Richmond Barracks on account of his age on about 12 May. As he made his way home to Rathmines he 'did notice the people were more friendly, much more so than when we marched into Richmond Barracks. The executions had turned the feelings of the people.'[36] In total, 3,149 men and 77 women prisoners passed through Richmond Barracks, which was the place for processing them all. By 11 July, 1,104 men and 72 women had been released, while another 23 men were acquitted by court martial. However, 160 men were convicted by court martial, with another 1,862 men and 5 women still interned. The majority of those in prison were rapidly sent to Britain within a fortnight of the end of the Rising. Four prisons initially took the bulk: between 30 April and 12 May, 1,267 prisoners were sent to Knutsford (467), Wakefield (381), Stafford (318) and Wandsworth (101). In time, more went to those prisons while some, including those sentenced to penal servitude, went to Lewes, Dartmoor, Portland, Pentonville, Wormwood Scrubs and Barlinnie. Some remained in Dublin at Mountjoy.[37] The final batch of women held ended up in Aylesbury.[38]

Arriving at Knutsford prison on Wednesday 3 May, an early group of prisoners found basic conditions. Charles Weston recalled 'we were put in single cells with bed board and a stool, but no bed. Next evening I got a pillow. After three days I got a very worn blanket. I was about a fortnight there before I got a mattress.'[39] Patrick O'Kelly of the 2nd Irish Volunteers spent four weeks 'in genuine solitary confinement' before release in early June. He described being in cells for all but half an hour each day and that 'silence was strictly enforced during the half-hour exercise in the Prison yard'. When his release came it was accidental, 'as I found out afterwards – in mistake for a Redmondite Volunteer who had the same name and who had been arrested in error'.[40]

Quite how many mistakes were made is an open question. Among those arrested was Octavus Hardy of 17 Belgrave Road. He was released shortly afterwards and a statement was issued by the War Office saying that he 'was a thoroughly loyal subject, and that his arrest was merely one of the unfortunate incidents which are bound to arise in the outcome of such military operations as those which took place in the Dublin area'.[41] If Hardy's arrest was a clear mistake, the authorities did not need actual proof of involvement in the Rising to arrest other likely suspects. It is possible to say definitively that of those arrested, between 1,585 and 1,613 people at least were from

Dublin.[42] These offer some insight into how many who were arrested had anything to do with the Rising, in which it has been argued almost half took no part.[43] Of 1,613, certainly 921 had taken some part in the Rising, while at least another 211 possibly had. Two certainly had not: Arthur Griffith and Eoin MacNeill. However, some of another 481 had probably not served since they cannot be found on any listings of those who were republican volunteers in the Rising. Of these, 212 were released by 7 June 1916 which suggests that the authorities found them of little interest although release did not necessarily mean that someone had not been involved: 110 Dubliners who had been in the Rising were out of prison by the same time. But 267 were imprisoned for longer, probably without having been active during the Rising.[44] Of course, some of them might have served in the Rising, and it is quite possible that by the time claims were made for medals or pensions for such service, and the material for service listings generated, some had died or moved away. They might even have lost interest in commemorating their past life and simply not applied for any recognition by the Irish Free State. However, the likelihood of substantial numbers of wrongful arrests remains.

It is clear that simply being an advanced nationalist could result in arrest after the Rising. That happened to Arthur Griffith, who had played no part in the Rising, and to Eoin MacNeill who had tried to stop it happening. MacNeill was rounded up and, at Richmond Barracks on 22 May, tried for eight charges of 'attempting to cause disaffection among the civil population', and four of 'acting in a way likely to prejudice recruiting'. He was convicted of all charges and told on 29 May that his punishment was penal servitude for life. Two days later he left Dublin for Dartmoor prison. Writing to his wife Agnes, known as Taddie, at Blackrock, he described his escort of Dublin Fusiliers as 'good decent men, a pleasure to meet'. A week later, Taddie received a letter from one of the soldiers, Private 25418 John O'Brien, a County Cork man serving in the 10th Dublins. He said that, 'I am one of the twenty Dublin Fusiliers who escorted Mr MacNeill and nine other prisoners to England last week. After travelling about half the journey Mr MacNeill asked me to write and let you know that he is all right.' O'Brien went on to say that he had later found paper for MacNeill, and had posted the letter himself in London. O'Brien wanted to check the letter had reached Taddie and added, 'I should have called upon you but thought it would be rather too great a liberty for a man in khaki.'[45] Just over five months later, John O'Brien was killed in the final days of the Battle of the Somme.[46]

MacNeill was at Dartmoor until early December 1916 and then at Lewes until June 1917. His work included sewing postbags and sandbags, making brushes and digging in the gardens. Food he described as 'repulsive to persons of a delicate appetite, and it was insufficient for the younger prisoners, some of whom were growing youths'. MacNeill received just one visit from his wife, which, by special application to the Home Office, took place in a room rather than through a grill. In his spare time, he said, 'I applied myself diligently to the study of languages, and by concentration on this I kept my mind free from the influences of the environment. Had I not done so, I have not the least doubt that I should have suffered mental injury.'[47]

Those interned in Knutsford and elsewhere were moved to Frongoch as part of a concentration of republican prisoners.[48] At least 300 Dubliners were interned there.[49] Charles Weston recalled, 'Frongoch was good. We were all together here in a big loft in an old distillery. We had straw mattresses and fairly good bedding. Food was better and camp routine was good ... We had plenty of hot water for baths and washing.' Whatever the British had in mind for this camp, it was not the university of republicanism it became. The men organised their own commandant and grouped themselves into companies. Irish sports were played, while there were classes in the Irish language and other subjects, including history. Richard Mulcahy, who had told Weston on the way to Knutsford of his pleasure at how events were developing, elaborated at Frongoch: 'By sending us to prison they have made heroes out of us. We will have men with us in the future who would never have touched us if they had sent us home after we surrendered.'[50]

During their time at Frongoch the prisoners were encouraged by their officers to behave in a disciplined manner. Frank Robbins recalled that in the early stages, where British rules were concerned, 'There was a tendency on the part of us in the camp to be rebellious and refuse to carry out orders.' However, the prisoners were persuaded by their officers that behaving as disciplined soldiers 'was something that we were doing for ourselves, that at least we should show discipline and do nothing that would prove to the British authorities that our officers could not control us'. In time this view was accepted, and that helped the men resist punishments or attempts to conscript them into the British army. Robbins recalled: 'Their task was made impossible by hunger-strikes and refusal to answer roll call, and it was the united action that brought these efforts to a successful conclusion.'[51]

During the summer, some men were taken to Wandsworth to appear before the Sankey Commission on the Rising, but the vast majority of the time was spent at Frongoch.[52] Meanwhile, in late July the release of nearly 900 men was announced, and by December there were no more than 600 still held.[53] When a general amnesty came in December and all those at Frongoch returned home – leaving just over 100 held elsewhere, including Mountjoy and Lewes – Mulcahy's prediction appeared to be coming true. Charles Weston remembered, 'There was a vast difference in the outlook of the people on our return and we got a grand reception on our arrival in the city and on our return home.'[54] Bernard McAllister recalled, 'I noticed a big change in the country on our return. The crowd who boohed us going away now … treated us as heroes and we got a grand reception on our arrival at Dublin.'[55] Whether any of the crowd were the same as those who had jeered in April is hard to know, but it is clear that there were a larger number of Dubliners ready to welcome the men back in December 1916 than had been prepared to cheer them in April.

Some who evaded escape had been on the run. Tom Byrne had left Liffey Street on Sunday 30 April. After some days hiding out in different parts of Dublin he headed for Balbriggan and a pub called the White Hart, run by Joe Kenney who was one of his comrades from the Irish Brigade in South Africa. He then headed north and recalled 'Any time I met police on my journeying I always tried to look very important and passed them without glancing at them.' Byrne eventually made his way to Belfast and worked in a cousin's spirit grocery business. He made his way back to Dublin just before Christmas 1916, once he was clear that there would be no further executions, and rejoined the volunteer movement, which was reviving as prisoners returned.[56]

The British Army

Other rebels had various encounters with the British army, some surprising. Among those released after only about a week of captivity, due to age, was Michael McCabe, who was just fifteen. He was one of 42 members of the Fianna held together at Richmond Barracks. A year later, he joined the British Army, serving as a private (29087) in the King's Own Royal Lancaster Regiment, and remaining in it until 1922, when he deserted and became part of the anti-Treaty forces at the Four Courts.[57] Patrick Dalton of the 1st Irish Volunteers spent a week in Richmond Barracks before returning to work at Dockrells in South Great George's Street. However, he was immediately dismissed for his part in the Rising and could not find another job. He went to England to seek work but 'getting stranded I was forced to join the British Army'. On his return to Ireland, he joined the National Army in June 1922.[58] Patrick O'Moore of the 2nd Irish Volunteers returned to Dublin to find that his unit had not fully recovered and 'after consultation with several officers of the Brigade I decided to join the British Army and secure all the training I could'. However, his past experience in the Irish Volunteers soon showed, and he was sent to France with the Machine Gun Corps. Like McCabe, he later served in the anti-Treaty forces at the Four Courts.[59]

A more unusual case was that of the Nunan brothers, Seán and Ernie. Like most members of the Kimmage Garrison, they were living in Britain until the early part of 1916. The authorities decided that they were therefore liable to conscription, and they were possibly not the only examples of this.[60] After spending some time at Frongoch, Seán and Ernie were taken to Wormwood Scrubs and then handed over to the British army. Seán was posted to the 6th London Regiment, immediately declared a deserter, found guilty and handed back to his regiment, then court-martialled for disobedience and sentenced to hard labour. When in London, being transferred between Winchester prison and Wormwood Scrubs, his army

escort suggested that we should go to the military canteen on the station and get a meal. Now my own home was only about fifteen minutes' walk from the station, and I suggested to the escort that, instead of eating in the canteen, they should come home with me and have a meal. They agreed, and the amazement of my parents can be imagined when I walked in with the escort. We had a meal, and sat around, talking, for quite a time, but eventually the escort said we had better be getting along.

They then arrived at the Scrubs to find the prison was full, so he was sent to Wandsworth. Eventually released back to the 6th Londons in March 1917, his regiment gave up and discharged him. After a brief stay with his parents, he was back in Dublin, joining the 2nd Dublin Irish Volunteers.[61]

Units of the Irish Volunteers had reformed as men were steadily released from Frongoch. In October 1916 Peadar McNulty assembled with his company of the 1st Irish Volunteers to elect officers and begin training. There were around forty men initially, joined by about another thirty by the end of the year.[62] They were building and planning to renew their war against the British. As Gerald Doyle recalled of his return from Frongoch, 'It was the Dawning of the Day, and a preparation for the next phase in the fight for Ireland's Independence.'[63] By this time the IPP had stepped up its criticism of the government's policies in Ireland.[64] But the political momentum increasingly favoured republicanism.

Yet despite this, at least five men who had been involved in the Rising as Republicans took the unlikely step of joining the British army. Michael McCabe, Patrick Dalton and Patrick O'Moore were mentioned earlier.[65] John McQuaid, who was a 'Pivot' during the mobilisation of the 2nd Battalion, joined, according to Frank Henderson, 'owing to difficulties at home following the Rising'.[66] Tim Finn, the former British soldier and IRB member, whose unit had not managed to engage in the Rising as he had wished, joined the 1st Irish Guards. Valentine Jackson recalled Finn's upset at not playing a bigger role in the Rising. He said, 'As the weeks passed he brooded on this until one evening, in what may well have been a fit of refreshed despondency, he re-enlisted, in the British army.'[67] There he saw the fight he had been deprived of in Dublin, only to be killed in action on 27 August 1918.[68] His story is a curious indicator of the reasons for which some men engaged in the Rising – not only the cause of 'Irish freedom', but in some cases simply a desire to do something adventurous or significant. In that sense, some British soldiers and Irish rebels had much in common.

11 THE OTHER 1916

The attack was preceded by the most formidable artillery preparation employed as yet in the History of the War, lasting as it did 7 days & 7 nights. The Battalion was allotted Pride of Place in the attack about to be launched . . .

War Diary, 9th Royal Inniskilling Fusiliers, 1 July 1916[1]

Jutland

Two British battles in the middle of 1916 might have been crucial to the outcome of war. Neither turned out to be, and neither looms large in Dublin's narrative of the war, dominated as it is by other events of 1916. The first was the major naval encounter of the war: Jutland, in the North Sea, around a hundred miles from the Danish and Norwegian coasts. Since the start of the war the German naval command had known that they should not seek a decisive battle with the Royal Navy's Grand Fleet due to numbers. However, during spring 1915 they had sought to draw parts of it into a more evenly matched fight, offering as temptation submarine warfare against merchants and assaults on British coastal targets. Meanwhile, the British did not believe they could satisfactorily draw out the German fleet by air raids or mining, and therefore felt that their only chance of engaging the High Seas Fleet was to wait for it in a part of the North Sea which was not mined. Throughout the spring of 1915 only a series of minor encounters was fought.[2]

At Jutland there was an 'almost accidental'[3] convergence of forces heading for their own planned operations along enemy coasts. This drew in ships held in reserve in case of the chance of a decisive action against the other side. Around 250 ships took part, with the Royal Navy having advantageous numbers, especially where the much-feared dreadnoughts were concerned (28 against 16). Fire was first exchanged at just before 2.30pm on 31 May.[4]

In the first phase of the battle, the 'run to the South', gaps between the Royal Navy's battlecruisers made it unable to take advantage of numerical superiority by concentrating fire, an error later blamed on Admiral David Beatty.[5] During this phase the single greatest loss of Dubliners on one ship occurred: more than a thousand crew were lost as the *Indefatigable* went down at around 4pm following a magazine explosion caused by at least four shell hits. One observer described 'huge funnels, turrets etc flying through the air, while the column of smoke must have been at least 1,500 feet high'. Just two of the entire crew survived.[6] At least twenty-seven from the city or county of Dublin were on the ship. Two of these were members of the Royal Marine Light Infantry: Private 16787 Francis Doyle whose mother lived in Phibsborough, and Private 15445 Patrick Sweeney, Dublin-born, with a brother living in the city.[7] The vast bulk were crew, principally stokers like 6614 Hugh Byrne, who had worked for the Dublin Corporation for twenty years and left a widow at Harold's Cross.[8] They also included two relatively young sailors, Boy 1st Class J/32856 Henry Mills and Boy Telegraphist J/31893 Robert Fegan, both aged seventeen.[9] Among the officers killed, Engineer Lieutenant Commander Patrick King's family from Drumcondra placed memorial notices in four different newspapers.[10] Less than half an hour after the *Indefatigable* went down the *Queen Mary* was sunk, with at least 13 Dubliners dead among a crew of nearly 1,300 of whom just 30 survived.[11]

In the next phase of the battle, as the battlecruisers engaged in a 'run to the North' there was no clear victor.[12] That helped shift the potential advantage to Admiral Sir John Jellicoe's dreadnoughts which had made their way from their base at Scapa Flow.[13] The first dreadnoughts opened fire soon after 6.15pm, with more general firing from the ships beginning a quarter of an hour later. Dubliners were killed in the losses of both the *Invincible* (five) and the *Defence* (eight).[14] Within fifteen minutes the Germans were beginning to withdraw, but that was not realised by the British and the Grand Fleet did not pursue them. Most firing was over by around 7.45pm, as darkness fell, but some exchanges continued into the early hours of 1 June.[15]

During the battle, factors which hampered the Royal Navy included signalling errors, gaps between ships, more effective German firing (including better ranging in the early stages), and German camouflage being more appropriate for the lighting they happened to have behind them.[16] Although Jellicoe's force did engage the Germans with some success, he was criticised for failing to pursue the High Seas Fleet in the final major phase of the battle. Yet he was conscious that if the Grand Fleet was decisively defeated it would pose serious risks for British security. With British superiority established there was no pressing need to destroy the German fleet, but a situation in which the Royal Navy suffered heavier losses posed serious risks for the UK so Jellicoe's caution was surely appropriate.[17]

Initial impressions suggested that the Germans had won. Certainly the Royal Navy's losses were higher: for example, 3 battle cruisers to the High Seas Fleet's 1, 3 armoured cruisers to none for the Germans, and 7 destroyers to 5. In total, the British lost 14 ships to 11 German, but the British casualties were much higher with 6,094 men killed compared to 2,551 Germans.[18] Of the dead, 56 were Dubliners. Some press coverage of the battle was initially unusually pessimistic with heavy British and German losses being mentioned in headlines.[19] However, the temptation to print propaganda asserted itself with the *Irish Independent* proclaiming 'A BRITISH VICTORY'.[20] This was not entirely false since much damage which took months to repair was inflicted on the High Seas Fleet. Moreover, British losses were nothing like those necessary to challenge the Royal Navy's overall dominance, which stayed in place for the remainder of the war.

Attention to the battle lasted only a few days, as the news of the HMS *Hampshire*'s sinking, with the loss of Lord Kitchener, came through and grabbed column inches.[21] Yet relatives of those whose ships had gone down continued to hope. The *Evening Mail* printed a picture of Stoker Petty Officer Robert J. Vernor from Courtney Place, North Strand. He was on the HMS *Nomad* when it was sunk and the paper said that he was believed lost, but pointed out that 'The Germans, however, saved a number of survivors of this ship, and it is possible he is one of them.' That was indeed the case, and he was held prisoner in Germany until repatriation in June 1918.[22]

Dublin's 1 July

Nobody in the UK imagined that a decisive victory at sea could rapidly end the war, but from late 1915 allied plans were set for a major initiative on the Western Front which could lead to victory. This did not

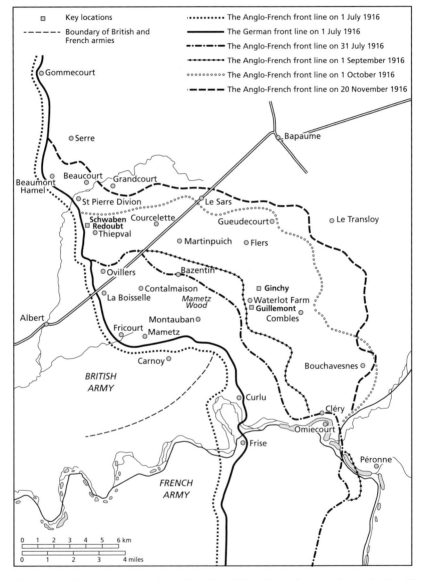

Key locations
Boundary of British and French armies

·········· The Anglo-French front line on 1 July 1916
━━━━━━ The German front line on 1 July 1916
━·━·━·━ The Anglo-French front line on 31 July 1916
×××××××× The Anglo-French front line on 1 September 1916
○○○○○○○○○ The Anglo-French front line on 1 October 1916
━ ━ ━ ━ The Anglo-French front line on 20 November 1916

Gommecourt

Serre

Bapaume

Beaucourt
Beaumont
Hamel
Grandcourt
St Pierre Divion
Le Sars
Schwaben Redoubt
Courcelette
Gueudecourt
Le Transloy
Thiepval
Martinpuich
Flers
Ovillers
Bazentin
Contalmaison
La Boisselle
Mametz Wood
Ginchy
Waterlot Farm
Guillemont
Albert
Montauban
Combles
Fricourt
Mametz
Carnoy
Bouchavesnes

BRITISH ARMY

Curlu
Cléry
Omiecourt
Frise
Péronne

FRENCH ARMY

0 1 2 3 4 5 6 km
0 1 2 3 4 miles

Map 11.1: Somme, 1916. Adapted by David Cox from the map drawn by David Appleyard in Grayson, *Belfast Boys*, 76.

necessarily mean securing a decisive breakthrough in one battle, but, through a process of attrition, forcing Germany to a point where it could not contain such a breakthrough. That plan was initially agreed in very general terms in December 1915 at the Chantilly Conference of allied generals. It was further developed in early 1916 in discussions between Haig (who had taken over command of the BEF in December 1915) and the French high command, with it steadily becoming clear that the centrepiece of the war on the Western Front in 1916 would be a joint Anglo–French attack in the summer of 1916. As the plan stood, after a meeting on 14 February 1916 between Haig and Marshal Joseph Joffre (in command of French forces at this time), 25 British and 40 French divisions would attack either side of the river Somme. However, a week after this agreement the German army attacked the French at Verdun, removing any possibility of a major French contribution on the Somme. In the months which followed, the plan evolved into a primarily British operation with the aim of taking pressure off the French at Verdun.[23] Writing in early June 1916 to the British Ambassador in Paris, Haig described his policy as 'attacking in order to draw pressure from Verdun' but 'not to think that we can for certainty destroy the power of Germany', instead 'improving our positions with a view to making sure of the result of [the] campaign next year'.[24] Crucially, the strategy on 1 July 1916 was a broad attack across the fronts of several divisions, aiming to open up large gaps in the line and restore mobile warfare to the Western Front. A more limited 'step by step' or 'bite and hold' approach – reaching and holding more limited goals before moving further afield – proposed by General Henry Rawlinson, was rejected.[25]

In Ireland's public memory of the First World War, and of the divisions which took part in the first attempted advance on the Somme, that first day of the battle belongs to Northern Ireland through the story of the 36th (Ulster) Division. Since at least the mid-2000s, the Republic of Ireland has made official efforts to include the Somme in a more inclusive all-Ireland narrative of the war, perhaps most notably when An Post produced stamps for the 90th anniversary of the battle's first day while the Royal Mail did not.[26] Despite that, no commemoration of 1 July which takes place in the Republic can compare to what happens in Ulster, and there is no sense in which any part of Dublin claims a special connection with the battle. Yet Dublin lost more men killed on 1 July 1916 than on any other day of the war. The 36th

Division was not solely recruited in Ulster, and Dubliners played a now-forgotten role in it, especially through the 9th Royal Inniskilling Fusiliers. Dubliners were also involved on 1 July in both the 1st and 2nd Royal Dublin Fusiliers, and in the 1st Inniskillings, plus a wide range of other units. Thus 1 July 1916 constitutes not only a forgotten battle for Dublin, it also points to a lost history of Dublin unionism.

Dublin's story of the 9th Inniskillings – the 'Tyrones' – began with the LDV, who had enlisted in the battalion in September 1914, taking their place alongside members of the Tyrone UVF.[27] Like the rest of the 36th Division the battalion arrived in France in early October 1915 and one of its companies was sometimes dubbed the 'Dublin Company'. LDV member Corporal 13494 Alan Browne was described as being a member of the Dublin Company in the press when he wrote home, 'In France at last! It is, as I anticipated, a beautiful country.'[28] The battalion was first in the trenches about a month after arrival, then occasionally in action between January and mid-March 1916, when they were periodically in trenches around Martinsart in the Somme area. They remained in that general location, rotating in and out of the trenches, occasionally carrying out raids, until the battle began on 1 July. During one period at the front, from 13 to 19 March, two Dubliners lost their lives, both being badly wounded and finally succumbing on 21 March: Sergeant 13492 Joseph Bayle and Private 16883 Michael Dalton, whose mothers lived respectively at Vavasour Square in Sandymount and Bishop Street. Bayle had been a drill instructor in the LDV. Alan Browne described how 'He was posting sentries in a thicket, when the same shell mortally wounded him and slightly wounded two others. He was a brave man and died game to the last.' It is possible that Dalton was wounded in one of the patrols which were the main recorded activity for the battalion in that time.[29]

Overnight on 28/29 June the battalion was relieved from the front and spent 29 and 30 June resting in Martinsart Wood preparing for the advance. At night on 30 June 22 officers and 680 other ranks took up their position in Thiepval Wood. Battalion war diaries are mixed in the level of detail they contain on morale and atmosphere within a unit – usually they contain little – but the 9th Inniskillings' diary is uncommonly elaborate in its discussion of such matters. It noted that the battalion was 'allotted Pride of Place in the coming attack ... being the leading Battalion on the right of the Division' and added that the men were 'determined to add fresh lustre to the name of the illustrious regiment to which they belonged'. It also referenced directly the historical coincidence with the anniversary (on the old Julian calendar which made it 1 July rather than 12 July) of the Battle of the Boyne, noting that the day was 'an old landmark in the history of ULSTER'.[30]

The target of the Ulster Division on 1 July as part of X Corps was identified as the 'D Line', about 3,000 yards from their position at the north-east of Thiepval Wood, just short of the village of Grandcourt. Capturing that line meant taking three earlier positions, the A, B and C lines, with the heavily defended Schwaben Redoubt sitting just behind the B Line. Those lines stretched along a divisional front which was just under two miles long, with 109th Brigade (including the 9th Inniskillings), half of 108th Brigade and part of 107th Brigade in the right and right-centre sectors. Behind this line, the rest of 107th Brigade was in reserve. In the left sector, north of the River Ancre, was the other half of 108th Brigade and 29th Division. Assembling for their attack the 9th Inniskillings had the 10th battalion (the 'Derrys') of their regiment on the left, and the 32nd Division to their right.[31]

Across the front the advance was due to begin at 7.30am, but Major General Oliver Nugent commanding the 36th (Ulster) Division sent his men out into No Man's Land a little earlier, while the final stage of the week-long artillery bombardment was coming to an end. That would give the Ulster Division a crucial advantage, allowing them to advance more rapidly and further than other parts of the British first wave.[32] The 9th Inniskillings took up their position there, just in front of the British wire at 7.15am. Fifteen minutes later the bugle sounded and the men advanced in good summer conditions, 'as if it was a parade movement'.[33] 'Pride of Place' in the advance was a dubious honour because it rapidly became clear that German positions in Thiepval village had not been destroyed in the bombardment, and the infantry of 32nd Division (the right of X Corps) were unable to advance in that direction.[34] This meant that German machine guns in the village could range over the fronts of both the 36th and 32nd divisions. At the same time, shell fire was coming from German lines 'and the ranks began to thin, men falling by the score'. Nevertheless, both the A Line and the B Line (also known as the Crucifix Line) were taken by the 9th Inniskillings and a push was made towards the C Line, specifically a point named 'Lisnaskea'. It was taken and held for about an hour by 'a mere handful of men', but the Germans were firing not only from the front but also from the right of the battalion, having exploited the failure of the 32nd Division to advance. Retreat was the only option and the battalion consolidated at the B Line. Machine-gun fire from Thiepval continued to rain down throughout the day, while ammunition and bombs ran short. The battalion war diary described the rest of the day:

> At about 3pm ... the enemy fiercely bombarded the piece of trench we were holding with High Explosives & Shrapnel attacking at the same time with bombs on our Right. Our bombs were at this time almost exhausted, nevertheless we held on to about 10pm that night, when we were compelled to face back to the German "A" Line & thence to our own trenches.

Over night, parties of the remnants of the battalion went into No Man's Land to find, treat and bring back the wounded.[35]

In the initial estimation of what had happened to the battalion on 1 July and into the early hours of the next day, of the battalion's 22 officers, 16 were casualties. Of these, 8 were already known to be dead, and another 4 were missing but would be confirmed dead at a later stage. So the battalion was left with just 4 officers. From the 680 other ranks who went into action on 1 July, 461 were casualties of some kind, leaving the battalion with little more than 200 men who were able to fight. It was already known that 51 were dead but all the 154 known to be missing would later be confirmed as dead. With a total of 221 dead, the battalion had among the highest number of fatalities in the Ulster Division on 1 and 2 July 1916.[36] Among the dead were at least 17 Dubliners. Among them was Private 16282 James Harvey, a former member of the LDV who lived at Gilford Place, North Strand.[37] Another was Monkstown barrister Lieutenant William Crozier, also an LDV member and among the older members of the battalion, at the age of 42.[38] Dubliners serving elsewhere in the Ulster Division included Private 5941 Samuel Russell and Lieutenant Edward Holland. Russell was working as a motor fitter living in Parkgate Street when he enlisted in the division's Army Cyclist Corps, but had been transferred to the 14th Royal Irish Rifles.[39] Dublin-born Holland had already seen service in the Royal Welch Fusiliers in 1908–12, but was working as a clerk in the Audit Department at the Guinness brewery and living in Rathgar Road when he enlisted. He served in the 9th Royal Irish Rifles formed from the West Belfast UVF.[40] Both men survived the Somme, and indeed the war.

To the left of X Corps, of which the Ulster Division was part, stood VIII Corps, including two battalions of the Dublin Fusiliers. The 2nd had been on the Western Front since the earliest days of the war. The 1st had been at Gallipoli from the first to the last stages of that campaign. It had then moved to Egypt where it spent some time in front line trenches at Darb-el-Haj, before reaching Marseilles from Alexandria on 10 March 1916, soon moving to northern France. The next three months saw the 1st Dublins training and being rotated in and out of various front-line positions in the Somme area.[41] The experience of the 2nd Dublins in the lead up to July 1916 was broadly the same.[42] Wilfrid Colyer, by now a lieutenant, said they dubbed their time training as 'fattening up for the slaughter'. During training, men initially worked at a platoon or company level 'to smarten up the men and correct the somewhat slouching habits which there was always a tendency to contract during a long spell in the trenches'. Activities included three to four days of exercises, such as bayonet-fighting and bomb-throwing. Then the men moved to battalion-level work, starting with parades, before 'rehearsals of the actual show'.[43] During this time, the composition of the 1st and 2nd Dublins was very different to the battalions of the New Army. Their experiences thus far meant that they contained battle-hardened soldiers. But their past losses meant that they contained a mix of the regulars and reservists who had fought in 1914 and 1915 alongside fresh drafts. These drafts were just as raw as those in the volunteer divisions, but tended to come from a wider range of backgrounds than those in the Ulster Division.

The front attacked by VIII Corps was different to that faced by X Corps, consisting of more uneven ground, including a series of ridges and valleys. Split into three sections, 31st Division was northernmost. Their part of the line was a little more advanced than the rest of the front and their role was to advance on the village of Serre forming a defensive flank for the rest of the Corps. Immediately south, 4th Division (including the 2nd Dublins) was to advance past the village of Beaumont-Hamel towards the Beaucourt Spur. South of them, 29th Division (including the 1st Dublins) would do the same, some of the division moving through the village itself. The plan of attack included specific mention of a 'creeping' barrage from the division's field artillery, based on the view that the infantry would advance at fifty yards per minute.[44] Colyer recalled, 'No great difficulty was anticipated in the successful accomplishment of these operations, for it was calculated that Beaumont-Hamel and the Hun front trench system would be practically obliterated by our artillery preparation.' Of the mood in the 2nd Dublins in the week before the advance Colyer noted 'The shadow of impending disaster certainly did not rest upon us.' He recalled how the men 'laughed and talked and smoked and sang and drank and retailed evil stories and won money at bridge (and lost it again at poker)'. However, a few days before the advance men of the battalion witnessed the aftermath of a direct hit on the bivouacs of a group of Seaforth Highlanders. Colyer remembered,

> Quite a number of the men, stout hearted fellows though they were, lost their nerve altogether, ran away from the camp, and spent the night wandering about the open country, some very scantily clad, just as they had been aroused from their sleep. They returned in two's and three's during the morning, quite exhausted with their walking, exposure and general fright.

According to Colyer, 'Our buoyant spirits were considerably reduced, and we began to take the offensive more seriously.'[45]

Neither the 1st nor 2nd Dublins were in the initial advance. The 1st Dublins were due to be in the second wave of the advance behind the 2nd Royal Fusiliers and the 1st Lancashire Fusiliers.[46] Those two battalions began their advance soon after 7.20am when a mine had been exploded at Hawthorn Redoubt close to Beaumont-Hamel. Colyer wrote, 'I was rather expecting a deafening roar as the mine went up, but rather to my surprise there is nothing of the sort; if there is any noise at all it is lost in the crashing of the artillery.'[47] Although causing much damage, the mine had alerted the Germans that an attack was coming and allowed them to reinforce their lines in advance of the main attack ten minutes later.[48] The 1st Dublins began to move to the British front line following the 7.20am attack. The plan was to move out behind the 2nd Royal Fusiliers by companies, reforming at the line called 'Station Road' and readying for an attack on the German second line. They found it hard even to reach the parapet of the British front line because it was blocked by men of the 2nd Royal Fusiliers and the 86th Brigade's Machine Gun Company. So the 1st Dublins did not even begin to go over the top until 8am.

Immediately they faced two problems. The first was that the British wire had been cut in intervals of roughly forty yards creating gaps through which troops could advance. However, the Germans had spotted these gaps and fixed machine guns on them. As the war diary said, 'the result being that our casualties were very heavy & only a few of our men ever got through the wire & still fewer of these succeeded in advancing more than 50x [yards] or 60x before being shot down'. If they made it through the gaps in the wire, they faced their second problem: the target of the German second line could only be even attempted if the first line had been taken, which the 2nd Royal Fusiliers had not done. This was largely due to German defences not being destroyed by the artillery and the German wire was largely undamaged.[49] At midday the attack was abandoned, with the battalion ordered to hold the British front line. At 7pm a party of one officer and twenty men ventured into No Man's Land to recover some mortars, returning without casualties; but there was no further thought of advance. The battalion remained in the line until 4 July when it was relieved, but suffered no further casualties after 1 July. Writing to Monica Roberts nearly a week later, Private 19543 Harry Loughlin talked up what had happened across the front, saying 'by now you shall have read all the victory we have gained'. But he conceded of the 1st Dublins' part of the line that 'owing to the imprignible position the Germans had, we could not do the wonderfull work in that sector'.[50] At the time the battalion estimated casualties on that day to be around 300 other ranks (including 18 killed and 63 missing), plus 4 officers killed, 7 wounded and one missing. It would later become apparent that there were 63 dead in the battalion, 5 of them officers and 58 other ranks.[51]

To the north in 4th Division, the 2nd Dublins fared no better. Their task, along with the rest of 10th Brigade and 12th Brigade, was to advance alongside the 2nd Seaforth Highlanders behind battalions of 11th Brigade once the first two German lines were secure. Despite some initial progress by the 1/8th Royal Warwickshires in entering the front line, machine-gun fire from Serre (which 31st Division had not captured) prevented any further advance by the 4th Division.[52] At 9am they began their attack from assembly trenches in which they had been overnight. Even before reaching the British front line they came under machine-gun fire from the village of Beaumont-Hamel which had not been taken by 29th Division. They also faced rifle fire and shells from the German front which they were due to attack. Five minutes later they received an order not to advance and most of the battalion was held back, but some were already in No Man's Land and all became casualties. At 12 noon orders were received to attack the German front but it was only possible to collect around 60 men.[53] News coming through was varied and unclear. Colyer had been wounded and separated from his unit, and later recalled thinking at the time that news 'varies considerably according to the character and imagination of the authority'. He added his recollection that 'All are agreed that our troops are far short of the objectives they were designed to reach.' Colyer remembered 'Some are confident that we are established in the Boche 3rd line; others doubt whether we have really got much past the 1st.'[54] All they could do was reorganise in their assembly trenches before being relieved at 5pm on 3 July. Three officers and 62 other ranks had lost their lives.[55] Colyer recalled, 'Many other battalions fared worse, true; but what made it so dispiriting in our case was that we had nothing to show for it.'[56]

At least 18 of the dead in the 1st Dublins and 20 of those killed in the 2nd were Dubliners, around a third of the battalion dead in each case, reflecting the slackening of local ties in battalions which had seen serious action and were supplemented by reservists. By the same token, Dubliners were serving in units beyond the 1st and 2nd Dublin Fusiliers and the 9th Inniskillings on 1 and 2 July 1916. Aside from the 55 Dubliners across those 3 battalions, another 61 lost their lives on the Western Front, all but 5 on the Somme. The largest single cluster was of 12 in the 1st Inniskillings serving in 29th Division alongside the 1st Dublins.[57] Another 8 were killed in the 1st Royal Irish Rifles, south of the Ulster Division.[58] Other Dubliners fell in battalions of the Border, East Yorkshire, London, Manchester, Norfolk, Sussex and Warwickshire regiments, along with the Machine Gun Corps, Highland Light Infantry, King's Own Yorkshire Light Infantry, Rifle Brigade, Royal Fusiliers, Royal Irish Rifles and Royal Irish Fusiliers. With 116 Dubliners dead in total, 1 July 1916 was Dublin's worst day of the war.

Newspaper coverage of the battle was initially unreservedly triumphal. Headlines on Monday 3 July included phrases like 'IMPORTANT STRATEGIC POSITIONS CAPTURED' and 'THE GREAT FRANCO-BRITISH DRIVE'. On 4 July it was reported that the German second line had been taken, but that the Germans had reinforced and were resisting strongly.[59] However, by 6 July the rather more measured phrase, 'FURTHER SLIGHT BRITISH ADVANCE' was used.[60] Indeed, there had been successes at some points of the attack. In the French sector – and in front of 30th Division who adjoined the French – artillery fire had been more intensive and caused much greater destruction of German lines and wire.[61] This meant relatively easy progress for the French and the capture of Montauban, La Bricqueterie and Pommiers Redoubt by the British by midday. However, in most parts of the front, surviving machine-guns posts resulted in enfilade fire and disrupted carefully planned timetabling of infantry and artillery operations.[62] The result was that any progress represented 'break-in' rather than 'breakthrough'[63] meaning that any ground gained would be very vulnerable to counter-attack. In later years, Colyer offered a veteran's reflection on the 'failure' of the attack:

> we know now that the attack was not really a failure ... We did not advance at Beaumont-Hamel, true; but our people did advance further south, very substantially. Their success would not have been possible if it had not been for our attack, which held a large force of Germans in the Beaumont-Hamel district and prevented them moving south to help in the defence down there.[64]

Yet, while this was correct, it was a charitable reading of what happened on 1 July: the attack in the Beaumont-Hamel area had never been conceived of simply as a diversionary operation to allow advances southwards.

Aftermath

There was a feeling among Haig and his colleagues that 1 July 1916 was a partial success with gains which could be exploited.[65] Consequently, operations after 1 July switched from attempts at advance across a broad front to both defending against

German counter-attacks and exploiting weaknesses in German lines. Some British soldiers were now consolidating new positions in captured German lines. Lieutenant Gerald Murphy was a medical officer attached to the 2nd Royal Irish Rifles. He wrote home about his new dressing station in former German lines. He said, 'It's about 40 feet deep underground, you go down by stair steps. The roof is supported by iron girders and crossed with wood. There are beds and rooms opening off the main passage. Electric light is installed and a system of alarm bells in case of attack.'[66]

At this stage of July, and into August, Dubliners saw action in a number of units. Having been in reserve on 1 July the 2nd Royal Irish Rifles were in bivouacs and billets in the first days of the battle, before marching through Albert on 6 July, to assembly trenches. They then successfully advanced at La Boisselle for the loss of 28 men and 2 officers killed, with another 5 officers and 116 men wounded, and 17 men missing. On 7 July, they faced difficult conditions. The battalion's Jesuit Chaplain was a Dubliner, Father Henry Gill, who noted that rain fell and, due to the soil being chalky, 'soon the hollows of the trenches began to fill up with a white liquid mud like thick whitewash'.[67] A further attack was launched the next day and a new position held overnight. However, that could not be maintained for long. In the first place, as the war diary recorded, on 9 July 'our troops in this position were subject to a continuous barrage from our own artillery, who owing to difficulty of communication were unaware of our presence'. At 4pm that day a German counter-attack was launched, forcing the battalion to retreat to their previous position from the day before. Over 7–9 July they lost 5 officers and 83 other ranks dead.[68] These included at least 13 Dubliners, such as Company Sergeant Major John Byers, whose wife Florence lived in the married quarters at Portobello Barracks. His posthumous award of the Military Cross was announced later in July. The citation read, 'For gallantry and devotion to duty on several occasions. In particular when, under heavy bombardment, his company suffered heavy casualties, his cool devotion to duty set a striking example.'[69]

The 2nd Royal Irish Rifles played their part in a series of piecemeal attacks between 7 and 13 July.[70] Immediately after, on 14 July, a new broad offensive on the Somme was launched – the Battle of Bazentin Ridge – with two crucial differences to that of

1 July: the artillery bombardment was far more intense, and many more men took up their attacking positions under cover of darkness in No Man's Land while the guns were still firing. The result was a successful attack on the German line between Bazentin-le-Petit and Longueval.[71] It seemed as if the tide had turned. Optimism was the public attitude of the soldiers: Private 11336 George Soper wrote of the enemy to Monica Roberts, 'I think we will finish him Between this and early next year.'[72]

Historians point to lessons learned from 1 July 1916 around the need to combine different elements of the army in any attack, even if this 'learning curve' would not be persistent and without regression until 1918.[73] Some of these were implemented on the Somme, but uneven advances could still cause significant problems. A cluster of Dubliners was serving in the 1st King's (Liverpool) Regiment when it went into action close to Guillemont on 8 August. They managed to secure some of their objectives, but came under fire from one side where another battalion had not been so successful, with some of the men encircled in forward positions. Aerial reconnaissance confirmed that the men had dug in, but reinforcements could not reach them. Thus 82 were killed including 5 Dubliners. Among those was one of the highest ranking Dubliners to be killed during the war, 26-year-old Lieutenant Colonel Charles Goff. Killiney-born Goff had joined the army in 1907 and at the outbreak of war was a lieutenant in the 1st King's (Liverpool) Regiment. He became a major in February 1916 and then took command of his battalion in March. On 8 August he went into action with his men. The 1st Liverpools initially gained and held their targets near Guillemont, but units either side of them did not advance and the battalion was overrun by a German counter-attack. Goff was initially declared missing, but many of his men had been captured and news of his death was sought through the Red Cross from those in prison camps. Only in December was his death confirmed by the War Office. Private 32990 William Kirkham 'saw Col Goff standing close to the entrance to the dugout, when a shell exploded between him & the dugout. No trace of him was to be seen after the shell had exploded.' By November, his widowed mother, living at Evergreen Lodge in Killiney, had herself accepted his death, placing an 'In Memoriam' notice in the *Evening Mail*. His body was never found.[74]

Overall, the attack on Guillemont was an almost total failure. That was partly because German defences had been recently strengthened but also because it was not fully understood that the key defences of the village were not front-line trenches but those hiding in shell holes or cellars.[75] A month later, Guillemont witnessed another attack, this time successful, during which the Dublin nationalists of the 16th (Irish) Division made their mark.

12 SUCCESS ON THE SOMME

The bombardment, destruction and bloodshed are beyond all imagination, nor did I ever think that valour of simple men could be quite as beautiful as that of my Dublin Fusiliers.
  Second Lieutenant Thomas Kettle, 9th Royal Dublin
  Fusiliers, early September 1916[1]

Guillemont and Ginchy

Not least because of much cross-community work in Northern Ireland, the role of nationalists on the Somme during September 1916 is much better known than it once was.[2] Dubliners played their part in particular through the 8th and 9th Royal Dublin Fusiliers, both battalions being members of the 16th (Irish) Division for which Parliamentary nationalists had been such active recruiters. However, Dubliners were also there in other battalions, including the 6th Connaught Rangers who were in the very first wave of the attack on Guillemont.

Allied attacks on the Somme which began in early September 1916 represented an increase in the French role in the battle, with six British and six French army corps on hand. However, the 3 September attack still saw the British dominate with eight divisions compared to four French.[3] Part of the attack was by XIV Corps on Guillemont. It was led by 47th Brigade from the 16th Division, temporarily attached to 20th Division, and another brigade of that division, the 59th.[4] 47th Brigade was part of a three-wave plan for taking what remained of Guillemont with battalions split into different waves. The 6th Connaughts took their position for the attack at 5am on 3 September. Their C and D companies were to be part of the first wave. Then, in the next two waves, platoons of B Company would fill gaps in C Company's lines, while platoons of A Company would play the same role for D. At 8am, bombardment of German lines began but some of the British heavy trench mortars fell short of their target onto 'Rim Trench' and the 6th Connaughts' C Company. Their casualties were nearly 200 by midday by which time it was clear that C Company could not be part of the first wave and troops from the second were ordered to replace them. At 12 noon the artillery set off 'an intense barrage' of the German front. Three minutes later the 6th Connaughts advanced and found 'Very little opposition... as the enemy surrendered at once' on the left of their advance – the area that was originally to have been attacked by C Company.[5] In the same brigade, the 7th Leinsters had not faced friendly fire. Its A and B companies were in the first wave of the advance near to the 6th Connaughts and they took their targets 'with comparative ease' after advancing at 12.03pm. Max Staniforth of the 7th Leinsters wrote to his parents about the advance: 'I concentrated my thoughts on keeping my pipe alight. It seemed to be the most important thing at the moment, somehow. Of course there was none of the "wild, cheering rush" one imagines. We stopped outside the parapet to straighten the line, and then moved forward at an ordinary walk.'[6] By 12.40pm Staniforth's battalion could attack its second target. The battalion's 'bombers did particularly good work by pushing forward through our own Barrage and clearing the village.'[7] Staniforth described how 'the air was just one loud noise – like moving in a kind of sound-box. And the machine-gun bullets snapped about your head rather like a swarm of angry hornets: all hissing and crackling.'[8]

In the early stages of the battle two Victoria Crosses were won, by Private 3/5027 Thomas Hughes, a County Monaghan man in the 6th Connaughts, and by Lieutenant John Holland of Kildare in the 7th Leinsters. Hughes took a machine-gun post single-handed. Holland led a bombing party into Guillemont.[9] Such heroism saw the 47th Brigade's first three targets taken by 1pm. Meanwhile, the 6th Royal Irish Regiment, including around 140 from the 6th Connaughts, and followed by the 8th Royal Munster Fusiliers, advanced at 12.25pm, with the 'Sunken Road' as their final objective. They 'went over the parapet with their pipes playing'.[10] By 3pm they had taken their target, though there was little left of the village which 'had been reduced to matchwood'.[11]

This success in taking Guillemont has been attributed to three changes from previous operations: the direction of attack (from new trenches close to the German lines), destruction of deep dug-outs, and thinner German defences than on previous occasions.[12] But success still had its cost: across the infantry battalions of 47th Brigade on 3 September, there were 1,147 casualties from around 2,400 who attacked.[13] The largest number of deaths was in the 6th Connaughts who lost 54. Among 7 of those dead with Dublin connections was Lieutenant Colonel John Lenox-Conyngham, the battalion commander, who had been killed while leading his men. Originally from an Ulster Protestant family, his mother was living in Dublin's Northbrook Road. So well-known and connected was he within Dublin Anglicanism that he would be remembered on three Dublin churches' memorials.[14] His brother, Dublin-born Hubert, also a Lieutenant Colonel (in the Army Veterinary Corps), would die of illness in March 1918.[15] Another man killed, Private 4699 Patrick Bolger, was a reservist with twelve years' service, working as a van driver before the war. He had been wounded in France in February 1916. His widow Mary Alice, of Lower Gloucester Street, was left with a nine-month-old baby, Josephine.[16] Dubliners were also killed in the 7th Leinsters and 6th Royal Irish Regiment

Overnight on 4 September, the part of the 16th Division attached to 20th Division which had been consolidating the line, was relieved. Other units of the Division were soon in action. On 5 September, the 7th Royal Irish Fusiliers were ordered to attack German positions alongside Leuze Wood, one of the ultimate but unreached targets on 3 September. After initial success they 'found themselves opposed by very thick barbed wire quite uncut'. As 'they gallantly attempted to break through', they 'were met by a withering fire from machine guns' and were forced to dig in. At dusk, they were forced to withdraw about 300 yards and dig in before being relieved the next morning. However, they were back in action on the evening of 6 September defending Guillemont, now facing heavy shelling from German lines. There they stayed until dawn on 7 September when they moved to divisional reserve.[17] The 7th Royal Irish Fusiliers lost 56 dead over those three days, among them 6 Dubliners, all killed in the attack on 5 September. The bodies of 42, the vast majority, were never identified so the men are remembered on the Thiepval memorial.[18]

The 8th and 9th Royal Dublin Fusiliers faced similar levels of fatalities over 6–8 September in their first engagements on the Somme, both as part of 48th Brigade which had been in reserve on 3 September. Their role at this time was partly simply to defend the gains made at Guillemont, facing bitter counter-attacks by the Germans. But they also took part in efforts to gain ground at Leuze Wood and close to Ginchy. Overnight on 5/6 September, the 9th Dublins became lost as they went forward to exploit gaps in the line, following a successful French attack on Leuze Wood. They returned to British lines as it became light. The next day they successfully entrenched part of the Guillemont–Combles road, though they were often under shell fire. Meanwhile, the 8th Dublins gained 300 yards of ground at Leuze Wood on 7 September, then held it in the face of a counter-attack and heavy shelling.[19] The 9th Dublins lost 42 men dead over those three days while the 8th would lose 48. The majority of these were Dubliners, 30 in the 8th and 26 in the 9th. These days seldom feature in the Guillemont–Ginchy narrative attached to the 16th (Irish) Division, yet they should be remembered as part of that phase of the Battle of the Somme, still marked by loss as well as by gain.[20]

Ginchy

The 9th Dublins spent much of 7 and 8 September digging assembly trenches in preparation for a new attack on Ginchy on 9 September.[21] This was a renewed attempt on one of the targets of 3 September. The 7th Division had repeatedly attempted to take it before being withdrawn. The task was now handed to the 16th Division. Some aspects of the attack were different to those on previous occasions. The advance would begin from the direction of Guillemont, rather than from Delville Wood, there would be a heavier artillery bombardment in advance, and there would be six battalions taking part (whereas 7th Division had used only two). Meanwhile, some German units which had arrived to support the defence of the village did not manage to make contact with their front line.[22]

As so often before, preparations for the attack on Ginchy began with infantry units taking up assembly positions overnight, under the cover of darkness. The first phase of the artillery bombardment began from 7am, lasting until 12.30pm. At that point, half the artillery continued firing on the German front while the other half began a creeping barrage 100 yards in front of the infantry. Battalions of 48th Brigade were in the first wave: the 7th Royal Irish Rifles and 1st Royal Munster Fusiliers (regulars who had joined the division in May 1916). Battalions of 47th Brigade were to the right of the 48th, with 49th Brigade due to enter the fray at a later stage, holding Ginchy if it was captured. Within 48th Brigade, the 9th Dublins were to follow the 7th Royal Irish Rifles on the left, and the 8th were behind the Munsters on the right.

The 8th Dublins took up their assembly place just after midnight on 8/9 September, which meant a long wait since the advance was not scheduled to begin until 4.45pm on 9 September. An order to delay the advance by two minutes, so that a further final intense barrage could take place, did not reach 48th Brigade, but that did not cause them any problems.[23] They mostly advanced about 100 yards behind the 1st Munsters. Movement was quicker than expected and at 4.52pm it had to be checked because the first and second waves had got too close to the artillery barrage. By 5.25pm the first objective within the village was secure and troops were pushing on to their second target. So enthusiastic was their advance that the battalion commander, Lieutenant Colonel Edward Bellingham, had to pull men back at 5.40pm to consolidate in the village. The 9th Dublins had meanwhile advanced at a similar time and by early evening they were mixed up in the village with the 8th Dublins. They had suffered heavy officer casualties and as objectives on the northern edge of the village were secured, elements of those battalions present in Ginchy effectively came under the command of Bellingham who led them in consolidating their positions before being relieved the next day.[24]

One of only two officers still standing in the 9th Dublins was 18-year-old Second Lieutenant (James) Emmet Dalton, who was born in the USA but had moved to Dublin aged two in 1900, becoming a naturalised British citizen in 1913. He had been involved with the Irish Volunteers from their formation, delivering rifles in County Mayo in 1914 on behalf of his father.[25] But he enlisted in the British army in November 1915 (having declared himself to be 19 rather than 17), after seeking advice from his father's friend Joseph Devlin, IPP MP for West Belfast and a supporter of recruitment for the 'Irish Brigade'.

Dalton had been living in St Columba's Road, and hoped to join the 7th Dublins. However, when he was commissioned at the end of the year he was sent to the 3rd Dublins for training. His commission came as something of a surprise to his father who, as Dalton arrived home in a British uniform, 'told me to get out, that no bloody redcoat would enter his house'. Dalton recalled, 'My mother was in hysterics, and after a time we subdued the old man, and I was received.' During the Rising he was training in Cork, rather then deployed on the streets of Dublin. He was then attached to the 9th in September 1916 (after Guillemont).[26] At Ginchy, in his first action, he earned the Military Cross, the medal citation reading: 'For conspicuous gallantry in action. He led forward to their final objective companies which had lost their officers. Later, while consolidating his position, he found himself, with one serjeant, confronted by 21 of the enemy, including an officer, who surrendered when he attacked them.'[27] Dalton was wounded a few weeks after Ginchy, spending a week away from his unit before returning, only to fall ill in October. He spent some time in hospitals in France and England, and then worked as a musketry and anti-gas instructor in the Dublin area in February and March 1917, before deployment to Salonika with the 6th Leinsters.[28]

Though Ginchy was taken, 47th Brigade to the right of the 48th had faced stiffer opposition with the artillery having been far less effective in its part of the line.[29] The plan as first formulated had the 6th Connaughts advancing with one company of the 7th Leinsters and two companies of the 11th Hampshires. However, the first wave of the 8th Munsters and 6th Royal Irish Regiment were so badly hit by snipers that many of their surviving men stayed in their trenches. Two companies of the Connaughts realised what had happened and did the same but two other companies along with the 7th Leinsters and 11th Hampshires did not. They noticed a pause in fighting and thought that it was their turn to advance. At 5.43pm a runner from the 6th Connaughts was sent back with a message for divisional HQ. It read, 'It appears that the trench opposite is full of Germans and that they were well prepared.' It was clear that in front of 47th Brigade the bombardment had done little damage to German positions.[30] The 6th Connaughts' commanding officer Rowland Feilding later wrote that part of the German front was 'hidden and believed innocuous', so it had been neglected by the preliminary bombardment. Instead, his men found it to be 'a veritable hornets' nest'.[31] Despite that, the advance of the 48th Brigade meant that Ginchy was secure.

It was a costly battle. On 9 September alone the 16th (Irish) Division lost 534 dead. The 1st Royal Munster Fusiliers suffered the heaviest losses in one battalion (71), closely followed by the Dublin battalions: 70 dead in the 9th and 67 in the 8th. Total casualties over the 16th Division's Somme campaign from 3 to 9 September saw more than 50 per cent of its officers killed, wounded or prisoners, and 40 per cent of its men. In numbers, from a strength of 435 officers and 10,410 men on 3 September, 224 officers and 4,090 were casualties by the time the campaign ended.[32] Among the dead on 9 September were two neighbours from Dublin's Newmarket. Thirty-one-year-old labourer Private 5761 George Deegan had previous service in the Dublins when he re-enlisted in August 1914. He had made his way to the 8th Dublins by a roundabout route, first seeing action in the regiment's 2nd battalion before being transferred. He left a widow, Sarah, at 46 Newmarket.[33] Close by at number 20 was John Callan, whose son, Private 5964 John Callan, aged twenty-two, was killed in the 1st Royal Munster Fusiliers.[34]

In the nationalist press, stories celebrating the 'valour' and 'great dash and gallantry' of Irish regiments at Guillemont and Ginchy abounded and by 14 September the *Freeman's Journal* specifically noted the nationalist role, reporting of 'The Irish Brigade' that it consisted of 'the regiments raised at Fermoy in accordance with the suggestions made by Mr. Redmond. They are largely, if not mainly, composed of the Irish National Volunteers from all over Ireland. The Brigade has more than fulfilled the high expectations of the Nationalists of Ireland, and its deeds are worthy of the great tradition its title recalls.'[35] This celebratory tone was soon tinged with sadness by news of one death in particular, which seemed to speak for all the losses, receiving major newspaper attention and providing Irish nationalism with a martyr: Lieutenant Thomas Michael 'Tom' Kettle. Kettle's wife Mary was left at 119 Upper Leeson Street. Dublin-born Kettle's death was such news because he was a former Irish Nationalist MP who had represented East Tyrone from 1906 to 1910. He was a significant figure in Irish nationalism, an Irish Volunteer and then a National Volunteer, and Chair of National Economics at University College, Dublin. He had covered the early stages of the war in Belgium as a journalist. Kettle's service in the war as a member of a British army was a symbol of the hopes of those nationalists who had enlisted in 1914, even though he had not gone to France until July 1916 having been in Ireland recruiting. Yet even before he died he knew that such hopes might well be dashed. His friend Robert Lynd said that Kettle regarded the 1916 executions 'with such horror', and was especially horrified by the murder of Francis Sheehy-Skeffington who was his brother-in-law. But Kettle also believed that the Rising's leaders had 'all but destroyed his dream of an Ireland enjoying the freedom of Europe'.[36] Yet he also commented on the executed leaders of the Rising, 'These men will go down to history as heroes and martyrs, and I will go down – if I go down at all – as a bloody British officer.'[37]

Kettle was at Ginchy with the 9th Dublins. He had two chances not to go into action that day, one due to illness and the other an offer of a staff appointment. However, he stayed with his men, writing to a friend on the eve of his battalion moving to Guillemont, 'The bombardment, destruction and bloodshed are beyond all imagination, nor did I ever think that valour of simple men could be quite as beautiful as that of my Dublin Fusiliers.'[38] The nobility of his comrades was a theme to which he returned when writing to his wife on 8 September: 'I have never seen anything in my life so beautiful as the clean and, so to say, radiant manner of my Dublin Fusiliers. There is something divine in men like that.'[39] This conception of the fight in which he was engaged was expressed in spiritual terms in the poem which became his best-known legacy. Written at Guillemont on 4 September 1916 it was entitled 'To my Daughter Betty, the Gift of God'. With his own possible death in mind, it was written to explain to his young daughter why he had fought. It became public after his death, though when it was published in newspapers at the end of October 1916 they were forced to apologise a few days later for having reproduced it without reference to Mary Kettle's wishes. It transpired that she had already refused to allow it to appear in a forthcoming volume of his poems 'on the grounds of its private character'.[40] Kettle wrote that in future years 'You'll ask why I abandoned you, my own', and said:

> Know that we fools, now with the foolish dead,
> Died not for flag, nor King, nor Emperor,
> But for a dream, born in a herdsman's shed,
> And for the secret Scripture of the poor.[41]

In response to the publication of the poem, Mary Kettle released a letter written by her husband on 3 September, which was his political testament. It said that had he lived he had meant to call his next book on relations between 'Ireland and England', *The Two Fools: A Tragedy of Errors*. He said that his experiences at the front had shown him that there were few differences between Britain and Ireland, and called for Colonial Home Rule for Ireland which he believed was 'essential as a prologue to the reconstruction of the Empire'. He also called for the end of martial law and the release of all Sinn Féin prisoners because 'If this war has taught us anything it is that great things can be done only in a great way.'[42]

The mystical and religious underpinnings of Kettle's war were seen in the moment of his death in command of his battalion's B Company. He had got to know Emmet Dalton briefly at the front. They had first met in France in early September, but had previously met in Ireland. Dalton explained,

> I was just behind Tom when [we] went over the top, he was in a bent position and a bullet got over a steel waistcoat that he wore and entered his heart. Well he only lasted about 1 minute, and he had my crucifix in my hands. He also said, "this is the 7th anniversary of my wedding" (I forget whether 7 or 8).

Dalton added, 'Tom's death has been a big blow to the Regt. and I am afraid that I could not put in words my feelings on the subject.'[43] A different account was sent to Mary Kettle by a member of the 1st Munsters, relaying information from a corporal in the 9th RDF, that Kettle had said, 'Oh my God, I'm struck', and died within ten minutes.[44] Plaudits for Kettle in the press described him as 'one of the most brilliant and versatile of the younger school of Irish Nationalists' and 'a representative figure – an exaggeratedly representative figure – of much of the suffering of the time'.[45]

Kettle could not have been more wrong in his hopes for Ireland's future. There was no question of Colonial Home Rule with agreement from Ulster. The release of prisoners did not result in a softening of opinion when it took place,[46] nor would side-by-side service in the British army lessen political differences at home. He was closer to predicting the future for the leaders of the Rising when he said that they would be remembered as martyrs.[47] Yet there was a clear tone of heroism in immediate verdicts on Kettle, perhaps seen most clearly in the verdict of his friend, Robert Lynd: 'He was one of those men who have almost too many gifts to succeed ... Had he only had a little ordinariness in his composition to harden him, he would almost certainly have ended as the leading Irish statesman of his day.'[48]

Although Kettle was buried, his grave was never properly marked and its location was lost. His fellow officer, Captain Maurice Healy, wrote to Mary Kettle in April 1917 that over a three-week period he had searched every cemetery in the relevant area with no success. He explained that,

> Tom may have been buried 'darkly, at dead of night'; with no time to do more than bury the dead and mark the grave with an anonymous cross. There are hundreds such. I myself have buried men under shell fire, and in the confusion have found it impossible to find the identity disc or any other identification. This is often done in the hope of an almost immediate re-interment. But it often proves impossible, through moves & c., to return to the same place, and then the grave remains anonymous.[49]

According to Emmet Dalton, Welsh Guards had buried Kettle,[50] and by November 1917, the grave had been found in the Carnoy area: Healy was sent details by Mary Kettle and arranged for it to be tended.[51] However, at some point it was destroyed or lost since Kettle was eventually listed on the Thiepval Memorial.[52]

Grinding On

Following Ginchy, the battle of the Somme ground on for over two months. Guillemont, Ginchy and some earlier operations from mid-July were essentially examples of the 'bite and hold' approach which had been rejected for 1 July. However, in mid-September, in the battle of Flers-Courcelette, the allies attempted a new breakthrough on a broad front from Combles to Thiepval, this time aided by tanks, though many broke down or were otherwise ineffective.[53] Dubliners took part in the battle in the 1st and 2nd Irish Guards in the Guards Division.[54] At least 15 Dubliners were killed at Flers-Courcelette, most of those (10) in the 2nd Irish Guards, which suffered around 300 casualties on 15 September. That was mainly due to machine-gun fire – as so often happened when artillery fire had not been heavy enough – but some men also advanced too quickly and got caught in the British barrage.[55] In the 1st Irish Guards 'Our men got their blood up and . . . our first wave went forward in an irresistible rush', but they too faced heavy German opposition. Ground was gained by the 1st Irish Guards and consolidated but at great cost with around 330 casualties.[56] Across a 1,500 yard front the Guards Division gained 2,000 yards.[57] There were also gains elsewhere but the German line was broken into rather than through, again because the artillery barrage had not been heavy enough.[58]

Later that month, there were further 'bite and hold' advances. Over 25–8 September there was success at Morval, aided by the effective combination of infantry and artillery, with the ranks following close behind a 'creeping barrage'. Over 26–30 September during the Battle of Thiepval Ridge, first Thiepval (on 27 September) and then the Schwaben Redoubt (on 28 September) were captured, nearly three months after the Ulster Division's assault. Later phases of the battle, such as at the Ancre Heights and Transloy Ridges continued to make gains, while Haig persisted in hoping for a breakthrough.[59] During this time, the British army saw some success from a devolved system of command, with more leeway for commanders on the spot.[60]

But some soldiers had had enough. Private 2974 Bernard McGeehan had enlisted in the 1/8th (Irish) King's Liverpool Regiment on 11 November 1914. Born in County Donegal, his own address was in Liverpool but his father, also Bernard, was living at Annesley Place in Dublin, and McGeehan had also lived in Dublin pre-war. McGeehan deserted from his battalion on the evening of 19 September 1916 in the Mametz sector on the Somme and was apprehended just over a week later. McGeehan's battalion commanding officer, Lieutenant Colonel Harry Leech said that 'In the trenches he was afraid and appeared incapable of understanding orders.' Leech added that he was 'of weak intellect' and 'worthless as a soldier'. Another officer said 'he was inclined to be rather stupid'. It is possible that McGeehan had what would now be seen as learning difficulties. In his own time, others in the battalion saw him as a figure of fun. At his court martial McGeehan described how, 'Ever since I joined, all the men have made fun of me, and I don't know what I was doing when I went away. Every time I join the trenches they throw stones at me and pretend it is shrapnel, and they call me all sorts of names.' Judged to have deserted in order to avoid going into battle, a sentence of death was passed on 21 October and confirmed a week later. At 6.16am on 2 November 1916 he was shot by a firing squad at Poperinghe. McGeehan was the only soldier with strong Dublin connections to receive this sentence. In 2006, he was one of the 306 British soldiers 'shot at dawn' for cowardice or desertion to receive a pardon from the government (though the 40 executed for murder were not pardoned). The certificate in McGeehan's record at the National Archives, signed by the Secretary of State for Defence, Des Browne, said, 'The pardon stands as recognition that he was one of many victims of the First World War and that execution was not a fate he deserved.'[61]

As McGeehan awaited execution late in October, the 2nd Royal Dublin Fusiliers went into action on the Somme again, at Le Transloy. There, at 2.30pm on 23 October the battalion advanced without being fired on until they were within ten yards of German lines. Then they came under heavy rifle and machine-gun fire, but being so close to the enemy they were able to throw bombs into the German trenches. As they entered the trenches 'heavy hand to hand fighting ensued, and it was the survival of the fittest', noted the battalion war diary. Nevertheless, the line was gained and held until the battalion was relieved two days later.[62] Writing to Monica Roberts, George Soper said, 'my God we had some fighting to do we used nothing else only Bombs and Bayonets It was proper hand to hand fighting'.[63] At least 47 were dead, including at least 23 Dubliners.[64] Among them was Monkstown-born Second Lieutenant Herbert Lemass, educated at Trinity College, Dublin, and Sandhurst. His second cousin, Seán, had been involved in the Rising and would serve as Taoiseach of the Irish Republic from 1959 to 1966.[65] One result of Herbert Lemass' death, not known at the time, was that in the autumn of 1917 his brother Edwin, already serving in the Army Service Corps, became exempt from infantry service under a ruling that if all sons except one had been killed in action, the remaining son would be exempt from infantry service.[66] The same ruling later saw Royal Field Artillery Captain Hugh Wilson of Carrickmines, withdrawn from the front. One of seven children (five boys and two girls), he had lost a brother in India in 1905, and three other brothers on the Western Front over 1916–17.[67]

Le Transloy was the 2nd Dublin's last major engagement on the Somme in 1916. As part of a reorganisation of many divisions they were transferred into the 16th Division on 15 November.[68] One other Dublin battalion saw action on the Somme that year: the 10th Dublin Fusiliers, the 'Commercials', who arrived in France in mid-August as part of the

63rd (Royal Naval) Division, though not all of the men were novices: Sergeant 14646 Charles 'Charlie' Findlater of Monkstown had joined the 7th Dublins and served with them at Gallipoli (with his brother, Herbert, who was killed) before being wounded. Returning home for treatment he was posted to the 10th Dublins.[69]

The 10th Dublins fought in the final stage of the Battle of the Somme known as the 'Battle of the Ancre', which ran from 13–18 November. The aim was to take a number of targets which had not been secured on 1 July from just north of Serre to east of Grandcourt.[70] Prior to November the 10th Dublins had spent only short periods at the front and when their baptism of fire came on 13 November it was costly. At 5.45am, 24 officers and 469 other ranks advanced with other units of the 63rd Division, targeting Beaucourt. Private 21755 Joseph Isaacs wrote home to his father in Dublin of the landscape they had to cross: 'The field was one mass of shell-holes, some big enough for a hundred or so men to fit into.'[71] Due to heavy mist obscuring them from the Germans, they faced little opposition until they were twenty yards from German lines. At that point machine gunners opened fire as did snipers. The 10th Dublins managed to take the German line, capturing 400 prisoners, suffering 227 casualties while doing so, and holding it until they were relieved on 16 November.[72] Of these men, 90 were dead, including at least 26 Dubliners, one of them the Gallipoli survivor Charlie Findlater.[73] Also dead was Private John O'Brien, who had helped Eoin MacNeill when he was being transported from Dublin to Dartmoor.[74] These were heavy casualties – more than 50 per cent of the strength of the battalion going into battle – and though part of wider gains, the Battle of the Somme was called off on 18 November. From 1 July to 18 November the allied front line had been extended as far as five miles into German territory. Dubliners had been in the battle from the first to its last days, making it their battle as much as that of anyone. But there was nothing like the breakthrough for which Haig had hoped and planned, and for the winter, it was now time to dig in.

13 SNOW AND SAND

...for eight days we marched over the most awful country ever known, marshes, ploughed soft land and high mountains, and rested at night simply by lying on a waterproof sheet with a blanket over, only to waken up stiff and soaked by the heavy dew ...

Lieutenant Harold Mellon, 5th Royal Inniskillings, on the retreat from Kosturino, December 1915[1]

Other Fronts

Throughout the war, Dubliners served and died on fronts and in conditions very different to France and Belgium, and different even to Gallipoli. They experienced extremes of weather, including great heat and monsoons. Drinking water could be scarce, and the terrain unfamiliar. They contended with diseases previously unknown to them and which often proved to be greater hazards – or at least more persistent and costly – than enemy action. Yet features of these fronts were also similar to some conditions on the Western Front: cold, wet and mud.

Mountains were a feature of different fronts in which Dubliners served, not least in Italy where a British force was sent in late 1917 to bolster the Italian fight against Austro-Hungarian forces.[2] Fourteen Dubliners were killed there, three as airmen and three in the Royal Garrison Artillery, the rest in a range of units. Germany's presence in East Africa provided other challenges. Lieutenant Henry McCombie took a roundabout route to service in Uganda from his roots in Monkstown. Aged fourteen in 1895 he was given a silver medal by the city of Dublin for his role in a sea rescue off the coast of Blackrock. Educated at Blackrock College, then King's College, London, he was a keen sailor, and shipwrecked twice, once in the Indian Ocean (in the Maldive Islands for three months) and then again off Nova Scotia. Basic training in the Cameron Highlanders at the outbreak of the Boer War was followed by transfer to the South African Constabulary and then later service in the police in British East Africa. When the First World War began he enlisted in the Uganda Volunteer Reserve, but was not released from the police until early 1915, at which point he was sent to the frontier as an intelligence officer. By that time, the initial German attempt to take British territories had been held off, but raids along the frontier were persistent.[3] In May 1915 McCombie and a small native force of 21 saw off a German raid numbered at 80, killing around one-third of the attackers. However, dangers lurked back at camp a few months later. The *Weekly Irish Times* recounted how McCombie 'and the other officers were at mess: hearing firing going on outside he went to the door, and was shot in the neck by a native policeman who had run amok'.[4]

Of course, Britain's major colonial interests in India were never threatened by the enemy, but the imperial presence in the region still took its toll. Some died through illness. Private 11791 William Leonard of Irishtown was serving in the 21st (Empress of India's) Lancers when he succumbed to the effects of a heatwave near Peshawar in today's Pakistan.[5] Private 20431 John O'Grady of Bishop Street died of heart failure at Thayetmyo in Burma, serving in the 1st Garrison Battalion of the Royal Irish Fusiliers.[6] Another death came more violently. Dr Percy Netterville Gerrard was a captain in the Malay States Volunteers and Colonial Medical Service in Singapore when part of the Indian 5th Light Infantry mutinied on 15 February 1915 for several days, killing 21 service personnel and a similar number of civilians.[7] Gerrard, whose brother Denison had already been killed in Belgium, was among the dead.[8]

Salonika

Beyond these isolated examples of service around the globe, for those soldiers who were not on the Western Front, service other than at Gallipoli was most likely to mean the Middle East (whether Egypt, Palestine or Mesopotamia) or the Salonika front (at Salonika itself or

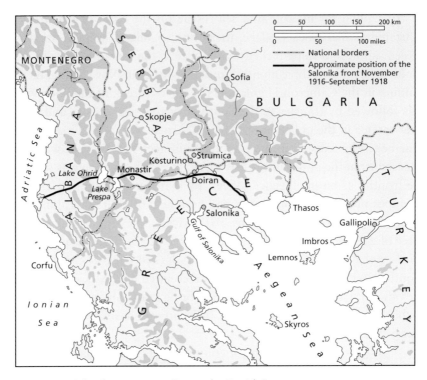

Map 13.1: Salonika, 1916–18. Drawn by David Cox.

in Serbia or Macedonia). Encounters with the Middle East often came very soon after Gallipoli for some men, with the wounded being evacuated there. Dublin teacher Reginald Ford of the 7th Dublins was sent to Alexandria after being wounded. He had been there on his way to Gallipoli and was able to renew his acquaintance with 'a strange combination of Western civilization with the mysterious aloofness of the East'. Ford visited the Pyramids and took a boat trip on the Nile, seeing 'inscrutable looking natives riding on camels'.[9]

However, most of the 10th (Irish) Division, including the 6th and 7th Dublins, did not visit Egypt after Gallipoli. They were taken to the familiar staging post of Mudros where they spent ten days, resting and re-equipping. Cecil Gunning in the 7th Dublins noted, 'We got out of our khaki drill and were issued with warmer clothing which was very welcome because it was now October and as we were feeling a bit washed out we were feeling the cold.'[10] From Mudros they took an overnight trip to Salonika on 9/10 October in crowded ships, disembarking over the course of 10 and 11 October.[11]

The British presence at Salonika arose from Bulgarian mobilisation in late September 1915. After flirting with the Central Powers and the allies, Bulgaria eventually joined the former. With some German support, Bulgaria threatened to invade Serbia (which was already fighting Austria-Hungary), partly because of its own territorial ambitions but also to help create a supply line to aid Turkey. A Greek request for allied troops in early October 1915 was met with the dispatch of British and French soldiers from Gallipoli. Much of the 10th Division was among the first to arrive, with the 6th and 7th Dublins in the very first shipment.[12]

Drury woke early on 10 October and 'saw the most magnificent morning with Mount Olympus on our Port hand. The top was covered with snow which was tinted salmon colour with the morning sun. No wonder the old Greeks thought and wrote such a lot about it.'[13] James McKenna of the 6th Dublins was from Carrickmacross in County Monaghan, but was studying at University College, Dublin, when he applied for a commission in the Dublin Fusiliers on the third day of the war.[14] He had been at Gallipoli with the battalion, but only began writing a diary as they headed for Salonika, keeping it for a few months. He recorded his first impressions while moored off the town that it 'looked awfully pretty in the distance'. However on landing, he found it looked different closer up: 'Hell of a march to camp; about 4 miles. Town damn dirty, also inhabitants.' His thoughts rapidly turned to the female population: 'Damn few women about the place, any there are have got older women or somebody like that with them. Saw some damn smart women but of course they are snapped up long ago by the French officers.'[15] Others had more practical concerns, with Cecil Gunning noting of the 7th Dublins' 'camp on the edge of town' that 'Tents were provided for us but they were few and far between. So long as the weather remained dry a good many of us slept in the open but when the weather broke as it very soon did the congestion in the tents was dreadful.' Equipment was left outside, only to sink in mud, and the effects of dysentery became more pronounced. Meanwhile, the arrival of conscripts from England did not necessarily help morale in the 7th Dublins. Gunning noted that with new arrivals there was a renewed effort from officers to instil discipline through marches and inspections. The conscripts were 'full of the joys of life' while all this took place whereas the Gallipoli veterans 'plod[d]ed along weary and washed-out'.[16] After three weeks near Salonika itself they headed north towards the enemy to relieve the French who were holding the front line.

Kosturino

The 6th and 7th Dublins began to move to the front with 30th Brigade on 28 and 29 October travelling, largely by train, nearly sixty miles north to Bogdanci, a village now in the Former Yugoslav Republic of Macedonia but which was then in Serbia. Rain fell heavily, and when the time came to march the 6th Dublins' war diary noted 'Road very indifferent, in some parts entirely washed away by floods, and in other parts under water.'[17] Drury had a horse but the treacherous conditions meant that he preferred to lead it. During the march he saw 'unfortunate natives' who 'were streaming along the road southwards all eager to get away from the invading Bulgar, and trying to carry away as much of their goods as possible'.[18] James McKenna noted, 'Reach our destination very tired and wet. Have some food and sleep. Damn cold.' Some of the men were soon supporting a French attack on the village of Memisli (two and a half miles south of Kosturino) on 3 November with 50 men from 6th Dublins, led by McKenna, carrying ammunition on mules up to the front. He described a 'Hell of a climb up and over three mountains'.[19]

For the 6th Dublins, much of the rest of November saw companies rotating to hold front-line positions, often under shell fire. A major challenge was obtaining food and water as the terrain made it hard to reach the front line with provisions. McKenna noted with some bitterness on 7 November, '6th Dublins only English Battalion doing any work and it's about time some other Battalion came up and did some. Rest of Brigade only a mile away and have done nothing since they arrived.' This was, in fact, not quite true, since the 7th Dublins were also holding the line from 1 to 11 November, but in a different position, so McKenna's belief was perhaps a reflection of poor communications in the area.[20] Drury was also disillusioned, noting on 19 November, 'Nothing special doing; indeed I don't know what we are hanging about here for. It doesn't seem possible to help the Serbs any more by staying in the country and it looks as if we might easily get into a bad mess considering there are large numbers of Bulgars behind us.'[21]

By late November 1915 it became clear that the Bulgarians were preparing to advance. The British and French general staff realised that they could not hold the positions they had, not least because of poor communications hindering the use of artillery, and by 2 December they had planned a general retreat. On 5 December, battalions were informed that it would take place over night on 11 and 12 December.[22] Meanwhile, the weather worsened, with snow falling and low temperatures. While in the line at Kajali, 4 miles south of Kosturino, the 7th Dublins 'had to endure great hardships, and hospital admission increased enormously'.[23] For Drury, cold was a constant concern, sometimes the main subject of his diary entry. McKenna's note on 22 November was typical: 'Very cold morning. Absolutely frozen. Rum issue which warms us up a bit.'[24]

As a prelude to a major attack, British lines were shelled on 30 November and 1 December in ways which suggested the Bulgarian artillery was working out its range for a major onslaught. Both the 6th and 7th Dublins were on relief in billets during that bombardment but D Company of the 7th Dublins were back in the line by 4 December and came under similar ranging fire.[25] Nearly a week later, on 6 December, the Battle of Kosturino began. The 10th Division was largely situated between Lake Doiran and, a few miles to the north-west, Kosturino. One company of the 7th Dublins was on the left of the line near Kosturino, but the rest of the battalion was held in reserve for 30th Brigade. The 6th Dublins were in divisional reserve, reflecting the fact that they had suffered much in their time at the front in late November and early December.[26] Also on the Division's left, Dubliners were serving in the 5th Connaught Rangers.

The 5th Connaughts (alongside the 10th Hampshires) had been in front-line trenches since 29 November having initially been due only for a three-day period there. After nearly a week they were tired and suffering due to the weather, and were told that they could be relieved on 6 December, but would have to return to the front by 10 December. Knowing that that would involve 'a very stiff climb up from Tatarli' (8 miles south of Kosturino), and that an attack was imminent, the commanding officers of both battalions asked to stay where they were until the main retreat.[27] It was a fateful decision. The Bulgarian lines opened rifle fire at 7.15am on 6 December, followed half an hour later by the artillery. That continued for several hours until it became more intense at 3pm as the infantry began to advance, massing in gullies out of sight. Attacks in the evening were repulsed but at 6.30am the next morning the Bulgarians secured 'Rocky Peak' which overlooked some of the line held by the 10th Division. That high ground gave the Bulgarians a crucial advantage and they sent in wave after wave of infantry. In positions named after places local to Dublin such as the Hill of Howth, Dollymount and Brayhead, the 5th Connaughts lost heavily. By 2.45pm B and C companies were 'practically wiped out by the enfilade fire' coming from positions captured by the Bulgarians. They had pierced the lines on Brayhead and were firing both ways along the Connaughts' trenches. With the line broken, at around 3pm the battalion began to retreat.[28] Among 98 members of the 5th Connaughts who lost their lives on 7 December were 6 Dubliners.[29]

Sections of the 6th and 7th Dublins were called up from reserve on the first two days of the battle. They mainly plugged gaps in the line following Bulgarian attacks which were targeted intensively at specific parts of the line before moving on to others. This confused officers, who expected attacks to be more sustained. The bemused adjutant of the 7th Dublins simply noted, 'Sometimes the fighting seemed more severe at one part of the line, and sometimes at another.'[30] The Bulgarians' chief advantage over the allies was superior artillery. They also had the advantage of the terrain which could help conceal their movements. One officer, Lieutenant Harold Mellon,[31] serving in the 5th Inniskillings, described to his father in Rathgar how he watched the Bulgarians 'through my glasses coming over the mountains in small bands and disappearing in the scrub and massing in the valleys'.[32] Once a major onslaught had been launched it was only a matter of time before the allies would have to withdraw. Drury wondered if this was clear to his superiors, noting on 7 December, 'The G.O.C. 31st Brigade seems perfectly useless, and when I saw him he was mooning about as if he didn't know nor care what was going on. He doesn't seem to realize that we are fighting about 10 times our number of Bulgars, and that only by keeping wide awake will he get his troops safely away.'[33]

Not until 8 December, while covering a general retreat, was either battalion engaged in heavy fighting, with the 6th Dublins facing a Bulgarian attack at Crête Rivet, four miles south of Kosturino. Two of the 6th Dublins' companies, A and C came under heavy attack on their right flank, the battalion war diary noting that the Dublins 'held on all forenoon', though some were 'unable to get away when Bulgars took ridge'.[34] The Bulgarians were aided by the fog which meant that firing blind was sometimes the only option for defenders. Drury noted how, on receiving a message that their enemy was massing in the fog,

> We hastily formed up the men and fired 5 rounds rapid along the ground into the fog ... We must have got a lot of Bulgars as we could hear their shouts and groans. The Bulgar then charged and we gave them another 5 rounds rapid as they loomed up in the fog. Some of our fellows even got at them with the bayonet. The old Bulgar was so shaken up that he retired into the fog to pull himself together a bit.

At that point, Drury's company retreated.[35] They had achieved their goal of providing some cover for other units before joining in the retreat themselves. The route back was arduous. Harold Mellon wrote how, 'for eight days we marched over the most awful country ever known, marshes, ploughed soft land and high mountains, and rested at night simply by lying on a waterproof sheet with a blanket over, only to waken up stiff and soaked by the heavy dew, and the two days before we reached Camp it rained for 24 hours.'[36] The men were tired after more than a month of hardship in Serbia, but by 12 December the entire 10th Division had reached Greek territory where the British army began to dig in around Salonika.

In the publicity which followed, the 10th Division was given credit for making the retreat possible: 'TENTH (IRISH) DIVISION TO THE RESCUE: BRITISH & FRENCH ARMIES SAVED' proclaimed the *Irish Independent*. The *Evening Herald* hailed the 'THE FAMOUS IRISH 10TH DIVISION Magnificent Stand That Saved the Allied Armies in Macedonia.' Both newspapers cited the War Office statement that, 'It was largely due to the gallantry of the troops, and especially of the Munster Fusiliers, the Dublin Fusiliers and the Connaught Rangers, that the withdrawal was successfully accomplished.'[37]

A month later the *Evening Herald* published an account of Kosturino from an unnamed Dublin officer of the 6th Dublins. Describing the retreat, he spoke of good morale because 'Remember we were a battalion of Dublin men practically, and all of us knew each other, and each other's families, and we could encourage each other in different ways.'[38] Certainly there were a large number of Dubliners in the 6th Dublins: of their 27 dead during their time in Serbia,[39] exactly one-third (9) had some Dublin connection, and another 7 were from another part of Ireland. Among them was Captain Charles Martin of Monkstown. He was initially declared missing rather than dead, and when his mother found that out, she began writing a diary which she hoped he would one day read and which included her account of the Easter Rising.[40] It ran from 1 January to 25 May 1916, its purpose never to be fulfilled.[41] Within the 7th Dublins, only 6 men died in Serbia itself, one of them a Dubliner. He was Private 13849 Robert Porter, whose parents lived in Clontarf. A letter home from a comrade, Lance Corporal 13847 Frederick McCabe, told how on 8 December 'Poor young Porter was hit with a shell and killed. Only a few seconds before he was talking about what he would do when we came home.'[42]

There were men from far beyond the Dublin area in the 7th Dublins, yet something of its 'Pals' character remained with men from the ranks rising to be officers in the battalion. Jasper Brett enlisted as one of the original Pals – a notable rugby star.[43] He was recommended for a commission while serving as a private at Gallipoli in September 1915 and took up his role at Salonika after spending some time in hospital suffering from enteritis.[44] Tipperary-born Allen Guest first joined the Royal Dublin Fusiliers in 1893 and served in the Boer War. By 1905 he was living in Dublin, and served as a reservist in the 4th Dublins from 1904 until June 1914 when his period of engagement ended, by which time he was a Company Sergeant Major. Joining the 7th Dublins in September 1914 he won the DCM at Suvla Bay and in July 1916 was commissioned in the battalion, leading men with whom he had enlisted as a Pal.[45]

The Salonika Front, 1916–17

The 7th Dublins emerged from Serbia relatively unscathed with around 900 other ranks and virtually a full complement of officers. However, the 6th Dublins were well below strength for the first half of 1916: when they left Serbia they had 9 officers and 417 other ranks, less than half the number with which they had entered the country, and they only approached full strength in early July.[46] Harold Mellon wrote of the relief of being out of Serbia. His 5th Inniskillings arrived in camp 'a bearded, dirty, torn lot of ruffians', immediately noticing how much warmer it was than in the mountains. On 29 December 1915 he described how 'The days here are wonderful, just at present, lovely sunshine and bright, just like an early Spring day in the "old country".'[47]

The Salonika front gained a reputation for inactivity, with the British force dubbed the 'Gardeners of Salonika' (as they did cultivate the land).[48] For most of the first half of the year the 10th Division laboured in trenches, on roads, building bridges and constructing drains. Occasional training was carried out from January, and by May it must have been clear that the division would be in Greece for some time, since the officers began Greek lessons. Special events were few and far between: St Patrick's Day saw a church service in the morning followed by sports in the afternoon. Competitions included a tug-of-war, machine-gun and transport contests and athletics events. In April, both rugby and football were played between battalions.[49] When summer came, such activities had less appeal: Drury noted on 5 July, 'Absolutely the hottest day I ever felt. The full heat of the sun is absolutely stunning and the air is so hot that it seems hard to breathe.'[50] Drury fell victim to malaria, leaving Salonika at the end of July, first for hospital in Malta then in Ireland.[51]

From arriving at Salonika until September, although disease continued to deplete the ranks, just 8 men died in the 6th Dublins, none of them killed in action, while from January to mid-August 1916 the 7th Dublins lost only 5.[52] The battalions were close to possible action when they moved to the front line in late May, holding and improving trenches and constructing strongpoints – one was called 'Dublin Castle'. However, not until late August, when both the 6th and 7th Dublins were posted to the front at the River Struma, were they in much danger, taking part in patrols and raids to gather intelligence about a feared Bulgarian attack.[53]

On 23 September, the 7th Dublins were part of an attack on the village of Karadzakoj Bala (about 100 miles north-east of Salonika), the orders for 250 men being to capture and burn it before retiring, alongside simultaneous operations close by. Following a one-hour bombardment, lines of 100 and 150 men, 100 yards apart, moved out across a front of about 350 yards at 4pm. They faced no opposition from about 800 yards, but when 700 yards from the village they came under a hail of machine-gun and rifle fire. They managed to advance another 300 yards or so but that meant they were under enfilade fire from Bulgarian positions. By 6.30pm they had retreated. As a result of the action 18 men died, with nearly 50 wounded. The village was taken five days later by 81st and 29th Brigades, with the 7th Dublins in support carrying ammunition.[54]

On 3 October, a further operation took place which was to be the last of the Salonika campaign for the 6th and 7th Dublins. Ordered to take the village of Zenikoj, just north of Karadzakoj Bala, they moved from the Karadzakoj area at 1.45am, crossing the Struma by the Jungle Island Bridge at 2.30am alongside the 7th Munsters. An artillery bombardment preceded the attack for about an hour prior to the village being captured by 6.20am. The 7th Dublins and 6th Munsters followed to consolidate defensive positions. Opposition was initially light, but on consolidating the village heavy fire came from Bulgarian lines on three separate occasions, at 9am, 12 noon and 4pm. The next day saw heavy shelling from 9am to 4pm but the village was held. As a result of the action 34 men were dead in the 6th Dublins and 25 in the 7th.[55] Across the whole division, 189 died between 30 September and 6 October.[56] Among the wounded – due to a shrapnel ball which pierced his helmet – was 2nd Lieutenant Francis Malley from Glasnevin. Part of a new draft for the 6th Dublins, he had originally joined the ranks of the 7th Leinsters in November 1914, before being commissioned in July 1915. He had arrived in Salonika in early September, so had been there only a month when wounded. For him, rapid evacuation to a hospital ship followed. Three weeks later, his wound was oozing pus and his scalp had to be opened to allow the flow. He survived, but saw out most of the rest the war in the 3rd Dublins, not fit for active service, before a transfer to the King's African Rifles in the summer of 1918.[57] His brother, Ernie O'Malley, became known for action elsewhere for a different cause.[58]

There was no repeat of such fighting at Salonika for the 10th Division, though they remained there for another year around the Struma Valley. During that time at Salonika the 7th Dublins lost 20 men and the 6th Dublins 18, around one-third of the deaths being due to illness. Only on five days between mid-October 1916 and their withdrawal from Salonika in September 1917 did the 6th or 7th Dublins lose men killed in action.[59] Days were taken up with similar activities to those carried out in much of 1916, with danger coming in the occasional patrol and sporadic enemy shellfire. In November 1916 the 7th Dublins had time to worry about the problems caused by stray dogs, with a corporal appointed as 'dog-killer'.[60]

Emmet Dalton (promoted to lieutenant on 1 July 1917) arrived in Salonika in July 1917 as the 10th Division's time there came to an end. He had recovered from wounds incurred on the Somme and completed his role training recruits in Dublin. He still did not join the 7th Dublins, the battalion he had originally sought to join, and was instead posted to the 6th Leinsters on 10 July. Dalton saw no action at Salonika but like Drury he succumbed to malaria which dogged him in months to come.[61] Back with his battalion in the summer of 1917, Drury once again suffered from malaria, and while in hospital outside Salonika he witnessed smoke from an accidental fire which destroyed two-thirds of the town.[62] In 1918 the British would fight again on the Salonika front, but on 2 September 1917 the 7th Dublins embarked for Egypt (followed a week later by the 6th) on their way to another theatre of war where they once again faced the Turks: Palestine.[63]

Suez and Mesopotamia

The 10th Division's engagement in Palestine in 1917–18 came after significant earlier conflicts in the Middle East against Turkey. A crucial interest for both Britain and France was the Suez Canal, vital for the route to India. Britain defended the canal from Egypt, but at the outbreak of war Turkey immediately deployed troops from Palestine in the sparsely policed Sinai desert, eventually concentrating around Beershaba from which an attack was launched in late January 1915. Though some Turks briefly crossed the canal they were repulsed by around 30,000 troops (mainly Indians) from a 70,000 strong force in Egypt.[64] Among the defenders was Lieutenant Henry Greene, whose parents lived in Clontarf and who was killed in action at Gallipoli later in the year. He had followed an Indian army career after education at public school in Cheltenham and then Trinity College. His initial service in the war was with the 92nd Punjabis in the Suez Canal area from November 1914 until July 1915 when he joined the unit of the Gurkha Rifles in which he was to be killed.[65]

The Suez area accounted for Dublin's oldest military death of the war: Major Joshua Fielding, once of the 4th (Royal Irish) Dragoon Guards, was a Rathgar Road resident who had fought in the Anglo–Egyptian war of 1882 and was later the Adjutant of the Royal Military Hospital at Kilmainham. Having been born in Merton, Surrey in December 1841 he was seventy-six years old when he died at Ismailia on 21 January 1917 while serving with the British Red Cross Society (which was formally considered as war service). Despite his age, his war had not been a comfortable one, having been captured by the Turks in Palestine (with one of his sons) only to escape after several months in prison in Jerusalem.[66]

In Mesopotamia, a British force was involved from November 1915 to protect British oil concessions in southern Persia. Basra was secured with relative ease but when a push was made on Kut-al-Amara, British and Indian forces became dangerously overstretched. On 7 December they were surrounded at Kut by Turkish forces and a siege began. In one attempt at relieving the siege, the Battle of Hanna on 21 January 1916, the 1st Connaught Rangers, which included many Dubliners, took part in the 3rd (Lahore) Division, recently arrived from the Western Front. Meanwhile, Lieutenant Arthur Hill Neale of the 1st Brahmans also served there, attached to the 6th Jat Light Infantry in the 7th (Meerut) Division. Neale's mother lived in Ormond Road, Dublin, and he had been to school at St Columba's in Rathfarnham, then attended Trinity College before joining the Indian Army in which he saw early action in France before going to Mesopotamia in December 1915.[67]

The attempt to relieve Kut through Hanna was a disaster. Physical conditions were difficult. The 1st Connaughts' official history recorded how 'The morning was bitterly cold, the wind blowing down strongly from the snow-capped Pusht-i-Kuh mountains on the Persian border not many miles away, sweeping across the treeless plain and cutting like a knife.' Meanwhile, heavy rain turned the ground into mud, while telegraphic communication broke down as signallers were hit and telephones did not work. Despite the Jats and another unit taking part of the Turkish front line, accurate rifle fire prevented advance in other areas, and they then faced counter-attacks before being forced to withdraw to British lines. There were nearly 3,000 casualties among the attackers.[68] Arthur Neale was among those killed.[69] The 1st Connaughts lost 53 men in total, of whom at least 7 were Dubliners. Just two of the 53 (and none of the Dubliners) have a known grave, the rest being commemorated on the Basra Memorial, erected on the edge of the city of Basra in 1929 but moved further away from the city in its entirety in 1997 due to political sensitivities, and now resting in a battleground from the Gulf War of 1991.[70] Later attempts at the relief of Kut also failed and it eventually surrendered on 29 April 1916 in a humiliation later seen as rivalling the surrender of Singapore in 1942.[71] Among those who became prisoners of the Turks was Driver 55904 James Sweeney of the Royal Field Artillery's 76th Battery, whose parents lived at Thomas Street in Dublin. He died as a prisoner just two months later, on 30 June, and was buried in Baghdad.[72] The 1st Connaughts remained in Mesopotamia until April 1918.[73] By that time another 25 Dubliners had lost their lives as a result of service in the battalion in Mesopotamia.

Egypt and Palestine

After their departure from Salonika, the 7th Dublins arrived in Alexandria on 6 September 1917 and the 6th nearly a week later. On arrival, both battalions left within a day by train for Moascar (about 60 miles north of Suez), the first of several stops along the Suez Canal, where they spent the rest of month, mainly training, before heading for Rafa on the northern coast of the Sinai peninsula. Training was thorough, including the use of runners and how to judge direction of fire, in addition to more routine practice of methods of

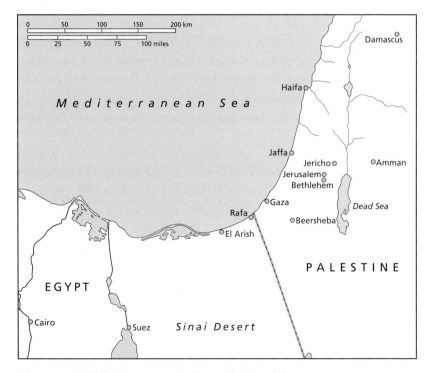

Map 13.2: Middle East, 1917–18. Drawn by David Cox.

attack. In Rafa for the whole of October, disease struck: having embarked at Alexandria with over 800 men, the battalion's fighting strength was down to nearer 600 six weeks later, despite having seen no action at all. Yet there was still the pleasure of swimming in the sea which the 7th Dublins found 'remarkably salty & buoyant and quite warm'. Their greatest challenge was a basic one: 'The principal difficulty everywhere appears to be water, more so the means of conveying it to places off the Railway.'[74] Consequently, water was piped in many places and significant attention given to guarding supplies to avoid the problems faced at Gallipoli.[75]

Held in reserve during the Battle of Beersheba on 31 October 1917, and the third Battle of Gaza in the days that followed, neither battalion took any part in the successful onslaught on both towns.[76] However, at least one Dubliner was involved in action shortly after, in another unit. When he enlisted in November 1915, Second Lieutenant Kevin Brayden was the London correspondent of the *Freeman's Journal*, born in Dublin with his parents living in Palmerston Road. His experience of service was a Dublin-diaspora story: enlisting in London he trained with the Artists' Rifles and was then commissioned in June 1916. He went to the Middle East in July 1917 with the 2/18th London Regiment (London Irish Rifles) as part of 60th Division. Held in reserve during the Battle of Beersheba, and then resting in the town in the days which followed, the battalion was in action on 6 November.[77] Writing to his newspaper on 19 November 1917 he described the campaign in southern Palestine surviving on 'a minimum of water'. The fighting itself 'was typical old-fashioned open warfare like what they had in South Africa, at least it was so after the taking of Beersheba', and mobile warfare was indeed part of the plan of General Allenby commanding the Egyptian Expeditionary Force.[78] However, Brayden was dead just a month later, killed in action on 23 December, in an attack on a Turkish position at Khurbet Adaseh outside Jerusalem. Assembling at 3am for an attack at dawn (just before 6am), the battalion faced machine-gun fire from the outset of their attempted advance. Fighting continued for six hours but the hill was not taken and the battalion withdrew having suffered around 130 casualties.[79]

The 6th Dublins relieved the 60th Division in positions outside Gaza on 8 November. The remainder of the month and well into December saw them and the 7th Dublins mainly engaged in working parties creating and enhancing defensive positions in the area around Gaza. During that time they came under fire from Turkish snipers, but also supported occasional attacks and took part in patrols.[80] The 6th and 7th Dublins took no part in the capture of Jerusalem, but provided two representatives each (other ranks) for Allenby's ceremonial entry into the city on 11 December 1917.[81] Drury noted, 'It is hard to imagine the Holy City in Christian hands again after so many hundreds of years.'[82]

Dangers lurked in unexpected places. Eight Dubliners died at sea on 30 December 1917 when the *Aragon*, the transport ship on which the 6th Dublins arrived in Egypt in September, was hit by a torpedo fired by German submarine *U-34* while anchored outside the harbour of Alexandria. Four of the dead were from the 7th Dublins, one from the 6th, two from the 1st Leinsters and one from the 1st Royal Irish Regiment. A total of 610 people, of whom 380 were soldiers, were killed. The next day, the *Osmanieh* was sunk by the same submarine: 198 people were killed, of whom 76 were soldiers. Whether the men were on the ships as wounded, or were travelling home on leave, is unknown, but they are all remembered on the Chatby Memorial in Alexandria.[83]

For the remainder of their time in Palestine, the two battalions took part in just one major action each. The 7th Dublins were involved in the 'Defence of Jerusalem', temporarily attached to 29th Brigade. There on 27 December the 7th Dublins were in close support to the 1st Leinsters. Three companies were deployed at different stages, one capturing a ridge known as Shamrock Hill. Four men were dead, including Lieutenant George Hare, originally an enlisted man in D Company of the 7th Dublins on 14 September 1915, commissioned a year later and remaining in the 7th Dublins. He was hit by a sniper after Shamrock Hill had been captured.[84]

Ten weeks later the 6th Dublins took part in the Battle of Tell 'Asur which followed the British capture of Jericho and the driving of the Turks across the River Jordan, the principal aim being to capture high ground.[85] In reserve on the first day of the battle, the 6th Dublins joined the fray on its second, 10 March. Though they came under some machine-gun and enfilade rifle fire the battalion captured its targets with only 'slight opposition' and suffered no fatalities.[86] Drury described how the battalion had to climb up a hill to their target: 'It was impossible to see over any terrace to the one above, and every moment we expected a shower of stick grenades on our heads.' It seemed as if the Turkish forces were putting up little resistance and withdrew rapidly. Drury noted how the 6th Dublins on reaching what they thought was their goal were 'laughing a little shame-facedly as if our little bit of sword rattling had been rather overdone. We were sure Johnny Turk would have waited for us and put up some scrap, and everyone was disgusted to find we had only to say "Boo" and he ran away.' However, it transpired that there was another crest and on that it seemed the Turks might offer more resistance. Yet once again they retreated almost on sighting the 6th Dublins, who then consolidated overnight.[87]

Emmet Dalton had meanwhile seen less action with the 6th Leinsters who had arrived in Egypt in mid-September and then played a supporting role at Gaza in late October and then in the advance on Jerusalem.[88] Regularly suffering from bouts of malaria, Dalton became assistant adjutant of the 6th Leinsters, with a range of administrative duties, and kept a diary from mid-January to early April 1918, giving some insight into the monotony and boredom of daily life in Palestine, especially while stationed at Suffa. Contact with home through letters was important, though some, he noted, took as long as four months to reach him.[89] Football offered some leisure, and he began to study the Russian language.[90] He also attended Mass regularly on a Sunday at 7.30am.[91] Yet the rain was a serious inconvenience, especially since he was living in a bivouac.[92] In early February Dalton became battalion Intelligence Officer which gave him a more varied workload, including map-making and reconnaissance.[93] Being exposed to news from the various fronts of the war made him wonder 'when all this perfect Hell will end'. He noted that he felt 'rotten' and that 'I don't think I would feel so fed up as I do, if I could only see the folks at home occasionally', while noting that there were men serving with him who had not been home for over two years. He showed signs of depression which only lifted when he took on instruction and intelligence duties at the Army Sniping School in El Arish. His mood was lightened by being able to play golf and getting a week's leave in Cairo.[94]

Some Dubliners saw action in the Middle East campaign towards its end in a range of units. The last two men with a Dublin connection killed in the Middle East before the Mudros Armistice of 30 October 1918 were both, coincidentally, serving in the 1/1st Dorset Yeomanry (Queen's Own). On 11 October, Meath-born Private 73062 George Grey whose parents lived in Phibsborough and who had originally served in the South Irish Horse, died of pneumonia.[95] On 13 October, Lieutenant John Mason, whose wife lived in Northumberland Road, died of wounds received in action about two weeks earlier, on 27 September.[96] A month later the Turks were driven from Palestine.[97]

However, mass involvement by Dubliners was over by the summer of 1918. Although the 10th Division remained in the Middle East until the war's end, the division was significantly reorganised in late April and May 1918 with all but three of the Irish battalions within it (regular units which had not been part of the original division) replaced by Indian ones. The 7th Dublins left the 10th Division on 30 April and the 6th on 27 May. The 7th travelled to France in early June where 26 of its 33 officers and 788 of its 814 other ranks were transferred to the 2nd Dublins. Its remaining cadre joined the 11th Royal Irish Fusiliers, a newly formed battalion in the 16th (Irish) Division.[98] Remaining in Egypt until early July, the 6th Dublins were destined for service in the 66th (2nd East Lancashire) Division on the Western Front.[99] Emmet Dalton, serving in the 6th Leinsters, made a similar journey, as his battalion headed for the same division before being disbanded in July. Dalton saw out the war in the 2nd Leinsters.[100] Though the men who had served in the 10th (Irish) Division fought to the end elsewhere, by the summer of 1918 the division was effectively no longer an Irish unit.

14 ATTRITION: 1916-17

*...semi fatal encounters shadow one's appearance and a strange
tyrant look indicates warfare in one's face...*
> Private 19543 Harry Loughlin, 1st Royal Dublin Fusiliers,
> 5 March 1917[1]

The Toll of War

In the wake of the Battle of the Somme and the repercussions of
the Easter Rising, changes in Dublin's engagement with the war were
seen in four key areas from late summer 1916 into 1917 and the summer
of that year. One was a renewal of recruiting efforts to fill gaps in the
ranks. Two others – mounting front-line losses and manifestations of
the war on the home front – demonstrated how the war was increasingly
attritional. The other, the release in June 1917 of the remaining Easter
Rising prisoners, gave a new impulse to republican politics in the city.

For soldiers, the war was taking an emotional toll. Private
19543 Harry Loughlin of the 1st Dublins wrote to Monica Roberts
in March 1917 of how 'semi fatal encounters shadow one's appearance
and a strange tyrant look indicates warfare in one's face'.[2] Rugby
international Jasper Brett of the 7th Dublins was diagnosed with
'neurasthenia' (shell shock) in April 1916 and was in hospital at
Salonika for about six weeks before being sent back to his unit.
A month later, on 21 June, he was sent back to hospital, his record
noting gastritis, monomania, melancholia and confusional insanity.
The severity of his mental illness was recognised and on 22 July he

was sent to England on the Hospital Ship *Valdivia*. Brett spent time at a psychiatric hospital for officers in Richmond, Surrey, before being discharged and sent home to Kingstown in January 1917. On the evening of 4 February, having gone for a walk, his body was found on track in a railway tunnel near Dalkey. The inquest revealed that he had 'committed suicide by placing himself on the rails ... the ten past ten p.m. train from Dalkey & Bray passing over him and severing the head from the body'. The inquest concluded that he should not have been discharged from hospital as 'he should not have been at large'. Brett's father said that his son was distraught at having been discharged: 'He was a soldier to the tips of his fingers & as brave as a lion & it simply broke his heart to be turned out in mufti.' A service medal arrived two weeks after his discharge, and he was wearing it when he died, but this was after he had been 'insulted as a "slacker" in a London Restaurant because he was turned out without anything to show he had served'. Brett's father made a claim for £2,000 in compensation for loss of earnings, but his claim was met with a gratuity of £69 and 15 shillings, plus remission of death duties.[3]

Some families felt the effects of multiple losses, and the fear that further might follow. With a fatality rate of 12 per cent across the British army, it was, on a purely statistical level, a very unlucky family which had anyone killed unless it had at least ten members serving. Yet many were especially hard hit. In Dublin's Golden Lane, Julia Carter lost her husband, Private 18816 Joseph Carter, on 6 September 1916 in the 9th Royal Dublin Fusiliers. Eight months later news came through that her son, Private 40323 John Carter was missing in the 10th Dublins since 24 April 1917. In July 1918 she was still seeking definite news in a newspaper appeal. His body was never found.[4] Some deaths occurred very close to each other with news reaching families almost at the same time. Lieutenant Arnold Fletcher of Shankill, County Dublin, serving in the Machine Gun Corps, died in hospital in Rouen on 30 April 1917 after an operation to amputate a leg. His father, George, was with him, and did not then know that just two days before he had lost another son, 2nd Lieutenant Donald Fletcher, serving in Macedonia with the 6th Leinsters.[5]

The losses for Michael and Mary Brennock of Shelbourne Road were more spread over time. Their first came in November 1914 when their 23-year-old son, Private 3258 William Brennock, was killed serving in the 1st Irish Guards.[6] A second son, Stoker 1719U Patrick

Brennock, was killed on the HMS *Europa* in August 1915. A third lost his life in February 1917 serving in the 1st Dublins, Sergeant 20432 Thomas Brennock.[7] Lance Corporal 9929 James Naylor of East James Place was killed in action with the 1st Royal Irish Rifles on 12 March 1915. His brother, Private 14578 John Naylor of Great Brunswick Street, was killed in the 8th Dublins on 29 April, his wife Margaret being wounded during the Rising on the same day. She died two days later.[8] A third brother, Private 24841 William Naylor of Lad Lane made it to within one month of the war's end, killed in the 1st Dublins on 14 October 1918.[9]

The Geraghty family of Middle Gardiner Street were a microcosm of Dublin's service across regiments. Six brothers, all privates, served in four different Irish battalions and in two English regiments.[10] Three of them were killed. 8019 Christopher Geraghty lost his life in April 1915 with the 2nd Dublins, and 23842 Francis Geraghty in June 1916 in the 9th. 5012 James Geraghty was killed in the 1st Irish Guards in December 1917.[11] The other three brothers were discharged before the war's end: 7485 Joseph Geraghty in the 1st North Staffordshires was unfit for war service in May 1915,[12] while 7365 John Geraghty of the 1st Royal Irish Rifles was discharged in October 1917 after service aggravated a glandular problem making one of his legs swell.[13] The other brother, 17150 Patrick of the 1st (and later 1/4th) King's Own (Royal Lancaster) Regiment was discharged in April 1918, probably wounded.[14]

Other individual cases brought home possible effects of war. In January 1917 the newspapers reported the tragic story of Private 5980 Robert Storey. He served in France with the 1st Royal Irish Rifles and was wounded. He was home on leave in early 1917, staying with his brother-in-law at Myrtle Street. His wife, Jane, and 6-year-old son were in temporary accommodation in North Strand, where it seems it was not possible for Storey to stay. Instead, Jane and her son visited Storey each day and were said to be on good terms. At about 5.20pm on 14 January, with Storey due to leave Dublin on a 6pm train, the Storeys left the kitchen where they had been having tea, apparently to say goodbye in the parlour. However, screaming followed and Jane Storey rushed from the parlour covered in blood, with a five inch cut on her throat. As she fell and died, Storey was observed to fall dead into an armchair having cut his own throat. The child had seen everything.

The coroner concluded that 'The only explanation to offer was that the deceased soldier had got a fit of insanity.'[15]

War in the Air

The air war became more visible as the death toll rose. Across the war, around 7,000 Irishmen served with either the Royal Flying Corps, the Royal Air Force (which replaced the RFC in April 1918), or the Royal Naval Air Service. Around 500 were killed.[16] As regards Dublin, 1,098 men can be identified as having served in the RFC or RAF at some point, and another 46 in the RNAS. Of these, at least 67 transferred into a flying unit after service elsewhere, usually the army; 90 of the Dubliners died. In line with the steady growth of air combat, none of the dead were killed in 1914, just 6 in 1915 and only 10 in 1916. However, in 1917 30 were killed, and 39 were dead in 1918, with another 5 over 1919–21 but listed by the Commonwealth War Graves Commission as First World War deaths.[17]

There were some obvious attractions to being in the Royal Flying Corps. Orlando Beater transferred from the Royal Dublin Fusiliers in July 1917. He had two weeks of leave, trained for a month before further leave, and was posted to France in mid-September. Training was so short because he was an observer rather than a pilot.[18] While awaiting posting to a squadron, having arrived at St Omer, Beater found a more relaxed atmosphere than in the army: 'It is rather amusing the different garbs some of the pilots affect at breakfast. One extraordinary sportsman comes in tastefully attired in none too fresh pyjamas, dressing gown and pumps.'[19] Yet the basic flying conditions were tough. Posted to 55 Squadron, flying in De Havilland 4s and carrying out bombing and reconnaissance, Beater noted of his first sortie, 'We were up at sixteen thousand feet and it was very cold indeed: the wind pressure was simply terrific. My fingers ached, and I lost two valuable silk handkerchiefs, which were literally sucked out of my overcoat pocket, and disappeared in a second'.[20]

Flying was initially quite frequent for Beater, usually every few days, with regular encounters with the Germans. However, low cloud and heavy rain prevented forays into enemy territory. In September 1917 Beater recorded thirteen and a half hours of flying, followed by just over fifteen in October. Although in constant danger while in the air, if only because of the risk of engine failure, few men in the infantry

faced little more than half a day of danger each month.[21] In November
and December operations became few and far between, with just three
bombing missions undertaken, twice to Mannheim and once to
Kaiserslautern, before more frequent missions were undertaken from
January 1918.[22]

Yet when danger came there was often little chance of escape,
and in some cases men were not even in combat. Second Lieutenant
Frederick Hoey of Ballsbridge was killed in an air accident while
training at Yatesbury in Wiltshire on 7 June 1917. He appears to
have lost control of the aircraft while coming out of clouds in
a spinning nose dive at 2,000 feet, with the engine full on. The aircraft,
an Avro 504A, hit trees and then overturned on the roof of a house.[23]
There were also hazards on the ground. Patrick 'Paddy' Devan, whose
mother lived in Dublin's St Mary's Road, was a General Post Office
telegraphist before his skills took him to the Royal Flying Corps
in January 1918 as a wireless operator. He died on 11 September
1918 of gas poisoning.[24]

However, most the fliers' deaths came in air combat, though
not necessarily instantly. On 11 April 1917 Lieutenant Martin Lillis,
a barrister from Monkstown, was serving in the Royal Flying Corps'
3rd Squadron flying over Lagnicourt during the Battle of Arras. He
was the observer in a two-seater Morane Parasol carrying out artillery
observation control. The German pilot who shot the aeroplane down,
Leutnant Fritz Bernert, claimed his nineteenth kill and was awarded
the Blue Max. Lillis was presumably still alive when the plane crashed
as he was recorded as having died from multiple fractures.[25]

Three Cruess-Callaghan brothers of Blackrock were killed
serving in the air, each roughly a year apart. Eugene was first,
a second lieutenant in 19 Squadron, aged just eighteen when he was
killed on 27 August 1916. Initially declared missing, not until April
1917 was he formally presumed to be dead.[26] His brother Stanislaus,
a captain in 44th Wing, aged twenty-one,[27] was killed on 28 June 1917.
He was in Canada at Camp Hoare, Ontario, training cadets in wireless
operations. Having planned to travel to RFC headquarters in Toronto
by train he was offered a seat in an aircraft flown by a cadet with 62
hours of flying experience. During the ascent the engine stalled, and the
plane crashed, 'the engine striking Callaghan in the back of the head and
pinning him to the earth'. He survived for less than an hour without
regaining consciousness. A local newspaper was at pains to point out

that a Roman Catholic chaplain was on hand to give him the last sacraments. The pilot was injured but survived.[28] Just over a year on, another brother, Joseph, a 25-year-old Major in 87th Squadron, was killed on 2 July 1918. He enlisted in the Royal Munster Fusiliers in December 1914 and transferred in August 1916 to the Royal Flying Corps on gaining a commission. He experienced some ill health during the war, including 'enfeebled heart action accentuated by overuse of tobacco'.[29] In addition to his parents, a sister and two brothers too young to serve in the war were left grieving.[30]

Peter and Marian Cowan lived in Ailesbury Road. They lost two sons in the Royal Flying Corps, Sidney and Philip, in both cases enduring long waits after their sons were initially declared 'missing'. Sidney was a 19-year-old captain who enlisted in July 1915 while studying engineering at Trinity. He earned the Military Cross with two bars, with the initial award coming in May 1916 when he brought down a German plane, fired on the downed crew as they fled for cover, and 'Although forced to land through his engine stopping he contrived to restart it and got back under heavy fire.' Bars were announced in October and November 1916. The first was for 'fine work in aerial combats' and the second for a 'long contest with seven enemy machines, finally bringing one down in flames'.[31] However, when Sidney Cowan went out on offensive patrol on 17 November 1916 in 29th Squadron he did not return and was reported missing. On 20 November his parents received a telegram stating that 'this does not necessarily mean he is wounded or killed'. Two days on, a further telegram said he was 'missing believed killed' but a day later a letter from the War Office offered some hope. It said that no report of his death had been received, and that his name would be placed on the missing list sent to the United States Embassy for circulation in hospital and prison camps in Germany. Cowan's file contained a note dated January 1917 from an officer in the RFC saying that those on the same patrol had reported Cowan killed, but that does not seem to have been conveyed to his parents. Then, in late March 1917 his parents received a notice from a Lieutenant H. A. Freeman of the 22nd Infantry Brigade Headquarters. It said that during a recent advance he had come across a German grave at Ablainzevelle 'In memory of a gallant English officer', Captain S. E. Cowan, killed in the air on 17 November 1916. Though Cowan was spelt with a K it seemed unlikely to belong to anyone else and Freeman's particular interest was explained when he added, 'unless I am mistaken this officer was at Marlborough College with me'. The War Office's initial view was that 'this evidence only points to a location of a grave, and no confirmation of burial is obtainable', but they formally declared in late June 1917 that Cowan was dead.[32] Five months later, Peter and Marian Cowan received news that Philip, also a captain, aged twenty-two, was missing on 8 November 1917, serving in the 56th Squadron after previous service in the 8th Manchester Regiment. Philip's body was never found and only in mid-July 1918 was he formally presumed dead. He is commemorated on the Arras Flying Services Memorial which marks those who died across the whole Western Front but have no known grave.[33]

Recruitment and Politics

Dublin saw little of conscientious objectors since there was no conscription in Ireland, but the city witnessed the effects of the policy introduced in early 1916 in Britain since a Non-Combatant Corps was based at the Royal Barracks. These men had been conscripted but refused to fight and were instead given non-front-line war work. Some accepted this but others objected even to, for example, being made to wear khaki uniforms, and refusal to accept military discipline was also an issue.[34]

In the absence of conscription, a renewed recruiting effort took place even while the Battle of the Somme was raging, and in Dublin men of the Ulster Division initially led the way. In late August 1916 around 40 men and 8 officers of the division were welcomed by the Lord Mayor of Dublin, James Gallagher. They were travelling after leave from Belfast to North Wall for embarkation to France and, even before the 16th Division was in action on the Somme (though possibly referring to the presence of Dubliners in the Ulster Division), an all-Ireland message was offered by Gallagher. He said, 'North and South had fought together like brothers', and hoped that 'they would find on their return an united Ireland and that North and South would share in the glory of the victory achieved for the British Empire'.[35] Major Robert Knox, a former UVF member in the 10th Inniskillings,[36] responded, closely echoing the sentiments, saying that 'no political or religious differences existed between them at the front, whether they came from the North or the South and that he too hoped to return in triumph to an united Ireland'.[37]

Similar appeals were at the heart of the City and County of Dublin Recruiting Committee's work. In mid-September 1916, it said that 'much anxiety is felt for the future of the Irish regiments, which, through individual and continued courage at the front, have become seriously depleted'. They tried to shed positive light on recruiting being down when compared to the same period in the previous year by saying that 'a steady flow of men was coming forward'. Their hope lay in 'new recruiting ideas, containing a well-considered appeal to Irish sentiment'.[38]

Others took a different view of the slowdown in Irish recruitment. In early October 1916, the *Evening Mail* wrote that while Irish regiments were in desperate need of fresh recruits, 'Practically none are forthcoming, certainly not enough to keep the Irish regiments Irish in anything but name.' The *Mail* argued for conscription saying, 'there are many young Irishmen who are willing to go, if all had to go'.[39] However, a more typical reaction to conscription plans – which John Redmond described as a 'most fatal thing' which would be 'resisted in every village'[40] – was outright opposition. The Dublin Corporation passed a resolution 'in most emphatic manner' condemning conscription, arguing that no authority other than an Irish Parliament had any right to introduce it. At the same time, the Corporation called for an amnesty for those arrested during the Rising and held in prison without trial.[41] This atmosphere led to the IPP tabling a motion in Parliament saying, 'That the system of Government at present maintained in Ireland is inconsistent with the principles for which the Allies are fighting in Europe'.[42] That was a significant change in the rhetoric of the nationalist leadership in Westminster and though the motion was defeated, Redmond's position against conscription meant that there was no question of the British government extending it to Ireland for the time being.[43]

The change in IPP positioning reflected wider changes in opinion. It should not be imagined that public opinion changed comprehensively after the Easter Rising. Much of Dublin's wartime activity continued well into 1917 in a way that was completely unaltered. Men joined the colours and visiting units were welcomed with celebrations, most notably the Duchess of Connaught's Own Irish Canadian Rangers in January 1917.[44] Fundraising for the wounded was hard for even republicans to criticise. September 1917 saw a military tournament at Lansdowne Road to raise funds for members of the Royal Dublin Fusiliers held as prisoners of war.[45] In October 1917 the same venue hosted a baseball match between teams representing the USA and Canada in aid of the Dublin Castle Red Cross Hospital.[46] However, tensions were rising, despite the fact that the vast bulk (around 500) of those still in prison following the Rising were released in December 1916.[47] In February 1917 there were further arrests of those believed to be active republicans, including Seán T. O'Kelly, the future President of Ireland, who had been arrested after the Rising but released in late 1916. The somewhat bizarre story of what happened to some of the men would not have helped the public feel that due process was being followed. One batch of ten was deported to Oxford, but having expected to be held in custody were told that they had to fend for themselves in the city. They had not been imprisoned, but merely removed from Ireland, without being put on trial.[48]

On Easter Monday 1917, 9 April, a crowd of around 2,000 people gathered in the city centre, marching and singing republican songs to mark the anniversary of the Rising. Someone hoisted a tricolour on the roof of the GPO and a police attempt to confiscate it after it had been taken down ended in 'a fiasco'. Stones were thrown at police but the day was otherwise without trouble.[49] A month later, there was broad nationalist opposition to partitionist proposals to settle the Irish Question in advance of an Irish Convention meeting in July,[50] though a major goodwill gesture was made in mid-June by the British when it released all 118 remaining prisoners convicted of offences during the Rising. In some cases this meant life sentences being lifted after only about a year in prison.[51] They arrived back in Ireland on the morning of 18 June, greeted by enthusiastic crowds at Kingstown, before a train journey to Dublin's Westland Row station. They were effectively if not formally given a civic reception, with the Lord Mayor visiting the prisoners at Fleming's Hotel in Gardiner Row where they were being entertained.[52] Tensions were already high in the city prior to the release, due to a 'riot' in Beresford Place (and other violence in Aungier Street) on 10 June during which police had been attacked. Inspector Mills was hit on the head with a hurley, suffering a fractured skull, and died the next day.[53] On the evening of 18 June, Union Flags were removed from shops and houses in Boyne Street and Townsend

Figure 14.1: Released republican prisoners surrounded by crowds on Westland Row, 18 June 1917. (Image Courtesy of the National Library of Ireland, KE 127).

Street and burned. Bridget Rooney, a soldier's wife from Kennedy's Court' was pelted with stones.[54] Two nights on and houses in Fitzwilliam Lane which were displaying Union Flags were attacked and windows broken.[55]

In this atmosphere the police continued to arrest republicans. On one occasion this resulted in the mistaken captivity of a Dublin University OTC veteran of the Rising. Paul Guéret joined the army in July 1916 for training as an officer and was at the front in January to April 1917 with the 8th Royal Dublin Fusiliers. Home on sick leave at Sandymount in the summer, suffering from varicose veins, his house was visited early one morning by British soldiers. They accused him of IRB membership and took him to Beggars Bush Barracks. His grandson recalled, 'Two days later he was released and driven back to his home in a Rolls Royce!' He had been mistaken for his brother Joseph who was in the IRB, and was at the house briefly that evening on the run.[56]

Meanwhile, the dwindling Redmondite National Volunteers, who by February 1917 were reckoned to have just 129 rifles in Dublin,[57] were in turmoil due to the calling of a Convention of the organisation. Such was the change of opinion even among that group that some of those involved said a Convention was impossible while John Redmond led the organisation as many battalions would not send representatives. Public spats between National Volunteers followed in the pages of newspapers on a variety of matters, from leadership to premises, though Redmondite supporters still seemed to be broadly in control.[58] A further opportunity for street politics – though orderly this time – came following the death of Thomas Ashe. He was released in June 1917 but was sent back to prison in August and soon demanded prisoner-of-war status, going on hunger strike. He died on 25 September 1917 and his funeral attracted 30,000 mourners along a route from City Hall to Glasnevin.[59] Ashe's death acted as a stimulus for Volunteer drilling across nationalist Ireland.[60] In Dublin, it was now clear that republicanism was gaining a major foothold among the public.

Western Front, Winter and Spring 1916–17

In October and November 1916, the first of four major reorganisations of the 16th Division (as part of changes across the British army) saw two regular battalions (the 2nd Royal Irish Regiment and the 2nd Dublins) join it, while the 7th and 8th Royal Irish Fusiliers were merged. The 1st Munsters had joined the division in May 1916 and they now absorbed the regiment's 8th battalion.[61] This was a prelude to relatively quiet winter months for the Dublin battalions on the Western Front. The 10th Dublins spent a lengthy spell from late November to mid-January well behind the lines at Noyelles-sur-Mer, about ten miles south of Boulogne on the coast, before heading back to the Somme's Beaucourt sector.[62] The 2nd Dublins became part of the 16th Division in mid-November 1916. With the 8th and 9th battalions, they spent much of the winter rotating in and out of trenches at the front in the Locre and Kemmel area. Losses were relatively low: deaths in these battalions after they left the Somme until late February 1917 were 19 in the 2nd, 15 in the 8th and 25 in the 9th.[63]

During the winter, the battalions (and especially their officers) were occasionally billeted with local families. Orlando Beater, of the 9th Dublins prior to joining the RFC, was promoted from lieutenant to captain in late October. He noted in his diary that his 'very dirty smelly billet, in little stuffy rooms' was visited by a 'large floating population of

Tommies who drop in for coffee, and incidentally I suppose, to flirt with the girl of the house.'[64] When at the front, the approach of the division was described to Beater and his fellow officers as,

> to keep on strafing the Hun and keep him in a constant state of uncertainty as to our intentions. Systematic strafes by the Heavies, Trench Mortars and Machine Guns would go on every second night, alternated by reconnoitering and fighting patrols, which would endeavour to cut off Hun wiring parties and generally cause terror and dismay among the opposing hosts.[65]

Yet much of most days was quiet, with practical matters such as 'the importance of seeing that the men rub their feet daily with whale oil' coming to the fore.[66]

The 1st Dublins moved to the Ypres area in late July 1916 and then to the Somme area in October. Over the six-month period from mid-August 1916 to mid-February 1917 the battalion lost the comparatively low figure of 33 dead. Of those, 13 came over the period of 20 to 28 October in Mametz Wood. During that time the battalion held a part of the front where the trenches were wet, muddy and needed much repair. The men fell not to a specific attack but the hazards of occasional German fire.[67]

In February 1917 as conditions allowed – or at least, were thought to allow – the British army once more sought to gain ground. On 28 February, as part of a process of strengthening British positions on the Somme, the 1st Dublins moved from Hardecourt (near Guillemont) to attack Potsdam Trench. The target was gained and held until relief came the next day, but they faced a number of problems: machine-gun fire from German lines; running into the British barrage; and thick mud, which meant that men took three to four minutes to advance a hundred yards. A further problem arose from a tape used in No Man's Land to indicate an assembly point. The battalion reached it, but at the wrong angle, so initially moved off slightly to the left of the intended direction. Meanwhile, despite the risks of being close to the British barrage, the men were keen to stay close to it because it offered protection against German attack. Consequently, planned waves of attackers became mixed up and it was hard to form up as necessary to attack German trenches.[68] Learning was taking place at the front, but by trial and error. On 28 February and 1 March 51 men died, the majority on the second day as the battalion held the trench in the face of heavy shell fire. At least 19 were Dubliners, demonstrating the strong local core to the battalion despite all it had been through and the many drafts it had received. One of them was Thomas Brennock, the third of three brothers to die in the war.[69]

There was no attempt to shift the 16th Division's front in February, but losses grew compared to previous months as German activity intensified. Across the month, there were 4 dead in the 2nd, 5 in the 9th and 6 in the 8th.[70] But February was grim for the 10th Dublins, rotating in and out of trenches around Beaucourt, and losing 59 men dead. During that time they did patrol, and the losses largely came from periodic German fire on British lines, both from artillery and snipers. The worst single day – on which 'Our artillery was quiet & retaliation when called for was poor' – was 8 February, with 7 dead.[71]

In April, a new major offensive was attempted around Arras as part of the planned 'Nivelle Offensive'. It should have been helped by a new focus on the 'creeping barrage' drawing on lessons learned on the Somme.[72] However, the attack was not only hindered by German partial withdrawal to the strongly fortified 'Hindenburg Line' in March, but also by artillery being ineffective in support of infantry. The battle began on 9 April with some initial advances, but the weather turned on 11 April with heavy rain causing problems for targeting of artillery. When the 1st Royal Irish Fusiliers advanced near Fampoux they found that their targets had not been destroyed and came under heavy fire. They did not secure their goal and lost 81 dead, of whom at least 10 were Dubliners.[73]

The next day, the 1st Dublins entered the battle. Their experience demonstrated just how essential was successful coordination between infantry and artillery, if any attack was to succeed. From 12 April over the next two weeks they periodically held the line, mainly at Monchy. By 23 April the battalion had lost 19 dead, but it was to lose even more in one day on 24 April in one of the most futile operations it carried out. Ordered to attack a German hill at 4pm the battalion did exactly that. However, as the war diary recorded, due to a messenger 'losing his way orders regarding change in time of barrage did not arrive until after the action'. Without any artillery support the battalion faced heavy rifle and machine-gun fire from German lines and 'After stubborn resistance they were compelled to fall back in our original front line.'

By this time, 36 men were dead. The officer who wrote in the battalion war diary noted bitterly, 'Thus, owing to there being no artillery support the task allotted to the Battn. was unaccomplished.' It was muted criticism, but even in that form a rare example in an official record of the finger of blame being pointed.[74]

A similar fate was endured by the 10th Dublins earlier on in the battle on 15 April. They were ordered to attack the village of Gavrelle without any preliminary bombardment – though the divisional war diary described their operation as a 'patrol' which would not usually be accompanied by artillery fire. The war diary noted, 'Owing to the very heavy Bosch artillery and machine-gun fire the attempt was unsuccessful.' Of these, 12 lost their lives and about 70 more were casualties.[75] Such operations were, at the core of an attritional approach to warfare. Yet successful aspects of the Battle of Arras such as the Canadians securing Vimy Ridge were undermined by the attack continuing well after there was any chance of significant gains.[76] There was still much to learn if attrition was to lead to victory.

15 LEARNING

Our chaps took the ridges from him in a couple of hours what he had fortified for two years. Our artillery was simply splendid they never left a part of his trenches but they didn't hit.
Private George Soper, 2nd Dublin Fusiliers, writing about Messines, June 1917[1]

Messines

Following Arras, the next major British initiative on the Western Front was at Messines Ridge on 7 June 1917. The battle has become central to cross-community initiatives in Northern Ireland and to all-Ireland work on the First World War because at Messines the 16th (Irish) and 36th (Ulster) divisions fought alongside each other.[2] Dubliners played a role, especially in the 2nd, 8th and 9th Royal Dublin Fusiliers. Messines was a prelude to the third Battle of Ypres, aiming to deprive the Germans of the view the ridge gave them over the Ypres area. If the allies held the ridge it would aid making covert troop movements in preparation for the attack. The battle was unusual for being seen, in the words of the *Dublin Evening Mail* as a 'complete success'.[3] This followed the effective combination of preliminary bombardment, control of the skies by the Royal Flying Corps, underground mines exploding at 'zero hour', and the immediate advance of infantry behind a meticulously timed creeping barrage produced by concentrated artillery fire.[4] Such coordination of

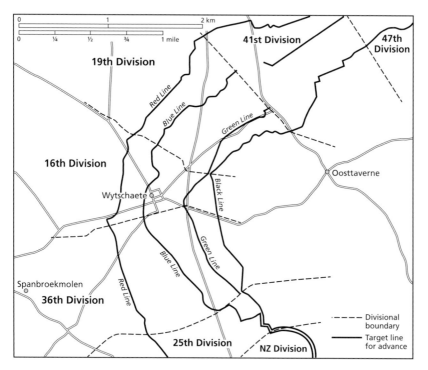

Map 15.1: Messines, June 1917. Adapted by David Cox from the map drawn by David Appleyard in Grayson, *Belfast Boys*, 110.

infantry and artillery was the army's principal lesson from the Somme and these developments were crucial in the British army's learning curve during the war.[5]

The battle began at 3.10am with nineteen mines exploding at eleven firing posts.[6] 2nd Lieutenant Arthur Glanville had been attached to the 2nd Dublins in March 1917. Writing home he described how 'The ground swayed in an alarming manner and the trench rocked like a boat on a sea.' However, the sound of explosions 'was completely drowned in the simultaneous burst of the hundreds of guns' and, in a diary written in 1918 as a prisoner of war, he recalled the mines as being 'like a chestnut burning in a fire in comparison to the war of the artillery'.[7] Minutes later, the infantry advanced behind a creeping barrage. The 16th Division was in the centre, attacking the village of Wytschaete. To their left was the 19th (Western) Division, and to their right the 36th. The attack was led by 49th Brigade adjoining the 19th Division with 47th Brigade next to the Ulster Division. As part of 48th Brigade, the 2nd, 8th and 9th Dublins were in reserve so did not play any part in the initial advance, though the 9th came under shell fire while waiting in reserve.[8] The 9th flanked the Ulster Division while the boundary of the 2nd and 8th Dublins touched the 19th Division.

47th and 49th Brigades took their targets with relative ease, proceeding through the red, blue green and black lines, taking the latter at 8am. Not until 11.55am did the 8th Dublins advance. A Company carried munitions for the brigade Machine Gun Company while B and C companies advanced leaving D Company in reserve. The war diary noted that 'Despite heavy hostile shelling ... casualties were slight' and the 8th was able to consolidate – in particular by erecting barbed wire – at the front by 2pm. The 9th Dublins performed similar roles advancing shortly after the 8th at 12.30pm, followed by the 2nd that evening. Having relieved other units of the 16th Division all three battalions held the front line on 8 June in the face of a German counter-attack which ultimately failed due to being broken up by British artillery fire.[9] However, further fighting continued for a week, not involving the 16th or 36th, and by 14 June the final objective of the Oosttaverne Line had been captured.[10]

Messines was a remarkable success, though perhaps its ease was felt most strongly by those who were not in the first wave of the attack. Just one man of the 2nd Dublins was killed at Messines, Private 11336 Edward Bannister, an English transferee to the battalion.[11] Members of his battalion wrote of the battle in enthusiastic terms. George Soper told Monica Roberts, 'Our chaps took the ridges from him in a couple of hours what he had fortified for two years. Our artillery was simply splendid they never left a part of his trenches but they didn't hit.'[12] Wilfrid Colyer's memoirs said that from the perspective of the 2nd Dublins 'the attack represented the first easy victory – an "absolute walk-over" – they had had for many a long day. They gained all their objectives, consolidated, withstood a few spasmodic counter-attacks, and were relieved next day happy and smiling.'[13]

The 8th and 9th Dublins fared worse. The 8th lost 8 men, all except one of those on 7 June. The 9th Dublins lost 18 men over 7 to 9 June, partly because they had come under fire while in reserve at the start of the battle (7 were dead that day), but they also suffered more in German counter-attacks on subsequent days.[14] Among the

Figure 15.1: After Messines. Royal Dublin Fusiliers and other troops of the 16th Division with souvenirs of the capture of Wytschaete. Near Bailleul, 11 June 1917. (©IWM, Q 5628).

8th and 9th Dublins' dead, 10 of the 26 were Dubliners, the remainder being from across Ireland and England. In total, the battle accounted for the lives of at least 46 Dubliners. Beyond the Dublin Fusiliers, 15 dead were serving in other battalions of the 16th Division including 5 in the 2nd Royal Irish Regiment which had been in the first wave of the attack; 5 were in the Ulster Division. The other 16 were in a range of units, including English, Scottish, Australian and New Zealand infantry battalions.

Aside from the success of the Battle of Messines, it is significant for how it is remembered as the place at which the 16th and 36th Divisions fought side-by-side. It has become a key site for commemorations which focus on reconciliation, whether between Britain and Ireland or communities within Ireland, with the opening of the Island of Ireland Peace Park at Messines in 1998.[15] The message of that was embodied in words spoken by President Mary McAleese at the park's inauguration:

> The men of the 36th Ulster Division and the 16th Irish Division died here. They came from every corner of Ireland. Among them were Protestants, Catholics, Unionists and Nationalists, their differences transcended by a common commitment not to flag but to freedom. Today we seek to put their memory at the service of another common cause ...[16]

This approach has its roots in some immediate attention after the battle to the story of Major Willie Redmond, who was Nationalist MP for East Clare and brother of John Redmond.[17] Serving in the 6th Royal Irish Regiment in the 16th Division, aged 56, he was discouraged from going into battle. However, he did so at Messines and was wounded. Collected on the battlefield by stretcher-bearers of the Ulster Division, he died at an aid post after being giving the last rites by a chaplain from the 36th. His death received massive newspaper coverage and there were requiem masses held in Dublin and London.[18] Within the story of his death, the nationalist press saw hope of Irish unity, the *Freeman's Journal* writing,

> If the prospect of a union with the men of Ulster today is brighter than it has been, it is due largely to the unmistakable ardour with which he pursued the ideal of a united, self-governing Irish nation, and the no less unmistakable sincerity of his generous tolerance. It is not too much to say that he gave his life for a united Ireland.[19]

Quite why the newspaper believed there was a realistic prospect of unity between north and south because of Redmond and his death is unclear. Certainly there were accounts of how a graveside volley was fired by men of the 16th and 36th divisions, and of course the circumstances of his death had seen the divisions intertwined.[20] During the battle there were reports of a 'friendly rivalry' between the two divisions: 'There was a race between the South and North Irish as to whether a green flag or an orange should be planted first above the ruins of Wytschaete. I do not know which won, but both flags flew there when the crest had been gained.'[21] Another correspondent wrote how 'Dublin men were going into the barrage, touching shoulders with their comrades of an Orange Lodge in North Ulster.'[22] Years later there was talk from veterans of how the two divisions had fought side-by-side.[23] But there was no sign of any shift in opinion in the unionist press, nor among unionist leaders.

Indeed, the composition of the two divisions had changed greatly since 1914. The 16th Division at Messines was about as Irish as it had ever been, but a significant number of those men were not part of the original division and therefore might not have shared politics with those who joined from the National Volunteers. Meanwhile, the 36th Division had changed more dramatically.[24] The chaplain of the Ulster Division who had given Redmond the last rites was in fact the division's Catholic chaplain,[25] a reflection of how post-Somme, the division had received drafts from a range of sources, many of them Catholic and many not part of the pre-war UVF. A Catholic Dubliner who found himself in the 36th was Private 5741 Joseph Symington of Ranelagh Road. He had joined the 3rd Royal Irish Rifles, a reserve battalion, in March 1916. He was posted to the Ulster Division on 8 July 1916, first to the 14th Royal Irish Rifles and then in February 1917 to the 109th Machine Gun Company in which he served out the war.[26] Symington's case was only typical later in the war: aside from some members of the 14th Royal Irish Rifles who had joined from the Young Citizens Volunteers (and *might* have been Catholic Unionists), Catholics were extremely rare in the division at its formation.[27] Overall, of those killed in the two divisions at Messines, no Irish connection can be found for around one-third of men, while those men do have a demonstrable connection to England, Scotland or Wales.[28] Does this mean that the story of Messines as one of co-operation, as told in connection with the Peace Park at Messines, is simply wrong? Not at all, and it makes an important contribution to reconciliation. But whether it reflects the battlefield experiences of those who fought there in the 2nd, 8th, 9th and Dublins, whose main contact was with their own division and were as likely to run into an English unit as an Ulster one, is questionable.

The Third Battle of Ypres

As the war ground on into the summer, Joseph Clarke of the 2nd Dublins continued to express optimism: 'there is still a chance of us all getting home before the year is out', he wrote to Monica Roberts.[29] Sergeant 9485 Edward Heafey of the 8th Dublins expressed anger about republicans: 'I wish I had my way with the Sinn Feiners I would put every one of them out here & make them do some real good fighting & make them realise what war is like.'[30] One man was overwhelmed by the pressure of war: Private 26212 Patrick Boylan of the 1st Inniskillings, whose mother lived in High Street, Dublin, died from a self-inflicted gunshot wound.[31]

British efforts on the Western Front were focused on the attempted advance around Ypres, to which Messines had been a prelude. The 1917 battle at Ypres is commonly called the 'Third Battle of Ypres' (or 'Third Ypres'), or simply 'Passchendaele', though the fighting at Passchendaele was just part of the wider battle. As Paddy Griffith argues, Third Ypres 'probably represented the most sophisticated of all the BEF's attack plans in the entire war'. Instead of attempting breakthrough in one effort, or just one 'bite and hold' operation, Third Ypres aimed at a series of 'bite and holds'. Messines showed that, with adequate artillery preparation, infantry could gain about a mile of ground with relatively light losses, and the plan was to repeat this every two to three days in a series of operations on the Ypres front.[32] That this was all to go horribly wrong did not mean that the British army – or at least parts of it – was not learning. Rather, at Third Ypres they faced the 'myriad of other concerns', not least the weather, which could hinder the best laid plans.[33]

The attack was launched on 31 July at Pilckem and there were initial gains. Among Irish units involved on that first day were the 1st Inniskillings, in which Francis Ledwidge lost his life. When news came through of the death of 'Ireland's Peasant Soldier Poet' it was much lamented in the Dublin press.[34] Part of the 16th Division – 47th Brigade – was in reserve for the initial attack behind the 15th (Scottish) Division. Yet after some initial progress the 15th were partially driven back, and heavy rain caused any further attack to be postponed. Before it began, the advance already faced one significant obstacle: the time between the success at Messines, while Haig pressed the government to authorise a further major offensive, allowed the Germans to strengthen their defences. There was still a three-week-long artillery preparation of the target, but the advancing infantry faced an enemy which was better entrenched than it might have been if the attack had followed hard on the heels of Messines. Meanwhile, whatever plans had been put in place, nobody had reckoned on the deluge of rain which made the battlefield a mud bath.[35] Nor was anyone prepared to call off the attack because of the weather.

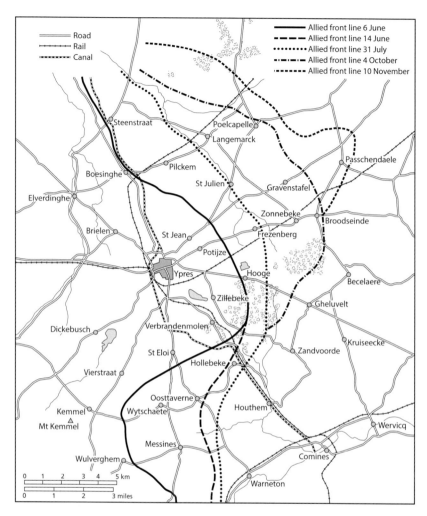

Map 15.2: Ypres, 1917. Adapted by David Cox from the map drawn by David Appleyard in Grayson, *Belfast Boys*, 121.

The 2nd, 8th and 9th Dublins took up positions ready to go to the front on 31 July, but ended up not doing so as the attack slowed. Instead, on various occasions until mid-August they defended the lines, in particular at Frezenberg, facing attacks by gas, artillery and aircraft machine guns. On 1 August, the 9th Dublins found trenches 'in a very bad condition and dug-outs and shelters very poor. The men were drenched with rain, the majority having been exposed the whole night.' Spending two to three days at the front at a time, the 2nd

Dublins lost 18 men, the 9th lost 28 and the 2nd lost 44.[36] The 2nd Dublins suffered so heavily from gas that the battalion was down to fewer than 300 men, and the battalion was supplemented by men from the 8th Dublins.[37] Arthur Glanville of the 2nd Dublins described it as '"Hell" all the time! Mud awful, no trenches, no shelters, no landmarks, all movement by night, shelling all the time & everywhere casualties enormous!'[38]

All three battalions were then part of the assault on Langemarck on 16 August, in which the 16th (on the right) and 36th Division (on the left) were at the forefront. Alongside the three Dublin battalions already in the 16th Division's 48th Brigade came the 10th Dublins who had joined the division in late June, though they were not involved in the fighting at Third Ypres.[39] 48th Brigade was on the right of the 16th Division's front, with the 9th Dublins and 7th Royal Irish Rifles leading, and the 2nd Dublins in reserve.[40] As they assembled in reserve the 2nd Dublins suffered casualties with the Germans bombarding their assembly positions at 4.30am. The 9th Dublins assembled late on 15 August, taking positions by 11.30pm, with zero hour set as 4.45am on 16th. They moved out at 4.45am under a barrage which made progress difficult. However, they secured their first target before grinding to a halt. Some confusing messages came through about progress of battalions alongside, while the chain of command was disrupted by message runners becoming casualties. Meanwhile, the 2nd Dublins' B Company moved forward behind the 9th Dublins and was 'wiped out before reaching its objectives by enemy Machine Gun and Artillery Fire, only Two Officers and 3 Other Ranks surviving'.[41] A Company moved up behind the 7th Royal Irish Rifles and had more success before digging in, though all their officers became casualties.

As early as 10am British artillery was falling short, and at 3.45pm a German counter-attack had some effect. The 2nd Dublins, who had made their way forward, had to fall back at 4.10pm as losses in the 2nd Middlesex Regiment weakened the line alongside them. C Company had gone forward at 9.30am supporting the 9th Dublins, and at 10.30am the attached company of the 8th Dublins advanced behind the 7th Irish Rifles. They eventually joined forces and held a position until 10pm the next day when they were relieved.[42] For the 9th Dublins, the night of 16th and the next day were 'comparatively quiet with the exception of intermittent shelling and sniping'. They held on until relief in the early hours of 18 August.[43]

The operations over 16 to 18 August at Langemarck were extremely costly for the 16th Division. Between 1 and 20 August, 221 officers and 4,064 men were casualties.[44] Among the Dublins, the 8th lost 13, while there were 36 dead in the 2nd. A staggering 98 were killed in the 9th.[45] Illustrating how the local character of the battalions was changing, just 6 of the 2nd and 3 of the 8th were Dubliners, though nearly one-third (30) of the 9th's dead were from the city or county. Among them was a veteran of the Easter Rising, 19-year-old Lieutenant William Brereton-Barry, who had been in the city with the 10th Dublins. Having been wounded, he was rescued by a stretcher-bearer, only for the stretcher to be hit by a shell. His parents lived at Glenageary and it would be March 1918 before an enquiry into their son's death led them to accept that he was not coming home.[46]

Another 30 Dubliners also died in other units of the 16th Division, and 8 in the Ulster Division. One death was especially high profile: Father William 'Willie' Doyle, the Jesuit chaplain, transferred from the 8th Royal Irish Fusiliers to the 8th Dublins in December 1916.[47] Doyle's bravery gave him a legendary status among the men and he won the Military Cross on the Somme.[48] Two days before he was killed, a fellow chaplain wrote to Doyle's father, 'Father Doyle is a marvel. They may talk of heroes and saints; they are hardly in it. He sticks it to the end – the shells, the gas, the attack.'[49] He was particularly famed for braving danger to give the last rites to dying men. A newspaper report described how on the day of his death, 'He went back to the field to administer to those who were glad to see him bending over them in their last agony. Four men were killed by shell fire as he knelt beside them, and he was not touched – not until his own turn came. A shell burst close and the padre fell dead.'[50] Another newspaper report pointed out how Doyle had been popular among both the 16th and 36th Divisions, citing an Ulster Protestant who said, 'He was as ready to risk his life to take a drop of water to a wounded Ulsterman as to assist men of his own faith and regiment.'[51] Doyle was buried on the Frezenberg Ridge though later fighting meant that his grave was lost.

The role of the 16th at Langemarck was later criticised by some generals, who believed it had become unreliable due to politics. However, as Denman points out, the Ulster Division had done no better and there was no question over its loyalty.[52] At any rate, the 16th Division played no more part in Third

Ypres, with all units moving to the Bapaume area on the Somme by the end of August.[53]

The 1st Dublins were drawn into Third Ypres in mid-August, placed in reserve on 15 August as 29th Division attacked Passerelle Farm, on the Pilckem Ridge. They were not required in the attack but did move into the line the next day, until relief on 20 August, during which time they faced very heavy shell fire, losing 23 dead, including 7 Dubliners.[54] They took part in just one more action at Third Ypres even though they had no need to. In early October, the battalion was told that it would transfer to the 16th Division later in the month. However, hearing at the same time that part of the 29th Division was due to attack at Langemarck, without the 1st Dublins, a battalion deputation was sent 'to the divisional commander requesting permission to make one more attack for the honour of the 29th Division, which all ranks were so grieved to leave'.[55] So, at 6am on 4 October, they followed a creeping barrage towards their targets near the Broembeek river, just north-west of Langemarck. Though units alongside them had problems securing their goals, all of the 1st Dublins' were reached and by early afternoon they were consolidating their positions. During the attack an English member of the battalion, Sergeant 10605 James Ockendon won the Victoria Cross having single-handedly taken on two machine-gun posts. However, they had faced problems learning how to follow a creeping barrage, the war diary noting, 'All ranks praise the accuracy and volume of the barrage though several admit that they were wounded by getting too close under it.' They also found that the lack of light made it 'extremely difficult at that hour to ascertain the line of the barrage after the first lift.' Expecting to be relieved overnight, no relief came and they remained there until 6 October by which time the 1st Dublins had lost 56 men dead, 8 of them from Dublin.[56]

The Dublin Fusiliers Brigade

The British army of the war's final year bore little resemblance to that of 1915–16, let alone of 1914. Casualties and reorganisations had all but destroyed the character of volunteer divisions. But the 16th Division was also facing other changes. From late August to November 1917 the second of four major reorganisations took place which greatly altered its character, already changed by the influx

Figure 15.2: The 8th/9th Royal Dublin Fusiliers. At the time of their merger, the battalion received a visit from Cardinal Francis Bourne, the Head of the Catholic Church in England and Wales, pictured with Major General William Hickie, the Commander of the 16th Division, at Ervillers, 27 October 1917. (©IWM, Q 6153).

of drafts. From its earliest days the division was never quite simply an army of Irish nationalists, as the label the 'Irish Brigade' would have had it. In September 1914 the 11th Hampshires had joined as divisional troops, while there were over 200 men from the Guernsey militia in the 7th Royal Irish Rifles when they were first formed.[57] In the late 1917 reorganisation, the 1st Dublins and the 7th Royal Irish Regiment joined the division, mergers took place between the 7th and 8th Inniskillings and the 8th and 9th Dublins, while the 7th Royal Irish Rifles left for the Ulster Division.[58] With the 2nd Dublins having joined post-Somme, and the 10th after Messines, this meant that all the Dublin battalions serving on the Western Front were now in the 16th Division. Indeed, they were altogether in what was effectively a Dublin Brigade – the 48th – and the phrase 'Dublin Fusiliers Brigade' would be used in the 1st Dublins' regimental history.[59]

Of course, men who had joined from political backgrounds were still serving. One of those in the 10th Dublins was Private 25713 John Kearns of Beaver Row, Donnybrook, a former member of the Irish Volunteers' 3rd Battalion. Though his battalion saw little in the way of enemy fire in their rotations at the front around Bapaume in September, snipers were active and it is possible that one of these accounted for Kearns, who died of wounds on 26 September.[60]

The 16th Division was in a series of actions over October and November. On 16 October, the 7th Leinsters raided Tunnel Trench in the Croiselles Heights area, establishing that the Germans had wired the construction so that it could be exploded if captured.[61]

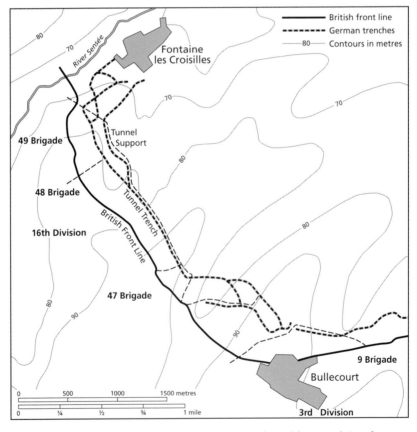

Map 15.3: Tunnel Trench, 20 November 1917. Adapted by David Cox from Johnstone, *Orange, Green and Khaki*, xxxi.

Further intelligence came from a raid by the 2nd Dublins on 21 October at the junction between Tunnel Trench and Prince Trench. They gleaned information about the state of No Man's Land and the condition of the German trenches. They also came face to face with six Germans who 'held up their hands, all were armed with revolvers, except two in rear who had rifles, and on getting to close quarters these men fired but missed, and then ran away'.[62] Such incidents made soldiers wary when the enemy appeared to surrender, and could lead to shootings of prisoners.[63]

The intelligence garnered in these two raids was vital because plans were being made for the 16th Division, along with the 3rd Division, to attack a 2,000-yard section of Tunnel Trench (and behind it Tunnel Support) as a diversion for a major action at Cambrai on 20 November. Armed with much information about the general area, the attack began at 6.20am on 20 November. All three brigades of the 16th Division were involved in the first wave, 49th Brigade to the left, 48th Brigade's Dublin battalions in the centre, and 47th on the right. It was a textbook operation. The lead units of 48th Brigade were the 2nd (on the left) and 10th Dublins (on the right). The 1st Dublins were in support, tasked with wiring positions gained, while the 8th/9th Dublins were in reserve. They advanced at 6.20am close behind a creeping barrage, reaching their objective four minutes later. Since smoke had been used in the British barrage the Germans feared they might be under attack by gas and put on gas masks which greatly hindered them as they fired rifles and machine guns. Bombers from the 10th attacked strong-points and gained Mebu Minerva, a key stronghold in the middle of Tunnel Trench, by 6.30am. Communication with battalion headquarters was established at the same time through signallers having laid a cable as they advanced. Consolidation of the main Tunnel Trench was being carried out by 6.40am, with all objectives captured by 7.10am. The 1st Dublins had wired the front by 7.30am. This allowed further repair of positions – necessary because of the British artillery bombardment – to take place behind some protection against counter-attack. In 48th Brigade there were 25 dead, 12 of them Dubliners, and around another 50 wounded.[64] Across the two divisions which had attacked there were 805 casualties in total, with 718 German prisoners taken.[65] The 10th's war diary attributed 'the lightness of our casualties to the excellent barrage put down by Artillery, Machine Guns, and Trench Mortar Batteries, and also to the fact that this barrage was very closely followed by the Assaulting troops'.[66] The British enjoyed similar success in the main action at Cambrai, with tanks taking a leading role, though initial gains of up to three miles were lost in German counter-attacks up to early December.[67] By then, as in previous years, attempts at a major advance were delayed until the spring due to the weather.

The 16th Division wintered in the Somme area, spending time at Ste Emilie, Hamel and Villers Faucon. They faced occasional enemy raids, shell fire and snipers. On 29 and 30 November the 2nd, 8th/9th and 10th Dublins suffered heavy bombardments, losing 27 dead between them. The 2nd Dublins also lost another 6 between 23 and 26 December for similar reasons. Otherwise, 48th Brigade only lost another 18 men dead between the start of December and the end of February 1918.[68] By that time, the 16th Division had been significantly reorganised yet again, and the men were within weeks of facing the prospect of losing the war.

16 VICTORY FROM THE JAWS OF DEFEAT

They all had the look of hounds whipped off just as they were about to kill.

> Lieutenant Noël Drury, 6th Royal Dublin Fusiliers, on how his men greeted the news of the armistice[1]

Changes

No year of the war saw so much change in allied fortunes as 1918. The trauma of Passchendaele in the summer of 1917 was followed by a bleak winter with little prospect of victory. There was then the spectre of defeat when the spring offensive from late March 1918 brought German forces within fifty miles of Paris. Yet after a month of bitter fighting, the German army was exhausted and the allies were on the brink of a decisive advance leading to victory – snatched from the jaws of defeat – in November. The USA had entered the war in April 1917 but the relatively small number of troops it sent from the summer of 1917 had little initial impact. That changed in the early summer of 1918.

During 1918, reorganisations meant only three Dublin battalions were still in existence at the end of the war. The most substantial changes in the 16th (Irish) Division took place in February 1918, with each infantry brigade cut from four to three battalions, as across the British army as a whole. All surviving battalions from the south of Ireland then on the Western Front were grouped together. The 10th Dublins and the merged 8th/9th were disbanded, with their members going to form the 19th and 20th Entrenching Battalions. In the 48th 'Dublin Fusiliers Brigade', the 1st and 2nd Dublins remained, joined by the 2nd Munsters. All were regular battalions originally, and no part of Redmondite recruiting for the 16th Division.[2] The 6th Dublins later arrived in France from Palestine in July 1918, placed in the 66th (2nd East Lancashire) Division, spending their early weeks, as Drury noted, on 'a special course of treatment to get rid of the malaria which a great many of us have'.[3] That all happened against a backdrop of radical political change in Ireland, as Sinn Féin emerged to replace the IPP as the major force in Irish nationalism.

The German Spring Offensive, 1918

During the winter of 1917 German forces on the Western Front were significantly strengthened as Tsarist Russia collapsed and the conflict in the east drew to a close: 48 German divisions headed west, making the relative strength of the Germans versus the allies 191 to 178 divisions.[4] This enabled the Germans to build for the *Kaiserschlacht* (known in English as the 'spring offensive'), which sought to exploit Germany's numerical strength before American soldiers arrived.[5] There were three separate phases to the offensive. From 21 March, Operation Michael took place around Arras. Then came an attack on the Lys in Flanders in April. Finally, there was an advance on the Aisne in May. 'Stormtroopers' were central to the first phase, using infiltration tactics to attack weaker rear positions on the allied lines, initially avoiding strongpoints which were then attacked by infantry once confusion had been sewn. Creeping barrages and gas supported the advance, and the cover of mist was also utilised. The attack initially took forty miles of allied ground, including land gained at such cost on the Somme in 1916. Before the tide of battle turned, they came within fifty miles of Paris meaning that the capital was within range of German artillery. The first day of the offensive saw more casualties than any other day of the war, nearly 40,000 each for the Germans and the British. More British were killed on 1 July 1916, but what made the day different was the number of prisoners captured by the Germans: 21,000, compared to just 300 taken by the British.[6]

On 21 March 1918, 16th Division held part of the front close to the Somme villages of Lempire, Épehy and Ronssoy, with 21st Division

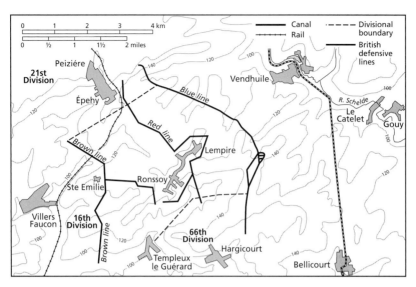

Map 16.1: 16th Division, 21 March 1918. Adapted by David Cox from Johnstone, *Orange, Green and Khaki*, xxxviii.

to their left at Épehy and 66th Division to the right, divided from the 16th by water. While the division held a front line around a mile north-east of the villages, a more strongly fortified 'battle zone' existed closer to the villages on the Ronssoy Ridge. Orders in the event of an attack were for a quick retirement from front-line posts (blue line), while strongpoints (red line) were held. The 16th Division's sector was divided in two, 48th Brigade to the left near Épehy, and 49th on the right. In 48th Brigade, two companies of each of its three battalions were in the front line, while two were behind the battle zone.[7]

On 20 March, the 1st Dublins believed attack 'now to be certain', even though 'on many previous occasions it was given out that this was about to take place'. At 4.45am next morning gas shells landed near 48th Brigade and 'Visibility was rendered impossible by a very thick mist.' British artillery replied, but was hampered by gas. The gas attack caused few casualties in the 1st Dublins because box respirators were put on quickly. Around four hours later high-explosives replaced the gas barrage until about 10.45am. Ten minutes later the Germans were through the abandoned blue line and into the red line. As parts of battalions retreated, those remaining came under enfilade fire and by early afternoon there was a piecemeal withdrawal to the 'brown line' in front of Ste Emilie. By 2.30pm the 1st Dublins could only muster 70 men to fall back and defend positions around the Lempire–Épehy road though about 30 stragglers arrived later. When the 2nd Dublins withdrew to the brown line at around 3pm they had 7 officers and 200 men, down from well over 600 earlier in the day. A further barrage was opened up on the division's positions at about 4.15pm, but the line was held by 48th Brigade until 8.45pm when they began to be relieved by 47th Brigade, a process which continued until the early hours of the next day.[8]

From then until 30 March the division took part in several retreats, defending different positions west of Ronssoy over a distance of around thirty miles towards Amiens. They delayed the Germans as far as they could, while occasional counter-attacks – causing further delays, if not halting the enemy – took place alongside them. Finally they found themselves at Hamel, a few miles east of Amiens, being relieved from there overnight on 3/4 April.[9] Losses continued to be heavy throughout this period. On 21 March the 2nd Dublins lost 112 dead, and the 1st a further 101. Between 22 and 5 April the 1st lost another 49 men and the 2nd another 29. Across the entire period of the offensive, from 21 March to 5 April, 329 men either serving in the Royal Dublin Fusiliers on the Western Front, or recently transferred to the 19th or 20th Entrenching Battalions lost their lives, at least 66 of whom were Dubliners. At least another 42 Dubliners were killed serving in other units of the 16th Division (around half of them in the 7th Royal Irish Regiment), and another 28 in the Ulster Division. Across the 16th division as a whole, the cost of the spring offensive was more than 1,000 dead, more than 3,000 wounded, and around 1,000 taken prisoner. There were similar figures for the Ulster Division.[10]

These levels of fatalities compared to any of the worst periods of the war. By early April the 16th Division was barely functional and it could not survive simply by replenishing battalions with drafts. Consequently the division was further reorganised over April to June 1918. The 1st and 2nd Dublins were briefly merged in April as a 'composite' battalion, before being reconstituted as a new 1st battalion, returning to 29th Division. The 2nd was reduced to cadre strength and operated as a training battalion, later re-emerging as a fighting-strength unit in June when their ranks were joined by men of the 7th Dublins returning from the Middle East. In June, the 16th Division was sent to England to reconstitute and while it was there the

2nd Dublins were transferred to the 50th (Northumbrian) Division. When it returned to France in late July it contained just one Irish battalion (the 5th Royal Irish Fusiliers), though during the summer of 1918 there were fourteen southern Irish infantry battalions on the Western Front.[11] Meanwhile, the 19th and 20th Entrenching Battalions which had briefly been a home for men of the Dublins were broken up in late March and the men sent to reinforce units of the 16th Division, especially the 2nd Munsters.[12]

The spring offensive effectively ended the 16th Division as an Irish formation, not only in terms of numbers. Writing in his diary on 22 March, Haig noted 'Our 16th (Irish) Division which was on the right of VII Corps and lost Ronssoy village, is said not to be so full of fight as the others.' This was not a view he changed with hindsight, adding in the post-war typescript version of his diary, 'In fact, certain Irish units did very badly and gave way immediately the Enemy showed.'[13] Haig was not the only person holding that opinion in March 1918 and the division's reputation was dogged by accusations even at the front – some perhaps merely banter – that it was full of supporters of Sinn Féin. However, when the Chief of the Imperial General Staff, Field Marshal Sir Henry Wilson, was asked to look into the matter in the context of Irish recruitment he found no evidence for the accusation. He also pointed out that the division's ranks were one-third non-Irish.[14] It is worth noting that Wilson was a supporter of conscription in Ireland and had no interest in suggesting that the Irish were less likely to fight than others,[15] but his verdict was one that was echoed in the British official history of the war.[16]

The 16th Division had played their part in halting the German offensive with the actions of battalions like the 1st and 2nd Dublins. However, the slowing of the German advance also depended on the allies co-operating more closely then ever before, with Marshal Foch put in command of all allied soldiers on 26 March. German gains continued, but following a counter-attack in Moreuil Wood on 30 March after the Germans failed to take Amiens, the first phase of the offensive was called off on 5 April. A renewed effort was made in the Battle of the Lys from 9 April but by the end of the month, despite gains, that halted. The 1st Dublins were periodically at the front during that battle, and though not in major action, casualties were incurred. A war diary entry resonant of *All Quiet on the Western Front* covering 16–18 May, while the battalion was in the line at Nieppe, noted 'Nothing unusual to report, usual patrols at night – weather fine.' But the battalion still lost seven men during that period at the front.[17] The Germans made one last heave on 27 May in the third Battle of the Aisne. By 6 June, they had reached the Marne, faced ever-growing supply problems, and could go no further. From then on, the Germans would only retreat.[18]

Home Front

Doubts about the 16th (Irish) Division's fighting prowess were linked to political changes at home. John Redmond's death on 6 March 1918, from heart failure after an operation, caused an outpouring of grief across nationalist Ireland. His body rested at Westminster Cathedral until being removed to Ireland for interment at Wexford on 9 March. Arriving by boat at Kingstown, the funeral party were met by members of the National Volunteers and a guard of honour from the Royal Irish Regiment.[19]

Redmond's death was a metaphor for changes taking place in Irish politics in the wake of the Easter Rising, the failure of the Irish Convention to reach a settlement on Home Rule, and the debate around conscription. Parliamentary by-elections demonstrated how Sinn Féin was steadily winning support from the Irish Parliamentary Party. From the war's start to the Rising there were seven by-elections in which the defending party was the IPP, and one also took place during Easter Week 1916. The IPP retained seven of those seats, losing one to an independent nationalist. Following the Rising to the end of the war, there were another eleven such contests, and though the swing to Sinn Féin was not universal, it was marked. The IPP held the first seat, West Cork, in November 1916, but in 1917 Sinn Féin won three of the four by-elections, including East Clare which had been vacated by the death of Willie Redmond. In 1918, there was a recovery for the IPP as they held three seats, and in a sign of how tough the government was prepared to be in the face of growing militancy, twenty-eight of Sinn Féin's members were arrested at the Ancient Order of Hibernians in Dublin's North Frederick Street on 19 February. They were charged with unlawful assembly and drilling. However, everything changed when, on 9 April, a bill for the introduction of conscription in Ireland was put before the House of Commons. Alongside it was a new bill for Home Rule, which did not satisfy nationalists while at the same time angering Unionists. In the wake of this, Sinn Féin took two seats previously held by the IPP, one of those unopposed.[20]

The conscription crisis might have divided the IPP and Sinn Féin.[21] However, when the bill was presented to the Commons, moves were already afoot to bring together nationalists and republicans in an 'Irish Covenant' against conscription, not least within the Dublin Corporation.[22] Emotions ran high, with the *Evening Telegraph* declaring that 'Lloyd George has declared war on Ireland.' The paper argued, 'Every man dragged out of Ireland by the alien power that has kept this country in chains would nurse in his heart a burning desire for revenge, and would strike back when and how he thought best.'[23] This was strong language from a constitutional nationalist publication. In mid-April, nationalist, republican and Roman Catholic opposition coalesced in a mass public pledge on which opposition could focus. Sunday 21 April saw a reported 150,000 Catholics sign the pledge in churches, while trade unions declared a 'labour holiday' (practically, a strike) for Tuesday 23 April. Dublin and many other places ground to a halt as the British government received a clear sign of the challenges of implementing conscription.[24]

Conscription received Royal Assent on 18 April but its terms delayed implementation until Home Rule was passed.[25] Until June, Irish conscription remained a goal for the British government, but they were considering a different approach due to the strength of opposition. On 16 May, under the guise of fears of a 'German plot', Sinn Féin leaders were arrested, though the arrests were really directed at anti-conscription agitation. Those arrested included Éamon de Valera, Arthur Griffith, Countess Markiewicz, and two MPs elected at recent by-elections, William Cosgrave and Joseph McGuinness. They remained in jail in England until early 1919, their imprisonment a powerful symbol of Ireland's republican struggle.[26] Over the next six weeks a series of repressive measures took place until, in early July, Sinn Féin and the Gaelic League were proscribed, while there was a ban on all meetings and processions across Ireland.[27] Further arrests took place later in the summer.[28]

At the same time, a voluntary recruitment scheme was launched, with some implication that if it was successful there would be no need for conscription in Ireland. Its target of 20,000 by 1 August and 3,000 a month thereafter was hopelessly optimistic and by October only 10,000 recruits had been raised (of whom nearly half joined the

Royal Air Force),[29] though the number of recruits raised from August until the end of the war was higher than in February to August 1916.[30] Efforts at recruiting in Dublin were sometimes disrupted, notably in late August when meetings in Kildare Street, James Street and Portland Row, addressed by the nationalist MP and former Boer, Colonel Arthur Lynch, were disrupted by protesters and were abandoned.[31] Of course, men could still have very personal reasons for enlisting: in October, at Dalkey, a Mr Page said that he was enlisting to avenge the sinking of the *Leinster*.[32] Members of the Davis Hurling Club had been killed on the ship while working for the post office and 'He appealed to all Gaels, with whom he had played hurling and football, to join up and avenge their murders.'[33] However, such efforts were not as necessary as they had appeared to be in the spring of 1918. The post-*Kaiserschlacht* manpower crisis had reduced in severity by the summer, partly due to the arrival of American troops on the front, but also because of recruitment in Britain.[34] This meant that from June there was no question of conscription being implemented in Ireland, even if it notionally remained on the table.

The War at Sea and the RMS *Leinster*

Over 1917 and 1918 the war at sea continued to affect Dublin. From the beginning of 1917 until the armistice there were 144 Dubliners killed in the Merchant Navy and another 84 in the Royal Navy. Many were on ships which did not contain other Dubliners. However, there were some clusters. On 9 July 1917, HMS *Vanguard* sank at Scapa Flow following the largest explosion in British history when a stokehold fire detonated the magazine. 824 died, including 12 Dubliners. Among them was Artificer Engineer Effizio Repetto of Rathmines. He had served in the Falkland Islands, at Jutland and off the coast of Gallipoli.[35] There were 7 merchant sailors from Dublin among 32 lost on the SS *Memphian* when it was hit by a torpedo from the German submarine U-96 7 miles from the North Arklow light vessel while *en route* from Liverpool to Boston. Two of the dead, James Austin and William Brien were from the village of Rush.[36] There were 6 Dubliners lost when 12 merchant sailors were killed on the SS *Hare* on 14 December 1917.[37] The SS *Adela* was a Dublin-based transport ship, and was 12 miles off Anglesey when it was sunk on 27 December 1917. Most of those killed – 17 of 24 – were from Dublin.[38]

On 2 April 1918 the *Evening Telegraph* carried news of two fishing boats, the *Geraldine* and the *St. Michan* which were fired on and sunk by U-96. The entire crew of 5 were lost on the *Geraldine*, all from Howth: Joseph Rickard, Joseph Gaffney, Patrick Rourke, Christopher Farren and Patrick Harford. But everyone on the *St. Michan* survived: 9 crew and 2 children who had gone on the boat with their father for a pleasure trip. It was fired on second, which meant those on board had more time to plan to escape, and they left the boat for a punt in which they rowed for several hours before being picked up by a patrol. One crewman, Patrick Caulfield attributed their survival to divine intervention. He was carrying a crucifix and said, 'I told the men to pray, and that the prayers and the crucifix would save us. I put the crucifix on the stern of the boat, and, though the timber all round it was torn away by the shells, the cross was untouched.' Having left the boat for the punt, the men held up the crucifix 'and told the Germans that now they could not sink us: that we had the Great Power on our side. All of us then joined in prayer, and it was through the intervention and by the mercy of the cross our lives were saved.'[39]

The greatest shock for the people of Dublin was the sinking of the RMS *Leinster* on 10 October 1918, an event dubbed by the *Freeman's Journal* as 'Ireland's Lusitania'.[40] The ship was the city's mail steamer, plying between Kingstown and Holyhead. It was outward bound when hit by a torpedo from UB-123 (which sank a week later with the loss of its crew of 36 after hitting a mine).[41] Sunk just outside Dublin Bay, over 500 died (the largest ever loss in the Irish Sea) as, aside from being the mail boat, it was a key route for people travelling from Dublin to Britain.[42]

At around 10am on 10 October UB-123 fired a torpedo which missed the *Leinster*, but a second followed shortly after. That hit the port side and the explosion also blew a hole on the other side of the ship. A few minutes later a third torpedo finished the job.[43] Florence Enright of Mountjoy Street was on board and described how

> Pieces of iron and wood flew about, hitting various people, many of whom were wounded, blood flowing freely from them. The boat immediately listed, and the deck went perpendicular, so that we could not stand. I jumped off into the water, and was sucked under the sinking vessel. On coming to the surface I swam away until I got hold of an upturned boat.[44]

The ship sank quickly and as lifeboats picked up those in the sea, Royal Navy vessels close by began to pick up survivors. News reached the shore fast and in both Dublin and Kingstown people gathered to find out about family and friends. The Press Bureau blundered and put out a message saying that all lives had been saved, only for the terrible truth to become more apparent as the evening approached.[45] At Kingstown, those waiting suffered the grim sight of bodies being brought ashore.[46] Yet there was hope for some, with around 200 rescued. Sister Mary Murphy, whose father lived in Findlater Street, was returning to her hospital in Nottingham following the funeral of a brother. She survived after spending three hours in the sea.[47]

Precise estimates of the numbers of dead vary, from 501 to an upper limit of 532 (21 postal staff, 37 crew, 134 civilians, and 340 military personnel).[48] Of Dubliners there were at least 24 civilians, 23 military, 20 postal staff and 14 crew. Among the civilians was Nurse Sophia Barrett of Carrickmines, a member of the Voluntary Aid Detachment who had been 'Mentioned in Despatches' in January 1918 while serving at Number 6 General Hospital in Rouen. She was returning to Rouen when the *Leinster* was hit. Her body was one of those recovered and she was buried at Kilternan Parish Churchyard.[49] Two members of the Irish Guards were killed, probably returning to their units after leave: Lance Sergeant 3881 James Brady of Santry and Private 7938 Patrick Halligan of St Paul Street. Both would be remembered on the Hollybrook Memorial in Southampton alongside others whose bodies were never found.[50] Among the Dublin civilians were Thomas and Charlotte Foley, on their way to visit Charlotte's brother Private 31906 Christopher Barrett, who was serving in the Northumberland Fusiliers but was said to be on his deathbed in a hospital in England.[51]

As funerals were held in the days which followed, the nationalist leader John Dillon asked in Parliament why the *Leinster* had not had an escort, which had been done in the past as part of anti-submarine measures. The government responded that it had done as much as it could, not least because it did not have any spare vessels which were fast enough to escort the *Leinster* in high seas, and that 'the Irish Sea has been rendered at least as immune as any of the waters around the United Kingdom'. The government also rejected Dillon's call for a special enquiry, saying that the Admiralty and Mercantile Marine already studied all such disasters.[52] With the war ending a month later, there was no further political fallout from the sinking, but bodies were still being washed ashore in December.[53]

The Hundred Days

The final phases of the war became known at the 'Hundred Days'. They were 'a succession of dour attritional struggles rather than a thrilling climactic battle'.[54] Much of the British army's learning came to fruition, though even then the application of, for example, combined arms tactics, varied enormously. Victory would also be based on the attrition of earlier years and the weaknesses of the German army.[55] During this time, Dubliners were scattered across many units of the British army and indeed other armies. The parents of Arthur Stokes lived in Kingtown's Maurice Terrace when he was killed in action on 30 August 1918 serving as a corporal in the 126th Infantry Regiment of the US Army's 32nd Division.[56] However, Dubliners played a particular part as members of the 1st, 2nd and 6th Dublins, and also the 7th Royal Irish Regiment. During the Hundred Days at least 39 Dubliners were killed in the 1st Dublins, 22 in the 2nd, 18 in the 6th, and a further 21 in the 7th Irish Regiment. The Hundred Days began on 8 August 1918 with the Battle of Amiens. Ludendorff declared 8 August 'the black day of the German Army' as around five miles of ground east of Amiens was gained in what Gary Sheffield calls 'truly a watershed battle, the turning point of the war'.[57] Then, until 11 November, the allies advanced as far as 90 miles into German lines (though not reaching Germany itself). The German army collapsed as the allies deployed the lessons of 1916 and 1917 alongside superior resources and manpower.

Although the largest initial gains were made in France, the British army also chipped away at German positions in Belgium along the Lys valley in the 'Advance in Flanders' from 18 August to 6 September.[58] The war was highly mobile, with both set-piece attacks on German lines and patrols probing for weaknesses to exploit. Sometimes movement was so rapid that units lost touch with each other and patrols were pushed out to re-establish some kind of coherent line. Yet without adequate artillery support, attacks could still be costly and unsuccessful, as the 7th Irish Regiment found on 2 September at Wulverghem, losing 22 men.[59] The 1st Dublins had a similar experience towards the end of the advance, on 4 September, in an attack on the village of Ploegsteert which was 'carried through with the greatest dash & gallantry'. The progress of the operation showed how far the British army could now adapt to the situation on the ground, though not without first testing the planned method of attack. The initial assault on the village was by an Australian method known as 'peaceful penetration' where patrols gradually occupied outposts, often from behind.[60] That began at 3am on 4 September but it became apparent by 4am that machine-gun fire was causing heavy casualties and artillery support was requested. When it could not be provided, the battalion was ordered once again to attack. Some advance was made until 9am 'when it was again reported that the enemy was too strong for further advance and our casualties were heavy'. A bombardment was then provided for half an hour from 8am, but made little impact on the Germans' front line at Ploegsteert and further attack by the 1st Dublins was halted. Their commanding officer ordered the battalion to halt, and following a brigade-level conference a creeping barrage was planned at 3pm. That barrage lifted 100 yards every three minutes and provided the cover necessary for the battalion to take the village by 4.10pm. Over the course of the day 31 of the 1st Dublins were killed (at least 8 of them Dubliners) and around another 80 wounded, mostly before 3pm. Around 100 Germans had been killed and about 170 captured.[61]

In late September the Final Advance in Flanders began with an offensive east of Ypres, towards Courtrai. The 1st Dublins and the 7th Irish Regiment were again involved, following periods of training in September, with the 1st Dublins engaged in heavy fighting in two phases. Success on 28 September – despite a British battery falling short and causing casualties in the battalion – was followed by further advance on 29 September before progress in the area was halted by German machine-gun fire from pill-boxes. The battalion then returned on 14 October when, alongside Emmet Dalton's 2nd Leinsters, they liberated the village of Ledeghem.[62] Meanwhile, the 7th Irish Regiment was advancing at Wervicq.[63] Targets were gained by the 1st Dublins at Heule on 16 October, before the crossing the Lys at Courtrai on 20 October. The crossing was by a temporary bridge erected by the Royal Engineers, the men walking over in single file at intervals of fifteen paces to reduce casualties if the bridge was attacked. That crossing was effectively the end of the battalion's war as it was withdrawn to support positions on 21 October and then behind the lines for rest and training.[64]

Figure 16.1: Emmet Dalton with other members of D Company 2nd Leinsters in 1918. Among them, front row from left, Capt Emmet Dalton MC, Sgt O'Neill VC, Capt Moran MC and Pte Moffat VC. (Photo: Audrey Dalton Simenz).

Meanwhile, both the 2nd and 6th Dublins were involved in the battles of the Hindenburg Line (12 September to 12 October) and the Final Advance in Picardy (17 October to 11 November).[65] At La Pannerie, while holding the line on 7 October, the 2nd Dublins came under heavy shell fire, losing 33 men.[66] The 6th Dublins moved to the Guillemont area in early October. Drury found the village had

> completely disappeared. There is not one complete brick even. Everything is shattered and scattered to the winds. The only thing that would indicate that a village had ever existed here is the tangled remains of the metal parts of a sugar factory. The place is absolutely alive with enormous rats as big as cats and we could get no sleep with them crawling over one.[67]

On 7 October the 6th Dublins were around Le Catelet preparing No Man's Land for an advance by laying tape to aid the assembly of soldiers. During this operation Drury had a near miss: 'there was a tremendous burst beside us and I got an awful crack in the back'. He first thought he had been hit in the back and might be paralysed, but soon found he could move all his limbs. He discovered that a piece of shell case 'opened out flat about 12 inches square' had hit his pack, which was mainly full of clothes. With some relief he noted that he 'felt very small then at my fright of trying to move lest I should find my back broken'.[68]

The next day the 6th Dublins advanced at 5.10am behind a creeping barrage and a smoke screen. Drury recalled how, 'the air was rent with a snap and crash of sound such as I have never heard before – one almighty deluge of sound poured over us as made it difficult to breathe. I could feel the air pulsating and almost buffeting the breath out of my body.' Then the Germans returned fire for a few minutes and the advancing 6th Dublins faced machine-gun fire but made steady progress, capturing Beaurevoir Farm and Villiers-Outereaux. They continued to advance in support of attacking lines until 11 October, spending nights in bivouacs. Drury recalled moving forward 'slowly along at a most leisurely speed, keeping in touch with the people on each side of us, but doing practically no fighting'. He noted. 'We were all itching to get on fast' but had to stay with other troops 'who were not used to open fighting'. Very few Germans were encountered, though Drury described the horrendous sight of a German 'cut in two at the waist by a shell and the upper part of his body was sitting upright on the ground with his legs about 100 yards away'. On 11th the 6th Dublins withdrew from the line to billets, having lost 64 dead and more than 200 wounded.[69]

Both the 2nd and 6th Dublins were soon in action again, crossing the Selle at Le Cateau on 17 October. After crossing the river by a bridge unhindered, the 2nd Dublins were in the first wave to attack German lines on the far bank, in conjunction with the rest of the 50th Division and units of American infantry. Thick fog made it hard to spot German machine-gun posts and hampered efforts to coordinate British troops. After limited progress and heavy casualties, the attack was cancelled at 12.30pm. A successful attack was made the next day although 51 men were killed in the battalion over two days. In that attack on 18 October, the 2nd Dublins earned another Victoria Cross, as Cornishman Sergeant 14017 Horace Curtis attacked machine-gun positions and captured around 100 prisoners.[70] Meanwhile, the 6th Dublins were mopping up at Le Cateau and met some of the hazards associated with taking prisoners. A particular problem was the town's system of interlocking cellars which, as Drury noted, meant that, 'As soon as we had cleared one street and driven all the Huns out of it and started down the next street, machine-gun fire would be opened on us from the very houses we had first cleared.'[71] The battalion war diary noted, 'The enemy were a very brave and stout lot of fellows and regret to say treacherous.' It described how a lieutenant and his Lewis Gun Section had walked along a street with two German prisoners in front of them and called on Germans inside houses to surrender. Ten men came out with hands up but then opened up with a machine gun, killing some of the Dublins. The diary noted, 'needless to say the prisoners in possession were promptly dispatched to another world'. Relieved the next day, the 6th Dublins lost 17 men in this, their final major action of the war.[72]

In the early hours of 4 November the 2nd Dublins were at Fontaine-au-Bois. Initially in reserve behind other battalions in their brigade, they advanced at zero hour of 6.15am ready to fill gaps in the leading units. Coming under almost immediate fire they lost 14 dead, but moved forward when ordered to make a further attack after the advance battalions had taken their positions. They secured a spurt overlooking Landrecies and enfilading the Sambre Canal. Meanwhile, they prevented a German field battery coming into action, shooting the horses and drivers and capturing the battery commander.[73]

Four days later the 2nd Dublins, who had been on the Western Front since August 1914, took part in their final action of the war. On 8 November, in taking the village of Floursies the battalion came under machine-gun fire. One officer and four other ranks were killed, including two Dubliners: Private 23555 James Byrne and Sergeant 13810 John Gregory. Byrne's wife lived in Ringsend, and Gregory's mother in Rathmines.[74] Lieutenant Eric Greaves, whose parents lived in Sandymount Avenue, was later described as having died of wounds 'received on the eve of the armistice' and of influenza, when he died at Number 8 General Hospital, Rouen. He too had been wounded in that action of 8 November, but survived until succumbing to his wounds on 21 November.[75] It is likely that Private 9680 John McAuley, a Clonsilla man also of the 2nd Dublins, was wounded in the same action. He died of wounds a week after the armistice.[76]

8 November was probably the last day on which Dubliners lost their lives on the Western Front, though that did not only happen in the

2nd Dublins. Close to the 2nd Dublins were the 5th Inniskillings, securing their objective on the Avesnes to St Aubin road 'after sticky fighting' which saw the death of Private 17058 John Griffin of Inchicore, killed in action.[77] The next day, two men with possibly only tenuous Dublin connections were killed in action in the Canadian Army. Private 3231310 James Buttimer was born in Dunmanway, County Cork, and his parents were living there when he enlisted in the Canadian Army in Toronto in January 1918, but by the time his grave came to be prepared (which could have been well after the war's end) they had moved to Sandymount. He was killed serving in the 19th Canadian Infantry as they took the town of Hyon on 10 November.[78] So too was Private 410970 Percy Carleton, in Princess Patricia's Canadian Light Infantry (Eastern Ontario Regiment) on the outskirts of Mons. All his family were in Montreal during and after the war, and he was born in Westmeath, but at some point he attended the Masonic Orphan Boys School in Dublin since he appears on their memorial.[79]

Over 9 to 11 November there were another ten war deaths involving people with a Dublin connection. Nine of these were people who died of illness or of wounds, some at home and some overseas, including in County Donegal on 10 November Worker 48257 Sheila Dunne of Queen Mary's Auxiliary Corps whose mother lived on Dublin's South Circular Road.[80] Private 3/3507 Robert McCombie died of wounds on 9 November serving with the New Zealand Medical Corps in France. His parents lived in Monkstown but he had left Dublin to be Rector of St Peter's in Granity, New Zealand.[81] On the day of the Armistice itself, Private 7003 Robert Connor of the 2nd Machine Guns Corps, whose parents lived in Lower Gardiner Street, died of wounds in France.[82] The same fate – though in Syria rather than on the Western Front – befell Driver M2/080226 George Grover of the Army Service Corps' 11th Light Armoured Motor Battery. He had once been a member of the Boys' Brigade in Clontarf.[83]

The tenth person to die over those last three days of the war was certainly the last Dubliner killed in action. There had been a Dubliner on board the HMS *Amphion* when it suffered the fate of being the first British naval loss of the war, and there was also one on HM Paddle Minesweeper *Ascot* which was the last such loss on 10 November, hit by a torpedo from UB-67 near the Farne Islands off the Northumbrian coast. Sunk with all hands, among 51 dead was 27-year-old Trimmer

2656ST Patrick Pender, whose mother lived in Upper Gloucester Street.[84]

When news of the armistice came, some units were still attacking. The 7th Irish Regiment continued to advance until the armistice was called, receiving news by telegram while on the march. The war diary noted that 'There was very little excitement amongst the troops when the news was made known.'[85] Other battalion war diaries made no mention at all of the men's reaction.[86] In the 6th Dublins, Drury noted mixed emotions. At 9am on 11 November, his commanding officer

> casually remarked 'Well, we stop to-day', so I replied 'Thank the Lord, we could do with a spell of a few days.' So he smiled and said, 'Oh, but we stop altogether, the old war's finished.' I thought he was pulling my leg so I asked him was I to tell the men. He said 'Yes, certainly, an Armistice has been signed and all fighting will cease at 11.00 exactly.'

Drury could, 'hardly believe it. I don't know what to feel, but somehow it's like when one heard of the death of a friend – a sort of forlorn feeling.' His men 'just stared at me and showed no enthusiasm at all. One or two muttered "We were just getting a bit of our own back."' Drury recalled, 'They all had the look of hounds whipped off just as they were about to kill.' Nearby, Drury found celebrations among the local population: 'The French people are fairly off their heads, laughing and crying and singing, and clasping everyone round the neck and kissing them.' Drury's 'men got up a little better spirits' and there was a firework display once it was dark.[87]

The Armistice at Home

The new of the armistice was somewhat overshadowed in Dublin by the effects of the 'Great Flu': the Spanish influenza outbreak, which had hit Dublin in June with rapid effects. There were 5 dead in the city from flu in the week ending 29 June, but the weekly figure rose to 33 and then 78 in the next two weeks. The rate then slowed, though by early November there had been a total of 376 deaths in the city.[88] Across the whole of 1918–19, 2,866 in the city and county died from flu, from around 114,000 suffering from the illness.[89] Still in people's minds, as the armistice was marked, would have been recent warnings about avoiding the spread of flu in crowded places.[90] Yet that did not stop 'general manifestations of delight and jubilation'. The *Evening Mail* reported the display of Union Flags, British Ensigns, the Stars and Stripes and other flags of the allies on public buildings and offices, as well as on motor vehicles.[91] The *Freeman's Journal* said that American soldiers and sailors in the city received a particularly warm response. Meanwhile, students commandeered a laundry van and drove it about the city centre flying the Union Flag. Then at 3.30pm,

> A mock funeral took place through the streets. In the hearse, which was an open one, was laid the 'remains' of the Kaiser, wearing a gas-mask. The funeral, preceded by a number of students and followed by a large crowd of laughing soldiers and civilians, created general amusement, and added considerably to the hilarity of the proceedings.

Some businesses closed early to allow staff to celebrate. Those who did witnessed an aerial display from a number of aircraft performing acrobatics over the city. There was also conflict: some Trinity College students demonstrated outside the Sinn Féin headquarters in Harcourt Street, attempting to enter. The *Freeman's Journal* said, 'A scuffle ensued in the hall, and some blows were exchanged. Eventually the students were forced out, and, forming up, marched along Stephen's Green into Grafton Street, cheering and singing.' In the evening there was further violence as Sinn Féin supporters left a meeting at the Mansion House and clashed with crowds in Grafton Street and on O'Connell Bridge.[92] Far worse might have been expected.

With the war's end, moderate nationalists saw a chance to press Ireland's case in the peace talks to come. On the day the armistice was announced the *Freeman's Journal* published details of the IPP's appeal to President Woodrow Wilson for Ireland's 'free self-determination' in line with Wilson's 'Fourteen Points' for peace.[93] A new struggle was about to start, but it would begin with violence rather than diplomacy.

17 WAR OF INDEPENDENCE

... only a disciplined organisation could achieve results ...
Harry Colley, 2nd Dublin IRA[1]

Recovery

During the War of Independence, former British solders took up some crucial roles in the IRA. They provided military expertise, insights into discipline, and the ability to pose as British officers. Those who remained in the army could also be an important source of weapons. However, when they returned to Dublin in 1919, the IRA they joined or supported had already been developed from the Irish Volunteers of 1916 by veterans of the Rising and new recruits. Over 1917 and 1918 the Irish Volunteer movement steadily recovered and formed the basis of the post-war IRA.[2] When Oscar Traynor returned from Frongoch at the end of 1916, he found that 'My old Company, while meeting from time to time, was very much below strength.'[3] However, Harry Colley recalled that the release of the final batch of prisoners in mid-1917 'had a wonderful effect on morale and led to a very large influx of recruits'.[4] Tom Byrne found himself elected Commandant of the 1st Battalion.[5] Following Thomas Ashe's funeral in September 1917, Richard Mulcahy became commandant of the Dublin Brigade, a role he held until March 1918 when he became the IRA's Chief of Staff. At that point, Richard McKee took over in the city, running an organisation whose structures had been re-established by Mulcahy.[6]

The campaign against conscription also had an effect. Nancy de Paor sold 'No Conscription' flags to buy arms for the Dublin Brigade which 'became risky later when the Government made a regulation that it could not be done without a permit, and a good many members in Dublin and elsewhere were arrested and given short terms of imprisonment for contravening the regulation'.[7] The money helped to obtain arms from British soldiers at barracks. Enough had their price to have already provided Peadar McNulty's unit with about twenty Lee Enfields plus ammunition by late 1917.[8] Other soldiers supplied arms because they sympathised with the cause, including Dublin Fusilier Edward Handley who had been wounded in France. Posted as a storeman at Portobello Barracks, he secured weapons and ammunition by altering paperwork so that it did not appear anything was missing.[9] There were also new recruits during the conscription crisis. Vincent Byrne described 70 or 80 men in a unit of his battalion being dubbed 'the Conscript Company' by older hands, but the company 'fell away after the conscription scare was over'.[10]

However, the 1918 general election showed that the growth of support for radical republicanism in place of the IPP was not temporary. In December 1910, the IPP had won all 4 of the Dublin city seats, and both of those for the wider county. Unionists won the 2 Dublin University seats. In the December 1918 election the number of seats allocated to Dublin rose to 7 for the city and 4 for the county, in addition to the 2 university seats. Unionists held on to the latter, and won 1 of the county seats (Rathmines), but the other 10 were all gained by Sinn Féin. Among those elected were Constance Markiewicz in the St Patrick's city seat, and Frank Lawless of the Fingal Battalion, representing North County Dublin. Across the island, although Sinn Féin received slightly under half the popular vote they won 73 of 105 seats, though 25 of those were unopposed, which reduced their total of votes cast. Unionists were the second largest bloc, with a quarter of the popular vote and a total 26 seats (all in Ulster except the two Dublin University seats). The once dominant IPP fell to just 6 Irish seats and 1 in Liverpool, from their 74 in December 1910.[11]

During the election the IRA played a part in Dublin supporting Sinn Féin candidates. Peadar McNulty's company worked for Michael Staines in the city's St Michan's constituency. They canvassed, worked in tally-rooms as agents, ensured the vote was got out, and acted as 'personation officers'. At election meetings they provided 'protective units' in case of trouble.[12] Their presence was a sign of things to come: despite Sinn Féin's sizeable majority of Irish seats, the British government had no intention in 1919 of granting an 'Irish Republic', and instead offered a devolved Parliament within the UK. So following the 1918 general election, the Sinn Féin MPs refused to attend at Westminster and established their own Dáil Éireann, an independent Parliament in which they sat as if there was no question that Ireland was already fully independent from the UK. Inevitably, after the peace of November 1918, the British government would soon face war again in Ireland.

Preparing for War

In late 1918 and early 1919 the IRA, which had taken an Oath of Allegiance to the Dáil, continued to gear up for war, particularly by obtaining arms, sometimes from soldiers in Dublin but also through purchases in England which were brought over by sailors on ships routinely travelling from Britain to Ireland.[13] Other arms and munitions were secured through raids of private houses. During raids at Rathgar and Ranelagh, Gerry Byrne's unit faced little opposition: 'The two revolvers we got were more or less handed over. In fact, the owner told us if we had asked him for them in the first instance, he would have given them to us.'[14]

In late 1918 the IRA was on the streets of Dublin carrying out unarmed street patrols and 'intelligence work', observing movements and contacts of Crown forces then reporting back to officers.[15] It was clear in 1919 that the IRA would eventually strike at the British state, but some wanted action sooner rather than later. Harry Colley recalled that during 1919, 'we had trouble with some of our men who thought we were moving too slowly'. The response was that 'only a disciplined organisation could achieve results'. Colley and others 'urged them to use the time they had to perfect themselves as soldiers; and that they would, before long, get plenty of opportunities to meet the British Army'.[16] In the meantime, the IRA was forging itself into a force able to take on the British, and in Dublin that meant some reorganisation. In the city, the existing units were rebadged as part of the Dublin Brigade with the 1st to 4th battalion covering broadly the same areas as designated to them in the Irish Volunteers, while the 5th were 'engineers'. In early 1921, new 6th and

7th battalions were formed in the county and in 1921 the Dublin Brigade became part of the 2nd Eastern Division. The Fingal Battalion was no longer part of the Dublin Brigade, operating in its own right as the Fingal Brigade, later in 1921 joining the 1st Eastern Division across parts of counties Kildare, Louth, Meath and Westmeath.[17] This was the basic structure during the War of Independence, though most operations would be carried out by units far smaller than a battalion, such were the necessities of guerrilla warfare. For those reasons too, in time, the Dublin Brigade's fight against the British was enhanced by the creation of two units: the 'Squad' and an Active Service Unit.[18]

War Begins

If IRA units in Dublin were initially restrained, that was not the case across Ireland. On 21 January 1919, as the Dáil met and declared independence, an ambush was carried out at Soloheadbeg in County Tipperary, in which the IRA killed two policemen. Though it was many months before anything like a state of war existed, this was effectively the first act of the War of Independence. In February, the organ of the Irish Volunteers declared that the Dáil's existence meant that their members could treat the British army and the police 'exactly as invading enemy soldiers would be treated by the native army of any country'.[19] Soon, Dublin (the city not the county) would see some of the highest levels of violence of the conflict.[20]

In Dublin, the first IRA operation of the war was at Collinstown Aerodrome (now Dublin Airport), with a raid beginning late on 20 March. Participants included about 30 men of the 1st Battalion and a small number of men of the Fingal Brigade acting as drivers, including Joseph Lawless. He recalled, 'It was a bright moonlight night with a nip of frost in the air.' Because of the light, men approached the aerodrome 'bent double in the shadows on either side of the road towards the entrance to the camp'. Lawless became concerned when 'after a considerable time there was nothing but dead silence'. He and other drivers moved closer to the gate when they met IRA men who said that cars were needed at the guardroom which was now in the hands of the IRA. This was a change of plan as originally the raiders aimed to take British vehicles and load them up with arms, but the British had disabled the vehicles. As a result, the arms haul 'was limited to what two touring cars could carry and the remaining cars had to carry the men back to the city'. However, 75 rifles and 5,000 rounds of ammunition plus other equipment still represented a sizeable cache for an operation in which no shot was fired. The four cars went off in various directions, gradually dispersing arms and men. Lawless took his car to his garage in Dominick Street, and 'got home to my digs in Drumcondra as quickly as I could on my bicycle, taking care that my arrival there was unnoticed by any possible watch'.[21]

The IRA were again in action in County Dublin in late May 1919 when they raided a British field kitchen at Ticknock in the Sandyford area, stealing two mules.[22] At the end of July, the IRA carried out its first killing of the war in Dublin. Michael Collins was directing much of the IRA's war from Dublin, though it was said he never slept in the same place more than two nights in a row.[23] He had been pressing for action for some time when, in July, he was authorised to carry out the killing of Detective Sergeant Patrick Smith, who was tracking down and arresting Republicans. The authorisation came from the IRA's Chief of Staff, Richard Mulcahy, and the Dáil's Minister for Defence, Cathal Brugha.[24] To carry out the murder, Collins put in place the foundations of what became 'The Squad': essentially an assassination unit focused on British intelligence agents. One of the first to join was Jim Slattery who had been at Jacob's during Easter 1916, and was later held at Knutsford and Frongoch. In mid-July he was summoned to a house on North Great George's Street where he found 'a fairly big number of Volunteers present'. Some, including Slattery, were selected and invited into an inner room where they were addressed by the commandant of the Dublin Brigade, Richard 'Dick' McKee. Slattery recalled, 'Dick McKee addressed those of us who had been selected and asked us if we had any objection to shooting enemy agents. The greater number of Volunteers objected for one reason or another. When I was asked the question I said I was prepared to obey orders.'[25]

The Squad's first attempt on Smith was aborted. Having decided to shoot him as he went home to Millmount Avenue, Slattery and others waited on Drumcondra Bridge 'for about five nights' before they thought they had identified him. Unsure as to whether they had the right man they did not shoot, but later it became clear that it had been Smith. They left their next attempt for a week, fearing that Smith might have noticed them and become suspicious. Whether he had or not, he did not change his route home and Slattery described how, on 30 July,

> we shot Smith. We had .38 guns and they were too small. I thought that the minute we would fire at him he would fall, but after we hit him he ran. The four of us fired at him. Keogh and myself ran after him right to his own door and I think he fell at the door, but he got into the house.

Smith lived for another five weeks before succumbing to his wounds.[26]

On 12 September the Dáil was formally outlawed by the British government,[27] and a week later a meeting was summoned to expand and formalise 'the Squad', using that title for the first time.[28] Numbering a core of twelve, its initial members were nicknamed 'The Twelve Apostles'.[29] It was made clear that the Squad would take orders directly from Collins, and that they would be employed full-time by the IRA with a wage, since Squad members would have to give up any other paid work so as to be available at any hour. A factor driving this, as Vincent Byrne recalled, was that 'All operations carried out by the unofficial squad took place under cover of the dark evenings and, naturally, the British authorities knew this. Therefore, their agents and officials made sure that they would not be caught out after the fall of evening but would carry on with their dirty work during the daylight.'[30] Over time the Squad was reinforced, with one of the new recruits at some point in 1920 being ex-British soldier, Joseph Byrne. Byrne had been sent to France shortly after the Rising and only returned to Dublin after demobilisation.[31]

The Squad's first operation after its formalisation ended in failure and the death of a volunteer. On 19 December 1919, the Squad (supported by others including Dan Breen, who was on the run from Tipperary) attempted to kill the Lord Lieutenant of Ireland, Field Marshal Sir John French, as he travelled from Ashtown station to the vice-regal lodge in Phoenix Park. However, a plan to block the road with a farm cart failed when French's four-car convoy took less time to reach the park than expected. Meanwhile, IRA fire focused on the second car, in which they expected French to travel, but he had in fact travelled in the first. Vigorous fire was exchanged between the IRA and the convoy, but French escaped unharmed. Two policemen were wounded as was Dan Breen, while IRA volunteer Martin Savage was killed. Vincent Byrne recalled, 'I heard Martin Savage saying something, and it sounded like this: "Oh, lads, I am hit". The next moment, he was dead, lying on the road.'[32]

Following the failed attempt to kill French, the Squad focused on operations with a specific format, one that took advantage of knowing the streets of Dublin, being able to meet victims at close quarters, and making a quick getaway. One such killing was of Detective Inspector W. C. Forbes Redmond. The Squad was told that on 21 January 1920 Redmond would be attending a conference at Dublin Castle, and they set up groups of men at key positions outside. In Harcourt Street were Patrick O'Daly, Joseph Leonard and Seán Doyle. It was they who found themselves closest to Redmond as he left the Castle and O'Daly described how 'When Redmond was about two yards from me I fired and he fell mortally wounded, shot through the head.' Meanwhile, Thomas Keogh, who had been following Redmond, shot him in the back. He was soon dead, for the head shot had severed his spinal cord, while the other hit a lung, his liver and his stomach.[33] The sort of operation which had killed Redmond became the norm for the Squad.[34]

Meanwhile, regular units of the IRA widened their war. Harry Colley recalled that early in 1920 his 2nd Battalion was ordered to hold up a train which was carrying British military and munitions, at Newcomen Bridge. This 'first attempt at a big military operation in the 2nd Battalion' failed, partly because 'The information about it was only received a very short time before the train was due and arrangements were very rushed.' But there was also indiscipline on the part of one volunteer, who opened fire prematurely and provided warning of the attack.[35] Discipline soon became even more necessary as the British brought the 'Black and Tans' into action.

The Tan War Begins

The 'Black and Tans' were one of two special police units raised by the British government and deployed in 1920, the other being the Auxiliaries. The Black and Tans were formally the Royal Irish Constabulary (RIC) Special Reserve, recruited especially in urban areas of Britain among working-class war veterans. Their name came from their uniforms initially being a mix of khaki army surplus and black or very dark green police clothing, rapidly noticed by the local population when they arrived in Ireland from late February. By the middle of 1921 they numbered over 8,000.[36] A smaller and more elite force was the Auxiliary Division of the RIC, recruited from former army officers and specialising in intelligence and raids. They were more 'military' than 'police' and were headed initially by Brigadier General Frank Crozier who had commanded the 9th Royal Irish Rifles on the Somme in July 1916. The Auxiliaries' F Company were based in Dublin Castle and became effective at targeting the IRA's leadership in the city.[37] Around 2,200 men served in the Auxiliaries, a small number of them from Ireland. Of these, 14 living in Dublin had war service (all as officers between 2nd lieutenant and captain), and another 2 were new to the Crown forces; 6 of them were Roman Catholic.[38]

Harry Colley recalled how the Auxiliaries' arrival was seen by the IRA: well-armed, the Auxiliaries 'swaggered and bullied and appeared utterly reckless', so 'one does not wonder that, for a while, some of our people were rather downcast'.[39] They arrived in a city in which the tempo of the war had been raised in preceding months. A curfew was enforced between midnight and 5am from 23 February, as the Squad continued its work.[40] In early April, an IRA hunger strike began with over 100 prisoners at Mountjoy demanding prisoner-of-war status.[41] It lasted until the middle of the month when a general strike on 13 and 14 April raised the stakes, with as many as 60,000 people striking in Dublin on its first day.[42] Meanwhile, tensions remained high with the killing of Detective Constable Henry Kells on 14 April by the Squad in Camden Street.[43] The strike led to the release first of 66 prisoners, and then a steady stream.[44] The IRA also began to target tax offices and their employees. Peadar McNulty's company burned the head office in Beresford Place on the evening of 3 April, while five other Dublin tax offices were attacked by the IRA.[45] Homes of tax inspectors were also targeted for the destruction of documents.[46] Such events did nothing to harm support for the IRA beyond the immediate republican movement. A sign of that came on 20 May when a strike was held at Dublin docks with dockers refusing to handle British military equipment, soon joined by train drivers who would not transport British troops.[47]

Not all IRA prisoners were held in Dublin. Tom Byrne was in Wormwood Scrubs. He was arrested at home in Upper Eccles Street in late 1919. Byrne recalled, 'I had been staying at home as my wife was after having her first baby.' His wife was Lucy Smyth, another Rising veteran as a member of Cumann na mBan. She was involved in arms smuggling prior to the Rising and in the GPO had tended to the wounded, including James Connolly.[48] Byrne had probably been courting her since 1913, when he had a rival in love, Con Colbert, who was executed after the Rising. Colbert's sister said years later, 'I think he was in love with her and might have married her if he had lived.'[49] Instead, Lucy Smyth had married Tom Byrne in 1919. After time at the Scrubs, Byrne was transferred to Brixton Prison where he and others threatened a hunger strike, only to be released before they could act on the threat. Byrne was again arrested in 1920 when he was sent to the Rath Camp at the Curragh.[50]

Meanwhile, the net which the police and military sought to cast over the IRA was not without holes. Nancy de Paor described how Cumann members were persistently overlooked by the police 'unless caught red-handed in the commission of some offence'. She remembered with amusement that despite herself and her mother being widely known republican activists, the IRA's Adjutant-General had an office in their house for over six months without any police raids.[51] In the summer of 1920 the IRA even managed to obtain details of those whom the security forces were due to raid and give them some warning.[52] Yet in the autumn, the war became more bloody.

Bloody Autumn

On 20 September 1920, both sides in the conflict made clear their intentions. That morning, about twenty men from H Company of Peadar McNulty's 1st Battalion attempted to take arms from soldiers who were escorting bread supplies from Monk's Bakery in Church Street. A bakery employee told the *Evening Mail* how four IRA men 'held up the office staff with revolvers, and destroyed the telephone'. Shots were exchanged and three of the British soldiers were killed, the first in Dublin since the Rising. The *Mail* reported, 'The noise was deafening, and bullets could be heard whizzing on every side. There was much excitement in the locality, and throughout the city the incident created a profound sensation.'[53] Among the IRA, 18-year-old university student and resident of South Circular Road, Kevin Barry, became detached from his unit and was captured while hiding under a lorry.[54] On 1 November, after being tortured, he was hanged, the first republican executed since Roger Casement. He became the stuff of IRA legend.[55] Tom Byrne, commanding the 1st Battalion, had thought the operation unwise, believing the British would have good vantage points. He cautioned against the plan and had no knowledge that H Company would carry it out. There was a tone of regret in his 1951 recollection that 'three harmless British tommies were shot'.[56]

On the evening of 20 September the head constable of the RIC, Peter Burke, stopped at a bar in Balbriggan on his way to visit Black and Tans at Gormanstown. There was an altercation in the bar, with the police called to restore order. They did so, but rowdiness occurred again and an IRA unit appeared. It is not clear exactly what happened but Burke was shot dead, and his brother was badly wounded.[57] As a reprisal, 5 lorries full of police and Black and Tans arrived at about 11pm and began what became known as the 'Sack of Balbriggan'. Local people fled, 49 houses were damaged or destroyed, 4 pubs were looted and burned, a factory was burned to the ground, and 2 men were killed (both suspected by the police of IRA membership).[58] The *Evening Mail*, no supporter of the IRA, reported the 'pitiful spectacle' of the area being 'sacked by uniformed, armed men' who caused 'the wildest disorder'. They reported 'Men, women and children, some of them only scantily attired ... fleeing to the country for refuge' and described how a 'poor woman experienced great difficulty in getting her baby from its cot before her house was fired'.[59] It must have been hard for neutral observers to see the Crown forces as the representatives of law and order.

Two months later, worse came on 'Bloody Sunday', 21 November. At least 35 were killed, 3 in the IRA, 16 in, or linked to, Crown forces, and 16 civilians, in Dublin's worst single day of the War of Independence. All the dead were shot and most came in three specific incidents: a co-ordinated IRA attack on intelligence operatives at several city centre locations, firing by Crown forces on a Gaelic football crowd at Croke Park, and the deaths of 3 prisoners in custody.[60]

The IRA members who took part in the killings on the morning, which were intended to be 'the destruction of the Secret Service',[61] came from across the Dublin IRA units but of course included members of the Squad. Oscar Traynor described the evolution of the operation as a response to the fact 'that a number of English Military Intelligence Officers had been introduced into the city ... operating entirely as civilians and [who] were thus regarded as spies'.[62] Among those taking part was Vincent Byrne who led an attack on 38 Upper Mount Street, targeting intelligence officers Captain Peter Ames and Lieutenant George Bennett.[63] Byrne went to the front door with four or five others, one of whom was Tom Ennis. On ringing the bell, a servant girl answered. They asked where the two officers were and were pointed to their rooms. Byrne captured Bennett in the nearest room and Ennis took Ames at the back of the house. They then heard shooting outside and a ring at the door. On answering they found a British dispatch rider whom they held at gun point. Byrne described Ennis and Bennett facing a wall in a back room: 'I said to myself "The Lord have mercy on your souls!" I then opened fire ... They both fell dead.'[64]

At 117 Morehampton Road, the IRA attacked the home of Thomas Smith, reportedly a 'captain', and considered an agent even though he was probably not. He was expecting a registered letter and his young son was waiting to welcome the postman. When the boy opened the door to find armed men he cried, 'Don't shoot my daddy!' However, the IRA entered, gathered Smith and two lodgers, a member of the Rifle Brigade, Captain Donald MacLean, and his brother-in-law, John Caldow. These three were taken to a room away from the women and children and shot. MacLean died instantly and Smith before an ambulance could arrive, while Caldow survived.[65] Over the rest of the morning, not all the IRA's operations were successful, not least because targets could not always be found.[66] However, another ten members of the Crown forces were killed by the IRA, along with two civilians and one other who might or might not have been a British agent. Though targeted at British intelligence, it is likely that only six of the dead were involved in such work.[67]

In the afternoon, British forces responded. Harry Colley's 2nd Battalion had often acted as stewards for the GAA on a Sunday but for obvious reasons had been directed elsewhere. However, at about 2.30pm Colley and others learned news which had come from a Dublin police sergeant who was horrified about what was about to happen and had tipped off the IRA. He had relayed 'word that the Auxiliaries and military were already mobilised and under orders to proceed to Croke Park to mow down the people'.[68] Reaching the ground with the news, so as to try to stop the game, Colley and others were not persuasive enough to send people away. When the British forces arrived, it was not clear whether they opened fire first or whether fire had come from the crowd, but 'mow down the people' was more or less what they did, with ten killed in the park immediately, and another four dying of wounds in subsequent days. One of those at the game told the *Evening Mail* that the Crown forces had 'rushed in as though they were attacking the Germans'. He described people taking refuge where they could, whether inside the pavilion or under the banking around the pitch where they 'were huddled up on top of one another'. It was, he said, 'a scene of terror'.[69] Three of the dead were children. Three were members of the IRA but one was there to play in the match and the other two were watching.[70]

That evening, two republican prisoners (Dublin commandant Dick McKee and his deputy Peadar Clancy) were shot, along with another man who had been arrested on suspicion of being a 'Sinn Feiner' but was not a member of the IRA. They were reportedly trying to escape.[71] Further 'reprisals' were seen outside the city, in the villages of Swords, Skerries and Rush, which faced a 'Night of Terror and Burning' as Crown forces raided, burned and looted several houses and shops.[72] Raids continued in Dublin itself the next day.[73] Oscar Traynor replaced McKee as head of the Dublin Brigade.[74] Inside the IRA, Tom Byrne and Michael Collins fell out, 'owing to the failure of the 1st Battalion to carry out certain operations on Bloody Sunday'. Byrne was relieved of his command, though that did not stop Collins putting forward Byrne to be Captain of the Guard at Leinster House after the Irish Free State had been established.[75] For now, it was becoming increasingly clear that the British were losing their grip on the situation.

18 CROSSOVERS

You have been fighting for a foreign country long enough. It's up to
you now to fight for your own country.
Words spoken to ex-Dublin Fusilier Peter Gough by his
brother in 1919, which encouraged him to join the IRA.[1]

Shifting Loyalties

As the War of Independence intensified, the value of former
British servicemen became apparent. The Squad's work rested on intelligence information. Some came from former British soldiers whose
military service allowed them to cross over between the worlds of the
British military and the IRA, securing positions of use to the IRA.
On demobilisation in October 1919, Bernard Golden joined the IRA
in Dublin and was told to find civilian employment. He was first
attached to the Royal Garrison Artillery as a schoolmaster and provided
information on their movements.[2] In early 1921, he became a clerk at
Dublin Castle, smuggling out files whenever possible.[3] Meanwhile,
British army veteran William Beaumont, whose brother Seán was
already in the IRA (while also being a Communist),[4] had been angered
by being roughly handled by British soldiers searching a tram. They
found on him a notebook containing details of how to use a machine
gun. Beaumont eventually persuaded them that he had made the notes in
France and was set free. Beaumont had been very hostile to Sinn Féin
and to Michael Collins in particular, but his experience changed his

views and his brother recalled, 'He came home furious with indignation about the way that he and the other passengers, particularly the women, had been treated and the first thing he said to me when he came in was that, if I got him a gun, he would shoot some of the Auxiliaries.' Rather than do that, Seán suggested, 'he should cultivate their acquaintance and pass on any information he might get to me. He did so and got to know some of them through the fellow who had searched him and in other ways.' Seán recalled,

> From then until the Truce, my brother spent almost every night in their company, drinking. Sometimes they started in pubs or hotels and sometimes they finished up in the Castle to which he accompanied them, after curfew. They used to leave him home in an armoured car about two or three o'clock in the morning. When he came in I used to write down as much as he could remember of their conversation when it had any bearing on the war.[5]

The intelligence which led to the IRA's Bloody Sunday attack came from a number of sources, including civilian clerks. Lily Mernin, a typist in the Women's Auxiliary Army Corps, was crucial. She was the confidential secretary to the second in command of British military intelligence in Dublin, Major Stephen Hill-Dillon.[6] However, William Beaumont made a significant contribution and Seán Beaumont said that his brother's nights spent drinking with Auxiliaries meant that 'He was able to give me the names and addresses of all the Intelligence Corps of the Auxiliaries, that is, all the men that were shot on Bloody Sunday and a couple who escaped.'[7]

The highest-profile crossover from the British army to the IRA was Emmet Dalton, who was drawn into training because of his First World War experience. His time in the British army ended in April 1919, demobilised as a captain, a rank he had held since July 1918. He then returned to Dublin using a British grant to study engineering at the Royal College of Science (which he did for about a year) and, due to his military record, was given a job as a temporary clerk at the Office of Public Works.[8] It is not clear exactly what turned him towards the IRA. In one fictionalised account of his own life, his own character joined simply because he was 'he was so fed up after four years in France'. IRA legend, Tom Barry of the West Cork Flying Brigade, famously described how he had joined the British army in 1915 'for no other reason than that I wanted to see what war was like, to get a gun, to see new countries and to feel a grown man'. He stressed that 'Above all I went because I knew no Irish history and had no national consciousness.' Later, the 'beauty' of the words of the Proclamation of the Republic 'enthralled' him and he became an ideological republican. There is no evidence of Emmet Dalton having such a conversion and Pádraig Yeates sees him as a 'hybrid patriot who came from a strong Home Rule family background'. Dalton's choice of service at different times was, he says, 'almost instinctive' and responded 'to the national mood'.[9] Certainly Dalton was well versed in Irish nationalism and culture, having attended the Christian Brothers' O'Connell School in North Richmond Street, a school which contributed about 125 rebels to the Rising, including three of the executed leaders, though Dalton's father was very much a mainstream constitutional nationalist.[10] At any rate, Dalton certainly had a strong service ethic, and a record of putting his life on the line for others by joining armies, beginning with the Irish Volunteers. It is not exactly clear when he joined the IRA, but he was involved by the middle of 1919 giving lectures to IRA officers. Such work became central to his role in the immediate post-war years: by the summer of 1921 he was Assistant Director of Training, and then soon the overall Director. His way in was through his brother Charles who had joined the Irish Volunteers at the end of 1917 and was involved in intelligence work. It was he who recommended Emmet to Oscar Traynor. Such work meant he soon fell under the gaze of the authorities: in early December 1920, the family home was raided by Auxiliaries and the army, with Emmet and his father arrested (and held from 9 to 18 December).[11]

Former British army service was no protection when it came to searches because of the number of crossovers. One IRA member, Seán Prendergast, remembered an incident when an IRA man was searched and remarked that he was a former British soldier: '"What!", said the British soldier who was paying him all attention, "another bally ex Army Man! Blimmie, they must be all ex soldiers around here."' Prendergast made it clear that of course sometimes such claims were falsely made, but the problem for Crown forces was that it was 'hard to differentiate in a situation where any civilian might be a potential I.R.A. man' so 'they had no other recourse but to treat all citizens alike'. Meanwhile, 'Quite a number also were members of the I.R.A. or were related to I.R.A. men.' This meant that in early 1921, Prendergast believed 'the average ex British soldier was neutral at the time and wanted to remain so' and there were 'a fair number of them sympathetic to our cause for several reasons, one of which was because of the brutal atrocities and the harsh inhuman reprisal policy carried out by the British'.[12]

Overall, there were at least sixteen former members of the British military with First World War experience who joined or worked closely with the IRA in Dublin, whose story Steven O'Connor has done so much to document.[13] John J. Doyle, whose British service had ended in 1915, had seen action in the Rising.[14] Another Rising veteran was Michael McCabe. He had not, in 1916, been in the British army but joined it in 1917 and would rejoin the IRA at the outbreak of the Civil War,[15] where he would serve with fellow British veteran Patrick O'Moore.[16] Edward Handley had supplied weapons to the IRA while in the British army.[17] Bernard Golden and William Beaumont were both spying for the IRA.[18] Others included Jim Donnelly, Patrick Garrett, Anthony Lawlor, William 'Jack' McSweeney (or MacSweeney), Charles Russell, and Billy Walsh.[19] Another, William Warren, enlisted in the 2nd Royal Irish Fusiliers in 1913, was in India when war broke out and arrived in France with them in December 1914. He served all through the war and was discharged in August 1920, joining the IRA later that year.[20] In addition to the British veterans working with the IRA, Robert Barton focused on politics through Sinn Féin and as a Minister of the Dáil. This led to him being arrested by the British twice. In February 1919 he was arrested and held at Mountjoy, escaping in the middle of March by sawing through bars using tools smuggled in by Richard Mulcahy, who visited disguised as the clerk to Barton's solicitor. Re-arrested in January 1920, Barton was tried by court martial the next month and spent a year and a half in prisons in England before release in June 1921.[21]

Active Service Units

Less than a month after Bloody Sunday, the IRA began a new phase of its war in Dublin, attacking Auxiliaries at Ballsbridge Post Office on 14 December. The raid was carried out by about a dozen men of the 3rd Battalion from 9am. It depended on meticulous planning, with the usual patterns of the Auxiliaries carefully observed beforehand. Advance lookouts signalled the arrival of the Auxiliaries at the post office. As they collected their mail and left, a group of IRA volunteers opened fire with revolvers and threw a grenade (which fell short). Soon joined by men from the rest of the party, who fired shots and threw grenades, the IRA forced the Auxiliaries back into the post office, after they had abandoned the mail. The IRA then left, taking an Auxiliary car, the mail and one captured rifle. One of those present recalled, that in a seven-minute attack, 'The element of surprise had been most successful; the terrific din created by ... the explosion of grenades gave the Auxies ... to understand that they were attacked by a much larger party.'[22]

Around this time the police had increased their activity with the formation of the undercover 'Igoe Gang', led by Head Constable Igoe from Galway. Oscar Traynor recalled that the men of the Gang 'were regarded as being the type who would be prepared to shoot I.R.A. men on sight', and they were very effective.[23] One response came on the first day of 1921, when the Dublin Brigade was strengthened by the formation of an Active Service Unit (ASU). Its role went beyond the assassinations detailed to the Squad, and drew together men from across the Dublin battalions, twelve from each (mainly officers), plus two commanding officers. They were paid, £4 10s a week (around £190 now), and though active across the city, in principle men only operated in their own battalion area.[24] Detailed procedures for their behaviour were set down, including strict daily routines, and even a recommended reading list including British army classics such as *The Art of Reconnaissance* and *The Defence of Duffer's Drift*.[25] They were truly seeking to know their enemy.

If the Squad were the IRA's special forces in the city, the ASU is best thought of as something akin to commandos in a regular army. Patrick Mullen of the 4th Battalion was one who joined and recalled, 'the purpose of our joining the unit was to attack British forces in Dublin city at any time during the day or night when the opportunity presented itself'.[26] In the early days of the ASU, each of its four sections had to seek approval from ASU headquarters for proposed operations. However, that was difficult to implement because possible targets were not regularly in the same location which hindered planning. Men would gather for seven or eight hours, and end up playing cards rather than engaging in action. Eventually, authority for planning small operations was left with the sections themselves. That allowed the IRA to be more fleet of foot, hitting targets when opportunities arose. Sometimes that involved patrols, which were significantly increased at company level from January 1921.[27] On other occasions, sections would station themselves in positions from which there were many avenues of escape, and await a target.[28] From January to May 1921 there was a tenfold increase of IRA operations in Dublin.[29]

The ASU's first operation took place on the evening of 12 January in Bachelor's Walk, which Harry Colley described as the first daytime ambush in which the IRA used bombs.[30] Eyewitnesses saw 'a veritable hail of fire' across a distance of around 100 yards from the junctions with Loftus Lane to the Metal Bridge as a group of fourteen or fifteen IRA members attacked an Auxiliary lorry with four bombs and revolver fire. Civilians were caught in the fire: shop assistant Fanny Walsh had 'a remarkably narrow escape' when 'a bullet passed under her chin, grazing her neck'. Nobody was killed, and the IRA fled after Auxiliaries returned fire.[31]

By this time, many members of the IRA, whether paid or not, had had to give up their daily lives. Peadar McMulty noted, 'Many men were on the run, and could not reside in their homes.'[32] Soon after the Bachelor's Walk ambush, at midnight on Saturday 15 January, Crown forces hit back in an area bounded by Capel, Church and North King Streets and the quays, by raiding buildings looking for arms and IRA members. Nothing was found despite residents being held within what the *Evening Herald* described as 'a ring of steel' which represented 'new military tactics' in the city.[33] However, further such raids took place in the weeks and months to come, sometimes with more success. Squad member William Stapleton described one such raid in the Mountjoy Square area in February, which had a huge impact on those living there. From tenements with over a thousand residents, the British 'brought down to the square all the occupants, male, female and children. They lined them up or allowed them to sit about on the roadside while the search was in progress.' During this raid, some members of the Squad 'at first felt that we should attack the British with all we had got'. However, this option was rejected, partly because of fears of reprisals and a concern that there might be civilian casualties, but also for the pragmatic reason that 'it might attract too much attention to the aims of the raid, and might only intensify their searchings, and probably result in the finding of our important dumps off Charles St'.[34] As it was, the British did not find the Squad's stash of arms.

At this time the Dublin IRA numbered around 1,050 Volunteers, with 250 in each of the 1st, 2nd and 3rd battalions, 300 in the 4th and 100 engineers in the 5th. They were supported by munitions factories around the city, organised by Seán Russell, the IRA's Director of Munitions. Arms were described by Traynor as consisting of 'automatic pistols, revolvers, hand-grenades and landmines. There was a number of rifles and a limited number of Thompson machine guns.' The latter had only arrived in Dublin in late 1920, while rifles were of limited use in street fighting, so grenades and small arms were the weapons of choice for ambushes in the city. Brigade 'Special Service' units including intelligence, first aid, transport, armoury, training and the Republican Police were supervised by the brigade. Meanwhile, operations were planned by a Brigade Council, consisting of each battalion commander and brigade-level officers. They met at least weekly, considering reports of previous operations before planning future ones. In February or March 1921 three battalion commanders were replaced, and a plan was agreed to increase the level of activity. At the same time, new units were formed, the 6th covering the south of the county while the 7th battalion operated in areas to the west and south-west of the county, including Clondalkin, and Tallaght, and into parts of Wicklow.[35]

The IRA's reorganisation was accompanied by an increase of its activities on Dublin's streets. In January, some kind of IRA action took place in Dublin on average every three or four days. In February, action became more intense. The use of bombs in ambushes was by now well-established.[36] IRA attacks took place on more than half the days of the month, including the escape from Kilmainham Gaol of three IRA prisoners, Frank Teeling, Ernie O'Malley and Simon Donnelly. Sensational stories circulated in the press of how they had escaped, including one in which a lorry of about 16 men, dressed and equipped as British soldiers, had arrived at Kilmainham with documentation for the transfer of the prisoners. Without question, the three were said to have been handed over and driven away. However, they had in fact gained their freedom through an inside job, with a sympathetic member of the British army having used a bolt-cutter to open a gate.[37]

In early February, K Company of the 3rd Battalion carried out the only single-company operation to take place in Dublin: an ambush in the Merrion Square area. About 60 IRA volunteers took part, finding themselves unexpectedly fighting the British army. Laurence Nugent recalled, 'It was the Auxiliaries who were supposed to be in the lorries, and it was upon them that the attack was intended. But the lorries came along and it made no difference to the men of K. Company what section of the British forces they were attacking.'[38]

The fighting greatly increased in March, with IRA attacks on most if not all days, and a total of 53 across the month.[39] Growing sympathy for the republican cause was seen on the morning of 14 March as 6 IRA prisoners were executed at Mountjoy Prison for 'high treason by levying war'. Though traditionally no friend of the IRA, the *Evening Herald*'s report could only show sympathy as it described how up to 40,000 steadily assembled outside Mountjoy Prison. It told how early in the morning, 'a vast, silent mass of humanity was moving towards Mountjoy prison' who were 'above all … the very poor, women especially, who came from their humble homes to pray for the happy repose of the six whom the gallows awaited'. From around 7am masses were held across the city, and there was a strike from 8am to 11am which 'evoked a remarkable response and was not confined to any particular section of the city's population'. The *Herald* condemned the British government's 'folly' and 'unutterable barbarity' for executing men found guilty not by civil courts by 'extraordinary tribunals', adding that 'there is no limit to the action which the alien rulers of the country are capable'. It concluded, 'To-day the nation mourns many of its gallant young sons. But ever the darkest hour is that before dawn, and the final and glorious triumph of the cause of Irish freedom cannot be far distant. The soul of Irish nationality is indestructible. That is the lesson of history.'[40]

Later that day came the 'Battle of Brunswick Street'. It began with a routine patrol of the 3rd Battalion's B Company. They found a Black and Tan unit searching people in the Brunswick Street area and drew them into action by throwing a grenade. A fight ensued in which 3 IRA members were killed, along with 2 Auxiliaries and 2 civilians. Among the dead Auxiliaries was Dubliner James O'Farrell, a veteran of the First World War who had served first in the Dublin Fusiliers and then as an officer in the Tank Corps, and had been mentioned in dispatches.[41]

April 1921 saw a continued increase in IRA activity, with 67 separate attacks on Crown targets. They estimated that around £30,000 of property had been damaged (about £1.3m now), including 14 lorries and tenders, 4 horses, 4 mules, 2 motor cars, and, a little bizarrely, 350 pairs of breeches and 2,040 bed sheets. The IRA believed they had killed 5 Crown forces, compared to the loss of 3 of their own men.[42] Meanwhile, the IRA's record-keeping was developing to an extraordinary degree with the reports which survive in Richard Mulcahy's papers every bit as detailed as those produced by the British army at the front during the First World War. A patrol report dated 12 April 1921, from 4 Section of the ASU, described how a patrol towards the Guinness Brewery from Donore Avenue apprehended 'two enemy wagons' and shot four horses.[43] Another report, the day before from E Company of the 2nd Battalion, described an attack on the London and North Western Railway hotel at North Wall. At 7.45am that morning 29 men had set out to attack 60 men of the Auxiliaries. The report went on to outline the disposition of enemy forces, how much fire was exchanged, how many grenades were thrown, and the casualties incurred.[44]

Such reports illustrate the mentality of the IRA: they saw themselves as an army, with a chain of command which was part of a state to which they were accountable.[45] It also illustrates much of their confidence that they were on a path to eventual victory. Such attitudes were seen in the way in which the increasing numbers of IRA prisoners behaved in British camps. Gerry Byrne of the 4th Battalion had been arrested in late 1920. He described how at Ballykinlar the volunteers made representations that they 'should be allowed to appoint our own cooks and our own line captains', a request which was agreed.[46] The prisoners also tunnelled to escape. At Ballykinlar the tunnels were discovered.[47] Another, at Collinstown, would eventually allow several to escape.[48]

Month of Fire: May 1921

The peak of the War of Independence in Dublin came in May. That month saw 107 separate operations carried out by the IRA's Dublin Brigade, more than any other month of the war.[49] These often included the now-familiar pattern of IRA attack followed by Crown forces reprisals. On the evening of 4 May, ten men of 4 Section of the ASU attacked a lorry and a car returning from escorting workmen from Baldonnel aerodrome at the Half-way House on the Naas Road. The 'Ambush Report' described how the lorry appeared and two grenades were thrown, one of which exploded inside the lorry. The other bounced off, exploded on the road, wounding the section leader who was rendered unable to give orders. The section continued to attack with both grenades and rifle fire, but had been told to await orders before finally charging the lorry to take rifles held on it. Not knowing that their commander was wounded, the men waited as 'the enemy were lying in the lorry moaning' and 'blood was flowing out of the lorry on the road'. However, no order came and the vehicles managed to escape. Four of the Crown forces were dead and seven wounded, with one casualty for the ASU, while the chance to seize the rifles had been missed. Crown forces later returned and burned the Half-way House in reprisal.[50]

During May 1921, there was one especially prominent operation involving ex-British soldiers: the IRA's audacious mission to Mountjoy Prison on 14 May to rescue the Longford IRA's Seán MacEoin. Emmet Dalton was selected for the venture because Michael Collins' plan involved capturing a British armoured car and driving it into the prison. The crucial element was someone who could pose as a British officer. Aside from actually being a former British officer, Dalton 'was the typical British Officer, very neat, debonair, small fair toothbrush moustache, and spoke with a kind of affected accent, which was entirely suitable for the character which he had to impersonate'.[51] Ex-RAF man Jack McSweeney, who was known to Dalton, gave him and others on the mission advice on how use to use the Hotchkiss machine gun they expected to capture at the start of the operation.[52] Dalton was joined in British army uniform by Joe Leonard, who had inside knowledge from serving six months in Mountjoy. Other Volunteers on the operation included Dalton's brother, Charles and one other ex-British army man, former Private 8831 Peter Gough.

Gough had enlisted as a reservist in 1912, in the 4th Dublins, while working as an under-gardener, so had been mobilised at the outbreak of war. Transferred to the 1st Dublins in February 1915, he went to Gallipoli where he was wounded, returning home in June 1915. In September 1915 he was posted to the 6th Dublins, with whom he saw action again at Gallipoli and then Salonika. In March 1916 he rejoined the 1st Dublins and later served in Egypt. By the time he was demobilised in May 1919, he was a member of the Labour Corps and had seen further service in Egypt. Having been wounded on multiple occasions he was in receipt of a 20 per cent disability pension when he returned to

Dublin after the First World War.[53] At this time, he was told by his brother (a member of the ICA), 'You have been fighting for a foreign country long enough. It's up to you now to fight for your own country.' Gough reacted by joining the IRA, serving in a unit in the Baldoyle area. He had been a machine gunner during the war and when that expertise was discovered in the IRA it was put to use.[54]

On 14 May, Gough took part in the capture of a British armoured car as part of an IRA unit of five. Ambushing the car in the Abbey Street area, they ordered the occupants out at gun point and drove it away to collect Dalton and Leonard. On arriving at the prison, the armoured car drove in, and Dalton and Leonard entered the central part of the jail, carrying with them a false prisoner transfer document. Gough and the others waited with the armoured car, keeping the engine running. However, the prison governor wanted to confirm the order with Dublin Castle before releasing MacEoin. Dalton and Leonard took the governor and his colleagues prisoner, with MacEoin still in his cell. Meanwhile, a scuffle had begun outside the prison as other Volunteers tried to seize the gatekeeper's keys. Shots were fired and Dalton and Leonard aborted the mission and fled. In months to come, the authorities realised that Dalton had been involved and something of a myth surrounded him, including the mistaken belief that he had been involved in the Kilmainham escape in February.[55]

Dalton had not been, but he would on other occasions use his British military experience to talk his way out of situations. Oscar Traynor remembered a raid on the Dublin Brigade's Headquarters. Once documents had been hidden in a wall, Dalton had said, 'I think the best thing we can do is to go down and brazen it out.' Traynor and others agreed and they were halted at gunpoint by a soldier. He recalled how,

> Dalton went over and said a few words to him. What he said to the soldier I do not know, but the fellow nearly saluted him, put his rifle to the ground and went on talking. The soldier then went to the door and brought back a British officer, similar in type and appearance to Dalton himself. This officer and Dalton conversed for several minutes, and O'Malley and myself noticed that they had got to the stage of laughing at some event – probably something that happened in the Great War – which was being retailed. Eventually Dalton said, 'Come along, men', so we followed him out and down the steps.[56]

Figure 18.1: Custom House, Dublin on fire after the attack by Republicans, 5 May 1921. (Image Courtesy of the National Library of Ireland, HOGW 164).

Custom House

The most dramatic event of the war in Dublin was the occupation and subsequent burning of the Custom House on 25 May, described by the *Evening Herald* as the 'Custom House Cauldron'.[57] The IRA operation at the Custom House consisted mainly of men from the 2nd Battalion, since it was in their area. Commanded by Tom Ennis, they were assisted by men from the 1st, 3rd and 4th battalions, plus the Squad and the ASU, numbering about 120 in total. The aim was to attack a big target, and the Custom House was one of two sites under consideration since January, the other being Beggars Bush Barracks.[58] Entering the building just before 1pm, Squad member Vincent Byrne spread paraffin and paper around the building's second floor amidst shocked civil servants who were told to leave. After a whistle indicated that he should light the fire, Byrne recounted that he 'lit a ball of paper and, slightly opening the door, I flung it into the office. In a flick the whole office was ablaze.'[59]

The IRA managed to delay the arrival of the city fire brigade, which helped the fire take hold.[60] However, the building was already

Figure 18.2: Republican prisoners outside the burning Custom House, 5 May 1921. (Image Courtesy of the National Library of Ireland, INDH82).

under fire from Crown forces before matches had been struck because some of the regular Volunteers had opened fire themselves as they saw Crown lorries at Eden Quay. There had also been confusion inside the building as to whether or not the necessary paraffin had been spread, which caused a crucial delay of a few minutes. As a result, Joseph Byrne recalled, even before the building had been set alight, 'the Custom House was almost surrounded with Black and Tans and Auxiliaries'. This prompted the arrival of Auxiliaries and an armoured car which greatly hampered the evacuation by the Volunteers. Joseph Byrne recalled, 'It was a case of every man for himself and I escaped through the back entrance and got safely away.'[61] Vincent Byrne described how as he tried to leave, Auxiliaries blocked his passage and he fired on them until he ran out of ammunition. However, he then walked out of the building and managed to persuade the soldiers who captured him that he was in fact just a passer-by, and had been delivering a message for his boss while on the way to buy some timber. As a ruse, he carried with him a carpenter's rule and paper replete with notes about timber. These persuaded the officer and he was allowed to leave the area.[62] His case was unusual, since at least 80,[63] and possibly virtually all, of the IRA Volunteers who were in the building, were arrested. Later in the day, Joseph Byrne and another Volunteer escorted Michael Collins to view the fire. Byrne recalled, 'We walked down from the Engineer's Hall in Gardiner's Row and mingled with the people. Collins did not say anything but smiled when he saw the place was still burning, and then moved off.'[64]

However, in terms of the fighting strength of the IRA in Dublin the burning could have been literally a Pyrrhic victory had it not been for a rapid reorganisation within the ranks. Oscar Traynor described how 'it was found necessary to carry out an almost complete re-organisation of the various units' in Dublin.[65] The Squad was reduced to about half its size. The ASU was also badly affected and significant amounts of arms and ammunition were lost. However, Harry Colley believed that because the IRA scraped together men and arms in every way possible, the Crown forces did not realise that they had captured so much of the ASU. Over the next few days as the Custom House continued to burn, units of the Dublin Brigade provided men to keep up operations in the streets while a new ASU was formed. As part of that, the Squad was amalgamated with the ASU as the Dublin Guard.[66] To the outside world, the change was not visible: in May, the IRA had carried out 107 operations in Dublin, and still managed 93 in June. The difference was that company patrols had stepped in to take the place of the ASU, which had carried out 21 of the May operations but just 5 in June.[67]

Truce

Flames burned at the Custom House until the evening of 27 May, and it smouldered for days longer.[68] The IRA lost 5 men dead, while 4 civilians were killed, including the caretaker of the Custom House, shot when he tried to alert the police.[69] Harry Colley believed that 'its destruction struck the mightiest blow yet delivered to the enemies' control in this country'. He also believed 'It was the main factor in bringing about the Truce' in July.[70] However, the British interest in a truce might have had just as much to do with the number of Crown forces killed in June – 22 in Dublin, from 93 IRA operations.[71]

The attacks continued as in previous months. In Dublin city, civilians did not offer the same kind of tacit support to the IRA as they did in more intimate rural areas.[72] However, civilians were becoming increasingly hostile to Crown forces due to raids,[73] and were also aware of how to avoid being caught up in operations in areas where they had become frequent. One notorious area was known as 'The Dardanelles' due to the persistence of attacks on British forces passing through, even though the actual number of attacks (about a dozen) might not have been significantly greater than in other areas.[74] The nomenclature reflected how important Gallipoli had been to Dublin. It covered an area within the 3rd Battalion's territory, west of St Stephen's Green, running for about three-quarters of a mile from South Great George's Street along Aungier Street to Kelly's Corner. It was patrolled nightly by different sections of the 3rd Battalion, with attacks taking place prior to the curfew. Mick Carroll led the battalion's 2 Section and described how, because people 'living in the vicinity got to know our faces they just made themselves scarce at our approach, leaving the Unit to stand out in bold relief'.[75] Meanwhile, the Dublin Guard continued where the Squad had left off, with targeted assassinations.[76] Yet the Dublin Brigade suffered from internment of significant numbers of its volunteers and successful Crown raids on arms dumps, and the curfew also limited operations.[77]

In these circumstances, with fighting continuing and international pressure on Britain to settle affairs in Ireland,[78] a truce became only a matter of time. King George V was influential behind the scenes in criticising British reprisals, and from mid-June did much to encourage the British government towards a settlement. His belief, influenced by Jan Smuts, was that offering Dominion status to Ireland as a whole could sway opinion there behind a settlement. On 24 June, Lloyd George secured the agreement of ministerial colleagues to invite both de Valera, as President of the Dáil, and James Craig, as the newly established Prime Minister of Northern Ireland, to London for talks. De Valera wanted a truce before talks and after a meeting in Dublin on 5 July with Smuts, unofficially representing the government, the diplomatic wheels turned. On 9 July, a truce was agreed, to come into force at noon two days later. Negotiations would then begin.[79] De Valera and a Sinn Féin delegation headed for London on 12 July for discussions preliminary to full negotiations.[80] For now, it was unclear how those would play out. Joseph Lawless, then a prisoner, recalled, 'The general feeling we had at the time was that the truce was most probably a temporary respite and that, when negotiations broke down, the war would begin with redoubled effort on both sides.'[81]

How effective had the IRA been in Dublin during the War of Independence? Writing in 1939, IRA veteran J. J. 'Ginger' O'Connell wrote, 'A very common assumption is that Dublin shot its bolt in 1916; and that the rest of the country bore the subsequent brunt.' However, he pointed out that for the first time in any of Ireland's struggles with Britain, 'military operations' were directed from Dublin, and that Dublin was crucial in leading the reorganisation of 1917–18. Meanwhile, as regards the military effectiveness of the Dublin Brigade itself, O'Connell rightly argued that it had 'elaborated a quite new technique for guerrilla fighting in a large city – and it applied that technique with far-reaching effect'. The result was that it pinned down at least a quarter of British forces in Ireland acting as 'a Containing Force'.[82]

During the Truce, some believed the war might soon resume and that arms therefore needed to be restocked. William Beaumont took part in a three-person IRA visit to Germany for that purpose, along with Jack O'Mara and James Connolly's son, Roddy. However, they were

Figure 18.3: Protest outside Mountjoy prison, 23 July 1921, as prisoners were held during the Truce. (Image Courtesy of the National Library of Ireland, HOG 165).

unsuccessful.[83] Meanwhile, IRA prisoners were retained by the British, a matter which attracted public protest, and so for them the war had not really stopped.

Joseph Lawless was one of about 1,200 prisoners held at the Rath camp at the Curragh. He described how the camp commandant 'went out of his way in many matters of detail to let us see that the truce had nothing to do with us and that he at any rate still looked upon us as malignant enemies whom he might punish at his pleasure'. This, Lawless said, 'merely made us more anxious than ever to escape'.[84] That meant continuing with the digging of a tunnel. In May, three had been under way but it was decided to focus on just one. Lawless' account of the escape inevitably draws comparisons with the so-called 'Great Escape' from Stalag Luft III in 1944. A tunnel was dug over many months, with bed boards used to shore up the ceiling and walls as it was constructed. Access was through a vertical shaft in one of the huts, with spoil from the digging moved in sacks and then distributed evenly under huts. A pump was constructed to provide air for the diggers. When the escape was eventually made in the early hours of 9 September, the diggers had decided to break through even if they had not reached the clump of furze which was their target, and they ended up being about twenty yards short of cover. Although the exit was beyond the usual range of the camp lights, and the night was dark, this inevitably reduced the number who could escape.[85] Tom Byrne was one of forty to fifty who escaped, making his way back to Dublin.[86] Lawless did not, though he and another prisoner later bribed a soldier to allow them to escape hidden on a swill cart leaving the camp.[87]

Escaped prisoners found the IRA continuing to organise during the Truce. They were following an order received from Richard Mulcahy by Oscar Traynor that the Dublin IRA must 'intensify' its training.[88] Peadar McNulty's 3rd Battalion took part in a camp at Mulhuddart in late July, and continued over the summer to obtain arms from wherever they could. The autumn saw them drilling, training and continuing to recruit.[89] They expected to fight again, and they would, though not in the way they would have hoped for or imagined.

19 CIVIL WAR

I could not imagine Irishmen fighting Irishmen on the issue involved, because in the end what was left would be mopped up by the British and all our efforts of past years frustrated and in its wake a trail of bitterness.

Seamus Pounch, IRA Assistant Quartermaster General in 1921, in 1949 recalling the outbreak of the Civil War

Treaty

As some form of independence for part of Ireland began to emerge, former British soldiers continued to play a role in republicanism. During the negotiation of the Anglo-Irish Treaty from October 1921, Emmet Dalton accompanied Michael Collins for some of his time in London, advising Collins on military matters and liaising with the British over observation of the Truce through talks at the Colonial Office with the Secretary of State for the Colonies, Winston Churchill. Dalton also made plans for Collins to escape by air if the negotiations fell apart and his liberty was threatened.[1]

The terms of the Anglo-Irish Treaty agreed in December fell far short of the 'Irish Republic' for which so many felt they were fighting. Certainly, most of Ireland would cease to be part of the United Kingdom, severing all legislative ties with Westminster, with a new Irish Free State established. Crown forces would leave the Irish Free State (except for the Royal Navy stationed at three treaty ports). Moreover, the new state would notionally cover the whole island.

Figure 19.1: The Irish delegation leaves 10 Downing Street after meeting with the British government, October 1921. Left to right: Emmet Dalton, a policeman, Arthur Griffith, Robert Barton, Michael Collins, unknown. (Image Courtesy of the National Library of Ireland, NPA MKN33).

However, Northern Ireland (as established by the 1920 Government of Ireland Act) had the right to opt out and inevitably would. Meanwhile, the Irish Free State would remain within the British Empire as a Dominion, with the King as Head of State represented by a Governor General. These proposals put Ireland on a par with Australia, Canada, Newfoundland, New Zealand and South Africa. The new state was by no means a 'Republic' due to the continuation of the monarchy, and it was, republicans felt, not truly 'Irish' since it enshrined partition.[2] The treaty was signed for the Dáil by Collins, Arthur Griffith, and former Dublin Fusilier Robert Barton, but it immediately sparked a conflict among republicans. Barton later repudiated it, falling in behind de Valera and the anti-Treaty cause.[3]

The Dáil ratified the treaty on 7 January 1922 (narrowly, by 64 votes to 57), setting up a Provisional Government a week later with Michael Collins as its chairman. De Valera resigned as President of the Dáil, after the Treaty vote, and narrowly lost to Griffiths in a new election. Meanwhile, perhaps because many had expected to resume the war at some point, some IRA members found it easy not to regard the

Treaty as the end of their struggle.[4] Following the Dáil's vote, discontent within the ranks rapidly emerged as the Dáil sought to make the IRA the new army of the state. Dublin Castle was taken over by the new government on 16 January, immediately raising the question of how to garrison such locations. Beggars Bush Barracks was taken over on 31 January by the Dublin Guard, and became the headquarters of the new National Army. As barracks were steadily handed over by the British across Ireland, some were taken by IRA members who were anti-Treaty, but all those in Dublin went to forces loyal to the Dáil. In February 1922, a convention of the Dublin Brigade was held at 41 Parnell Square. Peadar McNulty noted, 'by a large majority the Brigade renewed allegiance to the Irish Republic'.[5] By 'the Irish Republic' he meant not the regime being established by the Dáil. The brigadier, Oscar Traynor, was among those opposing the Treaty. Of all the Dublin battalions, only the 2nd backed it.

These local discussions were merely a prelude to an Army Convention of the IRA held in the Mansion House on 26 March at which outright opposition to both the Treaty and the Dáil's authority was agreed.[6] A second convention on 9 April agreed a new Republican Constitution and that the IRA would continue on the same basis as the pre-Treaty IRA.[7] The first action of the IRA's new Executive was to order the occupation of the Four Courts, which was done in the early hours of 14 April initially by 120 men.[8] For now, there was no direct conflict between the IRA and the National Army, not least because the IRA in Dublin outnumbered the National Army in both armaments and manpower (perhaps around 1,000 against 3,000 IRA in Dublin and at least 20,000 more in the country). Indeed, it has been argued that had the IRA immediately gone on the offensive with a guerrilla war in Dublin, they would have won easily. However, the IRA Executive did not wish to be the first to open fire and opted instead for the symbol of resistance provide by the occupation.[9] For a time, there was some prospect of agreement between the IRA and their former comrades in the National Army, with meetings held to build bridges. Meanwhile, the Dáil had called an election for 16 June. Efforts were made to bring the two sides together, not least through a pact between Collins and de Valera who agreed that pro- and anti-Treaty Sinn Féin candidates would stand on a joint slate. There was also a meeting of pro- and anti-Treaty officers at Mansion House on 8 May, to try to stem the rush towards fighting. However, the Collins–de Valera pact fell apart before the election and the two sides competed against each other in the ballot.

58 pro-Treaty candidates were elected, and 36 antis.[10] In Dublin city, the popular vote for the Treaty was seven to one, and in the county, ten to one, electing seven pro-treaty, three independents, one Labour and one anti-treaty Teachtaí Dála (TDs). This was a significant shift in the Treaty's favour, since prior to the election the TDs were seven anti and five pro.[11] However, armed conflict now looked inevitable.

The Battle of Dublin

Part of the anti-Treaty IRA's anger was focused on the continued presence of British troops in Ireland. The Free State was not established under the Treaty, merely planned, and the British army would not leave until it was operational. To work on the handover, the IRA had even appointed a 'Chief Liaison Officer' who knew both armies intimately: Emmet Dalton.[12] Meanwhile, the British were anxious that there might be renewed violence, which was indeed threatened by an Army Convention which met on 18 June. The British consequently put pressure on Collins to take action against the anti-Treaty IRA, while also making their own plans to attack the Four Courts. Historians, often influenced by their own pro- or anti-Treaty views, disagree over whether the Civil War was the inevitable consequence of long-standing divisions within the republican movement, or whether it was due to British pressure.[13] It is clear that when the Provisional Government decided to act, the British military facilitated their action through the provision of artillery. Late on Tuesday 27 June an ultimatum was issued for the Four Courts garrison to evacuate. When they did not, soon after 4am the National Army began their attack, which the provisional government claimed was being carried out because over previous days units of the IRA had raided businesses and demanded money from them. The government had, they said, 'received an emphatic mandate from the Irish people' and could 'no longer tolerate any interference with their liberty and property'.[14] An *Evening Herald* journalist went out to investigate and was 'almost deafened by thunderous bursts'.[15] Crucial to the attack was artillery, suggested by Emmet Dalton, who then obtained two eighteen-pounder field guns from the British.[16] Civil war, and more specifically the Battle of Dublin, had broken out.[17] Recent estimates of the numbers of dead in the conflict range from about 1,200 to about 2,000, much lower than an older figure of 4,000 to 5,000. In Dublin,

Figure 19.2: Fighting in the area of the Four Courts, late June 1922, looking down Winetavern Street. (Image Courtesy of the National Library of Ireland, NPA ASG11).

there were at least 258 (95 pro-Treaty, 84 anti-Treaty, 72 civilians, 6 British army and 1 police).[18]

The conflict posed dilemmas for men who were used to action. Seamus Pounch was at Jacob's during the Rising, and by the Truce was the IRA's Assistant Quartermaster General. He wanted no part of the Civil War, recalling, 'I could not imagine Irishmen fighting Irishmen on the issue involved, because in the end what was left would be mopped up by the British and all our efforts of past years frustrated and in its wake a trail of bitterness.' He decided to take no part.[19] Others felt more torn. Joseph Lawless had briefly joined the National Army but left in March 1922 over differences of opinion on how to run the Mechanical Transport Section. He described how 'it was with quite a shock I woke on the morning of Wednesday 28 June to the sound of heavy gunfire in the city'. Having established what was happening, 'I sat in my office at the garage in a state of mental upheaval.' Lawless discussed the matter with a friend, Conor McGinley, like Lawless a former Volunteer and a member of the IRB. They 'eventually agreed that civil war was an evil thing, that we should do nothing to spread or prolong'. Later in the day 'Although I had no heart in the fratricidal struggle', Lawless 'realised that I must make my contribution towards the supremacy of the Government of Dáil Éireann as representing the democratic majority of the people of Ireland'. The next day he went to Portobello Barracks and re-enlisted.[20]

Dalton's British guns shifted the balance in favour of the National Army, but inside the Four Courts was considerable expertise among men who had fought against the odds before. Some had British military experience. Michael McCabe, who was at Roe's Distillery during the Rising but was freed after capture due to his age, had enlisted in the British army in 1917 and remained in it until April 1922 when he deserted while stationed in Dublin. On his desertion in late April 1922, he met Liam Mellows, whom he had known in the Fianna, and followed him. McCabe was an instructor in arms drill in the Four Courts garrison and took part in raids for weapons. Present from a few days after the Four Courts were occupied was also Patrick O'Moore, who brought machine-gun skills learned on the Western Front.[21]

Following the attack on the Four Courts, IRA units occupied several buildings around the city, initiating the 'Battle of Dublin'. Oscar Traynor set up headquarters in Barry's Hotel in Gardiner's Row, drawing together volunteers from various battalions along with the ICA. The 3rd Battalion were based at 41 York Street, while the 1st Battalion operated from 44 Parnell Square.[22] Peadar McNulty recalled how on 28 June, the 1st Battalion 'endeavoured to relieve the Four Courts by breaking through the Cordon of the Free State troops'. However, the National Army held streets next to the Courts and the IRA's 'attacking force was greatly inferior in numbers.' No break-through was made.[23]

On Thursday 29 June, further shells were received from the British, procured by Emmet Dalton.[24] Throughout the day, artillery fire rained down on the Four Courts while fighting continued at other locations, but IRA attempts to relieve their garrison failed, while the National Army entered the grounds.[25] By early afternoon on Friday 30 June, the position in the Four Courts was untenable. It was on fire, and explosions had destroyed parts of the building (and historic records inside). In a message to the garrison Oscar Traynor said he could not get men through to assist, and told them, 'If the Republic is to be saved your surrender is a necessity.' Then 140 laid down their arms. Simon Donnelly was inside and described his comrades being told by their

Figure 19.3: The Four Courts burning, 30 June 1922. (Image Courtesy of the National Library of Ireland, HOG57).

Figure 19.4: Ruins of the Gresham Hotel, O'Connell Street, Dublin, July 1922. Scenes associated with the Easter Rising became apparent again during the Civil War. (Image Courtesy of the National Library of Ireland, INDH262).

leaders that 'while they were compelled to surrender their guns they would never surrender their principles'. During the fight, the IRA had lost 3 dead and 8 wounded. The National Army lost at least 7 dead and around 70 wounded.[26] Over the next days, as Emmet Dalton continued to direct operations,[27] the National Army steadily tightened the noose around Republican strongholds, which fell one by one, often largely destroyed like the Gresham Hotel, until the Granville Hotel was the last to stand. Those there, led by Cathal Brugha, surrendered soon after 7pm on 5 July, though Brugha charged into the street while firing and was hit. He died of wounds two days later. By that point there were 59 dead and 273 wounded across the city.[28] Michael McCabe was captured,[29] but key figures in the Dublin IRA escaped, including Oscar Traynor, though in his case not for long, since he was captured on 27 July.[30]

'Irregulars'

Following the fall of the Four Courts, the National Army was reorganised and expanded. Richard Mulcahy became Chief of Staff. Michael Collins was overall Commander in Chief. The Provisional Government sought an army of 20,000, with 15,000 reservists. For some roles, those with British army experience were targeted by Emmet Dalton, who was the commanding officer of the new Eastern Command which covered Dublin.[31] One of those who joined was George Geoghegan of Queen Street. He had served in the early stage of the First World War as a driver in the Army Service Corps, before being discharged in July 1916 to be a civilian driver in Dublin. He had taken no part in the War of Independence, but on joining the National Army in July 1922 was rapidly promoted to sergeant on the basis of his British military experience.[32]

Over the summer, the Civil War continued in Dublin, with the anti-Treaty IRA (dubbed 'Irregulars' by their opponents), using much the same tactics as used by the IRA against Crown forces, including targeted killings, bank and post office raids, and ambushes. There has been a view among some writers that after the Battle of Dublin conflict in the city all but ceased. However, as John Dorney points out, two-thirds of the conflict's fatalities in Dublin came after the battle. Moreover, the command centres of both sides were located there, so the city was at the centre of activity.[33]

A Provisional Government intelligence report described how in early September, the National Army was now 'faced with a guerrilla campaign which day by day becomes more effective. Very little damage is done in DUBLIN, but the sleep of the citizens is disturbed nearly every night by fierce fusillades in all quarters.'[34] The major initiative which the IRA planned was the isolation of Dublin through the destruction of communications. On the evening of Saturday 5 August they planned to blow up railway bridges and block roads, but the National Army had wind of the scheme and intercepted the IRA at various points of attack, capturing 160 men. Fighting took place until 3am on Sunday morning by which point the plot had been foiled.[35]

The key event of the wider Civil War in the summer of 1922 was the killing of Michael Collins by the IRA at Béal na mBláth in County Cork on 22 August.[36] In Collins' party were both Emmet Dalton (who was leading actions against the IRA in the Cork area) and Peter Gough. When the car carrying Collins and Dalton was hit, Dalton ordered the

Figure 19.5: Staff officers at the funeral of Michael Collins, 28 August 1922. Richard Mulcahy is on the far left, marked faintly on the original photograph with an X, with Gearóid O'Sullivan to his left, and Emmet Dalton on the right of the front row. (Image Courtesy of the National Library of Ireland, HOGW 177).

driver to 'Drive like hell', but Collins wanted to stay and fight so they left the car and took cover. Shots were exchanged for about twenty minutes, but Collins was hit in the head. Dalton was with him when he died.[37] Collins' funeral was held in Dublin on 28 August, and could be seen as a show of support for the Provisional Government. Tens of thousands lined the streets for 'one of the largest processions of the kind that has ever been seen in the city'.[38]

Fighting continued in Dublin, with regular raids and ambushes. A typical week in August saw twenty-two separate incidents, ranging from attacks on British troops and members of the National Army to a raid on a jeweller, and the destruction of two bridges far outside the city near Shankill.[39] By the autumn, there was a shift towards sabotage, such as cutting telephone and telegraph wires.[40] However, by September the National Army was very proficient at facing down the IRA in the city. It had two key methods for tackling them. First, it raided premises believed to be linked with the IRA: over 2,000 raids were carried out in Dublin between August 1922 and September 1923.[41] During this time, prisoners were taken, including former Dublin Fusilier Robert Barton, who was active in the city attending Republican Cabinet meetings. He escaped once, only to be recaptured.[42] Second, the IRA carried out daily patrols of the streets (usually 8–10 men on foot, or on bicycles or in vehicles), searching anyone deemed suspicious.[43] The National Army also benefited from intelligence about specific operations and was sometimes able to be in precisely the right place at the right time. Following an attack at Rotunda Rink on the evening of 17 September, an IRA operation report noted that as soon as the IRA attackers 'came into position they found that the enemy had anticipated them and had armoured cars etc., in readiness'. The same evening, the National Army had intelligence of a plan to take over police offices at Oriel House where the Criminal Investigation Department was based, and had an armoured car and armoured lorries in place outside.[44]

The IRA faced some local hostility. During an ambush in Parliament Street by six men from the ASU, six rounds were fired from revolvers and a grenade thrown, wounding three Free State soldiers. As the IRA withdrew, their report noted, 'They were followed by a mob shouting "Here's the murderers" "Here's the robbers". The locality is very dangerous for operations by our troops. It is a F.S. stronghold.' Inevitably, these attacks occasionally threw the remaining

British soldiers and the National Army together. An ASU attack on a British car in Dorset Street on 30 September was followed by two National Army soldiers getting into the car and continuing the journey with the British. A week later, on 7 October, members of the ASU were intercepted by Free State soldiers in Manor Street. Shots were exchanged and after five government soldiers were wounded an IRA report noted, 'A British soldier came out of a house close by and picked up the rifle of one of the F.S. soldiers and commenced using it against our men.'[45] During such operations, civilians obviously faced significant risks. Former British soldier George Geoghegan, by then a sergeant in the National Army's 16th Infantry Battalion, led a raid on a shop in his own street, Queen Street, on 11 November 1922. On leaving the scene, Geoghegan shot an onlooker in the stomach, 22-year-old John Crosbie, who died a week later. It is not clear why Geoghegan fired the shot, but he was convicted of manslaughter (after being charged with murder) and spent eighteen months with hard labour in Mountjoy Prison.[46] When three young anti-treaty republicans (Edwin Hughes, Brendan Holohan and Joseph Rogers) were killed on 6 October, the finger was pointed at Charles Dalton, who with his brother, Emmet, had grown up only streets away from where the three had lived. A case was made for Dalton having been nearby the site of the killing in a National Army open-topped Lancia, but there was other evidence that he could have been nowhere near. The verdict of the inquest was death by 'person, or persons unknown'. Such cases pointed to how violence had become, as Pádraig Yeates says, 'intimate and local'.[47]

Meanwhile, the IRA was weakened by the wounding and capture of Ernie O'Malley on 4 November when the house at which he was staying in Ailesbury Road was attacked by government forces.[48] A National Army report described how the boards of a hiding place had almost been broken in when a man inside opened fire and the soldiers retreated downstairs. Further shots were fired and the man captured, at which point his identity was realised.[49] O'Malley had not joined the Irish Volunteers until after the Rising, but was accepted to have taken part in the Rising on his own initiative as a sniper, and later served in the IRA outside Dublin during the War of Independence. Though Castlebar-born he had grown up in the city and his family lived there. He had taken part in the Four Courts occupation and in early July was made Assistant Chief of Staff of the IRA, a role which included command over a large area including Dublin.[50] Three of his brothers were in the IRA, Charles, Cecil and Patrick, with Charles already killed during the Civil War.[51] However, his brother Frank had served in the British army during the First World War and died in 1921 while serving with the King's African Rifles in Dar-es-Salaam.[52] Indeed, he himself had intended to join the British army in the early stages of the war, and was ambivalent about the conflict before the Rising.[53]

Operations by the IRA in Dublin were reduced following O'Malley's capture, but did not cease. Wellington Barracks was attacked on 8 November by 11 men from the ASU, firing from 4 different positions which gave the impression of a larger mobile force; 3 men set up a Thompson machine gun in a house on the south side of the canal, from which Barrack Square could be fired on. They began the attack as National Army soldiers paraded on the square; 1 National Army soldier and 2 IRA members were killed (plus a further 22 Army wounded).[54] Meanwhile, the IRA also carried out operations targeted at individuals, with the apparent intention of inflicting wider collateral damage. A National Army report told of how, on 10 December, at around 9pm, men called at the Philipsburgh Avenue home of Captain Sean McGarry, a member of the Dáil. McGarry's wife opened the door. When she told the men that her husband was out, 'The place was then rushed' and 'Petrol was sprinkled about the place and fire set to it, the windows were broken in order to allow a breeze to fan the fire.' Mrs McGarry's request to get her children from an upper floor was refused, and when she did so, both she and the children suffered burns which put them in hospital.[55]

The Irish Free State

The Irish Free State was formally established on 6 December and the last British troops (around 3,000) left on 17 December. As they departed for North Wall, they were met at Beresford Place by at least 500 members of the Legion of Irish Ex-Service Men, carrying Union Flags and wearing medals.[56] Meanwhile, at the final British headquarters in Parkgate Street, Phoenix Park, a symbolic transition of military power was taking place. At around 9am, General Richard Mulcahy arrived by car, with fellow officers of the National Army. The guard at the gate changed at 9.17am. The *Irish Times* reported the National Army saluting the Wiltshire Regiment 'as the latter marched out – a little matter of presenting arms and commanding "Eyes right;" but a small detail that counted for much'. The Wiltshires headed for the Royal Barracks for one final ceremony at 9.50am. The *Irish Times* described how 'Green uniforms and khaki faced each other in that grey stark square of the Royal Barracks.' Then, the Wiltshires marched out, their regimental Colours saluted by Mulcahy and his staff, the Wiltshires offering 'Eyes right' as they passed the General. Mulcahy then addressed his troops, speaking first in Irish, telling his men that they had now taken over 'barracks in the capital of their country, that had for centuries been held by the enemies of their nation'. Continuing in English he concluded on the soldiers' part in the mission of making 'Ireland the country that they had always dreamed and wished it to be'.[57]

By the first months of 1923, the IRA's numbers had greatly reduced since the split over the Treaty. A National Army intelligence report from the start of 1923 estimated around 300 members in the city, and another 100 in the county unit (which also covered Wicklow).[58] However, it was able to continue its campaign in the city. A National Army patrol was attacked in Cork Street on 18 January and two days later a railway viaduct at Malahide was destroyed, hindering goods trains on the Dublin to Belfast route.[59] 26 January saw the burning of a barracks at Dundrum.[60] On 31 January, the Coast Guard station at Balbriggan was destroyed by mines.[61] Over the next weeks, to mid-April, there were raids (for money), attacks on homes of opponents, bombings of railway bridges, train ambushes and shoot-outs with the National Army.[62] On occasion, the National Army used tactics which would have been associated in the minds of local people with the British army during the War of Independence. For example, on 24 February, a National Army unit came under fire near City Hall, though could not be sure of the origin of the fire. There was some suspicion that it might be from roof tops around Castle Street. When it stopped, pedestrians and vehicles were searched. Later, fire opened again and a number of tenement houses in Castle Street were, in the words of the National Army report, 'raided'. Nothing was found.[63]

The discovery by the National Army of an IRA bomb factory in a house on the North Circular Road in late February[64] probably had some impact on IRA operations in the city, as patrols faced ambushes less frequently than they had done.[65] Further arms and ammunition were seized at Dolphin's Barn and Dalkey in mid-April.[66] The IRA was still able to carry out one of its most high-profile Dublin operations, blowing up the Grand Central Cinema in Lower O'Connell Street on 27 April.[67] However, that operation was the last significant one carried out by the IRA in Dublin. The commander of the IRA, Liam Lynch, was killed on 10 April, and his successor, Frank Aiken, rapidly called a ceasefire. By early May, peace talks had begun between the Dáil and de Valera.[68] At the end of May, the Civil War ended as the IRA leadership realised it could not win and ordered the dumping of arms.[69]

Since no terms were agreed, the Irish Free State continued to hold IRA prisoners – a staggering number of 12,000 at the war's end. In total, 14,023 were held at some point, including 2,438 Dublin men and 190 Dublin women.[70] A hunger strike of initially 300 prisoners (rising at its peak to 2,550) began on 15 October and lasted until 23 November 1923, both against prison conditions and as a protest about continued imprisonment. However, the strike collapsed and only in the summer of 1924 was the release of prisoners complete.[71] Among ex-British soldiers in the anti-Treaty IRA, Michael McCabe was released in December 1923 after being held first at Mountjoy and then Newbridge, but Patrick O'Moore was not set free until the general release in the middle of 1924.[72]

The end of the Civil War did not mean an end to organisation by the 'Irregular' IRA. In the summer of August 1923 National Army intelligence reports suggested preparations for an attack on government forces after the next election. However, by late October there seemed 'no immediate danger of the Die-Hards starting active warfare'. In November, their activities were focused on raising funds for prisoners. By early 1924, unit meetings were taking place under the guise of dance classes.[73]

During the Civil War, as many as 800 government forces were killed. Figures for 'Irregular' deaths are harder to verify, but are generally agreed to have been much higher. Certainly 81 of them were executed by the Irish government, including 12 Dubliners.[74] That total was double the number executed by the British during the Easter Rising and during the War of Independence.[75] Those figures alone explain why the 'peace' was an uneasy one, perhaps more uneasy for some veterans of the fight against the British or the Civil War than for veterans of the First World War.

One British veteran had already become too uneasy to see the Civil War to its conclusion. Following the death of Michael Collins,

Emmet Dalton, now with the rank of Major General, continued to lead actions against the IRA in Cork. During this time he was placed on a 'death list' by Ernie O'Malley, who knew the Dalton family, being only a year younger than Dalton with both having attended the O'Connell School.[76] Dalton married Alice Shannon, whom he had known since childhood, in Cork on 9 October 1922, and they went on to have three daughters and two sons.[77] As his army career continued, he became concerned about the execution of republican prisoners and resigned from the National Army on Armistice Day 1922.[78] He instead became Clerk of the Senate of the Irish Free State, playing football, golf and cricket in his spare time. His brother, Charles, was a leading figure in the National Army 'mutiny' of 1924. The mutiny was prompted by plans to reduce the size of the army, but was fuelled by grievances among former allies of Michael Collins who, despite being pro-treaty, did not believe that the government was sufficiently 'Republican'. The mutiny fell apart as the government stood its ground and Charles Dalton resigned his post to avoid punishment, later publishing his memoirs but suffering terribly from paranoid schizophrenia until his death in 1974. During the mutiny Emmet, as a public servant, had been forced to remain silent on issues affecting the army, but he had been involved in an initial meeting in January 1923 of the group who became the mutineers.[79] Following family financial problems which became apparent in 1925, he resigned from his role and worked first as a salesman and then a private detective, before working in England from 1941, first as a film salesman for Paramount, and then as a film-maker. Dalton rejected approaches to join British special forces during the Second World War, and his film work eventually took him back to Ireland with the opening of Ardmore Studios in 1958, though he retained his main home at Radlett in Hertfordshire through the 1960s before returning to live in Dublin. That world became a career for one of his children, Audrey, who began a film (and later television) acting career in Hollywood in 1952. Emmet Dalton's death in 1978 showed how the divisions of the Civil War lingered: his funeral with full military honours at Glasnevin, and burial in the republican plot, was attended by many from Fine Gael, but not a single representative of the Fianna Fáil government.[80]

20 PEACE

I have not had my statement witnessed out here, afraid it just wouldn't suit.

Michael McCabe, Royal West African Frontier Force, explaining that he had not asked anyone in the British army to witness his 1938 application for an IRA pension[1]

Returning and Serving

While some returning soldiers were active in the Irish Revolution, most were not. A different future beckoned, not connected to the fight against Britain or between republicans. Their first challenge was to get home. Released prisoners of war were often soonest home, but there were some tragic cases among them. Thomas Bennett of the 2nd Royal Irish Regiment was taken prisoner at Mons in 1914. He died on 14 November 1918 when on his way home to Dublin after release.[2] Yet the armistice of 11 November 1918 was not an end to the war, merely a halt, so there were no immediate mass returns. Lieutenant Allen Guest was unusual in successfully making a case for getting home a little earlier than most on the basis of his long service. He had been discharged in June 1914 after twenty-one years service, including the whole of the South African War and a period of four years away from his family. He re-enlisted in September 1914. Writing in mid-December 1918, Guest had served overseas from deployment for Gallipoli in July 1915 until June 1918 when the cadre of the 7th

Dublin Fusiliers returned to Aldershot, before being absorbed by the 11th Royal Irish Fusiliers and heading for France. During that three-year period, he had been at Aldershot for six weeks, and home on leave twice for 14 days. His wife, he said, due to having seven children, 'complains of being unable to manage the family and begs me to ask for transfer for home service where I could occasionally obtain short leave and be able to assist'. In January 1919, his request was agreed. Two months later he returned home to Church Avenue full-time after demobilisation.[3]

The return home was slower for others. A week after the armistice the 1st Royal Dublin Fusiliers began a 178-mile march across Belgium, directly eastwards to their eventual destination of Cologne. They arrived on 10 December, as part of the allied occupation force. The battalion's official history noted difficulty 'in making those men understand who were unavoidably detained with the Army of Occupation that a state of war still existed, that peace had not yet been declared, and that an army had still to be maintained in the field'. The battalion still numbered around 650 at the end of February but by the end of April the battalion, then in France, had fewer than 80 of all ranks. The final batch of men returned to the UK in mid-June.[4]

The 2nd Dublins were effectively demobilised rather more quickly, with only around 100 men remaining in late January. Most of those were sent in the next month to the 1st Dublins in Germany, with the cadre remaining in France and not heading back to the UK until June.[5] Meanwhile, the 6th Dublins were posted to the edge of the Belgian part of the Ardennes in late November, and were in that area until March. They were welcomed by the Belgian people displaying Union Flags, but perhaps not for the reasons they might have imagined. Noël Drury noted in his diary on 24 November that at Hastierre-sur-Meuse, people explained that the Germans had said, 'that the British were awful savages and would beat and burn all before them if each house did not show a flag. So they browbeat the people into buying an enormous stick of flags which were brand new and made in Germany for the occasion!'[6]

Drury's battalion had expected to go to Germany, but it was clear by late December that they would not, and they killed time in the Ardennes while the process of winding down the unit began.[7] 500 were demobilised in late February, leaving fewer than 200, of whom nearly half were posted to the 5th Royal Irish Regiment on the Rhine in early March.[8] Drury returned home on leave at the end of January, which was extended due to family illness and he never returned to his unit. His final diary entry, on 11 March 1919, simply noted, 'Doffed uniform and turned civilian again.'[9] Across the British army, by mid-July 1919, nearly 3,000,000 had been demobilised, leaving around 1,200,000 still serving.

While Drury relaxed in the Ardennes, soldiers elsewhere were continuing to suffer from wounds and lose their lives. Anne Young of Sandymount Road had lost a son in September 1914, when Private 6483 Charles Young was killed in action serving in France with the RAMC's 13th Field Ambulance. She then lost her husband, Captain Benjamin Young, in November 1916, also of the RAMC, who died serving at a military hospital in Cork, and was buried at Drumcondra. When the armistice came, Anne Young might have hoped that another son, Lance Corporal B/202230 Hector Young, serving in the 10th Rifle Brigade, would survive. However, he died in hospital in England on 30 December 1918 and was buried at Tidworth.[10]

Other deaths came because, beyond the Western Front, fighting did not cease. The replenished 2nd Dublins departed for Constantinople at the end of 1919 as part of the force occupying former Ottoman territories. They faced attacks from Nationalist Turks from the middle of 1920, and remained there until mid-November when they headed for India.[11] From the armistice until deaths stopped officially being recorded as 'First World War' by the War Graves Commission at the end of August 1921,[12] over 300 Dubliners lost their lives either in service or defined as 'war dead', due to death from wounds or illness incurred during the war. Of these, 92 were before the end of 1918, but there were then another 125 in 1919, 61 in 1920 and 23 in 1921. These men fell from the Baltic to East Africa. Private 11027 Henry Begley of Upper Dorset Street and a member of the 1st Connaught Rangers, was deployed to Russia as part of the British government's contribution to the fight against the Bolsheviks over 1918–19. He was killed in action on 27 July 1919.[13] Patrick Killeen died in Baghdad on 12 June 1920, there with the 2nd Royal Irish Rifles suppressing the Arab rebellion.[14] Former Dublin Fusilier, Lieutenant Frank Malley, brother of Eoin O'Malley, was in Dar-es-Salaam attached to the 2/1st King's African Rifles when he died of blackwater fever.[15] The final war deaths were closer to home, probably the result of lingering war wounds or illness. The last Dublin Fusilier considered a war death was Private 11938 Michael Callaghan of

Bride Street. He had been discharged in October 1917 suffering from tuberculosis but when he died on 29 August 1921 he was given a British war grave at Grangegorman.[16] A day later, the final war death of a Dubliner took place, when Private 49879 Michael Scully of St Michael's Hill and the Worcestershire Regiment died. He too was buried at Grangegorman.[17]

Meanwhile, the tradition of Irishmen serving in the British army continued. The 1st Dublins were deployed from Aldershot to London in April 1920, in case of possible disturbances following a strike in the coal industry. In the event, they were not needed.[18] Those stationed in India had opted for post-war service, but that did not mean that they paid no attention to developments at home. In late June 1920, members of the 1st Connaught Rangers at Jullundur mutinied in protest at the British army's activities in Ireland. Among them was Dubliner John Flannery. When he re-enlisted in February 1919, his mother was living in Castle Street, and he had already served ten years in the Connaughts.[19] There was support within the battalion for Ireland's 'fight for freedom' and concern 'against the atrocious deeds committed on the people of Ireland by the Black and Tans'. Flannery emerged as the leader of the mutineers, despite having initially advised against the rebellion.[20] Adopting a policy of 'passive resistance', a tricolour was hoisted over the barracks and the men wore Sinn Féin rosettes.[21] The mutiny spread to a unit of Connaughts about twenty miles away at Solon. It was there on 1 July that the mutiny turned violent as guards killed 2 mutineers. However, the mutiny continued until 11 July, when the authorities persuaded the bulk of the battalion to stand down. At Jullundur 33 were convicted, with 5 of them, including Flannery, sentenced to death. At Solon, 28 were convicted, 9 of them sentenced to death, though only one was eventually executed, James Daly. None of the Jullundur mutineers was ever executed.[22] Flannery was discharged from the Connaughts in April 1921 and sent to HM Prison Maidstone.[23] Those with short sentences were released following the Truce of July 1921, but others had to wait until January 1923, following an agreement between Britain and the Irish Free State.[24] By the time they emerged from prison, not only were the Connaught Rangers no more, but also all other southern Irish regiments, including the Dublin Fusiliers, were disbanded on the formation of the new state, their colours laid to rest at Windsor Castle on 12 June 1922.[25]

This was not the end of southern Irish service in the British military. For some, First World War service was followed by service in a second global conflict. John Day survived the sinking of the *Arabic* in 1916 then served in the Royal Flying Corps and the Royal Air Force. In 1942, he was aged 52 and Squadron Leader of the RAF's 24 Squadron, a transport squadron with the role of transporting VIPs, including Winston Churchill.[26] On 30 October 1942 he was a passenger on a Lockheed Hudson which took off from Belfast around lunchtime and crashed in woods close to RAF Halton at Wendover in Buckinghamshire. Everyone on board was killed.[27] He left a widow and son. A grandson born in 1969 was named after him.[28]

Life and Death

Commemorating the dead would become the highest-profile aspect of the lives of veterans in Dublin after the war, and the most politically charged.[29] But for most it was of little concern other than at a few points of the year. More pressing were matters of daily life. Among some soldiers returning to Dublin, adjusting to family life was a challenge. Private 1121 Daniel Hogan was discharged as medically unfit in the summer of 1917. In 1926, his wife, by then living in Canada, wrote to the War Office saying that she had not seen him 'for several years'. She was trying to find out where he was. It may have been a shock to her to receive the reply that he had died in May 1921.[30] Another case saw ex-soldier Michael Brophy of Peter Street sentenced in a police court in June 1922 'for wilfully neglecting to maintain his wife, Bridget Brophy, and their three children under the age of fourteen years'.[31]

Others struggled in the face of extraordinarily serious wounds. Thirteen members of the Royal Dublin Fusiliers were among those treated by Harold Gillies, the pioneer in the use of plastic surgery to treat facial injuries at the Queen's Hospital in Sidcup.[32] Among them at least four were Dubliners. One was Robert Callaghan, discussed later.[33] When he was discharged to Storey's Villa off School Street in September 1919, Private 11161 Joseph Fitzpatrick, age 29, had already been suffering from a gunshot wound to his lower jaw for nearly a year. A pre-war Dublin Fusilier, he served in France, Salonika and Egypt, before returning to France. He was hit in the face in October 1918 serving in the 6th Dublins and began treatment soon after, but did not go to Sidcup until March 1924. He was admitted suffering from a splintered lower jaw which had a piece sticking through his tongue. Two months of treatment followed.[34] Lance Corporal 12215 James Roche of Inchicore was wounded at Suvla Bay in August 1915 serving in the 7th Dublins, and was discharged in May 1916. He began treatment under Gillies in February 1920, then aged 34. He had already had six operations, three in Cairo and three in Dublin, to remove bone fragments and dead tissue from around a fractured mandible. After having some teeth removed to make way for a bone graft, operations followed in April, August and September to carry out the graft, followed by another in October to remove scars. Finally, at the end of November he was fitted with dentures and discharged two weeks later.[35] Gillies could do little to help Sergeant 25649 Robert Wheatman of Old Camden Street. Enlisting in the 6th Dublins in January 1916 he had been in Dublin at the Royal Barracks when the Rising broke out. Shot in the left jaw, he spent three months in the King George V Hospital before being transferred to a reserve battalion, the 11th Dublins. His service continued until February 1918 when he was eventually discharged from the army as being no longer fit for service. At this point, a medical board described him as being unable to eat solid food, suffering from weight loss and heart trouble, and having a discharge from his ears and nose.[36] When he attended Gillies' clinic in December 1920 he was suffering from partial paralysis on the left side of his face and 'great masticatory disability'. However, he did not want a bone graft, due to his underlying heart problems, and was simply fitted with dentures.[37]

The cases of the Gillies patients who travelled to Surrey for treatment were extreme examples of the sufferings of former soldiers. For others, support was available closer to home. Since at least early 1916, 'broken-nerved soldiers' had been treated at Dublin's Richmond Asylum.[38] The Ministry of Pensions was established at the end of 1916 to administer war pensions for the wounded and widows/dependants of the dead, with awards for the wounded covering both physical and mental injuries.[39] Local committees were set up across Britain and Ireland with Dublin's beginning work in May 1917.[40] Groups were formed to help veterans back into civilian life, and to make claims for benefits or land, the most prominent being the 'Comrades of the Great War' which held its first meting in Dublin in September 1918.

It continued to organise events until 1921 when it was subsumed by the British Legion.[41]

The establishment of the Irish Free State did not result in any change to the entitlement of disabled ex-servicemen to pensions since the British government maintained its obligations to those who had served in the British military. While there were significant problems in the organisation of pension claims in the early years, by all measures veterans in the Free State were more likely to receive a pension than their counterparts in Great Britain, and at a higher rate. For example, figures for 1926–7 show that 31.6% enlisted men in the Irish Free State received a pension, compared to 16% in Northern Ireland and 9.8% in Britain. Meanwhile, the value per pension to a disabled veteran was £17 7s 6d in the Free State, £9 19s 6d in Northern Ireland, and £5 0s 7d in Britain. Possible reasons for this include, for example, Irish soldiers having served longer (due to Irish recruitment having been mostly before 1916), the Ministry of Pensions possibly being more generous to Irish applicants knowing that they would not receive other support in the Free State, or Irish claimants simply being more effective in their applications.[42]

Pensions were also provided for former members of the IRA, by the government of the Irish Free State. These were not only for wounded veterans but also those who served, on the basis that IRA members missed out on career opportunities through the act of serving. The first pensions legislation, the Military Service Pensions Act of 1924, covered those who had served in both the pre-Truce IRA and in the National Army during the Civil War. This deliberately political act by the Cumann na Gaedhael government excluded anyone in the anti-Treaty IRA, but ranged beyond the Irish Volunteers to include the ICA, Fianna Éireann and the Hibernian Rifles. Later changes included paying pensions to those who had mutinied in the Connaught Rangers in 1920 and, in 1971, to widows of military service and the Connaught mutineers who had not remarried. Most significant was the 1934 act – again political, and passed by de Valera's Fianna Fáil government – covering those who had served in the anti-Treaty IRA, along with members of Cumann na mBan. Changes were also made in 1934 to cover those who served in only one of 1916 or the War of Independence. In total, over 80,000 applied for pensions, with around 18,000 awarded.[43] Among Dubliners to take advantage of the 1934 changes were two former British soldiers who fought in the anti-Treaty IRA: Patrick O'Moore and Michael McCabe. Remarkably, McCabe's correspondence address when he applied for his pension in 1938 was the Gold Coast Regiment of Britain's Royal West African Frontier Force. Writing to a friend who was assisting with the paperwork, he said, 'I have not had my statement witnessed out here, afraid it just wouldn't suit.'[44]

Employment prospects were a different matter and government support could only ever be piecemeal at a time when economic orthodoxy was against vast state involvement in job creation. The Dublin Corporation decided in early 1922 that when employing men it would ensure that 25% were from the pre-Truce Dublin Brigade of the IRA.[45] As regards British military veterans, in early 1920 there were 83,500 demobilised servicemen in Ireland, of whom 27,468 (one-third) were receiving unemployment benefits, compared to just under 10% in Great Britain. The Ministry of Labour believed this was due to the political situation leading to hostility towards ex-servicemen and the British government did provide some funding for public works schemes, some of which went to house-building in the Dublin area.[46] Houses were built through the Irish Sailors' and Soldiers' Land Trust, established in 1923 by the Free State but actually an imperial body since the British government retained responsibility for ex-servicemen. Of nearly 2,000 houses built by 1928 in the Free State, 526 were in County Dublin, nearly half at Killester, which became Dublin's first garden suburb. Rents were lower than in comparable housing elsewhere in the city but this did not prevent a rent strike by tenants over 1924–6.[47] Yet, despite this scheme being set up through fears that there might be problems for ex-servicemen finding work, former IRA member Peter Gough may still have believed that proving his British army service could help him find work: in 1937, for that reason, he wrote to the War Office requesting a copy of his discharge papers which he had 'lost'.[48]

Desertion continued to be dealt with, but relatively leniently, with cases generally only coming to light when a soldier made a request to the War Office, often for the issue of war medals. Private 25795 Patrick Caffrey had served in France with the 8th Dublins, but deserted in January 1918. He contacted the War Office in November 1924, then living in North Cumberland Street, to request his medals. He was told that he was a deserter and liable to prosecution, but that any sanction might be dropped if he made a full confession. Explaining his case, Caffrey said that he had arrived in Dublin on leave on Christmas Day 1917, and had only been home three days 'when I was visited by two unknown armed men who t[h] reatened my life on account of doing duty during the rebellion of 1916'. He said he was told not to attempt to leave Ireland and was shadowed during his stay. For that reason, and because his brother, Private 14620 Francis Caffrey, serving in the same battalion, had been killed on the Somme, Caffrey decided to desert. Whether there had been any threat from unknown men could have been open to dispute, but the War Office decided to take him at his word. He was formally discharged and his medals issued. Similar cases were still coming to light many years later. In December 1936, John Fitzgerald of Annmore Drive wrote to the War Office to request his medals. He had deserted not once, but twice, first from the Dublin Fusiliers in July 1917 and then, having re-enlisted fraudulently, from the Connaught Rangers in July 1919. He blamed family troubles for his first desertion. Then having re-enlisted, he said that a rumour reached him after the armistice that his deserter status had been discovered, so he decided to quit the Connaughts. The War Office did formally discharge Fitzgerald, but decided not to issue his medals.[49]

A body of the existing establishment continued to play a part in the running of the British Empire. For example, Lieutenant Edwin Lemass of Monkstown, who was a second cousin of future Taoiseach Seán Lemass, joined the Colonial Service after the war. He was based mainly in Tangier, and later became a judge in Egypt.[50] Others found their places in the Irish Free State. Bryan Cooper had been a Unionist MP in 1910 for South Dublin, elected in the January election and defeated in December. A prominent figure in the 10th (Irish) Division, and author of its first history, he was elected as a TD for Dublin County in 1923 as an independent, winning the seat twice in the 1927 general elections (first as an independent and then for Cumann na Gaedhael) and holding it until his death in 1930.[51] The first three appointments as legal officers made by former Republican Court judge, Cahir Davitt, when he was appointed Judge Advocate General of the National Army in 1922, had all served in the British military, Charles Casey and John Donovan in the army and Thomas Coyne in the RAF. Casey went on to become Attorney General of the Irish Republic in 1950, Coyne later became a diplomat and then secretary to the Department of Justice, while Donovan took on a senior role on the Electricity Supply Board.

In appointing them to their positions with the court of the National Army, Davitt had in mind their legal experience and their knowledge of military matters, the latter of which was amply proven (and not hindered) by their British military experience.[52] Davitt also appointed Eugene Sheehy, brother of Mary Kettle and Hanna Sheehy-Skeffington, and a former British officer.[53] After the Rising, he had briefly (from mid-July to mid-November 1916) served on the Somme with the 1st Dublins, before becoming an intelligence officer with an artillery unit. He served until demobilisation in March 1919 and returned to the bar in Dublin. Beyond protesting about the actions of Crown forces, Sheehy played no part in the fight against British rule, but that was no barrier to him working for the National Army, and he later took on other senior legal roles.[54]

Meanwhile, service in the Free State's National Army, was an attractive option for many British army veterans, with around half of the 55,000 men in the National Army in the mid-1920s reckoned to be British army veterans.[55] Some of those who joined the National Army were still serving when the Second World War – or the 'Emergency' as it was called in the south of Ireland – broke out. Among them was Arthur Neilan, the 1916 rebel whose brother Gerald had been killed in the British army during the Rising. He served with the 2nd Field Company of the Army Corps of Engineers from June 1940 until his death in November 1944.[56]

Debate continues among historians as to how far British veterans became targets of the IRA. Certainly, in November 1922 the anti-Treaty IRA were ordered by their commander, Liam Lynch, to kill British veterans in the National Army.[57] One recent study of three Munster counties shows that ex-servicemen faced much hostility during the Civil War, because of their past service, but also that this was part of much wider violence directed against Protestants.[58] Over 120 war veterans were killed by the IRA in various guises between 1919 and 1924 and it has been argued that most of these were 'killed simply as retribution for their part in the war'.[59] Such an approach is in line with writers who stress the sectarian nature of the IRA's activities during the Irish Revolution.[60] However, whether or not the IRA might have – at least on occasion – behaved in a sectarian manner in some parts of the country, the sheer number of veterans, not least in Dublin, suggests that any concerted campaign against them by the IRA would have run into difficulties. Moreover, as Paul Taylor argues, 'Their integration into society was not defined by war service. The term ex-servicemen implied a homogeneity which in reality, beyond attendance at remembrance ceremonies, did not exist.'[61] So what stands out more than 120 dead is the vast number who lived their lives free from IRA violence.

21 | COMMEMORATION

... real republicanism has a glowing centre of egalitarianism and how could it be very republican to ignore the deaths, the injuries and the families of the working people of Ireland and Britain who were sucked into a war that was not of their making.

President Michael D. Higgins, August 2014[1]

Commemorative Days

The dead of wars live on in the hearts and minds of those who knew them, and in the individual memorials which are constructed.[2] But the complexities of memory arise in how societies as a whole, or in part, commemorate war. How could a state which had emerged from a war with the British appropriately commemorate the dead of a military against which it had fought?[3] Part of the answer was in the collective acts of citizens of the new state who had been part of that army and had established rituals from the war's end. They did not need state sanction to commemorate as they wished. The first opportunity for mass commemoration in Dublin came on 19 July 1919, 'Peace Day'. This was a UK-wide event, though in Belfast it was marked a month later to avoid clashing with Orange events.[4] The Irish Nationalist Veterans Association (which was active in Belfast into the 1920s but had little profile in Dublin after 1919) boycotted the event. The general nationalist position was that Peace Day was a celebration of militarism.[5] However, the commemorations were still substantial. Crowds assembled from 9am as military units took up positions around Castle

Yard. They included all the Irish infantry regiments, along with English, Scottish and Welsh regiments serving in Dublin, and units such as the Royal Engineers. The Royal Navy and Royal Air Force were also represented, with tanks bringing up the rear. At 11.40am they left Castle Yard, with the salute taken by Lord French at College Green. The *Evening Mail* reported, 'As was only to be expected, the Dublin Fusiliers received an ovation all to themselves.' The parade took nearly two hours to pass. There was no outright opposition, but a sign of feeling among elected local politicians was that 'In contrast to practically every other building in Dame Street, no flag was flown over the City Hall – even the flag bearing the City arms was not hoisted.'[6]

Annual commemorations focused on Armistice Day. At the two minutes' silence at 11am on 11 November 1919, the *Evening Mail* reported, 'Thousands participated in the mute tribute of respect and homage'. The city's central gathering place was at College Green. The bell of Trinity College sounded at 11am and as traffic halted 'It was as though the chill hand of death had been suddenly laid upon the pulsating heart of the Metropolis, and that the life blood of her arteries had been petrified in their course and ceased to flow.' As the bell chimed again, along with factory and ship sirens, flags which had been lowered were raised and God Save the King was led by students at Trinity. However, a discordant note was struck with the singing of Sinn Féin's 'The Soldiers' Song' outside the party's headquarters in Harcourt Street after the end of the silence.[7]

Over 1919–22, there were plenty of incentives not to disrupt the anniversary of the armistice due to the tensions aroused by street violence and curfews. This meant that 1923 was the first armistice marked in 'genuine peacetime conditions'.[8] The focal points were parades and services in the city centre. The *Irish Times* reported, 'A good many members of the National Army wore the poppy in their caps'.[9] While the President of the Free State's Executive and the Governor General did not attend Armistice Day commemorations in Dublin, they sent representatives between 1924 and 1932 (after which point Fianna Fáil was in government led by de Valera and did not take part). The first wreath laid for the Free State government by Senator Colonel Maurice Moore, in 1924, carried the words in English and Irish, 'In memory of all the Irishmen who died in the Great War from the government of the Irish Free State'.[10] Also from 1924, a centre-piece of commemorations in Dublin was a twenty-foot-high wooden cross marking the role of the

Figure 21.1: Armistice Day, College Green, 11 November 1924. A Celtic Cross in memory of the 16th (Irish) Division was unveiled and later transported to Guillemont. (Image Courtesy of the National Library of Ireland, HOG131).

16th Division on the Somme. It had been resting between Guillemont and Ginchy since the autumn of 1917. When plans were made for a permanent stone cross (at Guillemont, which would be unveiled in 1926), the wooden cross was sent to Dublin and it was used annually until 1939 when it was placed at Islandbridge where it still rests.[11] The stone cross that was placed at Guillemont was also on display in Dublin prior to its erection in France, at the College Green events in 1924.[12]

The Irish Free State was represented at Armistice Day events in London in 1923 by two Senators, Lord Glenavy (at Westminster Abbey) and Bryan Mahon (at the Cenotaph). From 1924, when there was only a ceremony at the Cenotaph, the Irish High Commissioner in London participated, accompanied by Mahon, and the High Commissioner continued to attend until the outbreak of the Second World War when such ceremonies were suspended.[13]

The presence of the President of the Executive Council was periodically requested in London. When first invited, in 1924, William T. Cosgrave pointed out 'that it would be hypocritical for him' to attend

'having regard to the fact that he was imprisoned by the British government during the world-war'. Nor did Cosgrave attend the unveiling of
a tablet commemorating the Empire's dead in Westminster Abbey in
1926, when all Dominion Prime Ministers were in London for the
Imperial Conference in October and November. Cosgrave could not
attend the whole conference and might have used that as an excuse for
not being there on this occasion, sending instead the Vice-President,
Kevin O'Higgins, who had lost a brother in the war.[14] However, his
reasons were actually rather more complex than simply his own imprisonment, as he explained in a letter to the British Prime Minister, Stanley
Baldwin. Cosgrave said that he would 'personally feel very much honoured to be present', but that he faced 'a very real difficulty'. He wrote
that he had taken part in the Rising during which 'a considerable
amount of feeling was naturally aroused and bitter words were spoken'.
He pointed out that 'So far as those who were killed amongst my
companions are concerned, time and subsequent happy developments
have almost completely cicatrised the wounds.' However, he was concerned about those who had 'lost brothers and sons' in the British army
during the Rising. He argued that among them there remained 'and not
unnaturally – a feeling of, I shall not say, bitterness, but rather of pain'.
He added, 'I fear lest the personal presence at this ceremonial, in
memory of their beloved sons, of one to whom they attribute responsibility for their bereavement should re-open wounds that are not yet
quite healed. It is so easy to hurt and so difficult to heal.' Cosgrave
recognised that 'my absence may occasion comment amongst the
unthinking, but I feel that you will agree that if the price to be paid for
the absence of such comments were the infliction of pain upon the
relatives of the dead, silence would be too dearly bought'.[15] Baldwin
replied that he fully appreciated the reasons. So impressed was
Dominions Secretary Leo Amery that he wrote to Cosgrave asking if
'the chivalrous thoughtfulness' of his letter could be made public since
he had been 'greatly moved' by it and felt that it could 'do much to heal
old wounds'. Cosgrave agreed and publication in the British press was
well-received.[16]

Commemorations in Dublin were not free from controversy
and trouble. Tensions often arose between students from Trinity
College and University College, reflecting not only how their different
politics made them see the war in different ways, but also a general
rivalry between two groups of students.[17] Beyond that, there were other

efforts to hinder commemorations. In 1926, when it was said that 120,000 had gathered at a memorial to the 16th Division in St Stephen's Green, smoke bombs were let off.[18] A public meeting in 1927 organised by Fianna Fáil saw speakers protest against 'the flaunting of the English flag in Ireland'.[19] In the same year, a British Legion hall was opened at Inchicore on 5 November only to be burned down five days later.[20] In future years, the Union Flag continued to offend, with scuffles breaking out in 1930 as attempts were made by protesters to seize flags.[21] In 1932, there was a police baton charge on those protesting against the armistice commemorations and the display of Union Flags around O'Connell Street and at College Green. One poppy-snatcher got more than he bargained for with 'a nasty cut on the hand from a razor blade, which had been secreted by the poppy-wearer.'[22]

As remembrance in Dublin moved from the city centre to Phoenix Park in 1926, the government continued to be represented until 1932. With Fianna Fáil then in office, changes were made. Though no supporter of de Valera, police commissioner Eoin O'Duffy outlined concerns about Armistice Day providing opportunities 'to display anti-Irish and pro-British sentiments'. He urged the government to ensure that events were more processions than parades, with formal military commands not allowed. He also wanted Union Flags banned and suggested that poppies only be sold on 10 and 11 November. O'Duffy's general approach was agreed by the Cabinet, with the exception of banning military commands, and with an extra day allowed for poppy sales on 9 November. A year later, O'Duffy had been replaced as commissioner by Eamon Broy who sought further restrictions, which would have seen an end to any processions and no ceremony at Phoenix Park. Instead, there would simply be church services and the sale of poppies. These restrictions were rejected by the government, but they did decide to shorten the procession from Phoenix Park so that it started at Beresford Place. In a sign of the times, it was also felt necessary to ban British Fascist uniforms. The British Legion's response was conciliatory, assuring the government that 'the very last people who desired that the day should be one of disorder were ex-Service men'. Pointing out that it was the government's duty to ensure that peaceful assembly could take place, the Legion nevertheless agreed to the new rules. They remained in force until 1939, when the outbreak of World War Two saw the ending of Armistice Day parades, although processions to church services on the Sunday before were allowed, along with the sale of poppies and the erection of a cross in Phoenix Park at which there was a small ceremony on 11 November.[23]

Islandbridge

Some debates on commemoration were focused on groups and the maintenance of war graves.[24] Many memorials to individuals, especially in churches, aroused no controversy. However, plans for a memorial to Tom Kettle, initially approved in 1923 did not reach fruition until 1937. The memorial which was unveiled then contained no mention of the British army.[25] More widely, the focus of remembrance came to be the Irish National War Memorial Gardens at Islandbridge. An all-Ireland memorial in Dublin was first mooted towards the end of 1918, with specific proposals considered from the summer of 1919 by a War Memorial Committee initially led by the Lord Lieutenant of Ireland, Lord French and later by Andrew Jameson of the whiskey-distilling family and a Senator in the Free State. Initially, a Soldiers' Central Home, which would offer board and lodging to soldiers and sailors passing through the city, was proposed and agreed. As well as having a practical function, it would house Ireland's War Memorial Records.[26] However, by the end of 1919, the ongoing conflict in Ireland led to the idea being abandoned. Until 1923, the committee focused on producing the War Memorial Records, which contained nearly 50,000 names of supposedly 'Irish' war dead, but in reality was all those who had served in Irish regiments. With the end of the Civil War, thoughts again turned to a memorial. Merrion Square was proposed, with a memorial combining a public park 'after the manner of St Stephen's Green, with the addition of a Cenotaph in the centre'. The sum of £40,000 was raised by the Irish National War Memorial Fund.[27] A Senate debate in March 1927 voiced concerns about it as a site of conflict, and the effects of mass gatherings on the daily life of the area. Some felt that it would be wrong to mix solemn commemoration with a recreational park. Perhaps more surprising were issues raised by those linked to veterans, that the money would be better spent on employment and housing for veterans. Faced with a coalition of unlikely allies, the proposal was defeated in the Senate by 40 to 13.[28]

Phoenix Park emerged as an alternative during the debate, and although it was not chosen, ten acres at nearby Islandbridge were provisionally agreed by 1929. Edwin Lutyens, a central figure in the Imperial War Graves Commission's work, was employed a year later as chief architect. When a final decision was taken at the end of 1931 to begin work, the Irish National War Memorial Committee's funds had risen to over £50,000. The Free State government committed a similar amount, justified as being a form of unemployment relief.[29] The work was effectively completed by the spring of 1937, carried out by a workforce consisting half of British veterans and half of those who had served in the National Army.[30]

In the same year, de Valera spoke at the opening of a new Reading Room at Trinity College, Dublin. The entrance to the new building was a Hall of Honour listing the names of Trinity's war dead (of whom there were 471) and which itself had been opened in 1928 without any government representative in attendance. Although de Valera's presence marked a rapprochement between him and a bastion of the Anglo-Irish ascendancy, there was no mention of the war or the Hall of Honour in the opening speeches.[31] In November 1938, it looked like there might soon be more direct engagement with war commemoration, when de Valera met with Jameson and agreed in principle to a formal opening of Islandbridge in the summer of 1939. The government would be represented either by de Valera himself or a relevant minister who would declare the park open. In March 1939 a date of 30 July was set, but in April de Valera changed his mind. In a meeting with the British Legion, he said 'The tenseness of the international situation' had 'altered the situation'. In particular, the threat of conscription being introduced in Great Britain, and 'the possibility that an effort might be made to apply it to our fellow countrymen in the Six Counties', meant that a formal ceremony 'might evoke hostility and give rise to misunderstanding'. He suggested postponement or a lower-key opening. The Legion agreed with the former, saying that 'It was their desire to respect fully the wishes of the Taoiseach and the Government and to do nothing that would embarrass the government.' When it became clear the next month that conscription would not be introduced in Northern Ireland the Legion took it upon itself to announce that the opening would go ahead on 30 July, only to be called in to the Taoiseach's office for an explanation by staff that conscription was not the only difficulty. They were obliged to put out a press statement explaining that the announcement had been unofficial. In June, with the government now clear that 'far too much emphasis is laid on the imperial and military aspect of the function', the press were told that the opening had been 'indefinitely postponed'. Instead the park simply opened by default, with its gates unlocked during the day.[32]

In 1940, Islandbridge was opened for Armistice Day. Sensitive to Ireland's neutral status, the government retained rules against military parades, uniforms, and the display of Union Flags. Poppies could be sold only on 11 November, but the Memorial Park was open for a few days either side of the ceremony, and on the Sunday after, to allow for preparation and for public viewing of wreaths. These procedures remained in force for the duration of the war. For reasons which are unclear, 1943 saw the Ministry of Justice propose a relaxation of the ruling on flags. While they suggested still prohibiting the public carrying of any 'Union Emblems', they also proposed that furled flags could be taken into Islandbridge and unfurled once there. Perhaps Allied progress in the war against Nazi Germany made some in the Free State less cautious on the subject, but the change was not agreed until after the war had ended. However, the government had already allowed other smaller ceremonies at Islandbridge, such as in August 1942 when the Old Contemptibles Association was allowed to mark the Retreat from Mons, providing that no more than 20 people attended and simply laid a wreath. In the event, much larger numbers attended and in future years 100 men and their wives were allowed.[33] Yet, a symbol of the state's distancing from memorialisation of the war dead came in October 1941 when bound volumes of Ireland's Memorial Records were removed from Árus an Uachtaráin (the residency of the President, an office established as part of the 1938 Constitution of 'Éire') and placed in store by the Office of Public Works. These were originally a gift to the Governor General. A letter in August from a civil servant argued, 'There appears to be no reason why these articles should be retained in the official residence of the President.' In one simple act, it was declared that the names of the dead had no place at the heart of the state.[34]

After the 'Emergency', the British Legion expected that parades could resume and they planned to hold one in 1945 on what was now Remembrance Sunday instead of Armistice Day (though coincidentally it was 11 November in 1945). When it was cancelled by the police, there was an outcry in the *Irish Times* and questions in the Dáil. A year later, a procession from the city centre to Islandbridge was allowed, and poppies were sold from premises in Dame Street and Grafton Street.[35] That procession was the norm until the closure of Islandbridge in the early 1970s, though its length shortened as the veterans became older.[36] By the late 1950s, organisations supporting First World War veterans in Dublin included the British Legion, the Royal Air Force Association and the Soldiers', Sailors' and Airmen's Families Association.[37] There were some efforts to coordinate veterans from a range of regimental associations. When they met at a dinner in 1958, they toasted both Ireland and Queen Elizabeth II.[38] Royal Dublin Fusiliers veterans continued to meet for social events, until at least the late 1960s, though by then even the more active veterans' organisations were winding up due to the age of their members.[39] At Islandbridge, attendances at ceremonies steadily reduced and parts of the site fell into disrepair.[40] Remembrance could still attract controversy even prior to the outbreak of the Troubles, with a pipe bomb exploding at Islandbridge after the 1956 ceremony.[41]

Memorialising the Rising

Remembrance of the Rising and subsequent events of the Irish Revolution was no easier, and both remembrance of the First World War and of the Rising by the Free State are aptly described as 'a chronicle of embarrassment'. This was because the state 'emerged from four bitter conflicts', which included not only Britain versus Ireland and Catholic versus Protestant, but also constitutionalists versus radical separatists and pro- versus anti-Treaty.[42] It has been argued of First World War remembrance that issues arose around it not simply because people wanted to 'expunge the memory of the war' but because 'the war of ideas and ideological conflict' which had marked 1914–18 was not over.[43] Exactly the same could be said of 1916–23 as regards disputes within nationalism and republicanism. Consequently, a 'Partisan rivalry' marked annual Rising commemoration from 1924, with much controversy over who should be invited to the closed formal government events.[44] A focal point from 1923 included the commemoration of Michael Collins and Arthur Griffith on a temporary Cenotaph on the lawn at Leinster

House, to which Kevin O'Higgins was added in 1927. The Cenotaph would become an avowedly partisan pro-Treaty site of memorial, and when de Valera came to power in 1932 he ended formal government participation in events there. However, in the mid-1930s plans were initiated to add anti-Treaty heroes Cathal Brugha and Austin Stack to Leinster House through the commissioning of busts of both. These would not come to fruition until 1951, by which point the Cenotaph had been replaced with a permanent structure.[45] That was never formally unveiled, becoming 'merely a silent honour' and 'a monument to unease – an unease with a past that no longer seems to suit'.[46]

Work on Islandbridge was well under way when a memorial to the Rising was unveiled at the GPO by de Valera on Easter Monday 1935.[47] In that year, a proposal was made by Oscar Traynor and the Dublin Brigade Council of the Old IRA, for a memorial at Rotunda Gardens, 'dedicated to the memory of all those who gave their lives in the cause of Irish Freedom and to be known as The Garden of Remembrance'.[48] The site was symbolic, since the Irish Volunteers were founded at the Rotunda in 1913.[49] The Fianna Fáil government agreed the proposal, but many delays followed. The land was handed over to the Office of Public Works in September 1939, but the outbreak of the Emergency and the consequent financial constraints meant that work was suspended.[50] It was agreed in 1940 that there would be a design competition, but that was not announced until January 1946, and a winner found in August.[51] Even after the Emergency, there was no rapid progress. In 1949, with Fine Gael now in power, the site was temporarily allocated to hospital premises to tackle the problem of infant mortality, promoting angry questions in the Dáil as to whether the memorial project had been abandoned. Over 1951 to 1953, it looked like a start would be made, as statements were made that the temporary children's hospital premises could be moved.[52] Yet not until 1959 was a move of the hospital buildings possible, with work planned for completion in 1963, though later delayed by a year.[53] However, even though work on the main structures was largely complete in 1964, continuing discussions over a central statue meant that when the gardens were opened on the fiftieth anniversary of the Rising the statue was not present and indeed was not unveiled until 11 July 1971, the fiftieth anniversary of the Truce.[54]

1966 and the Troubles

Nothing symbolised the different priorities given to First World War and Rising commemoration in the Irish Republic so much as what happened in 1966. In that year an official programme of public events marked the Rising's fiftieth anniversary. The centrepiece was a parade in O'Connell Street on Easter Sunday, broadcast live by RTÉ on radio and television, with as many as 200,000 people in the surrounding area. That contrasted with the absence of any official consideration of the Somme's similar anniversary, other than in a minuscule manner through the inclusion of some of Thomas Kettle's poetry in official publications.[55]

Later, as the impact of the Troubles was felt, Islandbridge was closed between 1971 and 1988 over fears of IRA action against ceremonies. It reopened following criticism of the Irish government's attitude to remembrance after the Enniskillen bombing in 1987. Not until 1994 did an official government representative take part in a ceremony: Bertie Ahern, later Taoiseach but then Finance Minister.[56] By that point, President Mary Robinson had signalled a shift in the state's attitudes to remembrance when she became the first Irish President to attend the annual Remembrance service in St Patrick's, Dublin's Protestant cathedral in November 1993.[57] This landmark event was followed steadily by others which became possible following the Troubles ceasefires of 1994. In 1998 President Mary McAleese took part in the opening of the Island of Ireland Peace Park at Messines on 11 November, alongside the British and Belgian heads of state. On 1 July 2006, she was at Islandbridge for a Somme ninetieth commemoration.[58] In the same year, An Post issued stamps to commemorate the Somme, a move which was welcomed by the Orange Order, who criticised the Royal Mail's failure to do so.[59] In 2010, President McAleese, with the Duke of Gloucester in attendance, unveiled a new memorial to the 10th Division at Suvla Bay.[60]

A Queen and Two Presidents

A new chapter in commemoration of both the First World War and the Rising opened in May 2011, when Queen Elizabeth II visited the Republic of Ireland, paying tribute alongside President McAleese both to British war dead at Islandbridge, and the dead of 'the cause of Irish Freedom' commemorated at the Garden of Remembrance.[61] The Queen's visit rested on a new public mood which had developed

over many years through grassroots initiatives. In 1995, Tom Burke led
the formation of the Royal Dublin Fusiliers Association. This followed
a discussion with an elderly neighbour in Killester. The neighbour 'took
out a shoebox with his medals in it and he broke down crying. When
someone that age breaks down and then thanks you, because it's the first
time in his life he has been asked to talk about these things, it sticks with
you. It lit a light.' In the early days of his work, Burke was told by
a Loyalist from Northern Ireland, 'You guys have the Famine, leave us
the Somme.' A decade on, Burke's work was recognised with the award
of an honorary MBE of which he said, 'I'll wear it with my old hurling
medals'.[62]

Recently, local projects have resulted in discussions and websites,
aided by the growth of digital history,[63] and a Dublin branch of the
Western Front Association was inaugurated in February 2012.[64]
In July 2014, a Tree of Remembrance was unveiled at St Patrick's
Cathedral reflecting 'an increasing sense of confidence and security' in
taking part in First World War remembrance.[65] By this time the Irish
government was already planning extensive commemoration of the First
World War alongside that of revolutionary events as part of the 'Decade
of Centenaries'.[66] President Michael D. Higgins marked all the major
events of the UK's war, attending ceremonies at Liège to mark the war's
outbreak on 4 August 2014, at Gallipoli on 24 April 1915, and at
Islandbridge on 9 July 2016 to mark the Somme.[67] There was significant
government presence at events at Guillemont on 3 September 2016 and at
Tom Kettle's memorial six days later.[68] At the end of 2016, Michael
Jackson, the Church of Ireland Archbishop of Dublin could claim that
'North and South, we have taken back The Somme into our
self-understanding and identity.'[69] A year on, Sinn Féin for the first time
sent a representative to the annual remembrance service at St Patrick's.
Commenting on her attendance, the party's then deputy leader, Mary Lou
McDonald, said of the war's dead, 'It is right that we remember them.
The dead of World War One are part of our shared, and at times
contested, history.'[70]

Even if much First World War commemoration is broadly
'British' in tone,[71] President Higgins' words in August 1914, and the
next year in Turkey, revealed new departures in the analysis put forward
by the head of state. Previous Presidents had argued that remembering
WWI was part of reconciliation between different traditions. Higgins
effectively argued that remembering the war should not be about

recognising another tradition but about accepting that Irishness is multi-faceted. This became apparent following his dedication of a cross of commemoration at Glasnevin in a joint British–Irish ceremony on 31 July 2014. His actions, and the presence of both British and Irish soldiers, were targeted by a small group of protesters. He had spoken there about Irishmen in the British army in WWI having a 'multilayered sense of identity'. Protesters yelled abuse at British soldiers and during a minute's silence, they heckled and yelled 'Higgins, you traitor.' Responding to them a few days later he sought, for the first time by any Irish head of state, to draw the story of service in the First World War into a republican narrative. He said, 'real republicanism has a glowing centre of egalitarianism and how could it be very republican to ignore the deaths, the injuries and the families of the working people of Ireland and Britain who were sucked into a war that was not of their making'.[72] In Istanbul on 23 April 2015, he returned to the idea when, before he headed to ceremonies at Gallipoli, he spoke of how 'clouded versions of what true Irishness was stopped people's agony being appreciated'.[73] This was a notable step, but only time will tell how far the lost and wounded of 1914–18 take their place alongside those of the Rising.

Inevitably, in 2016, the Rising's centenary was *the* commemorative event of the year in Dublin. When the anniversary came, marked as always at Easter which was in late March, rather than on the precise dates in late April, the once-unionist *Irish Times* headlined its front page with the words 'Dignity and hope front and centre on the day the nation stood proud and remembered.' The journalist Miriam Lord described 'truly a great day to be Irish', as many thousands packed the city centre for a series of military and religious commemorations as part of the official State commemoration. Central to the events was the presence of 3,500 relatives of those involved in the Rising. Among them, one figure stood out, the oldest: Sheila O'Leary, the 94-year-old daughter of Tom Byrne and Lucy Smyth. She was their second child – their first having died shortly after the raid which saw Tom arrested.[74] Tom died in 1962 and Lucy ten years later. Sheila had a special place in the story of the Rising, being the only surviving child of two Rising veterans.[75] She brought her father's service medals with her in a wooden box and said at the end of the day, 'I feel very emotional when I think of the values of every one of those Volunteers. They all deserve to be honoured.'[76]

CONCLUSION: THREE MEN

We were surprised, annoyed and we thought that it was madness ...
we were at war in defence of this country and what we believed in ...
Former Royal Dublin Fusilier, IRA member and National
Army General, Emmet Dalton, asked in 1978 about his
reaction to the Easter Rising[1]

From 35,000 to 3

Across the First World War, somewhere between 35,000 and
40,000 Dubliners served in the British forces. Nearly 4,000 more,
90% of them women, saw voluntary service in the Red Cross.
At least 6,568 of the military were killed, putting Dublin's fatality
rate at 16–19%, more than the UK-wide figure of 12%, perhaps one
and a half times more. Part of that can be explained by the bulk of
Dublin's recruitment coming in the early years of the war, with there
being no conscription to ensure a continuous flow of men over
1917–18. Meanwhile, whereas across the entire war 54.8% of the
British army were infantry, 72.2% of Dubliners who served in the
army were in the infantry.[2] Both factors combined meant that
Dubliners served in units which were more likely to face danger, and
did so for longer, than the UK average.

The story of this service ranged globally, from the farthest seas
sailed by the Royal Navy and the Mercantile Marine, to every land
theatre in which the British fought. When veterans returned to Dublin,

they found it changed utterly, because of the conflict around Ireland's quest for some form of independence, a conflict which spoke to wider struggles for autonomy within the British Empire. Most would avoid any part in this conflict, but some played a central role. This put them in a tradition of militant Irish republicanism drawing on the services of former British soldiers from the earliest days of the Irish Volunteers and even during the Easter Rising.

Throughout this book, the experiences of the Royal Dublin Fusiliers, along with some other Irish battalions, have been central to exploring the role of Dubliners on the battlefield. Those men included not only the volunteers who flocked to the colours, but also the regulars and reservists who were already serving when war broke out. However, Dubliners also served throughout the British army, nearly one in ten of them in English, Scottish or Welsh infantry regiments. Stories of individuals have illustrated the lived experiences of a city and its surrounding county: people back home waiting for months to find out what 'missing' really meant; wounds and suffering which continued well after the war; and people who were executed or went to prison because they fought for their beliefs. In most cases, little is known about the people featured because the only footprint they have left on history is at one momentous moment such as their death, winning a medal, or when put on trial. However, three men stand out as embodying the story of Dublin's military service as a whole in 1912–23 – whether for Britain or as Irish Republicans – its conflicting loyalties, suffering and service.

Emmet Dalton: 1957, 1966 and 1978

Few would or could remember all sides equally. Perhaps only one man did, who had fought in both the British army and the IRA: Emmet Dalton. In the mid-1950s, he began to write a film script about Michael Collins, in which his own story featured, partly fictionalised. It never became a film and Dalton retained some wariness about aspects of revolutionary commemoration, claiming in 1957 that he was 'thoroughly fed up' with the way in which the Mountjoy raid's anniversary was commemorated year after year. He said there were many other incidents in which he was involved which were 'more daring and certainly more important' but were never referred to.[3]

Perhaps Dalton was thinking only of his past in the IRA but he was not ashamed of his role in the British army. Shortly before his death on 4 March 1978 he was interviewed by Cathal O'Shannon on RTÉ and made no apology for his views on the Rising. Describing those at Kilworth Camp in Cork when news came through, he said, 'We were surprised, annoyed and we thought that it was madness.' He defended that as, 'we were at war in defence of this country and what we believed in', and denied feeling any sympathy for the rebels.[4]

Twelve years before, as the Rising's 50th anniversary was marked, Dalton made a case for also remembering the Somme. He wrote to the *Irish Times* reminding readers that 1966 was 'also the 50th anniversary of the Battle of the Somme, where thousands of young Irishmen fought with great gallantry before losing their lives'. He made the bold claim that 'These young men were volunteers who answered the call of Ireland's political leaders of that day; they were motivated by a just cause', and cited his friend Tom Kettle's poem to his daughter Betty.[5]

Robert Callaghan: 1922, 1938 and 1948

Captain Robert Callaghan, born in Clontarf in 1886, was hit by a bullet in the Struma Valley in Macedonia on 3 October 1916, aged 30, serving with the 7th Dublins. The bullet entered his left cheek under the eye, ran through his nose and blew away almost the whole of his right upper jawbone. Both his eyes were lost. After much treatment, first on a hospital ship and then in Malta, he arrived at Southampton on the HS *Glenart Castle* in early December 1916. Further treatment followed and he was discharged from the army in March 1917, retaining the honorary rank of captain. He took up residence at his father's house in Drumcondra Road. Having had two artificial eyes inserted, Callaghan suffered from continued problems with his eyelids and nose. He was transferred from the Special Military Hospital at Blackrock to the care of Harold Gillies in May 1919. In his first operation, incisions and transfers of skin and muscle were made. Four months later he married Violet Hortense Hunter in Fulham. She was the daughter of a surgeon and it is possible that they had met due to his treatment.[6] He returned to Gillies in February 1921 for work on his nose. Then, in late 1921, it was clear that an eyelid needed attention so that it did not droop, and a further operation followed in February 1922.

17th May 1919   1st August 1919

20th February 1922   28th March 1922

Figure 22.1a-h: Captain R. W. H. Callaghan, 7th Royal Dublin Fusiliers. The photos were taken in relation to stages of his treatment. (Photos: from the Archives of the Royal College of Surgeons of England).

Along with the physical and emotional effects of his wounds, Callaghan faced a battle with bureaucracy over his pension. He initially received an annual wound pension of £200 and a £500 gratuity for the loss of his eyes. Possibly advised by staff in Sidcup (he wrote from there), he applied for another gratuity in February 1921 for facial disfigurement. The latter was because, as a medical board said in July, his lower right eyelid 'is drawn downwards which causes an unsightly appearance and necessitates wearing a shade'. Meanwhile, nasal obstructions hindered breathing. Callaghan was awarded a further gratuity, of £250, and an additional annual wound pension of £50.

These new awards prompted a Ministry of Pensions official to look again at Callaghan's case. The precise rate of daily 'retired pay' was partly determined by rank. When Callaghan was wounded, he held the rank of Acting Captain. To be paid a pension at the captain's rate one needed to have been in that role for fifteen days, but Callaghan had only held the rank for ten days when wounded. Despite that, the fact that he was a captain at the time of his injuries was communicated by the War Office to the Ministry of Pensions, and they paid him for some time at the rate for that rank – 7/- a day instead of the lower rate of 3/-. He had thus been significantly overpaid by £305 and was told that most of the overpayment would be deducted from arrears owing to him for his second annual wound pension of £50 per year. However, £117 was left to be recovered and that would be recovered from his second gratuity.

It is hard to take in what this must have meant to Callaghan. When news reached him, he was living in Booterstown, an area once represented in Parliament by Edward Carson. Callaghan wrote to Carson, by then in the Lords, in November 1921, saying that since the Ministry of Pensions had admitted the mistake was their fault, 'Surely this is not justice?' Carson immediately wrote to the War Office saying it was 'deplorable that a man blinded in the War should be put into such a state of anxiety through no fault or mistake of his own.' Over the course of the next year, three departments – the War Office, Treasury and Ministry of Pensions – sent letters back and forth to each other, partly trying to establish which department was responsible. The War Office took the view as early as January 1922 that the overpayment was not Callaghan's fault, and that only a limited recovery from the second gratuity should be made, proposing a deduction of £17 not £117. It would take until October 1922 to agree that, and in November Callaghan was told that he would receive a further £100 to make up for most of the second gratuity which he had not been sent. In the near future a daughter was born, for in 1931 he made enquiries about support for his daughter to attend the Royal School for Daughters of Officers of the Army in Bath.[7]

There was no expectation that Robert Callaghan would take part in a second war but he tried to do so. In late September 1938, at the height of the crisis over the Sudetenland, by then living in Blackheath, Callaghan wrote to the War Office saying, 'In the event of Great Britain becoming involved in war, may I, a war-blinded officer, now practising as masseur & medical electrician, offer my services in these capacities?' His offer was acknowledged, but it is not clear that he ever took up such a role.[8] He died in Greenwich in on 30 December 1948, age 62, from heart failure, bronchitis and phlebitis. His death certificate described him as a captain of the Royal Dublin Fusiliers (retired) and a 'blind pensioner'.[9] To the end, his service in the Dublins defined him.

Michael McCabe: 1938, 1941 and 1975

Michael McCabe took up service in the British army again in the 1930s and was in it when he applied for his IRA pension in 1938.[10] So when the Second World War broke out he was already serving as part of the Gold Coast Regiment. A June 1941 note from him held in his IRA pension file apologises for a delay in responding to a letter, stating that he had been on active service for the past year and was now 'somewhere in Abyssinia'. He survived the war, leaving the army in 1946, taking up residence back in Drumocondra, in Griffith Avenue. He lived until September 1975, when his home was in Portrane.[11]

How can McCabe's story be reconciled with any sense of logic or consistency? This man was so much against Ireland being part of the United Kingdom that in 1916 he took part in an armed rebellion against it. Yet a year later he was in the British army, surely knowing the risks of such a venture, and indeed he was wounded in 1918. He appears to have had no desire to go back to Ireland after the war to pursue the ideals of Easter 1916 – at least, he did not do so. It was only when in Dublin in 1922 that he came across his friend from the Fianna, Liam Mellows. Then, he deserted from the British army and took part in the occupation of the Four Courts. One might expect that a serving British soldier like McCabe was exactly the sort of man who might seek an accommodation with the British, but instead he took the anti-Treaty path and became a prisoner of the Irish Free State. Later, he again put his life on the line in wartime, for a country to whose rule in his own country he had been bitterly opposed.

There are no firm explanations for McCabe's actions. He left no detailed description of what he had done, beyond his IRA pensions file, let alone any explanation. We can speculate on the appeal of the excitement of 1916 to a fifteen-year-old member of the Volunteers, influenced by his father's membership of the IRB. Perhaps it was simply personal friendship that caused him to follow Mellows in 1922. If his joining the British army twice was simply for economic reasons, he was hardly the first Irishman to succumb to the lure or necessity of the King's shilling. We might also wonder if he was someone who simply enjoyed military life, whatever the army and whatever the cause. Perhaps at different times the opportunities open to him were extremely limited. None of this can be known. What we can be sure of is this: during the years 1912–23, British and Irish soldiers could be both the worst of enemies and the best of comrades. More than any other, Michael McCabe's life was a symbol of that paradox of British–Irish relations.

APPENDIX 1: POPULATION

Table A1.1: 1911 Census Data

Category	Dublin City	County Dublin	All-Ireland
Population (no.)	304,802	172,394	4,390,219
Denomination%			
Roman Catholic	83.1	71.0	73.9
Protestant Episcopalian	12.9	22.8	13.1
Presbyterian	1.4	2.5	10.0
Methodist	0.8	1.6	1.4
Other	1.8	2.1	1.6
Education%			
Read and write	92.6	95.1	87.6
Read only	2.1	1.5	3.2
Illiterate	5.3	3.4	9.2
Irish language%	3.9	3.4	13.3
Occupation%			
Professional	13.7	18.7	7.8
Domestic	13.5	24.1	9.4
Commercial	17.0	13.7	6.1
Agricultural	1.7	12.3	43.0
Industrial	54.2	31.3	33.8
Housing (families)%			
Occupying four rooms	10.4	10.7	16.9
Occupying three rooms	10.5	17.6	25.1
Occupying two rooms	21.0	18.5	21.3
Occupying one room	33.9	8.1	6.4

Table A1.1: (cont.)

Category	Dublin City	County Dublin	All-Ireland
One room tenements	21,133	2,844	58,334
(persons per room)			
One occupant	3,604 (17%)	1,031 (36%)	17,157 (29.4%)
Two–four occupants	12,277 (58.1)	1,380 (48.5%)	29,554 (50.7%)
Five–seven occupants	4,609 (21.8%)	382 (13.4%)	9,666 (16.6%)
Eight or more	643 (3%)	51 (1.8%)	1,957 (3.4%)

Sources: Cd. 6049-I, *Census of Ireland, 1911. County of Dublin* (London: HMSO, 1912), vi–vii & 45; Cd. 6049-II, *Census of Ireland, 1911. City of Dublin* (London: HMSO, 1912), vii–viii & 14; Cd. 6663, *Census of Ireland, 1911. General Report* (London, HMSO, 1913), xvii–xviii & xxvii–xxix.

Note: % will not always add to 100 due to rounding. Figures for education are for those age 9 and above.

APPENDIX 2: MILITARY SERVICE

Table A2.1: Service by Type of British Unit (first known unit of service)

Type of unit	Number	%
Irish Infantry Regiments	13,141	54.9
English Infantry Regiments	1,695	7.1
Artillery	1,526	6.4
Army Service Corps	1,142	4.8
Royal Flying Corps/Royal Air Force	1,085	4.5
Royal Army Medical Corps	922	3.8
Royal Engineers	875	3.7
Royal Navy	788	3.3
Colonial Army Units	644	2.7
Irish Cavalry Units	627	2.6
Other British Army Units	592	2.5
Scottish Infantry Regiments	374	1.6
Cavalry (Non-Irish)	227	0.9
Merchant Navy	216	0.9
Welsh Infantry Regiments	89	0.4
Foreign*	14	0.1
Total	23,957	

Source: all sources used (see bibliography).

* Armies of Belgium, France and USA. Note: % does not add to 100.0 due to rounding.

Table A2.2: Service by Irish Infantry Regiment

Regiment	Number	%
Royal Dublin Fusiliers	6,572	50.1
Royal Irish Rifles	1,567	11.9
Royal Irish Fusiliers	957	7.3
Leinster Regiment	823	6.3
Irish Guards	767	5.8
Connaught Rangers	767	5.8
Royal Irish Regiment	703	5.4
Royal Inniskilling Fusiliers	646	4.9
Royal Munster Fusiliers	326	2.5
Total	13,128	

Source: all sources used (see bibliography).
Note: the difference between a total of 13,128 and 13,141 in this table and Table A2.1 is because thirteen are known to have served in Irish infantry units without the regiment being known.

Table A2.3: Service by First British Division of Service

Division	Number	%
16th	2,039	24.2
4th	1,299	15.4
10th	1,253	14.8
29th	907	10.7
2nd	606	7.2
3rd	587	7.0
27th	304	3.6
63rd	297	3.5
8th	281	3.3
24th	227	2.7
Guards	213	2.5
7th (Ferozepore)	190	2.3
36th	177	2.1
1st	58	0.7
40th	1	0.0
Total	8,439	

Source: all sources used (see bibliography).

Table A2.4: Battalion of First Known Service, where Service is in an Irish Infantry Battalion

Type	Battalion	Number	%
Service	Royal Dublin Fusiliers, 2nd	1,055	10.2
Service	Royal Dublin Fusiliers, 1st	769	7.5
Service	Royal Dublin Fusiliers, 8th	708	6.9
Service	Royal Dublin Fusiliers, 9th	540	5.2
Service	Royal Irish Rifles, 2nd	438	4.2
Service	Royal Dublin Fusiliers, 7th	430	4.2
Reserve	Royal Dublin Fusiliers, 4th	421	4.1
Service	Irish Guards, 1st	414	4.0
Reserve	Royal Dublin Fusiliers, 5th	413	4.0
Service	Royal Dublin Fusiliers, 6th	354	3.4
Service	Royal Dublin Fusiliers, 10th	296	2.9
Service	Royal Irish Rifles, 1st	280	2.7
Reserve	Royal Dublin Fusiliers, 3rd	273	2.6
Service	Leinster Regiment, 2nd	228	2.2
Service	Irish Guards, 2nd	213	2.1
Service	Royal Irish Fusiliers, 1st	195	1.9
Service	Connaught Rangers, 2nd	192	1.9
Service	Connaught Rangers, 1st	190	1.8
Reserve	Royal Irish Rifles, 3rd	183	1.8
Service	Royal Irish Regiment, 2nd	149	1.4
Service	Leinster Regiment, 1st	141	1.4
Service	Royal Irish Rifles, 7th	132	1.3
Service	Connaught Rangers, 5th	116	1.1
Service	Leinster Regiment, 7th	101	1.0
Service	Connaught Rangers, 6th	98	1.0
Service	Royal Irish Fusiliers, 2nd	93	0.9
Reserve	Royal Irish Fusiliers, 4th	86	0.8
Service	Royal Inniskilling Fusiliers, 1st	85	0.8
Service	Royal Irish Fusiliers, 7th	77	0.7
Service	Royal Inniskilling Fusiliers, 9th	74	0.7
Service	Royal Irish Regiment, 6th	73	0.7
Service	Royal Irish Regiment, 1st	70	0.7
Service	Royal Inniskilling Fusiliers, 8th	69	0.7
Service	Royal Irish Fusiliers, 8th	69	0.7
Service	Royal Irish Regiment, 7th	65	0.6
Service	Leinster Regiment, 6th	59	0.6
Reserve	Royal Irish Regiment, 3rd	58	0.6
Service	Royal Munster Fusiliers, 2nd	58	0.6
Service	Royal Irish Fusiliers, 6th	57	0.6

Table A2.4: (cont.)

Type	Battalion	Number	%
Reserve	Leinster Regiment, 5th	56	0.5
Service	Royal Inniskilling Fusiliers, 7th	53	0.5
Service	Royal Munster Fusiliers, 1st	53	0.5
Service	Royal Irish Rifles, 6th	51	0.5
Service	Royal Inniskilling Fusiliers, 2nd	50	0.5
Reserve	Leinster Regiment, 3rd	48	0.5
Service	Royal Irish Fusiliers, 5th	47	0.5
Reserve	Connaught Rangers, 3rd	46	0.4
Service	Royal Dublin Fusiliers, 11th	44	0.4
Service	Royal Munster Fusiliers, 6th	34	0.3
Service	Royal Inniskilling Fusiliers, 6th	32	0.3
Service	Royal Irish Regiment, 5th	32	0.3
Reserve	Royal Irish Rifles, 4th	32	0.3
Reserve	Royal Irish Fusiliers, 3rd	29	0.3
Reserve	Royal Irish Regiment, 4th	27	0.3
Service	Royal Inniskilling Fusiliers, 5th	25	0.2
Reserve	Irish Guards, 3rd	24	0.2
Reserve	Leinster Regiment, 4th	24	0.2
Reserve	Connaught Rangers, 4th	18	0.2
Service	Royal Irish Fusiliers, 9th	16	0.2
Reserve	Royal Irish Rifles, 5th	16	0.2
Service	Royal Inniskilling Fusiliers, 7th/8th	14	0.1
Service	Royal Munster Fusiliers, 7th	14	0.1
Reserve	Royal Inniskilling Fusiliers, 3rd	13	0.1
Service	Royal Irish Fusiliers, 7th/8th	13	0.1
Service	Royal Munster Fusiliers, 9th	13	0.1
Service	Royal Irish Rifles, 12th	11	0.1
Service	Royal Irish Rifles, 15th	11	0.1
Service	Royal Irish Rifles, 11th	10	0.1
Service	Royal Munster Fusiliers, 3rd	10	0.1
Service	Royal Irish Rifles, 8th	9	0.1
Service	Royal Dublin Fusiliers, 8th/9th	8	0.1
Service	Royal Inniskilling Fusiliers, 10th	8	0.1
Reserve	Royal Inniskilling Fusiliers, 4th	8	0.1
Service	Royal Irish Rifles, 10th	8	0.1
Service	Royal Irish Rifles, 14th	8	0.1
Service	Royal Inniskilling Fusiliers, 11th	7	0.1
Service	Royal Munster Fusiliers, 5th	7	0.1
Reserve	Royal Inniskilling Fusiliers, 12th	6	0.1
Service	Royal Irish Rifles, 9th	6	0.1

Table A2.4: (cont.)

Type	Battalion	Number	%
Service	Royal Munster Fusiliers, 8th	6	0.1
Service	Royal Irish Regiment, 1st GB	5	0.0
Service	Royal Irish Regiment, 2nd GB	5	0.0
Service	Royal Munster Fusiliers, 4th	5	0.0
Reserve	Royal Irish Rifles, 17th	4	0.0
Service	Royal Irish Regiment, 8th	3	0.0
Service	Royal Irish Rifles, 13th	3	0.0
Service	Royal Irish Rifles, 16th	3	0.0
Service	Royal Irish Rifles, 1st GB	3	0.0
Service	Royal Munster Fusiliers, 1st GB	3	0.0
Service	Royal Irish Fusiliers, 1st GB	2	0.0
Service	Royal Irish Fusiliers, 2nd GB	2	0.0
Service	Royal Irish Rifles, 8th/9th	2	0.0
Reserve	Royal Inniskilling Fusiliers, 13th	1	0.0
Service	Royal Irish Fusiliers, 10th	1	0.0
	Total	*10,311*	

Source: all sources used (see bibliography).
Note: % does not add to 100.0 due to rounding.

APPENDIX 3: PHYSICAL

Table A3.1: Average Height of British Military Recruits by Unit Type

Unit type	Number	Height
Irish Guards	109	5 ft 8 & 9/10″
Irish Cavalry	162	5 ft 6 & 9/10″
Engineers	405	5 ft 6 & 1/4″
Medical	262	5 ft 6 & 1/5″
Average (all Dubliners)	*7,227*	*5 ft 5 & 4/5″*
Army Service Corps	525	5 ft 5 & 7/10″
Irish Infantry (Guards excluded)	3,474	5 ft 5 & 1/2″
Air	925	5 ft 5 & 2/5″
Artillery	697	5 ft 4 & 1/10″

Source: WO 363 & 364; *Airmen Died.*

Table A3.2: Body Mass Index of British Military Recruits by BMI Category

BMI Category	Number	%
Underweight (less than 18.5)	387	9.7
Normal (18.5 to 24.9)	3,476	87.0
Overweight (25 to 29.9)	124	3.1
Obese (30 to 39.9)	9	0.2
Total	*3,996*	

Source: WO 363 & 364.

Table A3.3: Average Body Mass Index of British Military Recruits by Unit Type

Unit type	Number	BMI
Artillery	473	21.2
Guards	109	21.2
Engineers	142	21.1
Irish Cavalry	93	20.9
Average (all Dubliners)	*3,996*	*20.8*
ASC	227	20.8
Irish Infantry (Guards excluded)	2,389	20.6
Medical	155	20.5

Source: WO 363 & 364.
Note: Airmen are excluded from the BMI tables because weight information exists for only two of the 925 for whom there is a height.

APPENDIX 4: OCCUPATION

Table A4.1: Occupation and Unit Type of British Military Recruits

	Air	% of Air	Army Service Corps	% Army Service Corps	Artillery	% Artillery	Cavalry (Non-Irish)	% Cav (Non-Irish)
Animal-related	20	2.2	84	14.4	78	10.9	18	23.4
Commerce	30	3.3	10	1.7	21	2.9	2	2.6
Communication	51	5.5	11	1.9	29	4.0	1	1.3
Food/drink	20	2.2	58	9.9	19	2.6	2	2.6
Other skill	37	4.0	22	3.8	33	4.6	3	3.9
Skilled – construction	6	0.7	3	0.5	8	1.1		0.0
Skilled – engineering	38	4.1	18	3.1	13	1.8	1	1.3
Skilled – manufacturing	48	5.2	31	5.3	20	2.8	3	3.9
Skilled – trades	81	8.8	14	2.4	47	6.5	4	5.2
Transport	66	7.2	158	27.1	55	7.7	9	11.7
Unskilled	347	37.7	90	15.4	347	48.3	20	26.0
White collar	177	19.2	84	14.4	48	6.7	14	18.2
Total	921		583		718		77	

	Engineers	% Engineers	England (Infantry)	% England (Infantry)	Ireland (Cavalry)	% Ireland (Cavalry)	Ireland (Infantry)	% Ireland (Infantry)
Animal-related	6	0.4	14	4.6	20	12.2	288	6.6
Commerce	12	0.9	4	1.3	10	6.1	116	2.7
Communication	919	67.9	8	2.6	3	1.8	279	6.4
Food/drink	6	0.4	12	3.9	5	3.0	97	2.2
Other skill	8	0.6	24	7.8	6	3.7	214	4.9

							Occupation total	% total
Skilled – construction	15	1.1	7	2.3		0.0	39	0.9
Skilled – engineering	34	2.5	7	2.3	3	1.8	55	1.3
Skilled – manufacturing	10	0.7	14	4.6	6	3.7	134	3.1
Skilled – trades	41	3.0	17	5.6	10	6.1	200	4.6
Transport	82	6.1	20	6.5	16	9.8	209	4.8
Unskilled	164	12.1	147	48.0	37	22.6	2373	54.6
White collar	57	4.2	32	10.5	48	29.3	339	7.8
Total	1354		306		164		4343	

	Medical	% Medical	Other Army	% Other Army	Occupation total	% total
Animal-related	8	2.9	11	7.9	547	6.2
Commerce	26	9.4	12	8.6	243	2.7
Communication	11	4.0	2	1.4	1314	14.8
Food/drink	13	4.7	3	2.2	235	2.6
Other skill	24	8.7	7	5.0	378	4.3
Skilled – construction	4	1.4		0.0	82	0.9
Skilled – engineering	4	1.4	4	2.9	177	2.0
Skilled – manufacturing	8	2.9	2	1.4	276	3.1
Skilled – trades	11	4.0	9	6.5	434	4.9
Transport	14	5.1	6	4.3	635	7.1
Unskilled	82	29.6	24	17.3	3631	40.9
White collar	72	26.0	59	42.4	930	10.5
Total	277		139		8882	

Source: WO 363 & 364.
Note: % will not always add to 100.0 due to rounding.

Table A4.2: Occupation and Royal Dublin Fusiliers Battalions

	No. 1st	% 1st	No. 2nd	% 2nd	No. 6th	% 6th
Animal-related	6	3.9	17	6.7	5	2.6
Commerce	4	2.6	8	3.1	2	1.0
Communication	11	7.2	23	9.1	5	2.6
Food/drink	5	3.3	1	0.4	4	2.1
Other skill	5	3.3	7	2.8	7	3.6
Skilled – construction	1	0.7	1	0.4	1	0.5
Skilled – engineering	3	2.0	3	1.2	0	0.0
Skilled – manufacturing	3	2.0	7	2.8	8	4.1
Skilled – trades	7	4.6	10	3.9	4	2.1
Transport	6	3.9	10	3.9	6	3.1
Unskilled	93	61.2	152	59.8	149	76.4
White collar	8	5.3	15	5.9	4	2.1
Total	*152*		*254*		*195*	

	No. 7th	% 7th	No. 8th	% 8th	No. 9th	% 9th
Animal-related	5	2.3	13	3.9	16	7.2
Commerce	1	0.5	3	0.9	2	0.9
Communication	5	2.3	7	2.1	5	2.2
Food/drink	4	1.9	10	3.0	6	2.7
Other skill	11	5.2	14	4.2	12	5.4
Skilled – construction	3	1.4	6	1.8	5	2.2
Skilled – engineering	5	2.3	6	1.8	2	0.9
Skilled – manufacturing	5	2.3	10	3.0	11	4.9
Skilled – trades	8	3.8	16	4.8	11	4.9
Transport	6	2.8	11	3.3	8	3.6
Unskilled	111	52.1	222	66.9	141	63.2
White collar	49	23.0	14	4.2	4	1.8
Total	*213*		*332*		*223*	

	No. 10th	% 10th	No. occupation	Occupation as % of all work
Animal-related	2	1.7	64	4.3
Commerce	14	12.2	34	2.3
Communication	12	10.4	68	4.6
Food/drink	3	2.6	33	2.2
Other skill	11	9.6	67	4.5
Skilled – construction	1	0.9	18	1.2
Skilled – engineering	0	0.0	19	1.3
Skilled – manufacturing	7	6.1	51	3.4
Skilled – trades	2	1.7	58	3.9

Table A4.2: (cont.)

	No. 10th	% 10th	No. occupation	Occupation as % of all work
Transport	4	3.5	51	3.4
Unskilled	5	4.3	873	58.8
White collar	54	47.0	148	10.0
Total	*115*		*1,484*	

Source: WO 363 & 364.
Note: % will not always add to 100.0 due to rounding.

Table A4.3: Occupation of Irish Volunteers and Irish Citizen Army, 1916

	Ranks no.	Ranks %	Officers no.	Officers %
Animal-related	15	2.5	4	6.1
Commerce	49	8.0	8	12.1
Communication	8	1.3	0	0.0
Food/drink	12	2.0	1	1.5
Other skill	48	7.9	5	7.6
Skilled – construction	8	1.3	2	3.0
Skilled – engineering	20	3.3	1	1.5
Skilled – manufacturing	37	6.1	1	1.5
Skilled – trades	95	15.5	8	12.1
Transport	39	6.4	1	1.5
Unskilled	169	27.7	7	10.6
White collar	111	18.2	28	42.4
Total	*611*		66	

Sources: Sinn Fein Rebellion Handbook; NAI: CSORP/1916/19265 & 1918/16627; 1911 Census.
Note: % will not always add to 100.0 due to rounding.

APPENDIX 5: RECRUITMENT

Table A5.1: Regular British Army Recruitment in Ireland, 1 October 1912 to 30 September 1913

Recruiting Area	Joining territorial regiment of Area	Joining other Infantry	Joining other corps	Total	Area% of all recruits	% of Infantry Recruits joining territorial regiment of Area
27th Regimental Recruiting Area, Omagh	32	5	21	58	2.2	86.5
83rd Regimental Recruiting Area, Belfast	8	16	12	36	1.4	33.3
87th Regimental Recruiting Area, Armagh	94	4	36	134	5.0	95.9
102nd Regimental Recruiting Area, Naas	46	21	86	153	5.8	68.7
Dublin Recruiting Area	163	323	346	832	31.3	33.5
Belfast Recruiting Area	40	141	199	380	14.3	22.1
18th Regimental Recruiting Area, Clonmel	117	31	109	257	9.7	79.1
88th Regimental Recruiting Area, Galway	72	16	27	115	4.3	81.8
100th Regimental Recruiting Area, Birr	72	22	92	186	7.0	76.6
101st Regimental Recruiting Area, Tralee	86	24	43	153	5.8	78.2
Cork Recruiting Area	110	94	147	351	13.2	53.9
Total	840	697	1,118	2,655		54.7

Source: The Army Council, Cd. 7252, The General Annual Report on the British Army for the Year Ending 30b September 1913 (London: HMSO, 1914), 47.

Table A5.2: British Army Recruitment by Irish Recruiting Area, 4 August 1914 to 9 November 1918

Area	1914 (from 4 Aug)	1915	1916	1917	1918 (to 9 Nov)	Total
Omagh	3,643	3,016	1,148	892	811	9,510
Belfast	20,900	13,734	5,307	4,452	3,635	48,028
Armagh	1,740	2,270	850	486	438	5,784
Naas	1,681	1,570	624	476	71	4,422
Dublin	7,283	9,612	4,292	3,089	2,262	26,538
Birr	1,318	3,022	851	476	422	6,089
Clonmel	2,285	4,761	1,487	1,035	933	10,501
Galway	1,472	2,203	1,136	623	382	5,816
Tralee	1,288	2,506	1,156	795	594	6,339
Cork	2,524	3,677	2,206	1,699	974	11,080
Total	*44,134*	*46,371*	*19,057*	*14,023*	*10,522*	*134,107*

Source: TNA, NATS 1/398, Statistical tables showing numbers of recruits raised daily.

Table A5.3: National and Ulster Volunteers Recruited to British Military in Dublin, 4 August 1914 to 15 January 1918

Month	National Volunteers	Ulster Volunteers	Volunteer status now known	Total
4.8.1914–15.12.1914	2,522		3,983	6,505
16.12.1914–15.1.1915	31		735	766
16.1.1915–15.2.1915	46		505	551
16.2.1915–15.3.1915	29		556	585
16.3.1915–15.4.1915	58		966	1,024
16.4.1915–15.5.1915	50		814	864
16.5.1915–15.6.1915	46		831	877
16.6.1915–15.7.1915	37		654	691
16.7.1915–15.8.1915	31	1	926	958
16.8.1915–15.9.1915	19	6	801	826
16.9.1915–15.10.1915	23		481	504
16.10.1915–15.11.1915	25	3	929	957
16.11.1915–15.12.1915	18		658	676
16.12.1915–15.1.1916	15	5	485	505
16.1.1916–15.2.1916	16		358	374

Table A5.3: (cont.)

Month	National Volunteers	Ulster Volunteers	Volunteer status now known	Total
16.2.1916–15.3.1916	7		444	451
16.3.1916–15.4.1916	13		409	422
16.4.1916–15.5.1916	10		187	197
16.5.1916–15.6.1916	9		490	499
16.6.1916–15.7.1916	4		361	365
16.7.1916–15.8.1916			360	360
16.8.1916–15.9.1916			341	341
16.9.1916–15.10.1916	3		316	319
16.10.1916–15.11.1916			308	308
16.11.1916–15.12.1916			223	223
16.12.1916–15.1.1917			178	178
16.1.1917–15.2.1917			236	236
16.2.1917–15.3.1917		1	221	222
16.3.1917–15.4.1917			194	194
16.4.1917–15.5.1917			337	337
16.5.1917–15.6.1917			388	388
16.6.1917–15.7.1917			356	356
16.7.1917–15.8.1917			276	276
16.8.1917–15.9.1917			359	359
16.9.1917–15.10.1917			236	236
16.10.1917–15.11.1917			206	206
16.11.1917–15.12.1917			150	150
16.12.1917–15.1.1918			152	152
Total	3,012	16	20,410	23,438

Source: NLI, Redmond MS 15,258.

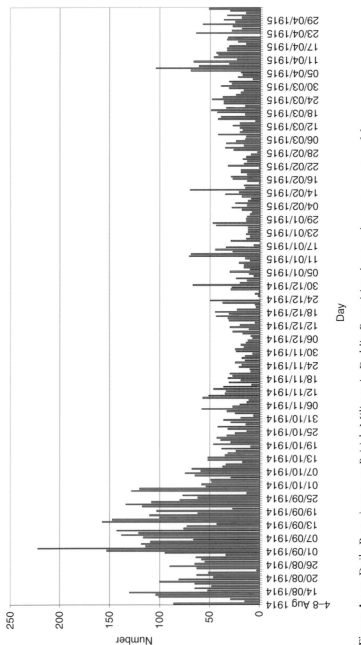

Figure A5.1: Daily Recruitment to British Military in Dublin Recruiting Area, 4 August 1915 to 4 May 1915. *Source:* TNA, NATS 1/398, Statistical tables showing numbers of recruits raised daily.

Table A5.4: Recruitment to Royal Dublin Fusiliers by Military Command, 24 January to 23 October 1915

Command	No.	%
Dublin	1,970	43.7
Other Irish	1,104	24.5
Scottish	640	14.2
Western	367	8.1
London	223	4.9
Northern	107	2.4
Southern	55	1.2
Eastern	42	0.9
Total	4,508	

Source: TNA, NATS 1/401: Consolidated Summary Tables.
Note: % does not add to 100.0 due to rounding.

Table A5.5: Recruitment of Dubliners to British Military by Place of Enlistment

Area	Number	%
Dublin (City and County)	5,911	86.9
England	371	5.5
Leinster (Other)	255	3.8
Scotland	78	1.1
Munster	67	1.0
Ulster	57	0.8
Wales	37	0.5
Connaught	17	0.3
Overseas	4	0.1
Isle of Man	1	0.0
Jersey	1	0.0
Total	6,799	

Source: WO 363 & 364.

Table A5.6: Recruitment of Dubliners to British Military by Denomination

Denomination	Number	%
Anglican	540	9.6
Baptist	5	0.1
Jewish	3	0.1
Methodist	24	0.4
Other Protestant	14	0.2
Presbyterian	48	0.9
Roman Catholic	4,981	88.7
Total	*5,615*	

Source: WO 363 and 364.

Table A5.7: Recruitment outside Dublin of non-Dublin residents to Royal Dublin Fusiliers

			Place of enlistment									
		England	%	Ireland*	%	Scotland	%	Wales	%	Other	%	Total	%
	Dublin	13	7.9	16	11.7	6	7.2		0.0		0.0	35	8.2
	England	107	64.8	3	2.2	1	1.2	5	11.6		0.0	116	27.1
Place of	Ireland*	32	19.4	114	84.7	32	38.6	15	34.9	1	50.0	194	45.3
birth	Scotland	9	5.5	1	0.7	43	51.8		0.0		0.0	53	12.4
	Wales	3	1.8		0.0		0.0	23	53.5	1	50.0	27	6.3
	Other	1	0.6	1	0.7	1	1.2		0.0		0.0	3	0.7
	Total	165		135		83		43		2		428	

Source: WO 363 and 364.

* Except Dublin.

Note: Only includes recruitment where RDF is first unit of service, and where both place of recruitment and place of birth are known.

Table A5.8: Home of British Military Recruits in County Dublin

Area	Number	%
Dublin City*	12,785	70.6
Pembroke	2,278	12.6
Kingstown	1,265	7.0
Blackrock	425	2.3
Shankill	245	1.4
Skerries	219	1.2
Swords	173	1.0
Rathfarnham	149	0.8
Clondalkin	128	0.7
Dundrum	122	0.7
Howth	88	0.5
Blanchardstown	81	0.4
Lucan	79	0.4
Tallaght	43	0.3
Total	*18,080*	

Source: all records used where there is information beyond a statement that someone is from 'Dublin'. The vast majority of records not used are newspaper casualty lists which simply state 'Dublin' whether for the city or county. See Map 2.1 for details of areas covered.

Note: % does not add to 100.0 due to rounding.

* Of this total, Inchicore contributed 477 (2.6%), Clontarf 473 (2.6%) and Glasnevin 363 (2.0%).

Table A5.9: Membership of Republican Units During Easter Rising by Residence in Irish Volunteer Area

	1st IV no.	%	2nd IV no.	%	3rd IV no.	%	4th IV no.	%	5th IV no.	%	GPO Garrison no.	%	Irish Citizen Army no.	%
1st Area	78	57.8	20	24.4	6	5.9		0.0	5	13.5	42	20.3	22	32.4
2nd Area	22	16.3	42	51.2	5	4.9	6	6.0	1	2.7	83	40.1	24	35.3
3rd Area	27	20.0	17	20.7	72	70.6	66	66.0	1	2.7	32	15.5	22	32.4
4th Area	8	5.9	3	3.7	19	18.6	28	28.0	2	5.4	43	20.8	0	0.0
5th Area		0.0		0.0		0.0		0.0	28	75.7	7	3.4	0	0.0
Total	135		82		102		100		37		207		68	

Source: all sources used for Republicans.

Note: Shows 731 members of Republican units during the Easter Rising, where both unit and precise place of residence are known, with residence divided into Irish Volunteer recruiting area. Unit's own area is highlighted in grey in each column. % will not always add to 100.0 due to rounding.

APPENDIX 6: RED CROSS SERVICE

(Source: British Red Cross Society, spreadsheet provided by
Dr Susan Hawkins, Kingston University)

3,979 Red Cross volunteers were identified with Dublin
addresses. The gender for 20 was not apparent, 3,459 women (2,188
not married, 1,159 married or widowed, 112 marital status not
apparent) and 500 men. Data on the year of joining is present for 366
men and 2,190 women, which shows 1917 to be the peak year.
Unfortunately data on the month of joining is only present for 306
men and 1684 women, with the peak year of 1,917 missing 211 of
637, and 1914's month missing for 111 of 367 (much higher proportions than are absent for 1915, 1916 and 1918). Even with that caveat,
these monthly figures show relatively even recruitment across the war
with peaks in August to October 1914, November 1915 to January
1916, and November 1917. Data on occupations is present for 2,962
women and 426 men.

Table A6.1: British Red Cross Society Occupations for Dublin Residents (% is per cent of each occupation by gender)

Occupation	Women no.	Women%	Men no.	Men%
Administration & Fundraising	144	73.1	53	26.9
Driving	12	46.2	14	53.8
Entertainment	5	83.3	1	16.7
Hospital Searcher	2	5.4	35	94.6
Irish War Hospital Supply Depot	955	98.9	11	1.1
Sphagnum Moss Association	144	98.0	3	2.0
Voluntary Aid Detachment	997	76.6	304	23.4
Work Party	703	99.3	5	0.7
Total	2,962		426	

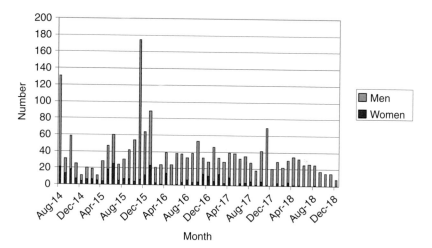

Figure A6.1: British Red Cross Society recruitment (Dublin residents) by month

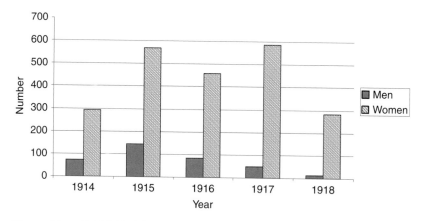

Figure A6.2: British Red Cross Society recruitment (Dublin residents) by year

Table A6.2: British Red Cross Society Occupations for Dublin Women

Type of work	Women	%
Voluntary Aid Detachment	997	33.7
Irish War Hospital Supply Depot	955	32.2
Work Party	703	23.7
Administration & Fundraising	144	4.9
Sphagnum Moss Association	144	4.9
Driving	12	0.4
Entertainment	5	0.2
Hospital Searcher	2	0.1
Total	2,962	

Table A6.3: British Red Cross Society Occupations for Dublin men

Type of work	Men	%
Voluntary Aid Detachment	304	71.4
Administration & Fundraising	53	12.4
Hospital Searcher	35	8.2
Driving	14	3.3
Irish War Hospital Supply Depot	11	2.6
Work Party	5	1.2
Sphagnum Moss Association	3	0.7
Entertainment	1	0.2
Total	426	

APPENDIX 7: DEATH

Table A7.1: War Deaths of Dubliners in British Military by Month, 1914–18

Month	Number
1914/08	41
1914/09	79
1914/10	138
1914/11	173
1914/12	38
1915/01	44
1915/02	52
1915/03	108
1915/04	235
1915/05	387
1915/06	118
1915/07	57
1915/08	264
1915/09	84
1915/10	60
1915/11	37
1915/12	63
1916/01	48
1916/02	35
1916/03	52
1916/04	249
1916/05	121

Table A7.1: (cont.)

Month	Number
1916/06	94
1916/07	286
1916/08	115
1916/09	332
1916/10	162
1916/11	110
1916/12	43
1917/01	44
1917/02	93
1917/03	90
1917/04	163
1917/05	108
1917/06	119
1917/07	94
1917/08	243
1917/09	79
1917/10	115
1917/11	135
1917/12	122
1918/01	35
1918/02	37
1918/03	250
1918/04	117
1918/05	89
1918/06	48
1918/07	40
1918/08	101
1918/09	182
1918/10	260
1918/11	107
1918/12	38

Source: all sources used.

Table A7.2: War Deaths of Dubliners in British Military by Theatre and Year, 1914–21

	France & Flanders	Home	Gallipoli	At sea	Salonika	Egypt & Palestine	Mesopotamia	Other*	Asia (South and East)**	Germany	Africa	Italy	Russia	Total
1914	414	15		32					2	2	4			469
1915	818	81	476	59	37	15	1	10	6	5	3			1,511
1916	1,310	112	2	75	71	10	55	6	5	2	7			1,656
1917	1,063	85		135	37	46	18	7	3	6	6	3		1,409
1918	893	216		82	22	42	9	10	12	9	9	10		1,314
1919	19	68		6		5	5	2	5	6	5	1	3	125
1920		40	2	1		2	5	5	4	1			1	61
1921		15					2	3	3		1			24
Total	4,517	632	480	390	167	120	95	43	40	31	35	14	4	6,568

Source: all sources used.
* Aden, Bermuda, Canada, Cyprus, Gibraltar, Malta, Netherlands, New Zealand, Persia, Persian Gulf, Syria
** India, Burma and Singapore

APPENDIX 8: SOURCES

Table A8.1: Location of Individual Dubliners in British Military by Source

Type of source	Number	%
From more than one source		
Duplicates	6,980	26.3
Possible duplicates	1,541	5.8
Found in only one source		
Newspapers	6,019	22.7
Service records	3,456	13.1
Pensions records	2,350	8.9
Irishwarmemorials.ie	1,647	6.2
AIR 79	910	3.4
CWGC	904	3.4
Books & book rolls	801	3.0
NAM post-war attestation	408	1.5
Soldiers Died	328	1.2
Wills	320	1.2
Presbyterian roll	258	1.0
Christmas 1914 PoW list	220	0.8
Skerries roll	86	0.3
Material from James W. Taylor	80	0.3
Sailors Died	74	0.3
Royal Naval Division service	43	0.2
Merchant Seamen PoW lists	29	0.1
Airmen Died	8	0.0
Auxiliary records	8	0.0
Gillies records	8	0.0
Other	6	0.0
PoW Interviews	5	0.0
Total	26,489	

Note: % does not add to 100.0 due to rounding. 6,980 is the number of individuals covered by more than one record. They appear at least once, but some several times, in the 12,225 duplicate records identified (see p.38).

ACKNOWLEDGEMENTS

I must begin with thanks for Tony Morris, who commissioned *Belfast Boys*, and, after it was published, first planted the idea that Dublin was the logical next step for my work. Nearly a decade on, here we are. That is partly due to support from the British Academy who generously provided a Small Research Grant to support my travels. The scheme is an excellent one and it is a shame that the Research Councils focus so much on large grants and do not behave more like the British Academy which makes a lot possible through targeted use of money aimed at the real additional costs of research. I am grateful too, to the Isobel Thornley Fund for University of London History graduates and staff, which provided a grant to fund the permission and reproduction costs of photographs.

At Cambridge University Press, I am grateful to Michael Watson for commissioning the book, and to Lisa Carter and Julie Hrischeva for guiding it through the production process. Gill Cloke must be thanked for carrying out the copy-editing with great diligence and insight, making significant improvements to the text. I am grateful to CUP's cartographer, David Cox, for his map-drawing and to Henry Maas for his proof-reading. Thanks are also due the publisher's reviewers of the proposal for this book and the manuscript, who made extremely helpful suggestions. Permission to cite archival material held by them is courtesy of the: Council of the National Army Museum; Dublin City Library and Archive, Royal Dublin Fusiliers Association Archive; Irish Jesuit Archives, Dublin; Military Archives, Dublin; National Archives of Ireland; National Library of Ireland; Archives of the Royal College of Surgeons of England; and University College, Dublin Archives. For permission to cite material held at the Imperial War Museum Archive I am grateful to: Julian Colyer (Wilfrid Colyer Papers); R. P. Glanville (Arthur Glanville Papers); and Anthony Beater (Orlando Beater Papers). Crown copyright material at the National Archives, Kew, is quoted within the terms of the Open Government Licence. Permission to reproduce photographs is stated alongside the relevant item. Thanks are also due to Glenn Dunne, Justin Furlong, Berni Metcalfe and Chris Swift at the National Library of Ireland for their friendly and efficient help with photographs. I am also grateful to Terri Dendy at the National Army Museum, Emma Harrold at the Imperial War Museum and Louise King at the Archives of the Royal College of Surgeons of England, for their assistance with photographs.

Thanks go to four researchers who have generously shared their information with me. James W. Taylor has provided a vast amount of material from his personal database on the Royal Irish Rifles. Dr Steven O'Connor generously shared material on British soldiers who were later connected with the IRA, and Neil Richardson did the same with regard to British participants in the events of Easter Rising. Michael Nugent drew my attention to the case of George Geoghegan and sent me all his material. Thank you all for your generosity of spirit.

Special thanks go to Dr Susan Hawkins of Kingston University for providing me with a download of data from the British Red Cross Society database. This saved me weeks of work in transcribing text from the online version, and I am very grateful for the time she spent on this. Other acts of kindness in providing material have also saved me much time and thanks are due to: Kate Swann, Alastair Massie and Kevin Blaney (National Army Museum); Ellen Murphy (Dublin City Library); Dr Lar Joye and Brenda Malone (National Museum of Ireland); Colm McQuinn (Fingal County Council); and Lisa Dolan and Commandant Stephen MacEoin (Military Archives, Dublin).

I would like to highlight the support of Dr Tim Bowman. He read draft material and was consistently generous in providing valuable advice. William Spencer at The National Archives, Kew, has been a constant source of expert advice and good conversation on First World War records. Ellie Grigsby performed a valuable role towards the end of the project in working as a volunteer Research Assistant on information related to Republican prisoners. Her support was crucial in getting the most out of that material in a timely fashion. I am grateful to Prof. Jane Powell, Dr Vivienne Richmond and Dr John Price for being supportive line managers over the past decade. As Warden of Goldsmiths, Pat Loughrey has been an enthusiastic supporter of this work, and history at Goldsmiths more widely, which has been much appreciated.

I am grateful to many other people for advice, support and conversation on Dublin in 1912–23 and the First World War more widely, in particular: Prof. Joanna Bourke, Tom Burke, Dr Marie Coleman, Siobhán Brennan Deane, Prof. Dejan Djokić, Harry Donaghy, Prof. David Fitzpatrick, Dr Brian Hanley, Prof. John Horne, Cllr Tom Hartley, the late, and much-missed, Prof. Keith Jeffery, Dr Heather Jones, Dr Rosie Kennedy, Dr Edward Madigan, Dr Emily Mayhew, Dr Fearghal McGarry, Dr Eve Morrison, Paul Nixon, Dr Daithí Ó Corráin, Seán O'Hare, Cormac O'Malley, Karen O'Rawe, Philip Orr, Dr Catriona Pennell, Prof. Jan Plamper, Dr Stephen Sandford, Prof. Gary Sheffield, Derek Smyth, Dr Paul Taylor, Dr Tom Thorpe, Dr Dan Todman, Dr Maurice Walsh, Prof. Alex Watson, Pádraig Yeates and the students of my third-year special subject at Goldsmiths, 'Life in the Trenches'. Thanks to my co-convenors of the 'War, Society and Culture' seminar at the Institute of Historical Research for providing an intellectual home for my work: Dr Tim Bowman, Dr Ambrogio Caiani, Prof. Mark Connelly, Dr Stefan Goebel, Dr Heather Jones and Dr Erica Wald. Sean Boyne and Conor Graham helped me to contact Emmet Dalton's daughter, Audrey Dalton Simenz, to whom I am grateful for permission to use a photo of her father. I am grateful to Coílín Nunan, great-nephew of Seán and Ernie Nunan and also a friend from my postgraduate days at The Queen's College, Oxford, for his help on the Nunan family story.

On a personal level, my Mum, Jannat, must be thanked for all her support over the years this work has been carried out, especially with childcare when I was travelling. My son, Edward, has steadily taken more interest in history as he has progressed through school and GCSEs, and accompanied me on my very last visit to an archive for this book, prior to a home defeat in the rain at Loftus Road. Finally, my wife, Lucy, made this book a much better one than it would have been through incisive comments on a draft. I am very much in her debt for this and for her love and support in all things.

NOTES

Introduction

1. Pádraig Yeates, *Lockout: Dublin 1913* (Dublin: Gill and Macmillan, 2001); *A City in Wartime: Dublin 1914–18* (Dublin: Gill and Macmillan, 2011); *A City in Turmoil, Dublin 1919–1921* (Dublin: Gill and Macmillan, 2012); *A City in Civil War, Dublin 1921–1924* (Dublin: Gill and Macmillan, 2015); and two chapters of David Dickson, *Dublin: The Making of a Capital City* (London: Profile, 2014), 425–501.

2. Fearghal McGarry, *The Rising, Ireland: Easter 1916* (Oxford University Press, 2010), 79 et seq. See also Diarmaid Ferriter, *A Nation and Not a Rabble: The Irish Revolution, 1913–1923* (London: Profile, 2015), 137–49; Michael Foy and Brian Barton, *The Easter Rising* (Stroud: Sutton, 1999), 15–36; Charles Townshend, *Easter 1916: The Irish Rebellion* (London: Allen Lane, 2005), 90–121.

3. Henry Hanna, *The Pals at Suvla Bay: Being the Record of "D" Company of the 7th Royal Dublin Fusiliers* (Dublin: Ponsonby, 1917); Arminta Wallace, 'The Dublin Pals Who Set off for Gallipoli's Killing Fields', *Irish Times* [IT], 9 February 2015, 13; Ronan McGreevy, '"It Was Magnificent ... We Called the Hill Fort Dublin"', and *IT*, 6 August 2015, 7; Tom Burke, 'All of Dublin Felt the Horror of a Single Brutal Weekend in Gallipoli', *IT Weekend Review*, 15 August 2015, 2.

4. See for example, the work of the Royal Dublin Fusiliers Association in covering all of the regiment's battalions: www.greatwar.ie (accessed 23 October 2017); and work ranging from Myles Dungan, *Irish Voices from the Great War* (Dublin: Irish Academic Press, 1995) to Philip Lecane, *Beneath a Turkish Sky: The Royal Dublin Fusiliers and the Assault on Gallipoli* (Dublin: History Press Ireland, 2015).

5. An exception is Keith Jeffery, *1916: A Global History* (London: Bloomsbury, 2015).

6. Keith Jeffery, *Ireland and the Great War* (Cambridge University Press, 2000), 2.

7. On the latter point, see Keith Jeffery, 'Commemoration and the Hazards of Irish Politics', in Bart Ziino, ed., *Remembering the First World War* (London: Routledge, 2014), 165–85, at 165–6.

8. Not least those listed in this chapter's first footnote.

9. See p. 163.

10. For example, *Soldiers Died* (www.ancestry.co.uk, and as a CD-ROM from Naval and Military Press) lists place of birth for the dead. However, if the place of

residence in that source is not also said to be Dublin, or another source has not verified their Dublin connection in 1914–18, they have not been included. Similar issues face the use of National Book of Honour Committee, *Dublin City and County Book of Honour* (Dublin: Book of Honour Committee, 2004). The book contains approximately 6,345 names of the dead. However, they have included people on the basis of being born in Dublin, even if living elsewhere, and did not have access to other sources which have become available since then. An estimate based on a sample of surnames beginning with A suggests that around 1,420 are included on the basis of being born in Dublin, even if they have an address elsewhere, and those were not included in this author's database. None of those otherwise in the book appear to have been missed by the author so if those born in the city were added, another 1,400 dead might be added to the author's total, while there are around 1,800 dead found in the author's database but not in the Book of Honour.

11. See p. 40.
12. Richard S. Grayson, *Belfast Boys: How Unionists and Nationalists Fought and Died Together in the First World War* (London: Bloomsbury, 2009, 2010 edition), 189–201; Richard S. Grayson, 'Military History from the Street: New Methods for Researching First World War Service in the British Military', *War in History*, 21, 4 (2014), 465–95.
13. The newspapers used to compile listings were, for each day they were published from 4 August 1914 to 31 May 1919: *Dublin Evening Mail* [DEM], *Evening Herald* [EH], *Evening Telegraph* [ET], *Freeman's Journal* [FJ], *Irish Independent* [II], *Irish Times* [IT], *Irish Volunteer* [IV], *The National Volunteer* [NV], *Saturday Herald* [SH], *Sunday Independent* [SI], and *Weekly Irish Times*[WIT]. As with the Belfast research, there was considerable duplication between newspapers, especially as the research progressed. Because of that, the final newspaper to be consulted, the *Dublin Daily Express*, was only sampled. In a sample of eight months (10 August to 16 December 1914, May 1915, 15 September to 14 October 1916, September 1917 and April 1918) not a single new piece of information was found, and so it was not used beyond that. It was essentially a London newspaper printed in Dublin with some local news and adverts, but it was not 'local' in the sense that the other papers were and did not pay any specific attention to Dubliners' role in the war beyond that also reported in other newspapers.
14. The National Archives, Kew [TNA], TNA, WO 329, also available on DVD-ROM from the Naval and Military Press.
15. For example, David Fitzpatrick, 'West Belfast Exceptionalism: Richard S. Grayson's *Belfast Boys*', *Irish Social and Economic History*, 38 (2011), 103–7, at 107, was critical of the apparent underuse of census data. It was also suggested by a reader of this book manuscript that the source might yield much data on the occupations of republicans, in addition to the *Sinn Fein Rebellion Handbook*. In fact, data from the National Archives of Ireland (CSORP/1916/19265 and 1918/16627) had already been used to supplement that, but a search was made of the 1911 Census. There were 260 individuals for whom no occupation had been found and for whom it was possible to search due to having a full address. Many could not be found because they were not at the same address in 1911 while there were too many people of the same name to make some matches reliable, and I make no apology for adopting high standards of accuracy in this process. Others did not show up at all, and some were children in 1911 without an occupation listed. Occupations were identified for 56. However, these occupations are only of use for comparison to previous work or work here on the British

army, if a rank for that republican can also be found through other records, and that was only the case for 38 of the ranks and 1 officer. In contrast, the CSORP data provided such information on 39 ranks and 10 officers, with the *Handbook* 534 and 55. Of course, many of these could also be found in the Census, but there is a danger of significantly overstating the value which it can have as a supplement to other sources. The limitations of using it for the British military are discussed in Grayson, 'Military History', 477–8, and for those reasons it was not used for that category other than for individual cases. There is also a danger that if one could find a large number of British soldiers' pre-enlistment occupations from 1911, this would distort the statistics in favour of social groups which were less likely to move. It is best then, to base soldiers' occupations on the 1914–18 figures found in their enlistment records which are a more comprehensive sample.

16. Key sources used were: Military Archives [MA], Military Service Pensions Collection [MSPC] (which includes four distinct categories: Pensions and Award Files; Organisations and Membership Files; Administration Files; and Medals) and Bureau of Military History Witness Statements; National Archives of Ireland, CSORP/1916/15564: Prisoners, 1926s: Courts Martial, and 1918/16627: Internees; *The Irish Times, Sinn Fein Rebellion Handbook* (Dublin: *The Irish Times*, 1917). For guidance on these see Marie Coleman, 'Military Service Pensions for Veterans of the Irish Revolution, 1916–1923', *War in History*, 20, 2 (2013), 201–21; Marie Coleman, 'Military Service Pensions for Civil and Public Servants in Independent Ireland', *Administration*, 60, 2 (2012), 51–61; Eve Morrison, 'The Bureau of Military History', and Marie Coleman, 'The Military Service Pensions Collection', both in John Crowley, Donal Ó Drisceoil and Mike Murphy, eds., *Atlas of the Irish Revolution* (Cork University Press, 2017), 876–80 and 881–5.

17. Listings and photos are at: www.irishwarmemorials.ie/Places (accessed 23 November 2017). Plenty of Trinity College, Dublin names feature in his text, but not all the names from the TCD memorial were included because those would obviously be from across Ireland and beyond.

18. The wider range of sources meant that there was more duplication of individuals than in the Belfast research. For Belfast, 81% of individuals were only found in one source, compared to around 70% for Dublin. See Grayson, *Belfast*, 194.

19. See for example, Gary Sheffield, *Forgotten Victory: The First World War – Myths and Realities* (London: Headline, 2001); William Philpott, *Bloody Victory: The Sacrifice on the Somme and the Making of the Twentieth Century* (London: Little, Brown, 2009). For a review of revisionism, see Peter Simkins, *From the Somme to Victory: The British Army's Experience on the Western Front, 1916–1918* (Barnsley: Pen and Sword, 2014), 38–58.

20. Ian Beckett, Timothy Bowman and Mark Connelly, *The British Army and the First World War* (Cambridge University Press, 2017), 4.

21. Aimée Fox, *Learning to Fight: Military Innovation and Change in the British Army, 1914–18* (Cambridge University Press, 2018).

22. See pp. 342–3.

23. Richard S. Grayson, 'A Life in the Trenches? Operation War Diary and Crowdsourcing Methods for Understanding Day-to-day Life in the British Army on the Western Front in the First World War', *British Journal for Military History*, 2, 2 (2015), 160–85.

24. Marvin Swartz, *The Union of Democratic Control in British Politics During the First World War* (Oxford: Clarendon Press, 1971).

1 Prelude: Dublin and Conflict, 1899–1914

1. MA, Dublin: Bureau of Military History [BMH], BMH.WS0391, 3: Molony, H.
2. BMH.WS0564, 1–5: Byrne, T. F.
3. BMH.WS0564, 5: Byrne, T. F.
4. Anthony J. Jordan, ed., *Boer War to Easter Rising: The Writings of John MacBride* (Westport: Westport Books 2006), 16–18.
5. BMH.WS0564, 5: Byrne, T. F.; Jordan, *Boer War*, 18–19; C. F. Romer and A. E. Mainwaring, *The Second Battalion Royal Dublin Fusiliers in the South African War* (London: A. L. Humphreys, 1908), 3–15. Byrne's account can be read as suggesting that the fight happened a few days earlier, but MacBride is clear that the first engagement for the Brigade was just outside Dundee on 20 October, while the same applies for the official history of the 2nd Dublins. See also Donal McCracken, *MacBride's Brigade: Irish Commandos in the Anglo–Boer War* (Dublin: Four Courts Press, 1999), 43–4.
6. Jordan, *Boer War*, 20–66.
7. BMH.WS0564, 6–13: Byrne, T. F.; Jordan, *Boer War*, 67–85.
8. H. C. Wylly, *Neill's Blue Caps*, vol. II, *1826–1914* (Aldershot: Gale and Polden, 1923), 168.
9. TNA, WO 363; Wylly, *Neill's*, II, 160–198; civilrecords.irishgenealogy.ie/churchre cords/images/birth_returns/births_1877/02999/2099411.pdf; civilrecords.irishgeneal ogy.ie/churchrecords/images/marriage_returns/marriages_1906/10136/5687890.pdf; and www.census.nationalarchives.ie/reels/naio00172918/ (all accessed 10 March 2017).
10. See p. 156.
11. Dickson, *Dublin*, 442.
12. Certainly sixty-six of those identified for this study who were killed had Boer War service. A further forty who survived were found, but due to the loss of war records in 1940 (see p. 38), and the possible non-linkage of WWI records with 1899–1902 records, this is likely to be the tip of an iceberg.
13. Richard Doherty and David Truesdale, *Irish Winners of the Victoria Cross* (Dublin: Four Courts Press, 2000), 99–100 and 198.
14. William Butler, *The Irish Amateur Military Tradition in the British Army, 1854–1992* (Manchester: Manchester University Press, 2016), 61–2 and 84–7.
15. Butler, *Irish Amateur*, 29 and 95–6.
16. Army Council, Cd. 7252, *The General Annual Report on the British Army for the Year Ending 30th September 1913* (London: HMSO, 1914), 47. I am grateful to Dr Tim Bowman for this reference. See also Table A5.1.
17. The Black Watch's Irish section included 144 Irish-born men in the pre-war years, of whom 61 would see First World War service: Ian Montgomery, 'Thoroughbred Irishmen: Black Watch Volunteers in Dublin Before the First World War', *The Irish Sword*, XXIX, 115 (Summer 2013), 41–61.
18. Dickson, *Dublin*, 379–80, 388, 385–6 and 404–7. See also P. J. Mathews, *Revival: The Abbey Theatre, Sinn Féin, the Gaelic League and the Co-operative Movement* (Notre Dame: University of Notre Dame Press, 2003); Yvonne Whelan, *Reinventing Modern Dublin: Streetscape, Iconography and the Politics of Identity* (Dublin: University College Dublin Press, 2003), 94–111. For use of 'O'Connell Street' See for example, *EH*, 1 April 1912, 1.
19. Dickson, *Dublin*, 391–401. See also Yeates, *Wartime*, 11–13.
20. The 'County' included rural areas plus eight 'Civic Areas' with a population of more than 2,000: Blackrock, Dalkey, Killiney and Ballybrack, Kingstown, Pembroke,

Rathmines and Rathgar, Balbriggan, and Terenure. See: Cd. 6049–I, *Census of Ireland, 1911. County of Dublin* (London: HMSO, 1912), vi.

21. Table A1.1.

22. Dickson, *Dublin*, 418; Yeates, *Wartime*, 8–11; Mary E. Daley, *Dublin: The Deposed Capital, A Social and Economic History 1860–1914* (Cork University Press, 1984), 314–15.

23. Senia Pašeta, 'Nationalist Responses to Two Royal Visits to Ireland, 1900 and 1903', *Irish Historical Studies*, xxxi, 124 (1999), 488–504. I am grateful to Dr Heather Jones for this reference.

24. *DEM*, 8 July 1911, 2; 12 July 1911, 5; *SH*, 8 July 1911, 1.

25. *DEM*, 11 July 1911, 5. See also *SH*, 11 July 1911, 1.

26. *FJ*, 10 July 1911, 6.

27. *ET*, 8 July 1911, 4. There was also some controversy over whether the Lord Mayor of Dublin should attend events, which he ended up doing only in part. See also *ET*, 4 July 1911, 3; 5 July 1911, 3.

28. BMH.WS0391, 1–2: Molony, H.

29. Senia Pašeta *Irish Nationalist Women, 1900–1918* (Cambridge University Press, 2013), 39–41.

30. BMH.WS0391, 3: Molony, H.

31. BMH.WS0482, 1–2: McNamara, R.; BMH.WS0391, 15–16: Molony, H.

32. *IT*, 17 February 1912, 15.

33. *EH*, 1 April 1912, 1; *ET*, 1 April 1912, 4; *FJ*, 1 April 1912, 6–10; *DEM*, 2 April 1912, 3; *II*, 1 April 1912, 4 and 7.

34. Fergus A. D'Arcy, 'Connolly, James' and Emmet O'Connor, 'Larkin, James', in James McGuire and James Quinn, eds., *Dictionary of Irish Biography* (Cambridge University Press, 2009), http://dib.cambridge.org/viewReadPage.do?articleId=a1953 and http://dib.cambridge.org/viewReadPage.do?articleId=a4685

35. Dickson, *Dublin*, 429–34; BMH.WS0391, 17: Molony, H. See also Yeates, *Lockout*.

36. See for example, James Plunkett, *Strumpet City* (London: Hutchinson, 1969; Dublin: Gill and Macmillan, 2013 edn), 547–8.

37. Grayson, *Belfast*, 3–4. See also Timothy Bowman, *Carson's Army: The Ulster Volunteer Force, 1910–22* (Manchester University Press, 2007).

38. *News Letter*, 11 April 2012, 20.

39. *ET*, 26 November 1916, 5.

40. BMH.WS: Byrne, T. F., 14; *IT*, 28 March 2016, 4.

41. Declan Brady, *Culture, Politics and Local Government in Fingal, 1891–1914* (Dublin: Four Courts Press, 2017), 40–1.

42. BMH.WS0376, 1: O'Kelly. See also Cathal Billings, 'Speaking Irish with Hurley Sticks: Gaelic Sports, the Irish Language and National Identity in Revival Ireland', *Sport in History*, 37, 1 (2017), 25–50.

43. BMH.WS04332: Donnelly, S. For the pre-war operation of the IRB in Dublin see David Fitzpatrick, *Harry Boland's Irish Revolution* (Cork University Press, 2003), 32–7.

44. J. B. Lyons, *The Enigma of Tom Kettle* (Dublin: Glendale Press, 1983), 238.

45. *FJ*, 26-11-113, 9; *II*, 26 November 1913, 5; *IT*, 26 November 1913, 7.

46. See for example, BMH.WS0282, 2: O'Grady, C. J.; BMH.WS0170, 2: Galligan, P. P.; see for example, *IV*, 7 February 1914, 9 and 18 April 1914, 8.

47. Cal McCarthy, *Cumann na mBan and the Irish Revolution* (Cork: Collins Press, 2007), 15–22; Pašeta, *Irish*, 131–8; *IV*, 9 May 1914, 13.

48. Damian Lawlor, *Na Fianna Éireann and the Irish Revolution, 1909 to 1923* (Rhode, Co. Offaly: Caoillte Books, 2009), 16–17; 'Fianna Eireann', in The National Association of the Old IRA [NAOIRA], *Dublin Brigade Review* (Dublin: Cahill, 1939), 65–70, at 65.
49. Dermot Meleady, *Redmond: The National Leader* (Dublin: Merrion, 2014), 274–8.
50. Meleady, *Redmond*, 296; Lyons, *Enigma*, 249–250.
51. M. A. Hopkinson, 'Childers, (Robert) Erskine', in McGuire and Quinn, *Dictionary of Irish Biography* (http://dib.cambridge.org/viewReadPage.do?articleId=a1649).
52. BMH.WS0267, 7: Pounch, J. See also *IV*, 1 August 1914, 9. For details See Francis Xavier Martin, ed., *The Howth Gun-Running and the Kilcoole Gun-Running 1914* (Dublin: Browne and Nolan, 1964).
53. BMH.WS0143, 3–4: Byrne, G.
54. BMH.WS0327, 5–6: Egan, P.
55. *EH*, 27 July 1914, 1; *ET*, 27 July 1914, 2.
56. *DEM*, 27 July 1914, 2, 3 and 4; *II*, 27 July 1914, 4; *IT*, 27 July 1914, 4.
57. *EH*, 28 July 1914, 2.
58. *FJ*, 27 July 1914, 6.
59. *EH*, 29 July 1914, 1; 30 July 1914, 1; 31 July 1914, 1

2 Dublin Goes to War

1. *IT*, 26 September 1914, 3.
2. Cited in Jennifer Speake, ed., *Oxford Dictionary of Proverbs* (Oxford University Press, 1982; 7th edn 2015), 92.
3. See p. 115.
4. *Hansard*, vol. 65 col. 1824, 3 August 1914.
5. *The Times*, 31 July 1914, 9; 1 August 1914, 8.
6. *Hansard*, vol. 65 col. 1828–9, 3 August 1914.
7. *FJ*, 4 August 1914, 3.
8. *The Times*, 19 September 1914, 9; Thomas Hennessey, *Diving Ireland: World War I and Partition* (London: Routledge, 1998), 73–8; Geoffrey Lewis, *Carson: The Man who Divided Ireland* (London: Hambledon, 2005), 167–9.
9. Grayson, *Belfast*, 11.
10. *IN*, 16 September 1914, 5.
11. *IN*, 21 September 1914, 5; Charles Hannon, 'The Irish Volunteers and the Concepts of Military Service and Defence 1913–24' (University College, Dublin, unpublished PhD thesis, 1989), 82–101.
12. *IV*, 8 August 1914, 1 and 15 August 1914, 1.
13. *IV*, 29 August 1914, 2.
14. University College, Dublin [UCD], Eoin MacNeill Papers, LA1/P/2; *BET*, 25 September 914, 6; *IV*, 3 October 1914, 10.
15. Hannon, 'Irish Volunteers', 105; National Library of Ireland [NLI], Redmond MS 15,258: Irish National Volunteers' Strength on 31 October 1914; Terence Denman, *Ireland's Unknown Soldiers* (Dublin: Irish Academic Press, 1992), 38.
16. *NV*, 17 October 1914, 5.
17. NLI, Redmond MS 15,258: Irish National Volunteers' Strength on 31 October 1914.
18. BMH.WS0340, 1: Traynor, O.; www.belfastceltic.org/oscartraynor.html (accessed 19 January 2017).
19. *IT*, 26 September 1914, 3–5; *FJ*, 26 September 1914, 5.
20. *FJ*, 28 September 1914, 9.

21. *FJ*, 26 September 1914, 5. See also Catriona Pennell, *A Kingdom United: Popular Responses to the Outbreak of the First World War in Britain and Ireland* (Oxford University Press, 2012), 185 and 187.

22. TNA, CO 904/94: RIC Report, Dublin, September 1914.

23. *DEM*, 2 November 1914, 5.

24. TNA, CO 904/94: RIC Report, Dublin, August 1914.

25. NLI, MS 9,620: Moylan Diary, 5 and 6 August 1914, 7–10.

26. NLI, MS 9,620: Moylan Diary, 12 August 1914, 17, 26 August 1914, 22, 1 September 1914, 24 and 8 October 1914, 30.

27. Pennell, *Kingdom*, 185.

28. *DEM*, 13 August 1914, 4.

29. *DEM*, 17 August 1914, 4.

30. *DEM*, 1 October 1914, 3.

31. *DEM*, 16 October 1914, 4.

32. *DEM*, 31 October 1914, 4.

33. UCD Archives, Papers of Thomas and Mary Kettle, LA34/364–77.

34. *FJ*, 31 August 1914, 6.

35. *IT*, 6 September 1914, 4.

36. *FJ*, 22 September 1914, 6.

37. William Buck, '"Come and Find Sanctuary in Eire". The Experiences of Ireland's Belgian Refugees During the First World War', *Immigrants and Minorities*, 34, 2 (2016), 192–209, at 192 and 195.

38. *DEM*, 18 September 1914, 3.

39. UCD Archives, Papers of Belgian Refugees Committee, P105, Minute Book 19 October 1914 to 27 October 1915.

40. *IT*, 21 October 1914, 6.

41. UCD, Belgian Refugees Committee, P105, Minute Book, 29, 6 January 1915.

42. *IT*, 25 July 1916, 4.

43. Buck, 'Sanctuary', 203–5.

44. *IT*, 5 December 1914, 5.

45. *IT*, 30 June 1915, 7.

46. *FJ*, 23 January 1915, 5

47. *DEM*, 20 September 1915, 3; H. D. Gribbon, 'Economic and Social History 1850–1921', in W. E. Vaughan, ed., *A New History of Ireland. VI, Ireland Under the Union, II, 1870–1921* (Oxford University Press, 1996), 260–356, at 347.

48. *DEM*, 13 October 1915, 5.

49. See for example, *II*, 18 February 1915, 3; *FJ*, 28 June 1915, 5; www.longlongtrail .co.uk/soldiers/a-soldiers-life-1914-1918/the-evacuation-chain-for-wounded-and-sick-soldiers/military-hospitals-in-the-british-isles-1914-1918/ (accessed 6 April 2018).

50. *DEM*, 22 September 1914, 2.

51. *II*, 23 January 1915, 3.

52. *DEM*, 24 August 1915, 3; *EH*, 16 September 1915, 2; adb.online.anu.edu.au /biography/smith-issy-8473 (accessed 5 October 2016).

53. *DEM*, 3 September 1915, 3.

54. *The London Gazette*, Supplement 29074, 16 February 1918, 1700; Doherty and Truesdale, *Irish Winners*, 107–8 and 225–6.

55. *FJ*, 24 June 1915, 8.

56. *DEM*, 3 July 1915, 4. See also *FJ*, 3 July 1915, 5 June 1915 and 5 July 1915, 6

57. *IT*, 4 December 1915, 6; Jane Leonard, 'Survivors', in John Horne, ed., *Our War* (Dublin: Royal Irish Academy, 2008), 209–23, at 219, ii.

58. NLI, MS 9,620: Moylan Diary, 6 August 1914, 10.
59. TNA, CO 904/14: Precis re secret societies, July 1914. Gosson, of the 2nd Dublins, died of tetanus on 4 May 1915 in hospital at Rouen: TNA, TNA, WO 363; www.cwgc.org/find-war-dead/casualty/514845/GOSSON,%20JAMES (accessed 23 March 2017).
60. TNA, CO 904/94: RIC Report, Dublin, August and September 1914.
61. IT, 3 September 1914, 6.
62. IT, 26 September 1914, 6; DEM, 26 September 1914, 3.
63. IT, 28 September 1914, 6.
64. IT, 16 October 1914, 6.
65. IT, 20 October 1914, 6.
66. See for example, II, 5 March 1915, 5; FJ, 26 March 1915, 7; DEM, 7 May 1915, 3; IT, 12 May 1915, 7; FJ, 17 May 1915, 6; IT, 22 May 1915, 9; IT, 31 May 1915, 8; FJ, 6 August 1915, 6; IT, 3 November 1915, 7.
67. Pennell, Kingdom, 190.
68. II, 17 February 1915, 7.
69. IT, 6 August 1914, 4. See also IT, 10 August 1914, 7.
70. IT, 25 August 1914, 3.
71. IT, 1 September 1914, 6.
72. Hanna, Pals, 13–14.
73. DEM, 11 September 1914, 2.
74. TNA, WO 339/11544: R. Tobin; Hanna, Pals, 236.
75. Stephen Sandford, Neither Unionist nor Nationalist: The 10th (Irish) Division in the Great War (Dublin: Irish Academic Press, 2015), 40.
76. David Fitzpatrick, 'The Logic of Collective Sacrifice: Ireland and the British Army, 1914–1918', Historical Journal XXXVIII (1995), 1017–30; Sandford, The 10th, 35–6.
77. Hanna, Pals, 17.
78. DEM, 16 September 1914, 3. See also IT, 17 September 1914, 6.
79. A newspaper reported that Hickman was promoted after joining the battalion: DEM, 28 August 1915, 3. However, his file contains an application for a commission in the 7th Dublins dated 11 September, three days before he enlisted. So it is likely that he was not clear how long a commission would take to be granted and decided to enlist anyway. See TNA, WO 339/12366: P. H. Hickman. See also Hanna, Pals, 20 and 196.
80. Stephen Walker, Ireland's Call: Irish Sporting Heroes who Fell in the Great War (Sallins: Merrion, 2015), 116–24; en.espn.co.uk/ireland/rugby/player/2502.html (accessed 5 October 2016).
81. TNA, WO 339/46640: J. T. Brett; Ken Kinsella, Out of the Dark, 1914–1918: South Dubliners Who Fell in the Great War (Sallins: Merrion, 2014), 346–51.
82. A rare example of coverage of the 10th Division as a whole prior to Gallipoli was FJ, 1 July 1915, 9.
83. Philip Orr, A Field of Bones: An Irish Division at Gallipoli (Dublin: Lilliput Press, 2006), 17 and 23; National Army Museum [NAM], Noël Drury Diary, Drury 1, 7–8; University of Dublin (Trinity College), War List (Dublin: Hodges Figgis, 1922), 56; TNA, WO 339/32747: Noël E. Drury.
84. NAM, 7607-69-1 to 4.
85. See p. 110.
86. See p. 109.
87. Table A4.1.
88. NAM, Drury 1, 14–15.

89. NAM, Drury 1, 28.

90. David Fitzpatrick, 'Militarism in Ireland, 1900–1922', in Thomas Bartlett and Keith Jeffery, eds., *A Military History of Ireland* (Cambridge University Press, 1996), 379–406, at 386; Fitzpatrick, 'Logic', 1017.

91. Some figures (NLI, Redmond MS 15,259) suggest only 568 reservists (exactly half of them Irish Volunteers) mobilised in Dublin, 3% of the Irish total. However, the army's annual report for 1913 shows that in that year, 31.3% of the regulars and 22.9% of the Special Reserve had been recruited in the Dublin area. Back to 1910, the figures were similar. So it is reasonable to assume that nearly one-third of the regulars and nearly one-quarter of the reservists were from Dublin. See War Office, Cd. 5481, *The General Annual Report on the British Army for the Year Ending 30th September 1910* (London: HMSO, 1911), 43; Army Council, Cd. 7252, *The General Annual Report on the British Army for the Year Ending 30th September 1913* (London: HMSO, 1914), 47.

92. It is not possible to be clear on wider Dublin County figures since they were recorded on a provincial basis, with only the Dublin Metropolitan Police district separated.

93. TNA, NATS 1/398, Statistical tables showing numbers of recruits raised daily; NLI, Redmond MS 15,259. See also Tables A5.2 and A5.3.

94. NLI, Redmond MS 15,259.

95. *EH*, 15 March 1916, 1. At least one other Dubliner would go on to serve in the French army – though for reasons which are unclear: Major J. B. Magennis, whose father lived in Harcourt Street, was reported to be serving in the French army in 1917. See *FJ*, 19 October 1917, 3. Two French soldiers had been schooled in Dublin: Louis Jammet at Belvedere College and Xavier de la Tour at St Vincent's, Castleknock. See *SH*, 18 March 1916, 5 and 15 April 1916, 5. One member of the Belgian army, who 'had been all through the war since the invasion of Belgium' was the stepson and son of Colonel and Mrs Fowle of the Royal Hospital, Kilmainham: Lieutenant Gaston De Pret-Roose de Calesberg. That was in 1918 when he was killed in action. See *II*, 22 January 1918, 2 and *DEM*, 26 January 1918, 1. However, in his record of death he is said himself to have lived in Antwerp: www .wardeadregister.be/fr/content/de-pret-roose-de-calesberg (accessed 6 October 2016). His brother, J. De Pret-Roose de Calesberg, served in the 21st Lancers and won the Military Cross: *II*, 23 July 1918, 2; www.haileybury.com/medals/militar y_cross%20h%20pre1912.htm (accessed 6 October 2016).

96. Given the front-line nature of their service, members of the Merchant Navy (217 in total) have been included in this figure.

97. TNA, PRO 1/387: Report of fire at Arnside Street repository, Walworth, 1940.

98. TNA, WO 363 and 374 service and pensions records accounted for 5,806 whose records could only be found in those sources. If that constitutes 36% of those records created (see Grayson, 'Military History', 481 n. 63), then the remaining 64% would be 10,321.

99. Many Royal Flying Corps officers' records would only be with army files and would face similar problems to searching through army officers' files. Naval records in ADM 188 in TNA do not include an address. They do include 933 individuals who were born in Dublin and who were not found in other records, but they are not included here for reasons stated earlier (see p. 4).

100. If the police figure of 26,538 in the city plus 6,500 regulars and 6,900 reservists are combined.

101. Army, Cd. 8168, *Report on Recruiting in Ireland* (London: HMSO, 1916), 3.

102. There are 609 men said to be dead in various sources, but where it was not possible to verify that in data from *Airmen Died, Sailors Died, Soldiers Died* or the CWGC. 353 were said in newspapers to be dead, 208 are names on local war memorials, while most of the other 48 are from various printed memorial rolls.

103. Table A7.1.

104. See p. 261.

105. Note that the 2nd RI Rifles have such a high figure due to data generously provided by the regiment's leading researcher, James W. Taylor.

106. TNA, NATS 1/401: Consolidated Summary Tables. See also Table A5.4.

107. Data used for the ranks calculation are solely from TNA, WO 363 and WO 364 service records. Much data was also gathered from, for example, church memorials of various types, but these are self-selecting and more likely to be Protestant, so are not as objective a set of figures as the service records. See Grayson, *Belfast*, 232–3, n. 7, on some of the difficulties of counting denomination. However, note that for soldiers joining in Dublin, there does not seem to have been the same absence of recording as 'Catholic' soldiers in known nationalist units as there was in Belfast, so at least Catholics have not been under-counted in Dublin service records.

108. Kimberley Jensen, 'Gender and Citizenship', in Susan R. Grayzel and Tammy M. Proctor, *Gender and the Great War* (Oxford University Press, 2017), 10–26, at 15.

109. I am very grateful to Dr Susan Hawkins of Kingston University, for her very substantial help in providing me with a spreadsheet of Dublin-related data from the British Red Cross Society resource, which is online at: www.redcross.org.uk /About-us/Who-we-are/History-and-origin/First-World-War. For the statistics, see Figures A6.1 and A6.2, and Tables A6.1, A6.2 and A6.3.

110. MA, MSPC/RO/609: Establishment of IRA 11 July 1921 and 1 July 1922, 3.

111. There are queries over ten more possible duplicates and another 216 whose service is difficult to verify but not possible to exclude (all men). Detailed studies are: Joseph E. A. Connell, *Who's Who in the Dublin Rising, 1916* (Dublin: Wordwell, 2015) and Jimmy Wren, *The GPO Garrison Easter Week 1916: A Biographical Dictionary* (Dublin: Geography Publications, 2015). The 1936 Roll of Honour identified 1,596 in Dublin, while current estimates range between 1,950 and 2,170. The total figure could be as high as 2,343 since another 6 are possible duplicates, and there are another 215 identified with possible service. See Connell, *Who's*, 2.

112. See p. 172.

113. Peter Hart, *The IRA at War 1916–1923* (Oxford University Press, 2003), 118–19 and 125.

114. Hart used a category of 'Un/semi- skilled' but it is not clear how he defined 'semi-skilled' so it is difficult to make comparisons with the categories used here.

115. Hart, *IRA*, 119.

116. See p. 163.

117. Tomás Irish, *Trinity in War and Revolution, 1912–1923* (Dublin: Royal Irish Academy, 2015), 90; Kinsella, *Out*, 337–40.

118. Hanna, *Pals*, 18–19, 176 and 202.

119. Hanna, *Pals*, 17–28; Bryan Cooper, *The Tenth (Irish) Division at Gallipoli* (London: Herbert Jenkins, 1918; Dublin, Irish Academic Press, 1993 edn), 28–9; Sandford, *The 10th*, 70–9; Tom Johnstone, *Orange: Green and Khaki: The Story of the Irish Regiments in the Great War, 1914–18* (Dublin: Gill and Macmillan, 1992), 89–92.

120. NAM, Drury 1, 12–13 and 25–6.

121. NAM, Drury 1, 17–20.

122. NAM, Drury 1, 22.
123. NAM, Drury 1, 25.
124. See for example, *II*, 1 January 1915, 5 and *II*, 3 May 1915, 3; Hanna, *Pals*, 17–31.
125. Hanna, *Pals*, 32–44 (quotation at 34); Sandford, *The 10th*, 79–82; Cooper, *Tenth*, 30–2; Johnstone, *Orange*, 94–7; NAM, Drury 1, 31–6.
126. NAM, Drury 1, 37–8.
127. *DEM*, 27 October 1915, 4; *DEM*, 9 November 1915, 3; *DEM*, 11 November 1915, 2; *FJ*, 6 January 1916, 7.
128. I am grateful to Dr Timothy Bowman for his advice on the LDV.
129. *IT*, 28 September 1914, 6 and 10 August 1915, 3. See *News Letter*, 11 April 2012, 20.
130. TNA, WO 339/21334: W. M. Crozier; see also Anthony Quinn, *Wigs and Guns: Irish Barristers in the Great War* (Dublin: Four Courts, 2006), 88–9.
131. *DEM*, 5 November 1915, 6.
132. *IT*, 3 October 1914, 6.
133. *II*, 3 February 1915, 3: a photo of officers and non-commissioned officers of the 6th Royal Irish Rifles was headlined 'GETTING READY THE IRISH BRIGADE'. A story on a fundraising event at the Abbey Theatre possibly refers to both the 10th and the 16th: *II*, 2 February 1915, 2.
134. *FJ*, 5 February 1915, 7; *FJ*, 6 February 1915, 5; *II*, 13 February 1917, 3, *II*, 19 June 1915, 3; *DEM*, 2 August 1915, 3; *FJ*, 3 December 1915, 6.
135. Imperial War Museum [IWM] 3385: Beater Diary; TNA, AIR 76/30/43: O. L. Beater. Beater was born in Stephen's Green in 1888 and grew up in Dublin. He had left by 1911 but the family was still resident. See: https://civilrecords .irishgenealogy.ie/churchrecords/images/birth_returns/births_1888/02528/1936799 .pdf, www.census.nationalarchives.ie/pages/1901/Dublin/Rathmines/ Terenure_Road/1297311/ and www.census.nationalarchives.ie/pages/1911/Dublin/ Rathmines___Rathgar_West/Terenure_Road/65306/ (all accessed 6 October 2016).
136. Johnstone, *Orange*, 188–200; Denman, *Unknown*, 39–58.
137. IWM 3385, Beater diary, 19 December 1915.

3 Outbreak, 1914

1. *DEM*, 7 January 1915, 3.
2. TNA, CO 693 Merchant seamen and fishermen detained as POWs in Germany, Austria-Hungary and Turkey; *Daily Express* (Dublin), 31 August 1914, 7. The Master of the SS *City of Hamburg*, G. J. Kirwan, had his wife and four children with him on holiday. They were all still held in mid-September 1914 (*DEM*, 16 September 1914, 3), but it is not clear whether the whole family were detained for the duration of the war.
3. Paul G. Halpern, *A Naval History of World War I* (Abingdon: Routledge, 1994), 26–7.
4. Halpern, *Naval History*, 27; *The Times*, 6 August 1914, 6.
5. *Times*: 7 August 1914, 6; 8 August 1914, 4; 10 August 1914, 2.
6. *Hansard*, HC Deb, 7 August 1914, vol. 65, col. 2154.
7. Halpern, *Naval History*, 34 and 344–5.
8. *EH*, 13 August 1914, 3.
9. *SH*, 16 October 1915, 5.
10. Halpern, *Naval History*, 33; www.wrecksite.eu/wreck.aspx?57, www.wrecksite.eu /wreck.aspx?56 and www.wrecksite.eu/wreck.aspx?62228 (accessed 9 May 2016).

11. www.wrecksite.eu/wreck.aspx?9850 and www.wrecksite.eu/wreck.aspx?386 (accessed 9 May 2016).

12. Halpern, *Naval History*, 482 n. 46; www.wrecksite.eu/wreck.aspx?10834 (accessed 9 May 2016).

13. Halpern, *Naval History*, 70–2 and 88–90.

14. TNA, ADM 188/380/216794: Edward Swords.

15. Cited in John Dixon, *A Clash of Empires: The South Wales Borderers at Tsingtao, 1914* (Wrexham: Bridge Books, 2008), 158.

16. *Sailors Died*; Robert Nield, *China's Foreign Places: The Foreign Presence in China in the Treaty Port Era, 1840–1943* (Hong Kong: Hong Kong University Press, 2015), 269; www.cwgc.org/find-a-cemetery/cemetery/2000318/SAI%20WAN%20 (CHINA)%20MEMORIAL (accessed 9 May 2016).

17. Halpern, *Naval History*, 92–3; 99–100; www.wrecksite.eu/wreck.aspx?138092 and www.wrecksite.eu/wreck.aspx?135896 (accessed 9 May 2016).

18. Rudyard Kipling, *The Irish Guards in the Great War*, vol. I: *The First Battalion* (London: Macmillan, 1923; London: Leonaur, 2007 edn), 17.

19. Johnstone, *Orange*, 17–40. The most detailed and reliable reference source for army structure and movements is Chris Baker's website 'The Long, Long, Trail'. Details of infantry regiments are at: www.longlongtrail.co.uk/army/regiments-and-corps/the-british-infantry-regimennts-of-1914-1918/ (accessed 29 April 2016).

20. Beckett et al., *British Army*, 208–9.

21. Ibid., 218.

22. Ibid., 212.

23. Ibid., 211.

24. *Soldiers Died*; www.cwgc.org/find-war-dead/casualty/2743587/RYAN,% 20JAMES (accessed 29 April 2016).

25. Terence Zuber, *The Battle of the Frontiers: Ardennes 1914* (Stroud: The History Press, 2014).

26. CWGC download, 3 May 2016.

27. Adrian Gilbert, *Challenge of Battle: The Real Story of the British Army in 1914* (Oxford: Osprey, 2013), 63–79; Peter Hart, *Fire and Movement: The British Expeditionary Force and the Campaign of 1914* (Oxford University Press, 2015), 84–123; Allan Mallinson, *1914: Fight the Good Fight. Britain, the Army and the Coming of the First World War* (London: Bantam Press, 2013), 296–319; Jerry Murland, *Retreat and Rearguard 1914: The BEF's Actions from Mons to the Marne* (Barnsley: Pen and Sword, 2011), 9–40; Terence Zuber, *The Mons Myth: A Reassessment of the Battle* (Stroud: The History Press, 2010)

28. A fourth man, Sergeant 5050 Charles Pearce was killed in the 1st East Surreys. Born and enlisted in London, his possible Dublin connection comes from the fact that post-war, his wife lived there. However, she had remarried and she might not have been there during the war. www.cwgc.org/find-war-dead/casualty/481885/ PEARCE,%20CHARLES%20EDWARD (accessed 29 April 2016).

29. Born and enlisted in London, he was possibly living in barracks in Dundalk in 1911, but *Soldiers Died* lists him as residing in Dublin. However, that could well have been a barrack address. Beyond that, no specific link to the area is apparent. See: www .census.nationalarchives.ie/pages/1911/Louth/Dundalk_Urban_No__4/ Military_Barracks/578700/ and www.cwgc.org/find-war-dead/casualty/878149/ CLOW,%20EDWARD (accessed 29 April 2016).

30. TNA, WO 95/1431: 4th Royal Fusiliers.

31. *Soldiers Died*.

32. Gilbert, *Challenge*, 68 and 71; TNA, WO 95/1421.

33. *EH*, 14 October 1914, 1. This was either 6816 or 8168 Thomas Whelan.
34. *DEM*, 7 January 1915, 3.
35. *EH*, 7 September 1915, 2. www.cwgc.org/find-war-dead/casualty/878242/CORRE, %20JOHN%20S (accessed 3 May 2016).
36. *Soldiers Died*; www.cwgc.org/find-war-dead/casualty/894941/WARD,%20T (accessed 3 May 2016).
37. www.cwgc.org/find-a-cemetery/cemetery/90801/st.-symphorien-military-cemetery/ (accessed 6 April 2018).
38. Holger H. Herwig, *The Marne, 1914: The Opening of World War I and the Battle that Changed the World* (New York: Random House, 2009).
39. See Table A2.4.
40. *EH*, 30 September 1914, 1.
41. Beckett et al., *British Army*, 216–18.
42. John Hutton, *August 1914: Surrender at St Quentin* (Barnsley: Pen and Sword, 2010), 127–43, 148–52 and 175–6.
43. TNA, WO 95/1481: 2nd RDF; H. C. Wylly, *Crown and Company, 1911–1922: The Historical Records of the 2nd Batt. Royal Dublin Fusiliers* (London: Arthur L. Humphreys, 1925), 17–25.
44. Wylly, *Crown*, 24 and 29.
45. *DEM*, 5 September 1914, 4.
46. *WIT*, 19 September 1914, 1.
47. www.cwgc.org/find-war-dead/casualty/572193/CLARKE,%20WILLIAM (accessed 3 May 2016); *EH*, 21 February 1916, 1.
48. TNA, WO 95/1481: 2nd RDF.
49. *EH*, 14 June 1915, 5.
50. *Soldiers Died*; TNA, WO 95/1134.
51. *Soldiers Died*; TNA, WO 95/1140: 12th Lancers.
52. *EH*, 15 October 1914, 2.
53. *The Times*, 3 September 1914, 8.
54. *The Times*, 5 September 1914, 9.
55. TNA, WO 95/1113; *The Times*, 18 September 1914, 4.
56. Gilbert, *Challenge*, 87. See also Mallinson, *Fight*, 329–30; Murland, *Retreat*, 43–4; David Kenyon, *Horsemen in No Man's Land: British Cavalry and Trench Warfare, 1914–1918* (Barnsley: Pen and Sword, 2011), 25–7.
57. Private L/7052 Alfred O'Brien did not arrive in France until June 1915. Private L/855 Philip O'Brien was there sooner, but not early enough, on 9 September 1914. See TNA, WO 329.
58. Beckett et al., *British Army*, 219–21.
59. CWGC download, 3 May 2016.
60. TNA, WO 95/1481: 2nd RDF.
61. TNA, WO 95/1481: 2nd RDF.
62. Grayson, 'A Life in the Trenches?', 160–85.
63. TNA, WO 95/1481:2nd RDF.
64. TNA, WO 363. I am grateful to James W. Taylor for flagging this case to me.
65. Gerald Lowry, *From Mons to 1933* (London: Simpkin and Marshall, 1933), 18; James W. Taylor, *The 2nd Royal Irish Rifles in the Great War* (Dublin: Four Courts Press, 2005), 266–7.
66. CWGC download, 6 May 2016.
67. TNA, WO 95/1612L 2nd Leinsters.
68. TNA, WO 95/1375: 3rd Division General Staff War Diary: 'Report on the Operations of the 3rd Division from 11th to 30 October 1914'.

69. TNA, WO 95/1415: 2nd RI Rifles.

70. John Lucy, *Devil in the Drum* (London: Faber and Faber, 1938; Uckfield: Naval and Military Press, 1992 edn), 211. See also Grayson, *Belfast*, 26–7.

71. Alan Palmer, *The Salient: Ypres, 1914–18* (London: Constable, 2007), 57–8.

72. Palmer, *Salient*, 1.

73. Gilbert, *Challenge*, 241.

74. TNA, WO 95/1342.

75. Kipling, *Irish Guards*, 42–3.

76. CWGC download 5 May 2016.

77. Kipling, *Irish Guards*, 50.

78. Kipling, *Irish Guards*, 51.

79. CWGC download, 5 May 2016. One of these men, James Moyles from Ballina, Co. Mayo, became the subject of a BBC *Who Do You Think You Are?* documentary nearly a century on, as the great-grandfather of Radio 1 DJ Chris Moyles. See 'Chris Moyles's Tears for Great Grandad Jimmy, Victim of Ypres', *Daily Mail*, 12 July 2009.

80. TNA, WO 95/1342; TNA, WO 95/1347; H. F. N. Jourdain and Edward Fraser, *The Connaught Rangers, 1st Battalion, Formerly 88th Foot*, vol. I (London: Royal United Service Institution, 1924), 440–1.

81. TNA, WO 95/1342: 1st IG.

82. *DEM*, 19 October 1915, 1; *ET*, 18 October 1915, 1

83. See pp. 25–6.

84. CWGC download, 6 May 2016.

85. *EH*, 15 November 1915, 5; www.cwgc.org/find-war-dead/casualty/472429/ROBERTS,%20WILLIAM%20OWEN (accessed 6 October 2016).

86. *EH*, 25 March 1915, 4.

87. See for example, *DEM*, 16 October 1915, 3. Sergeant J. Cochrane of the Irish Guards wrote home to his mother in Dublin about how a bullet passed through photos and a pay-book in his breast pocket, but was stopped by a roll-book.

88. Beckett et al., *British Army*, 228–36.

89. Ibid., 234.

90. See Table A7.2.

4 Stalemate, 1915

1. *DEM*, 5 May 1915, 3.

2. www.wrecksite.eu/wreck.aspx?11823 and www.wrecksite.eu/wreck.aspx?366 (accessed 9 May 2016).

3. www.naval-history.net/xDKCas1915-02Feb.htm and www.wrecksite.eu/wreck.aspx?382 (accessed 9 May 2016).

4. Halpern, *Naval History*, 44; www.wrecksite.eu/wreck.aspx?405 (accessed 9 May 2016).

5. TNA, WO 339/24519: W. T. Colyer.

6. IWM 7256: Wilfrid Colyer Papers, Part II, no number.

7. TNA, WO 95/1481: 2nd RDF.

8. Palmer, *Salient*, 113–7; Arthur Banks, *A Military Atlas of the First World War* (London: Heinemann, 1975; Barnsley: Leo Cooper, 1989 edn), 140.

9. Beckett et al., *British Army*, 253.

10. Tim Cook, *At the Sharp End: Canadians Fighting The Great War, 1914–1916*, vol. I (Toronto: Penguin, 2007), 146.

11. *DEM*, 5 May 1915, 3

12. IWM 7256: Colyer, Part III, 56.
13. IWM 7256: Colyer, Part III, 115.
14. TNA, WO 95/1481: 2nd RDF; Wylly, *Crown*, 43–4.
15. TNA, WO 95/1481: 2nd RDF; Wylly, *Crown*, 44–50.
16. TNA, WO 95/1481: 2nd RDF.
17. TNA, WO 161/98/479.
18. CWGC download, 10 May 2016.
19. See for example, *II*, 29 April 1915, 4.
20. *EH*, 30 August 1915, 2.
21. www.cwgc.org/find-war-dead/casualty/1621671/McDONNELL,%20PETER, www
.cwgc.org/find-war-dead/casualty/910395/McDONNELL,%20PATRICK and www
.cwgc.org/find-war-dead/casualty/1621670/McDONNELL,%20JOHN (accessed 10
May 2016).
22. Taylor, *2nd*, 59–84.
23. TNA, WO 95/1730: 1st RI Rifles; James W. Taylor, *The 1st Royal Irish Rifles in the
Great War* (Dublin: Four Courts Press, 2002), 53–7.
24. Kipling, *Irish Guards*, 94.
25. Source: data gathered from all sources used, but principally service records, newspapers and 1914 Christmas PoW List database created by Paul Nixon.
26. www.nationalarchives.gov.uk/help-with-your-research/research-guides/prisoner-of-
war-interview-reports-1914-1918/ (accessed 12 May 2016).
27. Patrick McCarthy, 'Casement's Irish Brigade', *The Irish Sword*, XXXI, 124 (Winter
2017), 203–11.
28. *ET*, 25 January 1916. 6.
29. *EH*, 3 November 1915, 2; *SH*, 13 November 1915, 1.
30. *ET*, 26 January 1916, 2.
31. *EH*, 30 September 1914, 1.
32. *EH*, 6 November 1914, 4.
33. TNA, WO 161/98/470.
34. Heather Jones, *Violence Against Prisoners of War in the First World War: Britain,
France and Germany, 1914–1920* (Cambridge University Press, 2011), 14.
35. TNA, WO 363. For a similar account, later in the war, see TNA, WO 161/96/36, for
2nd Lieutenant James Scott from Sydney Parade in Dublin, captured at Wytschaete
on 27 May 1917.
36. TNA, WO 161/98/479.
37. Jones, *Violence*, 371–6.
38. See for example, TNA, WO 161/98/647: Lance Corporal 15654 William Douglas,
8th RDF; TNA, WO 161/99/111: Private 4624 Bernard Murphy, 2nd RDF; TNA,
WO 161/98/460: Private 11309 William Casey, 2nd RDF; TNA, WO 161/98/616:
Private 8681 Michael McQuirk / McGuirk, 2nd RDF (listed as McQuirk on interview and McGuirk on medal card).
39. Substantial information, including intelligence material, is at TNA, WO 141/9.
40. TNA, WO 161/98/470; TNA, WO 161/99/11; TNA, WO 161/98/616; BMH.
WS0741: Kehoe, M. J.
41. TNA, WO 161/98/616.
42. TNA, WO 161/98/470.
43. BMH.WS0741, 10: Kehoe, M. J. The Dublin Committee of the Royal Dublin
Fusiliers certainly sent large numbers of parcels – 835 to men of the regiment at
Limburg and Giessen in April 1917 alone, for which acknowledgements were
received. See *IT*, 12 May 1917, 7.

44. Michael Keogh, *With Casement's Irish Brigade* (Drogheda: Choice, 2010), 195–9. I am grateful to Tom Hartley for providing this information. See also BMH. WS0741, Kehoe, M. J.

45. TNA, WO 161/98/470; TNA, WO 161/98/616.

46. See p. 121.

47. BMH.WS0741, 61: Kehoe, M. J.

48. See BMH.WS0741. All nine were born in Dublin: John Barnacle; Henry (Harry) Burke (probably service number 11438); Patrick Carr; John Collins; John Francis Kavanagh; John O'Curry; Michael O'Toole (probably service number 3964); John Stacey; and Thomas Wilson.

49. BMH.WS0741, 22: Kehoe, M. J.

50. *DEM*, 16 January 1919, 3.

51. BMH.WS0741, 62: Kehoe, M. J.

52. www.wrecksite.eu/wreck.aspx?10126 (accessed 10 May 2016).

53. www.wrecksite.eu/wreck.aspx?11110 (accessed 10 May 2016).

54. Halpern, *Naval History*, 298–9; Alexander Watson, *Ring of Steel: Germany and Austria-Hungary at War, 1914–1918* (London: Penguin, 2014), 239–40 and 416.

55. *FJ*, 10 May 1915, 5.

56. www.geni.com/projects/RMS-Lusitania-Saloon-passengers/14739; www.geni.com/projects/RMS-Lusitania-Victualling-Crew/14743; www.geni.com/ projects/RMS-Lusitania-Engineering-Crew/14744; www.cwgc.org/find-war-dead/casualty/2887011/GERAGHTY,%20M; www.cwgc.org/find-war-dead/casualty/2972969/ORANGE,%20JOHN and www .cwgc.org/find-war-dead/casualty/2979364/BARRY,%20W (accessed 10 May 2016); *DEM*, 15 May 1915, 1.

57. *SI*, 16 May 1915, 3.

58. *FJ*, 10 May 1915, 5. See p. 50.

59. *FJ*, 10 May 1915, 6.

60. *FJ*, 11 May 1915, 4.

61. *FJ*, 20 August 1915, 5.

62. *FJ*, 21 September 1915, 5; DEM, 4 January 1916, 3.

63. See p. 319.

64. Nick Lloyd, *Loos 1915* (Stroud: Tempus, 2006).

65. CWGC website (accessed 13 May 2016) search for those who died in 'United Kingdom forces' between 26 May 1916 and 30 June 1916, and are buried or commemorated in France (50,187) or Belgium (20,102).

66. Wylly, *2nd*, 55.

67. Dublin City Library and Archive, Royal Dublin Fusiliers Association Archive [DCLA, RDFA], 001/21: Elley to Roberts, 8 November 1915.

68. TNA, WO 95/1481: 2nd RDF.

69. DCLA, RDFA/001/21: Elley to Roberts, 9 December 1915. Redmond produced a newspaper account of his visit: *Irish Times*, 1 December 1915, 5.

70. DCLA, RDFA/001/21: Elley to Roberts, 20 November 1915.

71. DCLA, RDFA/001/21: Elley to Roberts, 12 January 1916.

72. DCLA, RDFA/001/77: Mordaunt to K. Roberts, 19 September 1915. It is interesting to speculate on what Mordaunt had seen himself since his TNA, WO 372 medal card suggests he first went overseas in the Balkan theatre on 25 April 1915. He had been transferred to the Western Front by July 1915 because his letters started to come from there then (addressed to 'Miss K. Roberts', Monica's sister). However, his scope for seeing Germans behaving badly towards civilians would have been limited, though he might have seen the after-effects.

73. DCLA, RDFA/001/18 and 21: Brooks to Roberts, 22 November 1915; Elley to Roberts, 20 November 1915.

74. *DEM*, 23 July 1915, 3.

75. www.cwgc.org/find-war-dead/casualty/583055/PRATT,%20WILLIAM%20JOHN%20ARMSTRONG (accessed 17 May 2016).

76. *DEM*, 28 September 1915, 4; *FJ*, 29 September 1915, 7.

77. *DEM*, 11 September 1915, 4.; 6 November 1915, 6; 2 December 1915, 5.

78. *IT*, 18 December 1915, 6.

5 Gallipoli: Helles

1. *FJ*, 25 May 1915, 5.

2. Philpott, *Bloody*.

3. Sheffield, *Forgotten*, 212.

4. Ibid., 94–5.

5. Edward J. Erickson, *Gallipoli: Command Under Fire* (Oxford: Osprey, 2015), 18–19.

6. Robin Prior, *Gallipoli: The End of the Myth* (London: Yale University Press, 2009), 242.

7. Jenny Macleod, *Gallipoli* (Oxford University Press, 2015), 13–22.

8. *EH*, 15 June 2015, 2.

9. Halpern, *Naval History*, 78, 145, 156 and 163–5; TNA, ADM 53/39479: HMS *Dartmouth* log book, 21 August 1914 to 30 April 1915.

10. Macleod, *Gallipoli*, 17.

11. Prior, *Gallipoli*, 241.

12. IWM, Rickus Papers: 94/7/1: E. E. Rickus to Mrs E. Hegarty, 7 May 1915.

13. H. C. Wylly, *Neill's "Blue Caps"*, vol. III (Aldershot: Gale and Polden, 1925), 1–15; TNA, WO 95/4310: 1st RDF.

14. Wylly, *Neill's, III*, 19–21.

15. Also at V Beach were parts of the 2nd Hampshire and the Royal Naval Division's Anson Battalion, along with support troops such as Royal Engineers. See Wylly, *Neill's, III*, 26. The 1st Dublins' two fellow battalions in 86th Brigade, the 2nd Royal Fusiliers and 1st Lancashire Fusiliers, landed at X and W beaches westwards around the coast.

16. For a detailed account see Lecane, *Beneath*, 152–73. See also Wylly, *Neill's, III*, 26 and 28–9.

17. *IT*, 19 May 1915, 4.

18. Peter Hart, *Gallipoli* (London: Profile, 2011), 144.

19. Nigel Steel and Peter Hart, *Defeat at Gallipoli* (London: Macmillan, 1994), 91.

20. Cited in Wylly, *Neill's, III*, 29.

21. *IT*, 19 May 1915, 4.

22. TNA, WO 95/4310: 86th Brigade.

23. Steel and Hart, *Defeat*, 92.

24. Wylly, *Neill's, III*, 33.

25. Prior, *Gallipoli*, 108–9.

26. Cited in L. A. Carlyon, *Gallipoli* (London: Doubleday, 2001; Bantam, 2003 edn), 40.

27. TNA, WO 95/4310: 1st RMF and 86th Brigade.

28. Macleod, *Gallipoli*, 29–35 and 40–1.

29. Wylly, *Neill's, III*, 31.

30. Lecane, *Beneath*, 165 and 173; Wylly, *Neill's, III*, 29.

31. O. Creighton, *With the Twenty-Ninth Division in Gallipoli* (London: Longman, 1916), 67; Lecane, *Beneath*, 171.
32. NAM, David French Papers, 1964-05-86: French to Lewis, 16 July 1915.
33. Cited in Wylly, *Neill's, III*, 31.
34. NAM, 1964-05-86: French to Lewis, 16 July 1915.
35. Wylly, *Neill's, III*, 34–5.
36. Wylly, *Neill's, III*, 33.
37. CWGC download, 24 May 2016.
38. Macleod, *Gallipoli*, 45–6; Field Marshal Lord Carver, *The National Army Museum Book of the Turkish Front, 1914–18* (London: Sidgwick and Jackson, 2003), 36–7; Steel and Hart, *Defeat*, 122–9; Prior, *Gallipoli*, 139.
39. CWGC download 24 May 2016; *Soldiers Died*.
40. TNA, WO 95/4310: 1st RMF and 86th Infantry Brigade; Creighton, *Twenty-Ninth*, 87; NAM, Henry O'Hara Papers, 1956-03-50: O'Hara to French, 15 May 1915.
41. The date is in doubt because, as Lecane discusses, although the CWGC records show 87 men in the 1st Dublins dead on 30 April, there is no evidence of any Turkish attack then. Meanwhile, there is plenty of evidence for an attack on 1/2 May. CWGC records do not list anyone dead in the 1st Dublins on 1 May, but show thirteen on 2 May. As Lecane suggests, there was probably a clerical error in attributing deaths. See Lecane, *Beneath*, 230.
42. Cited in Wylly, *Neill's, III*, 39.
43. NAM, 1964-05-86: French to Lewis, 16 July 1915.
44. TNA, WO 95/4310: 1st RMF and 86th Infantry Brigade.
45. Macleod, *Gallipoli*, 46–7; Carver, *Turkish Front*, 43–4; Steel and Hart, *Defeat*, 154–66; Prior, *Gallipoli*, 142.
46. Cited in Wylly, *Neill's, III*, 40–1.
47. TNA, WO 95/4310: 1st RMF.
48. NAM, 1956-03-50: O'Hara to French, 15 May 1915.
49. TNA, WO 95/4311: 87th Brigade; CWGC download 24 May 2016.
50. Macleod, *Gallipoli*, 48–9. See also Prior, *Gallipoli*, 152.
51. CWGC download 24 May 2016.
52. Dillon is listed as dead on 30 April, but this is more likely 1 May. See p. 93.
53. Alice Fagan's address is given as 18 Stafford Street by the CWGC for both her sons but this might only have applied post-war. In 1911, she appears to have been living just one street away from Stafford Street, in Jervis Street. See: www.census.nationalarchives.ie /pages/1911/Dublin/North_City/Jervis_St_/39140/ (accessed 24 May 1916).
54. *DEM*, 18 May 1915, 5; *IT*, 19 May 1915, 4.
55. *II*, 22 May 1915, 3.
56. *FJ*, 25 May 1915, 5; *EH*, 25 May 1915, 2; *DEM*, 10 June 1915, 5; *FJ*, 7 July 1915, 5.
57. *FJ*, 25 May 1915, 5.
58. CWGC download, 31 May 2016.
59. Carver, *Turkish Front*, 54; Macleod, *Gallipoli*, 48; Hart, *Gallipoli*, 264–5.
60. Frank Fox, *The Royal Inniskilling Fusiliers in the World War* (London: Constable, 1928), 187.
61. TNA, WO 95/4310: 86th Brigade.
62. CWGC download, 31 May 2016.
63. Macleod, *Gallipoli*, 48; Hart, *Gallipoli*, 258–64.
64. Fox, *Inniskilling*, 186.
65. Wylly, *Neill's, III*, 49–51.; TNA, WO 95/4310: 1st RDF.
66. Carver, *Turkish Front*, 62; Hart, *Gallipoli*, 286–91; CWGC download, 31 May 2016.

6 Gallipoli: Suvla Bay

1. NAM, Drury 1, 80.
2. Hanna, *Pals*, 49.
3. Hanna, *Pals*, 54.
4. TNA, WO 95/4296: 6th RDF and 7th RDF.
5. Hart. 304.
6. www.nationalarchives.gov.uk/pathways/firstworldwar/transcripts/battles/darda nelles.htm (accessed 14 November 2017).
7. Rhys Crawley, *Climax at Gallipoli: The Failure of the August Offensive* (Norman: University of Oklahoma Press, 2014), 242–3.
8. Hart, *Gallipoli*, 332–3.
9. Cooper, *Tenth*, 76.
10. Carver, *Turkish Front*, 73.
11. Macleod, *Gallipoli*, 57–9; Hart, *Gallipoli*, 330–45.
12. Macleod, *Gallipoli*, 57; see also Orr, *Field*, 68–9; Carlyon, *Gallipoli*, 512–3. See also Evan McGilvray, *Hamilton and Gallipoli: British Command in an Age of Military Transformation* (Barnsley: Pen and Sword, 2015), 140–2 and 193–4.
13. Sandford, *The 10th*, 142–5.
14. NAM, Drury 1, 80.
15. TNA, WO 95/4296: 6th and 7th RDF.
16. DCLA, RDFA/005: Tobin to his father, 13 August 1915.
17. *DEM*, 11 October 1915, 3.
18. Macleod, *Gallipoli*, 59–60; Hart, *Gallipoli*, 345–9.
19. NAM, Drury 1, 82.
20. *IT*, 8 October 1915, 4.
21. NAM, Drury 1, 82.
22. *DEM*, 31 August 1915, 5.
23. Hanna, *Pals*, 68.
24. DCLA, RDFA/005: Tobin to his father, 13 August 1915.
25. Cited in Kinsella, *Out*, 348. For Brett, see also Séamus Greene, '2nd Lieut. Jasper Brett', *The Blue Cap*, 18 (December 2013), 8–9.
26. DCLA, RDFA/005: Tobin to his father, 13 August 1915.
27. Cooper, *Tenth*, 49–50; Michael MacDonagh, *The Irish at the Front* (London: Hodder and Stoughton, 1916), 77; Hanna, *Pals*, 80.
28. DCLA, RDFA/005: Tobin to his father, 13 August 1915; TNA, WO 95/4296: 31st Brigade.
29. Cited in Hanna, *Pals*, 76.
30. David Fitzpatrick, 'Imperial Loyalties: Irishmen, Anzacs, and the Conflict of Empires at Gallipoli', *The Irish Sword*, XXX, 121 (Summer 2016), 305–31, at 319; Johnstone, *Orange*, 127.
31. DCLA, RDFA.018: Gallipoli Memories Diary.
32. MacDonagh, *Irish*, 76.
33. *The National Volunteer*, 1 January 1916, 5.
34. TNA, WO 95/4296: 6th and 7th RDF.
35. CWGC download, 17 June 2016.
36. Hanna, *Pals*, 202.
37. *DEM*, 11 October 1915, 4.
38. TNA, WO 95/4296: 6th RDF; Carver, *Turkish Front*, 79.
39. Cooper, *Tenth*, 92.
40. *DEM*, 31 August 1915, 5.

41. *DEM*, 11 October 1915, 4.
42. *IT*, 8 October 1915, 4.
43. NAM, Drury 1, 88.
44. NAM, Drury 1, 89.
45. NAM, Drury 1, 94.
46. *DEM*, 11 October 1915, 4.
47. *ET*, 4 September 1915, 5.
48. DCLA, RDFA/018: Gallipoli Memories Diary. See also Poole Hickman's account of capturing a female sniper in *DEM*, 31 August 1915, 5, and interview with Douglas Riddle: IWM interview 9345, Reel 2: www.iwm.org.uk/collections/item/object/80009134 (accessed 13 June 2016).
49. CWGC download, 17 June 2016; TNA, WO 95/4296: 6th RDF.
50. TNA, WO 95/4296: 6th RDF.
51. NAM, Drury 1, 98.
52. Hanna, *Pals*, 91–4.
53. NAM, Drury 1, 85.
54. Macleod, *Gallipoli*, 60.
55. NAM, Drury 1, 102.
56. TNA, WO 95/4296: 6th RDF and 7th RDF; Hart, *Gallipoli*, 361–5; Orr, *Field*, 121–6; *DEM*, 11 October 1915, 4.
57. *DEM*, 11 October 1915, 4. See also NAM, Drury 1, 103–4.
58. IWM 97/16/1: Ford Papers.
59. TNA, WO 95/4296: 6th and 7th RDF.
60. Hanna, *Pals*, 107; www.cwgc.org/find-war-dead/casualty/684461/WILKIN,%20ALBERT%20EDWARD (accessed 9 June 2016).
61. Hanna, *Pals*, 106; www.cwgc.org/find-war-dead/casualty/1735608/HARRISON,%20RICHARD%20SCORER%20MOLYNEUX (accessed 17 June 2016).
62. DCLA, RDFA/005: E. Hamilton to Dr R. F. Tobin, 19 August 1915.
63. CWGC download, 17 June 2016.
64. DCLA, RDFA/018: Gallipoli Memories Diary.
65. TNA, WO 95/4296: 7th RDF.
66. Hanna, *Pals*, 118.
67. Fox, *Inniskilling*, 194–9.
68. NAM, Drury 1, 111.
69. Ibid., 114.
70. Ibid., 115.
71. Ibid., 116.
72. Ibid., 116.
73. TNA, WO 95/4296: 6th RDF.
74. Cited in Hanna, *Pals*, 128.
75. Cooper, *Tenth*, 117 and 120. See also *ET*, 4 September 1915, 5.
76. NAM, Drury 1, 127.
77. Ibid., 128.
78. Ibid., 135.
79. Ibid., 144.
80. NAM, Drury 1, 143.
81. DCLA, RDFA/018: Gallipoli Memories Diary.
82. NAM, Drury 1, 152.
83. Hanna, *Pals*, 130. Hanna first floated the idea of a book about Suvla Bay in a letter to *The Irish Times*, in which he talked about the 10th Division generally rather than just the 7th Dublins or D Company. See *IT*, 7 December 1915, 6.

84. *ET*, 1 November 1915, 1; www.cwgc.org/find-war-dead/casualty/364896/FINN, %20P (accessed 20 June 2016).

85. *DEM*, 28 August 1915, 4; www.cwgc.org/find-war-dead/casualty/1735607/ GREENE,%20HENRY (accessed 20 June 2016); London Stamp Exchange, *Our Heroes* (London: London Stamp Exchange, 1988 edn, of 1916 publication), 116.

86. National Archive of Australia [NAA], First Australian Imperial Force Personnel Dossiers, 1914–1920, B2455: Ryan, Mitchell. Archives New Zealand, Wellington Office: Saunders, Thomas WW1 10/1329. For Saunders, see also Kinsella, *Out*, 106.

87. Australians: Private 1276 Joseph Guilfoyle, Private 1576 Thaddeus Coyne, Private 2003 Henry Smith, Private 146 Albert Stapleton, Corporal 1389 Frederick Merry, Private 1801 Thomas Lyons, Corporal 208 William Young and Lance Corporal 1294 William Mann. New Zealanders: Lance Corporal 970A Albert Bailey; Private 9771 William Moore. For Young see also Kinsella, *Out*, 140–1.

88. CWGC download, 17 June 2016. The figure for the 6th includes eight men who died having been ill or wounded and been evacuated from Gallipoli, while the 7th's figure includes nine such men. They died in Egypt, Greece or Malta.

89. Hanna, *Pals*, 148–50; CWGC download, 17 June 2016.

90. CWGC download 17 June 2016. Data in this download has been combined with that gathered from all the sources used for this book, plus further material from *Soldiers Died*. Of the 128 dead in the 6th Dublins, 80 seemed to have no Dublin connection at all, not even enlisting in the city, compared to 48 who were born, enlisted or resided in the city/county, or had a next-of-kin there. In contrast, of 115 dead in the 7th Dublins, 71 had such a connection, 41 did not and 3 were unclear. More widely, around one-third of the 10th Division at Gallipoli was probably not Irish. See Nicholas Perry, 'Nationality in the Irish Infantry Regiments in the First World War', *Irish Sword*, XII (1994), 65–95, at 79.

91. *DEM*, 28 August 1915, 3 and 31 August 1915, 5; *ET*, 31 August 1915, 3; *IT*, 31 August 1915, 5; *ET*, 3 September 1915, 3.

92. *DEM*, 28 August 1915, 3.

93. *IT*, 30 August 1915, 6.

94. *IT*, 29 August 1915, 4.

95. *IT*, 10 September 1915, 6 and *DEM*, 10 September 1915, 5.

96. *EH*, 3 September 1915, 1 and 2; *DEM*, 2 September 1915, 3 and 3 September 1915, 3; *IT*, 4 September 1915, 6; *DEM*, 13 September 1915, 3; *WIT*, 18 September 1915, 10; *EH*, 21 September 1915, 2; *EH*, 24 September 1915, 2; *EH*, 6 October 1915, 5; *DEM*, 9 October 1915, 3; *ET*, 25 January 1916, 5.

97. *SH*, 23 October 1915, 3.

98. *DEM*, 11 October 1915, 4.

99. See, for example, *IT*, 11 November 1915, 6; *WIT*, 23 October 1915, 8. There was a flurry of stories around the division as a whole in early 1916 when Hamilton's dispatch on Suvla Bay was issued: *FJ*, 7 January 1916, 7; *ET*, 7 January 1916, 6; *FJ*, 17 January 1916, 6; *ET*, 17 January 1916, 6. There was then a minor controversy through letters to *The Irish Times* about the apparent downplaying of the role of the 7th Dublins in Hamilton's narrative: *IT*, 22 January 1916, 6 & 25 January 1916, 7.

100. Hart, *Gallipoli*, 401, 413 and 435.

101. Wylly, *Neill's, III*, 54–5.

102. DCLA, RDFA/001/02: Harry Loughlin to Monica Roberts, 30 August 1915.

103. DCLA, RDFA/080: Andrew Horne to his mother, 14 January 1916.

104. Hart, *Gallipoli*, 435–51.

105. Fitzpatrick, 'Imperial', 317–18 and 331.
106. *FJ*, 21 August 1916, 7.
107. *FJ*, 9 March 1917, 6.
108. www.bbc.co.uk/history/british/easterrising/songs/rs_song06.shtml (accessed 20 June 2016); David Cooper, *The Musical Traditions of Northern Ireland and its Diaspora: Community and Conflict* (Farnham: Ashgate, 2009), 129.
109. NAM, Drury 2, 32.

7 Preparations

1. BMH.WS0923, 2: Callendar, I.
2. *IT*, 8 January 1916, 6; *DEM*, 14 January 1916, 4; *IT*, 16 January 1916, 5.
3. *DEM*, 8 January 1916, 3.
4. Tables A5.2 and A5.3.
5. *DEM*, 3 January 1916, 3.
6. Meleady, *Redmond*, 351–2; *DEM*, 11 January 1916, 5; *FJ*, 18 January 1916, 5.
7. *IT*, 17 January 1916, 6.
8. *FJ*, 11 February 1916, 5; *IT*, 12 February 1916, 6.
9. *FJ*, 19 February 1916, 5
10. *IT*, 17 March 1916, 3; *IT*, 20 March 1916, 3; *IT*, 10 April 1916, 7; *IT*, 17 April 1916, 6.
11. *DEM*, 11 March 1916, 6.
12. See for example, *NV*: 24 October 1914, 7–8; 7 November 1914, 7; 14 November 1914, 2 and 3; 21 November 1914, 7; 12 December 1914, 7; 19 December 1914, 2; 9 January 1915, 2; 16 January 1915, 2 and 7; 8 February 1915, 3; 27 February 1915, 5
13. *NV*, 23 January 1916, 3 and 30 January 1915, 3.
14. *FJ*, 5 April 1915, 5 and 6; *II*, 5 April 1915, 3 and 5–6.
15. *FJ*, 20 September 1915, 5.
16. TNA, CO 904/94 and 98.
17. TNA, CO 904/99.
18. TNA, CO 904/99.
19. Foy and Barton, *Easter Rising*, 1–39.
20. *IV*, 26 December 1914, Supplement; *IV*, 20 February 1915, Supplement.
21. Peter F. Whearity, *The Easter Rising of 1916 in North County Dublin: A Skerries Perspective* (Dublin: Four Courts Press, 2013), 20–1.
22. *IV*, 20 March 1915, 4.
23. Connell, *Who's*, 6; *IV*, 25 December 1915, 5.
24. UCD Archives, Papers of Éamon de Valera, P150/450: Volunteer Exercise, Finglas, 1915.
25. *IV*, 29 January 1916, 5.
26. BMH.WS0564, 15: Byrne, T. F.
27. *DEM*, 17 March 1916, 2.
28. Ibid.
29. *IT*, 28 March 1916, 5; *DEM*, 31 March 1916, 5; *IT*, 31 March 1916, 5.
30. *IT*, 12 April 1916, 4.
31. BMH MSP34REF56969, 30: McCabe, M.; UCD Archives, Papers of Ernie O'Malley, P17b/105/117: McCabe, M.
32. BMH.WS1758, 2: Burke, J. J.
33. BMH.WS0097, 1: Hayes, R.
34. Ann Matthews, *The Kimmage Garrison, 1916: Making Billy-can Bombs at Larkfield* (Dublin: Four Courts, 2010), 15–17.

35. BMH.WS1744, 1–2: Nunan, S.; see also www.rte.ie/archives/exhibitions/1993-easter-1916/2017-survivors/609028-the-survivors-sean-nunan/ (accessed 30 November 2016). For details of the Kimmage Garrison see BMH.WS0156, 10–12: Robinson, S.
36. *ET*, 8 January 1916, 5.
37. *IT*, 7 March 1916, 5; TNA, WO 339/17464: Barron, H.
38. www.cwgc.org/find-war-dead/casualty/732292/HOWARD,%20THOMAS (accessed 1 November 2016); *EH*, 2 February 1916, 6.
39. www.cwgc.org/find-war-dead/casualty/1763417/GALLACHER,%20JAMES (accessed 1 November 2016); Soldiers' Wills (http://soldierswills.nationalarchives.ie/search/sw/home.jsp).
40. CWGC download, 1 November 2016; TNA, WO 95/1974: 8th and 9th RDF; Johnstone, *Orange*, 207. 'Puits 14 bis' meaning, in effect, 'Mine shaft 14b'.
41. CWGC download, 1 November 2016; TNA, WO 95/1974: 8th RDF.
42. www.cwgc.org/find-war-dead/casualty/265580/BYRNE,%20PATRICK (accessed 1 November 2016); Soldiers' Wills; TNA, WO 95/1481: 2nd RDF.
43. DCLA, RDFA/001/01: Clarke to Roberts, 22 April 1916.
44. BMH.WS0340, 5: Traynor, O.
45. BMH.WS0923, 2: Callendar, I.
46. BMH.WS0585, 47: Robbins, F.
47. BMH.WS0564, 16: Byrne, T. F.
48. BMH.WS1687, 4 and 5: Colley, H. E.
49. BMH.WS1746, 2: Connolly, M.
50. BMH.WS0157, 19–20: O'Connor, J.
51. TNA, WO 95/1974: 9th RDF.
52. BMH.WS0716, 2: Molloy, M.
53. BMH.WS0541, 17: de Paor, N.
54. BMH.WS0585, 39: Monteith, R.
55. TNA, WO 363. I am grateful to James Taylor for alerting me to Bailey.
56. Townshend, *Easter*, 127–31.
57. BMH.WS0081, 11: Hobson, B.
58. BMH.WS0007, 9–10: O'Briain, L.
59. BMH.WS1768, 4: McDonnell, A.
60. BMH.WS1043, 45: Lawless, J. V. See also BMH.WS0263, 13: Slater, T.; BMH.WS1758, 2–3: Burke, J. J.; BMH.WS0564, 17: T. F. Byrne; BMH.WS1687, 6: Colley, H. E.; BMH.WS0428, 2: Devine, T; BMH.WS0585, 51: Robbins, Frank; BMH.WS0376, 2: O'Kelly, P.
61. BMH.WS0716, 3–4: Molloy, M. See also BMH.WS0323, 5: O'Brien, L., who heard Connolly say, 'If we can continue fighting for three days, being a uniformed force, we may be able to invoke the terms of the Geneva Convention.'
62. BMH.WS1746, 3–4: Connolly, M.

8 Rising

1. BMH.WS0327, 19: Egan, P. See also BMH.WS0282, 4: O'Grady, C. J.
2. See p. 163.
3. Connell, *Who's*, 12, 13, 143, 169, 192, 228, 239 and 251; McCarthy, *Cumann*, 52–72. For details of the fighting in Dublin see Derek Molyneux and Darren Kelly, *When the Clock Struck in 1916: Close-Quarter Combat in the Easter Rising* (Wilton: Collins Press, 2015). Thorough maps of the Rising are found in Fearghal McGarry, 'The Easter Rising', in Crowley et al., *Atlas*, 240–57.

4. Neil Richardson, *According to Their Lights: Stories of Irishmen in the British Army, Easter 1916* (Wilton: Collins, 2015), 3–4.

5. Richardson, *Lights*, 190 and 220.

6. Richardson, *Lights*, 245, 246, 262 and 264.

7. TNA, WO 339/47808: Eugene Sheehy; Richardson, *Lights*, 248; Daire Hogan, 'Sheehy, Eugene', in McGuire and Quinn, *Dictionary of Irish Biography* (http://dib .cambridge.org/viewReadPage.do?articleId=a8028).

8. TNA, WO 339/64722: P. Guéret; Richardson, *Lights*, 358–9.

9. Richardson, *Lights*, 282–4. See also Michael Pegum, 'The Gorgeous Wrecks and the Opening Shots in the Battle of Mount Street Bridge', *The Irish Sword*, XXXI, 123 (Summer 2017), 75–86.

10. Glasnevin Trust, *1916 Necrology: 485* (Dublin: Glasnevin Trust, 2016), 6.

11. TNA, WO 95/1974: 9th RDF.

12. www.cwgc.org/find-war-dead/casualty/563423/COLGAN,%20B (accessed 1 November 2016); *FJ*, 19 May 1916, 4.

13. TNA, WO 95/1481: 2nd RDF.

14. BMH.WS0249, 21: Henderson, F.

15. BMH.WS2433, 11: Donnelly, S.

16. BMH.WS0409, 24–5: Jackson, V.

17. BMH.WS1687, 6–8: Colley, H. E.

18. BMH.WS0340, 9–10: Traynor, O.

19. UCD Archives, Papers of Peadar McNulty, LA9: Manuscript of a short history of the 'A' Company, 1st Battalion, Dublin Brigade IRA by Peadar McNulty.

20. www.bbc.co.uk/taster/projects/easter-rising-voice-of-a-rebel/share (accessed 30 November 2016). See also BMH Pensions MSP34REF21506.

21. BMH.WS1744, 2: Nunan, S.

22. http://the1916proclamation.ie/ (accessed 15 November 2017).

23. BMH Pensions 24SP2824: Dalton, P.

24. BMH.WS0748, 7–9: Doyle, J. J.

25. BMH.WS0428, 2–3: Devine, T. W.

26. www.bbc.co.uk/taster/projects/easter-rising-voice-of-a-rebel/share (accessed 30 November 2016).

27. BMH.WS0461, 1–2: Byrne, J.

28. BMH.WS0191, 4–5: Reynolds, J. F.; BMH.WS0533, 2–3: Dowling, Thomas; BMH.WS0755, 118 and 122–3: Prendergast, S; BMH.WS0800, 16–18: O'Flanagan, M.; BMH.WS0800, 19: O'Flanagan, M.

29. www.grantonline.com/grant-family-individuals/grant-charles-1881/CW-Grant.htm (accessed 8 December 2016); TNA, WO 71/351: Heuston, S.

30. TNA, WO 339/26261: G. A. Neilan; *DEM*, 12 May 1916, 1; *II*, 8 May 1916, 2; *WIT*, 29 April 1916, 12; *IT*, 13 May 1916, 5; Richardson, *Lights*, 85–87; Ronan McGreevy, *Wherever the Firing Line Extends: Ireland and the Western Front* (Dublin: History Press Ireland, 2016), 130; Stephen Gwynn, *John Redmond's Last Years* (London: Edward Arnold, 1919), 227; www.dublin-fusiliers.com/battaliions/10-batt/officers/neilan/neilan.html and www.dublin-fusiliers.com/battaliions/10-batt/officers/neilan/family/neilan-family.html (accessed 8 December 2016); Ronan McGreevy, 'An Irishman's Diary', *IT*, 28 March 2016, 17; Ronan McGreevy, 'The Easter Rising Family Rift That Never Healed', *IT Online*, 24 April 2016, www.irishtimes.com/news/ire land/irish-news/the-easter-rising-family-rift-that-never-healed-1.2622619 (accessed 8 December 2016); BMH, MSP34REF1756: Neilan, A. Other brothers on different sides were the Saurins and Malones, and William Kent (TNA,

WO 363: Kent, William Luman 6425), brother of Éamonn Ceannt, discussed in: Tom Burke, 'Attitudes of Irish Soldiers Serving in the British Army During and After the 1916 Easter Rising in Dublin', *The Blue Cap*, 16 (December 2009), 1–17, at 3. Burke says that the Saurin brother in the British army was not in Dublin during the Rising whereas Richardson says he was: Richardson, *Lights*, 87. It is not clear whether Joseph Guéret was a runner for the Irish Republican Brotherhood during the Rising, but he was in mid-1917, when his brother Paul, an officer in the 8th Royal Dublin Fusiliers, was arrested in a case of mistaken identity while home on leave. See Richardson, *Lights*, 359 and p. 283.

31. *WIT*, 8 July 1916, 1; www.cwgc.org/find-war-dead/casualty/899851/BRENNAN, %20FRANCIS%20A (accessed 8 December 2016).
32. BMH.WS0249, 20: Henderson, F.
33. BMH.WS0267, 11: Pounch, J.
34. BMH.WS0822, 4 and 6: Stapleton, W. J.
35. BMH.WS0423, 2: Byrne, V.; BMH.WS0139, 4: Walker, M.
36. BMH.WS0139, 5: Walker, M.
37. BMH.WS1768, 4: McDonnell, A.
38. BMH.WS1768, 6: McDonnell, A.
39. BMH.WS1637, 5: Banks, H.; BMH.WS0166, 3: Doyle, S.
40. BMH.WS1768, 11: McDonnell, A.
41. BMH.WS1511, 29–30: Doyle, G.
42. BMH.WS243, 4: Foran, J.
43. BMH.WS0327, 19: Egan, P. See also BMH.WS0282, 4: O'Grady, C. J.
44. BMH.WS1758, 5–6: Burke, J. J.
45. BMH.WS1758, 5–6: Burke, J. J.; BMH.WS1511, 8–10: Doyle, G.
46. BMH.WS0352, 2: Murphy, W.
47. TNA, WO 339/15968: A. L. Ramsay.
48. *SH*, 5 February 1916, 5; *II*, 5 May 1916, 1; *EH*, 8 June 1915, 5; Richardson, *Lights*, 31–3 and 37–8.
49. Richardson, *Lights*, 149 and 157; www.cwgc.org/find-war-dead/casualty/899558/MULHERN,%20JOHN and www.cwgc.org/find-war-dead/casualty/900385/NOLAN,%20J (accessed 8 December 2016).
50. BMH.WS0871, p0-3–4; *DEM*, 5 May 1916, 1; *IT, SF Handbook*, 58. Glasnevin Trust, *1916 Necrology*; Richardson, *Lights*, 289–92.
51. B. P. McCann, 'The Diary of Second Lieutenant A. V. G. Killingley, Easter Week, 1916', *Irish Sword*, XX, 81 (Summer 1997), 246–53, at 247.
52. BMH.WS0097, 3–4: Hayes, R.; Jane O'Keeffe, ed., *The 1916 Rising Oral History Collection, Parts 1 and 2* (Tralee: privately published, 2015), 193 and 218; BMH.WS0149, 5–6: Weston, C.; BMH.WS0097, 4: Hayes, R.
53. Fearghal McGarry, *The Abbey Rebels of 1916: A Lost Revolution* (Dublin: Gill and Macmillan, 1915), 247–63.
54. BMH.WS0391, 32–3: Molony, H.
55. Ibid., 33.
56. BMH.WS1746, 5: Connolly, M.
57. BMH.WS0391, 34–5: Molony, H. See also BMH.WS1746, 6: Connolly, M.
58. BMH.WS0391, 36: Molony, H.
59. BMH.WS1184, 6: Costello, E.
60. Valerie Jones, *Rebel Prods: The Forgotten Story of Protestant Radical Nationalists and the 1916 Rising* (Dublin: Ashfield, 2016), 233–40.
61. BMH.WS0391, 37: Molony, H.
62. BMH.WS1746, 9 and 11: Connolly, M.

63. BMH.WS0357, 6: Lynn, K.
64. BMH.WS0357, 6: Lynn, K.
65. BMH.WS1746, 12–14: Connolly, M.
66. BMH.WS0391, 39: Molony, H.
67. BMH.WS0357, 6: Lynn, K.
68. BMH.WS0391, 40: Molony, H.
69. TNA, WO 97: Michael Mallin; Connell, *Who's*, 252; BMH.WS0382, 1–2: Mallin, T.; Brian Hughes, *16 Lives: Michael Mallin* (Dublin: O'Brien, 2012), 20–40. For Mallin, see also O'Keeffe, *1916 Rising*, 318–19.
70. BMH.WS0585: 18–19: Robbins, F. Of these, Vincent Poole was at the GPO rather than on St Stephen's Green (see Connell, *Who's*, 66).
71. BMH.WS0733, 44–5: O'Shea, J.
72. BMH.WS0585, 57–61: Robbins, R.
73. BMH.WS0585, 66–7 and 87: Robbins, R.
74. Glasnevin Trust, *1916 Necrology*, 6.
75. Johnstone, *Orange*, 211.
76. TNA, WO 95/1974: 8th and 9th RDF; CWGC download 7 December 2016.
77. *Soldiers Died*; *WIT*, 4 November 1916, 8. In Parker's case, the most recent action had been on 21 April on the right bank of the Tigris (see TNA, WO 95/5161: 8th Cheshires), while for Downey it had been on 18 April at 'Twin Pimples' (see TNA, WO 95/5105: 7th Indian Infantry Brigade).
78. Jourdain and Fraser, *Connaught Rangers, I*, 510–15.
79. *IT*, 26 April 1916, 5.
80. NLI, MS 9,620: Moylan Diary, 25 April 1916, 70–7.
81. *SH*, 3-6-1916, 3; Richardson, *Lights*, 20.
82. *WIT*, 29 April 1916, 10; www.cwgc.org/find-war-dead/casualty/899858/BROSNAN,%20PATRICK (accessed 8 December 2016); Richardson, *Lights* 105.
83. Richardson, *Lights*, 224 and 227.
84. BMH.WS0646, 6: Christian, W.
85. BMH.WS0923, 9: Callendar, I.
86. See p. 214.
87. dh.tcd.ie/martindiary/site/xscan.xq?id=martindiary_19160425 (accessed 9 December 2016.)
88. *IT*, 25 April 1916, 4; see also 5.
89. *IT*, 26 April 1916, 5; 27 April 1916, 2.
90. BMH.WS0270, 6–7: O'Reilly, E.; Conor Kostick, *16 Lives: Michael O'Hanrahan* (Dublin: O'Brien, 2015), 20 and 78.
91. BMH.WS0564, 18–21: Byrne, T. F.
92. McCann, 'Killingley', 247.
93. BMH.WS0461, 2–3: Byrne, J. See also Richardson, *Lights*, 195–6.
94. BMH.WS0097, 4: Hayes, R. See also BMH.WS1043, 61: Lawless, J. V.
95. BMH.WS0631, 1–2, Byrne, B. C.
96. BMH.WS0585, 70: Robbins, F..
97. BMH.WS748, 9: Doyle, J. J.
98. BMH.WS0359, 5–6: de Burca, A.
99. BMH.WS1687, 17: Colley, H. E.
100. BMH.WS0423, 3–4: Byrne, V.
101. BMH.WS0208, 8: Kavanagh, S.
102. BMH.WS0043, 5–6: Foran, J.; BMH.WS0327, 28–30: Egan, P.
103. BMH.WS0282, 6: O'Grady, C. J.

104. BMH MSP34REF56969, 30 and W34E7757, 27: McCabe, M.; UCD, O'Malley, P17a/105/116: McCabe, M.
105. BMH.WS0733, 47–8: O'Shea, J.
106. BMH.WS0733, 51: O'Shea, J.
107. BMH.WS0340, 12–14: Traynor, O.
108. McGarry, *Rising*, 99–100.

9 Falling

1. TNA, WO 95/1974: 8th RDF.
2. See p. 163.
3. Glasnevin Trust, *1916 Necrology*, 6.
4. TNA, WO 95/1974: 8th RDF.
5. TNA, WO 95/2247: 2nd RI Rifles; Taylor, *2nd*, 81–82; *EH*, 13 June 1916, 4; www .cwgc.org/find-war-dead/casualty/64922/BYRNE,%20THOMAS%20JOSEPH (accessed 8 December 2016).
6. Jourdain and Fraser, *Connaught Rangers, I*, 518.
7. NLI, MS 9,620: Moylan Diary, 79–82.
8. McCann, 'Killingley', 248.
9. Richardson, *Lights*, 230–1 and 291; TNA, WO 363 (Hare).
10. TNA, WO 363, Service Records.
11. BMH.WS0348, 6: Gerrard, E; Richardson, *Lights*, 296–7. Gerrard's uniform is now on display in the reading room of the Military Archives at Cathal Brugha Barracks (source: author's visit, 16 February 2017).
12. SH, 27 May 1916, 5; Richardson, *Lights*, 293 and 302; IT, *SF Handbook*, pp, 58 and 252.
13. BMH.WS0979, 1 and 9: Barton, R. C.; TNA, WO 339/56863: R. C. Barton.
14. BMH.WS0755, 136: Prendergast, S.
15. BMH.WS0755, 136: Prendergast, S.
16. BMH.WS0733, 80: O'Shea, J.
17. BMH.WS0585, 89: Robbins, F.
18. *DEM*, 12 May 1916, 3; James W. Taylor, *Guilty but Insane, J. C. Bowen-Colthurst: Villain or Victim?* (Cork: Mercier Press, 2016), 89–90 and 230–3. See also *FJ*, 17 October 1916, 5.
19. BMH.WS0428, 4: Devine, T.
20. BMH.WS0541, 26–7: de Paor, N.
21. BMH.WS0268, 8: Cosgrave, W. T.
22. BMH.WS482, 5: McNamara, R.
23. BMH.WS0167, 8: Byrne, C.
24. BMH.WS1043, 69–70: Lawless, J. V. See also O'Keeffe, *1916 Rising*, 176.
25. BMH.WS0097, 4–5: Hayes, R.
26. BMH.WS1043, 74: Lawless, J. V.
27. BMH.WS0263, 20: Slater, T.
28. www.thebikecomesfirst.com/the-irish-olympic-cyclist-who-fought-in-the-easter-rising/ (accessed 2 December 2016).
29. BMH.WS0139, 6: Walker, M; Connell, *Who's*, 162 and 166.
30. DCLA, RDFA 001/75: Monica Roberts Diary, 24 April 1916.
31. http://mountstreet1916.ie/ (accessed 1 December 2016).
32. In fact, while Louise Nolan was awarded the Military Medal, Kathleen Pierce was not. Such an award was made to Florence Williams for actions elsewhere in the city. See *SH*, 27 January 1917, 1.

33. BMH.WS0198, 19–21: Walsh, T.
34. BMH.WS0646, 7–10: Christian, W; BMH.WS208, 10–11: Kavanagh, S.
35. Brian Hughes, Billy Campbell and Susan Schriebman, 'Contested Memories: Revisiting the Battle of Mount Street Bridge', *British Journal for Military History*, 4, 1 (2017), 2–22.
36. Glasnevin Trust, *1916 Necrology*, 6.
37. NAM, Drury 2, 130.
38. Privates 8282 David Kirwan and 10284 Edward Murphy: www.cwgc.org/find-war -dead/casualty/629125/KIRWAN,%20D and www.cwgc.org/find-war-dead /casualty/629621/MURPHY,%20EDWARD (both accessed 8 December 2016); Jourdain and Fraser, *Connaught Rangers, I*, 518.
39. www.cwgc.org/find-war-dead/casualty/124896/JORDAN,%20T (accessed 8 December 2016).
40. Johnstone, *Orange*, 209.
41. TNA, WO 95/1974: 8th RDF.
42. Cited in Carole Hope, *Worshipper and Worshipped: Across the Divide – An Irish Padre of the Great War, Fr Willie Doyle Chaplain to the Forces 1915–1917* (Brighton: Reveille, 2013), 251.
43. TNA, WO 95/1974: 8th RDF.
44. TNA, WO 95/1974: 8th and 9th RDF.
45. CWGC download, 7 December 2016.
46. *FJ*, 22 May 1916, 4; *EH*, 12 July 1916, 3; *FJ*, 22 August 1916, 3; TNA, WO 161/98/647: Lance Corporal 15654 William Douglas.
47. BMH.WS0149, 9: Weston, C.
48. BMH.WS0097, 5, Hayes, R.
49. BMH.WS0147, 5: McAllister, B; BMH.WS0149, 9–10: Weston, C. McAllister suggested six or seven while Weston said only two and named them as Duke and O'Reilly from St Margarets.
50. NLI, MS 9,620: Moylan Diary, 82–3.
51. Private 2743 William Walker of the 5th (Royal Irish) Lancers lost his life that day. He was born in Glasgow but is listed in *Soldiers Died* as having resided in Dublin.
52. McCann, 'Killingley', 248.
53. BMH.WS0263, 21: Slater, T.
54. BMH.WS0585, 78: Robbins, F.
55. BMH.WS0533, 2–3: Dowling, T.
56. BMH.WS0923, 21–2: Callendar, I.
57. BMH.WS0208, 12: Kavanagh, S.
58. BMH.WS268, 8: Cosgrave, W. T.
59. BMH.WS0243, 8: Foran, J.
60. BMH.WS0340, 17: Traynor, O.
61. BMH.WS1687, 20–4: Colley, H. E.
62. BMH.WS0359, 16: de Burca, A.
63. BMH.WS0541, 27–8: de Paor, N.
64. BMH.WS0359, 13–14: de Burca, A.; BMH.WS748, 10: Doyle, J. J.
65. Glasnevin Trust, *1916 Necrology*, 6.
66. *FJ*, 1 June 1916, 5; www.cwgc.org/find-war-dead/casualty/629110/KINAHAN,%20J (accessed 8 December 2016).
67. TNA, WO 95/1974: 8th and 9th RDF.
68. McGarry, *Rising*, pp. 203–4.
69. BMH.WS0800, 21: O'Flanagan, M.

70. Richardson, *Lights*, 342–3; Foy and Barton, *Easter Rising*, 184–5; Joseph E. A. Connell, *Dublin Rising, 1916* (Dublin: Wordwell, 2015), 167–71.

71. BMH.WS1511, 14: Doyle, G.

72. BMH.WS0409, 25: Jackson, V.

73. BMH.WS0564, 22–3: Byrne, T. F.

74. BMH.WS0097, 5–8: Hayes, R.

75. BMH.WS1043, 113: Lawless, J. V. On the Battle of Ashbourne, see also Whearity, *Easter Rising*, 30–9; Paul O'Brien, *Field of Fire: The Battle of Ashbourne, 1916* (Dublin: New Island, 2012).

76. BMH.WS0097, 7: Hayes, R.; BMH.WS1043, 91–2: Lawless, J. V.

77. BMH.WS0149, 13: Weston, C.

78. BMH.WS0340, 18–19: Traynor, O.

79. BMH.WS0428, 7–8: Devine, T.

80. BMH.WS0359, 21: de Burca, A.

81. BMH.WS0428, 9–11: Devine, T.

82. BMH.WS1744, 3–4: Nunan, S.

83. BMH.WS0340, 21: Traynor, O.

84. Glasnevin Trust, *1916 Necrology*, 6.

85. TNA, WO 95/1974: 8th RDF.

86. TNA, WO 95/1974: 9th RDF.

87. TNA, WO 95/1974: 8th and 9th RDF.

88. www.cwgc.org/find-war-dead/casualty/1770936 (accessed 22 November 2017); see p. 11.

89. Johnstone, *Orange*, 212; Denman, *Unknown*, 70–1.

90. *DEM*, 28 October 1916, 3; TNA, WO 363.

91. TNA, WO 95/1974: 8th and 9th RDF; CWGC download 1 November 2016.

92. See p. 226; www.cwgc.org/find-war-dead/casualty/1765573/NAYLOR,%20JOHN (accessed 1 November 2016).

93. The Glasnevin Trust, *1916 Necrology* gives her date of death as 29 April, as do many other sources, but see the gravestone at: www.findagrave.com/cgi-bin/fg.cgi?page=gr&GRid=100954630 (accessed 8 December 2016). See also *EH*, 13 June 1916, 1; *FJ*, 23 May 1916, p. 4; /www.cwgc.org/find-war-dead/casualty/1765573/NAYLOR,%20JOHN (accessed 8 December 2016); Frank McNally, 'An Irishman's Diary', *IT*, 3 July 2014, 15.

94. dh.tcd.ie/martindiary/site/xscan.xq?id=martindiary_19160429 (accessed 9 December 2016).

95. BMH.WS0147, 9: McAllister, B.

96. McGarry, *Rising*, 209. John Lowe might have hoped for a more peaceful posting in Dublin after time at Gallipoli with the 15th Hussars. He later served on the Western Front, and was captured by the Germans in 1918, returning to Dublin in early 1920 to mid-1922 with the 15th Hussars. Post-war, he found minor fame in Hollywood as John Loder, not least as the third husband of 'the most beautiful woman in the world', Hedy Lamarr. See *The Times*, 30 December 1988, 14; Ruth Barton, *Hedy Lamarr: The Most Beautiful Woman in Film* (Lexington: University Press of Kentucky, 2010), 63; His Majesty's Stationary Office, *Army List*, February 1920, cols. 253–4 and January 1922, cols. 284–5.

97. BMH.WS0428, 12: Devine, T.

98. BMH.WS0359, 24–25: de Burca, A.

99. BMH.WS0800, 25: O'Flanagan, M.

100. BMH.WS1758, 6–7: Burke, J. J.

101. Compiled from Glasnevin Trust, *1916 Necrology*.

102. *IT*, 16 May 1916, 5; TNA, WO 339/59798: R. L. Valentine.
103. BMH.WS0585, 81: Robbins, F.; Máirtin Ó Cathain, 'A Land Beyond the Seas: Irish and Scottish Republicans in Dublin, 1916', in Ruán O'Donnell, ed., *The Impact of the 1916 Rising: Among the Nations* (Dublin: Irish Academic Press, 2008), 37–48, at 46. Byrne's granddaughter discusses the case at: www.youtube.com/watch? v=NY_asteHzyE (accessed 9 December 2016). See also Connell, *Who's*, 254.
104. BMH.WS0585, 80–1: Robbins, F.
105. BMH.WS0376, 3–4: O'Kelly, P.
106. BMH.WS0822, 9: Stapleton, W. J.
107. BMH.WS0423, 4–5: Byrne, V.
108. BMH.WS0139, 7: Walker, M.
109. BMH.WS0377, 19: O'Mara, P.
110. BMH.WS1140, 9: Ward, P.
111. BMH.WS208, 13: Kavanagh, S.
112. BMH.WS0097, 9: Hayes, R.; BMH.WS0147, 9–10: McAllister, B.; BMH. WS0149, 14: Weston, C.
113. BMH.WS0482, 7–8: McNamara, R.
114. BMH.WS0167, 8: Byrne, C.
115. BMH.WS0428, 13: Devine, T. See also BMH.WS1746, 16: Connolly, M.
116. BMH.WS0340, 24: Traynor, O.
117. BMH.WS0585, 82–3: Robbins, F. See also BMH.WS0733, 55: O'Shea, J.
118. Richardson, *Lights*, 391; TNA, WO 364; TNA, WO 339/13301: P. A. Purser.

10 Consequences

1. BMH.WS0382, 4–7: Mallin, T.; TNA, WO 71/353: Michael Mallin; Hughes, *Mallin*, 171–85.
2. See p. 129.
3. Richard S. Grayson, ed., *At War with the 16th Irish Division, 1914–1918: The Staniforth Letters* (Barnsley: Pen and Sword, 2012), 104.
4. Johnstone, *Orange*, 212–13.
5. Cited in Hope, *Worshipper*, 275.
6. DCLA, RDFA/001/01: J. Clarke to Roberts, 11 May 1916; RDFA/001/14: C. Fox to Roberts, 31 May 1916. See also: RDFA/001/14: C. Fox to Roberts, 12 May 1916; DCLA, RDFA/001/22: G. Soper to Roberts, 20 May 1916; RDFA/001/18: J. Brooks to Roberts, 14 June 1916; RDFA/001/02: H. Loughlin to Roberts, 17 June 1916.
7. www.cwgc.org/find-war-dead/casualty/899879/BYRNE,%20JAMES (accessed 8 December 2016); TNA, WO 372; Soldiers' Wills; Richardson, *Lights*, 115. I am very grateful to Neil Richardson for sharing with me material from his database of casualties. This was especially helpful in clarifying the links to Dublin of some victims. He also answered very specific questions which provided further assistance.
8. Richardson, *Lights*, 390.
9. Glasnevin Trust, *1916 Necrology*.
10. NLI, MS 9,620: Moylan Diary, 2 May 1916, 96.
11. *FJ*, 10 May 1916. 3.
12. *DEM*, 8 May 1916, 3.
13. BMH.WS482, 8: McNamara, R.
14. BMH.WS0147, 10: McAllister, B.
15. BMH.WS0149, 15: Weston, C.
16. BMH.WS0203. 5: O'Neill, E.

17. Charles Townshend, *Political Violence in Ireland: Government and Resistance since 1848* (Clarendon, 1983), 410.
18. DCLA, RDFA/001/45: H. Harrington to Roberts, 21 June 1916.
19. BMH.WS1687, 27–8: Colley, H.
20. Cited in Lyons, *Enigma*, 293.
21. Jane Leonard, 'The Reaction of Irish Officers in the British Army to the Easter Rising of 1916', in Hugh Cecil and Peter H. Liddle, eds., *Facing Armageddon: The First World War Experience* (London: Leo Cooper, 1996), 256–86, at 264 and 266. Forthcoming work by Peter Barton points to new information on desertions, though in very small numbers. See Ronan McGreevy, 'Secret Files Reveal How Deeply the Easter Rising Affected Irishmen Serving in First World War', *IT Online*, 6 May 2018, www.irish-times.com/news/ireland/irish-news/secret-files-reveal-how-deeply-the-easter-rising-affected-irishmen-serving-in-first-world-war-1.3486276 (accessed 9 May 2018).
22. www.taoiseach.gov.ie/eng/Historical_Information/State_Commemorations/The_Executed_Leaders_of_the_1916_Rising.html (accessed 06 April 2018).
23. *Hansard*, HC Deb, 11 May 1916, vol. 82, cols. 935-51; *FJ*, 11 May 1916, 3.
24. *Hansard*, HC Deb, 11 May 1916, vol. 82, cols. 952–60.
25. *DEM*, 12 May 1916, 3; *FJ*, 13 May 1916, 7.
26. *DEM*, 2 May 1916, 3.
27. BMH.WS0382, 4–7: Mallin, T.; TNA, WO 71/353: Michael Mallin; Hughes, *Mallin*, 171–85.
28. BMH.WS0979, 1–7: Barton, R. C.; TNA, WO 339/56863: R. C. Barton.
29. See pp. 286 and 301.
30. *FJ*, 16 May 1916, 3.
31. *DEM*, 26 August 1915, 3. See also *FJ*, 26 October 1915, 5 and *WIT*, 1 January 1916, 1.
32. TNA, WO 161/98/447. I am grateful to James Taylor for alerting me to Egan.
33. *IT, SF Handbook*, 128–49. Police file: TNA, MEPO 2/10668; Irish Brigade papers; TNA, WO141/9.
34. TNA, WO 363.
35. BMH.WS0423, 6–7: Byrne, V.
36. BMH.WS1768, 21: McDonnell, A.
37. *IT, SF Handbook*, 79–91.
38. BMH.WS0391, 41: Molony, H.
39. BMH.WS0149, 15: Weston, C.
40. BMH.WS0376, 5–6: O'Kelly, P.
41. *IT, SF Handbook*, 87.
42. The range is due to possible duplication which cannot be resolved.
43. Leonard, 'Reaction', 258. Leonard says that 'a massive 3,500 were arrested' and that 'Almost half had taken no part in the rising and were subsequently released. The remaining 1,800 were sent to internment camps in England and Wales.'
44. An intriguing case is the listing of Private T. Parker of Holles Row, described as a private in the 2nd Leinsters when he was shipped to Stafford on 8 May, yet the only reference to him appears to be in the deportations lists. See *SF Handbook*, 79.
45. UCD Archives, Papers of Eoin MacNeill, LA1/G/132: MacNeill to his wife 31 May 1916; UCD LA1/G/134: John O'Brien to Agnes MacNeill, 8 June 1916.
46. See p. 205.
47. UCD, MacNeill, LA1/G/158: Eoin MacNeill, Completed Penal Reform League 'Questionnaire for Ex-Prisoners', n.d. See also BMH.WS1511, 38–85: Doyle, G.

48. On life at Frongoch, see Derek Molyneux and Darren Kelly, *Those of Us Who Must Die: Execution, Exile and Revival after the Easter Rising* (Wilton: Collins Press, 2017), 226–42.
49. NAI, CSORP/1918/16627.
50. BMH.WS0149, 16: Weston, C.
51. BMH.WS0585, 104–5: Robbins, F.
52. BMH.WS0585, 108–10: Robbins, F
53. *IT, SF Handbook*, 69.
54. BMH.WS0149, 16: Weston, C.
55. BMH.WS0147, 11: McAllister, B.
56. BMH.WS0564, 25–7: Byrne, T. F.
57. BMH MSP34REF56969 30: McCabe, M.; UCD, O'Malley, P17a/105/116: McCabe, M. See pp. 286, 305, 307, 313, 322 and 344–5.
58. BMH 24SP2824, Dalton P.
59. BMH MSP34REF55705: O'Moore, P. M.
60. BMH.WS1043, 195–7: Lawless, J. V.
61. BMH.WS1744, 5–8: Nunan, S.
62. UCD, McNulty, LA9.
63. BMH.WS1511, 96: Doyle, G.
64. *FJ*, 19 October 1916, 5.
65. See p. 175.
66. BMH.WS0249, 28: Henderson, F.
67. BMH.WS0409, 25: Jackson, V. Other IRB members from Dublin to join the British army (though at the oubreak of war) included Robert Page and Stephen Barry. See BMH.WS0307, 1: McCarthy, T.; BMH.WS1765, 140: O'Kelly, S. T.
68. www.cwgc.org/find-war-dead/casualty/569134/FINN,%20T%20M (accessed 3 February 2017).

11 The Other 1916

1. TNA, WO 95/2510.
2. Halpern, *Naval History*, 310–4; Nigel Steel and Peter Hart, *Jutland, 1916: Death in the Grey Wastes* (London: Orion, 2003), 11–44.
3. Halpern, *Naval History*, 317.
4. Halpern, *Naval History*, 317–25.
5. Steel and Hart, *Jutland*, 147.
6. Steel and Hart, *Jutland*, 95–6; Halpern, *Naval History*, 118–19; John Brooks, *The Battle of Jutland* (Cambridge University Press, 2016), 458–9.
7. *Sailors Died.*
8. *EH*, 19 June 1916, 3.
9. *Sailors Died; DEM*, 8 June 1916, 1 and 9 June 1916, 1; *II*, 13 June 1916. ADM/188/712/32856: H. C. Mills; TNA, ADM 188/710/31893: R. E. Fegan.
10. *EH*, 5 June 1916, 3; *DEM*, 6 June 1916, 1; *II*, 6 June 1916, 1; *WIT*, 10 June 1916, 8.
11. Steel and Hart, *Jutland*, 103–8; Brooks, *Jutland*, 205–6.
12. Steel and Hart, *Jutland*, 164–5.
13. Steel and Hart, *Jutland*, 166.
14. See Steel and Hart, *Jutland*, 200–1 and 230; Brooks, *Jutland*, 281 and 288.
15. Overnight, one Dubliner was killed on the *Turbulent*, and two more on the *Black Prince*.
16. Halpern, *Naval History*, 317–25.
17. Steel and Hart, *Jutland*, 166–7 and 434–5.

18. Halpern, *Naval History*, 325–7.
19. See for example, *II*, 3 June 1916, 3.
20. *II*, 5 June 1916, 3.
21. *II*, 7 June 1916, 3.
22. *DEM*, 9 June 1916, 3; *II*, 13 June 1916, 3; TNA, ADM 188/494/303949: R. J. Vernor.
23. Philpott, *Bloody*, 56–87.
24. Gary Sheffield and John Bourne, eds., *Douglas Haig: War Diaries and Letters, 1914–1918* (London: Weidenfeld and Nicolson, 2005), 189.
25. Gary Sheffield, *The Somme* (London: Cassell, 2003), 22; J. Harris, *Douglas Haig and the First World War* (Cambridge University Press, 2008), 216–23.
26. 'Order Welcomes Somme Stamp Plans', BBC online 17 February 2006, at: http://news.bbc.co.uk/1/hi/northern_ireland/4723946.stm (accessed 5 November 2016).
27. See p. 47.
28. *DEM*, 5 November 1915, 6.
29. *IT*, 1 April 1916, 5; TNA, WO 95/2510: 9th Inniskillings; W. J. Canning, *A Wheen of Medals: The History of the 9th (Service) Bn. The Royal Inniskilling Fusiliers (The Tyrones) in World War One* (Antrim: W. J. Canning, 2006), 66–84.
30. TNA, WO 95/2510. On the Boyne anniversary, see Grayson, *Belfast*, 80.
31. TNA, WO 95/2510; Grayson, *Belfast*, 80; Peter Hart, *The Somme* (London: Weidenfeld and Nicolson, 2005), 150–62.
32. Simkins, *Somme*, 30.
33. TNA, WO 95/2510: 9th Inniskillings.
34. Robin Prior and Trevor Wilson, *The Somme* (London: Yale University Press, 2005), 87–9.
35. TNA, WO 95/2510; Grayson, *Belfast*, 80.
36. TNA, WO 95/2510; CWGC download, 5 July 2016.
37. *DEM*, 31 March 1916, 3.
38. CWGC; TNA, WO 339/21334: William Crozier; Quinn, *Wigs*, 88–9.
39. TNA, WO 363.
40. Arthur Guinness, Son and Co Ltd, *Roll of Employees* (Dublin: Arthur Guinness, 1920); Roll, 7; TNA, WO 339/29339: E. J. F. Holland.
41. Wylly, *Neill's*, III, 64–5; TNA, WO 95/4310 and 2301.
42. Wylly, *Crown*; TNA, WO 95/1481.
43. IWM 7256: Colyer, Part IV, 199–201.
44. Martin Mace and John Grehan, *Slaughter on the Somme, 1 July 1916: The Complete War Diaries of the British Army's Worst Day* (Barnsley: Pen and Sword, 2013), 85–7; Hart, *Somme*, 132–50.
45. IWM 7256: Colyer, Part IV, 211, 214 and 219–21.
46. TNA, WO 95/2301: 1st RDF.
47. IWM 7256: Colyer, Part IV, 243–4.
48. Mace and Grehan, *Slaughter*, 88–90.
49. Prior and Wilson, *Somme*, 80.
50. DCLA, RDFA/001/02: Loughlin to Roberts, 6 July 1916.
51. TNA, WO 95/2301: 1st RDF; CWGC download, 7 July 2016.
52. Mace and Grehan, *Slaughter*, 94–5.
53. TNA, WO 95/1481: 2nd RDF. See also IWM 7256: Colyer, Part IV, 247–9.
54. IWM 7256: Colyer, Part IV, 261–2.
55. TNA, WO 95/1481: 2nd RDF; CWGC download, 7 July 2016.
56. IWM 7256: Colyer, Part IV, 284.
57. TNA, WO 95/2305: 1st Inniskillings.

58. TNA, WO 95/1730: 1st RI Rifles.
59. *DEM*, 4 July 1916, 5.
60. *FJ*, 3 July 1916, 5; *DEM*, 3 July 1916, 3.
61. Beckett et al., *British Army*, 286 and 288.
62. Philpott, *Bloody*, 168–9, 178, 180 and 181–2.
63. Ibid., 208.
64. IWM 7256: Colyer, Part IV, 206.
65. Philpott, *Bloody*, 215.
66. *DEM*, 15 July 1916, 5.
67. Irish Jesuit Archives, Gill Papers, CHP1/28, 93. On Gill, See Taylor, *2nd*, 240–2. See also TNA, WO 374/27281: Henry Gill.
68. Including one officer temporarily attached from the Connaught Rangers. TNA, WO 95/2247; CWGC download, 8 July 2016.
69. *London Gazette*, Supplement 29684, 25 July 1916, 7444; *WIT*, 29 July 1916, 8; Taylor, *2nd*, 337.
70. Hart, *Somme*, 237–60.
71. Philpott, *Bloody*, 237; Hart, *Somme*, 260–82.
72. DCLA, RDFA/001/22: Soper to Roberts, 3 August 1916.
73. Philpott, *Bloody*, 252 and 264.
74. TNA, WO 95/1359; CWGC download, 8 July 2016; www.cwgc.org/find-war-dead /casualty/748893/GOFF,%20CHARLES%20EDWARD (accessed 8 July 2016); *DEM*, 23 November 1916, 1.
75. Hart, *Somme*, 330; Prior and Wilson, *Somme*, 160–2.

12 Success on the Somme

1. Cited in Robert Lynd, 'The Work of T. M. Kettle', *New Statesman*, 30 September 1916, 614–15.
2. Michael Hall, *A Shared Sacrifice for Peace* (Belfast: Island Publications, 2007); Connaught Rangers Research Project, *The 6th Connaught Rangers: Belfast Nationalists and the Great War* (Belfast: 6th Connaught Rangers Research Project, 2008). See also Denman, *Unknown*, 78–103.
3. Philpott, *Bloody*, 347.
4. TNA, WO 95/1969: 47th Brigade.
5. TNA, WO 95/1970: 6th Connaughts.
6. Grayson, *Staniforth*, 127.
7. TNA, WO 95/1970: 7th Leinsters.
8. Grayson, *Staniforth*, 127.
9. Doherty and Truesdale, *Irish Winners*, 121–2.
10. TNA, WO 95/1970: 6th RI Regiment.
11. IWM 80/25/1: W. A. Lyon, *Memoirs*, 64.
12. Prior and Wilson, *Somme*, 170
13. Denman, *Unknown*, 82.
14. St Mary's, Anglesea Road; Christ Church, Leeson Park; and St Columba's, Ranelagh. See www.irishwarmemorials.ie (accessed 11 July 2016). See also Denman, *Unknown*, 82; *FJ*, 13 September 1916, 1.
15. Cookstown District Council, *Cookstown's War Dead: 1914–18, 1939–45* (Cookstown: Cookstown District Council, 2007), 247; www.cwgc.org/find-war-dead/casualty/900633/LENOX-CONYNGHAM,%20HUBERT%20MAXWELL (accessed 19 September 2016).
16. TNA, WO 363; *SH*, 4 March 1916, 2 and 28 October 1916, 5.

17. TNA, WO 95/1978: 7th RI Fusiliers; see also Johnstone, *Orange*, 247.
18. CWGC download, 12 July 2016.
19. TNA, WO 95/1974: 8th RDF.
20. Exceptions include Denman, *Unknown*, 83 and Johnstone, *Orange*, 248.
21. TNA, WO 95/1974: 9th RDF.
22. Prior and Wilson, *Somme*, 170–1; Philpott, *Bloody*, 348.
23. Johnstone, *Orange*, 250.
24. TNA, WO 95/1974: 8th and 9th RDF.
25. Sean Boyne, *Emmet Dalton: Somme Soldier, Irish General, Film Pioneer* (Sallins: Merrion, 2015), 14–16.
26. TNA, WO 95/1974: 9th RDF; NLI, Emmet Dalton, MS 46,687/1: Army Pay Book; TNA, WO 339/53226: J. E. Dalton; Boyne, *Emmet Dalton*, 6–7, 23 and 27–8; www.rte.ie/archives/exhibitions/1011-ireland-and-the-great-war/1012-call-to-arms/315175-emmet-dalton-remembers/ (accessed 21 March 2017).
27. *London Gazette*, Supplement 29802, 24 October 1916, 10394; *II*, 20 September 1916, 2; *EH*, 20 September 1916, 1; *DEM*, 21 October 1916, 3.
28. TNA, WO 339/53226: J. E. Dalton; TNA, WO 95/1974: 9th RDF; Boyne, *Emmet Dalton*, 30; NLI, Emmet Dalton, MS 46,687/1: Army Pay Book. See pp. 216–17.
29. Sheffield, *Somme*, 108; Hart, *Somme*, 343–4.
30. TNA, WO 95/1970: 6th Connaughts.
31. Jonathan Walker, ed., *War Letters to a Wife: France and Flanders, 1915–1919* (Staplehurst: Spellmount, 2001), 70.
32. Johnstone, *Orange*, 253.
33. TNA, WO 363; Soldiers' Wills.
34. www.cwgc.org/find-war-dead/casualty/762819 (accessed 23 November 2017).
35. *FJ*, 9 September 1916, 5, 11 September 1916, 5, 12 September 1916, 5, 13 September 1916, 5 and 14 September 1915, 5.
36. Lynd, *Kettle*, 614–15.
37. Cited in Lyons, *Enigma*, 293.
38. Lynd, *Kettle*, 614–15.
39. Cited in Michael MacDonagh, *The Irish on the Somme* (London: Hodder and Stoughton, 1917), 162.
40. UCD, Kettle, LA34/19 and 20.
41. Gerald Dawe, ed., *Earth Voices Whispering: An Anthology of Irish War Poetry, 1914–1945* (Belfast: Blackstaff Press, 2008), 55. See also Boyne, *Emmet Dalton*, 24. The original manuscript is in UCD, Kettle, LA34/404–5.
42. UCD, Kettle, LA34/22: 4 November 1916.
43. UCD, Kettle, LA34/417: Dalton to MK, 14 October 1916. Kettle married on 8 September 1909.
44. UCD, Kettle, LA34/418.
45. *FJ*, 19 September 1916, 5; *DEM*, 21 September 1916, 4.
46. See p. 232.
47. See p. 167.
48. Lynd, *Kettle*, 614–15.
49. UCD, Kettle, LA 34/413: Healy to MK, 11 April 1917. See also UCD, Kettle, LA 34/420: W. Browne to his mother, 10 March 1917, and various letters in UCD, Kettle, LA 34/421–2.
50. UCD, Kettle, LA34/417: Dalton to MK, 14 October 1916.
51. UCD, Kettle, LA 34/413: Healy to MK, 27 November 1917.

52. www.cwgc.org/find-war-dead/casualty/798121/KETTLE,%20THOMAS% 20MICHAEL (accessed 15 February 2017). See also UCD, Kettle, LA34/423: Imperial War Graves Commission to MK, 5 July 1924.
53. Prior and Wilson, *Somme*, 229–38.
54. TNA, WO 95/1216: 1st IG; TNA, WO 95/1220: 2nd IG.
55. TNA, WO 95/1220: 2nd IG.
56. TNA, WO 95/1216: 1st IG. See also Kipling, *Irish Guards*, 170–80.
57. Prior and Wilson, *Somme*, 233.
58. Sheffield, *Somme*, 112–24.
59. Sheffield, *Somme*, 126–50.
60. Simkins, *Somme*, 93.
61. TNA, WO 71/513: Bernard McGeehan; TNA, WO 363: Wills. See also Stephen Walker, *Forgotten Soldiers: The Irishmen Shot at Dawn* (Dublin: Gill and Macmillan, 2007), 84–9.
62. TNA, WO 95/1481: 2nd RDF.
63. RDFA/001/22: Soper to Roberts, 28 October 1916.
64. CWGC download (18 July 2016). This shows 63 men dead in total in the battalion over 23 to 25 October 1916, but 16 of those are recorded as being remembered on the Menin Gate. It is possible that they were in another battalion as they should be on the Thiepval Memorial, being missing on the Somme.
65. www.dublincity.ie/main-menu-services-press-and-news-read-press-release-press-releases-2012-press-releases-may-2012-8 (accessed 18 July 2016); *DEM*, 30 October 1916, 1; *FJ*, 30 October 1916, 1; *WIT*, 4 November 1916, 8; *II*, 30 October 1916, 1; RDFA/035/02/06: Information Relating to Site of Death of Herbert Lemass; Kinsella, *Out*, 357–60.
66. TNA, WO 339/44144: E. S. Lemass.
67. Kinsella, *Out*, 116–23.
68. TNA, WO 95/1974: 2nd RDF.
69. *DEM*, 12 December 1916, 4. See also Kinsella, *Out*, 376–80.
70. Sheffield, *Somme*, 144–5.
71. *DEM*, 6 December 1916, 4.
72. TNA, WO 95/3118: 10th RDF.
73. *DEM*, 12 December 1916, 4; *DEM*, 27 November 1916, 3.
74. See p. 172.

13 Snow and Sand

1. *DEM*, 28 January 1916, 5.
2. For the Italian campaign, see Mark Thompson, *The White War: Life and Death on the Italian Front 1915–1919* (London: Faber and Faber, 2008).
3. Edward Paice, *Tip and Run: The Untold Tragedy of the Great War in Africa* (London: Weidenfeld and Nicolson, 2007), 30–1; Ross Anderson, *The Forgotten Front, 1914–18: The East African Campaign* (Stroud: Tempus, 2007), 44–5.
4. *WIT*, 25 September 1915, 6; www.cwgc.org/find-war-dead/casualty/905213/ McCOMBIE,%20L%20H%20D (accessed 31 August 2016).
5. *SH*, 10 August 1918, 3; www.cwgc.org/find-war-dead/casualty/1437433/ LEONARD,%20W (accessed 31 August 2016).
6. TNA, WO 363; Service Records.
7. *The Times*, 24 February 1915, 8; See R. W. E. Harper, *Singapore Mutiny* (Singapore: Oxford University Press, 1984).

8. *II*, 27 February 1915, 4.

9. IWM 97/16/1: Ford Papers.

10. DCLA, RDFA/018: Gallipoli Memories Diary.

11. TNA, WO 95/4836: 6th and 7th RDF.

12. Johnstone, *Orange*, 161–2; Kristian Coates Ulrichsen, *The First World War in the Middle East* (London: Hurst, 2014), 93.

13. NAM, Drury 2, 10.

14. WO 339/910: J. O'N. McKenna.

15. DCLA, RDFA/006: James C. McKenna, Observations, 10 October to 6 December 1915.

16. DCLA, RDFA.018: Gallipoli Memories Diary.

17. TNA, WO 95/4836: 6th RDF.

18. NAM, Drury 2, 26.

19. DCLA, RDFA/006: McKenna.

20. DCLA, RDFA/006: McKenna. See also TNA, WO 95/4836: 6th and 7th RDF.

21. NAM, Drury 2, 51.

22. Johnstone, *Orange*, 173–4; H. F. N. Jourdain and Edward Fraser, *The Connaught Rangers*, vol. III (London: Royal United Service Institution, 1918), 108 and 110.

23. TNA, WO 95/4836: 7th RDF.

24. DCLA, RDFA/006: McKenna. Drury was much concerned with the cold from mid-November, see NAM, Drury 2, 51 et seq.

25. Johnstone, *Orange*, 174; TNA, WO 95/4836: 7th RDF.

26. Johnstone, *Orange*, 175.

27. Jourdain and Fraser, *Connaught Rangers*, III, 110–11.

28. Jourdain and Fraser, *Connaught Rangers*, III, 117–23; Cyril Falls, *Military Operations Macedonia, from the Outbreak of War to the Spring of 1917* (London: HMSO, 1933), 69–70.

29. CWGC download, 6 September 2016. The six were: privates 5297 Michael Digan, 11076 J. Foy, 8980 John Gallagher, 9661 Patrick Murphy, 5480 John Scott and 5029 Joseph Walsh.

30. TNA, WO 95/4836: 7th RDF.

31. TNA, WO 339/21685; Harold Mellon.

32. *DEM*, 28 January 1916, 5.

33. NAM, Drury 2, 74.

34. TNA, WO 95/4836: 6th and 7th RDF; Johnstone, *Orange*, 175–80.

35. NAM, Drury, 2, 80.

36. *DEM*, 28 January 1916, 5.

37. *II*, 13 December 1915, 5; *EH*, 13 December 1915, 2.

38. *EH*, 10 January 1916, 5.

39. CWGC download, 6 September 2016.

40. See p. 138.

41. http://dh.tcd.ie/martindiary/ (accessed 6 September 2016). See also Kinsella, *Out*, 315–25.

42. *EH*, 22 January 1916, 5.

43. See p. 36.

44. Kinsella, *Out*, 350–1; TNA, WO 339/46640: J. T. Brett.

45. TNA, WO 364; TNA, WO 374/29700: A. Guest.

46. TNA, WO 95/4836: 6th and 7th RDF.

47. *DEM* 28 January 1916, 5.

48. Ulrichsen, *Middle East*, 94.

49. TNA, WO 95/4836: 6th and 7th RDF. See also NAM, Drury 2, 118–22.

50. NAM, Drury 2, 160.
51. NAM, Drury 2, 162–7; Drury, 3, 1–4.
52. CWGC download 7 September 2016. On malaria see Johnstone, *Orange*, 260.
53. TNA, WO 95/4836: 6th and 7th RDF.
54. TNA, WO 95/4836: 7th RDF; CWGC download, 7 September 2016.
55. TNA, WO 95/4836: 6th and 7th RDF.
56. Johnstone, *Orange*, 265.
57. TNA, WO 339/33638: F. L. Malley.
58. See p. 310.
59. The 6th: 17 November 1916 and 26 March 1917; the 7th: 31 October 1916, 24 February 1917 and 1 June 1917.
60. TNA, WO 95/4836: 7th RDF
61. NLI, Emmet Dalton, MS 46,687/1; TNA, WO 95/4579: 6th Leinsters; Boyne, *Emmet Dalton*, 31.
62. NAM, Drury 3, 9–10.
63. TNA, WO 95/4836: 6th and 7th RDF; TNA, WO 95/4583: 6th and 7th RDF.
64. Carver, *Turkish Front*, 8–9.
65. London Stamp Exchange, *Our Heroes*, 116; *DEM*, 28 August 1915, 4; TNA, WO 95/4428: 92nd Punjabis.
66. *II*, 30 January 1917, 2; www.cwgc.org/find-war-dead/casualty/110932/FIELDING,%20JOSHUA (accessed 31 August 2016); TNA, WO 372; TNA, WO 76/1/29: 4th Dragoon Guards.
67. *IT*, 21 February 1916, 6.
68. Ulrichsen, *Middle East*, 135; Ron Wilcox, *Battles on the Tigris: The Mesopotamian Campaign of the First World War* (Barnsley: Pen and Sword, 2006), 101–3; Jourdain and Fraser, *Connaught Rangers*, I, 493–5; TNA, WO 95/5139: 6th Jat Light Infantry; TNA, WO 95/5106: 1st CR.
69. www.cwgc.org/find-war-dead/casualty/1660035/NEALE,%20ARTHUR%20HILL (accessed 7 September 2016).
70. CWGC download, 7 September 2016; www.cwgc.org/find-a-cemetery/cemetery/88400/BASRA%20MEMORIAL (accessed 7 September 2016). The seven Dubliners were all privates: 9248 William Brophy, 8670 Patrick Cassidy, 9611 Patrick Evans, 1002 James Gallagher, 7844 William Hann, 7896 Christopher Rock and 10713 Christopher Walsh.
71. Ulrichsen, *Middle East*, 136. See also Wilcox, *Tigris*, 122–31.
72. *FJ*, 24 October 1916, 5; www.cwgc.org/find-war-dead/casualty/635419/SWEENEY,%20JAMES (accessed 7 September 2016).
73. Johnstone, *Orange*, 400–1.
74. TNA, WO 95/4583: 6th and 7th RDF.
75. Johnstone, *Orange*, 322.
76. Ulrichsen, *Middle East*, 111.
77. TNA, WO 374/8716: Kevin Brayden; TNA, WO 95/4670: 2/18th London.
78. Jeremy Stanley, *Ireland's Forgotten 10th: A Brief History of the 10th (Irish) Division, 1914–1918, Turkey, Macedonia and Palestine* (Ballycastle: Impact, 2003), 80.
79. *FJ*, 28 December 1917, 2 and 4; TNA, WO 95/4670: 2/18th London Regiment; TNA, WO 374/8716: Kevin Brayden.
80. TNA, WO 95/4583: 6th RDF.
81. TNA, WO 95/4583: 6th and 7th RDF.
82. NAM, Drury 3, 102.

83. *Aragon*: www.wrecksite.eu/wreck.aspx?134801 and *Osmanieh*: www.wrecksite .eu/wreck.aspx?99051; Chatby Memorial: www.cwgc.org/find-a-cemetery/ceme tery/142020/CHATBY%20MEMORIAL (all accessed 8 September 2016).

84. TNA, WO 95/4583: 7th RDF; www.cwgc.org/find-war-dead/casualty/647064/ HARE,%20GEORGE (accessed 8 September 2016).

85. Johnstone, *Orange*, 333–5.

86. TNA, WO 95/4583: 6th RDF.

87. NAM, Drury 3, 150–2.

88. TNA, WO 95/4835: 6th Leinsters.

89. NLI, Emmet Dalton, MS 46,687/3: Diary, 16 January 1918.

90. Ibid., 19, 22, 26 and 30 January 1918.

91. Ibid., 20 and 27 January 1918.

92. Ibid., 26 and 27 January 1918 and 5, 7, 8 and 9 February 1918.

93. Ibid., 1, 4 and 13 February 1918.

94. Ibid., 2, 3, 14, 17 and 24 February 1918 and 2, 3 and 25 to 27 March 1918.

95. *WIT*, 26 October 1918, 6; www.cwgc.org/find-war-dead/casualty/654187/GREY, %20GEORGE%20ROCHFORT (accessed 8 September 2016).

96. *DEM*, 26 October 1918, 1; www.cwgc.org/find-war-dead/casualty/476769/ MASON,%20JOHN%20NORMAN (accessed 8 September 2016); TNA, WO 95/4513: 1/1st Dorset Yeomanry.

97. Ulrichsen, 116.

98. TNA, WO 95/2831: 2nd RDF.

99. TNA, WO 95/3140: 6th RDF.

100. TNA, WO 339/53226: J. E. Dalton; Boyne, *Emmet Dalton*, 42–3. See p. 264.

14 Attrition: 1916–17

1. DCLA, RDFA/001/02: Loughlin to Roberts, 5 March 1917.

2. Ibid.

3. TNA, WO 339/46640: J. T. Brett. See also Kinsella, *Out*, 347 and 351.

4. Soldiers' Wills; *SH*, 14 October 1916, 5; *SH*, 20 July 1918, 3; www.cwgc.org/find-war-dead/casualty/548958/CARTER,%20J & www.cwgc.org/find-war-dead/casualty/743829/CARTER,%20JOHN%20J (accessed 13 September 2016).

5. *FJ*, 3 May 1917, 3; *ET*, 7 May 1917, 2; *FJ*, 7 May 1917, 2; www.cwgc.org/find-war-dead/casualty/514700/FLETCHER,%20ARNOLD%20LOCKHART and www .cwgc.org/find-war-dead/casualty/333158/FLETCHER,%20DONALD% 20LOCKHART (accessed 12 September 2016). See also Kinsella, *Out*, 172–5.

6. See pp. 66–7.

7. *DEM*, 19 October 1915, 1; *ET*, 18 October 1915, 1; *FJ*, 10 April 1917, 8; www.cwgc.org/find-war-dead/casualty/929021/BRENNOCK,%20WILLIAM, www .cwgc.org/find-war-dead/casualty/3033388/BRENNOCK,%20PATRICK and www .cwgc.org/find-war-dead/casualty/767671/BRENNOCK,%20THOMAS (accessed 12 September 2016). For Thomas, see p. 236. The Brennocks had two other sons and a daughter: www.census.nationalarchives.ie/pages/1911/Dublin/ Pembroke_West/Shelbourne_Road/61286/ (accessed 12 September 2016).

8. See p. 157.

9. www.cwgc.org/find-war-dead/casualty/48226/NAYLOR,%20JAMES, www.cwgc .org/find-war-dead/casualty/1765573/NAYLOR,%20JOHN and www.cwgc.org/find-war-dead/casualty/99418/NAYLOR,%20WILLIAM (accessed 12 September 2016).

10. *SH*, 4 March 1916, 2.

11. www.cwgc.org/find-war-dead/casualty/930677/GERAGHTY,%20CHRISTOPHER, www.cwgc.org/find-war-dead/casualty/4020095/GERAGHTY,%20FRANCIS and www.cwgc.org/find-war-dead/casualty/255553/GERAGHTY,%20J (accessed 12 September 2016).

12. TNA, WO 329.

13. TNA, WO 364.

14. TNA, WO 329.

15. TNA, WO 372: Medal and Award Rolls Index; *DEM*, 15 January 1917, 3.

16. Joe Gleeson, *Irish Air Aces of the RFC and RAF in the First World War: The Lives Behind the Legends* (Stroud: Fonthill, 2015), 9.

17. Airmen's records are not digitised and searchable by place, which makes them much harder to find than those in the army, unless they were dead. With a 7% fatality rate for the air services as a whole, compared to 12% across all services, it means that even fewer are found in the death records. See Gleeson, *Air Aces*, 12.

18. IWM 3385: Beater diary, 13 July 17 to 10 September 1917.

19. Ibid., 15 September 1917.

20. Ibid., 20 September 1917.

21. Ibid., 13 November 1917.

22. Ibid., undated pages towards end.

23. *WIT*, 16 June 1917, 8; TNA, WO 339/87276 and AIR 76/233/4: Frederick Hoey; www.cwgc.org/find-war-dead/casualty/405563/HOEY,%20FREDERICK%20CYRIL (accessed 23 September 2016).

24. TNA, AIR 79/498/54503; *DEM*, 18/09/1918, 1 and 11 September 1919, 1.

25. TNA, WO 339/56718: M. Lillis; Quinn, *Wigs*, 102–3; www.cwgc.org/find-war-dead/casualty/271610/LILLIS,%20MARTIN%20MICHAEL%20ARTHUR (accessed 23 September 2016); Kinsella, *Out*, 341–4.

26. *II*, 3 July 1917, 1; www.cwgc.org/find-war-dead/casualty/743456/CALLAGHAN,%20EUGENE%20CRUESS (accessed 23 September 2016); TNA, WO 339/5602: E. Cruess-Callaghan.

27. TNA, WO 339/71689: S. Cruess-Callaghan. His age comes from his record of birth: civilrecords.irishgenealogy.ie/churchrecords/images/birth_returns/births_1895/02196/1830229 (accessed 29 September 2016).

28. *Northern Advance*, 5 July 1917, cited at: www.veterans.gc.ca/eng/remembrance/memorials/canadian-virtual-war-memorial/detail/425405; www.cwgc.org/find-war-dead/casualty/425405/CRUESS-CALLAGHAN,%20STANISLAUS (accessed 23 September 2016); *WIT*, 7 July 1917, 8. TNA, WO 339/71689: S. Cruess-Callaghan.

29. *Airmen Died*; www.cwgc.org/find-war-dead/casualty/81156/CALLAGHAN,%20J%20C (accessed 23 September 2016); TNA, WO 339/5349: J. Cruess-Callaghan.

30. TNA, WO 95/56025: S. Cruess-Callaghan. On the family, see also Kinsella, *Out*, 188–93.

31. *The London Gazette* (Supplement), 29602, 30 May 1916, 5408; *The London Gazette* (Supplement), 29793, 20 October 1916, 10196; *The Edinburgh Gazette*, 13012, 16 November 1916, 2107.

32. TNA, WO 339/88606: S. E. Cowan.

33. *DEM*, 21 April 1917, 1; www.cwgc.org/find-war-dead/casualty/314159/COWAN,%20SIDNEY%20EDWARD and www.cwgc.org/find-war-dead/casualty/745725/COWAN,%20PHILIP%20CHALMERS (accessed 23 September 2016). TNA, WO 339/88608 and 15942: S. E. and P. Cowan; *II*, 19 November 1917, 2 and 15 July 1918. Sidney and Philip's parents also had a daughter, Hilda, and an older

son, Frederick, who was serving in the Egyptian government's Irrigation Department and appears not to have enlisted.

34. *DEM*, 28 February 1917, 3; 24 May 1917, 4; 8 June 1917, 4.
35. *FJ*, 25 August 1916, 7.
36. *The Times*, 28 January 1963, 12.
37. *FJ*, 25 August 1916, 7.
38. *IT*, 13 September 1916, 4.
39. *DEM*, 4 October 1916, 2.
40. *DEM*, 7 October 1916, 3.
41. *DEM*, 9 October 1916, 3.
42. *DEM*, 10 October 1916, 3.
43. Meleady, *Redmond*, 396.
44. *DEM*, 26 January 1917, 3 and 27 January 1917, 3.
45. *ET*, 14 September 1917, 3.
46. *ET*, 27 October 1917, 1.
47. *IT, SF Handbook*, 69.
48. *ET*, 23 February 1917, 1; *ET*, 2 March 1917. 2.
49. *DEM*, 9 April 1917, 3 and 10 April 1917, 3. See also BMH.WS0391, 42–7: Molony, H.
50. *DEM*, 22 May 1917, 3.
51. *DEM*, 15 June 1917, 3; *ET*, 15 June 1917, 1.
52. *ET*, 18 June 1917, 1; *EM*, 18 June 1917, 3.
53. *EH*, 11 June 1917, 1; *DEM*, 21 June 1917, 3; *DEM*, 4 August 1917, 3.
54. *DEM*, 19 June 1917, 3.
55. *DEM*, 1 June 1917, 3; *ET*, 7 August 1917, 3.
56. Richardson, *Lights*, 359.
57. TNA, CO 904/29: Return of Arms for Month Ending 28 February 1917.
58. *IT*, 28 May 1917, 3; *ET*, 19 July 1917, 2; 10 August 1917, 2; 18 August 1917, 2; 29 September 1917, 6.
59. *EH*, 1 October 1917, 5; *DEM*, 10 October 1917, 3.
60. Joost Augusteijn, *From Public Defiance to Guerrilla Warfare: The Experiences of Ordinary Volunteers in the Irish War of Independence, 1916–1921* (Dublin: Irish Academic Press, 1996), 65.
61. www.longlongtrail.co.uk/army/regiments-and-corps/the-british-infantry-regiments -of-1914-1918/royal-irish-rifles/ (accessed 16 September 2016).
62. TNA, WO 95/3118: 10th Dublins.
63. TNA, WO 95/1974: 2nd, 8th and 9th RDF; CWGC download, 13 September 2016.
64. IWM 3385: Beater diary, 5 October 1916.
65. Ibid., 14 November 1916.
66. Ibid., 9 December 1916.
67. TNA, WO 95/2301: 1st RDF; CWGC download, 13 September 2016.
68. TNA, WO 95/2301: 1st RDF; Wylly, *Neill's, III*, 81.
69. See p. 236.
70. CWGC download, 13 September 2016.
71. TNA, WO 95/3118: 10th RDF.
72. Paddy Griffith, *Battle Tactics of the Western Front: The British Army's Art of Attack 1916–18* (New Haven: Yale University Press, 1994), 85–6.
73. TNA, WO 95/1446: 4th Division Narrative of Operations, 9th to 21 June 1917; CWGC download, 13 September 2016.
74. TNA, WO 95/2301: 1st RDF; CWGC download 13 September 2016.
75. TNA, WO 95/3118: 10th RDF; TNA, WO 95/3093: 63rd (Royal Naval) Division.

76. Beckett et al., *British Army*, 320.

15 Learning

1. DCLA, RDFA/001/22: Soper to Roberts, 15 June 1917.
2. Richard S. Grayson, 'Ireland's New Memory of the First World War: Forgotten Aspects of the Battle of Messines, June 1917', *British Journal for Military History*, 1, 1 (2014), 48–65.
3. *DEM*, 8 June 1917, 3.
4. Griffith, *Battle Tactics*, 86; Ian Passingham, *Pillars of Fire: The Battle of Messines Ridge, June 1917* (Stroud: Sutton, 1998), 39–71.
5. Griffith, *Battle Tactics*, 65.
6. Passingham, *Pillars*, 95–6.
7. Letter cited in Tom Burke, *Messines to Carrick Hill: Writing Home from the Great War* (Cork: Mercier, 2017), 244; IWM 77/72/1: Lt. A.E. Glanville Diary, 6 and 7 June 1917. See also TNA, WO 339/67134: A. E. Glanville.
8. TNA, WO 95/1974: 9th RDF.
9. TNA, WO 95/1974: 2nd, 8th and 9th RDF.
10. Passingham, *Pillars*, 154–65.
11. *Soldiers Died*.
12. DCLA, RDFA/001/22: Soper to Roberts, 15 June 1917.
13. IWM 76/51/1: Colyer, vol. 5, Part V.
14. CWGC download 14 September 2016.
15. Grayson, 'Messines', 49–52.
16. www.president.ie/en/media-library/speeches/remarks-by-president-mary-mcaleese-at-reception-on-occasion-of-the-inaugura (accessed 14 September 2016).
17. Terence Denman, *A Lonely Grave: The Life and Death of William Redmond* (Blackrock: Irish Academic Press, 1995). For an account of the 6th Royal Irish Regiment at Messines See Burke, *Messines*, 239–58.
18. *SH*, 9 June 1917, 1; *ET*, 11 June 1917, 3; *FJ*, 11 June 1917, 4 and 5; *ET*, 13 June 1917, 1; *ET*, 22 June 1917, 3.
19. *FJ*, 9 June 1917, 5.
20. *ET*, 12 June 1917, 3.
21. *IT*, 12 June 1917, 5.
22. *DEM*, 9 June 1917, 3.
23. Grayson, 'Messines', 64–5; Grayson, *Belfast*, 103.
24. Grayson, 'Messines', 60–3.
25. *ET*, 13 June 1917, 3.
26. TNA, WO 363.
27. Grayson, *Belfast*, 188.
28. Grayson, 'Messines', 61.
29. DCLA, RDFA/001/01: Clarke to Roberts, 10 July 1917.
30. DCLA, RDFA/001/16: Heafey to Roberts, 18 July 1917. See also 15 August 1917.
31. Wills; www.cwgc.org/find-war-dead/casualty/439736/BOYLAN,%20P (accessed 15 September 2016).
32. Griffith, *Battle Tactics*, 86–7.
33. Fox, *Learning*, 9.
34. *FJ*, 9 August 1917, 4; *ET*, 15 September 1917, 3; www.cwgc.org/find-war-dead/casualty/101111/LEDWIDGE,%20FRANCIS%20EDWARD (accessed 15 September 2016).

35. William Philpott, *Attrition: Fighting the First World War* (London: Little, Brown, 2014), 277; Griffith, *Battle Tactics*, 87–8; Palmer, *Salient*, 168–9.
36. CWGC download, 15 September 2016; TNA, WO 95/1974.
37. TNA, WO 95/1974: 2nd RDF.
38. IWM 77/72/1: Glanville, 31 July 17 to 12 August 1917.
39. TNA, WO 95/1974: 10th RDF.
40. Johnstone, *Orange*, 288.
41. TNA, WO 95/1974: 2nd RDF.
42. TNA, WO 95/1974: 2nd and 8th RDF.
43. TNA, WO 95/1974: 9th RDF.
44. Denman, *Unknown*, 123.
45. CWGC download, 15 September 2016.
46. *II*, 18 March 1918, 1 and 2; *WIT*, 23 March 1918, 6; Richardson, *Lights*, 119–22; WO 339/54104: W. R. Brereton-Barry.
47. Hope, *Worshipper*, 381; www.cwgc.org/find-war-dead/casualty/1630374/DOYLE,%20The%20Rev%20WILLIAM%20JOSEPH (accessed 15 September 2016). See also Kinsella, *Out*, 288–98.
48. Hope, *Worshipper*, 387–8.
49. *ET*, 27 August 1917, 2.
50. *ET*, 22 August 1917, 1. See also Hope, *Worshipper*, 615–24; Michael Moynihan, *God On Our Side: The British Padre in World War I* (London: Leo Cooper, 1983), 174–210.
51. Cited in Moynihan, *God*, 209–10.
52. Denman, *Unknown*, 123–4.
53. TNA, WO 95/1974.
54. TNA, WO 95/2301: 1st RDF.
55. Wylly, *Neill's, III*, 88.
56. TNA, WO 95/1974: 1st RDF; Wylly, *Neill's, III*, 88–91; CWGC download 15 September 2016; https://livesofthefirstworldwar.org/lifestory/3318672 (accessed 7 November 2017).
57. Denman, *Unknown*, 54.
58. www.longlongtrail.co.uk/army/order-of-battle-of-divisions/16th-irish-division/ (accessed 16 September 2016).
59. Wylly, *Neill's, III*, 97.
60. National Museum of Ireland: Records of 3rd Battalion, Irish Volunteers; *Soldiers Died*; TNA, WO 95/1974: 10th RDF; www.cwgc.org/find-war-dead/casualty/178810/KEARNS,%20J (accessed 16 September 2016); *EH*, 8 October 1917, 2; *FJ*, 25 October 1917, 2.
61. Denman, *Unknown*, 125; Grayson, *Belfast*, 126.
62. TNA, WO 95/1974: 2nd RDF.
63. This was not only an issue later in the war: See Jones, *Violence*, 72–87.
64. TNA, WO 95/1974: 1st, 2nd, 8th/9th and 10th RDF.
65. Denman, *Unknown*, 128.
66. TNA, WO 95/1974: 10th RDF.
67. Bryn Hammond, *Cambrai 1917: The Myth of the First Great Tank Battle* (London: Weidenfeld and Nicolson, 2008), 423.
68. TNA, WO 95/1974: 8th/9th and 10th RDF; CWGC download 16 September 2016.

16 Victory from the Jaws of Defeat

1. NAM, Drury 4, 56–7.

2. Denman, '16th', 154; www.longlongtrail.co.uk/army/order-of-battle-of-divisions/16th-irish-division/ (accessed 16 September 2016); Johnstone, *Orange*, 354; TNA, WO 95/905: 19th and 20th Entrenching Battalions.

3. NAM, Drury 4, 1 and 3.

4. Watson, *Ring*, 517.

5. David Stevenson, *With Our Backs to the Wall: Victory and Defeat in 1918* (London: Allen Lane, 2011), 35.

6. Stevenson, *Backs*, 55.

7. Johnstone, *Orange*, 354–5; Denman, *Unknown*, 157–9.

8. TNA, WO 95/1974: 1st and 2nd RDF. See also Johnstone, *Orange*, 360–2; Denman, '16th', 156–66; Wylly, *Neill's, III*, 101–4; Wylly, *Crown*, 99–103.

9. TNA, WO 95/1974: 1st and 2nd RDF. See also Johnstone, *Orange*, 378–88; Denman, '16th', 168; Wylly, *Neill's, III*, 104–8; Wylly, *Crown*, 103–9.

10. Johnstone, *Orange*, 389.

11. Denman, *Unknown*, 172.

12. TNA, WO 95/905: 19th and 20th Entrenching Battalions.

13. Sheffield and Bourne, *Haig*, 390.

14. Denman, *Unknown*, 168–9. See also Terence Denman, 'The 16th (Irish) Division on 21st March 1918: Fight or Flight?', *Irish Sword*, 69 (1999), 273–87.

15. Keith Jeffery, *Field Marshal Sir Henry Wilson: A Political Soldier* (Oxford University Press, 2006), 222–3.

16. Johnstone, *Orange*, 390.

17. TNA, WO 95/2301: 1st RDF; CWGC download, 27 September 2016.

18. Grayson, *Belfast*, 135–8.

19. *ET*, 6 March 1918, 1–3; *FJ*, 7 March 1918, 5–7; *ET*, 9 March 1918, 1.

20. *ET*, 7 February 1918, 1; F. W. S. Craig, ed., *Chronology of British Parliamentary By-Elections, 1833–1987* (Chichester: Parliamentary Research Services, 1987), 299–301; F. S. L. Lyons, 'The New Nationalism, 1916–18', in W. E. Vaughan, ed., *A New History of Ireland: VI, Ireland Under the Union, II, 1870–1921* (Oxford: Clarendon Press, 1996), 224–39, at 226–36; Hennessey, *Dividing*, 220–1.

21. See for example, tensions highlighted in *FJ*, 1 April 1918, 4.

22. *ET*, 8 September 1918, 1.

23. *ET*, 10 April 1918, 3.

24. *DEM*, 16 April 1918, 3; *ET*, 15 April 1918, 2; *DEM*, 18 April 1918, 3; *ET*, 19 April 1918, 2;. *FJ*, 19 April 1918, 3; *ET*, 22 April 1918, 1; *ET*, 23 and 24 April 1918, 1. See also Jérôme aan de Wiel, *The Catholic Church in Ireland, 1914–1918: War and Politics* (Dublin: Irish Academic Press, 2003), 203–30.

25. Alan J. Ward, 'Lloyd George and the 1918 Irish Conscription Crisis', *The Historical Journal* 17 (1974), 107–29, at 114.

26. *ET*, 18 May 1918, 1; *DEM*, 18 May 1918, 3; *FJ*, 20 May 1918, 3; Ward, 'Lloyd George', 120; Diarmaid Ferriter, *Judging Dev: A Reassessment of the Life and Legacy of Eamon de Valera* (Dublin: Royal Irish Academy, 2007), 33.

27. *FJ*, 4 July 1918, 3; *ET*, 5 July 1918, 1.

28. *FJ*, 27 September 1916, 3.

29. Denman, *Unknown*, 174; Gleeson, *Air Aces*, 11.

30. Ward, 'Lloyd George', 121–3; Jeffery, *Ireland*, 7–8.

31. *IT*, 26 August 1914, 4

32. See pp. 261–2.

33. *FJ*, 14 October 1918, 4.

34. Ward, 'Lloyd George', 123–4.

35. *II*, 20 July 1917, 2; www.cwgc.org/find-war-dead/casualty/3044197/REPETTO,%20EFFIZZIO and www.wrecksite.eu/wreck.aspx?10477 (accessed 23 September 2016).

36. www.wrecksite.eu/wreck.aspx?10520; www.cwgc.org/find-war-dead/casualty/2979197/AUSTIN,%20JAMES; www.cwgc.org/find-war-dead/casualty/2979887/BRIEN,%20WILLIAM (accessed 23 September 2016).

37. www.wrecksite.eu/wreck.aspx?13220 (accessed 23 September 2016).

38. www.wrecksite.eu/wreck.aspx?12755 (accessed 23 September 2016).

39. *ET*, 2 April 1918, 3; www.wrecksite.eu/wreck.aspx?66820.

40. *FJ*, 11 October 1918, 2.

41. www.wrecksite.eu/wreck.aspx?1664 (accessed 23 September 2016).

42. www.wrecksite.eu/wreck.aspx?10319 (accessed 23 September 2016).

43. Philip Lecane, *Torpedoed! The R.M.S. Leinster Disaster* (Penzance: Periscope, 2005), 51–2 and 57–8.

44. *FJ*, 11 October 1918, 4.

45. *FJ*, 11 October 1918, 2.

46. *FJ*, 11 October 1918, 3; *ET*, 11 October 1918, 1 and 3.

47. *ET*, 14 October 1918, 3.

48. www.wrecksite.eu/wreck.aspx?10319 (accessed 23 September 2016); Lecane, *Torpedoed*, 127, 142, 164 and 194.

49. www.cwgc.org/find-war-dead/casualty/2894248/BARRETT,%20SOPHIA%20VIOLET (accessed 23 September 2016); British Red Cross Society Records. See also Kinsella, *Out*, 139.

50. *II*, 14 December 1918, 2 and 18 December 1918, 2; www.cwgc.org/find-war-dead/casualty/2894315/BRADY,%20JAMES and www.cwgc.org/find-war-dead/casualty/2894594/HALLIGAN,%20PATRICK (accessed 23 September 2016).

51. *FJ*, 12 October 1918, 3; *ET*, 14 October 1918, 3. Barrett did indeed die, on 13 October.

52. *ET*, 14 October 1918, 3; *Hansard*, HC Deb, 15 October 1918, vol. 110, cols. 18–21.

53. *DEM*, 14 December 1918, 4.

54. Jonathan Boff, *Winning and Losing on the Western Front: The British Third Army and the Defeat of Germany in 1918* (Cambridge University Press, 2012), 243.

55. Boff, *Winning*, 245–7.

56. *WIT*, 16 November 1918, 8 and 30 November 1918, 1; www.abmc.gov/node/346129#.V_Zg5dQrKHs (accessed 6 October 2016).

57. Sheffield, *Forgotten*, 237–9. See also Banks, *Atlas*, 181.

58. www.longlongtrail.co.uk/battles/battles-of-the-western-front-in-france-and-flanders/the-advance-in-flanders/ (accessed 27 September 2016).

59. TNA, WO 95/2330: 7th RI Regiment; CWGC download, 27 September 2016.

60. Nick Lloyd, *Hundred Days: The End of the Great War* (London: Penguin, 2013), 31.

61. TNA, WO 95/2301; CWGC download 27 September 2016; see also Wylly, *Neill's, III*, 115–8.

62. TNA, WO 95/2301: 1st RDF; TNA, WO 95/2308: 2nd Leinsters; Boyne, *Emmet Dalton*, 43.

63. TNA, WO 95/2330: 7th Irish Regt.

64. TNA, WO 95/2301: 1st RDF; Wylly, *Neill's, III*, 119–22.

65. www.longlongtrail.co.uk/battles/battles-of-the-western-front-in-france-and-flanders/the-battles-of-the-hindenburg-line/ and www.longlongtrail.co.uk/battles/battles-of-the-western-front-in-france-and-flanders/the-final-advance-in-picardy/ (accessed 27 September 2016).

66. TNA, WO 95/2831: 2nd RDF; Wylly, *Crown*, 115–6.

67. NAM, Drury 4, 12.

68. NAM, Drury 4, 17–18.

69. TNA, WO 95/3140: 6th RDF; NAM, Drury 4, 19–26; CWGC download, 27 September 2016.

70. TNA, WO 95/2831: 2nd RDF; CWGC download, 27 September 2016; Wylly, *Crown*, 117–9.

71. NAM, Drury 4, 32–3.

72. TNA, WO 95/3140: 6th RDF; CWGC download, 27 September 2016.

73. TNA, WO 95/2831: 2nd RDF.

74. *II*, 23 December 1918, 2; www.cwgc.org/find-war-dead/casualty/286979/BYRNE, %20J and www.cwgc.org/find-war-dead/casualty/286980/GREGORY,%20JOHN (accessed 26 September 2016).

75. *II*, 25 November 1918, 2; *WIT*, 30 November 1918, 6; TNA, WO 95/2831: 2nd RDF; www.cwgc.org/find-war-dead/casualty/517920/GREAVES,%20E (accessed 26 September 2016); TNA, WO 339/42051: E. Greaves.

76. www.cwgc.org/find-war-dead/casualty/481122/McAULEY,%20J (accessed 26 September 2016). McAuley is listed on *Soldiers Died* as DoW on 11 November itself. He was said to be missing in June: *II*, 10 June 1918, 2.

77. TNA, WO 95/3140: 5th Inniskillings; *II*, 23 December 1918, 2; www.cwgc.org/find-war-dead/casualty/2914911/GRIFFIN,%20JOHN (accessed 26 September 2016).

78. data2.collectionscanada.ca/e/e039/e000958814.jpg, www.cwgc.org/find-war-dead/casualty/894458/BUTTIMER,%20J%20C and http://central.bac-lac.gc.ca/.item/?op=pdf&app=CEF&id=B1354-S001 (accessed 26 September 2016).

79. data2.collectionscanada.ca/e/e043/e001073410.jpg, central.bac-lac.gc.ca/.item/?op=pdf&app=CEF&id=B1490-S027, www.cwgc.org/find-war-dead/casualty/482075/CARLETON,%20PERCY%20WAINWRIGHT and www.irishwarmemorials.ie/pdf/322.pdf (all accessed 26 September 2016).

80. www.cwgc.org/find-war-dead/casualty/662655/DUNNE,%20SHEILA (accessed 26 September 2016).

81. www.cwgc.org/find-war-dead/casualty/571849/McCOMBIE,%20ROBERT%20HERCULES%20BRIDEOARE (accessed 26 September 2016).

82. www.cwgc.org/find-war-dead/casualty/516704/CONNOR,%20ROBERT (accessed 26 September 2016).

83. www.cwgc.org/find-war-dead/casualty/897245/GROVER,%20G (accessed 26 September 2016); *DEM*, 15 July 1916, 3.

84. *Sailors Died*; www.wrecksite.eu/wreck.aspx?64179 and www.cwgc.org/find-war-dead/casualty/3040152/PENDER,%20PATRICK (accessed 26 September 2016); *WIT*, 30 November 1918, 1.

85. TNA, WO 95/2330: 7th RI Regiment.

86. See for example: TNA, WO 95/2301 and 2831: 1st and 2nd RDF.

87. NAM, Drury, 4, 56–7.

88. *DEM*, 27 June 1918; *ET*, 16 July 1918, 1; *DEM*, 8 November 1918, 4.

89. Ida Milne, 'Stacking the Coffins: The 1918–19 Influenza Pandemic in Dublin', in Lisa Marie Griffith and Ciarán Wallace, eds., *Grave Matters: Death and Dying in Dublin, 1500 to the Present* (Dublin: Four Courts Press, 2016), 61–76, at 62. See also Caitriona Foley, *The Last Irish Plague: The Great Flu Epidemic in Ireland 1918–19* (Dublin: Irish Academic Press, 2011).

90. *ET*, 26 October 1918, 1.

91. *DEM*, 11 November 1918, 4.

92. *FJ*, 12 November 1918, 3.

93. *FJ*, 11 November 1918, 3.

17 War of Independence

1. BMH.WS1687, 41: Colley, H.
2. John Borgonovo, 'Reorganisation of the Irish Volunteers', in Crowley et al., *Atlas*, 313–18.
3. BMH.WS0340, 26: Traynor, O.
4. BMH.WS1687, 34: Colley, H. See also BMH.WS0340, 27: Traynor, O.
5. BMH.WS0564, 28: Byrne, T. F.
6. Risteard Mulcahy, *My Father, the General: Richard Mulcahy and the Military History of the Revolution* (Dublin: Liberties Press, 2010), 32–3; Oscar Traynor, 'Foreword', in NAOIRA, *Dublin Brigade, Review*, 9–11.
7. BMH.WS0587, 8–9: de Paor, N.
8. UCD, McNulty, LA9: November 1917.
9. BMH.WS0625, 1–5: Handley, E. See also BMH.WS0668, 5–6: Byrne, G.
10. BMH.WS0423, 8–9: Byrne, V. See also BMH.WS1687, 36–7: Colley, H; UCD, McNulty, LA9: April 1918 and January 1919.
11. www.ark.ac.uk/elections/h1918.htm (accessed 5 January 2017).
12. UCD, McNulty, LA9: December 1918.
13. UCD, McNulty, LA9: November 1918. See also BMH.WS0668, 5: Byrne, G.
14. BMH.WS0668, 5–6: Byrne, G.
15. BMH.WS0668, 7: Byrne, G.
16. BMH.WS1687, 41: Colley, H.
17. www.militaryarchives.ie/collections/online-collections/military-service-pensions-collection/search-the-collection/organisation-and-membership/ira-membership-series (accessed 5 January 2017); BMH.WS1773: Brennan, Patrick J., 2. See also Dominic Price, *We Bled Together: Michael Collins, the Squad and the Dublin Brigade* (Wilton: Collins Press, 2017), 39–42.
18. See pp. 275–7 and 286–8.
19. *An t-Óglác*, 1, 10 (February 1919), 2.
20. Hart, *IRA*, 37–42 and 46.
21. BMH.WS1043, 256–7: Lawless, J. V.; UCD, McNulty, LA9: 20 March 1917.
22. BMH.WS1773 10: Brennan, Patrick J.
23. Joseph E. A. Connell, *Michael Collins: Dublin 1916–22* (Dublin: Wordwell, 2017), 1.
24. T. Ryle Dwyer, *The Squad and the Intelligence Operations of Michael Collins* (Cork: Mercier, 2005), 45.
25. BMH.WS0445, 2: Slattery, J.
26. BMH.WS0445, 4–5: Slattery, J.; Dwyer, *Squad*, 46–8.
27. *IT*, 13 September 1919, 5.
28. Dwyer, *Squad*, 52.
29. Tim Pat Coogan, *The Twelve Apostles* (London: Head of Zeus, 2016).
30. BMH.WS0631, 32–3: Byrne, Bernard C.; BMH.WS0423, 32: Byrne, V.; BMH.WS0547, 1: Leonard, J. See also BMH.WS0822, 32: Stapleton, W. J.; BMH.WS0461, 4: Byrne, J.
31. BMH.WS0461, 3–4: Byrne, J. See pp. 129–30. See also Price, *Michael Collins*, 82–3.
32. BMH.WS0423, 8: Byrne, V.; BMH.WS0547, 6: Leonard, J.; BMH.WS0225: McDonnell, M.; Dwyer, *Squad*, 70–3.
33. BMH.WS0387, 23–4: O'Daly, P.; Dwyer, *Squad*, 81–2; *EH*, 22 January 1920, 1.
34. BMH.WS0822, 35: Stapleton, W. J.

35. BMH.WS1687, 43: Colley, H.
36. D. M. Leeson, *The Black and Tans: British Police and Auxiliaries in the Irish War of Independence* (Oxford University Press, 2011), 24–30.
37. Leeson, *Black and Tans*, 30–8. See also Paul O'Brien, *Havoc: The Auxiliaries in Ireland's War of Independence* (Wilton: Collins Press, 2017).
38. Material on fourteen of these men comes from the detailed research on David Grant's website www.theauxiliaries.com (accessed 10 November 2017). I am grateful to Dr Tom Thorpe for this reference. The site shows 182 Irish-born Auxiliaries from a total of 2,214, of whom 37 were born in Dublin, but only 14 were in the city or county at the relevant time. The fifteenth man is James O'Farrell (see p. 290).
39. BMH.WS1687, 45–6: Colley, H.
40. *DEM*, 21 February 1920, 5; Dwyer, *Squad*, 95.
41. *DEM*, 5 April 1920, 3.
42. *EH*, 13 April 1920, 1; *IT*, 14 April 1920, 5–6.
43. Dwyer, *Squad*, 101–2; *EH*, 14 April 1920, 1.
44. *IT*, 15 April 1920, 5; 17 April 1920, 5; 19 April 1920, 5; *DEM*, 14 April 1920, 3; *EH*, 15 April 1920, 1; 16 April 1920, 1.
45. UCD, McNulty, LA9: 3 April 1920; *EH*, 5 April 1920, 1.
46. BMH.WS0668, 8: Byrne, G.
47. *DEM*, 21 May 1920, 5; 24 May 1920, 3.
48. Wren, *GPO*, 330.
49. BMH.WS0856, 3: Colbert, E. M.
50. BMH.WS0564, 28: Byrne, T. F.
51. BMH.WS0587, 16: de Paor, N.
52. BMH.WS1687, 49: Colley, H.
53. *DEM*, 20 September 1920, 3. See also W. H. Kautt, *Ambushes and Armour: The Irish Rebellion, 1919–1921* (Dublin: Irish Academic Press, 2010), 193.
54. UCD, McNulty, LA9: 20 September 1917; BMH.WS0885, 21–2: Kennedy, S.; BMH.WS0486, 5: McDonnell, D.; Dwyer, *Squad*, 139 and 154–6.
55. 'Kevin Barry Tortured by his Captors', in NAOIRA, *Dublin Brigade, Review*, 72–3.
56. BMH.WS0564, 29: Byrne, T. F.
57. Dwyer, *Squad*, 139–40.
58. Dwyer, *Squad*, 139–40; Leeson, *Black and Tans*, 25–6 and 172–5; Marie Coleman, 'Leinster', in Crowley et al., *Atlas*, 579–87, at 580. See also Maurice Walsh, *The News from Ireland: Foreign Correspondents and the Irish Revolution* (London: I. B. Tauris, 2011), 84–5; Maurice Walsh, *Bitter Freedom: Ireland in a Revolutionary World, 1918–1923* (London: Faber & Faber, 2015), 198–89.
59. *DEM*, 21 September 1920, 3.
60. Eunan O'Halpin, 'Counting Terror: Bloody Sunday and *The Dead of the Irish Revolution*', in David Fitzpatrick, ed., *Terror in Ireland, 1916–1923* (Dublin: Lilliput, 2012), 141–57, at 141–5. Another essay in the same volume lists 36 dead on 21 November: Jane Leonard, '"English Dogs" or "Poor Devils"? The Dead of Bloody Sunday Morning', in Fitzpatrick, ed., *Terror*, 102–40, at 140.
61. Frank Thornton, 'The Pre-Truce Intelligence Department', in NAOIRA, *Dublin Brigade Review*, 83–5, at 84.
62. BMH.WS0340: 51: Traynor, O.
63. Leonard, 'Bloody Sunday', 113–15.
64. BMH.WS0423, 53–7: Byrne, V. See also Dwyer, *Squad*, 181–5.
65. *DEM*, 22 November 1920, 4. Dwyer states that Smith was considered an agent but Leonard's more detailed biography does not suggest that he actually was. See Dwyer, *Squad*, 178; Leonard, 'Bloody Sunday', 109–10.

66. BMH.WS0642, 7: Byrne, C.
67. Leonard, 'Bloody Sunday', 120–4 and 130.
68. BMH.WS1687, 53: Colley, H. For a detailed account, see Michael Foley, *The Bloodied Field: Croke Park. Sunday 21 November 1920* (Dublin: O'Brien Press, 2014).
69. *DEM*, 22 November 1920, 3.
70. Dwyer, *Squad*, 187–90; Leonard, 'Bloody Sunday', 139–40. For a map of events, see Pádraig Yeates, 'Dublin', in Crowley et al., *Atlas*, 588–95, at 593.
71. *DEM*, 23 November 1920, 3; Yeates, *Turmoil*, 198–9.
72. *EH*, 22 November 1920, 3.
73. *EH*, 23 November 1920, 1.
74. BMH.WS0340: 33: Traynor, O.
75. BMH.WS0564, 29: Byrne, T. F.

18 Crossovers

1. BMH.WS0401, 1: Gough, P.
2. This probably means that his war service had been as gunner and later corporal 27055 in the Royal Garrison Artillery who were first deployed overseas to France in August 1915. Two other Bernard Goldens served in the British army in 1914–18.
3. BMH.WS0281, 1–4: Golden, B. J.
4. Emmet O'Connor, *Reds and the Green: Ireland, Russia and the Communist Internationals, 1919–43* (Dublin: University College Dublin Press, 2004), 48–9.
5. BMH.WS0709, 1–2: Beaumont, S.; Tim Pat Coogan, *Michael Collins* (London: Arrow, 1991; 2015 Penguin edn), 132, claims that 'Collins literally charmed Beaumont into joining the British Secret Service', but there does not appear to be any evidence that he did become a member.
6. See for example, Paul McMahon, *British Spies and Irish Rebels: British Intelligence and Ireland, 1916–1945* (Woodbridge: Boydell, 2008), 40; J. E. B. Hittle, *Michael Collins and the Anglo-Irish War: Britain's Counter-Insurgency Failure* (Washington, DC: Potomac Books, 2011), 77, 150, 160 and 164; MA, MSPC, MSP34REF4945: Mernin, L.
7. BMH.WS0709, 2: Beaumont, W.
8. Boyne, *Emmet Dalton*, 48–53; Yeates, *Civil*, 179–80.
9. NLI, Emmet Dalton, MS 46,687/6: Film script, n.d; Tom Barry, *Guerrilla Days in Ireland* (Dublin: Irish Press, 1949; Dublin: Anvil, 1962 edn), 2–5; Yeates, *Civil*, 312.
10. Boyne, *Emmet Dalton*, 9–12.
11. TNA, WO 95/53226: Dalton, J. E.; BMH.WS0434, 1: Dalton, C.; BMH, 24SP13470: Dalton, J. E.; TNA, WO 35/206/52: J. E. Dalton. In his IRA pension application he claimed to have joined the Irish Volunteers in either December 1918 or June 1919, which is an odd distinction to make, yet close examination of the handwriting does suggest an abbreviation to be Jun rather than Jan 1919. It is possible that he had joined before leaving the British army: while he was in France and Germany from 26 November 1918 to 4 January 1919, he had sick leave (with influenza) from 31 October for nearly four weeks and though he appears to have been in France all that time he might have been home to Dublin. Meanwhile, one 1926 referee in his application said that Dalton was lecturing 'about the end' of the 1 April 1918 to 31 March 1919 period. However, he was certainly in France/Germany in January to March 1919, so that is in all likelihood a mistake, and it seems more likely that he joined after demobilisation in April 1919. Charles Dalton said he had 'introduced' Emmet 'into the Volunteers on his return from the European

War'. See Charles Dalton, *With the Dublin Brigade: Espionage and Assassination with Michael Collins' Intelligence Unit* (London: Peter Davies, 1929; Dublin: Mercier, 2014 edn), 166.

12. BMH.WS0755, 485–6: Prendergast, S.

13. His paper '"It's Up to You Now to Fight for Your Own Country": The Recruitment of Ireland's Great War Veterans into the Irish Republican Army and the Royal Irish Constabulary, 1919–21' (http://sciences-po.academia.edu/StevenOConnor (accessed 21 February 2017)) says that around 1,500 ex-servicemen joined the RIC and 121 the IRA. 19.8% of the latter were in Leinster, and Steven was kind enough to provide the names of the 10 from Dublin. I am very grateful to Steven for sharing information from his database with me, in particular because when he did so, I had not myself identified 5 of his 10: Donnelly, Garrett, Russell, Walsh and Warren. In addition, he told me about two others (Lawlor and McSweeney) who were born outside Dublin. The difference between Steven's 10 and my 16 comes partly from the fact that 3 of my 'Dubliners', Dalton, Lawlor and McSweeney were not born there (which is how Steven has linked men to an area). Meanwhile, Steven's 10 do not include the two spies, Golden and Beaumont, while the file for one man, O'Moore, only became public after his research was carried out.

14. See p. 129.

15. See pp. 117, 141, 176, 305, 307, 313, 322 and 344–5.

16. See p. 175.

17. See p. 272.

18. See pp. 283–4.

19. BMH.WS0476, 3: Kinsella, J.; BMH.WS0396, 1: Sexton, S.; BMH.WS0641, 1 and 2: Dalton, E.; BMH.WS1280, 143: Broy, E.; BMH.WS1768, 58: McDonnell. A.; NLI, Warren, W., MS 44,6481–5; TNA, AIR 76/290/91: A. T. Lawlor; TNA, AIR 79/747/82335: W. J. McSweeney; TNA, WO 339/108026: W. J. McSweeney. McSweeney was born in Manchester, to an Irish father, and was living in Waterford in 1917, but appears to have been in Dublin after the war.

20. NLI, Warren, W., MS 44,648/1 and 5; TNA, WO 372.

21. BMH.WS0979, 13–14: Barton, R.

22. UCD, de Valera, P150/507: Souvenir Programme for the 1948 Annual Reunion Dinner of 'A' Company, 3rd Battalion, 24–5. See also *EH*, 14 April 1920, 1.

23. BMH.WS0340, 38: Traynor, O.; Dwyer, *Squad*, 200–5.

24. BMH.WS1687, 58: Colley, H. See also BMH.WS0340: 33–4: Traynor, O.; Padraig O Conchubhair and Paddy Rigney, 'The Active Service Unit', in NAOIRA, *Dublin Brigade Review*, 75–82. See also Augusteijn, *Public*, 139–40.

25. UCD Archives, Papers of Richard Mulcahy, P7/A/17/119–128. See also Ernie O'Malley, *On Another Man's Wound* (London: Rich and Cowan, 1936; Dublin: Anvil, 1990 edn), 48–9.

26. BMH.WS0621, 4: Mullen, P. For a list of ASU members, see Price, *Michael Collins*, pp. 307–9.

27. Augusteijn, *Public*, 164–9. See also Kautt, *Ambushes*, 186.

28. O Conchubhair and Rigney, 'Active', 75–7.

29. Augusteijn, *Public*, 171.

30. BMH.WS1687, 59: Colley, H.

31. *EH*, 13 January 1921, 1; *IT*, 13 January 1921, 5.

32. UCD, McNulty, LA9: January 1921.

33. *EH*, 17 January 1921, 1.

34. BMH.WS822, 44–6: Stapleton, W. J.

35. BMH.WS0340: 40–6, 78–9 and 83: Traynor, O. See also Augusteijn, *Public*, 25 and 102–5.

36. See for example, *EH*, 1 February 1921, 1, for an attack in Merrion Square.
37. UCD, Mulcahy, P7/A39; BMH.WS0340: 58–66: Traynor, O; *EH*, 15 February 1921, 1. See also 'Irish Republican Prisoners' Escape from Kilmainham Jail', in NAOIRA, *Dublin Brigade Review*, 104–6.
38. BMH.WS0907, 221: Nugent, L.
39. UCD, Mulcahy, P7/A39.
40. *EH*, 14 March 1921, 1, 2 and 3.
41. UCD, Mulcahy, P7/A39; Yeates, *Turmoil*, 238; *EH*, 15 March 1921, 1; 16 March 1921, 1; 17 March 1921, 1; *IT*, 15 March 1921, 5; 16 March 1921, 5. See also Kautt, *Ambushes*, 205–9.
42. UCD, Mulcahy, P7/A39.
43. UCD, Mulcahy, P7/A39.
44. UCD, Mulcahy, P7/A39.
45. *An t-Óglác*, III, 4 (15 April 1921), 1–2.
46. BMH.WS0668, 12: Byrne, G.
47. BMH.WS0668, 13: Byrne, G.
48. BMH.WS1043, 381–7: Lawless, J. V.
49. UCD, Mulcahy, P7/A21, 98.
50. UCD, Mulcahy, P7/A39 and P7/A19, 185; *IT*, 7 May 1921, 5; *DEM*, 5 May 1921, 3.
51. BMH.WS0340, 80: Traynor, O.
52. BMH.WS1280, 143; Broy; E.; BMH.WS0641, 1: Dalton, E.
53. TNA, WO 363.
54. BMH.WS0401, 1–2: Gough, P.
55. Boyne, *Emmet Dalton*, 61–8; BMH.WS0547, 15–19: Leonard, J.; BMH.WS0434, 34–7: Dalton, C.; BMH.WS0401, 1–2; TNA, WO 35/206/52: J. E. Dalton.
56. BMH.WS0340, 81–2: Traynor, O.
57. *EH*, 25 May 1921, 1.
58. BMH.WS0423, 63: Byrne, V.; BMH.WS0547, 20–3: Leonard, J.; BMH.WS0564, 30: Byrne, T.; BMH.WS0340, 67–71.
59. BMH.WS0423, 64: Byrne, V.
60. BMH.WS0547, 22: Leonard, J.
61. BMH.WS0461, 9: Byrne, J. See also BMH.WS0340, 73: Traynor, O.
62. BMH.WS0423, 65–7: Byrne, V.
63. Michael Hopkinson, *The Irish War of Independence* (Dublin: Gill and Macmillan, 2002), 103.
64. BMH.WS0461, 8–9: Byrne, J. On the Custom House operation see also BMH. WS0822, 77–80: Stapleton, W. J.; BMH.WS0621, 10–11: Mullen, P; UCD, Mulcahy, P7/A17, 272–4; UCD, McNulty, LA9: 25 April 1921.
65. BMH.WS0340, 85: Traynor, O.
66. BMH.WS1687, 83: Colley, H.; BMH.WS0822, 86: Stapleton, W. J.; Hopkinson, *Independence*, 103; UCD, Mulcahy, P7/A19, 192–3; Dwyer, *Squad*, 250; O Conchubhair and Rigney, 'Active', 80–1.
67. UCD, Mulcahy, P7/A21, 98; Augusteijn, *Public*, 172: Augusteijn suggests 103 operations in May and 92 in June.
68. *SH*, 28 May 1921, 1.
69. *EH*, 30 May 1921, 1; UCD, Mulcahy, P7/A19, 192.
70. BMH.WS1687, 84: Colley, H.
71. UCD, Mulcahy, P7/A21, 98.
72. Augusteijn, *Public*, 327.
73. Augusteijn, *Public*, 274 and 329.

74. BMH.WS0487, 19: O'Connor, J.; James Durney, 'How Aungier Street / Camden Street Became Known as "the Dardanelles"', *The Irish Sword* XXVII, 108 (2010), 243–51; 'The Third Battalion', in NAOIRA, *Dublin Brigade Review*, 25–33, at 32.

75. UCD, de Valera, P150/507, 29.

76. UCD, Mulcahy, P7/21, 103 and 105–6.

77. Augusteijn, *Public*, 181–2 and 244..

78. Dwyer, *Squad*, 249–50.

79. Ronan Fanning, *Fatal Path: British Government and Irish Revolution, 1910–1922* (London: Faber and Faber, 2013), 257–62; *SH*, 9 July 1921, 1; *EH*, 11 July 1921, 1.

80. *EH*, 12 July 1921, 1.

81. BMH.WS1043, 384: Lawless, J. V.

82. J. J. O'Connell, 'The Role of Dublin in the War of Independence', in NAOIRA, *Dublin Brigade Review*, 99–101.

83. BMH.WS0709, 4–5: Beaumont, S.

84. BMH.WS1043, 384–5: Lawless, J. V.

85. BMH.WS1043, 385–7: Lawless, J. V.

86. BMH.WS0564, 28: Byrne, T.; *DEM*, 10 September 1921, 3.

87. BMH.WS1043, 389–93: Lawless, J. V. See also *IT*, 12 September 1921, 3 and 13 September 1921, 5.

88. BMH.WS0340, 85: Traynor, O.

89. UCD, McNulty, LA9: July–December 1921.

19 Civil War

1. Boyne, *Emmet Dalton*, 79–84.

2. Fanning, *Fatal*, 277–311.

3. BMH.WS0979, 34–47: Barton, R. C.; UCD, O'Malley, P17b/99/50–61: Barton, R.

4. For police monitoring of the Truce, see TNA, CO 904/152.

5. UCD, McNulty, LA9: February 1922.

6. *IT*, 27 March 1922, 5.

7. *IT*, 10 April 1922, 5.

8. *IT*, 15 April 1922, 7.

9. Bill Kissane, *The Politics of the Irish Civil War* (Oxford University Press, 2005), 77–8.

10. *IT*, 8 May 1922, 5; Liz Gillis, *The Fall of Dublin* (Cork: Mercier, 2011), 19–39; Michael Hopkinson, *Green against Green: The Irish Civil War* (Dublin: Gill and Macmillan, 1998; 2004 edn), 34–44. 60–2, 66–9, 72–6, 93–104, 105–10.

11. *IT*, 21 June 1922, 5; 20 June 1922, 5. The votes were 72,285 to 10,929 in the city, and in the wider county 46,936 to 4,819.

12. Boyne, *Emmet Dalton*, 90–111; Yeates, *Civil*, 15.

13. Kissane, *Politics*, 203–4.

14. *EH*, 28 June 1922, 1.

15. *EH*, 28 June 1922, 1.

16. Hopkinson, *Green*, 115–17; Gillis, *Fall*, 40–8; Boyne, *Emmet Dalton*, 139–42. One of the guns was recently tracked down. See Kenneth L. Smith-Christmas, Lar Joye and Stephen McEoin, 'Possible "Four Courts" Irish Field Gun Returns Home', *ICOMAM Magazine*, 16 (December 2016), 28–32; Yeates, *Civil*, 77.

17. For maps of the conflict in Dublin, see Michael Hopkinson, 'Civil War: The Opening Phase', in Crowley et al., *Atlas*, 675–87.

18. Andy Bielenberg, 'Fatalities in the Irish Revolution' in Crowley et al., *Atlas*, 752–61, at 759–60; John Dorney, *The Civil War in Dublin: The Fight for the Irish Capital*

1922–1924 (Newbridge: Merrion, 2017), 323–8. Dorney's study provides a detailed narrative of events in Dublin.

19. BMH.WS0294, 9–10: Pounch, J.

20. BMH.WS1043, 417–18: Lawless, J. V.

21. BMH, MSP34REF56969 30: McCabe, M.; MSP34REF55705, 21: O'Moore, P. M.; UCD, O'Malley, P17a/130/5: List of 3 Section, Guards Company, Four Courts, 28 June 1922; P17b/85/11–18: O'Moore, P.; P17b/105/117: McCabe, M. See p. 175.

22. Gillis, *Fall*, 57–60.

23. UCD, McNulty, LA9: 28 June 1922.

24. Gillis, *Fall*, 60–3; Yeates, *Civil*, 81.

25. Gillis, *Fall*, 62–72.

26. Gillis, *Fall*, 73–83; Ernie O'Malley, *The Singing Flame* (Dublin: Cahill, 1976; 1987 Anvil edn)., 116; *DEM*, 1 July 1922, 3; NLI, MS 33063, 8: Account by Simon Donnelly, 1923.

27. NLI, O'Malley, E., MS 10,973/11/7 and 15: Reports from Emmet Dalton, 3 July 1922.

28. Gillis, *Fall*, 87–116; *DEM*, 3 July 1922, 3; 4 July 1922, 3; 5 July 1922, 3; 6 July 1922, 3.

29. UCD, O'Malley, P17b/105/118–19: McCabe, M.

30. *DEM*, 28 July 1922, 3.

31. Patrick Taaffe, 'Richard Mulcahy and the Irish Civil War', *Irish Sword*, XXX, 120 (2015), 193–216, at 196, 198, 200 and 213; Boyne, *Emmet Dalton*, 161–2; Yeates, *Civil*, 101.

32. I am grateful to Michael Nugent for providing information form his detailed research on Geoghegan. See also MA, VR1457 George Geoghegan.

33. Dorney, *Civil*, 2.

34. UCD, de Valera, P150/1646: Dublin District Weekly Intelligence Summary No, 176, 5 September 1922.

35. *IT*, 7 August 1922, 5. See also UCD, Mulcahy, P7/B/59/129–37: newspaper cuttings and intelligence reports; UCD, O'Malley, P17a/82/33: Material Lost 5/6 August 1922.

36. Hopkinson, *Green*, 176–9. For a map See T. Ryle Dwyer, 'Michael Collins and the Civil War', in Crowley et al., *Atlas*, 725–9, at 729.

37. Boyne, *Emmet Dalton*, 214 and 219–32; Meda Ryan, *The Day Michael Collins was Shot* (Swords: Poolbeg Press, 1989), 46, 114 and 154; *FJ*, 22 August 1923, 5. The death of Collins is much debated: see Gerard Murphy, *The Great Cover-Up: The Truth About the Death of Michael Collins* (Wilton: Collins Press, 2018).

38. *IT*, 29 August 1922, 5.

39. See for example, UCD, O'Malley, P17a/77/22–3: Operations Week Ending 26 August 1922.

40. UCD, O'Malley, P17a/77/44–53: Operations Weeks Ending 30 September 1922 to 14 October 1922.

41. MA, CW/OPS/07/028, Eastern District Command, Raids, Numerical Index, August 1922 to 7 September 1923. See also CW/OPS/07/024–27 for reports of raids.

42. BMH.WS0979, 46–7: Barton, R. See also UCD, O'Malley, P17a/99/50–61: Barton, R.

43. See for example, daily Operation Reports in MA, CW/OPS/07/01.

44. UCD, O'Malley, P17a/77/31–2: Operations Week Ending 23 September 1922. On Oriel House, see Yeates, *Civil*, 146.

45. UCD, O'Malley, P17a/77/44. 45 and 48: Operations Week Ending 30 September 1922.

46. Information provided to author by Michael Nugent, *IT*, 21 November 1922, 3 and 23 November 1922, 3.

47. Yeates, *Civil*, 140–5.

48. *DEM*, 4 November 1918, 3.

49. MA, CW/OPS/07/01, Daily Bulletin, 4 November 1922, 2–3.

50. Hopkinson, *Green*, 144; O'Malley, *Singing*, 180–9; Richard English, 'O'Malley, Ernest Bernard ("Ernie")', in McGuire and Quinn, eds. (dib.cambridge.org /viewReadPage.do?articleId=a6885); Richard English, *Ernie O'Malley: IRA Intellectual* (Oxford: Clarendon Press, 1998), 7; MA, MSPC, W34A6: O'Malley, E. B.

51. *DEM*, 4 November 1922, 3; English, *Ernie*, 19.

52. See p. 317.

53. O'Malley, *On Another*, 23–43

54. UCD, O'Malley, P17a/77/83: Report of Attack on Wellington Barracks; MA, CW/ OPS/07/01: Operation Report, 8 November 1922; *WIT*, 18 November 1922, 1; *DEM*, 8 November 1922, 3.

55. MA, CW/OPS/07/01: Irregular Operation Report, 10 December 1922. See also *IT*, 11 December 1922, 5.

56. *IT*, 18 December 1922, 4.

57. *IT*, 18 December 1922, 7 and 8.

58. MA, CW/OPS/07/15, Daily Intelligence Report, 11 January 1923.

59. *EH*, 19 January 1923, 1; *SH*, 20 January 1923, 1.

60. *EH*, 26 January 1923, 1.

61. MA, CW/OPS/07/02: IO Dublin District to OC Publicity, 1 February 1923.

62. *SH*, 27 January 1923, 1; *EH*, 30 January 1923, 1; *EH*, 31 January 1923, 1; *EH*, 6 February 1923, 1; *EH*, 7 February 1923, 1; *EH*, 10 February 1923, 1; *EH*, 15 February 1923, 1; *EH*, 16 February 1923, 1; *EH*, 21 February 1923, 1; *EH*, 6 March 1923, 1; *EH*, 7 March 1923, 1; *EH*, 15 March 1923, 1; *EH*, 24 March 1923, 1; *EH*, 27 March 1923, 1; *EH*, 29 March 1923, 1; *EH*, 2 April 1923, 1; *EH*, 4 April 1923, 1; *EH*, 9 April 1923, 1.

63. MA, CW/OPS/07/02: Special Report, 24 February 1923.

64. MA, CW/OPS/07/02: Operation Report, 21 February 1923.

65. MA, CW/OPS/07/03: Operation Reports, 1 March 1923 to 19 April 1923.

66. *EH*, 13 April 1923, 1; *EH*, 16 April 1923, 1.

67. *EH*, 27 April 1923, 1; *IT*, 28 April 1923, 8.

68. *EH*, 9 May 1923, 1.

69. *EH*, 29 May 1923, 4; *IT*, 29 May 1923, 7.

70. Figures compiled from MA, Prisoners' Location Books, CW/P/01/01 and 02.

71. *IT*, 16 October 1923, 5; *IT*, 3 November 1923; *IT*, 24 November 1923, 8; Hopkinson, *Green*, 256–8 and 268–71.

72. BMH, MSP34REF56969 29–30: McCabe, M.; MSP34REF55705, 21: O'Moore, P. M.; MA, CW/P/01/01: Prisoners' Location Book.

73. MA, CW/OPS/07/16: General Weekly Report No. 18, 17 August 1923; Fortnightly Report, 23 October 1923; General Survey, 15 November 1923; General Survey, 1 February 1924.

74. UCD, de Valera, P150/1657: Executed Irregulars.

75. Following the Rising 16 were executed. For the 24 executed from 1 November 1920 to 7 June 1921 see Seán McConville, *Irish Political Prisoners, 1848–1922, Theatres of War* (London: Routledge, 2003), 697–8.

76. Boyne, *Emmet Dalton*, 9 and 272.

77. Boyne, *Emmet Dalton*, 269–70.

78. BMH, 24SP13470: Dalton, J. E.; Boyne, 277–9.
79. Yeates, *Civil*, 282–6, 300, 312; Boyne, *Emmet Dalton*, 294–8, 363.
80. Boyne, *Emmet Dalton*, 284, 300, 306, 309, 310, 314, 319, 326, 346, 361 and 365–6.

20 Peace

1. MSP34REF56969, 24: McCabe, M.; MSP34REF55705, 30: O'Moore, P. M.
2. *EH*, 30 January 1919. 3.
3. TNA, WO 374/29700: A. Guest.
4. Wylly, *Neill's, III*, 125–133; TNA, WO 95/2301: 1st RDF.
5. Wylly, *Crown*, 125–9.
6. NAM, Drury 4, 67.
7. NAM, Drury 4, 78.
8. TNA, WO 95/3140: 6th RDF.
9. NAM, Drury 4, 82.
10. *WIT*, 18 November 1916, 1 and 8; www.cwgc.org/find-war-dead/casualty/900627/YOUNG,%20BENJAMIN%20POYNTZ; www.cwgc.org/find-war-dead/casualty/325867/YOUNG,%20CHARLES%20ROBERT and www.cwgc.org/find-war-dead/casualty/406238/YOUNG,%20HECTOR%20ALBERT (all accessed 7 February 2017).
11. Wylly, *Crown*, 130–3.
12. www.cwgc.org/about-us/faqs (accessed 7 November 2017).
13. Wills; *SD*; www.cwgc.org/find-war-dead/casualty/471613/BEGLEY,%20HENRY%20FREDERICK (accessed 7 February 2017).
14. www.cwgc.org/find-war-dead/casualty/634104/KILLEEN,%20P (accessed 7 February 2017); Taylor, *2nd*, 132.
15. www.cwgc.org/find-war-dead/casualty/123728/MALLEY,%20F%20L (accessed 7 February 2017); TNA, WO 339/33638: F. L. Malley.
16. www.cwgc.org/find-war-dead/casualty/899888/CALLAGHAN,%20M (accessed 7 February 2017).
17. www.cwgc.org/find-war-dead/casualty/900495/SCULLY,%20M (accessed 7 February 2017).
18. Wylly, *Neill's, III*, 139–40.
19. NAM, Irish Attestation Records at: www.nam.ac.uk/soldiers-records/persons?ss=%7B%22q%22:%22John%20Flannery%22%7D (accessed 7 February 2017).
20. BMH.WS0287, 3–10: Flannery, J.; Anthony Babington, *The Devil to Pay: The Mutiny of the Connaught Rangers, India, July 1920* (London: Leo Cooper, 1991), 6 and 9.
21. BMH.WS0287, 15 and 18: Flannery, J.; Babington, *Devil*, 16 and 27.
22. BMH.WS0287, 37–46: Flannery, J.; Babington, *Devil*, 51–56.
23. NAM, Irish Attestation Records at: www.nam.ac.uk/soldiers-records/persons?ss=%7B%22q%22:%22John%20Flannery%22%7D (accessed 7 February 2017).
24. BMH.WS0287, 46–7: Flannery, J.
25. Wylly, *Crown*, 151–6.
26. J. D. R. Rawlings, 'History of No. 24 Squadron', *Air Pictorial*, 34, 4 (1972), 144–7 at 145–6.
27. TNA, AIR 27/294/43 and 44: 24 Squadron Operations Record Book; www.cwgc.org/find-war-dead/casualty/2762389/DAY,%20JOHN%20FORBES%20ANDRE (accessed 10 February 2017).
28. www.thepeerage.com/p45854.htm#i458535 (accessed 10 February 2017).
29. See Chapter 21.

30. TNA, WO 363: Hogan, D.
31. *EH*, 20 June 1922, 1.
32. Gillies Archives: search.findmypast.co.uk/results/world-records/harold-gillies-plastic-surgery-archives-from-ww1?unit=royal%20dublin%20fusiliers (accessed 9 February 2017). See also Andrew Bamji, *Faces from the Front: Harold Gillies, The Queen's Hospital, Sidcup, and the Origins of Modern Plastic Surgery* (Solihull: Helion, 2017).
33. See p. 341–3.
34. TNA, WO 363; Royal College of Surgeons [RCS], Gillies, 709, Fitzpatrick, J.
35. RCS, Gillies, 1771, Roche, J.
36. TNA, WO 363 and 364.
37. RCS, Gillies: MS 0513/1/1/39 ID 2191, Wheatman, R.
38. *DEM*, 20 January 1916, 5.
39. Edgar Jones, Ian Palmer and Simon Wessely, 'War Pensions (1900–1945): Changing Models of Psychological Understanding', *The British Journal of Psychiatry*, 180, 4 (2002), 374–9.
40. *DEM*, 21 May 1917, 4.
41. *IT*, 25 September 1918, 2. For assistance on land see *WIT*, 17 August 1918, 2, and for assistance offered by the *Irish Times* through a servicemen's bureau see *WIT*, 8 March 1919, 1. For fundraising by the Comrades, See for example, *IT*, 9 September 1920, 6 and 26 August 1921, 3.
42. Paul Taylor, *Heroes or Traitors? Experiences of Southern Irish Soldiers Returning from the Great War 1919–1939* (Liverpool: Liverpool University Press, 2015), 111–22.
43. Coleman, 'Veterans', 201–21. See also Marie Coleman, 'Civil', 51–61; Diarmaid Ferriter, '"Always in Danger of Finding Myself with Nothing at All"', in Diarmaid Ferriter and Susannah Riordan, *Years of Turbulence: The Irish Revolution and its Aftermath* (Dublin: University College Dublin Press, 2015), 191–207.
44. MSP34REF56969, 24: McCabe, M.; MSP34REF55705, 30: O'Moore, P. M.
45. *IT*, 25 February 1922, 5.
46. Taylor, *Heroes*, 98–110.
47. Taylor, *Heroes*, 140–8.
48. TNA, WO 363.
49. TNA, WO 363.
50. TNA, WO 339/44144: E. S. Lemass; DCLA, RDFA/035: Lemass Papers.
51. Taylor, *Heroes*, 200; Cooper, *Tenth*.
52. BMH.WS1751, 15-16: Davitt, C.
53. See pp. 124–5.
54. TNA, WO 339/47808: Eugene Sheehy; TNA, WO 95/2301: 1st RDF; Richardson, *Lights*, 248; Hogan, 'Sheehy'.
55. Leonard, 'Survivors', 219. A 1923 analysis of officers, possibly incomplete, showed 244 National Army officers with former British army service: MA, SDG (1) List of ex-Britishers in Commands and Services.
56. MA, W34E747, 38–43: Neilan, A. See also McGreevy, *Wherever*, 130.
57. Taylor, *Heroes*, 210.
58. Gemma Clark, *Everyday Violence in the Irish Civil War* (Cambridge University Press, 2014), 84, 125, 152, 194 and 199.
59. Leonard, 'Survivors', 218.
60. For a useful summary of the debate see Matthew Lewis, 'Sectarianism and Irish Republican Violence on the South-East Ulster Frontier, 1919–1922', *Contemporary European History*, 26, 1 (2017), 1–21, at 3–4.

61. Taylor, *Heroes*, 233.

21 Commemoration

1. *IT*, 1 August 2014, 3; *IT*, 5 August 2014, 5.
2. Individual memorials can be very visible and public, such as stained-glass windows: Martin Staunton, 'Saint Ann's Church, Dublin', *The Gallipolian*, 74 (Spring 1994), 37–8.
3. For many of the issues raised here, see Richard S. Grayson and Fearghal McGarry, eds., *Remembering 1916: The Easter Rising, the Somme and the Politics of Memory in Ireland* (Cambridge University Press, 2016).
4. Grayson, *Belfast*, 168.
5. *IT*, 17 July 1919, 6; Grayson, *Belfast*, 168–9. See also Jane Leonard, 'The Twinge of Memory: Armistice Day and Remembrance Sunday in Dublin since 1919', in Richard English and Graham Walker, eds., *Unionism in Modern Ireland: New Perspectives on Politics and Culture* (Basingstoke: Macmillan, 1996), 99–114, at 101.
6. *DEM*, 19 July 1919, 3.
7. *DEM*, 11 November 1919. 3.
8. Leonard, 'Twinge', 102.
9. *IT*, 12 November 1923, 5. On poppies in Dublin, see Heather Jones, 'Church of Ireland Great War Remembrance in the South of Ireland: A Personal Reflection', in John Horne and Edward Madigan, eds., *Towards Commemoration: Ireland in War and Revolution, 1912–1923* (Dublin: Royal Irish Academy, 2013), 74–82.
10. *IT*, 12 November 1924, 7.
11. Catriona Pennell, '"Choreographed by the Angels"? Ireland and the Centenary of the First World War', *War and Society*, 36, 4 (2017), 256–75, at 260; McGreevy, *Wherever*, 215 and 226.
12. *IT*, 12 November 1924, 7.
13. Leonard, 'Twinge', 105–6; NAI, DFA 34/169: Foreign War Memorials, 1924–36.
14. NAI, Taoiseach S3370A: Armistice Day, 1923–31.
15. NAI, Taoiseach S5276: Unveiling of Memorial Tablet in Westminster Abbey (Cosgrave to Baldwin, 13 October 1926; Baldwin to Cosgrave, 14 October 1926; Amery to Cosgrave 15 October 1926).
16. *IT*, 20 October 1926, 7.
17. Leonard, 'Twinge', 102.
18. *IT*, 12 November 1925, 7.
19. *IT*, 12 November 1927, 9.
20. *IT*, 7 November 1927, 5; 11 November 1927, 9.
21. *IT*, 12 November 1930, 7.
22. *IT*, 12 November 1932, 9.
23. NAI, Taoiseach S3370B: Armistice Day, 1932–44.
24. NAI, Taoiseach/S3743: Bar Memorial, 1924; NAI, DFA/239/89: IWGC, 1924–31. The Imperial War Graves Commission contacted the Free State government about the maintenance of graves (of which there were 917 in Dublin city and county) in early 1924, though it took four years for the government to agree to take on the costs of British graves in their territory.
25. Heather Jones, 'Cultures of Commemoration: Remembering the First World War in Ireland', in Crowley et al., *Atlas*, 838–47, at 842.

26. *DEM*, 18 July 1919, 3. For the Irish National War Memorial Comittee's records see DCLA, RDFA/020/1–168.

27. NAI, Taoiseach, S4156A: War Memorial, Selection of Site, 1924–29 (note dated 24 November 1924).

28. Nuala C. Johnson, *Ireland, the Great War and the Geography of Remembrance* (Cambridge University Press, 2003), 84–94. See also NAI, Taoiseach, S4156A: War Memorial, Selection of Site, 1924–9.

29. NAI, Taoiseach, S4156B: War Memorial, Selection of Site, 1929–40; Taoiseach, S4156C: War Memorial Islandbridge, Opening Ceremony, 1938–41.

30. Johnson, *Geography*, 108–10.

31. Trinity College, Dublin, *Official Unveiling of a Memorial Stone* (booklet for ceremony of 26 September 2015, in author's possession); Irish, *Trinity*, 262–6.

32. NAI, Taoiseach, S4156C: War Memorial Islandbridge, Opening Ceremony, 1938–41.

33. NAI, Taoiseach S3370B: Armistice Day, 1932–44.

34. NAI, PRES/1/P/2026: Ireland's Memorial Records.

35. NAI, Taoiseach S3370C: Armistice Day, 1945–7; *IT*, 9 November 1946, 4.

36. NAI, Taoiseach S3370D: Armistice Day, 1948–50; Taoiseach, S3370E: Armistice Day, 1951–8; Taoiseach 96/6/111, Armistice Day, 1959–69.

37. NAI, DFA, 316/27/979: Ex-servicemen's organisations.

38. *IT*, 12 November 1958, 5.

39. DCLA, RDFA/022: RDF Old Comrades Association, Reunion Dinner, 21 October 1967; Jason R. Myers, *The Great War and Memory in Irish Culture, 1918–2010* (Palo Alto: Academica, 2016), 217–18.

40. Leonard, 'Twinge', 107; Myers, *Great War*, 209.

41. NAI, JUS/90/116/727: Armistice Day, 1945–60.

42. David Fitzpatrick, 'Commemoration in the Irish Free State: A Chronicle of Embarrassment', in Ian McBride, ed., *History and Memory in Modern Ireland* (Cambridge University Press, 2001), 184–203, at 186 and 203.

43. Johnson, *Geography*, 78.

44. Fitzpatrick, 'Commemoration', 196–7.

45. Fitzpatrick, 'Commemoration', 199–203. Anne Dolan, *Commemorating the Irish Civil War: History and Memory, 1923–2000* (Cambridge University Press, 2003), 6–56. See also: archiseek.com/2013/1951-cenotaph-leinster-house-dublin/ (accessed 28 February 2017).

46. Dolan, *Commemorating*, 56.

47. Fitzpatrick, 'Commemoration', 197–8.

48. NAI, Taoiseach, S8114A, Garden of Remembrance: Memorandum, 20 September 1935.

49. See p. 19.

50. NAI, Taoiseach, S8114A, Garden of Remembrance: Memorandum, 27 February 1940.

51. NAI, Taoiseach, S8114B, Garden of Remembrance: Competition for Designs, January 1946.

52. NAI, President, P2270; NAI, Taoiseach, S8114B, Garden of Remembrance.

53. NAI, Taoiseach, S8114B/2–3 and S811C/61–3, Garden of Remembrance.

54. *IT*, 12 April 1966, 1 and 11; *IT*, 12 July 1911, 8; NAI, Taoiseach, 96/6/193, Garden of Remembrance and 2002/8/471: Truce Commemoration; Roisín Higgins, *Transforming 1916: Meaning Memory and the Fiftieth Anniversary of the Easter Rising* (Cork University Press, 2012), 41–3 and

147–52. See also Margaret O'Callaghan, 'Reframing 1916 after 1969: Irish Governments, a National Day of Reconciliation, and the Politics of Commemoration in the 1970s', in Grayson and McGarry, eds., *Remembering*, 207–23; Rebecca Graff-McRae, *Remembering and Forgetting 1916: Commemoration and Conflict in Post-Peace Process Ireland* (Dublin: Irish Academic Press, 2010).

55. Higgins, *Transforming*, 30–56 and 168.
56. Johnson, *Geography*, 110; Leonard, 'Twinge', 109–11; Jane Leonard, 'Lest We Forget', in David Fitzpatrick, ed., *Ireland and the First World War* (Dublin: Trinity History Workshop, 1988), 59–68, at 64–7; *IT*, 2 July 1994, 11.
57. *IT*, 12 November 1993, 1 and 15 November 1993, 1.
58. *IT*, 12 November 1998, 10; *IT*, 3 July 2006, 7.
59. See p. 181.
60. Jeffery, 'Commemoration', 175.
61. *IT*, 18 May 2011, 1 and 6; 19 May 2011, 7; 20 May 2011, 6.
62. *IT*, 29 December 2004, 7. See also www.greatwar.ie/ (accessed 24 February 2017); and Tom Burke, 'Recovery and Reconciliation: The Royal Dublin Fusiliers Association', in Horne and Madigan, eds., *Towards*, 98–104.
63. See for example, http://eastwallforall.ie/?s=first+world+war (accessed 24 February 2017).
64. wfadublin.webs.com/ (accessed 10 November 2017).
65. Pennell, '"Choreographed"', 268.
66. www.decadeofcentenaries.com/ (accessed 24 February 2017).
67. www.decadeofcentenaries.com/4-august-2014/, www.decadeofcentenaries.com/ 24-april-2015-commonwealth-and-ireland-commemoration-service-for-gallipoli-campaign-cape-helles-turkey/ and www.decadeofcentenaries.com/9-july-2016-state-ceremony-to-mark-centenary-of-the-battle-of-the-somme-irish-national-war-memorial-gardens-islandbridge-dublin-8/ (accessed 24 February 2017).
68. Pennell, '"Choreographed"', 267 and 269.
69. https://dublin.anglican.org/news/2016/12/Christmas-Day-Sermon-of-the-Archbishop-of-Dublin (accessed 21 November 2017).
70. www.sinnfein.ie/contents/46990 (accessed 13 November 2017).
71. Pennell, '"Choreographed"', 267.
72. *IT*, 1 August 2014, 3; *IT*, 5 August 2014, 5.
73. *IT*, 24 April 2015, 10. See also Jenny Macleod, 'The Gallipoli Centenary: An International Perspective', in Brad West, ed., *War Memory and Commemoration* (London: Routledge, 2017), 89–106.
74. See pp. 278–9.
75. Her brother had already died, as had former Taioseach, Garrett Fitzgerald, whose parents were both in the GPO.
76. *IT*, 28 March 2016, 4; Wren, *GPO*, 25–6 and 330; www.storiesfrom1916.com /1916-easter-rising/tom-and-lucy-byrne (accessed 21 November 2017).

Conclusion: Three Men

1. www.rte.ie/archives/exhibitions/1011-ireland-and-the-great-war/1016-easter-rising/315378-emmet-dalton-remembers/ (accessed 21 March 2017).
2. Data on the British army are from Army Council, *Cmd. 1193*, *General Annual Reports on the British Army for the Period from 1st October, 1913, to 30th September, 1919* (London: His Majesty's Stationery Office, 1921), 17–21. Figures used are those for 1 October in each of 1914–18 for the army

as a whole excluding the RFC, Colonial Corps and Indian Native Troops. In October 1914, the infantry and foot guards constituted 70.5% of the army, in 1915 62.8%, in 1916 58.9%, in 1917 50% and in 1918 45.4%. Dublin's infantry numbers (which include foot guards) are taken from the infantry lines in Table A2.1.

3. NLI, Emmet Dalton, MS 46,687/6: Film script, n.d; **Boyne**, *Emmet Dalton*, 341–2.
4. www.rte.ie/archives/exhibitions/1011-ireland-and-the-great-war/1016-easter-ris ing/315378-emmet-dalton-remembers/ (accessed 21 March 2017).
5. *IT*, 9 September 1966, 3.
6. Marriage certificate, copy in author's possession.
7. RCS, Gillies, 3766: Callaghan, RWH; TNA, WO 339/30779: R. W. H. Callaghan; civilrecords.irishgenealogy.ie/churchrecords/images/birth_returns/births_1886/ 02615/1965374.pdf; https://churchrecords.irishgenealogy.ie/churchrecords/dis play-pdf.jsp?pdfName=d-833-2-3-012.
8. TNA, WO 339/30779: R. W. H. Callaghan.
9. Death certificate, copy in author's possession.
10. See p. 322.
11. MA, MSP34REF56969 39: McCabe, M.; W34E7757, 20 and 30–3: McCabe, M.

BIBLIOGRAPHY

Primary Sources

Archives

Archives New Zealand, Wellington Office (http://archives.govt.nz/world-war-one)

Thomas Saunders

Dublin City Archive

Royal Dublin Fusiliers Association (including Irish National War Memorial), and the Monica Roberts collection (databases.dublincity.ie/monicaroberts/)

Imperial War Museum

Arthur Glanville
Douglas Riddle (www.iwm.org.uk/collections/item/object/80009134)
E. E. Rickus
Orlando Beater
Reginald Ford
Wilfrid Colyer

Irish Jesuit Archives, Dublin

Henry Gill Papers

Military Archives, Dublin (www.militaryarchives.ie)

Administration Files (online)
Bureau of Military History, Witness Statements (online)
Civil War Captured Documents
Civil War Internment Collection
Civil War Operations and Intelligence Reports
Medals (online)
Organisations and Membership Files (online)
Pensions and Award Files (online)

National Archive of Australia (https://discoveringanzacs.naa .gov.au/series-info/b2455/)

First Australian Imperial Force Personnel Dossiers, 1914–1920

National Archives, Kew

ADM 53: Ships' Logs
ADM 188: Naval Service Records
AIR 76: Air Officers' Service
AIR 79: Airmen's Service
CO 693: Merchant Seamen and Fishermen Detained as POWs in Germany
CO 904: Royal Irish Constabulary Reports
MEPO 2/10668: Irish Brigade
NATS 1: Recruiting Statistics
WO 71: Courts Martial
WO 95: Unit War Diaries (see also CD/DVD Resources)
WO 141: Registered Papers, Special Series (Intelligence)
WO 161: Returned Prisoner of War Interviews
WO 329: Medal and Award Rolls (see also CD/DVD Resources)
WO 339: Army Officers' Service
WO 363: Army Service (available at www.ancestry.co.uk)
WO 364: Army Pensions (available at www.ancestry.co.uk)
WO 372: Medal and Award Rolls Index
WO 374: Army Officers' Service

National Archives of Ireland, Dublin

Census of Ireland, 1901 and 1911 (www.census.nationalarchives.ie)
Chief Secretary's Office (files on Republican Prisoners)

Department of Foreign Affairs (files on ex-servicemen)
Office of the President (files on commemoration)
Office of the Taioseach (files on Armistice Day, Garden of Remembrance and War Memorials)
Soldiers' Wills (http://soldierswills.nationalarchives.ie/search/sw/home.jsp)

National Army Museum, London

Attestation Books of Disbanded Irish Regiments (www.nam.ac.uk/soldiers-records/persons)
David French
Henry O'Hara
Noël Drury

National Library of Ireland, Dublin

Emmet Dalton
Ernie O'Malley
John Redmond
Simon Donnelly
Thomas Moylan (online at: catalogue.nli.ie/Record/vtls000577015)
William Warren

National Museum of Ireland, Dublin

Records of 3rd Battalion, Irish Volunteers

Private Collection

Christmas 1914 Prisoners of War (Paul Nixon, http://armyancestry.blogspot.co.uk/p/researchers.html)

Royal College of Surgeons of England, London

Patients of Harold Gillies (index at www.findmypast.co.uk)

University College, Dublin Archives

Belgian Refugees Committee, P105
Éamon de Valera, P150
Thomas & Mary Kettle, LA34

Eoin MacNeill, LA1
Peadar McNulty, LA9
Richard Mulcahy, P7/A
Ernie O'Malley, P17b

CD/DVD Resources (from Naval and Military Press)

Airmen Died
First World War Campaign Medals (see also, National Archives, Kew, WO 329)
Sailors Died
Soldiers Died (also available at www.ancestry.co.uk)
War Diaries, Western Front (see also, National Archives, Kew, WO 95)

Newspapers and Periodicals

An t-Óglác
Blue Cap, The
Daily Express (Dublin edition)
Dublin Evening Mail
Evening Herald
Evening Telegraph
Freeman's Journal, The
Irish Independent, The
Irish Times, The
Irish Volunteer, The
London Gazette, The
National Volunteer, The
News Letter
Saturday Herald
Sunday Independent
Times, The
Weekly Irish Times

Official Publications

Army Council, Cd. 7252, *The General Annual Report on the British Army for the Year Ending 30th September 1913* (London: HMSO, 1914).

Cmd. 1193, *General Annual Reports on the British Army for the Period from 1st October, 1913, to 30th September, 1919* (London: HMSO, 1921).

Cd. 8168, *Report on Recruiting in Ireland* (London: HMSO, 1916).

Cd. 6049-I, *Census of Ireland, 1911. County of Dublin* (London: HMSO, 1912).

Hansard.

HMSO, *Army List*, various editions.

War Office, Cd. 5481, *The General Annual Report on the British Army for the Year Ending 30th September 1910* (London: HMSO, 1911).

Secondary Sources

Books

aan de Wiel, Jérôme, *The Catholic Church in Ireland, 1914–1918: War and Politics* (Dublin: Irish Academic Press, 2003).

Anderson, Ross, *The Forgotten Front, 1914–18: The East African Campaign* (Stroud: Tempus, 2007).

Augusteijn, Joost, *From Public Defiance to Guerrilla Warfare: The Experiences of Ordinary Volunteers in the Irish War of Independence, 1916–1921* (Dublin: Irish Academic Press, 1996).

Babington, Anthony, *The Devil to Pay: The Mutiny of the Connaught Rangers, India, July 1920* (London: Leo Cooper, 1991).

Bamji, Andrew, *Faces from the Front: Harold Gillies, The Queen's Hospital, Sidcup, and the Origins of Modern Plastic Surgery* (Solihull: Helion, 2017).

Banks, Arthur, *A Military Atlas of the First World War* (London: Heinemann, 1975; Barnsley: Leo Cooper, 1989 edn).

Barton, Ruth, *Hedy Lamarr: The Most Beautiful Woman in Film* (Lexington: University Press of Kentucky, 2010).

Barry, Tom, *Guerrilla Days in Ireland* (Dublin: Irish Press, 1949; Dublin: Anvil, 1962 edn).

Bowman, Timothy, and Connelly, Mark, *The British Army and the First World War* (Cambridge University Press, 2017).

Boff, Jonathan, *Winning and Losing on the Western Front: The British Third Army and the Defeat of Germany in 1918* (Cambridge University Press, 2012).

Bowman, Timothy, *Carson's Army: The Ulster Volunteer Force, 1910–22* (Manchester University Press, 2007).

Boyne, Sean, *Emmet Dalton: Somme Soldier, Irish General, Film Pioneer* (Sallins: Merrion, 2015).

Brady, Declan, *Culture, Politics and Local Government in Fingal, 1891–1914* (Dublin: Four Courts Press, 2017).

Brooks, John, *The Battle of Jutland* (Cambridge University Press, 2016).

Burke, Tom, *Messines to Carrick Hill: Writing Home from the Great War* (Cork: Mercier, 2017).

Butler, William, *The Irish Amateur Military Tradition in the British Army, 1854–1992* (Manchester University Press, 2016).

Canning, W. J., *A Wheen of Medals: The History of the 9th (Service) Bn. The Royal Inniskilling Fusiliers (The Tyrones) in World War One* (Antrim: W. J. Canning, 2006).

Carlyon, L. A., *Gallipoli* (London: Doubleday, 2001; Bantam, 2003 edn).

Carver, Field Marshall Lord, *The National Army Museum Book of the Turkish Front, 1914–18* (London: Sidgwick & Jackson, 2003).

Clark, Gemma, *Everyday Violence in the Irish Civil War* (Cambridge University Press, 2014).

Connaught Rangers Research Project, *The 6th Connaught Rangers: Belfast Nationalists and the Great War* (Belfast: 6th Connaught Rangers Research Project, 2008).

Connell, Joseph E. A., *Dublin Rising 1916* (Dublin: Wordwell, 2015).
Who's Who in the Dublin Rising, 1916 (Dublin: Wordwell, 2015).
Michael Collins: Dublin 1916–22 (Dublin: Wordwell, 2017).

Coogan, Tim Pat, *Michael Collins* (London: Arrow, 1991; 2015 Penguin edn).
The Twelve Apostles (London: Head of Zeus, 2016).

Cook, Tim, *At the Sharp End: Canadians Fighting The Great War, 1914–1916*, vol. I (Toronto: Penguin, 2007).

Cookstown District Council, *Cookstown's War Dead: 1914–18, 1939–45* (Cookstown: Cookstown District Council, 2007).

Cooper, Bryan, *The Tenth (Irish) Division at Gallipoli* (London: Herbert Jenkins, 1918; Dublin, Irish Academic Press, 1993 edn).

Cooper, David, *The Musical Traditions of Northern Ireland and its Diaspora: Community and Conflict* (Farnham: Ashgate, 2009).

Craig, F. W. S., ed., *Chronology of British Parliamentary By-Elections, 1833–1987* (Chichester: Parliamentary Research Services, 1987).

Crawley, Rhys, *Climax at Gallipoli: The Failure of the August Offensive* (Norman: University of Oklahoma Press, 2014).

Crowley, John, Ó Drisceoil, Donal, and Murphy, Mike, eds., *Atlas of the Irish Revolution* (Cork University Press, 2017).

Creighton, O., *With the Twenty-Ninth Division in Gallipoli* (London: Longman, 1916).

Daley, Mary E., *Dublin: The Deposed Capital, A Social and Economic History 1860–1914* (Cork University Press, 1984).

Dalton, Charles, *With the Dublin Brigade: Espionage and Assassination with Michael Collins' Intelligence Unit* (London: Peter Davies, 1929; Dublin: Mercier, 2014 edn).

Dawe, Gerald, ed., *Earth Voices Whispering: An Anthology of Irish War Poetry, 1914–1945* (Belfast: Blackstaff Press, 2008).

Denman, Terence, *Ireland's Unknown Soldiers* (Dublin: Irish Academic Press, 1992).

A *Lonely Grave: The Life and Death of William Redmond* (Blackrock: Irish Academic Press, 1995).

Dickson, David, *Dublin: The Making of a Capital City* (London: Profile, 2014).

Dixon, John, *A Clash of Empires: The South Wales Borderers at Tsingtao, 1914* (Wrexham: Bridge Books, 2008).

Doherty, Richard, and Truesdale, David, *Irish Winners of the Victoria Cross* (Dublin: Four Courts Press, 2000).

Dolan, Anne, *Commemorating the Irish Civil War: History and Memory, 1923–2000* (Cambridge University Press, 2003).

Dorney, John, *The Civil War in Dublin: The Fight for the Irish Capital 1922–1924* (Newbridge: Merrion, 2017).

Dungan, Myles, *Irish Voices from the Great War* (Dublin: Irish Academic Press, 1995).

Dwyer, T. Ryle, *The Squad and the Intelligence Operations of Michael Collins* (Cork: Mercier, 2005).

English, Richard, *Ernie O'Malley: IRA Intellectual* (Oxford: Clarendon Press, 1998).

Erickson, Edward J., *Gallipoli: Command Under Fire* (Oxford: Osprey, 2015).

Falls, Cyril, *Military Operations Macedonia, from the Outbreak of War to the Spring of 1917* (London: HMSO, 1933).

Fanning, Ronan, *Fatal Path: British Government and Irish Revolution, 1910–1922* (London: Faber and Faber, 2013).

Ferriter, Diarmaid, *Judging Dev: A Reassessment of the Life and Legacy of Eamon de Valera* (Dublin: Royal Irish Academy, 2007).

A *Nation and Not a Rabble: The Irish Revolution, 1913–1923* (London: Profile, 2015).

Fitzpatrick, David, *Harry Boland's Irish Revolution* (Cork University Press, 2003).

ed., *Terror in Ireland, 1916–1923* (Dublin: Lilliput, 2012).

Foley, Caitriona, *The Last Irish Plague: The Great Flu Epidemic in Ireland 1918–19* (Dublin: Irish Academic Press, 2011).

Foley, Michael, *The Bloodied Field: Croke Park. Sunday 21 November 1920* (Dublin: O'Brien Press, 2014).

Fox, Aimée, *Learning to Fight: Military Innovation and Change in the British Army, 1914–18* (Cambridge University Press, 2018).

Fox, Frank, *The Royal Inniskilling Fusiliers in the World War* (London: Constable, 1928).

Foy, Michael, and Barton, Brian, *The Easter Rising* (Stroud: Sutton, 1999).

Gilbert, Adrian, *Challenge of Battle: The Real Story of the British Army in 1914* (Oxford: Osprey, 2013).

Gillis, Liz, *The Fall of Dublin* (Cork: Mercier, 2011).

Glasnevin Trust, *1916 Necrology: 485* (Dublin: Glasnevin Trust, 2016).

Gleeson, Joe, *Irish Air Aces of the RFC and RAF in the First World War: The Lives Behind the Legends* (Stroud: Fonthill, 2015).

Graff-McRae, Rebecca, *Remembering and Forgetting 1916: Commemoration and Conflict in Post-Peace Process Ireland* (Dublin: Irish Academic Press, 2010).

Grayson, Richard S., *Belfast Boys: How Unionists and Nationalists Fought and Died Together in the First World War* (London: Bloomsbury, 2009; 2010 edition).

    ed., *At War with the 16th Irish Division, 1914–1918: The Staniforth Letters* (Barnsley: Pen and Sword, 2012),

Grayson, Richard S., and McGarry, Fearghal, eds., *Remembering 1916: The Easter Rising, the Somme and the Politics of Memory in Ireland* (Cambridge University Press, 2016).

Griffith, Paddy, *Battle Tactics of the Western Front: The British Army's Art of Attack 1916–18* (New Haven: Yale University Press, 1994).

Guinness, Arthur, Son & Co. Ltd, *Roll of Employees* (Dublin: Arthur Guinness, 1920).

Gwynn, Stephen, *John Redmond's Last Years* (London: Edward Arnold, 1919).

Hall, Michael, *A Shared Sacrifice for Peace* (Belfast: Island Publications, 2007).

Halpern, Paul G., *A Naval History of World War I* (Abingdon: Routledge, 1994).

Hammond, Bryn, *Cambrai 1917: The Myth of the First Great Tank Battle* (London: Weidenfeld and Nicolson, 2008).

Hanna, Henry, *The Pals at Suvla Bay: Being the Record of "D" Company of the 7th Royal Dublin Fusiliers* (Dublin: Ponsonby, 1917).

Harper, R. W. E., *Singapore Mutiny* (Singapore: Oxford University Press, 1984).

Harris, J., *Douglas Haig and the First World War* (Cambridge University Press, 2008).

Hart, Peter (a), *The IRA at War 1916–1923* (Oxford University Press, 2003).

Hart, Peter (b), *The Somme* (London: Weidenfeld and Nicolson, 2005).

    Gallipoli (London: Profile, 2011)

    Fire and Movement: The British Expeditionary Force and the Campaign of 1914 (Oxford University Press, 2015).

Hennessey, Thomas, *Dividing Ireland: World War I and Partition* (London: Routledge, 1998).

Herwig, Holger H., *The Marne, 1914: The Opening of World War I and the Battle that Changed the World* (New York: Random House, 2009).

Higgins, Roisín, *Transforming 1916: Meaning Memory and the Fiftieth Anniversary of the Easter Rising* (Cork University Press, 2012).

Hittle, J. E. B., *Michael Collins and the Anglo-Irish War: Britain's Counter-Insurgency Failure* (Washington, DC: Potomac Books, 2011).

Hope, Carole, *Worshipper and Worshipped: Across the Divide – An Irish Padre of the Great War, Fr Willie Doyle Chaplain to the Forces 1915–1917* (Brighton: Reveille, 2013).

Hopkinson, Michael, *Green against Green: The Irish Civil War* (Dublin: Gill and Macmillan, 1998; 2004 edn).

The Irish War of Independence (Dublin: Gill and Macmillan, 2002).

Horne, John, ed., *Our War* (Dublin: Royal Irish Academy, 2008).

Horne, John, and Madigan, Edward, eds., *Towards Commemoration: Ireland in War and Revolution, 1912–1923* (Dublin: Royal Irish Academy, 2013).

Hughes, Brian, *16 Lives: Michael Mallin* (Dublin: O'Brien, 2012).

Hutton, John, *August 1914: Surrender at St Quentin* (Barnsley: Pen and Sword, 2010).

Irish Times, The, *Sinn Fein Rebellion Handbook* (Dublin: The Irish Times, 1917).

Irish, Tomás, *Trinity in War and Revolution, 1912–1923* (Dublin: Royal Irish Academy, 2015).

Jeffery, Keith, *Ireland and the Great War* (Cambridge University Press, 2000).

Field Marshal Sir Henry Wilson: A Political Soldier (Oxford University Press, 2006).

1916: A Global History (London: Bloomsbury, 2015).

Johnson, Nuala C., *Ireland, the Great War and the Geography of Remembrance* (Cambridge University Press, 2003).

Johnstone, Tom, *Orange: Green and Khaki: The Story of the Irish Regiments in the Great War, 1914–18* (Dublin: Gill and Macmillan, 1992).

Jones, Heather, *Violence Against Prisoners of War in the First World War: Britain, France and Germany, 1914–1920* (Cambridge University Press, 2011).

Jones, Valerie, *Rebel Prods: The Forgotten Story of Protestant Radical Nationalists and the 1916 Rising* (Dublin: Ashfield, 2016).

Jordan, Anthony J., ed., *Boer War to Easter Rising: The Writings of John MacBride* (Westport: Westport Books 2006).

Jourdain, H. F. N., and Fraser, Edward, *The Connaught Rangers*, vol. III (London: Royal United Service Institution, 1918).

The Connaught Rangers, 1st Battalion, Formerly 88th Foot, vol. I (London: Royal United Service Institution, 1924).

Kautt, W. H., *Ambushes and Armour: The Irish Rebellion, 1919–1921* (Dublin: Irish Academic Press, 2010).

Kenyon, David, *Horsemen in No Man's Land: British Cavalry & Trench Warfare, 1914–1918* (Barnsley: Pen and Sword, 2011).

Keogh, Michael, *With Casement's Irish Brigade* (Drogheda: Choice, 2010).

Kinsella, Ken, *Out of the Dark, 1914–1918: South Dubliners Who Fell in the Great War* (Sallins: Merrion, 2014).

Kipling, Rudyard, *The Irish Guards in the Great War,* vol. I: *The First Battalion* (London: Macmillan, 1923; London: Leonaur, 2007 edn).

Kissane, Bill, *The Politics of the Irish Civil War* (Oxford University Press, 2005).

Kostick, Conor, *16 Lives: Michael O'Hanrahan* (Dublin: O'Brien, 2015).

Lawlor, Damian, *Na Fianna Éireann and the Irish Revolution, 1909 to 1923* (Rhode, Co. Offaly: Caoillte Books, 2009).

Lecane, Philip, *Torpedoed! The R.M.S. Leinster Disaster* (Penzance: Periscope, 2005).

Beneath a Turkish Sky: The Royal Dublin Fusiliers and the Assault on Gallipoli (Dublin: History Press Ireland, 2015).

Leeson, D. M., *The Black and Tans: British Police and Auxiliaries in the Irish War of Independence* (Oxford University Press, 2011).

Lewis, Geoffrey, *Carson: The Man who Divided Ireland* (London: Hambledon, 2005).

Lloyd, Nick, *Loos 1915* (Stroud; Tempus, 2006).

Hundred Days: The End of the Great War (London: Penguin, 2013).

London Stamp Exchange, *Our Heroes* (London: London Stamp Exchange, 1988 edn, of 1916 publication).

Lowry, Gerald, *From Mons to 1933* (London: Simpkin & Marshall, 1933).

Lucy, John, *Devil in the Drum* (London: Faber & Faber, 1938; Uckfield: Naval & Military Press, 1992 edn).

Lyons, J. B., *The Enigma of Tom Kettle* (Dublin: Glendale Press, 1983).

MacDonagh, Michael, *The Irish at the Front* (London: Hodder and Stoughton, 1916).

The Irish on the Somme (London: Hodder and Stoughton, 1917).

Mace, Martin, and Grehan, John, *Slaughter on the Somme, 1 July 1916: The Complete War Diaries of the British Army's Worst Day* (Barnsley: Pen and Sword, 2013).

Macleod, Jenny, *Gallipoli* (Oxford University Press, 2015).

Mallinson, Allan, *1914: Fight the Good Fight. Britain, the Army and the Coming of the First World War* (London: Bantam Press, 2013).

Martin, Francis Xavier, ed., *The Howth Gun-Running and the Kilcoole Gun-Running 1914* (Dublin: Browne and Nolan, 1964).

Mathews, P. J., *Revival: The Abbey Theatre, Sinn Féin, the Gaelic League and the Co-operative Movement* (Notre Dame: University of Notre Dame Press, 2003).

Matthews, Ann, *The Kimmage Garrison, 1916: Making Billy-can Bombs at Larkfield* (Dublin: Four Courts, 2010).

McCarthy, Cal, *Cumann na mBan and the Irish Revolution* (Cork: Collins Press, 2007).

McConville, Seán, *Irish Political Prisoners, 1848–1922: Theatres of War* (London: Routledge, 2003).

McCracken, Donal, *MacBride's Brigade: Irish Commandos in the Anglo–Boer War* (Dublin: Four Courts Press, 1999).

McGarry, Fearghal, *The Rising, Ireland: Easter 1916* (Oxford University Press, 2010).

The Abbey Rebels of 1916: A Lost Revolution (Dublin: Gill and Macmillan, 2015).

McGilvray, Evan, *Hamilton and Gallipoli: British Command in an Age of Military Transformation* (Barnsley: Pen and Sword, 2015).

McGreevy, Ronan, *Wherever the Firing Line Extends: Ireland and the Western Front* (Dublin: History Press Ireland, 2016).

McGuire, James, and Quinn, James, eds., *Dictionary of Irish Biography*. (Cambridge University Press, 2009).

McMahon, Paul, *British Spies and Irish Rebels: British Intelligence and Ireland, 1916–1945* (Woodbridge: Boydell, 2008).

Meleady, Dermot, *Redmond: The National Leader* (Dublin: Merrion, 2014).

Molyneux, Derek and Kelly, Darren, *When the Clock Struck in 1916: Close-Quarter Combat in the Easter Rising* (Wilton: Collins Press, 2015).

Those of us Who Must Die: Execution, Exile and Revival after the Easter Rising (Wilton: Collins Press, 2017).

Moynihan, Michael, *God On Our Side: The British Padre in World War I* (London: Leo Cooper, 1983).

Mulcahy, Risteard, *My Father, the General: Richard Mulcahy and the Military History of the Revolution* (Dublin: Liberties Press, 2010).

Murland, Jerry, *Retreat and Rearguard 1914: The BEF's Actions from Mons to the Marne* (Barnsley: Pen and Sword, 2011).

Murphy, Gerard, *The Great Cover-Up: The Truth About the Death of Michael Collins* (Wilton: Collins Press, 2018).

Myers, Jason R., *The Great War and Memory in Irish Culture, 1918–2010* (Palo Alto: Academica, 2016).

National Association of the Old IRA, The (NAOIRA), *Dublin Brigade Review* (Dublin: Cahill, 1939).

National Book of Honour Committee, *Dublin City and County Book of Honour* (Dublin: Book of Honour Committee, 2004).

Nield, Robert, *China's Foreign Places: The Foreign Presence in China in the Treaty Port Era, 1840–1943* (Hong Kong University Press, 2015).

O'Brien, Paul, *Field of Fire: The Battle of Ashbourne, 1916* (Dublin: New Island, 2012).

Havoc: The Auxiliaries in Ireland's War of Independence (Wilton: Collins Press, 2017).

O'Connor, Emmet, *Reds and the Green: Ireland, Russia and the Communist Internationals, 1919–43* (Dublin: University College Dublin Press, 2004).

O'Keeffe, Jane, ed., *The 1916 Rising Oral History Collection, Parts 1 and 2* (Tralee: privately published, 2015).

O'Malley, Ernie, *On Another Man's Wound* (London: Rich & Cowan, 1936; Dublin: Anvil, 1990 edn).

The Singing Flame (Dublin: Cahill, 1976; 1987 Anvil edn).

Orr, Philip, *A Field of Bones: An Irish Division at Gallipoli* (Dublin: Lilliput Press, 2006).

Paice, Edward, *Tip and Run: The Untold Tragedy of the Great War in Africa* (London: Weidenfeld and Nicolson, 2007).

Palmer, Alan, *The Salient: Ypres, 1914–18* (London: Constable, 2007).

Pašeta, Senia, *Irish Nationalist Women, 1900–1918* (Cambridge University Press, 2013).

Passingham, Ian, *Pillars of Fire: The Battle of Messines Ridge, June 1917* (Stroud: Sutton, 1998).

Pennell, Catriona, *A Kingdom United: Popular Responses to the Outbreak of the First World War in Britain and Ireland* (Oxford University Press, 2012),

Philpott, William, *Bloody Victory: The Sacrifice on the Somme and the Making of the Twentieth Century* (London: Little Brown, 2009).

Attrition: Fighting the First World War (London: Little Brown, 2014).

Plunkett, James, *Strumpet City* (London: Hutchinson, 1969; Dublin: Gill & Macmillan, 2013 edn).

Price, Dominic, *We Bled Together: Michael Collins, the Squad and the Dublin Brigade* (Wilton: Collins Press, 2017).

Prior, Robin, *Gallipoli: The End of the Myth* (London: Yale University Press, 2009).

Prior, Robin, and Wilson, Trevor, *The Somme* (London: Yale University Press, 2005).

Quinn, Anthony, *Wigs and Guns: Irish Barristers in the Great War* (Dublin: Four Courts, 2006).

Richardson, Neil, *According to Their Lights: Stories of Irishmen in the British Army, Easter 1916* (Wilton: Collins, 2015).

Romer, C. F., and Mainwaring, A. E., *The Second Battalion Royal Dublin Fusiliers in the South African War* (London: A. L. Humphreys, 1908).

Ryan, Meda, *The Day Michael Collins was Shot* (Swords: Poolbeg Press, 1989).

Sandford, Stephen, *Neither Unionist nor Nationalist: The 10th (Irish) Division in the Great War* (Dublin: Irish Academic Press, 2015).

Sheffield, Gary, *Forgotten Victory: The First World War – Myths and Realities* (London: Headline, 2001).

The Somme (London: Cassell, 2003).

Sheffield, Gary, and Bourne, John, eds., *Douglas Haig: War Diaries and Letters, 1914–1918* (London: Weidenfeld and Nicolson, 2005).

Simkins, Peter, *From the Somme to Victory: The British Army's Experience on the Western Front, 1916–1918* (Barnsley: Pen and Sword, 2014).

Speake, Jennifer, ed., *Oxford Dictionary of Proverbs* (Oxford University Press, 1982; 7th edn 2015),

Stanley, Jeremy, *Ireland's Forgotten 10th: A Brief History of the 10th (Irish) Division, 1914–1918, Turkey: Macedonia and Palestine* (Ballycastle: Impact, 2003).

Steel, Nigel, and Hart, Peter, *Defeat at Gallipoli* (London: Macmillan, 1994).

Jutland, 1916: Death in the Grey Wastes (London: Orion, 2003).

Stevenson, David, *With Our Backs to the Wall: Victory and Defeat in 1918* (London: Allen Lane, 2011).

Swartz, Marvin, *The Union of Democratic Control in British Politics During the First World War* (Oxford: Clarendon Press, 1971).

Taylor, James W., *The 1st Royal Irish Rifles in the Great War* (Dublin: Four Courts Press, 2002)

The 2nd Royal Irish Rifles in the Great War (Dublin: Four Courts Press, 2005).

Guilty but Insane, J. C. Bowen-Colthurst: Villain or Victim? (Cork: Mercier Press, 2016).

Taylor, Paul, *Heroes or Traitors? Experiences of Southern Irish Soldiers Returning from the Great War 1919–1939* (Liverpool: Liverpool University Press, 2015).

Thompson, Mark, *The White War: Life and Death on the Italian Front 1915–1919* (London: Faber and Faber, 2008).

Townshend, Charles, *Political Violence in Ireland: Government and Resistance since 1848* (Oxford: Clarendon Press, 1983).

Easter 1916: The Irish Rebellion (London: Allen Lane, 2005).

Ulrichsen, Kristian Coates, *The First World War in the Middle East* (London: Hurst, 2014).

University of Dublin (Trinity College), *War List* (Dublin: Hodges Figgis, 1922).

Walker, Jonathan, ed., *War Letters to a Wife: France and Flanders, 1915–1919* (Staplehurst: Spellmount, 2001).

Walker, Stephen, *Forgotten Soldiers: The Irishmen Shot at Dawn* (Dublin: Gill and Macmillan, 2007).

Ireland's Call: Irish Sporting Heroes who Fell in the Great War (Sallins: Merrion, 2015).

Walsh, Maurice, *The News from Ireland: Foreign Correspondents and the Irish Revolution* (London: I. B. Tauris, 2011).

Bitter Freedom: Ireland in a Revolutionary World, 1918–1923 (London: Faber & Faber, 2015).

Watson, Alexander, *Ring of Steel: Germany and Austria-Hungary at War, 1914–1918* (London: Penguin, 2014).

Whearity, Peter F., *The Easter Rising of 1916 in North County Dublin: A Skerries Perspective* (Dublin: Four Courts Press, 2013).

Whelan, Yvonne, *Reinventing Modern Dublin: Streetscape, Iconography and the Politics of Identity* (Dublin: University College Dublin Press, 2003).

Wilcox, Ron, *Battles on the Tigris: The Mesopotamian Campaign of the First World War* (Barnsley: Pen and Sword, 2006).

Wren, Jimmy, *The GPO Garrison Easter Week 1916: A Biographical Dictionary* (Dublin: Geography Publications, 2015).

Wylly, H. C., *Neill's Blue Caps*, vol. II, *1826–1914* (Aldershot: Gale and Polden, 1923).

Neill's "Blue Caps", vol. III (Aldershot: Gale and Polden, 1925).

Crown and Company, 1911–1922: The Historical Records of the 2nd Batt. Royal Dublin Fusiliers (London: Arthur L. Humphreys, 1925).

Yeates, Pádraig, *Lockout: Dublin 1913* (Dublin: Gill and Macmillan, 2001).

A City in Wartime: Dublin 1914–18 (Dublin: Gill and Macmillan, 2011).

A City in Turmoil, Dublin 1919–1921 (Dublin: Gill and Macmillan, 2012).

A City in Civil War, Dublin 1921–1924 (Dublin: Gill and Macmillan, 2015).

Zuber, Terence, *The Mons Myth: A Reassessment of the Battle* (Stroud: The History Press, 2010).

The Battle of the Frontiers: Ardennes 1914 (Stroud: The History Press, 2014).

Articles and book chapters

Bielenberg, Andy, 'Fatalities in the Irish Revolution', in Crowley et al., *Atlas* (2017), 752–61.

Billings, Cathal, 'Speaking Irish with Hurley Sticks: Gaelic Sports, the Irish Language and National Identity in Revival Ireland', *Sport in History*, 37, 1 (2017), 25–50.

Borgonovo, John, 'Reorganisation of the Irish Volunteers', in Crowley et al., *Atlas* (2017), 313–18.

Buck, William, '"Come and Find Sanctuary in Eire". The Experiences of Ireland's Belgian Refugees During the First World War', *Immigrants and Minorities*, 34, 2 (2016), 192–209.

Burke, Tom, 'Attitudes of Irish soldiers Serving in the British Army During and After the 1916 Easter Rising in Dublin', *The Blue Cap*, 16 (December 2009), 1–17.

'Recovery and Reconciliation: The Royal Dublin Fusiliers Association', in Horne and Madigan, eds., *Towards* (2013), 98–104.

'All of Dublin Felt the Horror of a Single Brutal Weekend in Gallipoli', *IT Weekend Review*, 15 August 2015, 2.

Coleman, Marie, 'Military Service Pensions for Civil and Public Servants in Independent Ireland', *Administration*, 60, 2 (2012), 51–61.

'Military Service Pensions for Veterans of the Irish Revolution, 1916–1923', *War in History*, 20, 2 (2013), 201–21.

'Leinster', in Crowley et al., *Atlas* (2017), 579–87.

'The Military Service Pensions Collection' in Crowley et al., *Atlas* (2017), 881–5.

D'Arcy, Fergus A., 'Connolly, James', in McGuire and Quinn, *Dictionary of Irish Biography*, http://dib.cambridge.org/.

Denman, Terence, 'The 16th (Irish) Division on 21st March 1918: Fight or Flight?' *Irish Sword*, 69 (1999), 273–87.

Durney, James, 'How Aungier Street / Camden Street Became Known as "the Dardanelles"', *The Irish Sword XXVII*, 108 (2010), 243–51.

Dwyer, T. Ryle, 'Michael Collins and the Civil War', in Crowley et al., *Atlas* (2017), 725–9.

English, Richard, 'O'Malley, Ernest Bernard ("Ernie")', in McGuire and Quinn, *Dictionary of Irish Biography*, http://dib.cambridge.org/.

Ferriter, Diarmaid, '"Always in Danger of Finding Myself with Nothing at All"', in Diarmaid Ferriter and Susannah Riordan, eds., *Years of Turbulence: The Irish Revolution and its Aftermath* (Dublin: University College Dublin Press, 2015), 191–207.

Fitzpatrick, David, 'The Logic of Collective Sacrifice: Ireland and the British Army, 1914–1918', *Historical Journal* 38 (1995), 1017–30.

'Militarism in Ireland, 1900–1922', in Thomas Bartlett and Keith Jeffery, eds., *A Military History of Ireland* (Cambridge University Press, 1996), 379–406.

'Commemoration in the Irish Free State: A Chronicle of Embarrassment', in Ian McBride, ed., *History and Memory in Modern Ireland* (Cambridge University Press, 2001), 184–203.

'West Belfast Exceptionalism: Richard S. Grayson's *Belfast Boys*', *Irish Social and Economic History*, 38 (2011), 103–7.

'Imperial Loyalties: Irishmen, Anzacs, and the Conflict of Empires at Gallipoli', *The Irish Sword*, XXX, 121 (2016), 305–31.

Grayson, Richard S., 'Ireland's New Memory of the First World War: Forgotten Aspects of the Battle of Messines, June 1917', *British Journal for Military History*, 1, 1 (2014), 48–65.

'Military History from the Street: New Methods for Researching First World War Service in the British Military', *War in History*, 21, 4 (2014), 465–95.

'A Life in the Trenches? Operation War Diary and Crowdsourcing Methods for Understanding Day-to-day Life in the British Army on the Western Front in the First World War', *British Journal for Military History*, 2, 2 (2015), 160–85.

Greene, Séamus, '2nd Lieut. Jasper Brett', *The Blue Cap*, 18 (December 2013), 8–9.

Gribbon, H. D., 'Economic and Social History 1850–1921', in W. E. Vaughan, ed., *A New History of Ireland. VI, Ireland Under the Union, II, 1870–1921* (Oxford University Press, 1996), 260–356.

Hogan, Daire, 'Sheehy, Eugene', in McGuire and Quinn, *Dictionary of Irish Biography*, http://dib.cambridge.org/.

Hopkinson, M. A., 'Childers, (Robert) Erskine', in McGuire and Quinn, *Dictionary of Irish Biography*, http://dib.cambridge.org/.

'Civil War: The Opening Phase', in Crowley et al., *Atlas* (2017), 675–87.

Hughes, Brian, Campbell, Billy and Schriebman, Susan, 'Contested Memories: Revisiting the Battle of Mount Street Bridge', *British Journal for Military History*, 4, 1 (2017), 2–22.

Jeffery, Keith, 'Commemoration and the Hazards of Irish Politics', in Bart Ziino, ed., *Remembering the First World War* (London: Routledge, 2014), 165–85.

Jensen, Kimberley, 'Gender and Citizenship', in Susan R. Grayzel and Tammy M. Proctor, *Gender and the Great War* (Oxford University Press, 2017), 10–26.

Jones, Edgar, Palmer, Ian, and Wessely, Simon, 'War Pensions (1900–1945): Changing Models of Psychological Understanding', *The British Journal of Psychiatry*, 180, 4 (2002), 374–9.

Jones, Heather, 'Church of Ireland Great War Remembrance in the South of Ireland: A Personal Reflection', in Horne and Madigan eds., *Towards* (2013), 74–82.

'Cultures of Commemoration: Remembering the First World War in Ireland', in Crowley et al., *Atlas* (2017), 838–47.

Leonard, Jane, 'Lest we Forget', in David Fitzpatrick, ed., *Ireland and the First World War* (Dublin: Trinity History Workshop, 1988), 59–68.

'The Reaction of Irish Officers in the British Army to the Easter Rising of 1916', in Hugh Cecil and Peter H. Liddle, eds., *Facing Armageddon: The First World War Experience* (London: Leo Cooper, 1996), 256–86.

'The Twinge of Memory: Armistice Day and Remembrance Sunday in Dublin since 1919', in Richard English, and Graham Walker, eds., *Unionism in Modern Ireland: New Perspectives on Politics and Culture* (Basingstoke: Macmillan, 1996), 99–114.

'Survivors', in Horne, ed., *Our War* (2008), 209–23.

'"English Dogs" or "Poor Devils"? The Dead of Bloody Sunday Morning', in Fitzpatrick, *Terror* (2012), 102–40.

Lewis, Matthew, 'Sectarianism and Irish Republican Violence on the South-East Ulster Frontier, 1919–1922', *Contemporary European History*, 26, 1 (2017), 1–21.

Lynd, Robert, 'The Work of T. M. Kettle', *New Statesman*, 30 September 1916, 614–15.

Lyons, F. S. L., 'The New Nationalism, 1916–18', in W. E. Vaughan, ed., *A New History of Ireland: VI, Ireland Under the Union, II, 1870–1921* (Oxford: Clarendon Press, 1996), 224–39.

Macleod, Jenny, 'The Gallipoli Centenary: An International Perspective', in Brad West, ed., *War Memory and Commemoration* (London: Routledge, 2017), 89–106.

McCann, B. P., 'The Diary of Second Lieutenant A. V. G. Killingley, Easter Week, 1916', *Irish Sword*, XX, 81 (Summer 1997), 246–53.

McCarthy, Patrick, 'Casement's Irish Brigade', *The Irish Sword*, XXXI, 124 (Winter 2017), 203–11.

McGarry, Fearghal, 'The Easter Rising', in Crowley et al., *Atlas* (2017), 240–57.

McGreevy, Ronan, '"It Was Magnificent . . . We Called the Hill Fort Dublin"', *IT*, 6 August 2015, 7.

'An Irishman's Diary', *IT*, 28 March 2016, 17.

'The Easter Rising Family Rift That Never Healed', *IT Online*, 24 April 2016, www.irishtimes.com/news/ireland/irish-news/the-easter-rising-family-rift-that-never-healed-1.2622619 (accessed 8 December 2016).

'Secret Files Reveal How Deeply the Easter Rising Affected Irishmen Serving in First World War', *IT Online*, 6 May 2018, www.irishtimes.com/news/ireland/irish-news/secret-files-reveal-how-deeply-the-easter-rising-affected-irishmen-serving-in-first-world-war-1.3486276 (accessed 9 May 2018).

McNally, Frank, 'An Irishman's Diary', *IT*, 3 July 2014, 15.

Milne, Ida, 'Stacking the Coffins: The 1918–19 Influenza Pandemic in Dublin', in Lisa Marie Griffith and Ciarán Wallace, eds., *Grave Matters: Death and Dying in Dublin, 1500 to the Present* (Dublin: Four Courts Press, 2016), 61–76.

Montgomery, Ian, 'Thoroughbred Irishmen: Black Watch Volunteers in Dublin Before the First World War', *The Irish Sword*, XXIX, 115 (Summer 2013), 41–61.

Morrison, Eve, 'The Bureau of Military History', in Crowley et al. eds., *Atlas* (2017), 876–80.

O'Callaghan, Margaret, 'Reframing 1916 after 1969: Irish Governments, a National Day of Reconciliation, and the Politics of Commemoration in the 1970s', in Grayson and McGarry, eds., *Remembering* (2016), 207–23.

Ó Cathain, Máirtin, 'A Land Beyond the Seas: Irish and Scottish Republicans in Dublin, 1916', in Ruán O'Donnell, ed., *The Impact of the 1916 Rising: Among the Nations* (Dublin: Irish Academic Press, 2008), 37–48.

O Conchubhair, Padraig, and Rigney, Paddy, 'The Active Service Unit', in NAOIRA, *Dublin Brigade Review* (1939), 75–82.

O'Connell, J. J. 'The Role of Dublin in the War of Independence', in NAOIRA, *Dublin Brigade Review* (1939), 99–101.

O'Connor, Emmet, 'Larkin, James', in McGuire and Quinn, *Dictionary of Irish Biography*, http://dib.cambridge.org/.

O'Halpin, Eunan, 'Counting Terror: Bloody Sunday and *The Dead of the Irish Revolution*', in Fitzpatrick, *Terror* (2012), 141–57.

Pašeta, Senia, 'Nationalist Responses to Two Royal Visits to Ireland, 1900 and 1903', *Irish Historical Studies*, xxxi, 124 (1999), 488–504.

Pegum, Michael, 'The Gorgeous Wrecks and the Opening Shots in the Battle of Mount Street Bridge', *The Irish Sword*, XXXI, 123 (Summer 2017), 75–86.

Pennell, Catriona, '"Choreographed by the Angels"? Ireland and the Centenary of the First World War', *War and Society*, 36, 4 (2017), 256–75.

Perry, Nicholas, 'Nationality in the Irish Infantry Regiments in the First World War', *Irish Sword*, XII (1994), 65–95.

Rawlings, J. D. R., 'History of No. 24 Squadron', *Air Pictorial*, 34, 4 (1972), 144–7.

Smith-Christmas, Kenneth L., Joye, Lar, and McEoin, Stephen, 'Possible "Four Courts" Irish Field Gun Returns Home', *ICOMAM Magazine*, 16 (December 2016), 28–32.

Staunton, Martin, 'Saint Ann's Church, Dublin', *The Gallipolian*, 74 (Spring 1994), 37–8.

Taaffe, Patrick, 'Richard Mulcahy and the Irish Civil War', *Irish Sword*, XXX, 120 (2015), 193–216.

Thornton, Frank, 'The Pre-Truce Intelligence Department', in NAOIRA, *Dublin Brigade Review* (1939), 83–5.

Wallace, Arminta, 'The Dublin Pals Who Set off for Gallipoli's Killing Fields', *IT*, 9 February 2015, 13.

Ward, Alan J., 'Lloyd George and the 1918 Irish Conscription Crisis', *The Historical Journal* 17 (1974), 107–29.

Yeates, Pádraig, 'Dublin', in Crowley et al., *Atlas* (2017), 588–95.

Unpublished thesis

Hannon, Charles, 'The Irish Volunteers and the Concepts of Military Service and Defence 1913–24' (University College, Dublin, PhD thesis, 1989).

Selected Miscellaneous Websites

Auxiliary Division of the Royal Irish Constabulary: www.theauxiliaries.com

Commonwealth War Graves Commission: www.cwgc.org

Diary of Mary Martin: http://dh.tcd.ie/martindiary/

Irish Births, Death and Marriages: www.irishgenealogy.ie

Irish War Memorials: www.irishwarmemorials.ie/Places (all Dublin city and county memorials)

The Long, Long Trail (The British Army in the Great War of 1914–1918): www.longlongtrail.co.uk

Wreck Site: www.wrecksite.eu

Index